Letters of
Frank Sargeson

Letters of
Frank Sargeson

Selected and edited by SARAH SHIEFF

VINTAGE

creative nz ARTS COUNCIL OF NEW ZEALAND TOI AOTEAROA The assistance of Creative New Zealand is gratefully acknowledged by the publisher.

A VINTAGE BOOK published by Random House New Zealand,
18 Poland Road, Glenfield, Auckland, New Zealand

For more information about our titles go to www.randomhouse.co.nz

A catalogue record for this book is available from the National Library of New Zealand

Random House New Zealand is part of the Random House Group
New York London Sydney Auckland Delhi Johannesburg

First published 2012

ISBN 978 1 86979 333 3

Design: Carla Sy
Cover illustration: Alan Thornton, Portrait of Frank Sargeson, 1968, oil on hardboard, 795 x 603mm, Accession No: A527, given anonymously, 1968. Hocken Collections Uare Taoka o Hakena, University of Otago.

Printed in China by Everbest Printing Co Ltd.

Contents

Acknowledgements

This project would have been impossible without the good will of many people. At the hunting and gathering stage, friends, librarians and fellow scholars helped locate the letters from which the final selection was drawn; as the editing progressed, others offered advice and practical support. Finally, the appearance of each and every letter in this volume represents two and sometimes three separate acts of generosity: Frank Sargeson, via his executors, controls the content of the letters; the recipient or their executor controls the physical item, and the archives holding letters also have duty of care. My first debt of gratitude is therefore due to the late Dame Christine Cole Catley and the Sargeson Trust, who, as the guardians of Frank Sargeson's estate, honoured me with this responsibility and gave me unrestricted access to his papers. Kevin Ireland often provided information about the who, where and what of the letters — I am grateful for his sharp eye and his voluminous memory. Karl Stead allowed me access to his correspondence with Sargeson, helped decipher Frank's handwriting, and provided much helpful detail. Together, Karl and Kay Stead advised and encouraged, made items from their personal collection available, and helped reconstruct Frank's method for his famed risotto with pipis. Paul Millar generously shared insights and material deriving from his own research relating to James K. Baxter, Charles Brasch and Bill Pearson. Pamela Gordon and the Janet Frame Literary Trust made copies of Frank's letters available and offered contextual and biographical advice.

I would also like to thank a number of others who gave me permission to publish letters: John Baxter, Geoff Bertram, Elizabeth Caffin, Alison and Ray Copland, Raewyn Dalziel, Anna and Delia Davin, Father Felix Donnelly, Adam Dudding, Nick Duggan, Margaret Edgcumbe, Murray Edmond, Patrick Evans, Maurice Gee, John Geraets, Rupert and Pia Glover, John Graham, Martin Green, Duff Hart-Davis, David Hill, Alan Horsman, Lawrence Jones, Rachel and Jonathan King, Graeme Lay, John Macalister, Bill Manhire, Vincent O'Sullivan, Mary Paul, Brigid Sandford Smith, Margaret Scott, Donald Stenhouse, Catherine Styles-McLeod, Ngahuia Te Awekotuku, Peter Wells and Janet Wilson.

Still others pointed to items, made images available, allowed me to read letters under their control, or offered advice, assistance and kindness. They include: Peter Alexander, Ken Arvidson, Chris Bourke, Diana and Nick Bridge, Christopher Burke, Matthew Butt, Giselle Byrnes, Derek and Lynne Challis, Jenny Chamberlain, Jenny and Martin Cole, Megan and Nigel Cook, Max Cryer, Jeny Curnow, Wystan Curnow, William Dart, Rosamunda Droescher, Frances Edmond, Riemke Ensing, Norman Franke, Phyllis Gant, Peter Gibbons, Ray Grover, Linda Hardy, Stephen and Gail Hofmann, Anna Huang, Keri Hulme, Jan Kemp, Nancy Luther, Brigid Magner, Owen Marshall, O.E. Middleton, Gordon McLauchlan, James McNeish, Douglas MacDiarmid, Ann Monteith,

John Newton, W.H. Oliver, Ally Palmer, Jock Phillips and the team at Te Ara, David Roberts, Roger Robinson, Alan Roddick, Elizabeth Aitken Rose, Haru Sameshima, Sarah Schindeler, Colleen Singleton, Saffron Solley, Anne and Jeff Stack, Anthony Stones, Jane Strachan, Oliver Strewe, Terry Stringer and Tim McWhannell, Studio LaGonda, Terry Sturm, Alan Thornton, Michael Whittaker, Tanya Tinter, Denys Trussell, Mark Williams and Ian Witten. My colleagues at the University of Waikato supported the research in various practical and personal ways, including granting two vital periods of study leave (2008 and 2009), a research grant (2008–2009), and a summer research scholarship (2009–2010). Special thanks to Profs Roy Crawford, Dan Zirker and Doug Sutton, and to Alexandra Barratt, Tracy Bowell, Lex Chalmers, Athena Chambers, Delwyn Dellow, William Farrimond, Carolyn Henson, Craig Hight, Mark Houlahan, Katie Johnson, Anne McKim, Kirstine Moffat, John Perrone, Jan Pilditch and Alistair Swale.

Many libraries made copies of the letters available from their collections, and gave permission for them to be included here. Special thanks to those who not only offered practical help and advice, but who handled large requests efficiently and with unfailing courtesy: Susan Halpert and Leslie A. Morris of the Houghton Library, Harvard University; Richard Workman and Jean Cannon of the Harry Ransom Center, University of Texas at Austin; John Delaney, AnnaLee Pauls, Ben Primer and Don C. Skemer of the Department of Rare Books and Special Collections, Princeton University Library; Andrew Gray of Durham University Library Heritage Collection, Palace Green Library; Iain Sharp of Sir George Grey Special Collections, Auckland City Libraries; Kirsty Webb of Takapuna Library; Stephen Innes of Special Collections, University of Auckland Library; Jeff Palmer of University of Canterbury Library; Sharon Dell, Anna Blackman and Natalie Poland of the Hocken Collections, University of Otago Library; and David Colquhoun, Catherine Bisley, Gillian Headifen, Alison Jones, Merryn McAulay, John Sullivan and Amy Watling of the Alexander Turnbull Library, Wellington. The Turnbull Library holds Sargeson's literary papers, and the papers of many of his key correspondents. Much of the research for the book was therefore conducted in the Turnbull's reading room, directly under Toss Woollaston's portrait of Michael King. In many ways Michael has been the project's guiding spirit. His biography of Sargeson has been a constant reference throughout the life of this project.

Thanks also to the staff at Random House, especially to my publisher Harriet Allan for her early and sustaining faith in the book, and to Sue Lewis, Carla Sy and Alex Bishop.

Finally, I would like to thank my family, who have supported this journey — Jen Shieff and Heather Macdonald, Kate Bukowski, Rob Shieff and Fiona Moir, Maddy, Harry and Ben Shieff, Judith Macdonald, Octavia Calder-Dawe, Dorothy and Ian Calder, and my parents June and Bill Shieff. I reserve my last word of gratitude for my husband Alex Calder, Frank's best reader and my own best companion.

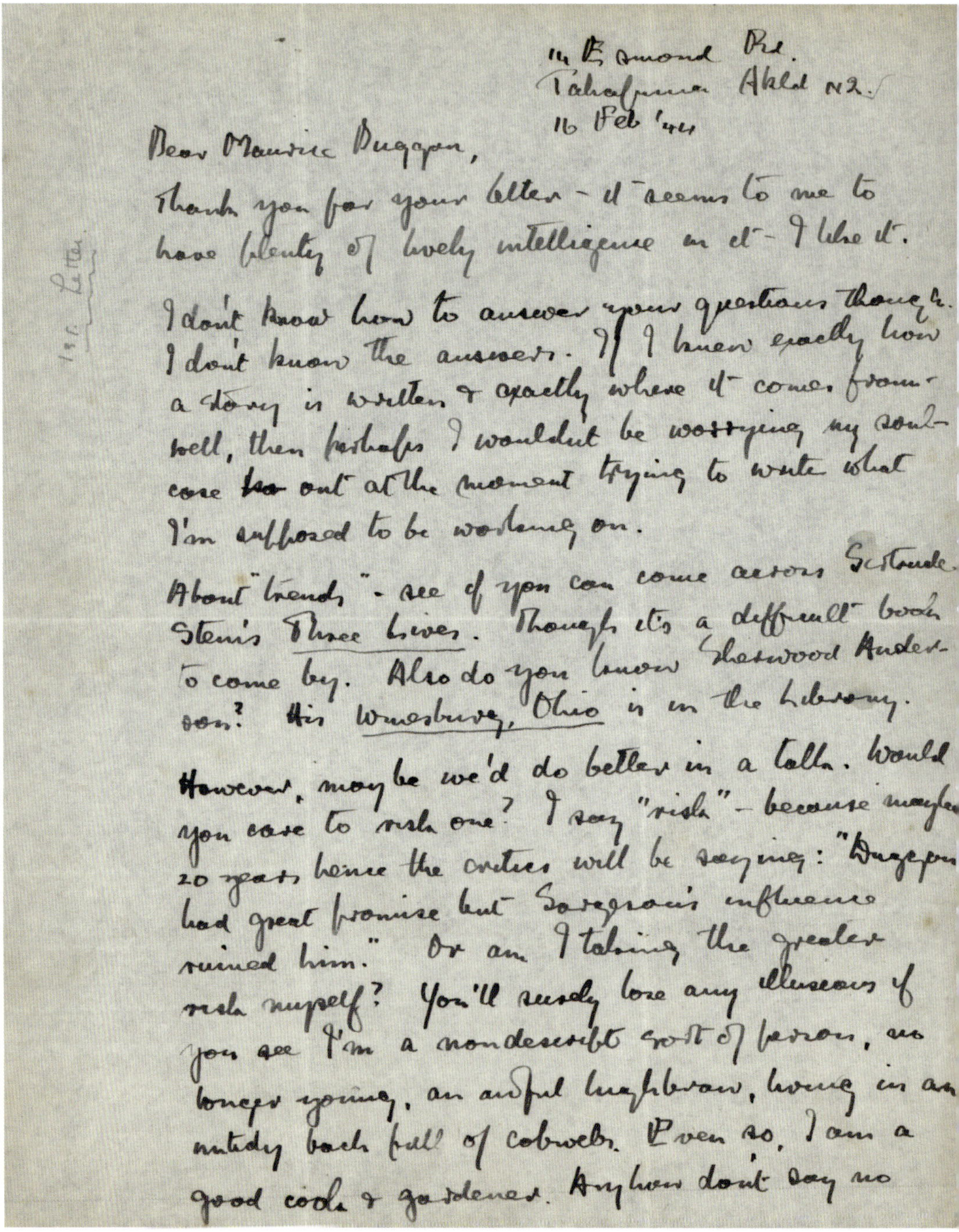
1st Letter

14 Esmonde Rd.
Takapuna Akld N2.
16 Feb '44

Dear Maurice Duggan,

Thank you for your letter – it seems to me to have plenty of lively intelligence in it – I like it.

I don't know how to answer your questions though. I don't know the answers. If I knew exactly how a story is written & exactly where it comes from – well, then perhaps I wouldn't be worrying my soul-case ~~too~~ out at the moment trying to write what I'm supposed to be working on.

About "trends" – see if you can come across Gertrude Stein's <u>Three Lives</u>. Though it's a difficult book to come by. Also do you know Sherwood Anderson? His <u>Winesburg, Ohio</u> is in the Library.

However, maybe we'd do better in a talk. Would you care to risk one? I say "risk" – because maybe 20 years hence the critics will be saying: "Duggan had great promise but Sargeson's influence ruined him." Or am I taking the greater risk myself? You'll surely lose any illusions if you see I'm a nondescript sort of person, no longer young, an awful highbrow, living in an untidy bach full of cobwebs. Even so, I am a good cook & gardener. Anyhow don't say no

3

just out of shyness – I'm easy-going – all the writers I know are – easy to meet & talk with. If you'd like to come over sometime let me know – or maybe you'd prefer a chat in town over a beer or a cup of coffee.

Apparently we have something in common. I'm supposed to be an invalid – bone T.B. – though I take little notice of it these days. But I've quite shamelessly exploited the situation so as to give me ample time for writing – the writing that, so often, even after so much trying, I don't do.

Best wishes anyhow

Frank Sargeson.

Introduction

Although I never met Frank Sargeson, our paths did cross in a way. When I was a young clarinetist, interested in any sort of gig, I received an invitation to play the slow movement of the Mozart concerto at a famous writer's funeral. It was early 1982. Sun streamed through the high windows of the Maclaurin Chapel. Tributes flowed; friends read from his work; an old mate kept up a slightly sozzled commentary from the front row. There was the ostentatious casket which, I learned much later, had been provided by a well-meaning funeral director in a misplaced gesture of propriety — and, more fittingly, a little table with a bowl of red peppers from his garden, and his favourite cap.

I came to know Sargeson on the page a few years later, when, as a graduate student of English, I was taught by his old friends Karl Stead and Bill Pearson. Sargeson's spare prose and laconic narrators repelled and fascinated me; the assurance that he had been a cat lover did nothing to dispel the terminal horror of 'Sale Day'. I now find myself teaching Sargeson's stories to students more alive to their sly winks and gender ambiguities than I ever was. And as the co-ordinator of the University of Waikato's Frank Sargeson Memorial Lecture, held annually to commemorate the legacy of Hamilton's most famous literary export, I've since come to meet others in the Sargeson circle — his heir and literary executor Christine Cole Catley; Kevin Ireland, who lived for a while in the army hut behind Frank's bach at 14 Esmonde Road; Lawrence Jones, who, as a young academic, reviewed Sargeson's novel *Man of England Now*; the writers Graeme Lay and Peter Wells, who came into contact with Sargeson in his later years; Frank's biographer Michael King. All are represented in this collection.

Norris Frank Davey was born in London Street, Hamilton, on 23 March 1903. Frank Sargeson, the writer he became, died in Auckland on 1 March 1982, and is probably still best known for his short stories. But Sargeson was also a novelist, a passionate but largely unperformed playwright, an autobiographer, a book reviewer and critic. He was also a prodigious correspondent. This collection presents just under 500 letters to 107 recipients, drawn from an archive of nearly 6000 letters to around 450 people. I have no doubt more will come to light. Not far into the collection phase, I began to wonder how Sargeson found time for all the letters, on top of his other writing, his garden, the friendships he nurtured and the quarrels he relished, his real and imagined poor health, and his genuinely terrible eyesight. The following email exchange — one of hundreds between friends and colleagues in the course of the editing process — is useful not only for the light it sheds on Sargeson's work habits, but as a reminder that letter-writing is far from a lost art, even if it has become more ephemeral:

From: Sarah Shieff
To: Kevin Ireland
Subject: A Frank question
Sent: Tues 16/09/2008 3:14 pm

Dear Kevin,

Frank Sargeson's letters are mounting up in drifts in my study. I'm beginning to wonder how he had (or made) time for all this activity — he must've written 10 letters a day on most days, and often more. From your knowledge of his routine, do you know if he had a regular time in the day for letter-writing?

Sarah

From: Kevin Ireland
To: Sarah Shieff
Subject: A Frank question
Sent: Sun 21/09/2008 12:17 pm

Dear Sarah,

Sorry, I've just got back from the east coast of Cape York, saltwater fly-fishing. Yes, Frank's routine was to take a small early breakfast while he read a few pages of Gibbon or Plutarch (instead of the morning paper), followed by work in the garden. Then creative work would start at about 9.00 am. He would 'enter the text' by revising what he'd written the day before, then he'd carry on with his daily quota of at least 300 new words. This usually occupied him until 12.00, when he would stop to collect his mail and eat a salad or a sandwich, or both. After lunch he would spend two or three hours industriously replying to letters and (if he had the opportunity) doing other writing to make a bit of money, such as radio talks, articles and book reviews. You will have noticed, as I soon did, that his daily writing schedule closely resembled school hours, though he usually laboured for six days, with Sunday as a day of rest (again, continuing a pattern usefully established in childhood). Late afternoons were for shopping and going to the library or doing more gardening. Then it was time for an evening meal, reading, listening to 1YC and occasionally 1YA, and for entertaining his many friends and callers.

All best wishes,

Kevin

The dates on Sargeson's letters, plus internal evidence, have subsequently revealed that he also regarded letter-writing as a 'rest' activity: many appear to have been written on Sunday afternoons.

The number of surviving letters suggests that Sargeson's correspondents were keenly aware of their importance: between them, Charles Brasch and Elizabeth

Pudsey Dawson alone kept over 600. But if Sargeson was a diligent and valued correspondent, he was also a meticulous keeper of his own and other people's letters. The Alexander Turnbull Library (ATL) holds 42 fat files of Sargeson's carbon copies of his own outwards correspondence, and hundreds of files of letters from other people survive in his papers. In reconstructing contexts and threads of conversation for this volume I drew on many of the latter, and came to realize that a good part of the significance of the Sargeson archive lies in its completeness in terms of its historical range (it spans 54 years, from 1927 to late 1981), in the number and complexity of the relationships it charts, and by virtue of the fact that both sides of so many conversations appear to have survived almost intact. This selection can only hint at its significance.

Sargeson's interest in the material value of his papers was piqued late in 1969 when he learned that Denis Glover had sold his own correspondence to the Turnbull Library for the princely sum of $550. Early the following year Sargeson made his own papers available for purchase, and also arranged for the Turnbull to acquire both sides of his correspondence with William Plomer. Subsequent sales supplemented Sargeson's always tenuous income stream, and, after his death, his executors salvaged further teetering piles of paper from his cottage and sent them on to the Turnbull. The collection is still growing.

The selection

After the letters had been located and xeroxed, I began my reading. This produced an index by recipient, and a preliminary selection of about 2000 letters, all of which have some claim to a place in a single volume with room for only a quarter of that number. Positive impressions had to give way to a steelier sorting. After transcribing and arranging the letters chronologically, I then ranked the 2000 contenders over five selection criteria: biographical interest, historical interest, literary interest in terms of Sargeson's career, general literary interest, and liveliness. The list of high scores was still too large for a single volume, so further cuts were made to produce a strong chronological sequence. I also wanted to strike a balance between important friendships conducted entirely or significantly by post and his care for 'one-off' correspondents, and to convey a sense of his friendships with women. Beyond that, the selection reflects the fact that Sargeson's friendships tended to wax and wane. Although I found myself mining key correspondences, only a few epistolary relationships seem to have been sustained for a lifetime: even the letters to E.P. Dawson trail off after her return to England in 1962. Others, for example with Maurice Duggan and Alec Pickard, are intense and relatively short-lived. If some friendships terminated towards the end of Sargeson's life, others took their place — Marcel Aurousseau,

Ralph Bodle, Toby Easterbrook-Smith and Dorothy Sutherland all entered (or re-entered) his life in his last ten years.

There are some significant and perhaps surprising gaps. For example, there are no surviving letters to his close friends D'Arcy Cresswell or R.A.K. Mason — perhaps due to fecklessness in one case, and proximity in the other. Mason lived near Sargeson in Takapuna; of necessity, the selection over-represents people who lived outside Auckland. That may also explain why there is a single surviving letter to Allen Curnow and none to Maurice Shadbolt. The only surviving letter to Robin Hyde already appears in *The Book of Iris: A Life of Robin Hyde*. My selection presents few letters to family, although there are copies of Frank's letters to his brother Harold Davey and his sisters Joyce and Phyllis in his outwards files. Some of these show him at his testy best. 'Look', he says to his sister Phyllis on 13 July 1973, 'I just can't take this business of people fixing their own time for calling. Monday is never a free day for me except for very special occasions, and I could manage a short visit about half past eleven in the morning.' (Less than three weeks later, this to his friend Murdie: '[W]henever you cared to call in it would be very pleasant to see you, more especially if you had a little time to spare.') The major contours of Sargeson's life must guide the selection, and in the end it seemed invidious to include letters to family simply because they were family. Letters to Renate Prince, the young architecture student who lived in Sargeson's army hut from June 1951 until her departure for England in July of the following year, also do not appear. Sargeson undoubtedly wrote to Prince — a single indicative letter survives in the outwards files — but when contacted in 2009 she expressed a wish not to be involved.

A note on the text

While Sargeson appreciated the personal touch of a handwritten letter, he was a quick and accurate typist and wrote about seventy per cent of his letters that way, often using the distinctive sheets of green typing paper he liked on account of his eyes. He would generally make corrections by hand, often adding marginal notes and postscripts. Whenever possible, these marginal additions have been silently incorporated into the relevant sentence; otherwise, a note in square brackets indicates that a marginal comment has been interpolated. Postscripts might sometimes appear on the side or top of the original page, but always follow the author's signature in this edition. Not all postscripts are consequential. An ellipsis after the signature points to a postscript elided for reasons of space.

Sargeson's hand-written letters tend to clump, especially when his typewriter was on one of its many visits to the pawn shop. 'It's true this typewriter is borrowed,' he told E.P. Dawson on 6 April 1942. 'The Jews have had my own since the end of November.' He was a great user of airmail letter-cards and aerogrammes, and during the war correspondents in England and the US would sometimes receive typed or hand-written airgraphs. (This process was devised to reduce the bulk and weight of airmail. Letters were typed or written on a special form, photographed, sent by air as negatives on rolls of microfilm, and printed at their destination.) Few letters from the 1930s survive, probably due to the increasingly unsanitary conditions in the original Davey bach, which Sargeson occupied from the time he moved to Takapuna in 1931 until its removal following the construction of the new house in mid-1948.

In presenting these transcripts of Sargeson's letters, I have endeavoured to strike a balance between conveying a lively sense of the original letter and readability. I have also tried to deliver the text in a form that would have pleased him. Sargeson was a careful proof-reader of his own work, including typed letters, and was always pained to discover overlooked errors in published work. In order to avoid the intrusive and patronising [sic], I have made silent corrections where words or letters have been omitted inadvertently and an intended meaning is clear. By the same token, I have also aimed to preserve Sargeson's idiosyncrasies and preferences, taking as my guide a series of letters to his editor Bill Pearson in which he passionately defends his right to inconsistency. 'Leave as is,' he says. 'If this upsets you read Paradise Lost in original text.' To this end, I have preserved his patterns of punctuation and any eccentric or creative mis-spellings — for example, his preferred 'develope' and the occasional 'antibotic'. I have used ampersands whenever they appear in the originals. For ease of reading, however, I have normalised underlinings to italics, both for emphases and for book titles. Again, in the interests of readability, I have normalised double quote marks to single. Sargeson often opened brackets without closing them. This tendency became more pronounced as he aged. This was such a determined and often uncorrected quirk that I have left them as they appear. On the rare occasion when Sargeson uses a square bracket, which was his habit with embedded parentheses, I have used an ordinary bracket, in order to distinguish them from my own editorial insertions.

Editors of letters have different ways of introducing annotations and contextual information. Some editors still regard the original letter as sacrosanct, and introduce no explanations of their own except through an elaborate apparatus of footnotes. I follow a more recent trend. Where the information I wish to supply occupies little space — the title of a work, a surname or first name — I have interpolated the information within square brackets. I am aware intrusions of this sort may annoy some readers, but since I find constant eye-skipping from text to footnote more annoying still, I have chosen the lesser evil. Where more substantial explanations are required, I have divided material between headnotes and endnotes. The former, sometimes quoting an incoming

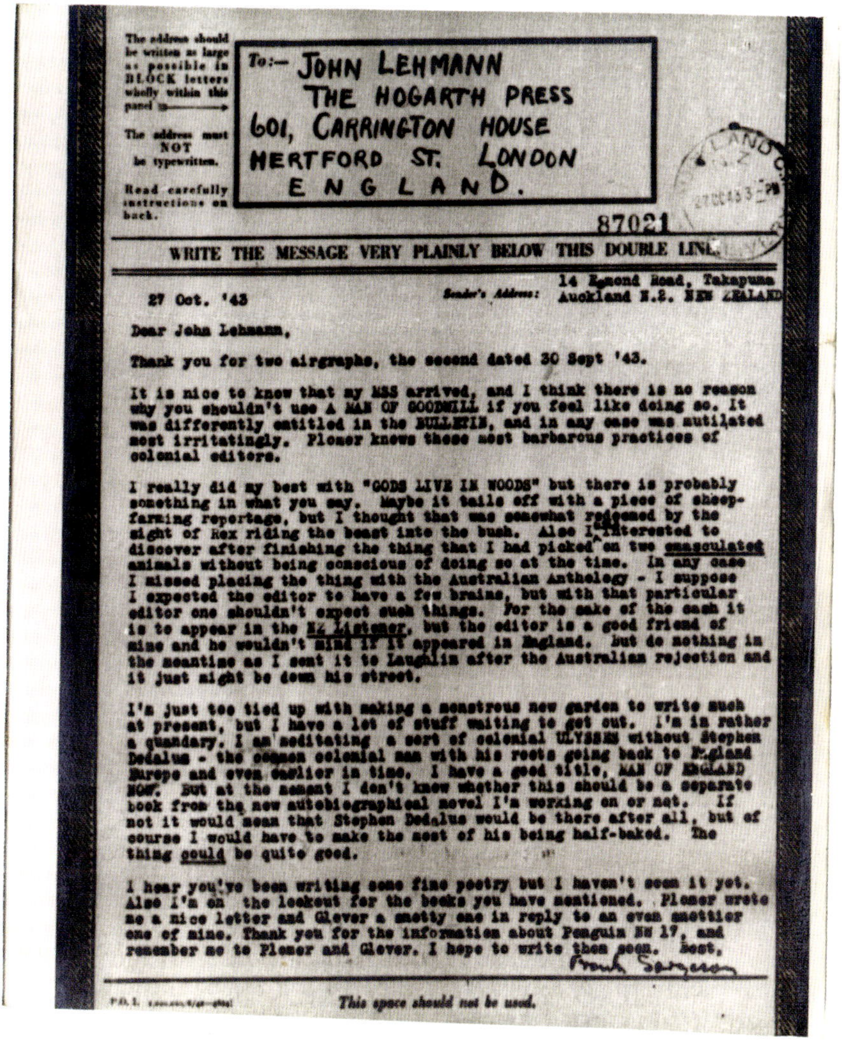

The address should be written as large as possible in BLOCK letters wholly within this panel

The address must NOT be typewritten.

Read carefully instructions on back.

To:— JOHN LEHMANN
THE HOGARTH PRESS
601, CARRINGTON HOUSE
HERTFORD ST. LONDON
E N G L A N D.

87021

WRITE THE MESSAGE VERY PLAINLY BELOW THIS DOUBLE LINE

27 Oct. '43

Sender's Address: 14 Esmond Road, Takapuna Auckland N.2. NEW ZEALAND

Dear John Lehmann,

Thank you for two airgraphs, the second dated 30 Sept '43.

It is nice to know that my MSS arrived, and I think there is no reason why you shouldn't use A MAN OF GOODWILL if you feel like doing so. It was differently entitled in the BULLETIN, and in any case was mutilated most irritatingly. Plomer knows these most barbarous practices of colonial editors.

I really did my best with "GODS LIVE IN WOODS" but there is probably something in what you say. Maybe it tails off with a piece of sheep-farming reportage, but I thought that was somewhat redeemed by the sight of Rex riding the beast into the bush. Also I was interested to discover after finishing the thing that I had picked on two emasculated animals without being conscious of doing so at the time. In any case I missed placing the thing with the Australian Anthology - I suppose I expected the editor to have a few brains, but with that particular editor one shouldn't expect such things. For the sake of the cash it is to appear in the NZ Listener, but the editor is a good friend of mine and he wouldn't mind if it appeared in England. But do nothing in the meantime as I sent it to Laughlin after the Australian rejection and it just might be down his street.

I'm just too tied up with making a monstrous new garden to write much at present, but I have a lot of stuff waiting to get out. I'm in rather a quandary. I am meditating a sort of colonial ULYSSES without Stephen Dedalus - the common colonial man with his roots going back to England Europe and even earlier in time. I have a good title, MAN OF ENGLAND NOW. But at the moment I don't know whether this should be a separate book from the new autobiographical novel I'm working on or not. If not it would mean that Stephen Dedalus would be there after all, but of course I would have to make the most of his being half-baked. The thing could be quite good.

I hear you've been writing some fine poetry but I haven't seen it yet. Also I'm on the lookout for the books you have mentioned. Plomer wrote me a nice letter and Glover a snotty one in reply to an even snottier one of mine. Thank you for the information about Penguin NW 17, and remember me to Plomer and Glover. I hope to write them soon. Best,

Frank Sargeson

This space should not be used.

letter, are reserved for contextual information it would be helpful to know prior to reading the letter; the latter supply explanations of content.

Where two copies of a letter exist I have tended to prefer the copy in the recipient files, which will include Frank's corrections, marginalia and postscripts. Sargeson's carbon copies of his own letters, generally indicated by the prefixes MS-Papers-0432 and MS-Papers-4261 in the index, are almost always unsigned. I have otherwise reproduced his signature as it appears.

All letters are from 14 Esmonde Road unless otherwise stated. Except in the case of 'official' or business letters, Sargeson didn't include his recipients' addresses on letters. As these locations are often important for context, I have deduced the whereabouts of his correspondents from envelopes and 'inwards' letters where they survive, and from internal evidence and other biographical sources where they don't. I have standardised the formatting of dates, and speculative locations and datings on undated letters appear in square brackets. Sargeson sometimes made mistakes with dates, and occasionally put the wrong year on January letters. Such emendations also appear in square brackets.

I have aimed to use complete letters wherever possible but have been obliged to introduce some elisions, always indicated thus [. . .] in the text. Sometimes I have felt a need to cut to the chase, and have reproduced one or two golden paragraphs from material that otherwise would not strongly merit selection. Elisions also allow me to avoid repetitions on Frank's part (he recycled his best anecdotes) and space-wasting explanations on mine; sometimes an elision marks a point where the author is replying in detail to a letter that has not survived. Only one such cut is 'censoring': for legal reasons, I suppressed the name of a living person who had been involved in alleged criminal activity. I have been tempted to censor Sargeson's opinions where they are obviously cruel or unfair, but in the end decided to leave them in the interest of presenting a full sense of his character. I apologise for any offence they might give.

Every effort has been made to contact Frank's living correspondents and copyright holders. In some cases, the trail ran cold; in others, the recipient details are so sketchy that the intervening years have done their own work of erasure. I apologise for any omissions or oversights.

Sarah Shieff is a senior lecturer in English in the School of Arts at the University of Waikato. She edits the *Journal of New Zealand Literature*, and writes about New Zealand literature and cultural history.

Notes on key correspondents

These notes include the people Frank Sargeson (FS) wrote to most often, but also include some correspondents with whom he exchanged few letters but who are nonetheless mentioned frequently in the archive.

Marcel Aurousseau (1891–1983), Australian geographer and writer whom FS met in London in 1927. Aurousseau had recently returned from a walking tour through France and Spain and was at work on his travel memoir *Highway into Spain (*1930). FS wrote to Aurousseau intermittently and mostly without acknowledgement until 1966 when the correspondence revived as Aurousseau awaited the proofs of his monumental edition of the letters of Ludwig Leichhardt. 13 letters (1968–1978) survive in FS's outward files.

David Ballantyne (1924–1986), novelist and journalist, met Sargeson in early 1944. *The Cunninghams*, Ballantyne's first novel, was published in the United States in 1948 and seemed to promise much, but his five subsequent novels — including *Sydney Bridge Upside Down* (1968), the Gothic masterpiece on which his reputation now rests — received little critical attention during his lifetime. 24 letters survive, 1944–1979.

James K. Baxter (1926–1972), came to FS's attention in 1945 when the young poet reviewed *When The Wind Blows* for the Canterbury Students' Association Magazine. Four letters survive, all dated 1955.

Bruce Beaver (1928–2004), the Australian poet and novelist, lived in New Zealand between 1958 and 1962 when he returned to Australia with his New Zealand wife Brenda. 77 letters survive, 1963–1979.

James Bertram (1910–1993), journalist and academic, edited the first two issues of *Phoenix* magazine, studied at Oxford, and reported from China during the Civil War until his capture by the Japanese in 1940. He returned to a lectureship in English at Victoria University in 1945 and helped found *Landfall* two years later. He was the general editor of Oxford University Press's 'New Zealand Writers and their Work' series. Six letters survive, 1971–1974.

Ralph Bodle (?1917–1991), bibliophile and amateur literary historian, lived on a small farm in Kaukapakapa. He met FS in December 1973, introduced by their mutual friend Murdoch McLean, Bodle's neighbour and FS's firewood delivery man. 64 letters (1974–1980) survive in FS's outwards correspondence files.

Charles Brasch (1909–1973), poet, editor and philanthropist, established *Landfall* magazine in 1947. The correspondence, begun the previous year when Brasch approached FS as a potential contributor, only terminated with Brasch's death in May 1973 and is largely intact: Brasch kept 374 of Sargeson's letters and Sargeson kept 253 of Brasch's. It offers an extraordinary record of their life and times.

14 Esmond Road, Takapuna, N.2

26 June '66

Dear Karl,

This business of getting Mason's play started is like one of the labours of Herakles. Also I'm about to approach the Ombudsman about Soc Sec's action in cancelling my Age pension owing to Katherine Mansfield and some other monetary assistance. Incidentally, you once spoke of the Oxford Pres as "that idiot organisation." I assure you they have nothing on Pauls-- who were asked by Soc Sec for details of payments to me over a twelve month period-- the incredible bastards included the advance of £100 paid many months before (which by the way Soc Sec accepted as correct without reference to me), and this bloody muck-up I think tipped the scales against me in Wellington. But forget it-- it's what I've been up to my neck in all my life.

About the New Poetic. My praise without reservations would be tedious, so if I seem all reservations don't believe it-- the praise is there all right-- the book is away out ahead of anything anyone else at present can or could do. But that of course doesn't mean I totally go along with you. So--

p 11 I've spoken of a point being an area-- this is a little troubling to my notions of geometry.

The 3 omissions which spring most to my mind are Hardy Housman and Bridges. Also Hopkins.

p 107 Shouldn't last word of footnote be dispens<u>a</u>ble ?

p158 It interests me that homosexuals who appear about the streets and beats from time to time are often called trade.

p 83 top of page. One of the most ify bits in the book. The comeback (equally futile) would be that Mr Stead was a poor boy verylimited etc....

I think somewhere you refer to Prufrock as "difficult" I must say I've never thought it that at all. Also I think it odd you don't draw attention to the lines beginning we have lingered in the chambers etc. Surely along with the concluding line of Byzantium these are as good as can be found in this century. I imagine the reason you <u>don't</u> draw attention to the lines is that you are not concerned with good great poetry as such (and by such, I mean without any concern for whether it's Image Discursive or anything else)-- all you are concerned with is your theory and the necessities of putting it over. In the largest sense this is of course bad-- though no doubt necessary to the making of your brilliant book.

(By the way, speaking of Byzantium, do you remember I pointed out Coleridge's Remorse Act IV Sc III - I stood in unimaginable trance/ And agony that cannot be remembered, as possibly connected with Dying into a dance/An agony of trance etc. It now strikes me that although the obvious connection of the Coleridge is with Yeats, the Coleridge tone is surprisingly like Eliot).

If I had been reviewing The New Poetic I think I would have had only trifling reservations about its brilliance, the work put into it, the logic of its argument -- all that. But what it finally amounts to is a most curious endeavour at limitation. Kubla Khan-- okay, who would want to disagree? But how many K K's can there be? One must be grateful for the Image when it turns up in Yeats and Eliot-- and Stead. But surely only a very young man would want virtually to say let's wipe most of the rest. I can only say you simply cannot do that. Also it is far far better that you should be yourself a poet who holds our attention (whether your poetry conforms to your theories or not) than that you should write the concluding half-page of your book. Too clever. No definition. A belief, a faith-- well and good, but you must risk eventual defeat by somebody who may turn up with a belief and faith in the Discursive-- Lucretius, and I can't explain the thrill I get even with my poor Latin. Or Milton, and you know how I admire there. Or

Is it the same old Puritanism?

Anyhow, let me be tedious with more congratulations-- and particularly that one watches for another book of poetry from you with breathless anticipation

Bestlove, F.S.

I went to a C.N.D. meeting & disturbed Dr Whittlestone by asking if he couldn't as a daring scientist keep the DDT & Christ knows what poison out of the milk & meat how did he suppose he was going to keep out the Strontium 90.

Christine Cole Catley (1922–2011), writer and publisher, met FS in 1947, introduced by her future husband John Reece Cole. FS made John Reece Cole his literary executor in 1953, but as Cole's health deteriorated in the 1960s FS transferred the responsibility for his estate to Christine Cole. In 1972 she divorced John and changed her name by deed poll to Christine Cole Catley, taking the surname of her new partner Douglas Catley. She established the Frank Sargeson Trust in 1982. 17 letters (1958–1980) were in her possession at the time of her death.

John Reece Cole ('Reece') (1916–1984), airman, short story writer and librarian, met FS in 1944. In his distinguished career as a librarian Cole served first with the New Zealand National Library Service, then as a UNESCO library advisor in Indonesia, and finally as the head librarian of the Alexander Turnbull Library. 231 letters survive, 1944–1975.

Rhondda Coleman ('Rhonda') (née Bosworth) (1944–), grew up in Takapuna, met FS in her mid-teens, and became part of the Bohemian set congregating around 14 Esmonde Road at the time FS was writing *Memoirs of a Peon*. Rhondda married Frank's 'bodgie' friend Andy Coleman in 1962 and moved with him to Christchurch. They are the dedicatees of FS's *The Hangover* (1967). 22 letters survive in FS's outward files.

Ray Copland (1918–2009), taught English literature at the University of Canterbury, and judged the BNZ Katherine Mansfield Award in 1965, the year FS's 'Just Trespassing, Thanks' took first prize. His *Frank Sargeson* appeared in Oxford University Press's New Zealand Writers and their Work series in 1976. 20 letters survive, 1965–1977.

James Courage (1905–1963), short story writer and novelist, lived most of his life in England. Courage's first five novels are set in his native Canterbury and focus on family conflict; his last two, *A Way of Love* (1959) and *The Visit to Penmorten* (1961), deal directly with the homosexuality that had been an implicit concern of the earlier books. The correspondence began when Courage wrote to FS to thank him for a review of his first novel, *The Fifth Child* (1948). 18 letters survive, 1949–1959.

Dan Davin (1913–1990), expatriate novelist, short story writer, historian and publisher. After military service in Greece, Crete, Egypt and Italy, Davin joined Oxford University Press, where, over a long and distinguished career, he rose from editor to Academic Publisher. The correspondence began in 1947 when FS wrote to congratulate Davin on his novel *For the Rest of Our Lives*; they first met in 1948 when Davin was in New Zealand interviewing veterans for his history of the Battle for Crete. 59 letters survive, 1947–1971.

Elizabeth Pudsey Dawson ('Peter') (1894–1986), English-born pacifist, philanthropist, self-identified lesbian and author came to New Zealand in 1925 and supported herself with a small inherited income and by working as a physiotherapist. She lived in Pelorus Sound in the 1930s and moved to Wellington at the outbreak of World War II, and from 1942 lived in a cottage near the beach at Mount Maunganui. The correspondence began in the late 1930s when Dawson wrote to FS about his sketches in *Tomorrow*; in return, Sargeson offered her criticism of her plays and stories. Dawson's work appeared in *Tomorrow*, *Arena*, *Art in New Zealand*, the Sydney *Bulletin* and the Christchurch *Press*; FS included her story 'Maria' in *Speaking for Ourselves*, and Helen Shaw included 'I Believe' in *The Puritan and the Waif*. FS and Dawson met in Auckland in 1942 and thereafter FS often visited her in Mt Maunganui. Dawson was unstinting in her generosity to other NZ writers: she supported the endeavours of Sargeson, A.R.D. Fairburn, Denis Glover and Janet Frame out of her modest means, and made Janet Frame the beneficiary of her will. Dawson returned to England in 1962. Her papers in the Hocken Library hold 278 letters from FS and a further dozen survive in the Turnbull. Together they span 1939–1976. Around 211 mostly undated letters from Dawson survive in FS's papers.

Felix Donnelly (1929–), Catholic priest, academic, and an early advocate for gay rights. He directed the Department of Community Health and Department of Psychiatry and Behavioural Science at the University of Auckland from 1972 until his retirement in 1994. Six letters survive in FS's outwards files, 1975–1980.

Robin Dudding (Bob) (1935–2008), journalist, teacher, and editor of several of New Zealand's most influential literary journals: *Mate* (1958-1966), *Landfall* (1966-1972), and *Islands* (1972–1987). *Islands* 21 (March 1978) paid tribute to FS at 75. 96 letters survive, mostly in FS's outwards correspondence files.

Maurice Duggan (1922–1974), short story writer and advertising executive, met FS early in 1944. Along with his future wife Barbara Platts and Barbara's cousin Una, Duggan formed part of the inner circle at 14 Esmonde Road, which at that time included Greville Texidor, Werner Droescher, Len and Gladys Salter and Renate Prince. Duggan kept his first 60 letters from FS in a numbered sequence, 1944–1954; a further five (1966–67) record increasing disaffection and emotional disengagement.

Toby Easterbrook-Smith (d. 8 August 1981), a lecturer at Hamilton Teachers' College, wrote FS a letter of appreciation on 16 March 1978, in time to wish him a happy 75th birthday. He wanted Frank to know how rewarding he had found teaching his fiction to classes of young adults 'picked from the farms and country towns of the King Country, the Waikato, and Bay of Plenty.' 20 letters survive, 1979–1981.

Patrick Evans (1944–), novelist, playwright, academic, wrote to FS in June 1975 asking him to confirm some general biographical information about Janet Frame for his book on Frame in the Twayne's World Authors series. Four letters survive, all from 1975.

A.R.D. Fairburn ('Rex') (1904–1957). Sargeson and Fairburn — poet, polemicist, designer, advocate for currency reform — first encountered each other in the pages of *Tomorrow* and met in 1935 when Fairburn was working for the Farmers' Union. Their close if combative friendship lasted until late 1947 when ideological differences drove them apart. Fairburn kept 11 of FS's letters, 1935–1950.

Roderick Finlayson (1904–1992), short story writer and novelist, grew up in Auckland and spent his summers working on farms in the Bay of Plenty, where he was welcomed into the whanau of Hone Ngawhika. For their time, the stories collected in *Brown Man's Burden* (1938) offer an unusually sympathetic representation of Maori experience. 83 letters survive, 1939–1980.

E.M. Forster (1879–1970). William Plomer brought *That Summer* and *I Saw in My Dream* to the English novelist's attention, and Forster wrote to FS in 1949 expressing interest in the latter especially. This selection presents the single letter to Forster surviving in Sargeson's outwards files. Three holograph letters from Forster (1949–1958) survive in FS's papers.

Janet Frame (1924–2004), poet, novelist, autobiographer. FS reviewed Frame's first collection of stories for the *Listener* in April 1952. At the time of their first meeting in late March 1955, when FS offered her the use of his army hut at 14 Esmond Road, Frame was living with her sister's family in Northcote. Frame recounts the months between April 1955 and her departure for England in July 1956 in *An Angel at My Table*, the second volume of her autobiography. They corresponded until the end of FS's life. 214 letters survive.

Maurice Gee (1931–), novelist, had known of FS since 1945, when Sargeson had included Gee's mother's story 'Double Unit' in *Speaking For Ourselves*. Gee and FS met in 1956, and kept loosely in touch from that time. 11 letters survive, 1969–1979.

Denis Glover (1912–1980), poet, printer, publisher, sailor, and another of the authors whom FS first encountered in the pages of *Tomorrow*. Glover founded the Caxton Press in Christchurch in 1935. Under his direction, and until his departure in 1951, Caxton was at the forefront of literary publishing in New Zealand. Caxton also enabled *Landfall*, which had its origins in conversations between Glover and Charles Brasch in London during the war. 83 letters survive, 1935–1978.

Eric Godley (1919–2010), FS's 'geneticist friend'. A distinguished botanist, reproductive biologist and botanical historian, Godley probably met FS through their mutual friends Maurice and Barbara Duggan. Four letters survive, 1952–1977.

John Graham (1922–), playwright, poet, horticulturalist, radio engineer. In the summer and autumn of 1957 FS spent long hours helping Graham on his market garden in Birkdale, but the packing-shed theatre they hoped to establish came to nothing. Graham was declared bankrupt and moved to the Bay of Plenty. 34 letters survive, 1956–61.

Martin Green (1932–), English writer, editor and publisher, first read FS when he was still at school, in John Lehmann's *New Writing*. He championed FS's work first at MacGibbon & Kee, and, from 1971, at his own firm of Martin Brian & O'Keeffe. 139 letters, 1963–1978, survive in FS's outwards files.

Lionel Grindlay (1906–1984), Invercargill-born civil servant, journalist and aspiring novelist, visited Auckland in 1944 and sought out FS, who had been writing supportively to Grindlay's fellow Southlander Alec Pickard. Grindlay's novel *Zig-Zag* remains unpublished. One letter, dated 1945, survives in FS's outwards files.

Max Harris (1921–1995), Australian poet, novelist, critic and publisher, and the driving force behind the literary journal *Angry Penguins* (1940–46). FS set the tenor of their correspondence in 1944 when he wrote to Harris affirming his decision to publish the 'Ern Malley' poems but admonishing him for the rashness of his blurb. FS included Harris's 'The Papeye and the Molacca' in *Speaking for Ourselves*. 11 letters from Harris and three from FS survive, 1944–c.1946.

Raymond Hawthorne (1936–), actor, director and teacher of drama. At the time of their correspondence Hawthorne was the director of Auckland's Theatre Corporate, which he had founded in 1973. Two letters from 1978 survive.

Joseph Heenan (1888–1951), senior public servant, writer, horse-racing enthusiast. As under-secretary for Internal Affairs (1935–1949) Heenan was responsible for cultural patronage in New Zealand. He oversaw the New Zealand Centennial Celebrations and the landmark historical surveys of 1939–40, and facilitated the establishment of the New Zealand Literary Fund in 1946. He was personally responsible for an additional Cultural Fund, which disbursed surplus art union profits, and drew the literary pension he arranged for FS in1947 from this source. Seven letters survive, 1947–50.

Kennaway Henderson (1879–1960), cartoonist, journalist and editor, Henderson founded the radical left-wing magazine *Tomorrow* in 1934. *Tomorrow* ran initially weekly, and then fortnightly until June 1940, when it closed under government pressure. Two letters survive, both from 1935.

David Hill (1942–), journalist, novelist, playwright and children's author, taught for fourteen years, including at Takapuna Grammar School (1967–1974), before turning to full-time writing. The selection presents both surviving letters, from 1971.

M. H. Holcroft ('Monte') (1902–1994), journalist, essayist, editor and novelist, joined the *Southland Times* in 1937, and wrote a positive review of *A Man and His Wife* for that paper in 1940. FS initiated a correspondence following the publication of Holcroft's *The Deepening Stream* in 1940. The relationship deteriorated after Holcroft succeeded Oliver Duff as the editor of the *Listener* in 1949. 17 letters survive, 1940–1966.

Alan Horsman (1918–), professor of English at the University of Otago and a friend of Charles Brasch, was the academic most closely involved in establishing the Burns Fellowship in 1959. Four letters survive, 1959–1978.

Kevin Ireland (né Jowsey) (1933–), poet and novelist, grew up in Takapuna, and first met FS while delivering newspapers to his next-door neighbours. He later became a frequent visitor, and lived for a time in FS's army hut. Ireland left for London in 1959, and spent most of the next 25 years overseas. 55 letters survive, c.1957–1979.

Lawrence Jones (1934–), academic and historian of New Zealand fiction, was born in Los Angeles and came to New Zealand in 1964 to take up a position in the English Department at the University of Otago. Two letters survive in FS's outwards files, 1972–73.

Rodney Kennedy (1909–1989), artist, drama tutor and theatre director. Dunedin-born Kennedy was a passionate advocate for contemporary New Zealand art and theatre, championing the work of Toss Woollaston and Colin McCahon in particular. He produced plays for amateur dramatic societies and, from 1948, tutored drama at the University of Otago. After his retirement in 1971 he was director at Dunedin's Globe Theatre. One letter survives, from 1955.

Michael King (1945–2004), journalist, historian, film-maker and biographer, met FS in 1977. Their friendship grew as FS's health deteriorated. King was a foundation member of the Sargeson Trust and FS's authorised biographer. Four letters survive, 1977–1980.

James Laughlin (1914–1997), publisher, editor, poet, was born in Pittsburgh, Pennsylvania, the son of a steel magnate. His New Directions publishing company, founded in 1936, was at the forefront of modern American letters. An annual anthology of new writing, *New Directions in Poetry and Prose*, began in 1936 and carried work by Ezra Pound, Gertrude Stein, William Carlos Williams and others; Sargeson appeared in several issues between 1938 and 1946. 38 letters from FS survive in Laughlin's papers in the Houghton Library, 1937–1980.

Graeme Lay (1944–), writer of short stories, novels, and non-fiction, grew up in Taranaki and attended Victoria University of Wellington. He approached FS for advice about his writing in 1975; his first novel, *The Mentor* — loosely based on his friendship with FS — appeared in 1978. He was a frequent visitor in Sargeson's last years. Two letters survive, both from 1975.

John Lehmann (1907–1987), English poet, editor and publisher, was editing the literary magazine *New Writing* for the Hogarth Press when he came across *Conversation with My Uncle*. FS became a regular contributor to various journals edited by Lehmann, including *New Writing* (1935–40), *Folios of New Writing* (1940–41), *New Writing and Daylight* (1943–1946) and the monthly *Penguin New Writing* (1940–50), which had a circulation of up to 100,000 copies. Lehmann established his own company in 1946 and published *That Summer and Other Stories* the same year; *I Saw in My Dream* followed in 1949. Through Sargeson, Lehmann met Denis Glover and Charles Brasch in London during the war, and eventually published poems and stories by Brasch, Glover, Roderick Finlayson, Allen Curnow and A.R.D. Fairburn. 78 letters (1938–1975) survive across Lehmann's papers in the Harry Ransom Research Center (University of Austin at Texas), the Princeton University Library, and in FS's outwards files.

E.H. McCormick (1906–1995), historian, archivist, curator and biographer, was born in Taihape and educated at Victoria University College and at Clare College, Cambridge. He returned to New Zealand in 1933, and in 1935 Joseph Heenan appointed him secretary of the National Centennial Historical Committee where he helped shape the centennial publication programme. His landmark *Letters and Art in New Zealand* (1940) was revised and updated as *New Zealand Literature: A Survey* in 1959. In 1951 he and FS selected the contents of the Oxford 'World's Classics' *New Zealand Short Stories*. Other works include biographies of Frances Hodgkins and Omai, an edition of Augustus Earle's writings, and the memoir *The Inland Eye*. 62 letters survive, 1940–1979.

Dennis McEldowney (1926–2003), author and publisher. FS initiated a correspondence in 1945 after reading McEldowney's story 'By The Lake'. They met briefly at the Christchurch Writers' Conference of 1951 and again the following year in Bayswater, where McEldowney was recuperating from surgery for a congenital heart defect. He became the first editor at Auckland University Press in 1966, and remained there until his retirement in 1986. 53 letters survive, 1945–1980.

Murdoch McLean ('Murdie') (?1912–2000), an impoverished subsistence farmer living on a decaying property in Kaukapakapa, began delivering firewood to FS in the early 1970s. From 1973 until his ill-fated marriage to a much younger woman in 1976, 'M' was the strongest thread in Sargeson's emotional life, and the steadiest drain on his resources. 14 letters survive, 1973–1980.

Ronald Hugh Morrieson (1922–1972), novelist, short story writer and musician. *The Scarecrow* and *Came a Hot Friday* were little noticed in his lifetime but are now regarded as New Zealand classics. FS wrote a prescient appreciation in *Landfall* in 1971. Five letters survive in FS's outwards files, 1971–1972.

Vincent O'Sullivan (1937–), poet, short story writer, novelist, playwright, academic. FS had noted O'Sullivan's poems and stories in *Landfall* and elsewhere, and wrote to him in August 1974 to congratulate him on his story 'Letter from Orpheus'. Five letters survive in FS's outwards files, 1974–1978.

W.H. Pearson ('Bill') (1922–2002), novelist, essayist and academic. Born on the West Coast, Pearson served in the army during the war, completed a PhD in London in 1952, and taught in the English Department at the University of

Auckland from 1959 to 1986. Pearson read 'That Summer' in 1943 in *Penguin New Writing* and had been greatly impressed, and FS knew of Pearson's essay 'Fretful Sleepers' (1951), but their first contacts, in letters and then in person in 1954, were inauspicious. That began to change following the publication of Pearson's novel *Coal Flat* in 1963. 63 letters survive, 1963–1977.

Alexander Gaskell Pickard ('Alec') (1913–2006), short story writer and teacher. Born in North Otago and educated in Southland and Dunedin, Pickard was already publishing under his pseudonym A.P. Gaskell when FS wrote to him in 1942 to congratulate him on his stories in the *Listener*. FS assumed an active mentoring role and reviewed Gaskell's *The Big Game and Other Stories* (1947) in the first issue of *Landfall*. They met for the first time at the Christchurch Writers' Conference of 1951 and infrequently thereafter: Pickard taught at Southland Boys' High from 1943–1960, and then at Fairfield College in Hamilton until his retirement in 1974. 72 letters survive, 1942–1978.

William Plomer (1903–1973), South African-born novelist, poet and editor, was a reader for Jonathan Cape in London when Sargeson sent him *Conversation with My Uncle* in about 1938. Plomer responded with a friendly letter, now lost. Both sides of the surviving correspondence (1942–1973) are held in the Alexander Turnbull Library: FS kept 91 of Plomer's letters (1945–1973) and Plomer kept 104 of FS's, 1942–1973.

H. Winston Rhodes (1905–1987), Australian-born professor of English at the University of Canterbury and a life-long socialist, was working with Kennaway Henderson and Frederick Sinclaire on the production of *Tomorrow* when he first encountered FS's sketches. Rhodes helped found the left-leaning *New Zealand Monthly Review* in 1960, which, under his editorship (1960–68), carried poetry and essays by Rewi Alley, James K. Baxter, Charles Brasch, Janet Frame, John A. Lee and others. 87 letters survive, 1968–1980.

Helen Shaw ('Hella') (1913–1985), short story writer, poet, editor and journalist. FS included her story 'Noah' in *Speaking for Ourselves*, and work also appeared in *Islands*, *Numbers*, *Landfall*, *Here & Now*, the *Listener* and elsewhere. Shaw edited and self-published *The Puritan and the Waif* (1954), a symposium of critical essays on FS. In 1941 she married the Czech photographer Frank Hofmann (1916–1989), who had arrived in Auckland in 1940 as a refugee from Nazism. 63 letters survive, 1948–1978.

Keith Sinclair (1922–1993), Auckland-born historian and poet. The first of several editions of his best-selling *History of New Zealand* appeared in 1957. Sinclair joined the Department of History at the University of Auckland in 1947, where he taught until retirement, and is closely associated with the development of a proudly nationalist school of New Zealand historiography based on empirical research. 14 letters survive, 1950–1967.

Kendrick Smithyman (1922–1995), poet, critic and university lecturer, recalled being provoked and puzzled by 'Sale Day' when he read it in James Laughlin's *New Directions*. He met the author first in 1943. After his war service Smithyman taught at primary and intermediate school, and in 1963 joined the English Department of the University of Auckland where he remained until his retirement in 1987. 13 letters survive, 1949–1952.

C.K. Stead ('Karl') (1932–), poet, novelist, short story writer and academic. Stead invited FS to talk to the Auckland University College Students' Literary Society in 1954. Stead and his wife Kay soon became close friends of FS, and were living nearby in Takapuna at the time Janet Frame was working in the hut at 14 Esmonde Road — a period recalled in Stead's novel *All Visitors Ashore* (1984). The Steads moved to Armidale, NSW in 1956, and from there to Bristol in the United Kingdom, where Stead undertook the doctoral research that would become *The New Poetic* (1964). Stead returned to the English Department of the University of Auckland in 1959, where he remained until his retirement in 1986. He was a foundation member of the Sargeson Trust. 142 letters survive, 1954–1977.

Dorothy Sutherland (1917–2010), the daughter of Dominic ('Don') Doran (1888–1950), who befriended FS in Wellington in 1928. 20 letters survive in FS's outwards files, 1971–1980.

Greville Texidor (1902–1964), English-born novelist and short story writer, arrived in New Zealand with her third husband Werner Droescher in 1940. They settled on the North Shore and became part of FS's inner circle. The family moved to Australia in 1948 and to Spain in 1954; Texidor returned alone to Australia in 1962 and died there in 1964. 10 letters survive, 1945–1950.

Phillip Wilson (1922–2001), novelist, short story writer and journalist, was born in Lower Hutt and attended Auckland Teachers' College at the same time as Kendrick Smithyman and Keith Sinclair. He served in the RNZAF during World War II, and became known as a short story writer in the late 1940s; during his lifetime he published five novels, two collections of stories, and two biographical studies of William Satchell. Wilson, David Ballantyne, Bill Pearson and John Graham — plus the sculptor Anthony Stones and FS's neighbour John Jenkins — were pall-bearers at Sargeson's funeral. 52 letters to Wilson survive, 1961–1977.

The Letters 1927–1939

To Joyce Davey, *Hamilton*

Alexander Turnbull Library

[A postcard to FS's younger sister sent at the start of a two-month walking tour of Europe, July–August 1927.]

12 Juillet [July] 1927, Paris

Dear Joyce

La vie Parisienne. Les vins! Les dîners! les theatre! Les folies! mais c'est très difficile tout seule. Never mind I am having a wonderful time & if I can survive the two months I can survive anything. It is hard to get enough to eat. Petit dejeuner is the most meagre meal I know of. Paris water is not fit to drink & it is absolutely necessary to drink wine or beer. The wine is good & cheap & the beer is very nice & very light. Taxis are cheap. Half an hour costs 10 francs — 1/8.

Love Norris

To Fred Bush, *London*

Alexander Turnbull Library

[FS made friends with Fred Bush and his wife Lucy soon after his arrival in London in April 1927. Frank and Fred became lovers in May.]

2 [August] 1927, Reconvilier, Switzerland

Dear Fred

Tonight I am sharing a hotel with half the Swiss Army. It has occupied every room except the one left over for me. I shall now be able to tell all my belligerent acquaintances to be sure & join the Swiss Army, because instead of camping out, it lives in hotels, sleeps in French beds feeds on Hors d'Oeuvres Pommes saute & salade, & dances in cabarets to the accompaniment of concertinas & violins played by callow youths from the sawmills.

You will see by the enclosed cards that I am amid fine scenery, but the walk today was not satisfactory. My tummy has the collywobbles again, there are ulcers in my throat & a large blister on a foot. Heavy rain fell overnight & this morning when I set out, the tops of the mountains were shrouded in heavy black clouds from which wisps would continually detach themselves, to float down the valleys and descend on one like a breath of wind off a snow-field. The ground was too sodden to enable me to take rests & in anycase, one becomes so soaked with perspiration that to stand still for even a few seconds is to feel the cold creeping into the flesh.

Just on 4 o'clock the sky suddenly dropped in a thunderstorm & I was lucky to be within reach of this shelter. The hotelkeeper is an Alpin Club member & as he speaks

English he has explained the whole route & tomorrow he is going to set me off on a track which goes over the top of the range. When I reach the top (if ever) I am to find some sort of hermit who I suppose will be dressed in sack cloth, have a beard to his ankles, white streaming locks, & carry a crooked stick in his hand. Anyhow this anchorite will guide me through the trackless forest & set me right for downstairs. Sounds rather exciting doesn't it? Perhaps the old man will ask me to live with him for ever, & every evening we will sit on some lofty crag & watch the sun go down. At any rate a robe of gunny sacking wouldn't bag at the knees would it? But I am so 'intrigué' by mine host's description of the view that I think I shall have a shot at it. He also tells me not to go to Lausanne but to pass through Berne & thence take a magnificent path which is impossible in winter but passable in summer. It enters the Bernese Alps at Spiez & comes out at Leuk & both upstairs & downstairs one can see the famous peaks of all the Alps. I am also inclined to be guided by him as to this portion especially as he assures me that the route I had intended taking is as hot as the road from Basle to Delémont & that was as hot as h__l. [. . .]

I have seen many cement & iron works today stuck in the valleys right between the sheer rock faces & at present I am in the midst of the district where all the watches & clocks are made. My own watch is a Swiss. What a journey it has had since it was first assembled. I shouldn't be surprised if it starts to play up as I draw it away once more from its native soil. Am sorry you didn't like my letter from Molsheim but can't remember what it was about. If you think I'm a pessimist you are mistaken. I am an optimistic pessimist who always looks on the bright side of gloomy things & the gloomy side of bright things thus maintaining a healthy insanity. To be healthily insane is the only way to get the best out of life. Most of us try to be sane, & only do reasonable things, but it makes us frightfully miserable & bores us to death — if we will only admit it etc etc etc . . . Quite enough.

Was glad to hear you have eaten all the peas but trust a few caterpillars were shrewd enough to eat a few also. Please note that I daily remove many caterpillars (& oftimes slugs about 9 inches long) from the danger zone of the roadway into the comparative safety (when you & Mrs Bush are in England) of the grass. What with the garden, your mother & work & whatnot I can see your hands must be full so I think I had better discontinue these distracting notes. During the past 3 weeks I have written 1½ chapters of my first, only, & immortal (immoral?) novel entitled — no I won't tell you the title but when it is published in 3 volume form you will receive a copy gratis.

I really think I will give you breathing space for a week or so, so farewell until then.

Yours as ever.

Frank.

['my first novel': FS abandoned 'The Story of Harry Weston' soon after his return to London.]

To Lucy Bush, *London*

Alexander Turnbull Library

15 August 1927, Milan

Dear Miss Bush,

(I really can't rack up the audacity to address you any other way) I received your letter & Fred's P.P.P.S. this morning; also the snaps, which do not do me justice. I am much worse to look at than they show me. However I was delighted to receive all; letters, p.scripts & snaps, & to know that you are all safe & sound. I can't give you any more addresses as my movements are extremely fickle. I am like the wind — liable to sudden changes, storms, tempests, & sudden calms. Florence is too far from London. Venice is likewise. Southern France is too hot. German railways are too dear. Switzerland I've seen. It looks as though I'll have to pass right round the world to get back. So I think instead of writing, you had just better wait for 4 sharp taps on your front door & listen for them on any evening after the 23rd & before the 31st. This morning I went to Cook's office to try & solve the problem, & after I had absorbed 20 minutes of one man's time I found that all quotes were for 2nd class travel. They do not deal in 3rd class tickets as they say no one ever demands them. I told them to make a note of my demand & said 'good day,' so now I can see I am in for a fine time obtaining a ticket from an Italian firm; but perhaps the office boy will speak English or French.

When I left Meina I walked to Sesto which is right on the edge of the endless plain of Lombardy. My miserable heart failed me, but I am not very ashamed, for it is flatter than a pancake, richer than a fruitcake, & seems to swelter & simmer under the sun like an omelet. So I took the train to find Milan in the very centre, & hotter almost than a tropical city. Nevertheless the mornings & evenings are not so unbearably hot & I have spent several hours in the cathedral ('duomo' they call it in Italian) which no doubt you have seen in pictures. It is Gothic architecture in what is called its decadent period, but for all that, it is a wonderful work, built all of white marble with (I should say) about 100 spires, each capped by a statue. The vastness of the interior is more than I can describe, likewise the windows. Besides the cathedral I am anxious to see the 'Last Supper' by Leonardo da Vinci, but everything is closed up today on account of a sort of Bank Holiday. I have found that for buying tickets, enquiring the way & obtaining food etc the Italian tongue is easier than either French or German, & it is delightful to listen to the natives speak. Vowels are not clipped off short, & each vowel has only one sound.

Well, well, this afternoon is a good time to get the washing done, so au revoir.

Yours sincerely,

Frank

P.S. Very glad to hear the garden is looking gay. Who will look after it during the holidays?

16.8.27. P.P.S.

Just another line to let you know I am going on to Genoa & perhaps Florence by train & foot, but *please don't write* as plans may be changed.

Today I was delighted to meet again my lovely lady of 52, of my Swiss travels, & we spent a splendid afternoon together. I hope I won't meet her again, because if I do I'm sure I shall go off my head & ask her to marry me.

Besides the post-cards I have sent on to you, I find I have 56 in my possession & I suppose a further dozen have been posted off to New Zealand. It has become a perfect mania & it was only by a superhuman effort I refrained from buying small reproductions of 'The Last Supper' which thrilled me with all sorts of emotions, as no other painting ever has done.

Well, well, farewell until near the end of the month.

F.

[There is a five-year gap between this pencil draft and the next surviving outwards letter, dated 9 July 1932. ATL MS-Papers-0432-140.]

To Kennaway Henderson, *Christchurch*

Alexander Turnbull Library

[Henderson, the editor of the left-wing fortnightly Tomorrow *(1934–1940), had written to FS thanking him for submitting 'A Piece of Yellow Soap': 'I have enjoyed this, all but the last three or four words. To me they rather spoil your sketch. [. . .] Isn't "he felt ashamed of himself" rather obscure?' Henderson had also asked FS to approach likely Auckland subscribers and contributors to* Tomorrow*. ATL MS-Papers-0432-168.]*

10 August 1935

Dear Henderson,

Your letter to hand. I will see [Prof. Arthur] Sewell [William Hollis] Cocker Fairburn and Mason and continue to try to do what I can. There are difficulties of course. I am often marooned on the North Shore for lack of finance.

About the sketch, I am at a loss to know how to alter it. It's ludicrous to try to explain these things. I try to get my effect through implication and suggestion. I imagine there are enough implications in the last paragraph to occupy the attention of a Bench of Bishops for six months. In the last few words what I imply, I suppose, is that no matter how life may be organised it is a dreadful business, and that the Creator (if any) might conceivably be quite overwhelmed and devastated by a woman entering heaven with a lump of soap. Symbolism of course. Use it or not as you please. I shan't take the slightest offence. So little of my writing has been published that I have grown a thick skin, and I am grateful indeed to Tomorrow for publishing such fantastic comments on life. [. . .]

I may say I am very 'left' in my views, but when I sit down to write whatever there is of the artist in me gets the upper hand. The business of seeing these more or less university people is rather difficult for me. I have never mixed much with such people. At the moment I am very unsettled. I am in touch with [the actor and director] Auriol Lee and [the London theatrical agents] A.D. Peters and there is, apparently, every chance of my getting a play produced in England. At the moment I am altering and developing my play to suit these people and have at least a month's solid work ahead, and may not find time to prepare my odd pieces for Tomorrow. I shall try to keep them going. My play by the way is a somewhat bitter comedy set in N.Z. (not so thin as [Merton] Hodge's [*The Wind and the Rain*], I hope) and if it is successful I shall follow it up with a hot 'left' one. I'm afraid I have the vice of keeping very much to myself. The few people that have encouraged me I know, in most cases, by letter only. Dr. Duncan for instance has been an immense source of encouragement for years, but I have never met him. I will keep on doing my best and report from time to time, and you will understand that if I do not contribute for a time, it is because my circumstances don't allow me the time.

Yours sincerely,

[FS's hopes for a production of his 'boarding house' play 'Secret Places' came to nothing. The correspondence between FS and Dr. John Donald Campbell Duncan (1881–1942), the Government Balneologist at Rotorua's Bath House, lapsed after their one brief meeting. The letters appear not to have survived.]

To the Rations Department, *Department of Labour, Auckland*

Alexander Turnbull Library

21 October 1935

Dear Sir,

[. . .] With reference to your memo of 1st. inst: I regret having to refer to you again but I do not see any chance of my being self-supporting at the end of this month. All my available spare cash has been expended in manure and tomato plants. 160 plants have been put in and another 160 will be planted immediately it rains again.

Would it be possible to continue the sustenance payments in the meantime.

Otherwise I do not see any alternative but to offer myself for camp work in which case my work will have been wasted and my chances of being self-supporting until May of next year destroyed. I am faithfully showing each week the money I receive for my produce, and until I show that I am receiving an amount sufficient to pay my way I should be grateful if the sustenance payments could be continued.

Will you please advise me.

Yours faithfully,

To Denis Glover, *Christchurch*

Alexander Turnbull Library

[By November 1935 several of FS's stories had appeared in Tomorrow; *the parodies of New Zealand prose writers to which he refers were published in 1937 and 1938. Glover to FS, 9 November 1935: 'By all means let me see your play.' ATL MS-Papers-0432-166.]*

13 November 1935

Dear D.G.

Thanks for the letter. Only one or two of the sketches really satisfy me. I've been thinking of changing over to some parodies. 'Boys & Girls' by Isabel K. Peaton. 'How I Write' by Alan B. Multanga 'The Teeny Land' by James Bluffby etc.

I certainly think the Press has done outstanding work. I see it in the Library of course.

To get the bouquets over: I get a great kick out of your verse & Fairburn's. Curnow's worries me, as Auden's & Spender's worries me — makes me feel obtuse & dated. Frankly I think Mason has done the best in N.Z. Queerly he's not in quite the same tradition. He writes *clichés* but he gets there. There's a piece — Fragment in one of his penny broadsheets that's a real skull-lifter. The P.K. squibs are a delight. [Glover's *Tomorrow* pseudonym, Peter Kettle.] It's along those lines my mind runs. I'm so fearfully shy & tongue-tied that I feel I have to get my own back somehow & that's why I write.

Well I am sending the play ['Secret Places'], and you must say what you think. Marris read it. He said it wasn't up to publication standard; that I'd evidently never lived in a boarding house (Oh God!)

Some years ago I ventured to write a novel ['Blind Alleys'] & Jonathan Cape got me to alter it for him; then he said conditions were too hard. I'd only consent to publication now on the condition that I'd be free to violently attack it in all the literary journals in the Empire. Of course I've a dozen or so short stories & I'm putting one in with the play for you to see. I think however the best work I've done so far is in the play.

You must get a heap of fun out of running the Press. I've been farm-labourer, milkman, whatnot, & my garden is in such a sorry plight at the moment that I can see a Relief Camp ahead if Peters doesn't hurry up & get a production.

Tomorrow really is a quite too noble effort. Henderson must be one of the world's great enthusiasts. I'm always on the point of getting new subs but never quite get there.

If you did decide to reprint any of the sketches I'd like to make a few alterations here & there.

Yours sincerely,

Frank Sargeson

P.S. The layout of the play in the typescript is I think, fairly satisfactory. For printing my idea is, brackets & italics for stage directions inside the dialogue: italics without brackets for directions etc. outside the dialogue.

I'm not the prolific writer that you might think from the above. I began writing in 1929 am 32 now & feel 60. (Too much 'I', I think).

To Sherwood Anderson, *[USA]*

Alexander Turnbull Library

[An unsigned and undated manuscript.]

[1935]

Dear Mr Anderson,

This letter has to be written. I have tried not to write it, struggled with myself, but it is no good struggling.

I have never written to a writer before, nor tried to see or talk to one. A year ago Mr Bernard Shaw came to New Zealand but although I have read him all through I did not trouble to take a look at him. Why should I write to you? I haven't read you all through — some of your books are hard to come by in this country. Well, you are not like Mr Shaw. Lots of people must write to Mr Shaw but somehow I think he would never care if nobody ever wrote to him. Lots of people must write to you, but not so many. I wonder what they say. Horrible terrible things I know a lot must, but others would tell you of their love for you, though they mightn't say it openly.

I wish I wasn't a writer fellow myself. (Perhaps you have already guessed that I too can work with words. Perhaps not) I'd rather I was a farmer, farming in the middle of one of our swamps, who had read something of yours, perhaps only a few pages, & had just written you a few ridiculous lines, in pencil perhaps, leaving off ploughing to squat on a stump, and addressing them 'Sherwood Anderson Esq., Author, U.S.A.'

Well, I don't know what I've got to say. Why should the words you have written come into my life as they have, come right deep into my life, & why should the words of other writers never have come so deep? There it is. Before I had ever read anything of yours I had beaten out my way of bringing out my words something like you do. But it is much deeper than that. When I cry over my reading I don't cry because any tragedy has happened to the characters, I cry because of the craft of the writer, because his craft has lighted him through a life that has been so complicated, secret, disguised. It is a sacred thing. And there are people who say: 'why don't you —' 'you ought to —' To hell, I say, with such people. You would understand that. Then scraps of conversation are where I jump off from very often, and sometimes people say strange things to me. A few days ago the little man who brings bread to my bach looked at me and said a strange thing. He knew he could say it to me, and he knew that because he wanted to say it, even though we should never see each other again, there would always be something between us. And he wanted there to be something between us. Sometimes I wish your characters would talk more. I like plays that are all talk. I have written a comedy and I prove what a brilliant, witty, wise, sophisticated fellow I am — oh, I assure you. But I know you are right. All this talk is trickery. It doesn't happen in life, and even though the inside life of your characters can never be proved to be true (it will always be thought of in relation to your name) it is nevertheless far nearer to truth than the playwrights can ever get.

Of course we have our writers in this country. Such pretty pretty fellows, yet when they run away from their country and like Mr Bolitho squeeze literary juice out of Royal Personages it is hard to blame them. How would you have felt, Mr. Anderson, if you had known that in your own country there was not one paper or magazine that was looking for anything except shoddy stuff. If you had dropped your MSS. in the post & known that it would be weeks & weeks before an editor would see them and weeks & weeks & weeks before they would come back. Would even you have fallen down — I mean permanently? I know you wouldn't have, but — well next door is Australia. There is nothing much there and month by month over there, as here, your terrible magazines, back-dated ones, are dumped in their thousands. They are sort of missionary magazines, they try to convert everybody to a belief in writing as just a matter of great quantities of printed paper.

No, there is nowhere to send out M.S.S. to but your own country & England, and that means if they are published, less than a score, perhaps of our own countrymen will ever read them. Once Mr Squire (now Sir John of course) said he nearly took a story of mine for the London Mercury, one of the editors of New Stories (I think it must have been Mr. H.E. Bates) said 'please send some more of your work' but if these stories had been published how many of my own countrymen, those that I try to understand and write about, would read them? Not any, as likely as not. A novel would stand more chance and once I nearly knocked myself out getting one finished (and such a bad one too) and Mr. Jonathan Cape asked me to make some alterations: then he said conditions were too bad.

But I am complaining too much. There is nothing to this letter. I have never written to a writer before & I don't suppose I ever will again. Read it, Mr Anderson, because of something in me that your words have stirred up over years, something passionate, something that will not give me peace, but perhaps may if I post this away. It is with pain that I tell you I cannot give you my name and address. You might think I am asking for help, you might send me a line or two, you might not. No, it is impossible. It is enough if, because I have written this, you may, now & then, hold your pen the faintest bit firmer, draw your line the faintest bit sharper. I know the way you put your words together will make a sort of music at the back of my heart all my life.

[Hector Bolitho (1898–1974) was best known for his popular biographies of royalty.]

To Denis Glover, *Christchurch*

Alexander Turnbull Library

[FS's first collection of stories, Conversation with My Uncle and Other Sketches *was published in 1936 by Bob Lowry at the Unicorn Press, Auckland.]*

3 June 1936

Dear Glover,

Disappointment over not being able to make the Tamaroa that sailed 22nd last month [for London] caused me to decide on bringing out the sketches. A very sudden decision. I pawned my typewriter & got a bit of backing & the job was put in hand right away. Estimated cost £9.6.7 for 500 copies. 32 pages, stapled. I thought of you of course, but decided to rush it on here. Have to sell them myself & through booksellers — price 1/- or 1/6 — haven't decided yet. I must get my typewriter back & pay my backers back. Have had to let a chance of sailing on Trojan Star on the 6th slide, but it was only passage-working. No wages. At the moment however I have a kitchen job in a restaurant & after it shall have better chance of getting signed on in the ordinary way.

I feel I've simply got to go & find out definitely if my play can get produced. I want to know one way or the other & if after pestering various people in England I find it's the other, well, I suppose I shall come back here. But personal pestering does produce results as I've recently found with the 'Star.'

I saw the poem you did of Mason's ['End of Day']. A very nice job. And I believe you're doing something of [D'Arcy] Cresswell's with a crackerjack title — I can't remember what just now ['Eeena Deena Dynamo']. I don't see Cresswell much. I believe I'm the only person besides himself who's read his Anthology & Thesis in their final forms. Oh God! The man will always have my admiration because he's a man of spirit, obviously; but I have the idea that at the root of his theory of life & poetry there isn't anything more exciting than a psychological mess. Psycho. messes are valuable, doubtless, but not valuable enough to produce the earth-quaking work that Cresswell thinks he's producing. [. . .]

All the best

F.S

To Denis Glover, *Christchurch*

Alexander Turnbull Library

[Glover's story 'Death and the Maiden' appeared in Tomorrow, *20 January 1937.]*

26 January [1937]

Dear Glover,

I enjoyed so much your story of Mr. Death that I must write you a letter. You & I, of course, are the only people in N.Z. who can write short stories. Place either of us beside, say, Mr Holcroft, & what have you? (Don't, though, repeat this to Holcroft). His mediocrity is appalling. And his technique! My God! Isn't there a bit in Tchekov about if you have a gun hanging on the wall on the first page of a short story it must be most excitingly discharged on a succeeding page? Well, in that story of Holcroft's 'The Trees' [*Tomorrow*, Sept. 1936], what became of the telegram? I was irritated beyond words. But anyhow there's nothing even faintly interesting that I can see about Holcroft's people.

Of course with you & me, besides our people, there's you & me, your bright & eager exuberance & my — but modesty won't let me carry on.

You took me in, though. For all my suspicions until the 7th paragraph I really did expect a tale of passion. Though I should have known better, because no one who's writing a tale of a great passion says that he is. Do you know Maupassant's story, The Chair-mender? Only a few pages but maybe the greatest thing about passion ever done. Did you, though, when you began, intend to write the real thing, & then drift off into an 'idea'? Is this my old criticism about your stories not being 3 dimensional? I don't say that the highest literature can't be the 'idea' sort. Nearly all Shaw's plays are, & God knows, I've read the lot often enough, & Shaw's certain enough of a rock well up towards the top of Parnassus in my opinion. The queer thing about myself is that although I've always been enormously attracted to the 'idea' of writing, right from my earliest attempts I always tried to make something out of the things that I'd seen happen or guessed had happened in the lives of the people I'd known. Perhaps it's all a matter of temperament. D'Arcy [Creswell], of course, maintains that to understand the common passions of men you must be subject to uncommon passions yourself, in order that from your detached point of view you can see clearly what you wouldn't see if you were involved yourself. There may be something in it. If, for example, Somerset Maugham is very much of a homosexual as so many people have told me that he is, it's a case in point. His detachment & his comprehension are both highly developed, yet possibly he has a great deal of experience that he never taps & probably would make a mess of it if he did. [Marginal note: About Maugham. Have you ever read 'Of Human Bondage'? It's on the same scale as 'The Way of All Flesh' & no less powerful.] Anyhow this is getting away from the point. There's no one in N.Z. who can do 'idea' writing of the quality of 'Plot & Counterplot' [*Tomorrow*, Oct. 1936] & 'Death & the Maiden' & both, I think, are a great advance on your '3 Stories'. The first, of course, came nearest to being lifelike of anything of yours I've read, but I liked the 2nd the better.

I've at last read [Robin Hyde's] 'Passport to Hell' [1936]. It's an obscene book. Where's the point? Thousands of soldiers had the same experiences but why write them up ('write-up' is a good word to describe the book) if you can't infuse some profound & tragic significance into them. And Iris [Wilkinson/Robin Hyde] hasn't the faintest ability to do that. Stark may be quite a decent fellow. She has turned him into an animal, and I find her sentimental caressing of this animal revolting. And the bad prose!

About the Catholic Church. What exactly is happening in Spain I don't know. But I do know that if you add the Catholic understanding of human experience to the Greek you get something valuable. I can't make my mind up about machines & Karl Marx & Russia yet. Communist attempts to deal with anything beyond the mechanics of existence seem to me on a level with Y.M.C.A. summer camps.

No more this time,

Yours,

F.S.

To Denis Glover, *Christchurch*

Alexander Turnbull Library

27 June [1937]

Dear Glover,

[. . .] I'd certainly ask Cresswell for a contribution [possibly to *Verse Alive* No. 2] if [Cresswell's verse play] The Forest appeals to you. He's supposed to be paying off his debts, but I believe he's getting £4.4.0 a week for his [radio broadcast] hour. His tree-planting is over long since. He couldn't keep out of pubs & so was frequently not on the job & unfit for it when he was. The Forest is the best he's done but I think one of his troubles is that when he's writing he hears his words so clearly, (& in his own voice,) that he's deluded into thinking that he has achieved better poetry than he really has. Nevertheless particularly in places where he is stating his own faith he has achieved something very good indeed, if not, so far, genuinely great. That is the main thing about the work — his faith. His characters aren't real, they're simply inventions which he can either caress or hate according to his faith. Iris says he's not sure of his faith & that's where he breaks down. But I don't agree. He could never have kept going so long if he had ever doubted. He really does believe that after death he will find himself lying in Apollo's lap. The omens are all there. Herrings chase him out of the sea & leap up into his hands, & hares sit down in the fields & let him stroke them. Poor D'Arcy (which, of course, sounds patronising). I should say in temperament he's very close to what Marlowe must have been. Let's hope they both find their Ganymedes in the next world, & of such incredible beauty as to make up for the buttonses and bellboys of this.

Iris, by the way, has finished her 6th (I think it's 6th) book [*The Godwits Fly*]. She's living in a bach near to Cresswell & has the entire neighbourhood terrorized. A mooing cow has caused her agonies, but the woman owner has recently tied up the cow's mouth with a piece of rope, so Iris can now begin a new MS in peace. [. . .]

Nothing more just now,

Yours

F.S.

To Denis Glover, *Christchurch*

Alexander Turnbull Library

9 August [1937]

Dear Glover,

I got letter & 3 copies Verse Alive — thanks & this time I must sell the goods sharply & send you the money & no hanky-panky.

I'll be posting Hart Crane & the photo. Read the essay at the end of the former, also I've marked a page — your jaw will probably drop off & you'll be proclaiming yourself a re-incarnationist. Don't look at the photo too close or in a strong light & it's not so bad. I'd like a snap — I've been told you're a Prussian type, also pure Greek, & write me often so that I can feel I am doing the set books for 1937. Coleridge — Jeremy Taylor — Dryden — I get snatches from Sewell too. [Glover was an assistant lecturer in English at Canterbury University College.]

That bit 'faith in any better order of things' worries me. Would any other order of things alter [R.A.K.] Mason or any of us — much? Dostoevsky, I'm afraid, has had the last word on human nature for long years to come yet. We're all Dostoevskian up here — Mason, Cresswell, Robin Hyde, myself, even Fairburn. Mason of course is the last person in the world who should ever be a Marxist. Those two uncut umbilical cords of his — one leading to his mother & one to his poetry. If there is any fault in his poetry that's it. With Emily Bronte & Emily Dickinson you do feel that they did get out beyond themselves, but Mason never. 'Who touches this book touches a man'. Well, when I take up a book I don't quite want to touch a man. Both Mason & Cresswell are a little different from the rest of us in this way — that whereas life tortures all of us & it is delight & pain, Mason tortures himself & Cresswell tortures other people, & that gives them a new delight & pain that most of us realise, happily, only in the imagination.

Robin Hyde, the silly bitch, is, I believe, going to tear Verse Alive to pieces in the Observer. I must get a copy & write in if she deserves it — She interprets your Chestertonian piece as a sneer at G.K.C. I'm fed up with her — do you see the pieces she has in the Star — Star-Sun lately? Each is a sort of orgasm in 3 stanzas. I wouldn't mind so much if they weren't so obviously masturbatory orgasms. By the way, do you know Robert Frost? Some of his short poems are good but our Robin has picked on some of his longer & duller pieces to make that Husband & Wife thing out of in your Miscellany. There's yourself with no time to read & myself some days reading myself blind. I've been re-reading Ulysses for an article & Show Down by M[argaret] Escott that [Dr Frank] Birkinshaw put me on to. And isn't [the English poet] Ruth Pitter a trimmer?

Though unlike Fairburn I think she gets better epithets when she's blessed by the Comic Muse — and you have to add to that her characterisation — 'the curate big with fruity voice'. Now I'm getting tired & incoherent. [. . .]

F.S.

To Denis Glover, *Christchurch*

Alexander Turnbull Library

28 August [1937]

Dear Glover,

You're a dirty dog wanting me to return the very snap I want to keep, but I'm too honest not to comply. Anyhow I like your picture. Wholesome's the word — 'I'm not being rude, merely candid'. Evidently the Boy Scouts produce such people occasionally, but I'm afraid it's just by accident. That bit is in Scouting for Boys (1909 Edition) & my brother did join & I didn't. And my brother said if I joined he'd leave — he was always scared of my crying in the wrong places, & unfortunately I nearly always did. Incidentally he's now the asst. manager of the N.Z. Coop Dairy Coy — his insensitivities having enabled him to get there, while I've advanced as far as relief work and sustenance. But I wouldn't change places with him no matter how many quids I was offered for a quo. All the same he has his good points — has the typical Sargeson good-nature, though curiously enough we're not Sargesons — that's our mother's name — but all that's another story & I'd better say pardon the family genealogy.

Last week's been a bit of heaven. Rex Fairburn & wife & 3 children & 1 unborn have been in the local motor camp, so I've been there nearly all the time blissfully happy playing with the children. And of course the evenings were just delightful stretches of obscene conversation between Rex & myself with the wife modestly listening in. My God, though, it hurts just to be an uncle — I've been indulging in so many sentimental reveries that I feel like writing a lyric entitled Reverie & I believe I could make it pretty good Robin Hyde — by the way there's a story attached to that name which I wish I could tell you but I can't. And also by the way Fairburn has had a Hollywood still taken too. Shall I suggest that he send you one? It's fairly good & he's a most attractive-looking bloke — just under 6'4" as I suppose you know.

O Bathos! Tomorrow night I've got to stand in the queue for tickets for the Springbok Test. Reward 10/-. I did the same for the last match here, so do you wonder at my jeering remarks? And as I've quarrelled with Cresswell I won't be able to make the night go fast by looking him up in Gleeson's pub, where doubtless he'll be with the sailor boys seeing the entire navy's concentrated here at the moment. [. . .]

Good luck,

F.S. [. . .]

To Denis Glover, *Christchurch*

Alexander Turnbull Library

26 September [1937]

Good Glover,

I'm sorry I didn't make the 2 more sales of Verse Alive I thought I would. But I've still hopes. Unfortunately the people I'm mainly mixing with aren't susceptible. It's queer — I live mainly with the people I draw my material from, but these people read True Detectives. And as far as the people who (I hope) read my writing, a whole heap of gold clocks wouldn't drag me into mixing with them if I could possibly avoid it. [. . .]

I haven't been working much — reading piles of books instead. I always do that when I'm working outside as I am at present, navvying & digging people's gardens. I'm too tired to write. I was, however, bushed to get £4.15.0 from the Sydney Bulletin. I'll send you the story ['A Great Day'] when it comes out. It's not one of my best, but it has its points. And the money got my typewriter out of the pawn shop for the umpteenth time so I'm nearly out of debt again & happy on that score.

I saw the proof page of Fairburn's poem ['Dominion'] & it looks fine. I hope you won't be losing too much over it. Has Cresswell sent you The Forest yet? I never see him now — only faint echoes of his persistent interference in my personal affairs. I'd stick up for him with my dying breath as a writer, but the man's quite unfit for personal relations. Someday you may hear that I've broken his neck.

One day a week I dig up at Mt Pleasant Hospital — it's slapbang up against A.U.C & I'm always poking my head up over the wall to look at the stoodents. I think of you & the austere H.W.R. [H. Winston Rhodes]. But it's the A.U.C. gardener I'm interested in mostly. It annoys me that he can dig & grow things better than I can. I've found a man who has the last Beethoven quartets on the gramophone. So I'm off.

F.S.

To James Laughlin, *Norfolk, Connecticut*

Houghton Library

[Laughlin's New Directions Publishing Company published William Carlos Williams's novel White Mule *in 1937.]*

26 December 1937

Dear James Laughlin IV,

Many thanks for your letter. WHITE MULE and the Christmas card haven't turned up yet but no doubt they will.

Yes, I would like to contribute to NEW DIRECTIONS. I gave Fairburn some typescript to send you some time back, but whether he sent it on I don't know. He's away on holiday just now.

Thanks for being kind to my booklet. It's mainly kicks on the arse I get. Yes, I know Saroyan. I missed his first though I know the title-story THE DARING YOUNG MAN ETC. I've read his 3 books since and I think he's mainly fine. What shall I say, about the clearest spirit I know of in modern American letters. Maybe I appreciate him most when he's quite concrete (things like THE SUNDAY ZEPPELIN come right along my street).

When I sent you my little book I was in a big hurry over the tomatoes I grow for the living I don't get, and didn't have time to say anything. Now I must say I liked very much your prose that started with the young people on the beach and ended with the wild ride in the car. I wonder if you've brought out that novel yet. About your poetry: I've found it difficult except the one about your rich old Scot grandfather. I must get that copy of NEW DIRECTIONS [No. 1, 1936] again. When Fairburn or I get a book like that it goes into circulation among our friends and it's hard to say where it is at any given moment. There were great things in it. That Cocteau thing, and what a trimmer of a story by W.C. Williams ['A Face of Stone'] — the one about the couple and the baby.

Reading the Life of Hart Crane sent me back to his Collected Poetry. You know how he apostrophizes Whitman as Panis Angelicus. Well, if you can translate that as angel cake didn't he get fairly close to something American after all?

William Plomer's another person overseas who's interested in my writings. He's Cape's reader, he succeeded the late Edward Garnett. Cape would like to publish a collection of mine but he wants a novel first. The only luck I've had has been with a few things in TIME AND TIDE. I think Sherwood Anderson's influenced me more than anyone, and through him your great Mark Twain.

All the best, and I'll write again,

Frank Sargeson

['That Cocteau thing': 'The Laic Mystery: an essay in indirect criticism' translated by Olga Rudge.]

To Denis Glover, *Christchurch*

Alexander Turnbull Library

29 December 1937

Dear brother in Christchurch (in case ARDF who said he was going to address you so has forgotten to — only don't tell him I pinched the brilliant thought)

[. . .][C.A.] Marris [the editor of *New Zealand Best Poems* and the butt of Glover's satirical poem 'The Arraignment of Paris'] reveals himself as the swine that he is. The mere suggestion of legal action should be sufficient to make him lose caste with every writer of the Antipodes. I hope you broadcast the news as widely as possible. In a way I wish he'd sue you (though of course he won't): his appearance alone would damn him with the jury, and there'd be you as fresh and blooming as the plaintiff in a seduction or breach of promise case. Shed a tear or two and he'd never even get a farthing and costs. And I'd be prepared to come and give expert evidence. From my privileged position in the witness box I should describe Marris's work and anthologies as the productions of an intellectual leper.

As a matter of fact I'm fast becoming the *doyen* of NZ *litterateurs*. A bloke named Laughlin who each year issues NEW DIRECTIONS IN PROSE AND POETRY in America has asked me to contribute to the issue of 1938. I've seen a copy and it's full of Cocteau, Stein, Carlos Williams, Kay Boyle, Henry Miller, Pound etc. Nicely got out of course.

Reading over that last paragraph I can only ask you to overlook such damnable conceit. There are things that even a cad shouldn't say, or even do. [. . .]

Have been toying with Auden and MacNeice's Letters from Iceland. The Letter to Byron is good, likewise their Last Will and Testament.

My God, the material going to waste in this country. Coming down Victoria street early the other morning I found the street choc-a-bloc with Jugo-Slavs. Never heard a word of English from Hobson street to Queen street. I immediately decided to go to their picnic on Pine Island, but unfortunately mistook the date.

Can you tell me why Walpurgisnachts don't purge and love doesn't satisfy? I suppose it's better being an artist. All artists are sensualists as you know. They should remain so. They should never fall in love. For any ordinary young person to fall in love is a tragedy. For two ordinary young persons to fall in love with each other is a worse tragedy. For older persons it is even worse than that. For an artist it is like death without being dead. For elucidation of this see Dostoevsky.

A rotten dirty morbid letter. Don't show it to anyone.

F.S. [. . .]

[Walpurgisnachts: the eve of 1 May, on which, according to German legend, a witches' Sabbath took place on the Brocken, the highest peak in the Harz Mountains.]

To James Laughlin, *Norfolk, Connecticut*

Houghton Library

17 January 1938

Dear James Laughlin,

Thank you for WHITE MULE. When I saw it was a Williams I expected a lot and I wasn't disappointed. He's certainly one of the best you've got. With children and animals I don't suppose there's anyone to touch him. I was most interested in the technique he's used — the way he externalises mainly but doesn't hesitate to get inside a character if he thinks it will help. As a matter of fact I've always doubted whether a completely externalised novel could be written — maybe it could be done writing in the 1st person (I mean everything could be external except the narrator who needn't necessarily count).

If I could pick any fault I think it was that occasionally the dialogue and certain scenes didn't imply enough — didn't light up American civlization as perhaps it could have done. That's what I felt about his story in 1936 NEW DIRECTIONS — every sentence lit up your whole box of tricks. But could you possibly get such concentration right through a novel? The reader would be exhausted and knocked flat anyhow.

A nicely got out book too. I liked your little P.S., particularly the bit about the word being holy. People ask me what the hell I think I'm doing and I mumble something about loyalty to the word and they think I'm properly cracked. [. . .]

Shortly I'll be sending you one or two N.Z. publications. [. . .]

Best wishes for writing, publishing, and everything else,

Frank Sargeson

To Denis Glover, *Christchurch*

Alexander Turnbull Library

2 February 1938

Dear Glover,

[. . .] I am sending the NEW DIRECTIONS man various of your booklets. But the poetry he publishes is so frightfully difficult I haven't an idea what he'll think. He sent me WHITE MULE a novel by William Carlos Williams, and I'll let you have it eventually. Do you know his verse? I remember him from the old TRANSITION days. Have you followed up Saroyan, by the way? There are lovely stories in his recent LITTLE CHILDREN.

I very much admired your invention in PRAYERS IN PREJUDICE

[*Tomorrow*, Jan. 1938]. Also the sensual delight in:

beans

and big ripe fruits and crops good earth convenes

is right in my line. Of all our poets you are the most accurate observer. You'd appreciate the sight and touch of my tomatoes — even as I do myself. But there's a big problem in PRAYERS IN PREJUDICE. There's the gap between the two parts. To my mind you've made the people of the first part rather less than human, and those of the second, rather more than human. Say you were writing a story about some of the people in the first part — you could make it straightout satire, and leave it at that (it's what I'm very often tempted to do myself). Yet in the man, say, whose hopes are horses, mightn't you feel something of 'the infinitely gentle, infinitely suffering thing' that Eliot speaks about? Why, for instance, are his hopes in horses? Has he or has he not any intimations of other things that his hopes might be in? And if he has isn't that just where the everlasting human tragedy and comedy comes in? [. . .]

I've been closely re-reading ULYSSES and wishing to God I hadn't written that damned article in the Press before I *had* re-read the thing. It's fine without a doubt, particularly the joyousness and high spirits that *will* come through. And Bloom moves me ineffably. The whole thing's a powerful argument for Catholicism. And 'the ineluctable modality of visible things' that Joyce has so much to say about is very suggestive. *THAT's* why people put money on racehorses, and why they believe in God — because they have instinctive feelings against ineluctable modalities. I've rolled thousands of cigarettes and always get cigarettes, but say I looked down and saw that I was holding two mountains in my hands, yes, two mountains without a valley in between.

The best advice I could think of for Iris on her departure was, to mind the Steppes, not to drink too many rickshaws, and not to put her foot in the Po, also to say damn to all the Rotters in Rotterdam. She's a trying old thing. I described all her writing as fairytale writing and she was pleased. We had a tender goodbye under a vine growing down an alleyway behind the Regent Theatre. I'm glad she called Marris off in a way — I don't think he was bluffing, she has a lot of influence with him. But a Court case would have been a tidy bit of publicity. I went over big with Iris during the last few days. She thought I left a toy train and a pair of stockings for her nipper on her doorstep. I didn't, but the opportunity was too good to miss seeing I had to induce her to behave while she was meeting a few friends of mine. [. . .]

I am writing a new novel now. Really only a series of sketches linked together by heat. A hot summer if you get me. Title THAT SUMMER. Perhaps I can bring it off, perhaps not. If I have any luck selling stories this year I'll try to use the money to get you to bring out another booklet. I've not been decently printed yet. Rod Finlayson is getting Lowry to bring out some of his stories. If I'd known I'd have asked him to give you the job. TOOTHACHE, so a note from England informs me, is to appear in TIME AND TIDE, so Henderson if he wants to use it had better get in first.

About booksellers: as you say they're not much good. Whitcombes in all centres rather surprisingly sold all copies I sent them. I shall ask the NEW DIRECTIONS man to name a shop in New York that would display your publications. Fairburn could get you Australian agencies through a fellow called Jasper Brett who used to be on the Sun. Blackwood Paul in Hamilton would always do his best for you I'm sure.

Still have hopes of wandering off down south, particularly today. Heavy weather, headache, 1 cwt of good sound unsaleable tomatoes lying on floor. Can I survive this afternoon? A year's easy to get through, but an afternoon can be the devil.

F.S.

Do I detect your hand in some of Tomorrow's editorials? — A Ministry of Humour e.g.

['1 cwt': one hundred weight, approximately 50kg.]

To John Lehmann, *London*

Harry Ransom Humanities Research Center

23 March 1939

Dear Lehmann,

[. . .] About NEW WRITING, A GREAT DAY has appeared in the Sydney Bulletin so that can't be used. But AN AFFAIR OF THE HEART is O.K. I wrote it for a competition but a piece of imitation Mansfield won. Our Kathie has had a bad influence on people who try to write out here. Our kicking-off point should have been something resembling Huckleberry Finn — our material is somewhat similar to Twain's. But Kathie, who should have been born in England and only come out here on comfortably conducted tours, has led practically everyone down the garden path. Maybe I'm treading on dangerous ground saying this, because I've been amusing myself playing a game of trying to identify the 'Chalmers' of Isherwood's LIONS AND SHADOWS, and this letter may be going to 'Chalmers' for all I know. Anyhow a good essay by a New Zealander doing a little gentle debunking of Kathie, so far as her colonial significance goes, wouldn't be out of place, and sooner or later it will come.

Well, consider AN AFFAIR OF THE HEART by all means. And/or you might consider the enclosed piece THE MAKING OF A NEW ZEALANDER, just lately written.

A few coupons enclosed to cover any postages on my account.

Cheers and the best from,

Frank Sargeson [. . .]

['An Affair of the Heart' was awarded second place after 'It's Christmas Afternoon' by 'Dorian Gray' in the Auckland Star's *Christmas story competition of 1936. Lehmann took it for* New Writing 3, *Christmas 1939. 'The Making of a New Zealander' appeared in* Penguin New Writing 13, *June 1942.]*

The Letters 1940–1949

To E.P. Dawson, *Wellington*

Hocken Library

14 January 1940

Dear E.P.D.

[. . .] I was very interested to read your comment on my New Writing story ['An Affair of the Heart'] — you've given me a new slant on myself. I'd always judged that piece to be one of my best and maybe I'm all wrong. Yet I feel I've got to say a bit to try and justify my judgment. [. . .] I think I can answer along these lines. Life on its surface these days has become very tough, but underneath surely there's still tenderness (Lawrence, for instance, is held up for execration as the writer of the most obscene novel of the century, yet he considered entitling that novel TENDERNESS). Well, if life is tough on the surface yet tender underneath, it surely follows that that tenderness is going to be forced into strange channels. To let you into the mechanics of the thing, let me say that that story had no counterpart that I know of in real life — I mean it didn't grow out of any similar case that I have observed. No, I wanted to say something that would express the need for tenderness, and after searching about for some time I hit on the old woman and her son — both inventions. I didn't want to take a theme too well-worn, lovers, husband and wife, etc. — I thought an old woman and her son would suit me better, yet would find a human response almost anywhere the story happened to be read. And when the story was written I tried it out on a man who I knew was very attached to his mother, and had had quite a struggle to detach himself sufficiently to achieve a quite happy marriage. And I was fearfully embarrassed to find at the end of my reading that he was in tears — which in spite of my embarrassment I regarded as quite an achievement on my part — so devious and even devilish are the ways of artists. Well, I thought I'd achieved something, because I hold that art should move, rather than provoke to thought. Maybe though here I'm a bit old-fashioned. Maybe the art that moves is done for — anyhow it's quite obvious that great numbers of modern artists do try to provoke you to thought rather than move you. [. . .] Willy-nilly, I want to write something that will touch people. [. . .]

Tomorrow has been very much in the news lately I see. Heaven knows how Henderson keeps it going. Besides Defoe I'm very interested at the moment in Boswell's tour of the Hebrides with Dr Johnson. And have you ever read Henry James 'The Turn of the Screw'? — I think it's the most truly horrible story I've ever read. I still don't know what to think about the war — I suppose I'll have to think shortly if I'm conscripted. Two close friends I've said goodbye to — they went with the first echelon — one I went to the

Papakura Camp to see — but I think I'll have something to say about that in Tomorrow.

All good wishes to you and for your writing.

Yours,

F.S.

To John Lehmann, *London*

Princeton University Library

9 May 1940

Dear Lehmann,

Thank you for your letter and I'm glad to hear that NEW WRITING is carrying on in the meantime. I don't know what to say about the war. It's trying enough out here, so I have some idea of what it must be like in England, especially since the Norwegian business. So far conscription has been warded off, but I don't know for how long. Everything is muddle. Even the fire-eaters are dubious about sending too many of our young men abroad, because of the Japs. And our Labour Cabinet Ministers who were either C.O. in the last war or imprisoned for sedition are now making recruiting speeches. No doubt politically the Marxist position is the only one that makes any sense, but personally I feel like building a stockade for myself in the middle of the bush and keeping a gorilla to look after the door.

Recently I have had a little luck. In some Centennial Literary Competitions held here I received an award of £30 for a short story ['The Making of a New Zealander']. Of course I blew it in on a holiday in the Alps down South, but now I feel like a box of birds and have come back to my bach to finish my novel ['That Summer']. And a young fellow who does a good job of printing is bringing out a book of my stories. I'll send you a copy when it's out.

By the way when writing I always intended to say I saw Storm Jameson's review of NEW WRITING in FACT where she slated that first sketch of mine you printed ['White Man's Burden']. I was much amused. I've always thought her very much of a conservative as regards writing, and that's made me a bit suspicious about her up-to-the minute politics. Good luck to her anyway, but I've always thought that the Twain, Anderson, Hemingway line is the genuine Colonial line, and we're colonials out here — at least I am, all my grandparents were just young people when they landed here.

I wonder if you persevered with the Proust as wartime reading. I intended to do the same, but got onto Gibbon which went down well, and now I'm just finishing Boswell, both the Hebrides Tour and the Life, and they've gone down even better. I pick up modern books but throw them aside, though up in the mountains I did read my first Sayers. If the lady wasn't so preposterously pretentious I'd put her down on my list of pernicious people, along with John Gunther and Philip Gibbs. By the way I never noticed before how well Boswell anticipates some of the most important moderns. The bit in the Tour about how the Duke of Argyll sends an earl on a footman's errand and the earl carries it out but comes back whistling with his hands in pockets just to show everyone that he *isn't* a footman is pure Proust.

Lately there've been a few young New Zealanders living round here not long back from Europe. There's one named [J.A.W.] Bennett who began in a local suburb as an earnest young Plymouth Brother but became a Fellow in Medieval Literature at Oxford. (I asked him what the progression was — Brother, Fellow, Regular Fellow, Guy?) Anyhow the war caught him out here on leave, and since I've been away I hear he's chucked the Fellowship and gone to Columbia Univ. Then there's been J.M. Bertram who was in China and had two books published, but now seems to be rather unhappily kicking up his heels in these barbarous surroundings.

Thank you for telling me not to forget you, bombs or no bombs. I suppose I'll be kept very busy with the novel for some months, but if I write a story that I think is good I'll let you see it. I haven't heard from Plomer for a long time. I daresay he feels very badly over the war, but from what I know of him I shouldn't say it will drive him into the Left Camp,

Best of wishes,

Frank Sargeson

P.S. I'd like to write a letter telling you just what I think of the political situation in this country (and in others) but it would probably be censored, particularly if I used the language that would express it most forcibly.

['The Norwegian business': the failed Allied counter-offensive following the German invasion of 9 April. FS's 'The Making of A New Zealander' and E.A. Midgley's 'The River' shared the £30 first prize in the short story section of the Centennial Literary Competition of 1940. Denis Glover published A Man and His Wife *in September 1940.]*

To E.P. Dawson, *Wellington*

Hocken Library

[In the winter of 1939 FS had started to display the symptoms of what turned out to be tuberculosis, occasioning operations in the winters of 1939 and 1940.]

13 May [1940]

Dear E.P.D,

Two letters from you to hand, both like your article in Tomorrow full of all sorts of things that make me lean back and THINK. But let's get on with the good news. I'm on the top of the world. Douglas Robb really is a good fellow, he's the only doctor I know that I care a damn for, and he thinks the slight swelling and pain in my chest is simply owing to my constitution trying to get rid of something that I've become allergic (is it two l's or one, and don't you — like me — half like, yet half abominate that new American word) to. [. . .]

There are one or two points about your first letter. About not being sure about what I mean in my letters always — I suppose this is inevitable now and then. The reason for writing that is good writing, or one reason anyhow, is that there is no mistake about the meaning. When I've written anything that is good I always feel I've got it as clear as I possibly can. But letter writing is quite different. In letter writing I never feel that I've isolated some tiny little problem with the intention of making it crystal clear, rather do I feel that I've indulged the pleasure of communicating with a friend. Every friendship is different from every other one, but all are, to my mind anyhow, tremendously complicated. It would require a whole novel, probably a number of novels to simplify all those complications, hence letter-writing, with me nearly always a hasty business, can rarely, I should say, produce any great clarity. I am not always clear about your own meanings, but it does not worry me much. In your letters you throw off, and much more spontaneously than I do, such a lot of suggestions that start me thinking. And that's how it should be. I prefer the *poetic* (if I may use the term) people who make you expand to the *scientific* people who try to tie you down. The difference to my mind is the difference between Shakespeare and Bernard Shaw. [. . .]

[A]bout Kennaway [Henderson]: I think I'm right about fin de siecle. There is a Whistlerish touch about him; in spite of his politics and his undoubted sincerity, you can't help but feel that he's very remote from the real dinkum worker. So natty his shoes, and so expensive; a sort of shoes for shoes sake, and not shoes produced out of the blood sweat and tears of the workers, so to exaggeratedly speak. [. . .]

About the dedication [to *A Man and His Wife*], I meant that any way you helped me would also help my book. Glover will be put to a lot of expense in getting it out, though I hope he won't be out of pocket as regards actual cash; indeed he's realist enough to say bluntly that he has no intention of being. So although we're getting it out by subscription I told him that any cash I could rake up I'd let him have, and with your help it will be possible to let him have a few more notes than I would otherwise have been able to, if indeed I had been able to let him have any at all. So why not let me have the book say simply that it is dedicated to E.P. Dawson as a mark of appreciation? The actual wording of course will have to be thought out, and, again of course, it only goes in if you approve. After all you would have never have known of me or met me if it hadn't been for my writing, and if a book of the best of my writing so far is brought out largely because of you, or partly because of you, why not let us make our grateful acknowledgements?

You raise all my doubts and misgivings again when you mention sending me an extra amount, and also the mention of an extra year. PLEASE PLEASE, put the latter, for the time being anyhow, right out of your mind, but if you insist on the former it will nearly all go into getting the book moving. Feeling on the top of the world as I do at the moment I scorn the thought of cold and the necessity of fires or any creature comforts except the simplest. I have one idea at the moment — I MUST devote the next few months to finishing this novel I'm working on. I'm going to think of nothing else, I'm going to be rude to people who interfere with me, in short I'm going to be utterly selfish, because at the back of my mind is a feeling I've GOT to be. And because I also feel that there's a chance of the book turning out good, and so curiously justifying all my rudeness and selfishness. [. . .]

All good wishes,

F.S. [. . .]

To E.P. Dawson, *Wellington*

Hocken Library

10 June [1940]

Dear E.P.D.

Elizabeth Pudsey — how I chuckled over and relished the flavour of that. So very English, I mean I thought of what I would be fighting for if I were fighting for England in France at the moment. Chaucer, Shakespeare, Elizabeth Tudor, Dr Johnson, Dickens. Yes, that England counts a hell of a lot, and it's just God's own pity that it all got tangled with the Bank of England and the Rothschilds etc. Never mind, you can kill the Bank of England, but you can't kill the Chaucers and the Shakespeares — and the Elizabeth Pudseys. So look out Adolf, you've got hold of the wrong end of the stick, and some of us know something better than even the right end of a stick. [. . .]

My delay in writing has been owing to doctors and X ray reports etc. The X ray report is good. No lesions can be found anywhere in the chest, so it is thought there is merely a small focus of disease somewhere in the ribs. This sounds contradictory, but apparently it is so as the swelling persists and the sample taken by Dr Robb showed the appropriate bacilli to be present. What's to be done? Well nobody seems to have made up his mind yet, so I'm just left a little bit unbalanced (as evidenced by this rather incoherent letter), with a feeling of tiredness and apathy. I'm afraid at the moment, for really no reason at all, I've given in. It's the tiredness that has got me. All the last year in doing my garden jobs I'd come home absolutely bone tired, and I used to wonder why. Now I've adopted the easy explanation — this damned disease has got into my bones. But of course I'll snap out of this. T.B. or no T.B. I've got this thrice plaguey novel to finish, it's an intolerable burden but it's got to be got rid of, and the things I've been planning to write for weeks past and never touched! I suppose it's natural to feel tired thinking of it, but oh for the strength, even fake strength, to do the DEED. Incoherent? Mad? Both I think. I put off writing in the hope I'd be able to write sense. Too bad.

Yes, I do agree about Salute being too close to Heil. We've got to avoid that. As last resource we could always have just:

To
E.P. Dawson

But I think a brainwave will eventuate.

Now what with headache and incoherence I've got to finish today. Don't think I'm making fun of you by coming back to Elizabeth Pudsey. I'm really glad you told me. It really suits you perfectly, fits in with my picture of you asking me whether I thought your hat matched. Well there is such a thing as an Elizabeth Pudsey hat and you wear it, and it's probably bicycling round Wellington at this moment. A BRAVE ENGLISH HAT.

Best,

F.S.

[Dawson met the printing costs of A Man and His Wife, *and FS dedicated the book 'To E.P. Dawson'. FS to Dawson, 1 November: 'Glover writes to say my book is at present leaving his despatch department like the feathers from the tail end of a moulting hen'. Hocken MS-2404/001. It went into three printings in less than four years.]*

To E.P. Dawson, *Wellington*

Hocken Library

Thursday [June 1940]

Dear E.P.

[. . .] As for the fast aging F.S. with his T.B, his falling hair, his opening pores and (to be quite revoltingly low) his persistent B.O. he decided at the end of last week that he'd had enough of the Auckland Pub. Hosp. and walked out. Really though what with lack of sleep nerves etc. I was being reduced to a hopeless wreck. [. . .] That surgeon Spedding is a smug little creature. He did his best to scare me by saying and insisting that my bosom should not be opened or allowed to discharge (I only of course write these revolting details because your professional experience probably enables you to bear them) under any circumstances whatsoever. My troubles would only then really begin, he said. Well, what with their sun treatment etc. I could see the surface of the thing becoming thinner and thinner each day, and as nobody seemed to have the least idea what they were going to do except inject specimens into guinea pigs etc. I got sick of it and walked out. I walked straight along to Robb and he said they hadn't done any harm except delay a fairly urgent operation by a little over a week. I'm afraid I have to agree with him. The Hospital were afraid of creating a sinus, but as Robb says it will only be a few weeks before I have a sinus anyhow, so why not have a go and try to root out the focus of disease while the going's still fairly good. This means of course a private Hosp. but I suppose it can't be helped. I was conserving my assets (strictly speaking your assets) for the assistance of my novel, but I suppose I'd better like Mr Chamberlain be a realist and admit that it would be as well to divert some of them to assist myself. Anyhow Robb assures me that I need only be a few days in Hospital, as he's going to trust me to do my own dressings as I did last year. Luckily I don't infect very easily or I don't think I do, so no doubt all will go well. Well, [Mt Pleasant] Hospital can't take me [. . .] until Monday next, so this week I've been marking time stuffing myself with Vitamins A B1 B2 C D (E, which I believe is the fertility one, I've thought unnecessary to bother with just at present) and trying to keep my chest from breaking. It's going to be a curious race against time, but I think it will hold. Now all this is too gruesome for words, and I ought to be sat upon for writing it. I've finished correcting the proofs, have written a fair bit, read Hardy's Mayor of Casterbridge, done all my washing, and steadily pinned down for consumption the required vitamins each day. My head however feels a bit fuzzy as this letter indicates, but I'm looking forward to a glorious future free from ill-health. [. . .]

Lots of the best,

F.S. [. . .]

[Douglas Robb removed 'a couple' of infected ribs under local anaesthetic in June 1940.]

To Denis Glover, *Christchurch*

Alexander Turnbull Library

8 July [1940]

To Darling Denis, me old farting faggot (from Ould Ireland)

[. . .] E.P.D. is causing me much perturbation. Her latest letter infers the most disturbing conclusions about my sex-life. Like E.P.D. Adolf Hitler and a few others I am apparently chaste. Dreams that she has had about me (and Adolf Hitler and a few others) have informed her of these facts. (God knows what will be revealed if she dreams about you — but perhaps she will inform you). But joking apart the woman genuinely worries me. And I have a genuine sympathy for the frightful and even frightening condition she's in. Think back to your teens and consider the time when you had dreadful thoughts about babies and girls and things, when you used to look down at that curious little appendage and felt at last a dreadful conviction that it wasn't just meant for piddling with. Well say you'd never NEVER in all the terrible years that followed been able to do anything ANYTHING about it, except read perhaps Dr. Sylvanus Stall and later on, perhaps with guilty horror, Dr Havelock Ellis. Well, that's the state of just one area of our E.P. D's consciousness. So bear up my boy and be sympathetic, kind, LOVING. It's love makes the world a merry-go-round . . . No, I can't go on. I'm in this mess with the lady, and remember you encouraged me to take the disastrous step which I feel sure is just going to top it off. But if you keep your own letters brief, pert, cynical (whether brilliantly so or not) and above all, business-like, you shouldn't come to any harm, and may even make some profit out of the pair of us. Leave the human side to me and I'll surprise you by proving myself one of the most eminent soul-doctors of all time. Anyhow I hope she's sent the money. [. . .]

About my health. Yes, as my publisher I suppose you're entitled to know something, which is practically nothing as that's all I know myself. By taking plenty of good food, codliver oil, fresh air and sunshine, by resting about eight hours each day and being happy and not worrying about anything we hope to resist the disintegration caused by the tubercles. At the moment I have an abscess on the chest which is shortly going to be drained and the scar of last year's operation has recently started to leak again, but as I'm still putting on weight there's no need for any immediate worry. There now, forget it. The visible manifestations cause me only slight annoyance, and the larger implications have been put away into the back of my mind for the time being. If only Hitler will put off invading England for a couple of months I will have my novel finished.

F.S.

[The tubercular sinus on FS's chest required dressing for the next eight years.]

To E.P. Dawson, *Wellington*

Hocken Library

8 July [1940]

Dear E.P.

[. . .] About your letter with the five pound note. I do so much want not to hurt your feelings, but you really must not do this. Sometime ago I told you I was buying a few things and this I did, not an overcoat it is true, but the one I have will do this year. [. . .] Sooner or later, however events turn out, I must face up to the fact that it is freakish and unreal to be trying to do what I am trying to do in this country. The £45 has given me a splendid opportunity to tell the tale I have in mind, and once I have done that then I must turn my energies in some other direction. Is not this what you are doing yourself? Though I have protested against it, and in spite of what I say about my own intentions still protest against it. Why? Well, perhaps because your more abstract approach gives you a place in modern society and a validity to your writing. I'm not *absolutely* sure about this, but I think it is so. My own writing from some points of view is proletarian, but where is the N.Z. proletariat that I would like it to be read by? (But I can't go on developing my argument. A glance at the clock tells me I must hurry if I am to catch the mail. A man nearby who works on the road has just been in with a tale of illness about his wife and family and I have been out to pick lemons for him, and a few of the oranges that haven't been taken — as I picked them I had a horrible thought that he may already have had some of them. Unworthy thought! But it came into my mind so I have to admit it).

Do you know it mightn't be Taumarunui I go to after all? Some years ago I carried on a long correspondence with Dr. Campbell Duncan the Government balneologist at Rotorua. He paints and writes and dilletants (if that is the right spelling?) Anyhow he won the Bledisloe prize for a landscape once, and I enjoyed his letters and met him once only for a few minutes when he was leaving for Europe for a tour of the Spas to bring his balneology up to date. We'd always agreed not to meet as we thought it might destroy our correspondence and the ideas we'd got of each other. Anyhow at the last moment before sailing *he* insisted on meeting and it turned out as we'd expected. I don't say we were both exactly disappointed but we gradually ceased to write. But I remember his saying if our correspondence ever flagged I must go to Rotorua to stay with him and his wife and perhaps we'd get new angles on each other. I never went, but Fairburn's brother who has visited him lately tells me he remembers me and wishes I would go up. But I don't know. Of course it would be considerably more comfortable and perhaps more healthy in Rotorua than in Taumarunui, but I still don't know. And I hate indecision. I'm having difficulty in making an appointment with the doctor, but once I've seen him I'll have to make up my mind. All the best E.P. and this is a muddled letter. Just take it lightly, toss the Eliz. Pud. hat in the wind and go for a cycle and say to hell with Frank Sargeson today.

F.S.

To E.P. Dawson, *Wellington*

Hocken Library

26 September [1940]

Dear E.P.

Here I am all behind like a cow's tail, as we used to say when we were children — or rather as we used to hear our less prim elders say. By the way I have thought up a brilliant scheme for writing letters. You just let them write themselves, all you do is address the envelope and put a piece of blank paper inside, then trust to good fortune that the letter will write itself on its way to the addressee. Now wouldn't you like to do that with some of your correspondents — I would, though of course I don't mean you, and it's just occurred to me you MAY think I mean you, and then think to yourself, this fellow, creature, hombre, buckaroo, ink-squirter et al. is a vile insulting wretch. But it was just a perfectly innocent and really brilliant idea that came to me this morning. Anyhow I AM going to make out a list of correspondents whom I'm going to try it on.

Three letters from you this week, all as full as eggs of things it does me good to read. [. . .] I have heard very little about the book [*A Man and His Wife*] — reviews are always terribly slow coming out. I did, however, get a personal note from the Editor of the Listener [Oliver Duff]. I met him in Wellington and we didn't hit it. He writes me to say he doesn't like me trust me or believe in me, but there are now two writers in N.Z. and I am one of them. (To soften it, by the way, he qualifies his insults by saying he knows I feel just the same way about him). Well, I don't exactly. And anyhow I'm not too thrilled as he doesn't say who the other writer is — it may be A.B. Chappell or the Editor of Truth. Nevertheless it should mean some favourable publicity in the Listener. Like you I think there may be quite a good chance of the book's selling really well. I hope so but authors are selfish, egotistical beasts, all they really care about is getting the work they think is fairly genuine and good, put into tidy and permanent form — they don't I imagine care a damn whether their publisher loses money or not. That is authors who know they're not and never can be really commercial propositions. All the same I hope the book sells for your sake — I mean that. You believed in the work sufficiently to sponsor it and I'd like to see your faith justified in every sense possible, including, of course, the best. I really do like the page with your name on it and the acknowledgements — it is the best-looking page in the whole thing. I too don't like the line on each page — its worst effect is to produce the appearance of a definitely New Zealand book. I should be pleased with that, but the average NZ book being what it is I'm not. Also the type is set in too long lines, but of course Glover was at a disadvantage there owing to the shortage of paper.

Of course there is much that I write that irritates you. I have felt the same way about some of your things. Isn't the point just this: Everybody who is worth a damn is preoccupied with certain momentous questions — man's life on this earth, the terror marvel pity of birth reproduction and death, the apparently insoluble contradictions of character temperament etc. the search for community life and a stable political and social framework, the staggering questions of time and space. BUT, everybody who is worth a damn approaches these questions from a different point in time-space (if that means anything). My own approach, as I've said before, and as my book shows is almost entirely concrete — realistic, perhaps — and it is justified if sufficient power is infused to raise the finished thing to symbolical level. Sometimes, some places I think I've succeeded — most often I feel I've failed. On the other hand you with your (to me) amazing fluency (hesitating too, as is shown by the corrections addenda etc. in your letters) in dealing DIRECTLY with such (to me) frightfully difficult abstract ideas such as time, space, peace, etc. excite my wonder always, my irritation sometimes. I don't, and I don't suppose I ever will, feel quite *at home* with you. My predilection in life is definitely for characters who know nothing about what either of us are trying to deal with, but who by the blind intensity of their concrete living demonstrate all (or much of) that we're trying to get at. But of course all that is fearfully muddled. [. . .]

About the enclosure with the last letter. This was a shock. I thought all that was settled. Oh dear I'm not going into it all again. The nightmare at the back of my brain in connection with it all is that I may not be able to help you when you may need that help. It came too at such an awkward time for me. [. . .] Oh damn it all I have cashed it and put away five pounds which I hope I shall be returning shortly, the remainder pays some bills and will probably take me up to Rawene. Have you heard of Dr. Smith of Rawene Hospital — he wrote a book Notes from a Backblock Hospital? The WEA man here has wangled an invitation for me to go and stay with him for a week or so, if I can get up there — he's supposed to be a tuberculosis expert. Anyhow now I can go and I suppose go I'd better — it won't be until some time next week. [. . .]

My scarf has been christened my pheasant's scarf. The weather here is dry hot and muggy. Real unpleasant Auckland weather. Am feeling very much better, though I calculate it will be after Christmas before the holes in my chest have healed.

F.S.

P.S. Now I've written I feel awful about this long letter — it looks as though it takes money to prime the pump. Oh HELL.

To E.P. Dawson, *Wellington*

Hocken Library

11 October 1940

Dear E.P.

Your more than usually interesting letter was waiting for me when I got back from Rawene. [. . .] Your further remarks on Bandy [in 'Old Man's Story'] interest me no end. I drew him from a well-known local reprobate who sometimes comes to the bach for something to eat or 'borrow' a shilling. He's really very intelligent and has very acute perceptions, and the incident I've credited him with would, I think, be possible with him, though of course I've never heard of anything like that in his life. Thinking my stories over sometimes I sometimes feel in reality they're about nobody but myself — what I mean is that every experience used is something that I have experienced myself, or something which I realise I have strong possibilities of experiencing, and in order to put over this personal experience I simply fit it to characters who I imagine can carry it over powerfully into the queer re-created life that you find in books. Anyhow the reviewer in the Free Lance (O.N. Gillespie, I think) has picked on Old Man's Story as well as Holcroft and you, and this is encouraging as it's the last completed story I've written — I mean it's nice to feel that one may possibly still be developing. Personally I think the story is fairly good, but it's a frightfully difficult theme to get away with and what with the indirect reporting of Bandy's story I've never felt really happy about it. You're right, technically it is one of the weaker ones. [. . .]

I enjoyed it up yonder. Dr Smith is a great character, I think. Among other things he sent me back armed with bottles of sterilized gauze etc. and some ointment (M. and B. 693 introduced into sterilized lanoline) and the effect on the sinus seems to be really remarkable. He doesn't seem to have much idea about what my physical future will be, but he says he has never known a European die of phthisis [TB] up at Rawene, though of course the Maoris do.

[. . .] He seems to think sanatoriums are all nonsense — you need still air, not windy. His Hospital is so remarkable it would take me too long to go into all the ins and outs of it. His wife is if anything nicer. A Scottish Hebridean woman (of superior breeding as you very quickly realise — without her giving any direct indication of it). She reads a tremendous lot and knows her stuff. They have, by the way fourteen cats and five (no six) dogs, one of them a very epileptic one, and these creatures are all over the house at all hours. Later on I may go back there as I seemed to hit it with both of them. [. . .]

What with the war (mainly because of the war, I think) everybody up here that I know seems to be sick or neurotic or both. Fairburn is in a queer state, seems to be under stress and strain continually, and I sometimes fear that terrible things will happen. You see, I am more fortunate than he is. The storywriter still has some sort of a place even in N.Z., but the poet, scarcely any at all. And with Fairburn's great abilities, wide range, impeccable taste etc. it is a major tragedy. [. . .]

Best,

F.S.

To M.H. Holcroft, *Invercargill*

Alexander Turnbull Library

[Holcroft's essay The Deepening Stream *won first prize in the essay section of the 1940 Centennial Literary Competition. At the time he was leader-writer on the* Southland Times.*]*

28 December 1940

Dear Holcroft,

I meant long since to write about your essay. I thought it a good piece of work, and had it been possible I should have liked to work out some ideas in a review. But the Listener was the only possibility and I understood Duff arranged for that, though I haven't seen anything appear. As Glover says, one misses Tomorrow.

Particularly I liked the section about (and the references, passim, to) the bush. All that was well said, and I think all N.Z. writers have felt something of what you express.

Possibly the only thing I could bring against you would be the reverse of the tendency to experiment with forms which I suppose is obvious in my own work. I may be wrong, but I feel that direct criticism is becoming played out along with a number of established forms. For some years now I've been in touch with James Laughlin and his New Directions centre in America, and although some of the work put out is definitely batty, there's nevertheless a lot that appeals to me. The material offered to the writer in N.Z. is closer to that of America than anywhere else I think, but I think it won't do to approach it in any manner earlier than that of Sherwood Anderson. I know the critical approach doesn't vary quite so much, but I was immensely taken with an essay in indirect criticism by Cocteau which New Directions printed some time ago. The Laic Mystery it was called, and although Cocteau was talking about the painter Chirico, his method did enable him to talk about an immense number of things at the same time. Certainly it seemed to me a method which disclosed quite interesting possibilities for the development of critical writing. If you'd like to have a look at it I could send you the copy of New Directions in which it appears [No.1, 1936]. That is, of course, if you haven't already seen it.

I trust you're not finding your work in Invercargill too incongenial. I've been lucky in managing to dodge regular work mostly, though for the past six months I've been getting some amusement out of doing the Ben Bolt radio page in the Observer. Now, however, I'm turning it in — the Invalidity Pension has been granted on account of my T.B. and I do want to get on with some fresh work.

Best wishes,
Frank Sargeson

To John Lehmann, *London*

Harry Ransom Humanities Research Center

22 January 1941

Dear Lehmann,

[. . .] I had two notes from you recently — very lucky, as much mail has gone down lately. I hope you got my book [*A Man and His Wife*] — I'm not quite certain from the wording of your note. There's only OLD MAN'S STORY in it that you hadn't seen previously. It had never appeared previously, and some critics seem to think it my best. If it appeals to you you are welcome to use it any place you like.

Glad you've met Brasch, never met him myself, but they say he's a nice fellow, and I like his verse. There *have* been extraordinary developments in recent years, but what will happen next is a question. You have to be out here to realise the N.Z. writer's dilemma. Any truly indigenous literature is hardly past its embryo stage. It's damned hard to accept this bloody brutal barbarous environment for better or worse. In my stories I've tried to do this, but of course I've had to go to Europe and America for technique.

After the war it's hard to say what will happen, I mean even assuming there's no complete world-breakdown. For one thing there'll probably be a lot of immigration — people trying to get away from it all just in case it happens again. Another thing is that, particularly as regards Auckland, we're continually drawing closer to America. Yet another point is the not very distant day when our soil will be completely exhausted through our ruinous export of it in the shape of butter meat etc. Then hell will be let loose when a complete changeover of our economy becomes necessary. Meantime, of course, particularly with the war on, things have been going swingingly. Watersiders I believe average about £7-15/- a week, though there's nothing to spend it on but *Kitsch* — extending the term beyond the arts.

But as regards writers I'm afraid most of them are paralysed. There's a brilliant fellow, A.R.D. Fairburn (probably Brasch or [Edgell] Rickword has told you about him — he used to knock about London with the latter), but since the war he's produced virtually nothing — or rather nothing except brilliant conversation about everything, and brilliant arguments for remaining in his present state of torpor. But damn it all, having struck off a little flicker from Old Man Europe's flame, we damn well ought to keep it alight somehow. What we want perhaps most at the moment is someone after the cut of E.C. Large, someone well versed in modern technics but intelligent enough to expose the stupid folly of our economy and prepare the community for the great changeover.

Personally I haven't been getting along badly. On account of my illness I've been granted an Invalidity pension of 30/- a week — I don't know how long it will last, but long enough I hope to get my novel completed, and until that is done I don't suppose I'll be writing many stories. For the past six months I've been writing a page of radio criticism — rocking it in as venomously as possible. It's amused journalists and a few other people, but the general public has been very resentful about the continual attack on the incredible bullshine, so dear to its great heart, that is put over by the Commercial Stations. As for the National stations they're just high-minded attempts at a sort of High School culture. Thank God I'm still able to live in my flimsy bach and cultivate my citrus trees, my tomatoes, sweet corn and rock melons. It can be damned miserable and uncomfortable sometimes in winter, but I don't miss the hundred and one pseudo-comforts that I've never experienced anyhow — I don't put the T.B. down to the lack of them, no, rather to the strain of trying to write something of some value in a community which is not the slightest bit interested. Nevertheless it may interest you to know that over 300 copies of my book have so far sold at 6/- a copy, and the Caxton Press regards this as quite gratifying.

I was glad of news of Plomer, and trust he weathers the bombs. I must write him — I suppose he can still be reached through Jonathan Cape. In some ways the war continues to seem incredibly remote, though the [German surface] raiders have recently altered things a little. None of my friends has suffered so far, though I have a few away in Egypt, and a German refugee friend [Odo Strewe] has recently been interned. D'Arcy Cresswell, it seems, actually enjoys being in London at the present time. So far as the actual discomforts go I don't think I'd mind, I imagine they wouldn't be so unlike what I've always been used to, but I *know* I'd never be able to stand the bombs.

All the best,

Frank Sargeson

P.S. By the way one thing that strikes me as most peculiar is the almost complete lack of news about French writers. Where are Malraux Aragon Gide Cocteau et al. One doesn't wonder at the lack of news in the ordinary press, but I've not yet struck any English or American literary paper that has given any information. It may be a case of no news being good news so far as personal safety goes — I simply couldn't agree with E.M. Forster in his recent broadcast about the fate that would overtake eminent British writers in the event of Hitler bringing off his invasion. I notice that Joyce is dead — and the local press gave a few inches of mis-information about him, while [the Irish portraitist] Sir John Lavery got a whole column. Ulysses, by the way, in the shape of a Modern Library Giant, with the text of the judgment allowing the book into the U.S.A. is fairly easy to buy in this country.

To E.P. Dawson, *Wellington*

Hocken Library

16 May [1941?]

Dear E.P.

[. . .] Auckland differs from all the other cities in being so spread out, nobody seems to be much in touch with anyone (I haven't seen Fairburn for about 6 weeks), everybody is vague and haphazard, poor Glover can build up quite good connexions everywhere but here, where so many of the cognoscenti hardly seem aware of the existence of his press let alone his publications. I don't know whether to put it down to the climate or our closer connection with America or not. I've kidded myself it doesn't matter, and that the only thing that does matter is to get on and do as well as you can the only job you've learned to do. But it won't wash. I've just read Eric Gill's Sacred and Secular and he blows a lot of the wind out of me. He's got a lot of time for art but none for Art. The first implies a small community where you have your place, the second implies a lot of abstract cosmopolitan rubbish. It's no good my kidding myself I'm doing or trying to do a good job of work when I live in a community but not of it — sitting on my tail hoping to get stories published in England or America to be read by a few highbrows and the people round me neither knowing nor caring about my work. [. . .]

By the way I've read some interesting things lately — Paris France, by Gertrude Stein. Very Steinesque. She's the founder of modern prose style all right. The School for Dictators by Ignazio Silone. Very good. The best written and the most amusing summary of post-Armistice Europe I've come across. I also read his Fontamara and enjoyed it, and it strikes me as extraordinary that one or two scandalous episodes in this book should be broadcast round the world in the form of a Penguin while if Glover and I dared to publish much milder episodes (Glover insists they come out of my novel) we'd probably be put in gaol.

I really enjoyed the last few days [on Oakley Sargeson's farm] at Okahukura. Did a lot of exploring into the remote valleys of abandoned farms, finding queer little patches of grass that had hung on on sunny slopes and where sheep that must have been lost for several years were grazing. Only means of access to these valleys is up slippery and to a certain extent dangerous creek beds. I tried to bring four sheep that were simply balls of wool (the staple must've been well over a foot long) down one creek, but two went over a fall about 70 ft high and broke their necks, but I got the other two out though one broke its leg which isn't serious in sheep. Sounds cruel, but coming to the fall I didn't know it was there with the tangle of secondary growth overhead and the silly things jumped before I could stop them. Then one day when we killed a sheep for the house I made a haggis which turned out one of the tastiest and most nourishing things I've ever concocted, though the abattoir smell while it was cooking wasn't too nice. [. . .]

I (mistakenly or not) envy you your life in Wellington, your bicycle, your getting from one person to another, your knowing people, and having so many contacts. Hope to write more often now I'm apparently settled in here for the winter with the novel to revise and some short things to write. Last week I had everything out of the bach and scrubbed and cleaned burnt mattresses etc. The rubbish was so mountainous it burned for days. The bach looks so clean now I'm distracted from any job by wanting just to sit and look at it.

Yours,

F.S.

To E.H. McCormick, *Egypt*

Alexander Turnbull Library

29 July 1941

Dear McCormick,

[...] Glover is going in for publishing in big licks just at present. R.M. Burdon's N.Z. Notables is out, Curnow's Collected Poems etc. and just about to come out are Dr Smith's new book [*More Notes from A Backblock Hospital*], Sutch's rejected Centennial Survey [*Poverty and Progress in New Zealand*], and a book of stories by G.R. Gilbert [*Free To Laugh and Dance: Stories*]. This young man visited me recently, much taking my fancy in a pair of golden-brown corduroy trousers. I think he may turn out the best yet. He is very much influenced by Saroyan and has a certain 'literary' quality that rather worries me. But he's exuberant, and a little loosening up and overwriting for a change won't do any harm. Then Fairburn's collected poems are coming out, and Mason's. As far as I can see Glover will go broke, or he will be called up right in the middle of it all and everything will fall to the ground. He's a little shy of my own short novel, so we're letting it lie a while while I try in America.

Health hasn't been so bad lately, and I've been quite well off owing to my reprints in the Penguin New Writing and the B.B.C. Listener. The money, much to my surprise, came to hand and amounted to more than 20 notes. If I can complete a fresh group of stories which I'd very much like to do I've the notion I'd like to turn to something of my own story. I've always held that Dreiser's Dawn yields nothing to his fiction, nor does Anderson's Storyteller's Story yield much to his (to my mind) incomparable tales. My trouble as always is to get down to the actual writing. In a country like this it's difficult to sustain the feeling that what you are doing with paper has any value or significance whatsoever. Hence sustained work seems to me out of the question. Then again I'd much rather read books than write them, and most of all I'd much rather be out in the garden getting things to grow. Even so this personal problem is no unusual one probably. All creative writers *must* experience these confused and divided interests which are really the highly valuable materials out of which they make their synthesis. But this sounds as though it's getting pretty high-falutin.

I have one or two friends in the Middle East, simple souls from whom I hear sometimes. One went away believing that Prof. Algie was a Labour M.P. That shows how well our boys know what they are fighting for. I have a Sargeson cousin who has come through Greece and Crete. Oliver Duff's son Gowan has been posted as missing since Greece and no news yet. Terrible shame. I don't know whether you knew him, but he was the best of the three boys, one right out of the box. I see a lot of his mother [Jess Whitworth], a very fine woman.

At least one stray English novelist has turned up in N.Z. lately. Anna Kavan. She lives quite near me and I see a lot of her. Glover rather unkindly describes her as one of those blondes who get round the world with their knees behind their ears. It has some truth in it, but she puts it to good purpose anyhow. If you see Asylum Piece (Cape) try it. And Glover will probably be publishing a curious travel book shortly for her — The Cactus Sign.

Randal Burdon's book by the way is very good. His approach to N.Z. history is about the most refreshing thing that's happened yet.

I'm quite snowed under with correspondence just now so this must end. I hope you won't dissipate your energies in letter-writing as I do. I'd like to see you get something as good, in its own way, as Letters etc. out of what's happening to you now.

With best regards,

Frank Sargeson,

[At the time McCormick was stationed in Egypt with the N.Z. Army. His Letters and Art in New Zealand *(1940) appeared in the Centennial Publications series. The conservative Ronald Macmillan Algie (1888–1978), Auckland University College's first Professor of Law, became an influential M.P. in Sidney Holland's National Government. Gowan Duff survived the war. The British writer Anna Kavan arrived in NZ in February 1941 with the socialist author and pacifist Ian Hamilton. She lived with him in Torbay until late 1942, returning to England when Hamilton was threatened with imprisonment as a conscientious objector.]*

To E.P. Dawson, *Wellington*

Hocken Library

1 September 1941

Dear E.P.

[. . .] I'm afraid my behaviour hasn't been of the best recently. It was, I think, that my chronic inability to accept, deal with, manipulate, and generally take by the throat, the 'reality' around me, suddenly developed into one of its acute states, and stayed round about like that longer than usual. It was all reflected in the way I was feeling physically. I arrived up at Rawene with temp of 102 and spent a couple of days in bed. Very unhappy days too, as the old lunatic doctor WOULD come and pace up and down and expect me to grapple with all his minor and major lunacies. But I like Mrs Smith very much. She's so completely aware of what the world, and incidentally her husband, is like. I don't exactly approve of her way out — books — but she at any rate does the job thoroughly. And as I can talk books we get on, as we did before, very well indeed. But the old doctor. He regards you just as an extension of himself, you feel you have to account to him for every minute of your time, and heaven help you if you sort out the people of the village differently from him. Of course he doesn't appreciate his or anyone else's position, but his wife does. His crazy book [*More Notes from a Backblock Hospital*] will be out shortly and he thinks it's a masterpiece, which of course it may well be, though I can't be sure myself.

Another plague has been a derelict Englishman — public school etc. He's been having a tough time, but I really didn't expect him to turn up here at midnight when I was leaving for Rawene the following morning, especially as he read me his verse until about 2 in the morning — very good verse by the way. Of course I had to leave him the key of the bach, but I warned him when I'd be back and warned him that my old friend Harry would shortly be up from the South. He was still here and is still here — three of us. It took me all day washing dishes and cleaning up generally. So far I'm down £3, pair of shoes, singlet, shirt, socks, and Harry's down an overcoat. Also gasman called and should have been 8/- in the meter, but there was only 3/-. Mystery, but I think I know. After all, when one's up against it etc. I've washed his underclothes for him once, but this week I cease being Christ and have told him so. Yet it plagues me no end. In his circumstances one has to do just as he is doing. I don't blame him, I'm just irritated with myself for being irritated.

Glover certainly did well with the second edition [of *A Man and His Wife*]. I like it better than the first. But apart from receiving a few copies I haven't heard from him for ages. [. . .] [He] should have Smith's Sutch's and Gilbert's books out any time now — I'm looking forward to Gilbert's. I've seen him again and he's been called up and is undecided what to do.

I KNOW I should be reading Shakespeare or somebody but lately I've struck some fascinating modern books. Jail Journey — Jim Phelan, Hodge's books — It's Draughty in Front and Cab, Sir? Connolly's Enemies of Promise, Isherwood's Mr Norris Changes Trains. At the moment I'm taking the plunge into Herbert's Capricornia, but really, I do prefer authors who use fewer words.

Your semi-typed letter was one of the best you've ever written. I've read it through many times and one thing it's done has stopped me from beginning a detective novel about a hospital which the old doctor insisted on working out with me on a couple of evenings. I don't think I could write the damn thing anyhow. And now the warm spring weather is coming it would be such a damn waste. If I can't get on with the things I want to write in the next weeks I'd be much better out in the garden — I'd feel I wasn't being wasteful anyhow. My 28 lbs of seed potatoes are coming through and my new citrus trees are sprouting.

Brenda had a birthday yesterday and Gladys [Salter] borrowed a Kodascope and rented some films. One was an old Chaplin in two reels. Easy Street. It was the purest pleasure that has come my way for a long time.

Will write again soon.

F.S.

Yes, I read the Stein Picasso & enjoyed it.

[Gladys and Len Salter ran a small 'mixed goods' shop in Lake Road, Takapuna. They held meetings of the Takapuna Workers' Education Association [W.E.A.] in their sitting room, extended credit to FS, and sold his garden produce in their shop. FS occasionally helped behind the counter. In 1943 the Salters closed the shop and moved to a 34-acre block at Forrest Hill further up the North Shore.]

To E.P. Dawson, *Wellington*

Hocken Library

5 November [1941]

Dear E.P.

Thanks for letters, as usual full of frontlights and sidelights on a world I don't know much about. One does seem to get about in Wellington and meet people (it's the same in Christchurch) but not here. At least I don't. Somedays when I'm feeling there's nothing worth a damn I sit in the bach and long for the days of the slump. Then people would call and talk. Now they hurry by morning and evening with little bags and hardly have time to say goodday. I think your feeling about the Pacifists is not wholly connected with pacifism. I feel like that about the WEA people. So, so, so, so. . . . . . But I enjoyed myself the other evening. There's an engaging lunatic woman down the street who has joined, she's just too too human and I much enjoy the embarrassment she causes. As a sample of the statements she's likely to make I append the following: The reason why the Maoris can sing so well is that they are English gypsies, but they could never get back because they didn't understand the shipping. Like me she's had bone trouble, but that was only because she was kidnapped. A great source of trouble to her is this: that standing by her window a flash of lightning will start underneath the house on the opposite side of the road leap over to her, alight on her arm and finally run down her leg. It hurts terribly, and she wants to know if I will go with her to the owners of the house and ask if we can look underneath. I've promised to do this if it happens again, and seeing it's happened three times already I'm afraid I'm for it. As a matter of fact I think she's a witch. I imagine she mounts the handle of her vacuum cleaner some evenings & weaves horrid spells all over the city.

The other day I was taken to see Eve Langley who was in a nursing home, having just been brought to bed with her third infant. I was most embarrassed as she's another Robin Hyde — even plus, she takes herself even more seriously. She won the Bulletin Prior prize last year and Angus and Robertson are just bringing the work out. She writes 7000 words a day. When I hear such astronomical figures I always wonder what the gallonage of the Orakei sewer is a day. But I mustn't be unfair as I've read only the lady's poetry. She's not sparing of words at all. She's a little wee wee thing. The book is called The Oberland Pea-pickers and I reserve judgment. [. . .]

You know this spring I've somewhat undone myself. The two previous springs I was nursing my operations and couldn't do much to the garden. This year with some assistance I dug up nearly the whole show. I couldn't see such good ground going to waste so I gradually got it all planted, trying to resist crops that would need time for nursing. But of course it was impossible. I have peas beans lettuce parsley corn tomatoes rock melons and I've just dug nearly two hundred weight of quite good kidney potatoes in the rottenest weather — they came out all caked with soil and each one had to be individually washed before I could take them round to Gladys's shop. Well, I do LIKE being in the garden, but the time, the time! But still I can't resist and now I'm getting the potato patch ready for kumaras. Meantime a longish story lies on my table and is having a very slow and painful parturition. It is a breech birth I'm afraid and may be stillborn. I'm trying to write in the third person both in order to use more words and presuppose a slightly higher level of intelligence. But it doesn't work out. [. . .]

Best,

F.S.

['A longish story': at the time FS was working on a story about a Methodist creamery manager he referred to as his 'idyll'. Michael King suggests this story was abandoned and destroyed.]

To E.P. Dawson, *Wellington*

Hocken Library

22 January 1942

Dear E.P.

[. . .] Your letter has interrupted my story. Your peregrinations round the Little Bethels etc. it was. I did all that while I was living at the Y.M.C.A. [in Auckland] in 1926. And over and over again I've tried to deal with my experiences. Your letter made me open a trunk & go through piles of MSS. It all made me feel melancholy. A score or more of MSS, some of them running into 60 to 100 pages before being abandoned. Intended novels stories & several plays. Besides making me feel sad many a page brought a hot flush to my cheek. How ever could one be so, (no, not serious), but solemn so *young*! I date my fist real step towards knowing how to handle material from Conv. With My U. That was written in 1935, & I'd been trying since 1927. But curiously enough I've never, since 1935, attempted to handle what I botched previously — I mean I chose other material. Yet how strange it is that right now I should be attempting to. The story is the longest short one yet, & it's about a creamery manager & what happened to him in the year 1900. Yet I'm putting into it a lot of myself as a young Methodist local preacher — did I ever tell you I did that? — I show him working, preaching, even kneeling down saying his prayers at night, & at last pouring out his heart's affection. It's going to be damn difficult to get away with, but I think I can do it. It should mark a development if I can & that's what I'm mainly after. But too much of ME.

[. . .] The MS. page of my story stands at page 21 — that's already about as long as An Affair of the Heart — but it will run out at about 40–50. But how can I get on with it? The weather is superb. I get up early and get the sun on my back — it's doing me good — & then manure & water the tomatoes — such huge bunches! & rock melons. I can't water the corn — it's too much — & it's dried up & withered to buggery. But do the kumeras love the sun! By the splits in the hills I'll have tubers as big as my head. Then by about 9:30 all this is done, dishes are washed & place tidied up. In *theory* I should then sit down & go ahead. But do I? No, I stroll up the back to see if the bees are pimping for the rock melons. I look at the tomatoes & stroke one or two if my neighbour isn't looking out the window. Then I come back & fill my pipe & sharpen a pencil. But no, I think I can detect B.O. so I set to work doing a wash. And afterwards I stand looking at my underpants spread on the grape-vine to see them whitening in the sun. Then I feel fagged & feel like a cup of tea. Perhaps by 11:30 I really have got a line written, but it's getting too hot for anything. I spend an hour or so writing another line & decide it really is too hot to write. Besides, after only milk for breakfast I'm getting hungry. So I eat, then a lie-down under a lemon tree & another pipeful becomes practically the whole end of life. Then of course if I don't get to the butcher's he'll be shut & there's the cat to consider. But I may dash off another line before going. Then when I come back I have to eat something substantial. It's a bore, but necessary, besides with a belly full I can sit & dream for an hour afterwards & maybe, perhaps, even probably I shall stroll round to the shop. But all this life is known as working hard on a story, so I am abstracted & unsociable, even rude to Gladys's visitors & critical of her & Len. They offer me first coffee & mugs of milk & I refuse. But ah, Len wants his hair cut. And my real predilection in life comes out. To be doing some job of work under my hands. But something easy like gardening, or cutting hair, or cutting the dags off sheep's bottoms. Something common, earthy, smelling of humanity or animals, something easy. Not something rarefied & highbrow like writing, something hard. If I do a good job I come home almost feeling happy.

How a story ever finally gets written I'm sure I don't know. It's a sort of minor miracle. And how to explain all that's happening to me mentally & emotionally while it's being done I don't know either. Of course nothing I write, ever, is ever the whole truth or anyway near it. But if you or anyone else can fill in all the missing colours you may get something like Anatole France's revolving wheel. I don't know. [. . .]

Best

F.S.

To Alec Pickard [A.P. Gaskell], *Invercargill*

Alexander Turnbull Library

17 February 1942

Dear A.P. Gaskell,

It's a damn dangerous thing to go encouraging writers, but here goes — I've seen two of your tales in the Listener & this 2nd one ['The Picture in the Paper'] seems to me very nicely done. Unlike the majority of the people who pester me with their MSS you seem to me to know exactly what you are doing & do it damn well.

It looks as if you have been reading my stuff, but maybe I'm flattering myself. I hope you know what you're in for if you keep on, yet I hope you do keep on & carry right on where I & others will never be able to go. In one way I'm a fool to be writing you this, but during the 10 or so years when I was learning to write & practically never getting printed I could have done with a little encouragement from outside now & then.

With best wishes,

Frank Sargeson

To E.P. Dawson, *Wellington*

Hocken Library

22 March 1942

Dear EP,

First let my ego have its fling. *An Affair* etc. I have a mixture of feelings over your taking the story so seriously. What are the facts so far as I know them? (Stop me if I've said all this before). The entire story & characters are *invented*. It's a story of waiting derived, I think, from a complex of experiences of my own. In one sense it's true to say that Mrs Crawley is myself (or an extension of myself), successfully disguised, I imagine. Joe is a *mélange* of numerous people I've waited for & who for the most part have seldom turned up. There are certain rhythms in the prose which don't exist in anything else I've written & these I think are derived from Liam O'Flaherty *Two Years* which I was reading at the time of writing. Now the mother-son business is as old & older than Adam. It may or may not be or become pathological. I don't think that the question whether it is or isn't interests me one scrap. If such a business exists that's enough for me. I'm neither for or against it, all I know is that I'm moved by it — its profundity may be terrifying yet at the same time beautiful — this is what I've tried to aim at in the story, & if I'd been a great enough story-teller I'd have brought off a catharsis in the reader & rendered him temporarily speechless — forced him, in other words, temporarily to accept a great fact of life, made him feel temporarily humble before one of the great mysteries of the human heart. (Obviously, of course, I'm not a great, even good, enough story-teller for that). But tell me, honestly, can you blame Mrs Crawley? I can & do in real life when I meet them (the Mrs Crawleys), but it's the reasoning W.E.A. side of me that does that; another side, the side that makes me write stories, knows that the impulses of the human heart are as varied & incalculable as the N.Z. weather. I very often find them terrifying, wonderful, beautiful.

I've been wondering over your use of the words 'shady' & 'pathological'. If you take a long enough view of human affairs I doubt whether you can fasten on any area of human activity, & call it either of those names. Or if you can, you can only by using as a criterion contemporary (and therefore transitory) ideas of what constitutes healthy *mores*. Mother-son love has always existed, so has homosexual love, so has heterosexual, yet at the present time the two former are discredited. It wasn't always so (as you know Plato's dialogues on love refer exclusively to homosexual love), nor will it always be so in the future. The point is surely this: that anything that *exists*, must always be carefully reckoned with, because *mores*, sound *mores*, are always built on what exists, not on what some people (for the most part second-rate people) think *ought* to exist. To an imaginative mind there is surely something delightful in contemplating *everything* that exists, because of the wonderful possibilities of new development. Let me go on with this argument just a little further. Obviously at this stage of modern society *mores* are in a state of flux. But the individual has to get through life. All right, let him make that life tolerable to himself by a *minimum* of conformity to what a decayed social organisation demands from him, and a *maximum* of obedience to what the impulses of his own heart demands. Concretely, if you love your own mother go on loving her & if need be only pretend to love your wife; if you are sufficiently familiar with your own nature to be completely aware that you are either homosexual or heterosexual, then don't pretend to yourself that you are anything but what you are, no matter how much social pretence & nonsense may be necessary. Looking at things in the largest possible way it seems to me to be just like this: none of us living now can ever be part of a *system* of sound *mores* (using the word in the largest possible sense), therefore we have a duty to the human tradition (I mean something pretty tremendous by that) to avoid any private faking. I invented Mrs Crawley, but at least I can say I didn't fake her. But God help the old girl now, because I feel I can't do or say anything more about her. [. . .]

I'll ask Fairburn to post you the Folios of New Writing. All the past week I've been working on Dr Smith's new book [*Medical Advice from a Backblock Hospital*] — the typescript was in a state of chaos & caused me no end of bother. I've also been to see Dr. Wolfskehl — an old blind Liberal German professor of Literature (& quite good poet & translator I'm told). It was a real privilege & treat to meet him. A scholar, a humanist, a friend of Rilke, Wedekind, Thomas Mann, Franz Kafka. He's incredible to look at, like something you've dreamed or perhaps seen on the films — a bit like Maurice Moscovitch crossed with George Arliss. I hope to see him again & possibly I shall offer to read to him a couple of hours a week. He moved me no end. He said: 'Kafka is wonderful, he is *full* of emptiness'. The real thing that.

Generally speaking I'm in a curious state just now. See practically nothing of Gladys or Len or the friends you know. I'm struggling & struggling with my Idyll, but it doesn't come right yet. I glance at the papers but take very little interest in war news or anything else. [. . .]

F.S.

To E.P. Dawson, *Wellington*

Hocken Library

10 October [1942]

Dear E.P.

[. . .] Various items of interest through the post recently. [. . .] Here's a curiosity from America. One of the editors of the Houghton Mifflin Coy ('an old publishing company of very excellent standing') writes to my N.Y. agent [Harold Ober]: 'I am crazy about Sargeson. The guy can write like a fool, but I am still trying to figure out what some of his words mean. Is a budgie a parrot or a monkey? And just what is a cobbler (sic)? Also, am I right in my conclusions about Maggie?' He goes on later: 'I think you are quite right in saying there's no chance of blowing this story ['That Summer'] up to a book-length novel. Also I don't think his first book over here should be a collection of short stories, but if we came out with a full length novel, properly annotated, I think we could sell Sargeson in a big way. Would you be willing to write him for an outline of a sample chapter'. Well, there you are, that's America. If the outline and sample chapter is satisfactory they'd consider making me a Houghton Mifflin Fellow which would mean an advance — amount unspecified. Of course I shall send the bloody outline and sample chapter — I'm merely irritated I haven't yet got down to it — the sample chapter will be easy — it will be labelled Chapter 20 — but the outline worries me a little.

I've had a note from Lehmann lately and he says he's negotiating with his Bank to settle his account with me right now. I'm feeling expectatious. Also he enclosed Penguin N.Ws. 12 and 13. 13 has my *Making of a NZer* in it and it is the first of the thing reorganized. It is not particularly interesting, but there are some very good war drawings by Keith Vaughan and some interesting ballet photos. In his note Lehmann mentioned he was accepting the little Maori story I sent on for the young fellow in Invercargill [Alec Pickard / A.P. Gaskell]. This amuses me in this way. Various people, self-conscious strivers in the arts — like myself — have asked me to send on things for them to Lehmann. But none of them has clicked so far. I offered to do something for the Invercargill fellow and he does click. What do I imply? Well, it is nice to have one's judgment confirmed of course, but that isn't exactly the point. It's that those who have the stuff in them are better off if they work blindly and in isolation. I was in that condition when I wrote my stories. Now I know people trying to do the same thing as myself I can't write a bloody thing that's any good. A further point of course is that by writing to the young Invercargillite I may be rapidly ruining him. But of course don't take this paragraph too seriously, and do see that whatever I am saying about fellow-writers I'm also saying about myself.

Bob Gilbert was with the Salters for some days again recently and I enjoyed his company. We played chess mostly. He was full of criticism of his own stories — a very healthy sign, particularly as he struck me as being quite genuine about it. He sees now that in his book he has sometimes mistaken the *idea* for a story for the story itself. But ultimately I think this won't matter. His looseness and uncertainty of conception has great possibilities — he will go on writing easily and prolifically and this will be a great advance from would-be, and therefore constipated, perfectionists such as myself. [. . .]

All these reports from overseas about my novelette ['That Summer'] have given me a little more confidence about it, so I am definitely going to start passing it round to one or two. The last copy is over in Sydney with Angus and Robertson just now, but it will come back soon and you shall have it soon after that.

Are you still in the servery? I'm worried about that too. Before I had my last bout mainly on my back I'd got the garden in good nick and have recently had the first fruits. Potatoes, but with 62 wet days out of the 90 they were in they got blighted and I got only a quarter the weight I should have done. I gave away a fair number and sold the rest. Now peas are nearly ready and there are a lot and they're quite all right. I've had broad beans too, but as usual they got the rust badly. Fine weather has tempted me to put in tomatoes, about 70 plants, and this year for the first time I'm trying them in compost right from the beginning. But I fear if the weather is damp and hot they'll grow to stem and leaf and take the Irish disease into the bargain. I've got corn up and rock melons, and the Chinese gooseberries I couldn't afford to buy but did are sprouting wonderfully. It occurs to me the only two things I've ever grown here that have seemed to be immune to disease are leeks and chokoes. My choko this year is growing like magic, but leeks aren't thrilling enough to attract me. Nor your love, silver beet. The best thrill I ever get out of the soil is growing good rock melons — the musky smell — I believe the Australian aborigine women smell like that — and the slightly rotten rich flavour — just like the flavour of the body social these days.

Best.

F.S.

To E.P. Dawson, *Wellington*

Hocken Library

10 December [1942]

Dear EP,

[. . .]I'm a bit unbalanced really at the moment. I've been buying clothes. But I forgot to tell you that about 4 weeks back the money from Lehmann turned up. It was less than half what I was expecting — just over a fiver, and I used it to get my typewriter out of pawn. Now with the fiver from [John] Drew [Glover's partner at Caxton] I have bought a beautiful pair of trousers, some jockey underpants which the salesman assured me did everything in the way of avoiding 'gape' etc. just as the advertisements claimed, and oh *pièce de résistance*, a Harris tweed jacket — though this last will require me to do a little fresh manoeuvring with the pawnbroker and the typewriter before I actually have it. (This doesn't matter a scrap — it worries me only after six months, the limit of a pawn ticket if you can't trust the broker, and you never can). But how strange it is. For almost, though not quite the first, time in my life I'm going to be elegant — or rather as elegant as my looks and figure will permit. I can't explain it. Are some of these apparent trivialities really very important in life? Shabbiness suits this bach very well, but if people like the Sewells live in a modern house they just can't have shabby people visiting them, or rather it makes them a little uncomfortable. I've noticed that this year and laughed at it, yet now I go and do this mad thing against all that I say to myself and other people I believe in. The clothes are not the man, certainly, yet no one would receive you naked, so just where is the true attitude? Elegantly dressed you feel confident, lord it over shabby people — bad! And what has one given in return for the right to wear Harris tweed supplied by underpaid farmers and sweated factory girls who are not only keeping me clad but providing a rake-off for the wholesaler and retailer as well. No I give it up. Yet I'm deriving pleasure from the thought of going out togged up. Perhaps I'll even feel impressive enough to be offhand with waitresses and suchlike as rich people are in films. Yet if I am impressive will the waitress still drop the remark she used to when my appearance made her feel she was as good as I was and a good deal better — the remark that had something *genuine* in it and which I gratefully accepted as the missing link in the story I was trying to write. The best sort of clothes for a writer would be ones that would make him invisible. Short of that it is best to be shabby and nondescript — why should I suddenly seem to deny what I know to be true? Underneath my amusement at the Sewells' embarrassment at introducing me to their tailored friends in their tailored house was there a wish to be like them? All I can say is that in this world it is terrifyingly easy to damn oneself — yet the ways that the parsons point out are so difficult. [. . .]

Best,
F.S.

To Alec Pickard, *Invercargill*

Alexander Turnbull Library

30 January [1943]

Dear Pickard,

Thanks for your note and I'm glad you've seen Holcroft. He's a good bloke I believe, and a good critic I know, and I've always envied him his fluency on paper. I only hope he doesn't do you any harm, which is what I'm so frightened of doing myself. [. . .]

When you say you don't know where the hell you are I can't help wondering what your background is. I wonder if some reference to my own may help you. I started to write about 1928, when I was 25. I was a Waikato boy and my father was a town clerk, so I had the usual sort of small-town middle-class upbringing, very strict Methodist by the way. I had 4 years at High School and then worked in law offices and eventually passed my solicitor's exams. Literature, except the Bible and Dickens and the usual sort of boys' stuff, never touched me until I was 22, that was, first, Arnold Bennett, then Shaw. I read everything of Shaw's. Then I discovered Tolstoy and Dostoevsky, and oh boy! Later came Tchekov and de Maupassant, and again oh boy! That, naturally, was the beginning of my interest in the short story. From then to this day I suppose I've been developing my flair for knowing all about books, even those that I haven't read — with the aid of a few literary periodicals that's easy. By the time all this had started though, I was boarding in Auckland with spells of baching in this bach — it still stands up, but God knows how or why. Visitors say it will be interesting to see how it stands an air raid. In 1927 I had some luck and got away to England, and friends I made there couldn't understand my coming so far to spend such a lot of time reading in the British Museum. The main thing about England and the Continent though was that I began to combine a little life with literature — my Methodism plus my native timidity had hitherto made it impossible. Back in NZ I became a Civil Servant in Wellington and why I didn't cut my throat I don't know. Instead I started to write, short stories influenced by Joyce's Dubliners. [J.C.] Squire was kind enough to say he nearly printed one in the London Mercury. Then I wrote a novel in beautiful

Galsworthian prose, and Jonathan Cape was kind enough to say he would have published it if England hadn't just then gone off the Gold Standard. Then I wrote a play which A.D. Peters nearly got a production in London of. Almost simultaneously I had my first article published (in the N.Z. Herald ['In France: Along the Road', 1930]), and my first story (in the Australian Women's Mirror ['Life is Like That', 1933]). Both were terrible, though eventually the story was transformed into Three Men of my book. By this time I'd spent a couple of years on an uncle's sheep farm in the King Country and was back in the bach here — and the slump was on. The slump and the Christchurch paper, Tomorrow, (and of course Denis Glover and the Caxton Press) were the makings of me as a writer — or should I say the makings so far as I can put my finger on them. I was on relief work and sustenance and doing all sorts of odd jobs, though mainly gardening, and at the same time writing my sketches and stories, and as many articles as I could get the papers to take. And everything, by the way, was written under the spell of a single and continuous emotion. But things changed as the war got nearer, and as Holcroft probably told you I turned out to be a T.B. subject — the quacks have taken out two of my ribs, yet don't know to this day just where the trouble is. However ribs don't matter (you can wear corsets if necessary — Pope did, according to Dr Johnson) so things aren't so bad. There's Social Security and 30/- a week. But most days particularly this hot weather I'm too damned tired to do much work except the usual household chores. And that's one NZ writer's story. Or a little of it. And perhaps there's no point in it and it will make you yawn. And my God, I turn 40 in March.

Holcroft by the way makes some good points about writing in N.Z. in his essay The Deepening Stream. My experience is that there's no place for the writer in NZ life unless you're a journalist. You're just a bum. Yet Anderson in his A Storyteller's Story says the same about America — did I tell you he never started to write until he was nearly 40? — and worse, there's no place for the poet anywhere (I've gradually become more interested in poetry than any other form of writing). Though perhaps I'm exaggerating a little too much. Still, a few of us feel that willy-nilly we've got to take up a burden. Culture, a tradition, a necessity for interpretation, call it what you will, has got to be preserved and developed. The poets are the worst off of the lot though, and personally I don't blame the great number of them who seem to have decided that the only thing to be done about poetry in the meantime is to take it into a sort of private laboratory, and do some very private and esoteric experiments with it there. Perhaps we story writers are a little more fortunate, people like Hemingway and Bates even make a fair pile of dough, though I don't suppose better craftsmen, such as Anderson and V.S. Pritchett (at his best), have ever made enough to feed a canary. And when you come to NZ . . . well, well . . . I'd like to talk to you about all this. [. . .]

Best,

F.S.

To Denis Glover, *London*

Alexander Turnbull Library

10 February 1943

Dear Glover,

I am quite overcome by your quite pathetic letter of 28 November. The simple country sailor boy lost in the great city — the cry from the heart really touches me. Many thanks anyhow and oh how my heart throbbed at and over the modest understating of exploits in the glorious and horrible arctic regions. Like Melville you will need 40 years of returement and anonimity to deal with all this, and what horned wales and tailless beasts (I think I'll just leave those spellings) may come of it in time. [. . .]

Well, (two wells) here is the news. Those boys in Christchurch, Curnow and [J.R.] Hervey have been pushing their barrows in the absence of the master brain. Another Whim-Wham and New Poems. Also Dawson sent your boys [at Caxton] another £50, of which they sent me 10 quid. I regarded it as an attempt to shoulder off any responsibility for doing anything about That Summer and sent 5 back. But letters to Chch go off into a great void now, and I haven't heard anything since the beginning of December. I've always intended sending you a copy of N.Z. New Writing (Kiwi Books) Oh hell! The kiwi looks like the 'copy this and send for free criticism' of the Commercial Art School. But it's significant as well as depressing that no one could think of a non-imitative title. Anyhow perhaps someone has sent you a copy (I haven't one by me at the moment), certainly [the editor of *NZ New Writing* Ian] Gordon coyly sent one to Lehmann so if necessary have a look at his. I may say that the best of the prose was scouted for by myself — Gaskell's ['The Picture in the Paper'], [Greville] Texidor's ['Home Front'] and Anna [Kavan]'s. I'm still coaching Gaskell along and eventually I think he'll come along quite nicely. Texidor's thing ['Ice-storm'] even with obvious defects is good. And with much free criticism from myself she's since produced several things that I think are really fine. You'll be delighted to meet her, the knees inclined to be behind the ears, Kavan-like, certainly, but the attitude different. And it's all in the attitude, yes it is now. A really fine woman, with a lovely dreamy grace. Her husband [Werner Droescher] a nice bloke too, and he's beginning to write nicely — also a refugee.

The most depressing feature of the summer has been the transference to Auckland of Birdlime Villa in toto [the Christchurch flatmates Jean Stevenson (later Bertram) and Helen Shaw]. Jean is working on the Listener here. I've kept her down to one visit to the bach so far, but boy, it's difficult. Next time she comes there's got to be a protective crowd, and there'll be a notice pinned up: 'All visitors welcome provided they don't talk about their souls, nor attempt to talk about anybody else's (NB this includes the host's).' The poor girl still takes some time to speak her pieces. Ah well, maybe it should be: To forgive is human to er divine.

I see dear old (as you say) Karl [Wolfskehl] at least once a week, and he's been over here several times. He went into the sea once and looked like an intellectual porpoise. I have a notion he may be doing me harm. After all I'm a colonial and have a job to do that only a colonial can do, but intercourse with him is so damned attractive I'm losing my grip. I'm degenerating into a second-rate European, all subjective, when I ought to be trying to draw the subjective out of objective colonialism. His perception and vitality are however marvellous. If I give him a choice of authors when I'm reading to him he always picks the most interesting of the young people. I feel on the day he dies he'll still be trying to find out what the young things of 20 or so are thinking and doing. We have a big translation job on hand but it proceeds slowly — a handful of NZ short stories and a few poems. Through him I've met others, and extraordinarily pleasant people some of them are, particularly some who are farming hereabouts. I've had some very pleasant brief holidays with them.

My big autobiographical novel [*When the Wind Blows*] proceeds slowly, but with the better weather my health improved. I'm pretty well now and I hope to swing it along a bit faster with the cooler autumn weather.

The Army has nabbed Rex and he's doing it hard, surprisingly hard I find, but it's probably due to turmoils of the heart. His poem ['Poem'] in NZ NW is a wonderful tour de force, but hell, at his age he shouldn't be writing straight love lyrics. I stick to my opinion that straight love poetry of the highest order can come only from the very young, equally it can only be fully enjoyed by the very young.

Give my regards to poor D'Arcy if you see him. Christ, I'm sore with myself for never writing, but the fag of skirting his prejudices and not hurting him too much is something I can never face up to. [. . .]

Best,

F.S.

To E.P. Dawson, *[Mt Maunganui]*

Hocken Library

26 May 1943

Dear EP,

Such things going on up this way. Luckily I was out of them for a week or so as I had a bad cold. Two days I stayed in bed and read Lady Chatterley's Lover aloud to myself in French. It has improved my French no end. But the business is this: Poor old Karl is now installed as a boarder and lodger a few streets away. The landlady is an old friend of mine — I almost wrote 'flame'. Anyhow she has a lot of bric à brac, but Karl is seeing to that, and by the time he is through the house will be a nice modern home without a single piece of bric à brac. The other evening he was explaining to me that he never broke things, and flung up his hands to emphasize the point, and down came showers of glass from a beautiful art lampshade. Then, at leave-taking he became entangled in the hall curtain and brought the rod down, and completely wrapped up flapped about in the dark like one of the monstrous vampires he believes in. The landlady tried to help with an electric torch, but that got dashed out of her hand, and it was goodbye to another item. Well, it is terrible to have an outsize body as well as an outsize soul. And nobody and nothing (particularly the bric à brac) seems to be able to resist either. I'm afraid I'm feeling very exhausted myself, but what can one do when there are blind geniuses around. Oh, you should, and I hope shall, see him in the bach. The floor groans and creaks as he paces it, the walls rock, the words mispronounced with grammar upside down come in an endless torrent. A wonderful old man! An impossible old man! How long I can stand it I don't know. Sooner or later I will explode, but just at what point and what will be the result I don't yet know. Today I am taking him to get his hair cut. The landlady says this is necessary as she's sick of people referring to his hair as evidence that he is obviously a female in disguise. No, the whole thing is incredible and you can fill in any gaps in this paragraph in any way you wish, and I'm sure won't get the feel of the extravagance of it all.

28 May

I've been making desperate efforts to go on with this for the past several days. At the point I was at Karl arrived to say he'd blown the fuse with his electric shaver. [. . .]

I think I told you about the last letter from Glover, and from what I hear from various people his exploits have caused him to be recommended for some sort of decoration. This depresses me. He's puffing up Christ's College when he knows damn well he should be puffing it down. And I just can't see the point of carrying on like an Elizabethan sea-dog out of time and place. But I don't know. Perhaps something both good and modern will come out of it, though I don't see how it can. [. . .]

Well, no more this time. I've just time to post this before I go for Karl, and the rest of the day will be his I'm afraid. Though I shouldn't say 'I'm afraid', as once the plunge is taken I usually enjoy it quite well. [. . .]

Best,

F.S.

To Denis Glover, *[London]*

Alexander Turnbull Library

9 September 1943

Dear Glover,

Your Tit of 24 July for my Tat of 24 May just arrived. I'm too tired at the moment to go on titting and tatting, but I note that date, 24 May as rather significant. The autumn had just broken, Karl had been turned out of his lodging, & after a long hunt I'd got him a place near me. Several nights a week in frightful rain I'd hear 'Fraank, Fraank' & go out & rescue him, knee-deep in the garden mud. All winter I had some great sittings with him, often from 2 pm until midnight & later if I counted the repatriating of him. I'll have much to tell you of him when we meet again. In big quantities he can be very trying, but I wouldn't have missed him for anything. [. . .]

If you go to USA. I think you should try to see Laughlin (of New Directions). As a side-line to publishing he runs a Skiing Lodge (Alta Lodge, Alta, Utah) & I've heard from him a fair bit lately. One of his contributors is out here as a crack psychiatrist for the Army. This bird, Merrill Moore is credited with having written *40,000* sonnets. I've seen 6 & they aren't too bad. For both positive & negative reasons it's been interesting meeting him — you get quite a line on American College Culture, Laboratory Poetry etc.

Quite a number of lads I know are back from the Middle East & I'm getting fresh lines from just listening to them talk with a question now & then that is supposed to be just on the points that I want information on — I have a theory that post-war literature comes not so much from those who actually took part as those who can digest part of the experience at a remove or two away. After all that's what Aldous Huxley seemed to do last time. Though of course I know that I myself am far too old to really get a decent understanding. [. . .]

Recently I sent Lehmann a few things including *'Gods Live in Woods'* the last story I've written — it's an important story for me, because it touches maybe on something larger than anything I've touched on yet. It should please D'Arcy. Also the novel continues to promise well, I think. [. . .]

With all the best,

F.S. [. . .]

To E.P. Dawson, *Mt Maunganui*

Hocken Library

7 November 1943

Dear EP,

At last I'm round to writing you a decent letter. [. . .] Well, honestly I have been working eyes out. I was so overcome with the deadness of my own soil (lack of animal manure in the compost I think would be the explanation) and the immense possibilities in that up at Forrest Hill Road, that I suddenly went mad and dug with Len [Salter] like a lunatic. Between us we have made a monstrously large garden — you would really be surprised. And the results even now are surprising indeed. Rock melons grow at twice the rate they do on my place etc. Also I suddenly got sick of my perpetual tobacco embarrassment and decided to grow my own. We have over a hundred plants — over 80 up the hill and over 20 down here and they are all looking promising so far.

Have you heard that Ian Hamilton has bought 36 acres up at Kerikeri and is starting what seems to be a New Life colony up there. Of course it will fail, but it should be respected as a gesture. I have no intention of going myself, but would you consider it yourself. If so, I'd put it to him. Werner [Droescher] is going — to take charge of the children. And Gladys [Salter] for a while to help get things started. I believe colonists get board and lodgings but no pay. Situation ideal, big house with verandah 80 feet long. Ian wants suitable people, but just between you and me he seems to be picking on the wrong ones at present. Tell me if you're interested. Greville [Texidor] is not going, not to begin with anyhow.

[. . .] Did you see 'Gods Live in Woods' in the Listener? I heard from Lehmann and he and Plomer liked it but thought I could have made more of it — I'm dying to hear what E.M. Forster thought of it, but perhaps I never shall. Lehmann liked the one about the tomato-grower ['A Man of Good Will'] best of all the small bundle of MSS that I sent him and wants to use it — it seems so strange to me, I never showed it to any one and somehow still feel it was far from the best I can do. Penguin NW No 17 with the first part of the novel [*That Summer*] is out but I don't suppose I'll get my copy until Christmas or after. Lehmann says he hopes one day to do all my stuff in one big collection — thank God perhaps he doesn't do it now as it would probably make me feel I could leave off writing for good. [The Australian anthology] COAST TO COAST by the way turned down 'Gods Live in Woods'. I suppose it was expecting too much to expect that particular editor (Frank Dalby Davison) to have any idea what I was getting at.

This bout of hard mad work has done me good. I feel the pressure of the stuff inside me waiting to get out much more acutely, also I have a better idea what form it is to take. I want to write a sort of colonial ULYSSES. I see now that two books I have in mind — my long semi-autobiographical novel [*When the Wind Blows*], and MAN OF ENGLAND NOW should be one book. The man of England now will be the colonial Bloom — will be an attempt to depict what European man gone to the colonies has become, and the autobiography, woven in, will be a demonstration of the colonial Stephen Dedalus — and seeing he will be so half-baked compared to the Dublin one I can make the most of wonderful opportunities for self-ridicule. As for the colonial Bloom I have the character ready to hand — none other than Johnny — you remember the notes I read you — though of course endless others will be thrown in and developed, and really the thing can be quite a good thing and I'm profoundly excited about it. What a labour though, the mere thought of it makes me feel faint. Yet I have a strange feeling that I will shortly get down to it and will be completely preoccupied with getting it out maybe for years. [. . .]

Yes, later on, I'll be down to see you sure enough if you stay on — I've seen Tauranga so far only from the top of the mountain at Te Aroha. Meantime to bed with Henry James — Honi soit.

F.S.

[Johnny (aka Jack): John Unsworth Whewell. FS met Johnny/Jack, a drifting Englishman of about his own age, 'soon after Pearl Harbour'. Never able to hold down a job for long, Whewell came and went from 14 Esmonde Road, sometimes overlapping with Harry Doyle. In 1948 FS moved an army hut onto his property with the intention of providing Whewell with a base and himself with help in the garden, but Whewell never occupied the hut and instead used a small inheritance to return to England. See FS, More Than Enough, *pp. 140–147. FS's* Man of England Now *was published in 1972.]*

To Alec Pickard, *Invercargill*

Alexander Turnbull Library

1 January 1944

Dear Pickard,

Many thanks for your letter. You must have been writing about the same time as I was. I was very interested in all you had to say — the provincial town life, school, cricket, — it was all so very much part of my own life once, and you remind me of it in a way that makes me think it was all just only yesterday. Well, I suppose my reaction when it came was a pretty violent one — I suppose it just wouldn't occur to an unsophisticated person who happened to read my writings what a thoroughly middle-class person I am really.

Anyhow I have a little further literary news. My Christmas box came in the shape of Penguin NW No 17 from Lehmann. Unfortunately just the one copy. He has printed a little more than one third of my THAT SUMMER and apologises in his foreword for cutting it up in this way. Also he has printed Greville Texidor's story from the local NW, and printed again Plomer's SOME BOOKS FROM NZ which first appeared in one of the Folios of NW. I am quite and even genuinely overcome. The whole thing seems to be splashed with Sargeson. I now feel like a conjuror who has led people into believing he can do his stuff — there I am right under the spotlight, and I haven't an idea for a single one of the tricks I'm expected to do. Anyhow I dislike very much the idea of your eventually reading the novel piecemeal, so as soon as I can get one of my typescripts back I'll send it to you to read if you will. How the devil it's getting printed God knows. Superficially it's just a simple lively tale of a boy throwing up a farm job in the slump and coming into town, picking up with an older man, also out of work, and sticking by the older bloke. Really of course it's about a great deal more than that. Mainly I suppose it could be described as a story about love — I suppose an attempt at demonstrating something of the faith trust responsibility confidence & belief that is the sine qua non of such relationships. But what will puzzle many readers and enrage some is the almost complete absence of heterosexuality in the thing. (Fairburn even mistook the sex of one of the characters). Of course I have many reasons for this. The heterosexual motif seems to me to be worn a little thin, for one thing — though it isn't, let me say, in such things as your Holiday story, because you give it all or a great deal of the freshness and naiveté of youth. Also in times of chaos such as we are living in now everything seems to me to tend to break down. Sex becomes indeterminate, there is still the need and the search for a decent human relationship, but it becomes uncertain desperate anxious and even frantic. Anyhow from my reading of E.M. Forster's writings I can see quite clearly why he would like my story, but how far the average reader will see into it I don't know. I am grateful to Lehmann for taking the risk of printing it, yet am a little troubled both on his behalf and my own. But this is a hell of a game, trying to interpret one's own writings — one should, of course, do the best that is in one always and when the thing is complete try to forget it. It then begins an independent life of its own, may grow and increase in stature or fade away and die. If it is any good at all someone sometime somewhere will appreciate it for whatever worth it has.

I thought Elizabeth Bowen's introduction to the Faber [Book of Modern] stories was very pretentious but some of the stories I liked. As I told you I haven't read the Holcroft [*The Waiting Hills*] — the Library still seems to be having it bound. Just recently I've had much pleasure out of Gertrude Stein's first — THREE LIVES — it was first published in 1908 and this simply amazes me. It seems so very modern, but of course that is because of the enormous influence the book had on such people as Anderson, and through them Hemingway and the rest. Unfortunately I can't send it to you as I had difficulty in borrowing it even for a short time.

Whenever you talk about being a fizzer you worry me no end. Let me say I feel you have in you greater potentialities than Bob Gilbert has. Bob is slick, it's no good denying it, and he wouldn't deny it himself. Of course he *may* develope. Naturally you are assimilating, much more so than you are at present aware of I should say. Don't worry, *try* your best until you feel you have *done* your best with that particular impulse and only give up then. If it is all in you, right in the inside core, it will come out eventually, never fear. Yet I confess I feel miserable in saying all this. The life of the writer in England where writing can be part of the social pattern is I imagine miserable enough. Out here it is just plain hell. I can't ask you to endure the burden of that hell — all I can do is to try and help you to make the freest possible choice, in the fullest knowledge possible.

By the way the loot from the novel when publication is complete should be about £45. Not bad. When it comes to hand I'm going to be moving about the country a bit. I hope to be seeing Gilbert in Westland. I hope maybe the three of us can fix a date.

Thermometer is nearly 80 — *warmest* wishes,

F.S.

4/1/44 P.S. Yours just arrived. I feel like writing some more but it's too hot. But will write again soon. W.B. Yeats was a virgin until over 40, so no need to worry.

Cheers,

F.S.

['loot from the novel': That Summer *was published in three sections in* Penguin New Writing *17–19, 1943–1944.]*

To Alec Pickard, *Invercargill*

Alexander Turnbull Library

14 January 1944

Dear Pickard,

[. . .] I don't know that these confessions & revelations are good for either of us, but I confess I was rather startled by what you told me last time. When I think of my own fevers — of the body as far back as I can remember — of the heart & the emotions from round about 13 to 14 — well, you seemed to be speaking from another world — one that I could hardly credit the existence of. I don't know — I suppose my experience from round about the age of 20 has its basis in a sort of pragmatism. If the heart is moved it is a fact that can't be got over — something has to be done about it — & for me that 'something' has always been something positive rather than negative. The same when there is desire of the body, or when the two are wrapped up together — the most tormenting & unbearable situation of all of these is frustration, & hardly less so if there isn't. But don't mistake me — at the same time as all this is 'fact' it's also illusion — or am I wrong? — is the fact I accept as fact no more fact, than the illusion that I come to name illusion not really illusion? I don't know. All I know is that I have to *act*. And worse I'm compelled to *over* act. All that energy discharged! No wonder my literary output is so small. It has its base in so much of this same energy, yet how little I have to spare when love & sensuality make such terrific demands. And what agonies when some one I love or desire, or both, won't or can't reciprocate — or vice versa.

Aren't we, in some curious way, in somewhat the same position? — both frustrated. The only difference that frustration to me is something larger & more terrible — more *ultimately* & *finally* terrible — than it appears to you. — to you it must sometimes seem very *immediately* terrible. Anyhow I repeat, if it is possible, don't worry. It's true about Yeats. And I remember it used to be an axiom of Cresswell's that nothing the artist experiences can ever be a disadvantage to him. We both have energy — our writings prove that — & whether it operates against a background of license or restraint is probably quite beside the point. Hemingway has done a lot of whoring no doubt, & Jane Austen probably died a virgin, yet poor old Ernest can't hold a candle to dear old Jane as a writer. (Perhaps Jane held a candle sometimes to herself, but that's also beside the point).

By the way have you ever struck Dreiser's *Dawn* — autobiography. A wonderful piece of work, & one very wonderful blunt candid chapter on these matters.

Anyhow all this is very much *entre nous*.

Every day I've been intending to get my teeth into what I hope to write, but so far nothing much doing. I've had such a lot of reading matter to get through. I read some Santayana essays & they sent me back to Plato & from there I drifted to Swift & Hazlitt & came to the surface again only to be submerged in *New Writing and Daylight* several numbers of *Horizon* (English) & *The Partisan Review* (American) & finally Henry Green's *Caught*. I like Green very much — *Party Going* was very good. Anyhow say if you don't ever see any of these & I'll try to send you a parcel. Also I have a few things here I've always intended to send you but somehow never get round to.

I agree with you about writing something *funny* — I agree with Henry Miller — we could do with a hell of a lot more of it.

I don't know about that 'feminine' touch. I'm terribly prejudiced against women authors — unless they're more than half men — like Gertrude Stein. Once in about 10 centuries a real woman puts it across — Jane Austen, for instance — but it's too rare to alter my conviction that most women writers are just frightful nuisances — when they're not something very mischievous. But it's just a prejudice of mine.

Well, I have to get out in the garden. Tons of tomatoes corn cobs peppers (or capsicum, chili, paprika, pimento — you can take your choice of names) beans. The rock melons (40 have set nicely) ripening nicely, the passion vine is loaded, lemons grapefruit & oranges are OK & the Chinese gooseberry will bear next year. The tobacco is OK too.

All the best.

F.S.

To Maurice Duggan, *Mt Eden, Auckland*

Alexander Turnbull Library

16 February 1944

Dear Maurice Duggan,

Thank you for your letter — it seems to me to have plenty of lively intelligence in it — I like it.

I don't know how to answer your questions though. I don't know the answers. If I knew exactly how a story is written & exactly where it comes from — well, then perhaps I wouldn't be worrying my soul-case out at the moment trying to write what I'm supposed to be working on.

About 'trends' — see if you can come across Gertrude Stein's *Three Lives*. Though it's a difficult book to come by. Also do you know Sherwood Anderson? His *Winesburg, Ohio* is in the Library.

However, maybe we'd do better in a talk. Would you care to risk one? I say 'risk' — because maybe 20 years hence the critics will be saying: 'Duggan had great promise but Sargeson's influence ruined him'. Or am I taking the greater risk myself? You'll surely lose any illusions if you see I'm a nondescript sort of person, no longer young, an awful highbrow, living in an untidy bach full of cobwebs. Even so, I am a good cook & gardener. Anyhow don't say no just out of shyness — I'm easy-going — all the writers I know are — easy to meet & talk with. If you'd like to come over sometime let me know — or maybe you'd prefer a chat in town over a beer or a cup of coffee.

Apparently we have something in common. I'm supposed to be an invalid — bone T.B. — though I take little notice of it these days. But I've quite shamelessly exploited the situation so as to give me ample time for writing — the writing that so often, even after so much trying, I don't do.

Best wishes anyhow

Frank Sargeson.

To E.P. Dawson, *Mt Maunganui*

Hocken Library

17 February 1944

Dear Peter,

[. . .] A fan-mail letter has just turned up — from a young man — 21 — artificial leg — & very flattering — very young — shy — intelligent — he makes one of the best comments I've seen on my *Sale Day*: 'When in S.D. Victor dumps the randy cat in the fire, one's mind wants to swing away on another tack, but the story does abruptly in 3 more sentences — When I read this I was left with a feeling as if I had been on a train & had seen the most horrible accident, & yet the train wouldn't stop. The whole thing seemed to become at once incidental & yet to occupy my whole mind'. Well, well, what have we here? Maurice Duggan the name & he wants to write. The problem is should I say: 'you intelligent young hound go ahead, but forget you ever read Sargeson'. Or should I have a talk with him, thus destroying all his illusions about authors & authorship, & maybe turning him into a competent shop-assistant, tolerably happy with a wife 2 children radio h. & c. etc. Well, it is a problem. Am I better or worse off for having had to work things out all on my pat right from the beginning? I don't know. If I get to know him will he have enough native grit bounce resilience independence to take what good he can from me & reject the bad. Or should I be an old devil & claim him if I can as an enslaved disciple, a sycophantic prop for my old age, a perpetual feeder of my pride conceit & arrogance. Anyhow I'll let you know the sequel. [. . .]

Many good wishes,

F.S.

To Alec Pickard, *Invercargill*

Alexander Turnbull Library

27 February 1944

Dear Pickard,

I'm writing you so suddenly after yours to suggest you collect all your stories together with *Holiday* & try them on the Progressive [Publishing Society] people in Wn. They're doing a hell of a lot of publishing, so why not give it a go now while there seems to be a good chance. I feel damn sorry for you, getting so many rejections — I always feel that way over my own stuff — so much tripe published all the time & the good & better stuff only getting a hearing now & then. Anyhow your stories with *Holiday* would make quite a sizeable volume.

Gilbert stayed with me a couple of days last week, but I think he's gone back to the Islands now. It rained, so we spent 2 days flat out on the beds discussing life & literature (smutty yarns mostly) & I made a few excursions out to stretch my credit a few inches further with the long suffering tradesmen (neither of us had any money) & return with coffee & tobacco (our main necessities — for the rest I did really wonderful things with rice tomatoes pimento garlic etc. And we ate about a dozen melons each). [. . .]

Not long back Rod Finlayson brought over young Ballantyne to see me — he wrote a thing in the NW No 2. He's a cheeky young hound — just 21 & a cub reporter on the Star. Very tall, nearly as tall as Fairburn who's 6'4" — long black hair, specs — almost looks like Aldous Huxley — yet if my ears don't deceive me he called 'pictures' 'pitchers'. Anyhow he's intelligent though pretty chaotic so far, doesn't know where he is — but I like his cheekiness & independence — refuses to accept the WORD from anyone — but overdoes it. He also has a bitter cutting humour which I didn't like much — probably because it was too close to what I've got myself.

Recently too I had a letter from a young bloke who'd read some of my stuff & he also came to see me. He *sounded* intelligent in his letter — he made about the best comment I've yet heard on my story, *Sale Day*, but he turned out to be a heavy Irish boy, very likeable young & keen but I'm damned if I know whether there's much to him really. But I enjoyed meeting him.

Recently Texidor & I had a spell down in Tauranga (her husband put us on our honour, yet it really wasn't necessary as we found ourselves too occupied with sea sun sand & eating, with a spot of reading thrown in, to bother about anything else. Besides we were both reading Hawthorne — *The Blithedale Romance, House of 7 Gables* & *The Scarlet Letter* — and so much SIN — or should I more accurately say, sense of sin, — on paper was quite enough). Anyhow I'm much better for the change & have cut myself off from people as much as possible to write first a story & then get into the heavy difficult work of the novel. It's like contemplating the Descent into Hades — with the bleak prospect of the Resurrection possibly an indefinite number of years ahead.

Bugger this nib — I haven't another.

The garden is nearly over & I'm letting the bloody thing slide anyhow as I'll never get any writing done if I don't. NZ is a strange country — your climate would be as alien to me as a foreign one. I know only the North & melons corn cobs mangrove flats pohutukawas etc are in my blood along with the remains of my mother's milk. I envy you though, such things as brussel sprouts black currants cherries etc. Also I envy you the more bracing air. Half the year here it's too heavy & muggy for mental brightness. With my 2 gardens this year I must have had going on for ½ an acre. I like the digging of it over best — I work at it like a lunatic, & I always hate spoiling its ever-renewed virginity by planting & sowing. Something Freudian there, perhaps.

Oh, I got Holcroft at last [*The Waiting Hills*]. I was interested & even moved & touched by it — he is so keen, so earnest & so lyrical — yet the last seems to get the better of him — he frequently seems to be feeling lyrical at the expense of his thinking — some of his sentences are obscure & inflated to me. Windy is what you said I think, & I think I agree. Also if he feels that way about racing how does he feel about the stock-exchange & trade & finance — it seems to me they're worse rackets — so is the press. No, if he's not careful he'll end up as the Complete Earnest Journalist. Still, he really did touch me — I feel the terrific odds he's been up against all through the piece & he's never let himself be quite thrown yet — and I couldn't blame him even if he had.

Hope things are well with you.

Warmest regards,

F.S. [. . .]

To E.P. Dawson, *Mt Maunganui*

Hocken Library

25 April 1944

Dear Peter,

I got your letter at the farm & meant to send you a hurried note but didn't. [. . .] I worked, got back in the bush & shot rabbits, a weasel & a quail, while on the farm. My first shooting. With a Remington & I was quite good even up to 70 yards. The bullet goes 'plop' when you hit & sometimes the rabbit squeals. I can understand now the thrill you must get when you've got as far as getting your sights on a human being. Hemingway understands too.

It was very very quiet down there. I read *Nicholas Nickleby*, *Moby Dick*, *The Importance of Being Earnest* & *Lady Windermere* & *Sense & Sensibility*. I also wrote another chapter of my novel [*When the Wind Blows*] & managed to solve in my mind one or two more problems connected with it. Also my uncle told me an anecdote which I've started to turn into a story. The pair of us ate a wether & a lamb in 3 weeks & I've put on 5 lbs in weight, but, rather unaccountably I've come back with a very sore chest. I think this was due to psychological causes — Hamilton — it was dreadful. I enjoyed a few days in Cambridge with my sister but Hamilton was there all the time, like the Grey Death. In spite of all my good resolutions I couldn't keep my peace with the old people. I could never explain the situation in a letter — you will have to wait for the novel to get my version of it. Hamilton as I know it is unbelievable. The Grey Death, puritanism, wowserism gone most startlingly putrescent. I had to get away & get away quickly — I didn't want to do the old man in if I could avoid it. So I made hasty tracks for here — home, perhaps I should say — I came by a train that left Frankton at 4 pm & didn't get here until nearly 10. [. . .]

Best,

F.S.

To Alec Pickard, *Invercargill*

Alexander Turnbull Library

25 April [1944]

Dear Pickard,

[. . .] If I were you I think I'd try to get a collection published. The trouble with periodical publication is that you're in the sitting-room one day & the lavatory the next. The public *may* sit up & take a little notice of a book, & it's certain to impress a few journalists. I don't know about guts or no guts — the *best* in what you write is very good — I still have a vivid memory of the brilliant first page of the *Holiday* story — & in one story you carried it right through without a let-down. And anyhow we don't want any more would-be constipated perfectionists (a sort of puritanism really) like Mansfield & myself. No. We want a *body* of literature — the warts the spinal curvature, the piles may be there, but the child may have a lovely head of hair & nice eyes. Just dump your stuff on the Progressive & say Now then, what about it? I'd say the Caxton, but with Glover away they're hopeless. The cover of Fairburn's pamphlet [*We New Zealanders*] is a crime, but that's what one has to put up with — though Fairburn's in a rage about it. [. . .]

Rod [Finlayson] [. . .] tells me that Ballantyne continues to lend him typescript after typescript of stories — all good & some very good. I suppose the risk is that he'll go too fast & use up too much material before he can do his best by it. So far he's mainly under the influence of Farrell (*Studs Lonigan*) whose perception always seems to me plenty wide enough, but too shallow in depth. Anyhow Ballantyne persuaded me to put together a scratch copy of *That Summer* for him to read (the only complete typescript I have has been with Angus & Robertson for nearly a year). It was a mistake — at least so I tell myself — also I repeat to myself that he's only 19. He prides himself on being genuinely proletarian & picks me (quite rightly) as middle-class. So he was rather hoity-toity about my proletarian characters. I don't think he saw though that I don't care two hoots for these proletarians as such, but was using them only to put something over. Anyhow, he's like you — one of our great hopes, & God bless him & save him — particularly from journalists & journalism. [. . .]

Good luck & all the best

F.S.

P.S. Gaskell is OK as literary name. What about Mrs Gaskell of *Cranford*? [. . .]

To John Lehmann, *London*

Princeton University Library

30 April 1944

Dear John Lehmann,

Your February airgraph turned up only quite recently. And then came NW and D. and the Penguin 18. Many thanks. No sign of the money yet, but no doubt it won't be long. [. . .]

Well, I'm a little worried at seeing so many semi-colons in instalment 2 [of 'That Summer'] — I've noticed that the sort of character I'm making use of rarely uses anything except commas and full stops. But maybe this is carrying a theory of naturalism too far. I guess I've just about finished with naturalism anyhow, though I still prefer *Redburn* to *Moby Dick* — maybe if it's intense or fantastic or grotesque enough it will always go over. Maybe in exploring — or should I say exploiting? — the primitive or simple you need a naturalist method. But maybe not so in tackling the profound. [. . .] In passing, a strange mistake — to a New Zealander — appeared on page one of the first instalment of *That Summer*. I wrote 'slab *whare*'. Whare (pronounced, usually, wharry) is Maori and means hut and is very commonly used out here. [. . .]

Anyhow, you spoke of one big collection of my stuff, one day, in an airgraph last year. But no doubt things are just about impossible for you, and that one day is a number of years off. How would you feel if I did let the Progressive do a second book for me? It would be That Summer plus the six stories and sketches you have, plus one that's on the way to you now. I'd try to hang on to the copyright. [. . .]

As ever,

Frank Sargeson

[The planned Progressive Publishing Society collection was a casualty of the Society's financial collapse in 1945. John Lehmann published That Summer and Other Stories *in 1946 and corrected the misprint.]*

To Maurice Duggan, *Auckland*

Alexander Turnbull Library

3 May [1944]

Dear Maurice,

Thinking it all over I don't know what to say. It's strange, but it was only a few weeks back that I had the same question put by young Ballantyne. But with him the answer was easy. Besides being quite promising as a writer he's got a flair for slick easy journalism, so when I advised him to throw over his various ICS [International Correspondence Schools] courses I don't think I was doing him wrong. He can make his living pro tem by his journalism (he has a job on the Star), and he'll have to take the chance that his journalism won't damage him. It needn't necessarily, though as a general rule I'd say, 'For wage-earning keep clear, well clear, of anything that at all *resembles* what you really want to do, etc.'

I don't know Maurice. Journalism and school teaching are what a lot of writers depend on for a living. In my opinion the first *may* be good, but is *more likely* to be bad. And of course the attraction in the second is the comparatively short hours and the long holidays. A job like the one you've got now [probably as a clerk at The Farmers' Trading Company] I imagine is immeasurably superior in point of *experience* etc., but the hours are too long, and so on. I've probably told you how it happened in my own case, but here are the main points again: Very middle-class puritan wowser home — High School and matric — swot night after night until qualified as solicitor — £200 and a trip to Europe — NZ Civil Service — 1st break-down in health and farm life in King Country — Auckland and slump — milkman, relief, fishing and hawking fish, gardening and selling produce, going out gardening and variety of odd jobs — 2nd breakdown in health and invalidity benefit. Writing since 1928 — novel (dud) play (not so bad) stories (one published, and re-hashed it was the only one of the period that I included in my book). Slump produced new outlook and style and stories in book were produced from about 1935 on. From about 1931 I did a fair amount of journalism (Herald Star Observer) and would have done more if I'd had the flair Ballantyne has. But what with skirting editors' prejudices, trying to write down but not too far down, found it cost more labour sweat and trouble than my stories did. Also did higher-grade journalism, but unpaid, for *Tomorrow* which also published my stories. Have pretty shamelessly used the second breakdown to try and achieve the comparative leisure quiet etc to go ahead, and this period has so far produced seven or so more stories and the short novel, *That Summer*, now coming out in England. Have never acquired any *facility* in writing — except just once, when I wrote the second half of *That Summer* in a fortnight. The new big novel starts and stops, and though in theory I have only to go ahead with it, it just doesn't happen that way. If I live long enough I know I will finish it and it will be a development on earlier work, but I have to submit to its control of me rather than my control of it.

So Maurice my friend I just don't know. All I can say is I have the highest regard for your intelligence and intentions. Just what makes the writer I don't know. But I do know that all you say about NZ is along the right lines. That's why I mentioned Fairburn's pamphlet [*We New Zealanders*]. It's all right, but what is wanted is someone who will present his vision of things *concretely*, that is, in a novel, that actually shows the thing as it is and works. If eventually you can do that you will have done something that has never been done yet, that is crying out to be done, and that I, for one, will be deeply grateful for. Football for instance. Its importance and meaning in NZ. [Alan] Mulgan made a balls of it in his novel [*Spur of Morning*, 1934], but in the last *Listener* there was a story ['The Big Game'] by a young Invercargill fellow I've been encouraging for years. It doesn't go far enough, but it's a wonderful start. And unlike Ballantyne Gaskell isn't so alarmingly young. The trouble with a precocious young writer is that he'll go too fast and use up material before he's in a position to do his best by it. So don't go too fast if you can help it, and don't worry about not going fast enough. And judiciously but persistently use your disability (pardon me for mentioning it) to achieve your own ends — knowing of course that your own ends are vitally different from the piddling ends that the majority of people use themselves up in trying to achieve. And that's all I can say. About swot and work and money and the rest I'll just have to leave you to decide for yourself.

I'd like to have a chat with you but not just yet. I came back feeling strangely unwell after my spell away, and now I have another abscess on my chest. Of course it's nothing new, but it means the old tubercule bacillus has been working overtime. The bloody thing will break soon and settle down again after a few weeks. But until then I'm not in the mood for company. Meantime write me or not just as you like, and I'll be pleased to see just one page of MS if you feel like you've achieved something. [. . .]

All the best,

F.S.

P.S. Bloody unsatisfactory letter this, but it's the best I can do.

To Maurice Duggan, *Auckland*

Alexander Turnbull Library

9 June 1944

Dear Maurice,

I got your letter some time back and my only excuse for my silence is the usual — the winter is always a difficult time for me — this bach gets cold — I get depressed — and if I can stick at my writing it takes my mind off immediate surroundings. Also I'm still not so good in health. However, I was glad to get your letter. It was full of interest to me. I was indeed quite moved by it, though perhaps I shouldn't say so. I was sorry to hear about those scars [on the stump of his left leg], and I agree that you should get the quacks to lay off if you can. Exactly the same as myself if it means anything to you. Because they don't heal the quacks say let's have another go, but nothing doing.

Now about [Ronald] Firbank. I like him for various reasons. Prancing Nigger is about his best. Of course all very stinking in one sense, but aesthetically he achieved a lot — showed us how to keep a narrative moving with scraps of conversation — very different from such people as James and Meredith and Wilde — where the conversation is always a set piece. Brilliant no doubt, but much more a technique for the theatre than for a story. Also Proust. I like him very much, mainly I think because only Dostoevsky has outdone him in psychological knowledge. Also of course very stinking in parts but that's not the point. Writing is an art, and Proust is a very great artist. The early parts of In Search of Lost Time are very good, some parts in between are very boring, such as Within a Budding Grove, I think, but in the last volume Time Found Again he excels himself — tells you all about his method and ideas of creation — it was all thrillingly interesting to me. Just get what you can from him at your present stage of development, plenty of time, I hope, he'll last a lifetime.

I am very glad to see the two pieces you sent me ['Flood' and 'Vance and Me']. I think they promise very well. So far as I'm concerned you're on the right lines. That is, Vance and Me, seems to me the start of Huckleberry Finn all over again. Such things as Huck Finn and Melville's Redburn seem to me to establish the right colonial tradition. Anderson carried it on, though it's gone slightly off the rails I think in Hemingway Steinbeck Saroyan Faulkner and one or two others. Neither piece seems to me completely satisfactory, but the best bits are quite satisfying. 'Water-fattened bodies' — that should show you what you can get words to do for you — suggestions, implications — knowing NZ and her stock-raising as we do that gives us a larger picture than just a bloated beast. And 'he was afraid of the gun, a bit'. The last two words are very nice.

Now broadly speaking I'd say these two pieces are more the work of a man with a camera than a man with a paint brush. You are a little uncertain of yourself yet, you don't quite know what to do with and what to make of your material, so you just photograph it. Well, lots of even mature writers do that — the American Farrell does it I think to a large extent. As for me I feel I want something more than that. I want to feel that the writer is a painter rather than a photographer — that he has selected, left out, re-arranged, and added. I don't say that you haven't altogether done this, but perhaps you will see what I mean. I don't know that I can make more than one or two concrete suggestions as regards the two pieces, because in their own way they are complete. I see what you are doing with the word "'cos" but I am a little doubtful. You need only to drop in a few such expressions to get the flavour of the boy's world, but I am a little doubtful whether you have picked on the right one. But perhaps I am wrong here. Just one or two technical points. Leave a bigger left hand margin, and always put your name and address at the end of your typescripts. Things look different in print so I'd try for print with these pieces if I were you. Of course later on you may feel you could have done more with them, but print is always encouraging. I'd suggest you try the Listener with Flood and N.Z. New Writing with Vance. Just put your name & address on and a stamped addressed envelope to yourself enclosed. No covering letter — it is better not to when you are beginning. And good luck.

I shall write to you within the next week or so, suggesting a meeting either over here or in town.

Best,

F.S.

To James Laughlin, *Norfolk, Connecticut*

Houghton Library

28 June 1944

Dear Laughlin,

[. . .] Do you see an Australian thing — Angry Penguins — I imagine from the text these people are in touch with you. So far they've only very badly assimilated these overseas influences. Harris, keeping in step well behind Miller, must do a Vegetative Eye [Max Harris's experimental novel published in 1943]. Hell! Anyhow, I sympathise with them and hope they have a damn good fling. Australia has quite a good tradition to build on, but no one seems capable of developing it — hence impatience, frustration, chaos, and vegetative eyes. Of course sometimes I feel rather overwhelmed by the chaos in America too. I've been re-reading Huckleberry Finn and Redburn, and a lot of Hawthorne. The first two books seem to me to establish the right colonial tradition, and in Finn particularly, what a lot of symbols there are — the river: time life the world — the raft: the private area you mark off for yourself — the nigger: well, something sinister here, the dark love who shares your private area — the duke and the king: the trash that the river throws up, you find it amusing enough but you disengage yourself eventually. The whole thing essentially pagan. Anyhow, I'd say that Anderson carried along this tradition nicely, injecting a sort of poetry and pathos into it, but along come such people as Hemingway Faulkner Steinbeck Saroyan, and it goes off the rails. (I much prefer Twain's home-made raft to the New York department store paraphernalia that Hemingway takes to *his* river). And of course you have only to read Hawthorne to see *why* it has gone off the rails. The Blithedale Romance, for instance — quite surrealistic, and with such an extraordinary piece of surrealism existing in American literature, why not hook off to Paris and make things fruitier by importing bagfuls of the European variety? Well, maybe I'm all wrong, but that's something of the way I see it. And I notice I've left out Poe. [. . .]

I'm handing your catalogue into a bookshop here that's interested in your stuff, and hope they do some business with you. Good luck to PHAROS [Laughlin's new but short-lived New Directions periodical] — sounds solid and rigid — may its tumescence never de-tumess!

Ever yours,

F.S.

[Angry Penguins (1940–1944), edited by the Adelaide poet Max Harris, was the journal of the vigorously modernist Angry Penguins group of poets and painters, notably Sidney Nolan, Albert Tucker, and Arthur Boyd.]

To John Lehmann, *London*

Princeton University Library

[25 November 1944]

Dear Lehmann,

[. . .] Glover came back with somewhat less éclat than one expects of him. He walked into my bach and refused to eat and drink with me — I couldn't make out whether he had become very food-fastidious, or whether he feared that I might starve if he ate. Anyhow he now has the DSC — very difficult to get in the Navy so I've always understood. I like the idea of his being a very gallant officer and gent. — after the war he will be able to publish quite safely everything we write, no matter how dubious, — as a very g.o. and gent. could never be prosecuted. Still what a dichotomy — contemplation and action — perhaps in the years to come he will resolve it, and write well in doing so. [. . .]

Just at present I'm engaged in a fight to get a collection of Gaskell's stories published (you remember, the young cove whose Picture in the Paper I sent you). He's been hiding his light under a bushel — although from time to time I've urged him to send you anything he thinks is good I believe he's never done so — now that I have his material (I shall write him a foreword) I see that some of his stuff is really first-rate and even when he's not quite successful he's always wonderfully readable. There are one or two other young people who are coming along very nicely, and besides this collection of Gaskell's I have notions of doing some sort of Aust. and NZ story anthology. I can probably persuade the Progressive Pub. idiots in Wellington or Harris in Adelaide or Glover — I think Glover is a little worried at much less intelligent publishing people getting ahead of him during his absence. [. . .]

Well, I haven't heard from Harris in Adelaide for so long now I'm thinking it quite likely the police have him in gaol on their absurd charge. The fake 'Malley' poems were by no means fake right through, and the hoaxers played nicely into the hands of the bloody philistines — the whole business is very nicely summarized in the last number of Meanjin Papers (Brisbane) if you ever see that. I suppose all this sounds as though things are moving out here, and we're growing up and getting independent. Actually we're not, and it all means very little yet, though I imagine the 'Malley' hoax may finally pay some sort of dividend. For the poets to be assured of a decently large number of readers who would be scrutinising their work very closely would be all to their advantage. [. . .]

Give my best to Plomer, and I hope that both of you are dodging the flying bums. The only thing flying out here is the Good Earth (Australian brand) — it's all over the things in my garden. Strange that night would appear to be falling on man so soon after he was imagining it was only falling on the gods.

Many cheers,

F.S.

[FS's proposed foreword for A.P. Gaskell's The Big Game and Other Stories *(Caxton 1947) instead became a review in the first issue of* Landfall. *The 'Ern Malley' affair was an elaborate ruse perpetrated by the conservative Sydney poets Harold Stewart and James McAuley. Curious to learn if the Angry Penguins could distinguish between 'real' modernist poems and verses they had cobbled together from randomly selected fragments, Stewart and McAuley invented the Malley persona and arranged for some poems they had constructed under his name to come to Harris's attention. Harris, then a twenty-three year old undergraduate at the University of Adelaide, published* The Darkening Ecliptic, *the group of sixteen pastiche poems, in* Angry Penguins. *A Sydney tabloid revealed the deception, and the affair became international news. Harris and his supporters argued that the poems had literary merit and that the hoaxers had succeeded in spite of themselves, but the debate was quickly overshadowed when the police charged Harris with publishing obscene material. He was convicted and fined £5 in lieu of six weeks' imprisonment.* Angry Penguins *didn't survive the scandal.]*

To E.P. Dawson, *Mt Maunganui*

Hocken Library

17 February 1945

[. . .] P.S. Look Peter, I manage with my meat coupons — or rather I do manage when you don't send me any — there's offal & fish & shouldn't oh shouldn't you be getting proteins & more proteins into yourself. Try it & see — yes I like salads with 10–12 ingredients, heaps & heaps of it, but I like liver & kidney & brains & fat chops & a fat steak & fat fish even more & what's a salad without one or more of those. And I can't understand about the constipation — how any bowel can hang on to food taken with plenty of oil raw carrots or peanuts is beyond my understanding. Hope it won't be so very long before I'll be seeing you — I *must* have a chance soon.

To Alec Pickard, *Invercargill*

Alexander Turnbull Library

29 May 1945

Dear Gaskell,

What a life — if you don't waken. Gales hail rain, the bach rocking, mud outside, no gas, no spuds, no tobacco, & I'd be put to it to find the money for a box of matches. Nevertheless god father-midwife Sargeson has been such a busy body, establishing the canon of his collection, consulting, interviewing, trotting about raising money — £60 required & nearly achieved now — in short it's reasonably certain the thing will go ahead, with maybe no more than the usual delays. *And* I've lost your last letter. *And* I've lost the stem of my pipe. *And* it's bloody well freezing in here tonight. *And* thanks for *Purity Squad*. [. . .]

NZ. NW No 4 — your piece of course, but — for the rest. My sweet firking aunt!! And nearly every one a school teacher too! [. . .] [M]y country oh my God my country — THIS is what its literature is & what all the education racket leads to. Simply makes me swear to go on & be old faithful — rags & worn-out shoes & borrowing half crowns — until I'm found dead with my throat cut on a broken beer-bottle — in some whore's bed with the bed-bugs in Freeman's Bay — BUT to do honest writing all the same, & twist the knackers of a few varsity bullsh-artists whenever I get the chance. [. . .]

Have you noticed — E.M. Forster's *Where Angels Fear to Tread* — his first & in some respects his best is now done in Guild Books for 1/9. I get into bed these nights & read Elizabethan plays. Tourneur, Dekker, Massinger, Jonson, Webster — & Shaks of course. Wonderful, wonderful stuff!! Christ, how we've declined! Will language ever be put to better uses than Marlowe puts it to at his best? Never!

Many cheers,

F.S.

[At the time FS was finalising the text of Speaking For Ourselves, *1945. This collection of fifteen short stories by New Zealanders — plus Max Harris — included A.P. Gaskell's 'Purity Squad'.]*

To Alec Pickard, *Invercargill*

Alexander Turnbull Library

16 June 1945

Dear Pickard,

That was a nice thought. Many thanks, & it's hardly been out of my mouth since I opened the parcel — no doubt I'll end up with sarcoma, but I suppose it might as well be that as the pox (I wish sometimes my thoughts didn't tend to be so low).

Still much much work on the collection. [. . .]

I'm still very much a 16–17th cent. drama fan, but I must pull myself together & try to get on with my new book. If only I could take myself really seriously as a professional writer! But there you are — I can't stand too much untidiness around me, and I much prefer to writing (a) scrubbing the floor (b) cooking nice meals (c) washing my clothes (d) sunbathing (e) digging (f) looking at anything that's living or growing (g) eating (h) playing chess (i) reading (j) reading poetry out loud (k) drinking anything with alcohol in it (l) being with anybody I'm fond of (m) and of course the best of indoor sports — better even than chess.

Cheers,

F.S

To John Lehmann, *London*

Princeton University Library

[FS completed his autobiographical novel When the Wind Blows *in February 1945 and sent copies to Denis Glover, James Laughlin, John Lehmann and the PPS. Laughlin rejected it; the PPS was on the verge of collapse; Lehmann wrote to FS in June saying that he would like to publish the novel in instalments in* Penguin New Writing. *Caxton published the book in October 1945. The Takapuna Borough Council had been threatening to demolish FS's increasingly decrepit bach since February 1945.]*

7 July 1945

Dear Lehmann,

Your airgraph 15 June: first, it is kind of you to enquire about my bach, but it is all too trivial to tell you about. My Fabian tactics so far compare very well with the modern use of wedges, pincers, panzers etc. The Minister of Health writes to say he understands my privy door is off its hinges and no proper seat is provided (just fancy what poor Anna Kavan had to put up with when she visited me). This is apparently a very serious matter, but I remain calm. Also inside the bach the cobwebs remain hanging from the ceiling (the place has lately been called Dracula's den), and the uncertainty gives me the excuse for not removing them. In any case the bach motto is inscribed on the wall for all to see: Out of mind, out of sight. To sum up, I have a notion that the place will remain for a few years yet.

Also I am cheered by your kind words about *When The Wind Blows*, and the crucial point is no doubt that you would like to use it as you did the last one. But this is the position (a) I am puzzled to see how it could be divided into 3 parts, though it would go easily into 2. (b) Glover has been engaged in the most terrific burst of publishing and after just finishing a most beautiful anthology of NZ poetry, with a long introduction by Curnow (I haven't gone through it yet, but I understand it is a piece of very careful Yeats [*A Book of New Zealand Verse, 1923–45*] he has recently started on *When the Wind Blows*. Also Reed and Harris in Australia (the Angry Penguins people) who have been after me ever since they apparently discovered *That Summer*, have ordered a 1000 copies. Glover says he wouldn't want you to go ahead with your idea until he was fairly on the market — I don't know what Reed and Harris's ideas would be, but I'll find out and let you know. [The planned Australian edition came to nothing.] Of course in these circumstances you might feel that to use the thing as you suggest wouldn't suit you at all — I would just have to leave it to you to decide. You will see my position though, I think. I am all the time tending to fall between two stools — the old world and the new, and recently I have grown a little tired of being chided for not having new work freely available out here. So *When the Wind Blows* must go on the market as a little book on its own to help do something about my somewhat sagging reputation out here.

Another point is that the situation seems to me to raise quite important implications concerning English and colonial publishing overlapping etc. I am thinking of putting some ideas about it all into a memorandum which I'd send you, and you might find it worth while discussing some of the points raised with your publishing colleagues. I told you about the American infiltration — well, just lately Australia and NZ have had visits, first from [Prof.] H.S. Canby [a founding editor of the *Saturday Review of Literature*] and now Whitney Darrow (of Scribners) and another whose name I forget. This is very significant, and so are the press reports that the decisions these people make will have far-reaching effects on book publishing and marketing in the Antipodes. I feel certain a literary D day is being planned from America, and it will be far from an unmixed blessing. Both as author and reader I fear and distrust those stream-lined New York publishers and the hold that they will try to get. Surely what is required is that some sort of reciprocal scheme should be worked out between houses such as your own and such as, say, Faber and Faber on the one hand, and presses like Glover's on the other, in order that values that are well established in England, and that Glover is developing out here, may not perhaps be weakened in England and completely lost out here. Anyhow, that is some idea of the way I see the situation.

Please don't go to the bother of writing me until I let you know about Reed and Harris's ideas on WHEN THE WIND BLOWS. Then you can let me know how you feel about the matter. In theory Glover's edition should be out quite soon — say before the end of September, and of course I shall send you a copy, also Plomer. Glover by the way is quite sure that he will be shortly sailing your way again, but I doubt it. I am certain I shall be able to get a copy of *The Sphere* etc quite soon [Lehmann's *The Sphere of Glass and Other Poems*, 1944]. Also before Christmas I hope to send you a copy of a little book of NZ stories I've been editing. Thank heaven the job is done — it's been holding up my getting on with my new book [*I Saw in My Dream*].

With many cheers,

Frank Sargeson

P.S. Although the new book will be related to *When the Wind etc* it should at the same time take shape as a separate entity complete in itself, if my plans work out right.

To Alec Pickard, *Invercargill*

Alexander Turnbull Library

5 September 1945

My dear Pickard,

I am always so pleased to see your writing on an envelope, yet at the same time the guilt-complex the size of a house I have over you, makes me frown. Let me say I frequently drop into my notes to Lehmann references to you — how I've seen something of yours, & hope you've been sending along something — I say everything except ask him when the hell he's going to publish *The Picture in the Paper*. I dunno — I think I told you Finlayson's in somewhat the same box — has been waiting years to see something appear that Lehmann liked in *Sweet Beulah Land*. Truth is he's probably lost the typescript — I refuse to believe he's punishing you or any of us for the mild shock he got over the 1st number of N.Z.N.W. — And that anaemic bastard of his is now, I believe, finally defunct. Not much loss, I'm afraid. [. . .]

Yes, Glover indicates he will be going ahead with your things [*The Big Game and Other Stories*] — I have no indication when — and at the moment he's pulling out of a 3 weeks drunk over V & B Day coinciding (B standing for Birth-of-a-Son-and-Heir). Hence at the moment we are sending each other insane telegrams over our literary affairs. What chaos! Out of it eventually will come 2 books — the book of stories I edited & my own little novel. Good God, did Jane Austen have all this bother over getting her books published? — and yes by heck I remember, she DID. Probably it killed her — that and cancer — or was it T.B.? Well, perhaps there's some connection, because I can't remember any other winter that I've had so many publishing trials — nor any other winter during which I've daily recognized infallible signs of malignancy (I don't like my colour, or my face, or my weight going down) syphilis (I can't stand on one leg with my eyes closed — but this might be): aural vertigo (I can hardly stand on one leg with my eyes open) tinea (my athlete's foot seems to have spread to my crutch) impotency (I notice I frequently go quite 4 hours with not even a sign of an erection — but this might be): old age (I'm going bald, my teeth continually need filling — and yes, I confess it — it has a tendency to bend in the middle). *Test Paper*: consider whether Jane Austen may have had similar symptoms — that is assuming she was either (a) an aggressive Lesbian (b) a hermaphrodite (c) a transvestist. But quit fooling for Christ's sake. When I get time I read. On the bach wall, beneath the bach motto: OUT OF MIND, OUT OF SIGHT, I have a note of the various books you've mentioned — I sadly confess I haven't got round to them yet — except the afore-mentioned Jane. *Northanger Abbey* is the only one I haven't read, and *Mansfield Park* is the only one I don't own — pity, because it's very nearly the best — even though as I think Somerset Maugham remarks, the heroine is a half-wit & the hero an insufferable prig. Recently I read for the first time *The Great Gatsby* (F Scott Fitzgerald) — very good. At the moment I'm re-reading Coleridge's *Biographia Literaria* — you see you afflict me with a frightful nostalgia when you talk about football & cricket. Ah well, if all that bodily exercise is beyond me now, I can at least try my mental hand at intellectual exercise — and I know nothing more suitable than the *Biog* — frankly it hits football to the leg & takes cricket for a line-out — it's even better fun than composing radio advertisements must be when you can talk about half an inch on a dry brush, & not mean an old couple celebrating their golden wedding. And another one I've re-read has been *Don Quixote* (the Motteux translation) & here again is something that makes you feel it's been worth while to have lived to have come across it — the saddest bitterest bravest tale ever written — and the old Don & Sancho (really the 2 halves of one man — almost every man) two of the most perfect characters ever created — there's nothing to touch this book except perhaps *Hamlet* & *Lear* & Beethoven's last 4 quartets, & maybe parts of Dostoevsky.

No, no, you're no imitation Sargeson. What have we in common? Mainly an intense interest in *people* (as distinct from ideas & theories), & a powerful impulse to observe them — & sympathise with their human condition. Apart from that your actual writing is freer, easier, more exuberant, looser, less strict & precise — everything in fact that makes for further development. I don't *really* begin something as some critics have said I do — I end it, — I sort of tie up into a stylistic knot, that can never be untied, something that was free & easy in Twain & Henry Lawson. I'll always be grateful to you for taking a friendly glance at Sargeson, stuck away up his blind alley (how strange that I should have called the first novel I ever wrote, *Blind Alleys*), but you move forward my friend along a broad road that leads to the most exciting country — that is if you have faith nerve trust etc., & if you're able to escape feeling & being crushed by immense desolations of solitariness, endless labour, failure, doubt — but I'm getting so damned abstract now, I'd better leave off. And I know that you know what I mean anyhow.

May God, or Apollo, or the Muses, or Bacchus, or Priapus, or just the spirits of Jane Austen & say Emily Bronte & Olive Schreiner be with you.

F.S.

To E.P. Dawson, *Mt Maunganui*

Hocken Library

19 October [1945]

Dear Peter,

You simply overwhelm me. No sooner had my last letter gone off than I am showered with your largesse. Well, if you must, you must, and why your asparagus should require only a few minutes cooking when the stuff you buy (or rather that I have bought in times past) doesn't cook even after a lot of minutes, I'm sure I don't know. Also the tobacco crisis here is at its apex, so I was very grateful, being right out of smokes — though I do wish I could cut out, or at least cut down this filthy vice. Anyhow, my grateful thanks for everything. [. . .]

Naturally I'm interested to collect all the comments on Speaking for Ourselves. Yours quite good, though I could have done with your trying to express the inexpressible. Do you notice the marked similarity between all the women with the exception of yourself and Greville? [Dawson's story] Maria *could* be written by a man if it wasn't obvious that it's a woman, and Greville though feminine is very individually so — but the other four are unmistakeably feminine, and all in the same way — and this seems to be one of the weaknesses of the collection — the inclusion of all these four stories results in a certain monotony which rather contradicts foreword. However, one thing I was anxious to do was to try to knock the idea that I collect a select little group around myself, and I think the book succeeds here. Personally I like best (as wholes) Finlayson Lyders and Dawson, but Gaskell (his farmers are marvellously lifelike) [Lyndahl] Gee Gilbert Ballantyne Shaw Cole Harris Texidor and Duggan all have really wonderful bits in them. The level of the writing I think is very very decent for NZ. [D.M.] Anderson I only put in because the idea of the boy running away from a good home took my fancy ['The Student']. Of course Harry's objection is to the highbrowism — quite a legitimate one from his point of view. He liked [E.M. Lyders's] On the Rocks best and after that [G.R. Gilbert's] Mrs Pornog. This latter is strange — I think it is because the lavish pulp story atmosphere that he's used to is there, so, paradoxically, he feels at home in it — and this, even though the writer twists it to his own acid purposes. I'm rather proud of the blurb, but it is not as good as the one I did for the novel which is a really shameless piece of laudatory self-criticism. A copy still doesn't by the way turn up even though Glover promised me one 3 weeks ago.

Well, off to the quack, but more anon.

F.S. [. . .]

To Lionel Grindlay, *Invercargill*

Alexander Turnbull Library

22 November 1945

Dear Lionel,

I was so relieved to get your letter — I feared you might be hurt by my apparent neglect of you, and particularly in my not having copies of the books available for you. DO understand that things really have been difficult — did I tell you I had to raise £45 before Glover would have *Speaking For Ourselves* on, and as it's very doubtful whether there will be any surplus for the contributors I had to let them each have 2 complimentary copies, also a copy each for the backers — all this absorbed 40 copies, and Glover was only in the mood to let me have the bare half doz complimentary copies of the novel, and these were all absorbed by people abroad — my agent in New York Lehmann Plomer etc. So do forgive me. And hell, the health is lousy. After getting over a dermatitis I found I was rapidly developing a fistula — I'm supposed to go into hospital, but bugger it, I'm not going, not until the autumn anyhow so I may give myself a chance to get my next book drafted. But it is very painful even walking about the bach let along crawling round the garden doing the shopping etc. — perhaps it will be less painful when the thing breaks, but I have a fearful neurotic infection complex — my other two damned [tubercular] sinuses [in the chest and groin] are enough trouble and worry, and with the prospect of carrying another one, in such an awkward place, I really am most of the time in a state of psychological collapse. But to hell with all this. [. . .]

I saw the notice of my *Wind* in the S.T. [*Southland Times*] and suspected the hand of Holcroft — and now I see the Listener one which is certainly an improvement — I am relieved to see that in the interval he has evidently concluded that the writing at least just doesn't stop. Of course I can take it, and Monte I know is so sincere and painstaking that one always respects his judgment. He MAY be quite right in what he says, and there's only one point I'd like to go into here. He says 'a human personality must be studied as part of its environment'. Maybe, but that is the exact opposite of my purpose — I don't say my purpose comes off, but it is surely obvious that I am trying to show an environment by concentrating it into a human personality, nor can I conceive of anybody using any other method when the environment is a dirty little commercial and decayed puritan community such as a Waikato town — really, to my mind an epitome of New Zealand — or at least the NZ that governs us waters our beer reduces all values to money and convention, and generally blights all the given elements of natural environment and natural man. (The core of the thing is of course protestant, puritan, and I was most interested in the early parts of [Dan] Davin's *Cliffs of Fall* [1945] where he showed up nicely the wowserish Jansenist taint of the Irish catholic church in NZ — in the *Wind* I tried to ignore this taint, and Cherry is intended to point to the true Catholic view of man as a compromise between an animal and a god, and be contrasted with that foul little bastard Henry who is a victim of the protestant-puritan illusion that man need not necessarily sin. As an aside let me say that to me a puritan — and in this sense very few N.Zders are not puritans — is a hundred per center, a no compromiser, he must have things *pure* — in me it comes out in my 'pure' writing, I *must* write prose free from any taint of journalism or inexactitude, I *must* keep my eyes on the object and find the *one* word that will evoke describe or fix it (like Coleridge I believe that there is no such thing as a synonym — and that there is is only a dangerous delusion of journalists and slip-shod people) — or again if it is an image or an idea, then nothing can be more dangerous or disastrous than to chuck words round as Davin does, or make a selection from the various terminologies offering as Monte himself on occasions does — but of course I don't agree with myself and what I'm doing, but it's the only thing I can do because I'm a puritan, a New Zealander — it's an evil thing I'm doing, but I have to do it, and the only hope is that I may show the thing in its pure essence so that nobody can possibly mistake it, it's seen for what it is — and then there's hope (Goethe talks about those who do evil in order that good may come), then the *true* compromise between good and evil may be made — not the bastard one that prevails in NZ right down from its government and its newspapers to its cooking). And if you get all that's in the brackets you'll see that in *that* sense the Wind *is* autobiographical, but I protest in no other sense.

All clear as mud no doubt, but providing exegeses of my own work isn't in my line. And one reason why it isn't is because I think my imagination is much closer to a musician's than to a painter's or a pictorial writer's (cf Greville's) — and whoever wrote anything about music that is worth reading. I am very happy to say my next book is coming along nicely, and recently I was delighted to find in *The Witch of Edmonton* the very motto I had been looking for, for it, 'Bob me off with a dumb show! no, I'll have life'. I agree about the *Wind*'s being episodic, that was part of my intention — a sort of Sketch (or Incidental Music to) of the Artist as a Young Man instead of a portrait — now I'm into my Ulysses, though again of course not on nearly such a comparable scale — oh, how terrible to think that I may live long enough to feel impelled to write my Finnegan's Wake!

And now, indeed, I must rush back to creation and achieve my one line per hour. And I've written this immediately on receipt of yours as I *do* tend to put off writing. Lying on my bed of pain recently I composed about a dozen limericks about my various friends — I'd love to send you these, but a little too much obscenery (more of my Puritanism — the thing turned upside down) to transmit by post.

Love,

F.S.

To E.P. Dawson, *Mt Maunganui*

Hocken Library

8 December 1945

Dear Peter,

I must say the first of your two letters started me thinking. I remember when I was living at the YMCA, aged 22, spending my spare time reading Shaw Wells and Tolstoy, I used to think that I too was capable of making profound generalizations about life and the cosmos. But when I tried to put them on paper they either wouldn't go, or else they looked simply hopeless. Platitudinous (if there is such a word), as you say, both in content and form. I was terribly puzzled and profoundly upset. And it wasn't until many years after that I realized that that type of comment wasn't for me to achieve — now I suppose it can be said that the type of stories I write is more or less the comment I tried so hard to make then. However, one goes on developing, apparently, and lately I've been toying with the idea what with years of ripe experience and wisdom behind me I'd like to blossom out in generalized comment in the form of essays and book critiques. I don't know though. Sometimes I think my only real ability with words is (a) to make them play a sort of music (b) to give the reader a sort of picture. But I am not nearly so good at (b) — Greville, Gaskell and others are much better — as I am at (a). I've never been able to decide exactly whether when I'm writing I see my characters at all clearly — I rather suspect I'm more inclined to hear them talking. In other words my ability is definitely *words*, and words *heard*. For instance last time I was writing I was worrying about writing my review for the Listener. I lay down and heard the words that expressed what I wanted to say about one of them inside my head. I got up and wrote them down with hardly correction, and very rapidly. Then I did the same with another — the last gave me more trouble, but taken all round I think it's true to say I hear myself writing. Also it strikes me that writing related to music must make it difficult for the critics — because you can listen to music or not, enjoy it or not, but there's simply nothing whatsoever of any value to say after it is over. [. . .]

What a lot of visitors! I am working practically all my waking hours at the novel, and write more than a 1000 words each day. But now Lehmann has upset me with a cable: 'May I negotiate French edition That Summer on your behalf Paris publisher interested'. Well! Can it be l'amour qui n'ose pas dire son nom? But I don't think so — the French with their good sense are not interested in anything erotic *as such*. I prefer to think of it as just a remarkable piece of good fortune for myself and what I have to say — with the franc as it is I suppose any money in it would be negligible. However, I intend to cable back to go ahead, but I'll have to follow it up with Air mail with almost line by line corrections of misprints and mispunctuations — and that's going to be a hell of a lot of work. But the excitement over the novel was already giving me acute indigestion, and now I feel as though my stomach is one large ulcer.

To work to work,

F.S.

*[*That Summer *appeared as* Cet été-là *translated by Jeanne Fournier-Pargoire, Paris: Editions du Bateau Ivre, 1946.]*

To E.H. McCormick, *Wellington*

Alexander Turnbull Library

[FS anthologised Duggan's 'Notes on an Abstract Arachnid' in Speaking for Ourselves; *Dan Davin's* Cliffs of Fall, *1945, concludes with the protagonist's nightmare vision of a spider with a woman's face.]*

20 December 1945

Dear McCormick,

I was rather hoping it would be your task to review my story collection in the *Listener*, but I see not. I was wondering after your remarks on Davin what you would think of Maurice Duggan. Isn't it rather strange that the pair of them would have the image of the spider? And strange that Duggan should be developing on the Joycean lines that you suggested — both of them Irish New Zealanders too. However, the book has sold quite well so far, and this is a comfort as I had to collect £45 before Glover would have it on. But I was keen to do it as there is a notion about that I am leading a little group that I train to write in words of one syllable. Dear oh dear, those who know me know that I am insatiably interested in a wide variety of writing — just too bloody wide I think sometimes.

Davin's book I was most interested in — it was a real explosion, and I am hoping for more. As he matures I think he might write the masterpiece we are all hoping for. Also the promising young people who bring or send me their MSS to read were most interested in him too. The five most promising seem to me to be Duggan Gaskell Gilbert Ballantyne and Cole. Duggan is hardly more than 20 and has lost an entire leg with osteo-myelitis — I think eventually he will discard much of his present style and approach, but what is left will be developed to a high degree of intensity. Moreover, he's determined to be a writer no matter what the obstacles might be. Gaskell who is said to be closely modelled on myself is not really, I think. He achieves really brilliant and lifelike pictorial effects that I don't think I can bring off — for the reason that I imagine my imagination is much closer to a musician's than a painter's. [. . .] However, Gaskell is very balled up in school-teaching, and I am very sorry as he has a looseness about his prose that I think would lend itself very well to a long work. Gilbert writes quite prolifically and has recently had a short novel taken by Reed and Harris in Australia (Harris is an awful fool and a shockingly bad writer most times, but he may turn out very handy to us with his publishing). Anyhow, Gilbert is very literary and derivative, but I think there is a lot to him. [. . .] Ballantyne who is also about 20 years has also had a novel taken by Reed and Harris — a long one — the first of a trilogy — and the second is now completed. He's fluent and rather thin. Regional, representational, and photographic rather like Farrell. His most extraordinary achievement is that he gives you a most horrifying feeling of emptiness and barrenness — his people seem to have accepted the surface of our shallow shoddy gadget civilization as reality — you feel that they have no souls. But I imagine later on in his career if he doesn't die of T.B. he might find it necessary to invent souls if he's convinced they don't exist any more. Cole is perhaps the most doubtful of this handful. He has a pleasant magazine style but he doesn't choose magazine subjects, so the result is he's inclined to fall between two stools — the highbrows will say his style isn't good enough, and the pulp-readers will be repelled by his subjects. The beautiful Texidor is I think quite an acquisition to this country — and she has assimilated it remarkably well considering.

Lehmann offered to publish *When The Wind Blows* in his Penguin NW, but long ago I had a conversation with Rod Finlayson about publishing, and we agreed that we should try to have our books published in this country even though it meant financial loss to us — I don't think we can hope to have the impact we want to have with overseas publishing, though it is necessary at times for reasons of prestige. I don't imagine my *That Summer* will ever be published here as apart from the difficulties of getting a publisher to take it on I could hardly expect the middle-class NZ reader to take kindly to it, let alone understand it. [. . .]

With all kind regards,

Frank Sargeson

[Reed and Harris folded late in 1946 before they could make good on their plans for G.R. Gilbert's 'short novel' or David Ballantyne's '41st Summer'. FS's 'That Summer' wasn't published in New Zealand until 1964.]

To Max Harris, *Adelaide*

Alexander Turnbull Library

[On 24 April 1946 Harris wrote enclosing an article he had just written about FS for a magazine Louis Johnson was 'trying to start', and invited FS to comment prior to publication. ATL MS-Papers-0432-198.]

1 May 1946

Dear Harris,

Thanks for letting me see the article, but I don't know what you are expecting me to say about it. From my point of view it seems a thoroughly conventional piece of work — the convention being the narrow contemporary one which personally I can't be bothered with very much. Yes, let Johnson print it by all means, and I hope his magazine goes well. [. . .]

I can offer you these few notes on the article if they are any use to you.

Is 'The Wind and The Rain' a joke? If not I think I prefer my eye to your heart.

Is 'literary gents' contemporary Australian literary vulgarity?

Why not give instances? Is 'O Absolom, my son, my son', corny in the quality of its 'emoting'? — I suppose my sketch Toothache would be then too. I know a Scotch doctor who spent hours one night burying his son under a tree in the backyard, while his wife held a lantern. Nothing was said until they'd finished, when he stood up and said, 'Jock, my Jock!' before they went inside again. Pretty corny what? And adolescent?

Ever read Jewish literature — in Jacobean English. I should think more than 60 per cent of the paragraphs and sentence begin with 'and'. One might suppose that boy Henry in that environment noticed that.

Do you really believe that I write 'realism'? And that no attitude is evoked in say, That Summer, When The Wind Blows or The Hole That Jack Dug. What are those stories about? Tabulate your answers. (You should be used to answering exam questions). I can understand the commercial press critics never saying, even if they see. They dare not say — not in print anyhow. But what about you? And better be careful with your indignant, 'Of course I see!' There are traps that even the wariest have fallen into.

Of course Gilbert and Texidor are good writers. But why be Bulletinese and assume the whole show is a sort of literary race-meeting, with all of us trying to get our noses in front. Do you derive this idea from Aristotle or Aquinas or Dryden or Coleridge or Arnold or Eliot — or Douglas Stewart? Sure there's a gap between my sensibility and the emerging contemporary one, and I agree that Gilbert and Texidor are closer to the latter. But the testing of the new one is still to be. So why arbitrarily say 'Dylan Thomas, far and away the best living English poet'. It would be just as silly of me (but not quite) to substitute T.S. Eliot. Put in a word for Smithyman certainly, but why ignore Glover's magnificent Harry Singing in Book 7.

And your cocksureness about *your* particular corner of the contemporary sensibility is pathetic. What about Duggan? I know these people personally, and if I were to compete with you as a public tipster at the literary race-meeting I'd tip Duggan any day.

However, enough, and I hope we're both going to keep our hair on this time.

Yours,

FS.

['a Scotch doctor': see letter to Bill Pearson of 12 July 1964.]

To A.R.D. Fairburn, *Auckland*

University of Auckland Library

[On 7 August Fairburn had asked FS if E.P. Dawson had 'any taste in pictures.' 'The point is that I've owed her £9 for a long time [. . .] and if two of my pictures would settle the thing to her satisfaction I'd make the suggestion. But if she has no interest in Art this would be merely an imposition on her'. ATL MS-Papers-0432-161.]

12 August 1946

Dear Rex,

I must leave it to you about Peter. My mind reels when I contemplate my own relations with her — it wouldn't stand the strain of trying to advise you. Like myself she tries very hard to have a taste in pictures, and she would be very hurt if it was suggested she had no interest in Art. [. . .]

I don't know so much about Lili Kraus. Is she quite up to her composers? Art-music can be put over with such undreamed of perfection — I remember Pachmann. Surely if it's Art-music every note counts and means something — so surely it doesn't do to play as though your composer had left a fair amount of dead matter about in his composition. Or am I all wrong? Some passages very lovely of course. But I look forward to the thumping Solomon (probably he doesn't thump now).

McCormick's praise of Holcroft [*Encircling Seas: An Essay*] may be all very well, but I shall continue to think of him as mellifluous Monte, Maoriland's metaphysical mandarin.

Besides Una Platts I had half a dozen others Sunday. This bach is far too accessible.

F.S. [. . .]

To Alec Pickard, *Invercargill*

Alexander Turnbull Library

1 November 1946

Dear Pickard,

[. . .] I'm a practised log-roller, and if you really want to know one or two points about how to roll them here they are. Some years ago I sent Lehmann a food parcel, but it didn't act, so I didn't send him any more. Of course I didn't blame him. I like to think of myself as the Compleat Anarchyst, but while capitalism lasts I don't blame blokes like Lehmann for hanging on to their money, and they can only hang on to it by being clever enough to shy off publishing too many of our books. However, at last he fell, and read carefully here's the point — as soon as he'd fallen I sent food parcels off regularly. Also this cost me a bit as I couldn't send to him without sending to Plomer as well. I believe this is known as gratitude — but no doubt you've observed it isn't a lasting emotion. Still, I really think the pair of them have been impressed by just one food parcel before, but lots after. Recently too, I've extended the process to France, and this has also led to complications, because I thought if I sent to the publisher I should send to the translator too. Anyhow they all admire my neat stitches on the parcels I sew up, and of course to a female translator I select feminine dainties not to mention soap powder and soap. Results (France): I am told that the book has been a very big success and I am promised copies of press articles soon. Unfortunately this seems to mean mainly success of esteem, as the American soldiers have been about with their chocolate funny papers Forever Ambers and assorted pieces of the American way of life. The French public wants to buy only THICK books now of at least 400 pages, and if I can send one of these it will be published *immediately*. Also, you will be pleased to learn that the translator recherche des 'short stories' pour des journaux, so among other things I have sent [Roderick Finlayson's] Brown Man's Burden, [G. R. Gilbert's] Free to Laugh and Dance, Speaking For Ourselves not to mention about a dozen of Glover's publications. It cost me a bit, but my pride in establishing cultural relations between this country and France will be my reward. It only remains to say that I ticked Purity Squad as a story of merit. English results aren't to hand yet, but Lehmann published the book on Oct 14, and Plomer wrote to say it is a very pleasant book to look at. And I calculate Lehmann is risking nearly a thousand pounds on it. He's to pay me £100 advance, the French advance came to £21 after all, and I got £47 for The Wind in Penguin New Writing. Of course he's right after my thick book too, and thank heaven the thickness steadily increases at the rate of one page longhand per four to five hours work per diem. I hope to have it completed early in the New Year.

Any questions?

[. . .] You seem to me to lead quite a social life down there. If you can assimilate all that life surely one day you will be able to do something with it on paper. Could you let me see one or some of your paintings and drawings? It may be your métier — I mean visual art may be. You're certainly a visual writer, and this, by the way should help you with the critics because they nearly all follow Conrad in saying the first duty of the novelist is to make the reader see. But as for me I say, all very well, but mayn't one also try to make the reader hear? For me there's nothing in the whole of Western art that I know of that can touch those four last Quartets of Beethoven. Those four are the absolute peak, the utterly never to be attained again by Western man on this earth. And although English poetry will stand comparison with Europe's best, I have never heard anything in it that comes anywhere near to approaching that dizzy region of the human spirit. [. . .]

Ever,

F.S.

To William Plomer, *London*

Alexander Turnbull Library

7 November 1946

My dear Plomer,

It is really galling again to read in a letter from you about how nice the appearance of *That Summer* is. My copies just don't turn up. No doubt they will, but shipping at the moment seems more chaotic than it ever got in the war. Strings of boats at anchor in the harbour waiting for days to get to the wharves. Still, I hope it is all helping to fill empty European bellies.

Thanks for the appreciation of the bit of food. But really, don't mention it. How can we expect people such as you and Lehmann to take an interest in our work if you are fainting with hunger? Actually, a rather strange situation has been created out here. In the last 6 months everybody has discovered a friend pen-friend distant relative and the rest who suffers from under-nourishment. The shops have been swept clean of tinned meat dried fruit cheese etc. The big wholesalers have woken up to the fact there's money in it — hence there is an enormous traffic in tailor-made parcels, and stuff that would normally be in the shops is held for these. The press says things are going too far etc. Schoolgirls abandon their tennis-rackets and cricket bats (and possibly the handles of both) to meet in groups and pack and sew. All very strange and moving in a way. And I hope somebody benefits beside the black market people. Anyhow I have asked a store to send you a small Christmas parcel, and I hope it may have something decent in it, though I doubt it. I hope you get it, and don't mention it, or rather, the barest mention any old time that you did get it will do. It is almost nothing compared to what is available here. But DO ask for anything you are badly in need of. Soap, for instance. Or cooking fat.

[. . .] With a bit of Lehmann cash I am about to have an orgy of book buying. I didn't think much of Camus's little book in translation. I was very very pleased to see *Billy Budd* on Lehmann's list — I've never been able to hunt it up out here. Also I approve of [Saul Bellow's] *Dangling Man* — I read part of it in Partisan

Review, and it seemed OK. A psychological situation exteriorised in family rows etc, that's the stuff. I try PL [Editions Poetry London] stuff and can't read it — I gave up [Vladimir Nabokov's] *The Real Life of Sebastian Knight*, and I got through [Elizabeth Smart's] [*By*]*Grand Central Station* [*I Sat Down And Wept*] but thought only the exterior parts came off. Of course the new Penguin Classics are going to be a godsend to a cash-short person such as myself. But Dante done by Sayers! Perhaps afterwards she could do *The Hound of Heaven* into Italian, calling it *Selling the Almighty a Pup*.

But how is Lehmann going to live by publishing such books? Of course I hope he gets by, but it is almost as though Fabers tried to get by on the poetry and prose of Mr Eliot.

I hope you go over with the undergraduates. Best to your cobber [Charles Erdmann], and good luck with your own work. I hope to have my long book completed early in the New Year. And many cheers!

Frank Sargeson

To William Plomer, *London*

Alexander Turnbull Library

[Plomer wrote to FS on 8 March telling him that a friend had seen a copy of That Summer *in a bookshop in Zürich, and that he was about to send FS a copy of Melville's* Billy Budd. *He had also told FS he felt 'troubled, perhaps unreasonably, by the political ambitions of Moscow and by the methods it uses to further them — in short, by the Red Menace'. ATL MS-Papers-0432-177.]*

29 March [1947]

Dear Plomer,

[. . .] Your long and generous letter turned up about a week ago. Shortly before I got the [Clifton] Fadiman book [*Reading I've Liked: A Personal Selection*] and now Billy Budd has arrived. All very pleasant for me. I am very glad to have the Fadiman — quite a number of pieces I hadn't seen, and many I'm glad to have by me. I'd rather hoped he might have liked something of your own. [. . .]

I read Billy Budd very eagerly, and of course I was moved by it — one gets the authentic thrill of terror and the rest. But I find it really difficult to penetrate his words and sentences — his way of writing seems to me the very opposite to what I believe in — that the words should be the thinnest possible veils between the reader and the people and objects in the story. Of course in Redburn he brought it off, but Moby Dick has always read to me like monstrously improvised notes for some book he one day hoped to write — just what sort, he never knew. Rather like Shakespeare's Lear. Say he had been able to see his way through the fog, or say he had had the experience of actively loving the sailors who fascinated him so deeply — what sort of books would he have written then? A rather interesting question, I think. His present-day parallel seems to me to be Henry Miller — I get the same feeling of bigness, strain, and the confusion of occasional very clear concrete images embedded in verbal fog. I do envy you though your enthusiasm for and knowledge of his work — and it is particularly interesting that it should place you so close to so many of the very young literary people of today. [. . .]

Very kind of you to cheer me with your remarks on That Summer and the readers it may have. Yes, I see what you mean. And while I was feeling so gloomy you were visiting E.M. Forster at Cambridge — it seems rather fitting to me that he should be back there — from his books I should say it would be the right sort of place to get back to eventually. And talking of Mozart by candlelight — that is one thing that one doesn't miss so much out here. Music, I mean. At least I don't, as I'm a most persistent searcher after people with stacks of records, electric gramophones, acoustic ones too — the last sometimes built by themselves and reproducing very beautifully. The number of enthusiasts there are to be found is really astonishing, and it delights me very much to be able to hear lots and lots of music — its range roughly marked by the Gregorian plainsong at one end, and what of Benjamin Britten is available at the other.

And about the Red Menace. At my age (and yours too), I just can't get het up about it. I suppose I'm far too much preoccupied with trying to defend myself against the menace from my immediate neighbours. They certainly do press on me from all sides. It's my way of life or theirs, and I suppose theirs will eventually win — for a few hundred years perhaps anyway, but during my lifetime I shall always be resisting resisting resisting . . . . In any case, even if I were younger and in the pink of health, I somehow just couldn't see myself waist-deep in the snows of Siberia defending the American way of life. Yes, I know how you feel. It all seems pretty inevitable doesn't it, but the theory of cause and effect is, I very often feel, no more than a theory. I have a hankering after miracles. And sometime I must tell you of the new religion I would like to propound — Bootism. I can make it sound very attractive. [. . .]

Well, an uncomplaining cobber is the right sort to have. My own is quite that way — a wonderful sense of life while it lasts and an Irish tongue. I don't see much of him as he is usually all over the country doing a variety of jobs. At present he is in the heart of what we call the King Country painting the cottages of a sawmill right in the bush. For about 20 years he's been returning here with lovely stories — I wish I could see the way to write just a fraction of them. Anyway I'm just on the point of getting off down to those regions myself for a fortnight's break. And by God I need it. Unlike Japan in the autumn (according to Paper Houses), our days are heavy hot and muggy, with a humid wind that tries me right to the core.

Spring greetings to you, anyhow,

Frank Sargeson

To The Manager, *State Advances Corporation*

Alexander Turnbull Library

[FS had been staving off the Takapuna Borough Council's threats to demolish the bach in Esmonde Road since February 1945. In March he tried to persuade his uncle Oakely Sargeson to lend him money to build a house on the assumption that Oakley would eventually want to retire there and be looked after by Frank. In April 1946 Frank's father Edwin Davey transferred the property to FS, meaning he could in theory raise a loan against it, and by October 1946 he could show the Council plans for a new house drawn up by the architect Vernon Brown. Sargeson may even have attempted to placate neighbours by measuring out foundations for the as yet phantom building. In May 1947 the Council announced that it was prosecuting. FS lodged the following loan application but was turned down on the grounds that he did not meet the lending criteria. Eric McCormick's landlady offered to marry Frank, thereby making him instantly eligible for assistance but this was averted when McCormick interceded with his former boss Joseph Heenan, the Under-Secretary for Internal Affairs, who arranged for FS to receive a 'Civil List' pension of £4 a week, effective from July 1947.]

3 June 1947

Dear Sir,

I enclose:

a. Application for Loan
b. Form 2a
c. 2 personal references
d. Builders' tender
e. Plan
f. Specifications

I would mention these points:

1. The property was acquired by me as a gift, but I am told the current selling price would be not less than £300. The section was bought by the donor about 1923 or 1924 for £400–£500 — though I am not quite sure about this. I understand the Valuation Dept is at present re-valuing. I would point out that the section is the 7th section from the main road, also that the

next street, Napier Avenue is the street that will lead up from the proposed harbour bridge.

2. With reference to form 2a, income and assets: as these are somewhat unusual I give you some details. My books have been published in England France Australia and New Zealand. In addition one book has been published in an English language Continental edition. Over the past twelve months I have made publishing contracts with advances of £100, £21, and £140 provided for. (For convenience all these amounts are rendered in English currency — add 25% for N.Z.) In addition I have received over £60 in fees. I have nearly completed writing a new long book, and have various undertakings from a number of publishers in regard to it. I have no difficulty in selling shorter pieces of writing to journals and periodicals, and I was recently invited to do a talk for the British Broadcasting Corporation. This was recorded and sent to England, and I have since been asked for more.

3. My builders say they hope they can begin the house very soon. But in case of delay I should be glad of information as to when the Corporation's interest would begin to accrue. That is of course, in the event of a loan being granted.

4. The Takapuna Borough Council will not allow me to continue to live in the bach on the section on the ground that it is unsuitable for habitation. It is therefore necessary for me to build.

Yours faithfully,

Frank Sargeson

To John Reece Cole, *Wellington*

Alexander Turnbull Library

5 June 1947

Dear Reece,

[. . .] Excuse the scrawl — I'm refusing to write letters at the moment. There are too many claims on my time & too many invasions of my seclusion. I've been distracted like hell over the bach — the damned Borough Council! But now I've made a £1200 contract with [the builder] George [Haydn], & I think with some luck the loan will go through with State Advances. But what a hell of a lot of bother & time spent. And within a few months the carpenters will be hammering outside my window — perhaps.

I'm glad you thought well of Gaskell. I've been chided for puffing him, but I don't know — I think one may do that with a living author whose work's good or at least promising. Encouragement is very necessary. Of

List of illustrations

course one should never, never, puff a dead author — valuation is the thing then. No, I haven't heard from Lehmann, & when I look at his list, or read the advertisements for his Chiltern Library I feel I should write him only brief notes which will be put on his table by somebody entering on tip-toes. Still, if one can deliver him the goods I imagine he'd be pretty smart in the up-take. Of course it all depends on what *are* the goods — & we all differ so much. Luckily, perhaps. Did I tell you though that he got an offer of £140 down for an Albatross (English continental) edition of *That Summer & Other Stories*! [. . .]

I'm interested in the Wellington news. [. . .] Bob [Gilbert] is waiting news of his lighthouse appointment, & Joy's time draw very near. Bob is still the world's champion classic-book buyer, & the pair of us are engaged in a conspiracy to rescue English fiction from its decline. My God! How I have enjoyed lately Fielding's *Amelia* & Smollett's *Roderick Random* — wonderful stuff! [. . .] Now I'm on to Fanny Burney's *Evelina*. Recently I bought a complete Havelock Ellis in 2 vols & it's been a wonderful investment. I simply hand it to visitors I don't want to be bothered with, & I don't get a word from them for hours. Greville is up under (though perhaps not) Dr. Smith. It was suggested to her that if a girl the child should be named Concepcion. She would then be known as miscon-pardon, Miss Concepcion Droescher.

Well. I can't turn my hand to letter-writing very satisfactorily these days. My typescript stands at page 145 now, & the end is in sight — though a bit dimly. The only way to write books, in my view, is first to kick about a bit, then when the time comes sit down & perform the infinite labour of writing them. It's grind & strain, & strain & grind, with a thousand impulses working for one's defeat, & a thousand outside influences assisting. And finally there may be defeat even though the work is done. Yet even though one tries & fails, there are always those who tried & didn't fail to give fresh courage — & delight! Long live such as Fielding & Smollett, & the literary glories they executed! (A bit rhapsodical, what!) Best of luck Reece old dear. As long as the urge stays there everything should be all right eventually.

F.S. [. . .]

To E.P. Dawson, *Mt Maunganui*

Hocken Library

12 July [1947]

My dear Peter,

[. . .] E.H. McCormick has been very kindly performing good offices on my behalf, & it seems as though I may be taken off Soc. Sec. & put on some sort of Civil List — at a rather increased rate. Also the difficulty with State Advances may be fixed for me too. Anyhow I'm to meet the Under-Secretary [Joseph Heenan] later on this month — and I do want to have a Memorandum ready to put to him — setting out what I think should be done for the writers, painters & the rest. A point about the Civil List, or whatever they call it, is that there'll be no tags — I can earn what I can in addition, & no questions asked. [. . .]

I've been virtually a prisoner in the bach for a week. Still the bellyache & a bad cold. The former is I think some digestive trouble, but a new one on me. Of course, the weather — tonight the bach is nearly floating. However, I've doggedly done my page a day & the typescript is just on 170 now. Also, naturally, imprisoned, I've nearly read my eyes out of my head — and struck some wonderful stuff too. Yes, I got to the Boyd Neel [String Orchestra] again — 3 rows from the front middle stalls — I crawled round Dan O'Connor for the ticket. Also I heard Braithwaite & the [NZBS Symphony] Orchestra which was well worthwhile. Then I finished with *The Shoemaker's Holiday* the Dekker play put on by the College students, & *that* was worthwhile too. There I met Prof. [Sydney] Musgrove who talks with a pretty Cockney accent unless I'm mistaken — maybe. And by the way, I managed to pick up a lot of talk about the Boyd Neel orchestra. One theory is that they play so well because they're *all* in love with Mr Neel, who, off the stage is very *very* fairy-like (his favourite is supposed to be Mr. Grinke.) Actually, it all rather pleases me (a) because I like to think of people being as happy as they can be (b) because sensible people like the Greeks would take it all for granted anyway, & people who are sensible are to be preferred to those who are not. But perhaps I'm all wrong — & the gossip is too. [. . .]

My God, the rain! I can barely hear myself write this. And I'm off to bed to read one more horror story (real horror) by Arthur Machen before I put the candle out. If you're any good at magic at all, please hurry the spring along — though that will only mean gloom & freeze for starving Europeans, won't it? [. . .]

Best,

F.S. [. . .]

To E.P. Dawson, *Mt Maunganui*

Hocken Library

17 January 1948

Dear Peter,

You know it is amazing how slow people who are supposed to be clever and quick in the uptake can be. I have only just realized that a lot of my trouble at the moment, real and imaginary, is that I am having my change of life. One notes of course the symptoms in other people, broadening of the beam etc., but one has little notion of the interior changes I imagine until one experiences them. Half the trouble I'm having in finishing my book is that I have been developing a changed set of ideas without my hardly realizing it. An awkward situation when one has work incomplete. What do you advise — a few doses of hormones to return me temporarily in statu quo? Or must I try to fake up an ending? [. . .]

In any case I am suffering from headaches lassitude pains upsets worries. Lately I have been clearing the site on the section for the new house, and shortly I suppose I shall be complaining because the carpenters are banging outside the window. What there is of the garden is pretty good because of the rain. Such rain, but it might rain without a week of wind with humidity at about 99 percent. A proper bastard of a climate. Of course there have been too many, far too many visitors around. I have done nothing except make cups of tea and coffee, and then when they stay on do a casserole to feed the brutes on. I like visitors, but too many and too often wear you down. Last Sunday I got out of it and went to the tennis finals. New Zealanders can't play tennis — they play it exactly like New Zealanders, that is believe in bullocking. Only McKenzie and Miss Attwood in my opinion touch international form. The latter is a glamour girl, and it was most strange to see her defeating the hefty cow-spanking Miss Beverley, the prim girls' school-shoulders-back-stomach-in physical culture instructress Miss Kerr, the steel-muscled nutcracker-faced Miss Potter. Yes, most strange. With her lipstick her sweet curls her coy little shrieks and her tiny weak little drum stick arms she came back with a forehand that was as good as a kick from a stallion. Of course the key to it was her brains. If you like she played tennis in the way that Jane Austen wrote. Likewise McKenzie, one might say, had something of the cunning of Henry Fielding. But the rest were just too depressingly Alan Mulgan and Nelle Scanlan. Nevertheless I got a nostalgic pleasure out of the afternoon. [. . .]

Greville at the moment is very neurotic about the polio and her baby. Nobody is allowed to approach the child, and nobody who has been over to town is allowed to approach *her*. Nevertheless everybody is accused of trying to murder her baby in spite of all precautions — it will be just too tragic if the infant becomes a victim after all this.

Let's know how you are popping up.

F.S.

To Roderick Finlayson, *Weymouth, Manukau*

Auckland City Libraries

12 March 1948

My dear Rod,

I think I failed to reply to your last note. Truth is my usual preoccupation with and concentration round, myself, have been raised to a sort of fever pitch over finishing my book [*I Saw in My Dream*]. It was finished this week, though a big typing job that will last at least a fortnight is ahead of me. You remember you helped me with some Maori expressions (I am still considering Eh-e, Ah-e, Wah-ee, etc.), I wonder whether you could tell me how to spell the exclamation over loss grief hopeless tragedy? Also how is plain yes spelt in Maori as the European has written it? And there is one other point — right at the end of the book the young married consumptive Maori says, 'Perhaps I die soon, Dave, then my wife will want somebody to be her man'. He is supposed to be speaking in English. The statement is enormously important for the book, but do you think it sounds improbable? I feel it is pretty right myself but I can't be sure. [. . .]

From Yours,

F.S.

[Finlayson to FS, 16 March: '"Yes" in Maori is spelt ae. The only exclamation (that I know how to spell) over loss, grief is aue — which you have been considering representing as Eh-e, Ah-e, Wah-ee, etc. Seeing these last typed I don't like the look of them. It's a bit of a problem. "Aue" is a Maori word and to spell it otherwise is like spelling say a French word in some outlandish way just to give the English reader a distorted idea of its pronunciation. Yet if it's left as "Aue!" I suppose the average pakeha won't make much of its proper sound. [. . .] [I]n grief or hopeless tragedy I should say that the Maori, especially the Maori woman, is more likely to break straight into a tangi — a wail like the Irish keen. It might be represented (as I think I have seen it) by Ai-eee! But of course no spelling can suggest the truly awful grief of the tangi wail. Anyway, I suggest you use Ai-eee! if it seems right to you. Regarding the sentence "Perhaps I die soon, Dave, then my wife will want somebody to be her man". This is pretty right, I think; but I might question the phrase "to be her man". You see, in Maori there is no

equivalent of the verb "to be", and altho' the young Maori is speaking in English the use of "to be" doesn't sound quite natural to one influenced by Maori constructions. He might put it "somebody for her man". Have you considered writing it "my wife will want another man."? (He would say it with a slight accent on "another". And this seems the most likely to me).' MS-Papers-0432-162. FS finally preferred 'Ah-e', 'Ai-eee', and 'Then my wife will want somebody for her man'.]

To E.P. Dawson, *Mt Maunganui*

Hocken Library

3 April [1948]

Dear Peter,

[. . .] I'm a bit fagged Peter. I feel like a dressmaker who's done nothing but faggotting for about three weeks — and I imagine it would wear you out even though it might happen to be your favourite stitch. I have three [typescript] copies [of *I Saw in My Dream*] done and one *had* to go to Glover for advice though I haven't heard yet. Lehmann at the moment is in America and won't be home until next month, so the super-copy that goes to him airmail is a very impressive looking object bound in thin apple-green cardboard. L. professes to be on tip-toe, so I can only hope the thing doesn't bring him down flat-footed when he reads it. But enough of it, I'm that sick of revisions emendations, glossaries, tentative titles, second thoughts and third and fourth, corrections etc etc., I would like somebody to take the thing away and never let me see it until it goes into its 2nd hundred thousand. Sometimes I think everything is there, others it seems arid and wooden and NBG [no bloody good].

And I have broadened out still further with so much sitting. Also I've developed a very sore backside, not to mention an attack of piles — so I intend over the next fortnight to be in the upright or horizontal position more often than not. And somehow, I don't know how, I've kept the house moving even raising £50 and paying it to the builder to encourage him, though still, so far, all that has been done has been done by myself. I fear I must encourage myself to endure another winter in the bach, though a miracle might happen. And are the rats bad — they've eaten through the lining at last and I managed to poison a bald-headed old horror that promptly went and died in the wall. After the maggots had eaten him out they advanced across the floor in squads for two days, and a visitor didn't know whether to stay or go at the sight of my sweeping them up every half hour or so.

I have some hopes of getting away for a change of air scene and faces, but the house makes it difficult. Also once the book is published it seems very likely that I shall never be able to visit the King Country again if it becomes at all widely known. As you know, people who fancy they recognise themselves in books, always recognise themselves by their vices, never by their virtues. [. . .]

From yours,

F.S.

To James Laughlin, *Norfolk, Connecticut*

Houghton Library

5 April 1948

My dear Laughlin,

I'm afraid I must seem to you an ungrateful cuss. About this time last year your letter turned up, and then Forster's Longest Journey and Isherwood's Memorial. Yet I never seemed to get round to dropping you a line. I was of course most grateful for everything, particularly the Forster — that one is most difficult to get out here. Then early this year I got your magnificent [anthology of New Directions experimental writing] Spearhead [1947]. Quite a monumental volume (or is that the wrong adjective?) and a great number of contributions (not all though) very valuable to have. I was particularly glad to see you had picked that chapter out of the Nightwood book [by Djuna Barnes]; and obviously you are getting bolder and bolder with what you dare to print from Miller. And by the way only the other day I looked over the shoulder of a girl with her nose glued to a book in a bus. What should it be but your edition of Nightwood. I don't though altogether agree with the encomiums on that book. It's more than a bit phony, and I think T.S. Eliot is sometimes rather simple and easily taken in by what he's willing to recommend. What strikes me as one of the most interesting features of the book is that it is in a most (by now) well-defined New England tradition — the tradition in which probably James's Bostonians is the most notable example. I think that is really one of the great novels that has come out of America — everything is in it. I mean everything that is inevitably there when puritanism is rampant or dormant. Or am I getting a bit highflown? Also some time ago I tried your Jean Stafford whom you recommended. I liked a story of hers I saw in Partisan, but on the evidence of Boston Adventure I'm afraid I can't agree with you. To me that is just not the sort of book that is going to pick the novel up out of the gutter brush it up and put it on its feet again.

Anyhow it was most generous of you to send me Spearhead, and I trust I am grateful. [. . .]

Of course one reason for my not writing was that I had narrowed myself down to making one concentrated effort to get my long book finished. It is done now, thank God, but sometimes I think at a cost hardly to be reckoned. I am trying to get over the reaction by strenuously helping the carpenters who are slowly pushing ahead with the little house I am at last to have. And once reasonably housed I hope to start on a new literary tack. Anyhow, I hope that eventually you may see the book and perhaps think it is not so bad.

John Lehmann tells me he is off to America about now, so I rather hope you hit it off with him. I believe it is his first visit so that is rather interesting to me, as it does give him some sort of a taste of NZ life and I don't imagine you get it anywhere in Europe.

With all my best,

Frank Sargeson

To E.P. Dawson, *Mt Maunganui*

Hocken Library

27 June 1948

My dear Peter,

Your letter: and it's not that I don't want you to see the typescript (though I *am* a little reluctant — as a simple friend of mine said the other day, I put in all the horrible stuff), but I have just two complete copies here, now. And I am expecting to be directed by Lehmann any day to send one off to America and the other to Paris. I did the corrections and they seemed very slight when they were finished, but they cost me a lot of time and trouble — so I hope L. will be satisfied. I then set to work on a radio talk on Katherine Mansfield I'd been asked to do. 13 minutes — 2700 words. It troubled me for a few days but I polished it off yesterday, though it took me from morning until midnight to do it. I think it will be recorded and on IYA 28 July at 7.15 pm. But of course it's nothing, and I had a hard job trying not to run the poor girl down too much.

I shall look for the Tomorrow articles though I'm not sure I have them, or can find them if I have. If I have they are somewhere in the chaos of the abandoned bach. And I feel damn sorry for that poor little place. It sheltered me for so many years, and the ceiling fell in almost immediately I left it. It cuts me to the quick that I can't find time to put it up again. I am slowly getting the house under control and feeling more confident about it. There is a wider area of housework to do, but cooking and washing up *is* simplified and made less troublesome. The hot water is of course a godsend. The test is whether I can write in it and I think I can. I find I prefer to write in my bedroom with the special writing-cum-typing table I had specially built in — in there I am away from any distractions of books etc., and I find my imagination is helped, rather than hindered, by the sight of a perfectly blank pinex wall. In other words, there is a challenge — one is engaged in a work of the imagination, and if the images and the music come — then one gets a kick out of realising that a whole world is coming to life in a bare little pinex room. But for reading I go to my other table or to the fireside, with all those wonderful friends my books thick against the wall near me — and I must say that in such an environment I am enjoying *Don Quixote* more almost than anything I have ever read.

Of course I am far from straight yet. The damn paint upsets my stomach so I have abandoned finishing all that for the time being. And the damn builder won't remove all his litter gear and left-overs, so what I can't burn is a frightful eyesore to my fairly tidy mind's eye. Also it prevents me from getting at the garden which is going to run very late the coming season, I'm afraid. Another trouble has been that a waif who turns up every few years turned up and stayed [probably Jack Whewell]. I had to take him in as he had been living in bus shelters and eating a rich diet of crusts out of rubbish baskets, helped down with cold water. He is not quite the full pound, but he's very charming — and seeing I had used him in my book and created the best character in it out of him — well, that was another reason for taking him. Fortunately he has now gone off to a job, but if he's able to hold it down a week I shall be surprised.

Yes, let's see how things shape for your visit. Sometime before early spring I have to get down to the King Country to try to find a solution for my financial tangle, but I can easily fit it in with Carmen the Oliviers and everything else that's on. No, the *Pastoral Symphony* [1946] was from Gide's little recit, *La Symphonie Pastorale*. How close it stuck to the book I don't know, but a Gidean idea came through all right — that we may do a good action and set in motion a train of events that leads to a great evil. It was a wonderful film, and most damning to pathetic little suburban lollipop tragedies such as Coward's *Brief Encounter*, about which such people as female school teachers and doctors' wives have been raving. [. . .]

All the best,

F.S.

[1YA: the Auckland frequency of the national radio network specialising in news, current affairs, cultural commentary and light music — the precursor of today's Radio New Zealand National.]

To John Reece Cole, *Wellington*

Alexander Turnbull Library

7 July [1948]

Dear Reece,

[. . .] As usual I have been balled up, but thank God am settling down nicely in the new house now. It is extraordinary snug and convenient (probably too much of both), and George [Haydn] and I really did quite a good job of designing — the place even has the approval of some very intelligent architectural students who are followers of Cristina [Droescher]. Anyhow, I can manage a dinner for seven now with less trouble than it took before for one. I seem to have everything to hand except a conservatory, and I can even *write* in the damn place. Of course I've landed myself in a nice financial muddle, but that was to be expected. [. . .] [F]inding I can write in this damn palace I've started a new book. Very much in the feminine tradition, I'm afraid. Letter and diary form, and all done very much as though by a girl somewhat like Una Platts [*I For One. . .*]. But it *can* be good. Apart from plugging away at it all I've done else is a broadcast on Katherine Mansfield to earn a bit of dough. It's nothing of course, and didn't take me long, and if they ask me again I shall probably accept. Though with my sixty feet of bookshelves and my books all up on them I wonder who in hell wants to write books when there are so many to read. Somebody said the place looks like a hunting lodge, though what there is to be hunted I don't know, as I stick very close to the fireside in the evening, and I must say in that favourable and comfortable position I've been astonished at the speed with which I've recently re-polished off Tom Jones and Don Quixote — the latter by the way the finer work. Indeed, I guess, the finest of all.

Yes, I see how you are right in on all that is doing in the modern book world. I must look out for Gore Vidal, as his name is only faintly familiar. I met [?Andor] Fischmann recently for the first time and he talked a lot about the Kinsey book of which he thought very highly. But I assume he is using an old idea — Freud again, and Gide used it in Corydon — that mankind tends to seek pleasure in sex matters and propagation is only incidental. Correct me if I am wrong. Yes, I should be pleased to have another look at the Edmund Wilson [*Memoirs of Hecate County*]. And do you know what Gide books there are translated and available? I've had The Counterfeiters, The School for Wives, The Immoralist, Lafcadio's Adventures (Les Caves du Vatican) and the Journal. And I hope soon to get Strait is the Gate. But are there any others?

Well, to my dinner. All my best to Chris, and may everything that is hanging fire, FIRE for you very soon.

Best,

F.S. [. . .]

To Maurice Duggan, *Auckland*

Alexander Turnbull Library

4 August 1948

Dear Maurice,

I've had several goes at answering your letter. None of them went, however.

It does though seem to boil down to this: (a) there's the problem of the work you want to do. And (b) there's your personal problem. I don't see that the first should worry you unduly. You have the faith and my belief is that you're justified in having it. Why? Because to be a writer of fiction you must (1) Feel people and things very strongly (2) Be interested in words and what can be done with them to express what you feel. All right, you have both 1. and 2. — the rest is faith, and you have that too. (I never forget my irritation with Gladys Salter once when she came round and wanted to know if I'd got any rock melons up yet. I showed where they had just come through and she made an exclamation and said, 'Those little things!') I don't completely agree with you about *Old Man*, because I feel there is a great deal in it generated not by the emotion springing from your contact with the old man, but from the particular virtuosity you could command with words at the time you were writing it. (Note: Arthur Sewell used to say this about my stuff. He claimed that even though I used only the simplest words what I wrote was sometimes the result of excitement at finding out what I could make them do).

But enough of (a). You have so far and while still very young produced an impressive body of material. You *may* now pause for years. (Rock melons very often seem to stand still — then they suddenly shoot away, and almost before you can believe it you see the first flowers. Very often the fruit doesn't set. When it does it swells very rapidly — but it takes a hell of a long time to ripen. Note: Very often before the fruit is quite ripe the plant begins to DIE.)

Admittedly (b) is more difficult, and I don't know there's anything I can say that might help you. I can't say, Do as I did. Because it probably wouldn't make sense without my motives. But I always tried to follow my heart and very often managed to. If you follow your heart in theory at least you can't go far wrong. The heart has its reasons as you know, and they're not the reasons of the head. But I doubt much whether the heart has any scruples. I sometimes fancy you listen to the scruples of your conscience much too intently. (Note: I think Barbara [Duggan's wife] is sounder on this point than you are.) Indeed, I think it is a highly developed conscience with many scruples that makes you write in your letter as you do. That is perhaps why you want to be so careful to explain so exactly — with latinised words, emendations, qualifications etc. Isn't it rather like the fathers of the Church? Shouldn't it be more typical of [Duggan's half-brother] Sid, than of you? How can one enjoy the world, people and things, with a sensuous enjoyment, as an artist must, if one erects a barrier of words and explanations between one and the objects of enjoyment? Isn't it the curse of the Church and the Christian faith? Haven't you a priest in you which you must either exorcise or give in to? And not an easy-going Mediterranean priest — instead, a puritanical Irish one.

But don't take that last paragraph too hard. I'm only trying to throw out possible hints that might lead to something. What, precisely? Enjoyment, satisfaction, serenity — simple pleasures that are as much common denominators as boredom restlessness or anxiety.

But I see it's not much good my going on. I know you feel your personal problem very strongly. But I have no means of knowing the degree of strength. It may be you feel it to such a degree that it is completely beyond my experience — and power to assist you in any way whatsoever. And I'm afraid I just have to leave it at that.

F.S. [. . .]

To Alec Pickard, *Invercargill*

Alexander Turnbull Library

10 October 1948

My dear Pickard,

The devil! I can't turn up your last letter. I seem to remember the parts of it that related to myself — yet not so well those about your own affairs. The spectacle of human egotism might very well be a spectacle in glorious technicolour, don't you think? But Katherine Mansfield? I did it for money. I also did the Davin and Brains Trust talks for the same reason, and got enough to pay my rates (£16) — though it seemed as always paying away money for nothing. I liked Davin very well, and we had much better verbal sparring matches off the air than on. Indeed I think our radio duet a very poor exhibition indeed. For me it meant a rush trip to Wellington and 3 appearances at the mike without any preparation at all — so it is a wonder it wasn't even worse (though it could hardly be very much). [These talks, chaired by Oliver Duff, had been broadcast nationally as 'The New Zealand Writer and His Craft']. Davin was to look you up in Invercargill but apparently didn't as he was only there 2 days. I think you know Lionel G's gossip about how [Davin's] mother is no more and his father re-married to a prosperous publicaness. D. told me his announced book *Roads From Home* has a railway background, which interests me. In theory it can be quite good. Anyhow, I admire his Irish energy and determination, I think his writing will certainly develope, and I enjoyed the contact with his capable and confident mind. If NZ is too small for him though, it doesn't seem *quite* right that he should be at Oxford — I can better imagine him as a very rich and successful Chicago Irish thug. I liked him very well indeed. He admires most *School Picnic* and *Fight the Good Fight* in your book. He professed not to admire the *Big Game* because you didn't describe the match — which is absurd and sounds rather like Douglas Stewart. I think I rather annoyed him by saying that the leave-taking in *Fight the Good Fight* is better than the similar scene in *The Cliffs of Fall* (which of course it is) — though if writing is good one should leave to the newspaper critics all the business of 'better than'.

But now I remember you told me in your letter about the fortunes of your painting. Yes. And you were turning to writing again. So I hope you have turned — not that I don't believe you are a good painter, it's just my affection for my own medium. Though affection at the moment is hardly the word. Disgust. I am writing a long short novel in letter and diary form — and it started off famously. Now I can't get the young woman who is doing the writing to note down a single thing that doesn't send me off into a bout of yawning. Result: I lie on my bed, I wander about aimlessly, I neglect to do my washing and cook decent meals, I suffer from headaches and biliousness, I plant seeds in the garden which don't come up, and I worry about my persistent habit of living beyond my means. (When I looked at what I owe for books recently I got really scared. By the way I have fallen for Joyce Cary — *Mister Johnson*, anyhow).

But have you been sending out MSS? What are your relations with Lehmann? So many people tell me they never hear from him or get their stuff returned. I think when I asked Plomer to speak a word on behalf of *School Picnic* or some other story L. was just on the point of leaving for America. So I shall ask Plomer again. I had quite a lot of letters to write before I could get L. to contract for my last book *as I wrote it*. All settled now, though it mightn't be out for a year or more. The title settled on is *I Saw In My Dream*. And oh yes, you told me of [Georgina McDonald's] *Grand Hills For Sheep*. Yes, I'll say it makes mine look sicklied o'er. Damn, why couldn't I have thought of that? It would have done fine — the sheep in the story and their two-legged counterparts. Anyhow, I long to hear that you have got stuck into fresh work with energy devotion and all the rest of it. Didn't you think the last Landfall somewhat of an improvement? Bob Gilbert's story had life, and so did Cole's in a dour and dogged way. The Candide piece was nice and sounded like Glover — he was good at that sort of thing in the old long-distance good old *Tomorrow* days. I met Brasch up here not long back and liked him well well. He is like a shy dark girl painted by some modern painter like Modigliani(?) — a change after the beef beer and bombast of the Colonial intellectual of the Glover school.

Poor Lionel G. continues to live beyond *his* means. Unfortunately it seems to make him unhappier than it makes me. However he says he's finished some stories, and Cresswell found him so queer he suspected he might be a genius. I put in a word for him with Davin who promised to try to take him under his wing if possible. And Monte? — UNESCO? Well! Why don't such jobs go to the up and coming like yourself instead of the? — but no, one mustn't be unkind.

Any chance of your appearing up this way during the hols?

Many of 'em,

F.S.

[Holcroft resigned from the Southland Times *in May 1948. He was a founder member of the New Zealand National Commission for UNESCO, and UNESCO commissions took him to Paris and Beirut later that year. In April 1949 he was offered the editorship of the* New Zealand Listener.*]*

To E.P. Dawson, *Mt Maunganui*

Hocken Library

[Oakley Sargeson and Frank's mother Rachel Davey each loaned FS £250 to help with the construction of the new house. Oakley reluctantly accepted a promissory note from FS, which came to light after his sudden death in early November 1948. Oakley's property went to his brothers and sisters and the Public Trust asked FS to make good on the loan.]

6 December [1948]

PeteroPetero,

Here I am running ever so late, and I had wanted to answer your letter ever so promptly. Let's take things in order (a) Johnny (b) my uncle (c) work. Johnny [Whewell] has really been incredible. One of the most interesting things about him is that he will stay in a job if he goes to it with a few pounds in his pocket, but not if he has nothing to go on with until payday. It took me a long time to work it out, but now I think I have it. He is an ex-(English) Borstal boy, and I think that, probably quite subconsciously, his psyche goes back 30 years if he has to stay in a place under a boss without any money — he is *confined*, back in Borstal again. He ran away over and over again in those days. Still, his money from England draws nearer, he's out in a job at Onehunga at the moment, and I have sold the bach for removal so that he may put in its place an army hut of his very own. In theory it will have his bed a table a gas ring a heater light and a wireless — and if he can be content in it, going out and working a few days a week to keep from drawing on too much of his money, there *may* just possibly be quite an improvement in his psyche. How about your putting another army hut on the section so that we may all live as one large happy family?

My uncle. Apparently the farm is to be sold about the end of February, and it will cost about £7000 to buy, including stock. Also, my uncle left about £4000 in cash in the bank. The five residuary beneficiaries are all over 70 — 2 uncles my mother and 2 aunts. Bert [Cook] a very nice lad who worked for my uncle for about 10 years until he decided to be a vet — he's just finishing at Sydney university. My uncle helped him with some cash — but oh, why didn't he follow his heart? Bert was fonder of him than anyone, and my uncle was quite fond of him — yet the lovely farm has to be sold for all those old have-beens to get their whack. However, we shall see whether Bert's father-in-law may make it possible for him. Very nice of you to offer to help, but offer firmly declined with thanks Peter old dear. Of course the Public Trustee has asked me to cough up, and I have politely told him to stick the P.N. up his jacksie. Of course he may sue me — but I doubt it as the aunts and uncles will have to consent, and I doubt whether they will. I've ceased worrying.

Work. Everything came in a rush. Brasch wanted a review of Courage's novel, The Fifth Child for Landfall. And Commercial radio wanted two three minute book reviews at the rate of a guinea a minute! Gerald Kersh and Liam O'Flaherty — I enjoyed the first one (The Song of the Flea) immensely. Still, I managed to plug along at my novel-diary at the rate of a page a day nothing and nobody notwithstanding. And goddam me it has life in it so far I don't care what anybody says.

Enormous thanks for a bundle of succulent asparagus. The weather has been the very devil, like winter, and without the time to put into the garden that it needs the weeds are over my head. My bad neighbours have been complaining to me of my untidiness and intend to complain to the Council if you please. It gives me no real satisfaction to mention suburban fatuities in my Landfall review. I got the Bellow [*The Victim*] thanks very much, also Dubliners. I shall read the Bellow again. Bob Gilbert is due on the 15th to instal my 9 valve radio, and Harry is due on the 24th for 12 days leave. Bob's wife came in the other day by the way with an extraordinary story. She is staying at the Hotel Auckland, and a commercial traveller there is determined to ravish her. He has possession of a master-key to her room and has so far got as far as kissing her on the navel. He has promised her opals, but I told her to stick out for diamonds — after all one shouldn't surrender one's 'precious jewel' without getting the highest-priced jewellery in return. But seriously, Joy is really incredible — I simply have no idea whether this is all fantasy or not.

Did you ever meet Ursula Bethell? I must say I am interested in the accounts of her in the current Landfall. And how are you doing with the School Journal stories?

But I shall drop off to sleep if I carry on.

Salud,

F.S.

PS. Of course you are not supposed to put army huts on your place for accommodation — but they are permitted for wash houses wood sheds etc. and with luck one may get away with it. Say if you decided against Tauranga you had a car and a caravan, and an army hut here as a headquarters (after all Johnny is so unstable he may very well not carry out the plan I've suggested to him — or would you like me to put it up to Maurice and Barbara — after all, they have tons of space up at their place. Also, how does the idea of working in with Barbara at your old profession [physiotherapy] appeal to you? — part time, like, relieving and so forth. She's damn nice and easy-going). [. . .]

[FS to Lehmann, 17 November 1948: 'Most interested in The Victim. *A few technical problems unsolved perhaps, but good solid work — and I'm astonished that I have seen no reviews mentioning the book's Jewishness. Why do Jews with their recorded* pastoral *history never seem to question their present-day urban existence? And when they go to Palestine, I'm told, they get skin cancer.' Princeton University Library.]*

To Joseph Heenan, *Wellington*

Alexander Turnbull Library

[As Under-Secretary for Internal Affairs Heenan was responsible for the care of visiting dignitaries; a royal tour planned for 1949 was postponed after King George VI suffered an arterial blockage in his right leg. Sargeson introduced Heenan to Greville Texidor's work and later said that her novel These Dark Glasses, *1949, owed its publication to financial assistance arranged by him.]*

29 December 1948

Dear Jo Heenan,

Many thanks for yours. Yes, I expect after so much labour to put Royalty into circulation it is annoying to be defeated by the Royal circulation. However, I assume all your work may be the foundation for the tour when it comes off eventually.

I'm afraid just at this time of the year, with so many people dropping in, I find it difficult to get on with my work — so I am giving the proofs of Texidor's book a final look over in the hope I may get them as near perfect as possible. 10 pt Fairfield — a very pleasant type, and I think Lowry will go ahead and machine without any more delay immediately he begins the new year. The final result should be very pleasing — I hope you may think so. Texidor is still in Queensland, and it's uncertain when she'll be back. She's trying, certainly — but women in their forties, you know. One must give them time to settle down for the last few furlongs. And if you've had T's looks, and kicked up your toes during the prelims and after — well, the settling down business may take a little longer. [. . .]

Apart from pressure of the work I'm trying to get done, a disconcerting thing happened about the end of November. My King Country sheepfarmer uncle died suddenly, and I was immediately involved in a financial matter with the Public Trustee. My uncle was holding an on demand promissory note I'd given him for £250 to help with the house. A legacy reduces the amount to £150, and at the moment I'm trying to persuade the residuary beneficiaries to agree to £30 being deducted from each of their shares to wipe the amount out. I think I shall bring it off, but of course I find it quite a lot of bother. Still, I've managed to put in my 5 or 6 hours at my writing table each day and work goes ahead fairly nicely. Lehmann has now announced my book for publication late next year (we finally decided to call it I SAW IN MY DREAM), so sooner or later you'll find a copy turn up in your letter box. Also Texidor's of course, and sooner than my own, pretty certainly.

I haven't yet seen Glover's typography book [*Printing Types: A Second Specimen Book of Faces Commonly Used at the Caxton Press, Christchurch, New Zealand*] as I rarely get to town these days, but I understand it's very good. But when is he going to stop playing? Of course *he* argues that there's no decent local stuff to print, or not enough. But if so I hope the next few years may change the position. From what I hear about the activities of the younger people there's plenty of talent developing. I think Davin's visit did us all good. Young Ballantyne in particular has been working very hard ever since.

For now, all the best,

From

Frank Sargeson

[FS appealed to his mother as one of Oakley Sargeson's residuary beneficiaries to liquidate the debt: '[I]t astonished and moved me that [she] agreed, and persuaded the others with the exception of my spinster aunt'. FS, More than Enough, *p. 136.]*

To William Plomer, *London*

Alexander Turnbull Library

16 January 1949

Dear Plomer,

[. . .] Since I have been in my house, [visitors] have been my undoing. Over Christmas & New Year I seemed to do nothing but get meals & coffee, & pour beer. I approve of N.Zders' informal way of dropping in & staying as a rule, but my God, lately, too many have been making it too hot, coming too early & staying too late. I have longed for the old bach (sold recently for removal, for £8, by the way), where the company was strictly limited by the limited space, & I could always drop a hint that I'd had enough of them by filling the bath tub & beginning a bath in the middle of the floor. Those who could stand the sight of my middle-aged nakedness usually couldn't stand being splashed, & left me in peace. Now of course if I enter my super shower-box I am asked not to use all the hot water, & if I lock myself in my bedroom I am disturbed by the clatter of cupboard doors as the last of my provisions are searched for, or the sudden failure of the electricity as some ass tries to run the radio, the electric jug, & the stove all off one power point. Still, mainly nice people — though why is it that all the nice people never seem to have a shilling between half a dozen of them? I suppose if they did have they wouldn't be nice — & indeed, that's just exactly how the matter, out here, usually is. Another disturbing factor of the new place is the radio. It is a super-instrument of 9 valves, built for me by a friend who is a lighthouse keeper [Bob Gilbert]. It looks like some lethal machine, concealed in a wicked-looking black resonant box (you expect that any moment Lon Cheney or somebody like him will look in to work the dials), & turned full on it sounds like 7 symphony orchestras. (When *The Rite of Spring* comes over it sounds like 70 elephants having a humping festival). Neighbours 3 doors away have complained, & don't seem to understand when I retort that I have to take their commercial radio (do you know what commercial radio is like? you just *can't* imagine it), not to mention their bird baths with fishing gnomes, & plaster rabbits peeping from behind the larkspur (some very sweet white ones sit up on their hind paws, & I often think need only a rich red raw carrot suitably affixed to be really interesting nature studies for suburban children). However. What is disturbing about this instrument is that of an evening it seriously interferes with my reading. If Bach Beethoven Mozart or Benjamin Britten is on, I just have to turn it on, & so far I've found that Montaigne, Ibsen, George Eliot or Penguin New Writing just doesn't stand a chance in comparison. Still, undoubtedly there is a remedy for everything but death, & I hope to find one. [. . .]

Yes, why hasn't E.M.F. been 'honoured'? He must have nothing less than an O.M. though. He must refuse to be lumped in with an assortment of black marketeers, white slavers, bad-booze makers, 'processed' food devisors, french letter profiteers — & Chamber of Commerce leaders who go to the strip-tease shows in trousers which have no insides to their pockets. [. . .]

Yours

F.S.

To Marie Insley, *Kumeu*

Alexander Turnbull Library

[On 7 January 1949 Marie Insley wrote to FS asking if she could interview him for a paper about him she was writing for her W.E.A. Writers' Group. Their subsequent correspondence covers the period 1949–1958 and records Sargeson's efforts to assist her with the publication of her stories. She and her husband Jim visited FS occasionally, bringing gifts of chicken, eggs and honey from their property in Kumeu.]

10 February 1949

Dear Marie Insley,

[. . .] When you say 'lovely' seaside suburb I do feel a little bit prickly. I suppose Takapuna *is* lovely from some points of view — at least I really do think it was 20 or 30 years ago. But what worries me is that you seem to imply that I live here from choice and like it. No. All along it has been simply because of the bit of family property that my father allowed me to live on in the bach. I've never really felt at home in Takapuna, and from time to time I'm conscious that the feeling goes pretty deep. No doubt it's too late to make any break now, but I never quite get over my wish that I could have lived somewhere with more of a feeling of being at home. Perhaps I'm talking nonsense, though. It may be just my own particular dilemma. After all, if you are of middle-class origins, yet incurably interested in waifs and strays and people who more or less live on the social fringes, you are bound to land yourself in some sort of dilemma that just hasn't got a solution. [. . .]

With kind regards to both of you. I am eating the honey with my youghert (if that's how you spell it) in the mornings, and it is superb.

Yours,

Frank Sargeson

To John Reece Cole, *Wellington*

Alexander Turnbull Library

19 May [1949]

Dear Reece,

[. . .] Have been in the house long enough now to know there are many catches. My expenses have shot up — just one. What I have managed to earn, apart from the basic £3 weekly (incidentally, dropping further & further into arrears these days), has mainly gone in books. I curse myself — yet it is necessary, as under the new system at the library, nothing is ever in when I go over there. And much that I want these days they haven't got, anyhow. Among other things I'm trying to teach myself Greek, & I don't think I'll get very far, but it's very fascinating. Of course, the house is a definite advantage all told, but the damn things I have to buy now which I'd never have wanted previously, astonish me. Just at the moment I'm out of firewood, for instance, & have resorted to taking up my coke path in the evening, getting it glowing with paper & rubbish, & returning it to the path in the morning. Wonderful idea, but I suspect there's a catch in it somewhere. [. . .]

I do hope you won't worry too much if you find a long work doesn't seem to go. I think I'd say persist in writing it nevertheless. Remember lots of us have written a long apprentice novel round about your age. I did, anyhow — and probably if I'd been married to Hemingway's first wife, she would have been shrewd enough to lose it for me on a train.

Many regards, and to Chris,

F.S.

To William Plomer, *London*

Alexander Turnbull Library

29 August 1949

Dear Plomer,

A letter from you not long back and the Gore Vidal [*The City and the Pillar*]. Many thanks for both. [. . .] I am a little worried about the thinness of the prose of some of the younger promising Americans — nevertheless there is life in it. Strangely enough, I could take the ending of Vidal's story — it quite moved me — it was so much else in the book that I was doubtful of. Sometimes I felt I was reading something like an elaborate case-history out of Havelock Ellis — or perhaps something not many degrees removed — and I feel that a good novel would have to be very many degrees removed. Also I was amused by what seemed to me little slips here & there — such as a ship's steward sweeping out a cabin, & making the bed *afterwards*. [Marginal note: I mean he sweeps the floor before he sweeps the cigarette ash out of the bed. Also, what is the appropriate reaction when one reads: 'the fo'c'sle was in the forward part of the ship' — or am I just a hypercritical bastard?] But mainly I agree with your remarks — it is something that doesn't seem ever to have been done quite like that before. And what a handsome young man of his kind on the jacket! [. . .]

My main trouble lately has been a bit of eye-strain, & it's put me in a bad temper waiting some weeks to see a specialist. All nearly fixed now, but going without my daily doses of literary drug was much more serious than I had imagined. To fill in time I've bought & built an army hut on the back of my section — & I have some hopes I may get some pensioner to live in it & lend a hand with the garden housework & cooking. If only I could acquire some facility in literary composition! Over the most trifling review or talk I stumble like some *Paterfamilias* with buried literary ambitions writing a letter to the press about some social abuse. And by the way, it was particularly annoying having the eye trouble — because to my astonishment I have at last fallen for Henry James & come down rather heavily. After all, if we all of us live long enough, we are all pretty certain eventually to turn into a lot of old women — & how comforting to feel that once upon a time there was such a marvellous old woman as Henry J.!

I didn't know that John L. had been in South America — though he's written now, & it seems my novel will be out in October. I somehow fancy you won't care for it very much. Never mind, one always hopes for something better next time. I shall be sending you a copy anyhow. Also I really must get round to sending you a few things that Glover has done recently. Among them a very beautiful, amusing, & rather costly book of printing types. I never see him, but his letters are amusing, & I picture him getting fatter & fatter, with a belly full of beer, & a headful of bombast.

Well, I fancy I'm sounding pretty dull. But my kindest wishes, & many thanks for many books.

From yours ever,

F.S.

To Helen Shaw and Frank Hofmann, *Remuera*

Alexander Turnbull Library

[Helen Shaw had been planning an edited collection of essays about FS since 1948, with FS's reluctant co-operation. Shaw and her husband the photographer Frank Hofmann visited FS in September 1949. The photographs mentioned below were taken that day.]

Tuesday [1949]

Dear Frank & Hella,

Thanks for letting me see the photos. I'm afraid though, I don't agree with you. I can't see you using either — definitely not, anyhow, the one you like. Frankly I think it is quite impossible — suggests a keen young Chamber of Commerce man taking today off to put together a pep talk on how to conserve dollars. The other one is a pretty excellent piece of work that doesn't *quite* come off. It is infinitely the better, & perhaps *should* be used — but I guess you'd never get it past the bold he Glover. I know there has to be some concession to the reader with his pre-conceptions, but I'd hate to be a party to the pep-talk slant — and it's a darn shame the other one goes a fraction too far in the opposite direction; though perhaps that's not quite right, as it's the touch of sentimentality that just succeeds in spoiling it, perhaps. [. . .]

All for now — shall probably ring you up.

F.S. [. . .]

*[It seems FS later agreed to a cropped version of the preferred photo. Thursday, undated: 'Yes, quite a good picture now. If Glover can fit it to a page without an overall reduction in size it should turn out quite nicely. Probably both sides could be cut to get it in. The point is to tell Glover that an overall diminishing mightn't make it look too good.' Sunday 11 May 1951: 'Glover says yes, he is definitely doing it [*The Puritan and the Waif*]. Unfortunately he doesn't say when, but hopes. He* does *say my picture is* not *going in (I suppose he means the one we've sent).' ATL MS-Papers-7642-131. Shaw was unable to find a publisher for* The Puritan and the Waif *and produced it herself in 1955, in a cyclostyled edition of fifty copies.]*

To Kendrick Smithyman, *Auckland*

University of Auckland Library

15 December 1949

Dear Ken,

Your note [about *I Saw In My Dream*] is just what anybody could wish for, I think. Many thanks. And it is particularly generous of you, since on many occasions I must have seemed very slow to indicate that I had even *read* your own work. What makes me slow with so many of the younger people is, I think, that so often I can't see that they are aware of what is entailed by their attempting to achieve something in poetry or prose. Suffering is probably the word, though it's one to fight shy of as a rule. Perhaps there is a difference between poetry & prose — there was undoubtedly Keats for example, & Chatterton; but what is such a torment when one thinks of Rex is that it *looks* as if there is no reason why there should not have been a steady development over many years. (I can imagine R. dying of many things, but not of consumption). His was never quite the student or even Celtic talent that goes up in a bonfire once & for all. Anyhow what I mean by this is that I have been very encouraged to see something by you in many things I pick up each year. At intervals I read your 7 sonnets & find I appreciate them more now than I did; & I don't despair that in time I may catch up with your latest work. And your prose: may I say that so far as I know, you are the only one of the younger people who can compare with what Rex used to be like in the days of his brilliant best. Howard [Sergeant] wasn't the only one who saw the points of what you said in Arena 21. (And incidentally, your notes in the *Listener* are surely distinguished by your wit, not to mention the aptness of what you have to say — for God's sake keep on about the damn-all recordings that should be scrapped). But of course the test of it all is staying power. Some do & some don't — like my old ewe in *I.S.I.M.D.* And if *you* do, the achievement eventually may be very great — and greater if you just don't have any illusions about what it's going to cost you. Whether it is in the big sum total of all things, worth it, I don't pretend to know — but what I particularly liked in your notes was your reference to a 'work of art'. The creation of works of art is something that is possible in a world where so many atrocities have become nearly meaningless — & if they can give some of us a very fine pleasure, then that is undoubtedly something. I was over six years writing I.S.I.M.D.; and I mean by that there was hardly a morning I didn't wake up & see the damn thing on my table waiting to have a few more lines added after hours of struggle. Nothing was to go in that shouldn't be there; & nothing was to be left out that should be. Finally I was satisfied I had done the best I was capable of — & now I have your note for which I am very grateful. Most of the English notices have been quite bad, which doesn't surprise me, but like yourself, one or two people (one, a very great name), have recognised a work of art when it has come under their noses. So I am quite satisfied.

I'm afraid I get out very seldom just now. With a return of the damn T.B. trouble I spend a lot of my time on my back; and with eye-trouble (temporary I hope), I can read only in snatches — so keep those radio boneheads up to it if you can.

With all fair greetings to yourself & Mary & pickaninny (or plural, if it should be plural, now).

Frank Sargeson [. . .]

*[*Arena *21, 1949, was edited by the British poet Howard Sergeant and carried Smithyman's essay 'Contemporary British Poets'. In the following issue Sergeant praised Smithyman's 'all-round grasp of the newest [British] work'. The image of a very dead ewe appears in* I Saw in My Dream, *p. 219.]*

To E.P. Dawson, *Mt Maunganui*

Hocken Library

29 December 1949

Dear Peter,

[. . .] I've been trying to keep it to myself, but it will come out: E.M. Forster wrote, and I'm telling you what he said. But please please never refer to it in print. I should feel such a worm — at least if any reference to the letter appeared in print until after the kind man was dead.

> Dear Mr S, I have been reading ISIMD, have indeed read most of it twice, and I felt I would like you to know how much your work interests me. Hence this letter. I suppose that the story That Summer is really more successful, but I find something extraordinarily haunting in this later novel, something which cannot be analysed or worked out logically, though no doubt the Freudians might have a shot at doing this. The strong-room, Marge's W.C. and Cedric's cave are the same and not the same; they set the imagination, not the intellect, going; they cannot be patted into a symbol. I don't think many people will understand your book, and I don't understand a good deal of it myself. I wish we could meet and talk, but of that there is no chance.
>
> Of the isolated scenes, I find so vivid that of the uncles, and that of poor Mrs Daley on Molly, and there is one passage (about Rangi and Cedric and the carving of their names) which I am going to copy out.
>
> With all good wishes — and with best wishes for Christmas, for this letter should reach you round about then.
>
> Yours sincerely

Well, there. [. . .]

Perhaps Forster is right — what little thing I achieve is accidental. I don't know any more than he does about the cave etc., but I suspect that occasionally, and accidentally from the conscious point of view, one taps something very deep inside one's self. Caves were man's first dwelling: of course a cave is about the most permanent place where you could inscribe something in the vain attempt to keep a memory alive. Cedric is imaginary, so is Rangi, and so is all the business of carving their names — did I when I wrote that, very mysteriously tap something down in the deepest layers, and is it there now to haunt a reader here and there with the faintest of stirrings of something buried away in millions of years of the subconscious? I don't know, but I hope I did — because *if* I did (to be brutally practical) it may help sales for a few years to come.

All the English reviews haven't turned out too bad by the way. Anthony Alpers's mistress, Sarah Campion, did me handsomely in John o' London. I owe it to Anthony no doubt — he was probably stroking one or other of her bosoms while she wrote it.

Good days, good reading, and good relaxing,

F.S.

The Letters 1950–1959

To Dan Davin, *Oxford*

Alexander Turnbull Library

19 January 1950

Dear Dan,

Your missus turned up with the McCormicks & very pleasant evening spent by all I think. What a nice one out of the box! [. . .] We have a drought, & until it's liquidated I can't rouse myself sufficiently to take much interest in anything. Too hot. I attend to my garden early morning, read until I go to sleep in the afternoon, rouse myself with *Lemora* (a good clean wine), & after an enormous meal of summer food listen to the music. A sort of Mediterranean life which only a summer now & then enables one to live. Not very creative, I'm afraid, but very pleasant while it lasts. I did though sit up & take notice some time back when a letter turned up from E.M. Forster. He went straight to the point about the book [*I Saw In My Dream*], seeing that the strongroom, Marge's W.C. & the cave are all the same & at the same time not the same. Well, that is the point, & of course I'm very grateful. I do wish however that I were more of a straight-from-the-shoulder fellow. [. . .] It astonishes me that nobody indicates any awareness that the title is from *Pilgrim's Progress*, & one University lecturer has even publicly referred to it as *I. S. I. M. Dreams*. Still. What can one expect? Forster says not many readers will understand, & a letter from Lehmann implies that it is not a financial success. And I see I'm being very egotistic, & wanting to justify myself in writing all this. Puritanism again, no doubt. [. . .]

I was interested to learn news of [Davin's World War II history] *Crete*, & do hope you rid yourself of the burden of it very soon. Glover made a great effort & brought out Cole's collection of stories [*It Was So Late and Other Stories*] just before Christmas. Probably he has sent you a copy, but if not I will. Cole is much better for the book's appearance anyhow.

Damn these bloody [airmail letter-]cards. It's not quite so hot today, & just as I'm finishing my space I feel in the mood to comment on some of the ancient & modern books I've been reading & re-reading. I find the clever young people think very highly of *The Naked and the Dead*, but I found I couldn't take it. Eric McCormick thinks it's pretty fine too.

Well, from the margin of things to the centre of things, off this goes. With fairest greetings,

F.S.

P.S. I have a strong feeling that events may before long make the colonial literary tradition very important.

To Kendrick Smithyman, *Auckland*

University of Auckland Library

[In January FS invited Smithyman, Bob Chapman and Keith Sinclair to join him for dinner: 'I'm afraid it's to be a no-women evening which I hope doesn't sound too unhealthy. I want you all mainly to discuss poetry with me (but mainly for me) — & if you'll read me some too I'll be pleased: your own, please, if you will'. The following was written the morning after.]

22 January 1950

Dear Ken,

As usual when I have these discussions I get my own peculiar and chaotic excitement. Instead of sleeping I lay awake most of the night with a lot of what was said popping in and out of my mind. Well, never mind — but I want to say a few words about your fable ['Ballad of the Laggard Mouse']. I said I saw that the mouse was Death, but that's not quite right. As so very often, what I see a thing to be differs so very much from what others seem to understand about it, that I feel extraordinarily inhibited. So often what I see a thing to be is, conventionally, very shocking. There is more than a touch of that about your fable. Your mouse is an old problem of mine. Why do such a large number of women act as they do at the sight of a mouse? I can only suppose that it is a symbol not of Death but *a* death — a particular death. Surely your 'Mannikin' supplies the key. Isn't that mannikin related to Tom Thumb, to Punch, to the husband no bigger than my thumb? Doesn't one see it, though not symbolized, in so much prose literature? The end of *Joseph Andrews* say — 'They pampered their imaginations with the much more exquisite repast which the approach of night promised them; the thoughts of which filled both their minds, though with different sensations; the one all desire, *while the other had her wishes tempered with fears*'. Anyhow, if you approach your fable in this way, how everything fits in. The knives for example. One of the memories of my law days is the extraordinary number of cases I struck (many reported, but several actual experience), of wives' attempting to emasculate their husbands. Wouldn't these be related to the larger spiritual emasculation that is going on throughout society? Again, 'she is alone, as she will always be left alone'. When facing that kind of death women are always alone, of course. But the poem is full of it. 'A thing so lewd'. etc.

All this may seem nonsense to you. But I'm not so sure. I think it is fatal if the poet or the novelist thinks of his symbol or his idea first. I think he must keep his eyes on the particular and let its impact on him do its work, probably away down on the deepest levels. But once the thing is on paper he may look for symbols, and then, but only then, a certain amount of manipulation may be an advantage. Anyhow, the poem as it stands is to me a 'pleasant' poem, because it is not concerned with Death, but with that other death that is always somewhat comical and ridiculous.

Well, that is all for the moment, but I hope we may resume the discussion sometime, though I have little hope of keeping my head any better than I did last evening. We never got round to discussing Mary [Stanley]'s extraordinary Sestina — though why so many poets feel they owe it to themselves at some stage or other to write a sestina is a mystery to me. It's not a form I admire. And I can't understand your not admiring Baxter's first poem. Shouldn't we admire those who can best control their words? One *must* get beyond the stage of being controlled by them.

With regards,

F.S.

P.S. I wish you didn't write your poems on the typewriter.

[Smithyman had been married to the poet Mary Stanley since 1946.]

To E.H. McCormick, *Auckland*

Alexander Turnbull Library

9 February 1950

Dear McCormick,

Did you say on phone those books have been posted? I thought so, but if so they never reached me. The woman who runs the apology for a Library here dug them out for me; and I must say I have been very impressed with the Mulgan [*Man Alone*]. It seems to have gained since I read it last. Or I have. But surely one can now see that Johnson is approaching the status of a pretty effective symbol. I think part of the merit of the book is in its (& probably the author's as well), simplicity. Simplicity out of simplicity — that's fair enough. Isn't it partly the difficulty with Davin that he too seems to be a pretty straightforward person who tends to be too complex on paper? I suppose a good example of what attracts me most would be Gide: perfect simplicity from the most damned complexity. But what I really wanted to mention is Satchell. I found the *Greenstone Door* tough going, yet I'm fascinated by a psychological interest that I was never aware of previously. Somebody sometime back (I think it was Eric Godley) told me my Cedric & his Maori cobber were out of *The Greenstone Door*, but I didn't pay much attention. But I'm paying attention now, & at first I was upset. But I decided that there was no need to be. If (to be stinkingly literary) Mr Eliot can draw together many threads of a culture with allusions, liftings (the other day, 'Desiring this man's art & that man's scope' in one of Shakespeare's sonnets somehow chimed with something — & there it is in *Ash Wednesday* with one word altered), & symbolical figures, then surely one may do something similar with our own meagre culture. But how strange that it should have been done unconsciously. I must have read the *Door* about 1935 when it was republished, & I've remembered the early parts best, & as best liked; but I'd forgotten the names Cedric & Rangiora & also the cave (though not the river & the bush). My own Cedric was so named, because it was the most absurd name I could think of for the son of a Dally woman & a Portuguese-Maori. But surely something must have been going on at a deeper level. Rangi was the real name of that Maori boy, now dead, whom I knew only by hearsay. The cave is more complex, but as far as I know derives from a boy (European) who was crazy over caves & dug them out if he couldn't find them. Also as far as I know it wasn't thought of *ad hoc* — it was only towards the end I saw it as a symbol, or rather as a double symbol (the point that has interested Forster). But never mind the cave: let me stick to Cedric & Rangi. What does it all mean? Can it mean that a persistently recurring myth for the colonial is the myth of the waif. (I remember [the sociologist] Erik Schwimmer has some such notion). But note: Huckleberry Finn: and in New Zealand Satchell's Cedric & mine (even the same name), Dave-Henry (surely the same thing), Mulgan's Johnson & my Johnny (variants), my Bill in *That Summer*, many others in my stories, numerous examples in J.A. Lee's novels. Could I go on? You would know more than I do. Usually the waif doesn't have a girl, he has a friend; usually is being hunted, with all sorts of variations. And now it has just occurred to me the friend is sometimes a *dark* friend: Huckleberry Finn (the negro), Satchell (Rangiora), me (Rangi). Etc etc etc. Does this bore or interest you? It interests me. As A.P. Gaskell wrote to me once, when he had discerned in yet another story he had killed a little man, 'this writing stories is a most revealing business'. That's true enough. One feels that what one consciously reveals is bad enough, but with that other immense revelation going on — well, almost any other job is to be preferred. And then, stinkers like J.C.R. sit in judgment on it all.

But I'm finishing off the ruin of my eyesight.

Yours,

F.S.

['stinkers like J.C.R': In a review essay of 1946 the academic and broadcaster John Cowie Reid (1916–1972) had noted FS's 'emphasis on violence, on mental aberrations, on the sordid, the cruel and the bitter in life', and that 'his selection of subject and the pessimistic implications in the reactions of his characters to circumstance, contribute to a total effect of cynicism from which health is absent'. Creative Writing in New Zealand: A Brief Critical History, *p. 61.]*

To Dan Davin, *Oxford*

Alexander Turnbull Library

5 June 1950

Dear Dan,

Many thanks for your April letter. Oh yes, a short impression of your wife was a damn good one. I still have spasms of shame when I think of the one I imagine I made on her. Still, even more important than forgiving others is forgiving one's self. My kindest wishes to her.

Afterwards came D'Arcy, and he too was a breath of life. Not the least of his virtue is his persistence. 54, yet still living like a waif, and quite convinced that he is a messenger of the gods. He had *The Forest* in his pocket — completed at long last, and when read aloud (he reads extremely well) some us were bowled over. When I read it myself I thought it a wonderful achievement and wrote off to Lehmann to do what I could to help. L. got a copy of the text from Michael Hamburger, whom D. claims he has 'converted' — but I've heard nothing since. I think D's sort of verse would stick in L's throat, but it shouldn't. It succeeds wonderfully in spite of its *passé* flavour. Anyhow, I'm doing all I know how to get Bob Lowry to bring it out here beautifully at least, so I hope you will be able to say what you think of it eventually.

And talking of waifs: you know my theory that a vast deal of colonial writing is writing about waifs. Recently I did some re-reading and re-discovered a waif called Cedric in *The Greenstone Door*. He has a maori cobber called Rangiora, and they bugger about in a secret cave. There must be some myth. *Man Alone* is a sort of combination of the waif theme with a temporary political situation. It needs some epic genius to come along and exhibit the myth in some verse form, I think. Have you ever struck Conrad Aitken's *The Kid*? It is a sort of attempt along that line.

I got away for a short holiday in March and since then I've managed to push on to the end of my novella [*I For One*. . .] (it runs out at about 33,000 words, alas). Much revision necessary yet, and I fear it may not amount to much even then. I fear I have shot my bolt, and must now leave it to you and the other younger people — though perhaps we may see when I am over my change of life troubles. In two years I will be beginning my 7th 7 year span — and I have a notion that if there is any late flowering it will be about then.

Barbara Duggan has gone off to England to stay with Lettice Ramsay — the widow of a Cambridge don — in Cambridge. And Maurice is living in an army hut we have fitted up for him at the back of my section. The arrangement works all right so far, and I'm hoping that M. may come to light with the beginnings of really mature work. I continue to be irritated by J.C. Reid, Pat Lawlor, the new Government and many others and much else. I expect someday to hear your voice on some of the BBC transcriptions. I've very much enjoyed the poetry readings, partly Dylan Thomas read by himself — and generally speaking it has surprised me how well the incantatory over-rich and sometime over-ripe people come off compared to those who are more precise. I can for instance take Sitwell quite nicely.

Have you by the way had time to look at Bob Gilbert's typescript [probably 'Glass Sharp and Poisonous']? Let me know about this eventually, but I'm not pressing you, for God's sake remember that, as I know how pressed you already are. It's a worry to think of your spending so much time and energy on *Crete* — nevertheless in the distant sum of things it may be all for the best. It will surprise me if you don't write better than ever before when you get back to what you want to write. My own book [*I Saw in My Dream*] by the way sold about 1500 copies in Britain and about 900 overseas up to Christmas. Not so good, but yet not so bad. That number just made the advance of £100.

Peter Llewellyn who wrote *Journey Towards Christmas* is getting a great build up here. He writes stories in the Listener talks on the air frequently, and is approved of by Alan Mulgan. He is going to write the great New Zealand novel, so he has announced. I think his intentions are quite good, but I suspect he may eventually discover he is a little mistaken about his talents. But if he can bring it off good luck to him.

Well, chores and tasks ahead of me, so, so long for now, and cheers,

F.S.

[The English-born soldier, historian, journalist and novelist Stephen Peter Llewellyn (1913–1960) arrived in NZ just before the outbreak of World War II. His official history of the New Zealand Army's Divisional Ammunition Company Journey towards Christmas, *1949, was widely acclaimed at the time; he also wrote an account of the troopships carrying the 2nd New Zealand Expeditionary Force, and three novels. Bob Lowry's Pelorus Press published D'Arcy Cresswell's* The Forest *in 1952.]*

To Greville Texidor, *Hazelbrook, NSW*

University of Auckland Library

[Greville Texidor and Werner Droescher and their daughter Rosamunda moved to Australia in 1948. Cristina (b. 1929), Greville's daughter from her first marriage and the dedicatee of FS's When the Wind Blows, *remained behind. She kept in close touch with FS, stayed in his hut from time to time, and introduced him to her friends, including her boyfriend the artist Keith ('Spud') Patterson and the young architecture student Renate Prince. Cristina left New Zealand with Patterson in December 1950.]*

16 October 1950

Dearest Greville you lovely Thing,

Pity I don't write, but you've somehow gone out of my Life. [. . .] Until Cristina goes out of etc. too I am keeping an eye on her. Two dear little girls — poor little Cristina and pretty little Renate — both of them may be coming to stay with me. And I shall intercept all prospective lovers for cross-examination. Do you think I should ask them to strip before I issue my certificate?

I've meant to send you lots of things — Landfalls etc. I get a most interesting monthly from Paris Les Temps Modernes, run by Sartre — full of existentialism Jean Genet and articles such as Avatars de la Garce — and my God how rapidly the matriarchal society is approaching. I listened the other day to a farming talk from Ruakura on A.I. [Artificial Insemination] Just A.I. — and 'material' and 'technicians'. I believe the material is obtained by 'prostatic massage' but I admit this wasn't mentioned. But it all ties up with what one reads — the male in all bred animals is of no importance except for the few chosen specimens — and eventually it will be the same in human society.

I finished my little novel [*I For One. . .*] but can't get the time to revise it. So much hack stuff to do to keep up with the costs. Also I've begun a new book which Brasch is going to run in Landfall as I write it — which I'm finding means hard work but good discipline. My eye-sight doesn't permit of much reading but I pick up one or two interesting things now and then — such as Ben Franklin's Autobiography, or Angus Wilson's new little series of cracks at cracking English society. The radio by the way has improved no end with BBC world theatre etc — and whenever I think of the music I've assimilated in the last two years I always remember your remark about my narrow devotion to old B. — or something. Anyhow, apparently the musical-susceptible part of me hasn't been old and stiff enough not to take new impressions — and I've just about taken in everything that recordings can give you now. [. . .]

Love to dear Werner and Rosie,

Fx.

P.S. My regards to Mrs F[oster, Greville's mother]. Not heard from Maurice yet, but he must be in Barbara's bosom by now.

['I've begun a new book': 'Up Onto the Roof and Down Again', the first section of FS's autobiography, was published in three instalments in Landfall *December 1950–June 1951. Maurice Duggan lived in FS's army hut from April 1950 until his departure for England in September that year.]*

To E.P. Dawson, *Mt Maunganui*

Hocken Library

[FS had invited Dawson to comment on the second instalment of 'Up Onto the Roof and Down Again' prior to its publication in March 1951.]

[November 1950]

Dear Peter,

I'm sorry I didn't write last week when I got your first note — but so many things to do. Among other things I've been asked again to do a ZB chairing and still can't make up my mind whether to return the scripts and say no or not. It means £5-5/- for Christmas so I suppose I shall do it, telling or kidding myself that I *have* to do it.

Anyhow all that you say is vastly interesting in many ways. In the first part [of 'Up Onto the Roof and Down Again'] I was mainly engaged with remembering and dealing very little with the present. In the second I deal mainly with the present — and of course I hadn't realised the difficulties I was bound to strike when I'm supposed to be taking a real journey and meeting real people. I've always longed to use place names freely and never have in fiction, but now the enormous difficulties they land you in are vividly apparent to me. At the moment I don't quite know what I shall do. Perhaps try to go on further from Tauranga and so make the people less identifiable and the place not at all. But I don't know. Anyhow some action will be taken on all the points you mention. How strange about the pipis. When getting the effect I was aiming at the beards never entered my mind once — I suppose because having seized on the image of water cactus they would have interfered with it. The Japanese water flowers though I mean are those wonderful little pieces of porous wood coloured bright red blue yellow etc. which you drop in water and watch expand into flowers of various shapes. I had them often as a child, but they don't seem to be about now. Anyhow, the difference between the objective reality and what my imagination made of it is very interesting and makes me think of Proust — someday you must read all my twelve volumes. I've finished three so far and sent them off to Mrs Smith as I finish each one. Exasperating though he can be there's no doubt he is one of the great giants of the modern world. He really does make most of the other people look a little silly and trivial. A worm of a man no doubt, but by the marvellous strength of his imagination and its transforming power he creates an overwhelmingly fascinating world of detailed reality which you simply have to believe in even though you know it's not the day to day world we live in. And the extraordinary way he gets effects which strike you as universal and eternal — there's no escaping the conclusion that if we build great cities and crowd human beings into them the sort of human society that will result will always more or less approximate to that which Proust depicts. But a digression, I'm afraid. Anyhow, I have noted all your points and some modification will be made in every case. Actually it was I who made the remark about the maoris in the Mental Hospitals, but Greville could have, and it's quite true. And about the It — mainly the remark was based on *The It and the Gospels*, and *A Sermon for Christmas* — but I can easily give it a twist in line with what you suggest. About Michael [Hodgkins] — I'll use all your suggestions, indicate poverty but leave out details, change elaborate, change army hut to bach etc. I want to indicate the relationship to Frances Hodgkins, but will explain to Brasch and leave him to strike it out if he likes.

But oh dear oh dear this business of writing when one is doing it in such a way that it involves more or less representing the people one has known. So long as there is no downright dishonesty one imagines it will be all right, but it isn't. Naturally one doesn't see people as they see themselves, and so much creeps in from other sources the results are bound to be queer to those involved.

Spud and Cristina are going on the same boat middle of next month. He has been painting some lovely pictures of her — and he has given me one of a cat and some ferns, one of the loveliest pictures I have ever seen among the classics or anywhere. Apparently Renate isn't going just yet.

A wet day today when the garden was beginning to dry up. Please yourself about coming up when and as long as you like. I can't get your way just yet.

Best,

F.S. [. . .]

[FS's description of using pipis to make a risotto-style dish for 'K' (Dawson) appears in Once is Enough, *pp. 22-29. He attributes to K. his own theories about the over-representation of Maori in gaol.]*

To Charles Brasch, *Dunedin*

Hocken Library

22 November 1950

Dear Brasch,

2nd. instalment typescript [of 'Up onto the Roof and Down Again'] enclosed. As I am using place names and appear to be meeting actual people I'd better explain one or two points.

1. Nobody up to page 8 has any right to identify himself with anybody represented. It has all 'happened' in my imagination.
2. The K. introduced on page 8 is a composite representation —

though mainly based on my friend E.P. Dawson who has read the typescript and approves of it.

3. The Matthew introduced on page 11 is a fairly close representation of Michael Hodgkins, a blood-nephew of Frances. One of my aims is to encourage sympathy for him if I can. He is certainly not an unattractive person, but I have made him much more attractive than the great majority of people find him. I fear that someday opposition to him will be so great that an attempt will be made to have him put into a Mental Hospital — and what I have written may just possibly help to resist this if such an evil day comes. Anyhow, I can't see that my representation of him will land us in any trouble. The one thing in what I have written that makes it possible for the reader to identify him with nearly complete certainty is on page 13. . . 'reminding me that he is a nephew of the one visual artist from New Zealand who has become widely famous'. If you liked you could delete this, placing a full stop at 'introduced' just previously. But I'd like to keep it if I can, as it might create sympathetic curiosity about him — and perhaps some sort of help for him. Quite frankly he is hardly to be believed — actually. His clothes are incredibly dirty rags, and so is he incredibly dirty as he never washes. Nevertheless I admire him, particularly his spirit, enormously.

I think that's all. I hope you like it, I suppose because of the strain of the concentrated work that it costs me to do these things — but don't hesitate to say so if you don't. And raise any points that occur to you.

Warmest wishes,

F.S.

P.S. Michael by the way owns two of Frances's paintings — not very good ones, I'm afraid.

[Marginal note in Brasch's hand: 'No deletion. Cheque for part 1 sent. Will keep space in June LF for part 3'.]

To Maurice Duggan, *London*

Alexander Turnbull Library

15 January 1951

Dear Maurice,

[. . .] Unfortunately I'm still mighty irritable — my old man has had another stroke, and my mother is determined to make me feel extremely guilty about this: also, although the garden has never been so lush with nothing but the best for years I haven't so far eaten a mouthful myself: just milk and rusks give me a bellyache. Nerves, fuck it, nerves! AND my God you've no idea just what Peter is like — the nicest person on earth and NZ's number 1 neurotic and neurasthenic: just at the moment she's away at Kumeu with her two ex-nurse friends who run a big garden and small farm: they came across, and were awfully damn nice — Peter realises they've worked things out better than she has, the same as she supposes I have — and can't stop herself from sucking us all dry in her desperate endeavour to discover the secret she supposes us to have but which we either can't or aren't willing to communicate to her. But for the space of this letter let me see if I can forget it.

Good about getting the application [for a State Literary Fund grant] off to Lawlor: I'll be writing him today with offers of help suggestions and samples of work. I have some hopes that something may happen without too much delay.

Spud and Cristina got away alright on the Waiwera (I think) from Wellington on (as far as I remember the 23 Dec). [Frank] McGorm goes next Wednesday from here on Matoaroa, but it seems very unlikely Renate will be on same boat. What irony! — she crashed in German III so didn't finish her degree. But I'll know more soon when Reece and Christine will be up here. [. . .] Spud did pretty well with the show at Lowry's before he left — getting about £80. [. . .]

Frankly I was disappointed in the Arts Year Book (don't tell L[ouis] J[ohnson]). I hope somebody sends you a copy. Reece thank God says he has written you with his quite bright suggestions. The best satisfaction I've had lately was to find that Bob Lowry has got D'Arcy's play [*The Forest*] into the hands of the linotyper at last. The SLF [State Literary Fund] coughed up £50 so there should be no more horrid delays. I am trying to persuade Glover to change type format and paper of Landfall. I was very disappointed by the sight of the first part of my Roof in the last number (apart from appearance, Brasch, for all his care, left out a few words in what I thought was my best sentence, and to my mind spoilt it: it put me in an additional rage to discover a wrong word in my Lawrence note, but to my amazement I discovered the fault was in my typescript — a word I must have read 20 times and read wrongly). The next instalment is finished and twice as long — and I was half-way through the third, sailing along (with some italicised patches of quite presentable Duggan) — when of course it was all fucked up by a dozen or so Christmas pressures, and now I can't find the thread again. I don't get the time to revise the little novel, and as the language in it is so very different, I'm very doubtful whether I shall ever be able to make it anything like what it should be. When headache doesn't come to give me a rest from these worries I resort to Amphojel [an antacid] and Proust — to both of which indeed at the moment I am indissolubly wedded.

I hope things improve somewhat in London. I have no idea what you will be doing for money, and find it too upsetting even to enquire. Still, who knows? London can do anything to you — make or break you and everything in between, so I'm hoping you both get a lot of enjoyment whatsoever.

I fancy I forgot to thank Barbara for the New Statesman. Very kind of her.

Remind me sometime to tell you a fantastic story I listened to the other day about a crown prosecutor in a large provincial town who had to prosecute a fairy picked up by the police — a fairy that a few days previously he had been entertaining in the double bed normally occupied by himself and his wife while his wife and 2 kids were away on holiday. I think it may be true — I had it from the fairy who was lucky enough to have the case dismissed. There's even stranger things happen in Proust I know, but I think P. would have been quite pleased to hear that one. By the way Maurois's Quest for Proust is well worth having a look at. [. . .]

[O.E.] Middleton's eyes by the way have got so bad he's just about had it — but he's worked feverishly and turned out some interesting stories. He's hell of a nice — and his wife who was Maida Jones of Pirongia is very nice too. No, pension hasn't stopped — just long overdue. Inflation is terrific. I've been to town once since you left — for Lemora and do a ZB thing in one blow.

Cheers,

F.S.

[Duggan applied to the State Literary Fund for a grant to support him while he was in London. On 12 February FS wrote to Duggan saying he had the fund's secretary Pat Lawlor 'by the balls': 'He is recommending an immediate grant to the Committee which meets very soon. Can't promise it will come off but am keeping fingers crossed.' ATL MS-Papers-1760-08. Duggan's application was turned down in April. Frank McGorm was a New Zealander who wrote detective novels under the pseydonym of Peter Campion. Renate Prince — a Jewish refugee from Hitler's Germany — didn't go overseas at this point: she moved into the hut in June 1951 and lived at Frank's until July of the following year.]

To Maurice Duggan, *London*

Alexander Turnbull Library

4 June [1951]

Dear Maurice,

I don't imagine I've answered a letter of yours which caught up with me somewhere on my travels. It's just occurred to me I never rubbed my glasses clean all the way to Invercargill and back — for five weeks that is I had them on only to read menus etc. A real holiday in other words!

Well, a great time, and the [writers'] conference [held in Christchurch in May] was more of a success than I'd ever imagined it could be. Afterwards Bob Gilbert and I went with Gaskell in his car down through Canterbury (McKenzie country, Mt Cook, and the amazing Colin McCahon Lindis Pass, etc etc) to Arrowtown. After a week there we went on to Invercargill. Dunedin was wonderful, staying with Brasch and Rodney Kennedy and being made a fuss of by everybody. Still, glad it's all over now — and a thousand things to catch up with of course.

But about the conference and the State L.F. We caused a great stir — we, that is, Lou Johnson (whom I liked very much) John Kelly and Smithyman leading and myself in support. Lawlor was shaken right to his bottom, and [G.H.] Scholefield had such a revelation that I hear that he is resigning his chairmanship — that might not be a good thing as we may get somebody worse. Nevertheless it was wonderful to see Mulgan and all the dead horses waking up to see that the literary paddock was full of colts and even fillies running about kicking up their heels, and not prepared to stand any more nonsense. What's come of it is that first we tried to form a Writers' Union, but that was abandoned in favour of all going into the P.E.N. en bloc in order to outvote the stuffies and put the liaison between P.E.N. and the S.L.F. on a better footing. This is happening now and we are all hoping. But in the meantime it has been impressed on the S.L.F. committee that many a writer who has applied for help has felt that his case has been thoroughly muddled by the secretary [Lawlor] — never represented to it as one expects it should be.

Anyhow, if you are not doing so already how about collecting all your energies for another thorough-going application. You must manage things with Lawlor this time, but get Davin to write Prof. Gordon certainly, and I will write confidentially some other member of the committee — the most promising one or perhaps two, say Ormie Wilson and Jo Heenan. You must forward all *published* material this time, and what you haven't got I shall try to dig up for you. Also, I do think it would be a great help if you could somehow manage a few thousand words that could be labelled chapter so and so of a work in hand. Have you the nerve energy etc. to set about this? I hope so. I should say that after Christchurch your chances are much brighter.

Renate hopes to be coming up next week to live in my hut for the rest of the year. Then England — so she says.

You will just have to forgive me for not criticizing the last things you sent. What do I know about these things? I thought the piece Brasch accepted a pretty good piece of prose — and so did Brasch.

But more than that I can't say. I am surrounded with all sorts of pieces of prose more than half of which I don't get the time to read. You either do these things or you don't — and if you do you go on doing them and what else is there to it than that? Occasionally a Rimbaud turns up — or a James Baxter — or a Maurice Duggan.

No more just now. Love to Barbara Cristina etc.

F.S.

[FS's lobbying of members of the SLF came to nothing.]

To Alec Pickard, *Invercargill*

Alexander Turnbull Library

7 July 1951

Dear Alec,

The book turned up but a hell of a while after you had posted it apparently. I suppose the bloody mails must have been upset. Thanks very much. I have been looking into it and of course it all means something to me now — I mean I must have been young enough to see Central more than just visually, as I'm still suffering from a sort of mental and emotional indigestion as the result of my trip.

Almost none of the jobs I'd been hoping to get on to have even got started. McCormick suddenly decided to get busy on a suggestion of Davin's that we have a book of New Zealand Stories in The World's Classics (sounds a bit pretentious, but an Australian companion volume is already out, and it's not nearly as well done by that old Professor Murdoch and Henrietta Drake-Brockman as one imagines it might be). Anyhow, under the necessity of having to earn a bit of money somehow I took on the typing job besides being general assistant to McC. All texts that mightn't be readily available to the Oxford Press in England have to be typed and in the past three weeks I must have knocked off about 90,000 words. We are thinking — or rather more than thinking, we are using your Picture in the Paper, and also either The Cave or The Big Game. I rather favour the Big Game myself but McCormick prefers the Cave — so it may be left to Davin to decide. Have you any objections? Or alternative suggestions? I also prefer School Picnic to the Cave and also perhaps to The Big Game — but it's unlikely we'll be able to squeeze in all 4 I have mentioned. I don't know yet what fees if any will be paid — possibly none at all, which will be monstrous as I am demanding something for the typing. But what would you? Apparently even something like the Oxford Press, a bastion of our precious civilization, hasn't the money to keep alive the people who *are* our precious civilization.

The weather has been cold wet and miserable, and I have to spend far too much time chopping wood to get at my garden. The wood at least warms me twice over, and is unbuyable owing to strike troubles even if one had the money anyhow. I have company for the rest of the year — a lovely little refugee girl, very sweet and intelligent, and good at cooking and housework thank god, who has established herself in my army hut. I never thought I could take such persistent feminine odours in my shower box (vide your Fire of Life), but in the last few weeks I've got quite used to them. When one has a sort of golden-headed little princess living at the bottom of one's garden one can take the aura — and anyhow, the little creature's name is Prince.

I suppose it is about mid-term, and before long no doubt, lucky dog, you'll be off to Te Anau or some such place. Anyhow, I have the book, and whenever I'm looking into it, I'm with you.

Best,

F.S.

[The editors finally settled on A.P. Gaskell's 'The Big Game' and 'School Picnic'.]

To Dan Davin, *Oxford*

Alexander Turnbull Library

[On 15 August Davin told FS he had been reading Jane Mander's The Story of a New Zealand River *for the first time. He had found no entry for her in the* New Zealand Dictionary of Biography, *and asked FS for some biographical information.]*

24 August 1951

Dear Dan,

[. . .] I'd better put down a few things about Jane Mander while I have a few minutes. She was very nervous but a wonderfully good old scout when I knew her. She was born in 1878 and died in 1949. Her old man was the big sawmiller of the North and member for a Northern district (Marsden I think), for many years. Brought up mainly in Whangarei, did reporting for some little paper up north, and got away to America in her thirties. Became a cobber of such as Glenway Wescott Munroe Wheeler and Lloyd Morris in New York, and worked for the American Red Cross during the war. Got on to London and had a pretty tough time (knew people like Cresswell there, and Vernon Knowles) doing hack journalism and rapid French translations. Returned here about 1934, did more hack work but could never get down to writing her last book which was to be an autobiography. Probably her best book is *The River* (1920 — published in England and America by John Lane) but *Allen Adair* (1925) runs it pretty close (see McCormick's remarks in his survey). *The Passionate [Puritan]* (1922) and *The Strange Attraction* (1923) are also about the North, but she wrote them with one eye on the films on the advice of her New York friends. *The Besieging City* (I don't know the date) is about New York, and *Pins and Pinacles* (?) was her last — written she used to say only to fulfil a publisher's contract — Hutchinson, I think — and I think it is about London. My view is that Jane belongs to the period when the first pioneering was over: she grew up when the latest emancipated ideas were beginning to replace the struggle for existence. Her work is like Dutch painting, daylight honest realism with no nonsense: apart from her very remarkable narrative gift and aesthetic qualities she has sociological and documentary value: nearly always there is a remittance man, and you can relate him if you like to the man alone the waif the unattached wanderer etc. who so often turns up in our fiction.

Eric and I are cleaning up the W.C. [World's Classics] job now. Eric's last decisions mean more typing for me to do. [Lady Barker's] *Grave at Rakaia* quite nice but we think Lady B's *Christmas Day* story much superior. Should you bother to send a Duggan story out? You could decide about it when you see the rest of the material. We shall be sending you some marginal stuff which you will have to decide on — pay particular attention to a short thing called *By The Lake*: it's by an invalid lad [Dennis McEldowney] and I've always thought it a near-masterpiece — but Eric doesn't agree. Also, I think Middleton's *Cooper's Christmas* should go in (see Landfall June 1950).

I definitely don't want my name in as a selector: you're further off from the ill-feeling there's going to be. And about the fee: Eric should and must get the biggest cut as the thing would be quite impossible without him: I've done a hell of a lot of typing, but a lot of it I suppose isn't strictly necessary — nevertheless it helps to put the thing into handy and definitive form. But never mind, no doubt we can fix this part of the business later.

I think some publisher out here has just re-issued some Lady Barker. (Jane's *River* by the way was re-issued by Robert Hale about 1939).

Ask Maurice about the blonde [Renate] — he admires her even more than I do — if that were possible. [. . .]

All the best,

F.S.

PS All this investigation into colonial literature has depressed me. What can one do but shrug one's shoulders? — the only one of us who has been devastatingly first-class was a nineteen year old half-English half-German South African girl. I've just read *The Story of An African Farm* for the third time. [. . .]

To E.H. McCormick, *Auckland*

Alexander Turnbull Library

25 August [1951]

Dear Eric,

I feel in a bit of a quandary about the typing. I agree about [John A.] Lee — we should have the first one ['Man's Inhumanity to Man'], though I'd suggest we delete the opening page and a half which seems unnecessary — but I can type the lot & we can delete afterwards if you agree. Also I think [Alfred A. Grace's] *The Ngarara* is OK and *Te Wiria's Potatoes* if you like, but not *The Poriro*. But it's [Douglas] Stewart that worries me most. I find I just can't agree with you. *The Girl With Red Hair* is too long but it's a balls of a story anyhow, and *The Whare* still seems to me the best of the others. I think it's because of our barrenness that one falls for this 'It's NZ!' stuff. Stewart is plugging away at his 'make the reader *see*', following Conrad — whom he always used to be cracking up in the *Bulletin*. Surely you have to make the reader see more than he can already see for himself. It's exactly the same sort of thing that I'd brought up in talking about Ballantyne's novel (though B. doesn't use Stewart's Royal Academy language — hence I find him superior) — representation that doesn't make you feel strongly about some point or meaning isn't of much value. There must be some sort of revelation. Stewart is against flat language, but his total effect is a depressing sort of flatness to me. If you agree to *The Whare* I don't think you should worry too much about too many Maori stories — the Maoris are the most interesting people here anyhow, and they're so rapidly increasing that shortly a large number of stories in the collection about them won't be thought at all odd. But if you want one of the others I'm damned if I know what to suggest — probably *Carnival*, and that's probably ruled out: so almost any of the rest except *The Bishops Shoot a Godwit* — which I confess despite all my efforts I haven't been able to read through. *The People Were Different* if you like. Forsyth with his *Roofs of Dargaville* I think superior to Stewart in some ways: his language is better, you can read it without being repelled — but he's got a story that's been too big for him to handle: it's turned out only an attempt, with a sort of amateur flavour that I don't like. I'd be against including it — though it can be a marginal one if you like — though I think I'd be against that too. And for a second Finlayson choice I'm right against the solemn tract-like *Pakapoo*. Why not *The Everlasting Miracle* (in *Speaking for Ourselves*)? I was amused by Keith Sinclair's *The Camp*, though I don't think we can use it (it reminds me very strongly of an American story by Ruth McKenney, *A Loud Sneer For Our Feathered Friends* — about a girls' camp and very well done). Just to make sure I'll read de Mauny's two stories in the Pen. NW series. Until I hear from you I'll be typing Grace and Lee.

Davin wrote in connection with some notes he wanted on Jane Mander. I've just asked him in the meantime to agree to your having the biggest cut out out of the fee.

Best,

F.S. [. . .]

To Dan Davin, *Oxford*

Alexander Turnbull Library

[Davin wrote to FS on 1 September requesting more biographical detail about Jane Mander: 'I suppose I am right in guessing Jane Mander to have been born in Marsden? And am I right in remembering her to have died in 1950?' ATL MS-Papers-0432-155. The following is an incomplete draft in FS's outwards files.]

13 September 1951

Dear Dan,

[. . .] Now, about the information you want. Jane Mander (died 1949, by the way) was born at Drury, near Auckland. Brought up in Whangarei and Auckland. There's a great deal I could tell you about Jane — I only hope somebody gets round someday to doing a biography of her. She was slim, rather short, blue-eyed, very attractive, and almost of perfect balance of masculine and feminine — but absolutely no nonsense either way. I once asked her how it was she didn't go off her head trying to fit in in these benighted parts when she was growing up. She said she was lucky enough to get hold of Havelock Ellis when she was quite young and that put her pretty right. Afterwards she became famous as a person people of all sorts could depend on for sensible sympathy in their difficulties. I'd be a bit careful of emphasizing too much the 'autobiography' of the *River*. When I knew her old man [Frank Mander] he was about 90, very mild and frail, always reading the Bible and scared stiff of dying — not at all like the blustering Tom Roland of the novel. After having destroyed most of the kauri forests of the north he used to annoy me by telling me if he was a young fellow like me he wouldn't stay in N.Z. — no opportunity any more. He was M.P. for Marsden (a northern electorate) for many years, afterwards M.L.C. [Member of the Legislative Council.]

To William Plomer, *London*

Alexander Turnbull Library

16 September 1951

Dear Plomer,

Very disgraceful my not writing: your letter is dated 29 Jan. So much has happened. Nearly 2 years ago the Labour Govt. was turned out, the effect has been a bit disastrous for those who managed to get by on small incomes — prices gradually increased, & then came the extraordinary & mad wool prices. Without the controls & subsidies a terrible inflation really got going. I don't know that anyone really believes it can be stopped now — at the most stabilized, & even that seems doubtful. I had imagined that I should always manage to plug along, but this year things have become quite impossible. Still, there are the bright spots. A Writers' Conference at Christchurch in May was an excuse for having a trip round quite a lot of the South Island — cadging rides in cars etc. All that plain & mountain country, with Cook going up to about 12,000 feet from pretty near sea-level, is pretty unique & wonderful — all rock, river, tussock, & so amazingly silent & empty — I can remember feeling nothing like it in Switzerland. Nothing as it were humanized — nobody, European or Polynesian, has ever had more than a tentative foothold. In this sub-tropical North, Nature is very often richly sinister, frightening certainly, actively hostile in a jungle sort of way — but I've never felt it half so frightening as the super-superb *indifference* of those Southern rocks & mountains. But why write you this third-rate lyrical stuff?

I *have* managed to write an 18,000 word thing that ran in *Landfall*, & I still have a short thing (30,000 words) to revise from last year. But mainly I've been engaged in helping to compile a book of N.Z. Stories over the last 100 years for the World's Classics (!!!) — the Oxford series. Actually, my colleague (E.H. McCormick) & I dug out some very good early things — I wonder if you have ever struck Lady Barker — she was pretty good. However restrain yourself from buying the book when it appears as I shall be asking Davin to send you a copy. I've had time to read very few things — except re-read Schreiner's *African Farm* — how true you were about that — the only thing indubitably first-class that has come from colonial writers. An extraordinary unexpected pleasure, though, was [Oliver Wendell Holmes's] *The Autocrat of the Breakfast Table* — & an antidote to the poisonous feelings one has about America these days — surely the spirit in the *Autocrat* is too tenacious to be completely dead yet.

But space gone & nothing much said. I seem to be out of touch. [. . .] I send you all my best wishes & recommend you don't write me until I write you a livelier letter than this.

Ever,

F.S.

To Maurice Duggan, *London*

Alexander Turnbull Library

4 October 1951

Dear Maurice,

[. . .] Renate thought from your remarks about cooking that a food parcel (rather food parcels) would be acceptable. We both of us financially buggered though. I've said this before so won't repeat. But I should say food costs just about double what it cost last year. I'm very panicky that after plugging along in the life of my choice for so many years I'm going to be forced into abandoning it. However the enormous garden I've put in will shortly be producing, and no doubt the help I'll get from it will enable me to put off making any decision meantime. Renate continues to excite my wonder — who can understand young girls? — except Proust, and he was really understanding young men. She's in the middle of her exams, but simultaneously in the middle of re-decorating the hut which really is beginning to look like a dream. She's covered walls and ceilings with scrim sized it and put on various water colours and battens — and all this when she's still determined to be off to Europe about next February. I think something has gone wrong about her tall dark handsome Arab-looking young man, so don't let me down by mentioning it when you see her. Sometimes I feel my responsibilities — how can she keep all that beauty for long when she gets about four hours sleep a night? I can't see that a complicated bathroom technique of about 2 hours a day is going to save things for long. The differences between her and Cristina continue to fascinate me — but I should still hate to choose which one I'd be prepared to keep a protective eye on (with of course a dash of sadism here and there) until the end of my days. [. . .]

One of Harris's angry penguins turned up here recently — a bloke called Wentworth — one of *the* Wentworths of Australia. When in his late teens and at school in Europe he fell in with Auden and Isherwood during their Brussels days. Also Gerald Hamilton, (son of Sir Ian Hamilton), alias Mr Norris. I got a lot of fascinating gossip. Wentworth has been running a taxi on Thursday Island (which is about a mile long and half a mile wide) and is now writing a book while he works on a bread van — think of that: from luxury trips round the Norwegian fjords with Mr Norris to a bread van in Onehunga. He must have been very charming when he was seventeen — still has traces of it, and at anyrate is bright and amusing and an addition to my list of visitors that I wouldn't want deleted.

Poor old Harry by the way is very crook and I'm a bit worried that he may be breaking up. He takes Renate pretty well, though in his letters he always refers to her as 'that female'.

Good luck to both,

F.S.

To Alec Pickard, *Invercargill*

Alexander Turnbull Library

12 October 1951

Dear Alec,

[. . .] Your brother turned up to see me the other evening. He was like a visitor from another planet — a sort of nice clean flying saucer. I cross-examined him closely about his football. That's his main interest obviously — but what eventually will take its place? The educational set-up of this country surely has a lot to answer for. Football & a few other field sports yes, but beyond that a feeling of emptiness & the starved heart. I told Tom he'd have a better chance of making the All Blacks if he went & saw the Ballet (which should be compulsory for all backs): he took it quite nicely & if the Company returns here I think he might go. Pity my little golden-head, the little German princess, wasn't here to meet him. She's exactly the same age in years — but about 20 years older than I am in understanding & nous. She would have liked Tom, as she likes all these young NZders, but as I sometimes think about myself as well, it's as though we're to her a lot of nice neuter kittens that it's pleasant to be nice to, because there's no other possible basis on which to take us. Of course I know that's not the whole story about N.Zders, but our slow & childish development is something to be deplored. After all, the Maoris are NZders too & they mature rapidly enough. However Tom will probably come again when it's warm enough for swimming, & I'll be interested to see what he makes of some of the young spades that Renate brings round here if he runs into a few of them. So long as he doesn't throw up his job & take to sitting in a shop all day drinking coffee & eating benzedrine as most of them seem to do I suppose it will be all right.

Cheers,

F.S

To Charles Brasch, *Dunedin*

Hocken Library

[late November 1951]

Charles

(1) the thing [*I For One. . .*] is supposed to be a sort of polar opposite to *That Summer* i.e. the conditioned person as opposed to the non-conditioned.

(2) the prim neutral style is deliberate.

(3) I attempt Inter-colonial relations, as it were — a sort of

attempt to develop James' European-colonial relations

(4) no idea at all whether the thing is any good. Tell me if it is not. Don't show it round. Nobody has read it except myself, & I'm sick of it.

(5) Sorry for the poor carbon copy, which is the only text in N.Z. — original has gone to Lehmann, but even if he likes it, it will be too short, I'm afraid.

F.S.

P.S. Perhaps it would be as well if you returned the thing to me reasonably soon, in case Lehmann raises any points about it. Use the same wrapper which is addressed & stamped on reverse side.

To Maurice Duggan, *London*

Alexander Turnbull Library

15 December 1951

Dear Maurice,

[. . .] I strongly recommend you go right ahead on the S.L.F. [State Literary Fund] idea — organize it as thoroughly as you can, & I'll help by writing members of the Committee, as I said. You stand every chance. [. . .] And Rex — take no notice. He's been more impossible than ever this year, following me on to Dunedin, & condemning N.Z. literature in a public talk for being epicene, proletarian & colloquial. I fear it may all be in this year's Arts YB. which I am avoiding, as I've heard that I am dismissed there by the ever-faithful J.C.R. [John Cowrie Reid] as a garrulous old man. All too unpleasant to bother with. [. . .]

Reece has got a sort of American scholarship for 3 months from March — all expenses paid & £60 a month. I recommended him, but never thought he'd get it — now I'm slightly piqued, as I can't see it necessary to his writing or any advantage to it. His pro-American anti-Russian preoccupation is approaching a sort of mania, & how on earth can he settle his mind for writing when he's so worked up over what he can't alter? He should use his freedom to write now, & stop worrying about whether he's going to have it in the future. Though of course I'm over-simplifying, & don't really intend to run him down — he can't help his nerves — but as somebody says, if our nerves mean suffering for us, we also have our intelligence to alleviate us & make us fruitful.

I think Renate will be off to England about March all right. It's been wonderful having her here. She's a woman now — not the child she was, though a child with a wonderfully developed intelligence & sensibility — and as a woman she's become involved in all that a woman must be involved in. It has been a marvellous advantage to me to see it all happening. You must try tactfully to see what you can get her to tell you when you see her. I've been down to see Smithyman twice this year on Pine Island, & have become quite interested in him — also several others of the younger generation. I was quite touched in Christchurch by their having some regard for me — but as I say, I can respond less & less. Soon, I must, of necessity, be quite out of touch.

I was never so determined in my life a few weeks back to get a piece of work finished as well as I could do it — the little Una novel. I called it *I, For One* . . . . 30,000 words, & it's now gone off to Lehmann, who I'm afraid will find it too short apart from what he might think of the content. So I sent the copy to Brasch who, although he's doubtful whether I bring it off, was so impressed by pace, readability & interest, that he's offered to publish it in a single number of *Landfall* next year if Lehmann turns it down. I think that's what will happen — and anyhow I must sell it if I can for the money, which I think I can get Brasch to agree, may be about £40. Both Renate & I are completely in the financial soup, & old Harry is the mainstay at present, as although he's pretty crook (he *may* have cancer of the lung), at least he has miraculously managed to have a few 100 pounds in the Bank — work & a bit of betting luck, I imagine. Anyhow, now I can take up the expanded version of the *Roof* thing, but after the big generalisation I rounded it off with, I'm having the devil's own job trying to find the thread again. The Davin — World's Classics job is dormant this end at present, thank God. I've had some good reading this year, Trollope, Firbank's last 5 novels, Boswell's London Journal, the American parts of Martin Chuzzlewit, & (surprisingly) the Autocrat of the Breakfast Table, but correspondence is the main snag. Letters, particularly in connection with the Authors' Peace Appeal pour in, & instead of letting them just pile up I worry about them. [. . .]

Many cheers & go right ahead in every direction,

F.S.

P.S. Bob Lowry hasn't got D'Arcy's *Forest* out yet, but the woodcuts are beautiful. Glover has drunk himself out of the Press at moment.

[Duggan's second shot at the State Literary Fund, without FS's lobbying, was successful. FS wrote to him on 4 February 1952: '[T]hings have changed a bit since last time, and I've had to decide the best service I can do you is remain silent unless I'm asked to speak. [. . .] The Committee, newly organised since the fuss we kicked up in Christchurch last May, is very sensitive about private lobbying, and it's said that applications have been turned down on account of this — even when lobbyists have been Ministers of the Crown!' ATL MS-Papers-1760-08.]

To Charles Brasch, *Dunedin*

Hocken Library

1 February 1952

Dear Charles,

Word from Lehmann now about *I, For One. . . .* and as I supposed he can't do it — the length is fatal he says without some very special boost to put it across.

He seems to have been quite interested, but I quote one paragraph:

> 'We all thought there were wonderful things all through the book, but I myself was worried by the "tone of voice" of the book. I see the point of giving it all through the girl's journal, but she is irritating and at this length I can't help feeling that some of the irritation she causes spills over the book as a whole. A very difficult problem'.

He's probably pretty right — but more from the English point of view, I think. As a sort of intercolonial affair the thing is bound to irritate people who are rather more civilized — or at least differently civilized from the colonial.

Anyhow Charles, it looks as though, if it doesn't appear in *Landfall*, it must wait until it appears in my Collected Works, issued by the publishing houses of the USSRs of the Pacific, issued as an item in the Literary Museum of Curious Bourgeois Antiques. Meantime however, I imagine it may attract quite a lot of attention in *Landfall*. [. . .]

A very amiable letter from [James] Courage — and I can see he's not out of the wood over his breakdown yet. [. . .]

All the best,

F.S.

*[*I For One. . .* was published in* Landfall *in June 1952 and by the Caxton Press in 1954.]*

To E. H. McCormick, *Auckland*

Alexander Turnbull Library

[Early 1952]

Dear Eric,

Cheque enclosed — & it leaves me worried my cash advantage in the matter exceeds yours.

Do you think we could try one of the Janet Frame stories on Dan? Which one? — I can get the Caxton Press to post off the typescript of any one to Dan

— save myself typing. I am also getting her date of birth. She's out at Avondale by the way, & I fancy a pretty serious case.

Yours

F.S.

[Caxton published Frame's The Lagoon and Other Stories *in March 1952. The World's Classics editors chose 'The Day of the Sheep'.]*

To James Courage, *London*

Hocken Library

23 March 1952

Dear James Courage,

Many thanks for your Jan. letter. I made up my mind not to write until I had read your book — *D.W.C.* [*Desire Without Content*]. I did so last week, & now I want to send you my congratulations, & say something of my pretty nearly unqualified admiration. I really do think it one of the most extraordinary things ever done by a N.Zder. Don't expect from me anything 'clever' about it. I just disagree with Bob Chapman & his approach to it. I don't think the 'surround' matters much with some books. Whether I'm right or wrong, yours seems to me to go into some sort of *Wuthering Heights* category. Perhaps you had found a way of making objective a personal situation — I don't know; but I do know that your story has gone over to quite a wide variety of readers around this place, & that surely indicates the tragic situation you deal with has transcended whatever personal origins it might have. (I may be all wrong about this, but never mind). Anyhow, I was held all through, there are some wonderful climaxes, & always the writing is very sure. Nobody from N.Z. could have done all this a few years back. I hope you draw all the attention you deserve abroad, but I like to think of you & your book as brilliant pieces of evidence (vile phrase!) that we are growing up out here. I only wish your name was shouted all through the country, which it won't be, but again, never mind. And that's that — & of course I'm looking forward to the next one.

Your story *After the Earthquake* is in our [World's Classics] collection all right — if you haven't heard from O.U.P. it's because they've written instead to the Caxton Press & *Landfall*. I wish I were well enough off to send to you some of the excellent things that appear out here from time to time. Some of the poets particularly are improving out of all sight.

I won't write of what you say about your illness — except to say I know it all — never quite so badly thank heaven, & also thank heaven, I too feel I've probably turned the corner now (after all I enter my 50th year today). But I'm hoping you too will have the good fortune to hang on & come right out into the light & write more & even better books.

I'm a bit tired after a hot & busy summer. Too much hack stuff — radio journalism etc. to distract me from my work. Charles is publishing my little novel in *Landfall* complete for June. I'm afraid it's not very good, but it's a bit 'different' & has its points, & I itch to finish expanding my *Roof* to book-length so I can begin work on a new long novel. But there's always the house & garden to keep going & many worries.

With all my best wishes,
Frank Sargeson

To William Plomer, *London*

Alexander Turnbull Library

[Plomer wrote the libretto for Benjamin Britten's Gloriana, *a three-act opera based on Lytton Strachey's* Elizabeth and Essex: A Tragic History. *It premiered at the Royal Opera House Covent Garden in June 1953 during the coronation celebrations of Queen Elizabeth II.]*

29 June 1952

Dear Plomer,

You must be one of the kindest people on earth. I very much appreciated your letter. And my best congratulations on the novel [*Museum Pieces*] before it appears — & in any case September will be here so very soon now. But what a very difficult & delicate task for the Coronation! I mean the libretto — Elizabeth & Essex!! I just can't imagine what feelings round the Court are going to be: perhaps the Duke of Edinburgh will be sent to the Tower immediately to pave the way for a succession of Royal Lovers — but I suppose I am exposing myself to a charge of High Treason by saying this. (Lord only knows what you & Britten are letting yourselves in for though). No, this benighted country doesn't seem to have got round to the *Billy Budd* recordings yet, but they'll turn up on the air eventually no doubt — I was surprised how well the Grimes opera came over when I heard it.

I shall send you a copy of *Landfall* with my 'small thing' in it complete very soon. Perhaps it doesn't come off, but parts of it may amuse you if you find you can read it at all. (It runs to a bit over 30,000 words).

And no, I've not seen the [Rupert Hart-Davis's biography of Hugh] Walpole yet, though I've seen a number of notices of it. I shall get round to it eventually.

At the moment I seem to read only the Brontes over the fire at night, & stay in bed waiting for the sun to come out in the morning. It is all very curious — all your sufferings which we escaped during the war seem to have caught up with us: fantastic power-shortages & blackouts — even certain food-shortages: of course we can't claim to rival you in bombings & such horrors, but with the change of Government a couple of years back, in addition to an Inflation more severe than your own, we can show more vulgarity, Philistine greed & insensitiveness, to the square mile, than anywhere else in the world: there is much to be said for Tory government in Europe I don't doubt, but in these parts, nothing at all: there *was* something that might have been described as a humane colonial spirit: not now, no spirit at all, just a shameless aping, devastatingly empty & tasteless, of what Mr. Winston Churchill is imagined to represent in England. You will infer from my spleen that I am one who hasn't benefited from all this ignorant & catastrophic stupidity. I haven't, but I'm still alive, still plugging away at the work I want to do at my usual slow pace — so all I've said is so much wind, as the work I want to do is the only thing that really matters to me.

I'm ashamed to say I haven't yet read van der Post's book [*Venture to the Interior*] even though it is on my shelves: great advertisements for it appear even in local papers, so I infer it is an immense success — & very pleasant for the author & his friends of which you are one of course.

But no more my good Plomer — I'll try to write more cheerfully soon, & many cheers for your novel your libretto & all your good & excellent works.

From yours,

F.S.

To Maurice and Barbara Duggan, *London*

Alexander Turnbull Library

26 July 1952

Dear Two,

Your letter turned up the day Renate left for Wellington to catch the *Monowai*: I fancy she has sailed all right, & the idea is to go on from Sydney on *Orontes*. Do what you can for her: I can't tell you about her troubles difficulties & handicaps I've become knowledgeable about, but you may find out something yourselves. It was wonderful having her here — of course the sound of washing & ironing long after midnight was disturbing at times, but it's such an immense privilege to know somebody, the like of whom may turn up only once in a hundred years, one must put up with petty irritations. I'm posting her wrist watch care of you.

On her side of course, she had to put up with my uncouthness, which, as I'm sure you both know, but are always too kind to mention, can be pretty terrible & embarrassing at times. She leaves 2 houses behind her half completed (one of them nearly opposite your own place at Forrest Hill) — & wonderfully designed, plus some excellently designed furniture.

I'm wondering if you confessed to the S.L.F. you are using the money for fares — if not, be as careful as you can, as I believe there's ill-feeling over D'Arcy's putting funds to what was regarded as improper uses. The delays in payment are heart-breaking. The Hubert Church prize still *not paid* — & the core of it all is supposed to be some dilatory incompetence on the part of Professor Gordon — pity when Lawlor is such a reformed character. I can't help in this matter until next Writers' Conference — when it looks as though Gordon is due for the doing over Lawlor got last time.

What I like best about the June *Landfall* is my own photograph by John Pascoe — I wear my hair longer than Maurice these days. Reactions to the novel have been pretty good, & best of all, Una doesn't identify herself with the diarist overmuch, & we are still the best of friends. The dreary complaints about money as usual — & I'm writing for the *School Journal* at good rates to make up a bit. This is very hasty after the chaos of Renate's departure — I'm all behind with everything.

Best love,

F.S.

To E.P. Dawson, *Mt Maunganui*

Hocken Library

14 September 1952

Dear Peter,

[. . .] A duller, but quieter life since R. went — yet it suits me — I've plugged along a bit faster at expanding the damned old *Roof*, & it's near as long again now — but that still leaves 30,000 words to go: still, they should go down pretty smoothly from now on, as I've reached the part I always had in mind, & never could reach previously. I take a day off now & then to cast round for the opening chapter of the Bohemian novel [*Memoirs of a Peon*], but can't as yet find out quite how the story is to be told. Damned difficult. I also want to refurbish my old 3 act play, & try it out on one of the local societies — though the unintelligent bumptious local producers will be a difficulty. [. . .]

Jess [Whitworth] took me to see Augusta Ford, who is very American

University, but very intelligent in the American way. I've enjoyed very much listening to Canon [Charles] Raven, his [radio] talks so beautifully composed: Oxford Xtianity, I suppose, but very civilised for all that. The highlight recently was Baxter's public reading of his own poetry. A drunken Calvinist — or a Calvinist drunk, whichever you like: he is a genius or the nearest thing to it I have ever struck: but he'll either be dead, or else locked up either for obscenity or religious mania within the next five years — you feel he's not yet quite certain whether he's Elected or not: but if he can be sure either way he can do what he likes — the Antinomian heresy, the basis of Hogg's *Memoirs of a Justified Sinner*, I fancy.

All the best Peter,

F.S. [. . .]

To Dan Davin, *Oxford*

Alexander Turnbull Library

23 September 1952

Dear Dan,

[. . .] I've not much news — an early good spring, & I'm behind with the garden: I stick very close to an expansion of the *Roof*, which may turn out to require more vols. than Proust. But hack work to meet the high living costs is the devil. It is the *School Journal*! now, but they pay well. My *Landfall* novella has gone over rather well out here, but I don't know. Cresswell's *Forest* came out at last, beautifully done, except for some overpowering bloomers on Bob Lowry's part. There's to be a cheap printing, but I don't think it's out yet — the ordered copies were a guinea, & even though a friend & myself put in £15, by an oversight we never got one! N.Z! — things like that happen. It's a very curious work, uneven, archaic, a bit too propagandist perhaps — but with moments of very great beauty, & of course, it's saturated with D'Arcy's passionate belief in Spirit — a point which some people, inexplicably, seem to miss, while they fasten on to what is merely ancillary. No doubt it's not quite in the same class as the *Phaedrus*, but hats off to D'Arcy for his guts, & let's all forget how trying the bastard can be.

Young Baxter has been here reading his poetry — that drunken young Calvinist is a genius compounded of obscenity & religious mania: a sort of Calvinistic St John of the Cross all buggered up, a sort of Antinomian heretic, who, if he can be sure he's Elected, can do what he likes — & will do what he likes anyhow. He reads poetry beautifully, & excretes it as easily & naturally as other men whose bowels are in perfect health do their jobs.

Wonderful news that you are at work on the new fiction. May all the Muses help & defend you!

All the best,

F.S.

P.S. My sweet precious Renate should be in England now. I commend her to the adorable Winnie if they should meet.

To Charles Brasch, *Dunedin*

Hocken Library

[Bill Pearson's essay 'Fretful Sleepers: A Sketch of New Zealand Behaviour and Its Implications for the Artist' was published in Landfall *in September 1952. 'A Transfer (extract from a novel)', a chapter from what would become* Coal Flat, *had appeared under the pseudonym Chris Bell in* Landfall *in December 1951.]*

3 October 1952

Dear Charles,

Just a line of congratulation on producing a very readable number. (By the way I meant before to inquire what devoted slave of yours produced the Index — can it be possible you did it yourself? — because if so I won't feel so bad about my damned hack work — I'm writing moralising stuff for the *School Journal* at moment, alas!). Of course [Phillip] Wilson's story ['The Wedding'] is the best thing, & I'm glad we have it in our Oxford vol. but I can take Pearson even though he's far too flatulent — & how amusing when he suddenly mentions our virtues & devotes a few lines to them! — did you insist on his inserting that bit? But how suspicious one is of these generalising strictures — one always suspects that some boy or girl friend has been unkind, or an abortionist has named too high a figure. I felt a similar irritation over [Fairburn's] *We New Zders.* After all, why generalise over the generality? — they're always much of a muchness at all times & places, poor souls — not caviare to them, but balls — though that's not to say if you sort them out as individuals you don't find there's very few who won't interest & even move you. But it's a job for the poets & story-tellers, & I hope Pearson plugs ahead with his novel, of which I suppose *A Transfer* was a part. How well J[ames] B[ertram] says what he says about J.M.M. ['Le Tombeau de Katherine Mansfield'.]

Courage very kindly sent me a copy of his new novel [*Fires in the Distance*]: I see that the English reviewers are inclined to shake their heads — I'm afraid this will be chronic in the future, i.e. from now on, the more exactly we manage to get N.Z. life, the less we're likely to be understood by English reviewers.

I hardly like to say how successful I think the book is: I'm a little dumbfounded & puzzled, but there's no question C. has an apparently effortless technical mastery that makes the story easy to read & absorbingly interesting: the re-creation of the scene completely fascinates me. I suppose what one misses (and it is surprising) is a sort of irony that would imply that the author is aware of values beyond the understanding of his characters: it is surprising that although they don't altogether take themselves for granted, the author does — but perhaps Courage is really being a bit over-cautious: that is, sitting apart from them in England, he fears he may be accused of looking down on them — & of course he very well might be if the irony were the wrong sort or even if it were the right sort, didn't permeate the story in the way I imagine it very well might. But perhaps you won't agree. Anyway I enjoyed the book, & I can't escape the conclusion that an extraordinary & valuable body of work is being steadily built up. [. . .]

All the best, Charles, from

F.S.

P.S. The mother & her Beethoven might appear to contradict what I say, but I don't think so — in fact she seems to prove my point — she's capable of being cultured but not civilized — which is as it is with all of us, alas, hence the need for irony.

To John Reece Cole, *Wellington*

Alexander Turnbull Library

5 November [1952]

Dear Reece,

[. . .] The first batch of Oxford proofs turned up — to page 320. About another 100 pages to come, and your story among them. Page proofs, so the thing is moving along. And it looks very nice — a bit patchy, as such collections must be, but the best work is wonderful. McC. and I think Janet Frame's *Day of the Sheep* is one of the most beautiful things ever done in NZ. (We have a chronological arrangement of *subject*, which accounts for its being the last story in the present batch). Of course you can imagine the work involved, and the disputes about responsibility — but it's been fixed now that Davin only, appears on the title-page, and McC. and I get acknowledgements — in this way the two of us have some protection from the outraged Mulgans etc. The thing is going to be quite an event for NZ, and I confess to being proud of my part in pushing it along. (Frame by the way is back in Seacliff, but simple little letters can be coaxed out of her.)

Just finished my third School Journal piece — one to go, and that will be forty guineas worth: and have just been asked to chair the ZB reviews for January. I find it requires terrific self-discipline to knock these jobs off one by one, and at the same time keep the 'real' work steadily moving along. (Today I'm having a day off like a business man, and reading an Eric Ambler thriller). The feeling of monotony is overpowering sometimes, but I immediately remind myself what does it matter — at my age? How does Cocteau put it? — the older and more ugly our bodies become, the more beautiful our works should be. The great thing I fancy, is to get to the fifties without having let all the bitterness and frustration destroy one's capacity for distilling out the essences one has always been after. I was greatly interested the other day to read an American interpretation of Beethoven's last super-great quartets — the point made was that these super-beautiful works are rooted in frustration. [. . .]

Well, to Chris and all, all the greetings,

F.S. [. . .]

To James Courage, *London*

Hocken Library

[FS to Courage, 29 September: '[I]f you won't come back [to NZ] under your own steam you should be brought back by the scruff of the neck'. Hocken MS-0999/111. Courage suffered from depression, and spent some time in Napsbury psychiatric hospital following a breakdown in 1950. Maurice Duggan developed TB in Mallorca; Courage too had been treated for TB.]

28 November 1952

Dear Courage,

[. . .] I seem to be very wooden — tired out, I'm afraid, after knocking my way through a heap of absurd hack work. And so many worries — I expect you have heard about poor Duggan & his serious illness while in Mallorca. Did I startle you with my 'scruff of the neck'? — you must forgive an uncouth N.Zder. Yes, I expect you need the care you mention, & you certainly wouldn't get it here — it is awful to think of Janet Frame, whose very fine story you will see in the Oxford book — only 28 years old, but about 8 of those, (the last 8), spent mainly in Seacliff. Of course I'm perpetually on the verge myself, but I cling to Groddeck & work & interest in every fascinating thing — & I've always liked that bit about the big St. Theresa, who, when somebody complained he was assailed by disturbing images even when he was on his knees praying, said, yes, she had experienced the same thing herself, but found it best to ignore it. Look forward to your fifties, my dear fellow, as I do — one settles down then — those 7 year periods are absolutely right & the 7th is the worst for all of us. I have a constant lesson & inspiration in my lifelong friend [Harry] who is 10 years older than I am: in his early fifties he got over his migraine — he never was more than a bit neurotic, & now he's not at all, as cheerful as a bird, & better for me than ever he was in 30 years — & he always was pretty good.

How amused I was by your hitting on that expression for Cresswell — pirate-like. Exactly. And yet our relations have always been pretty good. He's in no doubt how deeply I respect him & his work, yet he knows also he has never subdued me into being his slave & disciple, & never will — & in any case he has a faithful follower in Rod Finlayson, who is such pure gold he is almost too good for D'Arcy.

All my best to you — & we'll see you one day when you've settled down, you'll see.

F.S.

P.S. Reading this over I am repelled by a sort of radio doctor complacency — you will have to forgive me.

To Denis Glover, *Christchurch*

Alexander Turnbull Library

[Glover may have sent FS proof sheets of his poem sequence 'Arawata Bill', published by the Pegasus Press in mid-1953.]

22 April 1953

Dear Denis,

Your proof sheets turned up when I was smothered under a heap of Landfall award poesy: I put in a lot of work on it, but with your experience you will know only too well what it is like — turning over the mountains like your Arawata Bill in the hope of finding a few moderately sized nuggets. Nevertheless there was I think at least one good nugget.

I was shocked to find you had pilfered a fair flower from your garden to stick in the bonnet of your Listener jeep. But dear oh dear what are those tops in the dawn? — I hesitate to think they may be bottle tops. But good work you subtle old ex sea dog with your tenuous effects that come off so nicely, your nuzzles and drizzles etc. Strange that your 'shoulder of a boulder' should remind me of the Songs of a Sub-Man [by Patrick Barrington]:

> Cold cold cold is the melancholy mould
> Cold is the foam cold sea,
> Colder than the shoulder of a neolithic boulder
> Is the shoulder you show to me

(Would you like more)?

Deafer than a heifer to the sighing of a zephyr.

(or more)?

Bitter bitter bitter is the lemon to the fritter
Bitter is the salt to the sea,
But bitterer by far than these bitternesses are
Is your bitter scorn of me.

But you probably know them. The sequence is going to enrich your already rich reputation — and many thanks for it.

Do you know? — Basil Dowling thinks The Forest is our finest verse play (I suppose he means finer than Curnow's [*The Axe*]), and contains some of the best poetry written anywhere for a long time. High praise — but I cling to the notion that it is at least partly true.

I am up to the neck in work and never have a moment of any kind. The Roof now just on 3 times original size, but needs a lot more yet — and I'm itching to begin the novel about the young bohemians — Renate and her cobbers. (That divinely lovely creature is at present hanging on to some male architectural student's waist as they tear across France on a second hand motor bike. May she survive! and at the same time not be laid a greater number of times than she can really do with).

After Hella Hofmann plaguing the life out of me over her Symposium (I could never convince her it was none of my business), I now feel very indignant about the SLF's [State Literary Fund] turning down a subsidy. Perhaps John Moffett's and that Baptist bastard (an expert on Euripides forsooth!) [E.M.] Blaiklock's work. I'm afraid the entire business was badly handled all round, and none of us who had anything to do with it have anything to be proud of. But if only Hella had gone ahead on her own steam! — after all she had the drive and energy to get the material, then she stupidly relied elsewhere instead of pushing the barrow along herself. At the same time as I was supposed to be helping her I was also supposed to know nothing of the contents (a pleasant surprise for you!) — and I'm damned if I know a single thing about any of them except one to this day. But apart from being personally involved, it does seem a bit scandalous that the application was turned down.

I thought Curnow's poem in Listener ['Jack-in-the-Boat'] terrifically good. I never see him and he has never been here thank God — I imagine I would have more against him if I knew him better, but God rot me if I ever deny he's a poet of the highest order — such perfect finish, an ear that is never out by so much as a tenth tone, and an intellectual quality that irks me and yet doesn't ask for the highest admiration without getting it. Amazing that the whimwhamsical stuff hasn't ruined him, yet it hasn't.

All my best to you — I assiduously coach the Smithymans along in the hope they may one day approach your finest qualities. (Ah, but if only one of you could write poetry that might come anywhere near to Milton at his best!)

F.S.

To John Reece Cole, *Wellington*

Alexander Turnbull Library

16 May 1953

Dear Reece,

[. . .] Sometime this year I must try to get round to digging up an old Will of mine and making a new one. I wonder if you would mind if I appointed you my Literary Executor — this sounds high and mightily important, also slightly comic, but actually if my present book turns out all right I should put my papers in order as a few things among them may eventually be of some interest: I am astonished at big bundles of abandoned MSS, not to mention my first novel, *Blind Alleys* — 228 typescript pages, a full length 3 act play called *Secret Places* — 93 typescript pages and much of it single-space, a collection of short stories plus a dramatic version of *Blind Alleys* — 151 typescript pages. It wasn't until after all that that I started on the Conversation With my Uncle line, and the result to date seems to be:

Stories say	200 typescript pages
That Summer	100
Dream	326
I For One	100
	726

Add 165 pages Roof so far. Do you think I should aim at 1000 pages that may possibly be of some value and then turn my toes up? No, actually I am trying a scheme with the Caxton for the 726 pages of fiction to appear in a Collected Vol — though it won't be possible unless the SLF can be persuaded to cough up nearly £1000.

Well, I must get on. Did I tell you of the astonishing pleasure I got from Eckermann's Goethe Conversations? — among other things I can now make the most beautiful blue and yellow shadows with a candle flame.

My best to DW [David Wentworth] if he is still with you and to Chris and kids of course.

F.S. [. . .]

To E.P. Dawson, *Mt Maunganui*

Hocken Library

5 June 1953

Dear Peter,

[. . .] You must grant me my obsession. I seem to be always fighting my way *to* my ms as well as *through* it. I have the feeling sometimes of being surrounded by every kind of distress. A very curious variety indeed. What for example does one do about two young men who airily toss in jobs of more than ten pounds a week and then turn up with every hope of being housed and fed, and some hope of a bit of pocket money into the bargain? I must say I have never been quite able to work such matters out, and now I find myself losing patience. Poor Johnny is a different matter, and one or two others as well, but when there is health strength and youth, and brains into the bargain, but no apparent aim or purpose, just a dislike for present-day society — well, I never quite lose sympathy, but the day when I lose my temper there's going to be quite a fireworks display. But it's a depressing subject so I leave it. [. . .]

Did you see about that damned Coronation medal in the paper? I always thought one was approached before any of these so-called honours were dumped on one. Nobody will believe that I *wasn't* approached — but I never knew a thing until the list came out. I infer they just picked out one ageing author one ageing painter (John Weeks) etc. and lumped them in with mayors chairmen and lieutenant-colonels. What an insult! And they never had enough brains to understand that poetry should have been their choice! However, the thing may be a help to me in my skirmishes with M.I.5 or 10 or whatever it is — apparently the Authors' Peace Appeal plus some literature from Prague has at least drawn attention, and I am marked down as at least a fellow-traveller. [. . .]

No more Peter. I am all blear-eyed at midnight. [. . .]

F.S.

[The names of the 1000-odd Auckland regional recipients of the Coronation Medal appeared in the NZ Herald *of 2 June. 129,051 medals were awarded across the Commonwealth.]*

To E.P. Dawson, *Mt Maunganui*

Hocken Library

3 September [1953]

Dear Peter,

Yes, I intended to write but events were much too much for me and after all the excitement and upset when I at last got back [from the South Island] I took refuge in a bout of the old TB trouble which followed a frightful cold: I still have a very painful swelling in my groin but I get round with a stick and I think things are improving. Of course the bloody bloody weather hasn't helped matters: the full year's rainfall already: the garden is all behind and it's too wet to be got at much even if I had the energy or agility.

Just about everything that could went wrong. It turned out the students at Otago paid my air fare but didn't pay anything in addition, and the fee for my two AE [Adult Education] talks [in Invercargill] was rather less than I expected. To cap it all I looked up a decayed old friend in Wellington and found him barely alive in shocking circumstances. All this case on top of my father's death plus another sad business which in the meantime I have to keep under my hat [probably Maurice Duggan's July suicide attempt]. Still, on the brighter side there was the kindness of Charles Brasch and his companion Rodney Kennedy: they share the ground floor of what I think is an old family house — I mean Charles's family — and Rodney is a very delightful person: his legs are almost short enough to make him a dwarf but I suspect he would refuse legs of a more standard size even if they could be definitely offered him. He produces plays for Amateur societies all over Otago, and is deservedly very popular for his ability his extraordinary good-temper and his kindness and generosity. I met God knows how many other people, all very hospitable, but I don't know that the talk for the students which I had put so much work into went over very well. I had been expecting a closed society, and my paper was prepared on that assumption, but it turned out a fairly large public meeting with the press there. Anyhow, Charles may publish the paper in Landfall with arguments against it by a theologian and a sociologist, and if so you will have the opportunity of tearing it to pieces also. But how strange! — what stimulated me most in Dunedin was a reconstruction of an early settler's cottage in the Old Colonists' Museum: it somehow got tied up with the experience of flying which also stimulated me enormously — and I suddenly seemed to see the possibilities of writing a play which I have been attempting to get started ever since I returned. Lying on my back I have been re-reading Lady Barker, also [Randal] Burdon's studies [*New Zealand Notables*, 1941–1950] (what a marvellous advance he made from the first volume to the third!) for atmosphere. Talking about atmosphere though, it was a marvellous trip from Dunedin up to Wellington — the air crystal clear at first and the mountains with Sefton Cook and the Tasman group standing head and shoulders higher looking very very grand. We were flying I suppose about 20 miles out at sea and at a height of 8000 feet: then we came down through clouds to Christchurch where it was all mist and rain and not too good for landing: but we flew above the dirty weather up to Wellington with more superb views of mountains. But I don't like flying — it's not so much the overt danger as the general uneasiness of the plane, a sort of extreme deadly menace very insidious and very potent. I was delighted to discover that when the passengers are experiencing their worst bumps the pilot as likely as not is filing his fingernails and not even bothering to look ahead — something that I want to use with good effect in my play if I can.

I stayed for about 10 days with the Coles in Wellington — Chris was just having another baby which has turned out to be a boy. Reece is now assistant director of the Turnbull, and although still very nervous contrives to keep himself in control pretty well: it seems doubtful whether he will write any more and I think it worries him profoundly, but he manages to keep his grip and as always he was extremely kind to me. Also Chris. But I had a very stormy session with Prof Gordon about the SLF's turning down Hella's symposium and also my own application for a rather largish sum for a collected volume of fiction. Gordon himself is not so bad, the trouble is mainly Lawlor plus the bunch of ragbags which is the committee. Nobody could be more stupid than Lawlor, and nobody more ignorant and nonentical than these people.

[. . .] Renate has written at last — from Stuttgart: a good letter — she talks about a baron who has an enormous schloss without drains and uses a motor-bike to take him about in the corridors. I must tell you about old Harry though: he had his 60th birthday recently, and although he is as thin as a piece of paper he can't bring himself to leave off working: my argument has been that there is no point in his going to heaven for his reward now that he can go and get it from the Social Security department. He has never had a doctor's prescription or any benefit whatsoever so far.

Well I must leave off. I was very glad that the Aussies got cleaned up in the cricket — but even gladder that Hamilton got the Ranfurly Shield taken off them. Best of luck Peter. I haven't seen Jess for ages, but Ernest rode over last Sunday on his bike, and told me among other things that NY skyscrapers are built by Mohawk indians.

F.S.

[The Otago settler's house and flying appear as motifs in FS's play The Cradle and the Egg, *begun soon after his return. The text of his address to the Otago University Literary Society, 'What is the Question', was published in* Here and Now *in March 1954 and also appears in* Conversation in a Train and Other Critical Writing, *pp. 78–89.]*

To Charles Brasch, *Dunedin*

Hocken Library

16 September 1953

Dear Charles,

Yes, I meant to write about Maurice, but there's nothing to say as I haven't discussed the matter with him. I feel I have lost the opportunity to now and it seems pointless anyhow as I can't escape feeling it's a temperament one is attempting to deal with rather than a person. All I have learned is that he meant business (he took 40 capsules): perhaps his being recalled to life again has made some difference to him but it is difficult to detect — any great difference anyhow. I have an uneasy feeling that eventually it will happen again. It seems that he takes some pride in feeling that he had the courage to die, and one must grant him that — but how can one suggest that a little less pride and some humility over the courageous business of living might be more to the point? In a way I am disappointed that by some miracle nothing seems to have leaked out, because it seems to mean that he's not getting the stimulation of the challenge to the immense effort that is required of him. But I'm far from sure of all this, and must ask for your continued discretion in the meantime.

Wellington was so different from Dunedin — for me, I mean. I went slumming and discovered an old friend of mine aged 78 now living in shocking circumstances. He used to be a damn good organist and had many appointments, but he had completely lost his grip of things and I could do nothing with him even though I saw various people and tried to get him into a Home. The house he was living in was inhabited by drunken brawlers and a poor creature, a woman with elephantiasis of the leg — the sort of leg I never want to see again. Renate used to share my no doubt unhealthy interest in scenes of poverty and squalor, but not long before she left she systematically detached herself from any such thing on the grounds that in Europe one would be destroyed if one were interested. No doubt she was quite right.

[. . .] I was very depressed over my interview with the fantastically stupid Lawlor and the horribly philistine Gordon — G. I know was supposed to write you about Landfall, but I could bet he hasn't. I flew at Lawlor when he said that it would take Landfall a long while to recover from publishing Courage's story. The other evening I heard him say on the air that Wilde's father was dirty immoral and something else which I forget, and he had two sons one of whom was a pervert and the other something which I also forget.

I have heard from Lehmann at last who wants me to spread around that he is starting up a new magazine from 31 Egerton Crescent SW 3 provisionally entitled The London Magazine. He still sounds depressed and I hope he hasn't had to scratch for a living. [. . .]

I read hard in last century here and in England — all to help my play [*The Cradle and the Egg*], but so much to do with the garden all behind and electricity going on to my hut and my doing much of the work myself. Bob Gilbert turned up last weekend with a leg of pork and a shoulder of mutton all of which we ate in 2 days. Bob goes to Napier soon to run some sort of radar thing that is supposed to help the Queen's plane to get round the country in safety. It will be a temptation if Holland goes in the same plane.

Good luck Charles,

F.S. [. . .]

[John Lehmann revived the defunct The London Magazine *(first published in 1732) in 1954, and remained its editor until 1961.]*

To Keith Sinclair, *Auckland*

Private collection

4 October 1953

Dear Keith,

[. . .] I keep thinking about the problem of lecturing writing poetry reading Gibbon etc. I think my attitude is tied up with my early beginnings — that is, failing to pass examinations, trying to write verse and prose and hopelessly failing there too. I expect I had some notion that I had to prove to myself somehow that I wasn't just a good for nothing. So I started the reading habit without ever supposing that it could benefit me in any material way — until now I've ended up with a distaste for any reading that is going to benefit me in a material way, and a suspicion of anybody else's reading if it's tied up with a livelihood. This sounds extravagant I know, and in more ways than one, but at least it's the traditional approach or was until some time last century. Anyhow, with me it seems to have worked, because provided one can tie in all activities with this self-cultivation there never seems to be what other people would call a dull or spare moment. In any case ask yourself how different it is from your own and Bob [Chapman]'s and Ken [Smithyman]'s precocity — the 3 of you appear to have fingered dictionaries in your cradles. But what I ask myself is whether or not there could be a combination of what appear to be two different attitudes. Take Gibbon as an example. Say you read him for pleasure and for your own disinterested cultivation when for the purposes of lectures you should be reading last century German history in works which don't happen to be works of literature — couldn't you when asked an awkward question related to the syllabus cunningly open up a fascinating sidetrack which besides getting you by might be remembered by students long after they had forgotten the damned stuff that got them through their examinations? In that way you would be assisting in reviving the failing Spirit cultivating your Pleasure Garden and earning your salary all in one. And to end up with I'm portentous enough to say that there is no other way of providing for your middle and old age. [. . .]

F.S.

To William Plomer, *Sussex*

Alexander Turnbull Library

[William Plomer moved to Rustington on the Sussex coast in June 1953. FS to Dan Davin, 22 September 1953: 'Was Gloriana good — I am a little embarrassed in writing to Plomer as the critics seem to say it wasn't'. ATL MS-Papers-5079-131.]

14 December 1953

Dear Plomer,

I meant ages ago to write you, but perhaps just as well I didn't because the other evening I heard the recorded *Gloriana* on my radio. I must say it came through as beautifully as things do come on the radio, but even so, although I got a pretty good idea of the music there wasn't much of your text I could pick up. All I can really say is there were some very excellent moments, and the whole thing was done with wonderful assurance and finish. I was much amused by some of the controversy — the outraged clergymen etc. I hope you won't mind my using the word 'polish' about your introductory remarks — I heard every word of that, and in every way, what you said, timing, control of voice and all the rest, it was a most wonderfully finished piece of work. I expect I would have felt the same about *Gloriana* if I had been there, but as you know, with a work of such dimensions even the best radio is rather like trying to get a large-sized river through a garden hose-pipe.

It was very kind of you to write me when you were in the thick of the last rehearsals. I hope the Q. [Queen] and the D. [Duke] were pleased — I hardly expect to get even a sight of that couple in about a fortnight, but perhaps I should drop them a note saying don't forget about the accolade for Sir Ben and Sir Bill when you get back. There is by the way such a lot of balls going on here about this visit that I'm laying in a stock of tins which may enable me to stay inside my own boundaries until it's all over. But I don't need to tell you about what provincial life is like.

I've remembered I said I would send you a copy of our Oxford book of NZ stories — it came out in September, and on the whole it looks rather well (except for some irritating misprints — have you noticed? — the setting in proof may be right, and wrong on publication: it must be the monotype that's used now, I think). Anyhow I'll be writing to Davin at the Oxford Press shortly, and I know he will be kind enough to send you a copy.

The damned inflation goes on and on, but I've retaliated by thoroughly organizing my life — so thoroughly indeed that now it is summer I'm in bed for only about 4 hours a night: I have such an enormous garden to attend to, but wonderful things from it this season. I had a five hour air trip down to Dunedin in the winter to read a paper to some University students, and I enjoyed very much the outing: the worst flying country in the world, but it was a good trip. The paper was very subversive, all about how you can't have a Christian country with the Christian seasons upside down etc. It's supposed to be printed, and if it is I shall try to send you a copy.

Just at the moment I don't seem to get things finished. I have 2 (indeed 3) largish things on hand — and one (it sounds absurd I know), is a play. But we shall see — I mention Ibsen to the local skeptics and mutter something about *that* provincial dump.

I see you have been having some scandals — I must say I chuckled over the photo in the English Listener of Sir David Maxwell Fyfe leading an Oxford procession with J.G. [John Gielgud] coming behind. Just exactly what does a Home Secretary do when he meets one of his victims on a social occasion — I mean a subsequent social occasion?

Are you enjoying the Sussex coast? I wish I could send you some of our present superfluity of sunshine.

I was relieved to have a note from John Lehmann at last — though it was sad that he should still seem a little depressed. I look forward to his new paper. I have thought the first number of *Encounter* only moderately interesting. But isn't the Laughlin-Ford *Perspectives* a glossy piece of work? — I read it with great interest though. Mainly this year I've been making a study of George Eliot — she ties up so nicely with all our decayed Evangelicalism etc. I thought *Deronda* except for a few patches a most magnificent performance. My father died this year aged 81 — just about to lay down the burden of the bloody ego he looked like a Russian saint. My mother aged 84 is still going strong, a rather preposterous woman with enormous strength of stubborn will. If I have anything of her vitality, and can use it in my own way, I should be doing my best work when I'm about 75.

Many cheers,

F.S.

Can one describe George Eliot as a Victorian blue stocking which actually came off?

['Some scandals': probably a reference to the events of the summer of 1953 which saw Michael Pitt-Rivers, Lord Montagu of Beaulieu and Peter Wildeblood arrested and charged with homosexual offences. In the Cold War atmosphere of the 1950s the political climate in Britain was virulently anti-homosexual: Home Secretary Sir David Maxwell Fyfe had promised 'a new drive against male vice' that would 'rid England of this plague'.]

To Dan Davin, *Oxford*

Alexander Turnbull Library

[M.H. Holcroft had reviewed the Oxford New Zealand Short Stories *in the* Listener, *18 December 1953. FS's dispute with Holcroft stemmed from Sargeson's belief that Holcroft paid him considerably less for his reviewing than his predecessor Oliver Duff. The spat, some of which was conducted in the* Listener's *correspondence column, finally ran out of steam in November 1955.]*

6 January 1954

Dear Dan,

[. . .] Texidor has written, and [. . .] she told enough about [Maurice Duggan's suicide attempt] for us to know that the story got out through the one loophole we were very doubtful about. Maurice and Barbara are up North with Eric Lee-Johnson at present, but when they come back B. will have to tell M. that he can no longer assume that people don't know. This conceivably may be a good thing — I don't know: anyhow, I only hope Maurice won't be too upset. The really upsetting thing is that the story should be getting about so long after the event — it was generally understood among 3 or 4 of us that Maurice much preferred to carry on as though nothing had happened (an impossibility perhaps, but it has seemed to work quite well), and after such a time it really did seem as though all had been forgotten. What the future holds I have no idea.

Yes, I agree that Holcroft shouldn't be replied to, and the book will certainly sell itself. In anycase I am about to embark on a quarrel with H. over his preposterously low fees. I am afraid he will interpret this as resentment over his review, but I can't help it if he is one of those irritating people who imagine that because each of us is several sorts of bastard we are necessarily every sort of bastard. H's fees for long past have been a disgrace, and even though I completely bugger up my chances of any more income from the Listener, at least I will know I have the support of every writer who needs the dough he can earn that way.

The TLS with the notice not turned up yet, but it will soon. Oh, the Queen, there have been wild outbursts of patriotism over a young woman who apparently consents to be a dummy on which you hang frocks for typists. My spleen makes me suspect the D. sells the dresses as a sideline after he has disrobed the model. They say half a million is being spent — and half that amount would save the Campion's noble attempt to establish a local touring Theatre from collapsing. One could weep for the incredible stupid vulgarity of it all — if it wasn't for the vitality: the vitality ensures that something, something cultural will come out of it eventually — but not in my day, and not in yours: we must console ourselves with the thought that against all the pressures and the incredible strain we have had the guts to do our little bit: I don't exaggerate when I say that to live here as I do I must be prepared for almost daily insults from people who are unlikely to be remembered a fortnight after they are dead: one must even put up with jeers from kids not yet school age. I could fix things in a month by making a pretty-pretty garden and catching the bus in the morning regularly. But this is tedious commonplace stuff — and I'd never deny that the vitality *is* pretty much there — perhaps at this stage it's all that matters. [. . .]

As ever,

F.S.

To Dan Davin, *Oxford*

Alexander Turnbull Library

5 April 1954

Dear Dan,

[. . .] I'm in a muddle of the usual tensions at the moment. After re-reading Ibsen, and seeing that the 'social' plays are rooted in the historical ones, and those in turn rooted in the sagas, I decided the play I wanted to write was impossible in spite of the appearances (God's Own country a provincial dump not unlike Norway last century and no doubt this as well) — after all that, I suddenly went ahead and now have the thing half finished. Dialogue — it's what's easiest to me and most days I'm upset if my pencil doesn't move fast and steady enough to give me a cramp in the hand. I even felt confident enough to leave off for a fortnight to write 2 3600 word stories which astonished me by turning out so well ['The Undertaker's Story' and 'The Colonel's Daughter']. But all this is done in a mess of undone housework the garden getting behind quarrels over trying to get Harry established in the hut neurotics and psychopaths turning up without jobs or money and socks and shirts that almost certainly have never been washed this year — give me the old-fashioned bum who knows without ever having to be told that any sort of life needs a pattern: the bohemian bum whose girl is as hopeless over a few fundamental necessities as he is is just an old-fashioned pain in the neck. [. . .]

My quarrel with Holcroft came off, not at all creditably to either of us — though I fancy he displayed a much greater aptitude for putting his foot in it that I did. I have to prepare a Memorandum now to put to the Minister through the PEN. It will do no good and I've virtually cut my own throat but it was at least a gesture. My Dunedin talk came out in Here and Now, but it did not altogether please me to see it in print — and I had similar feelings about the talk on the book of stories which Charles has printed in Landfall. Apart from the hope of getting work completed the best hope this year is the possibility of a few weeks up at Arthur's Pass [. . .]. I was 51 the other day, but I still want to write stories novels plays — and an enormous extension of the Roof. I do NOT want to be another sort of Cyril Connolly. [. . .] We all know what we should be doing and it's not what Connolly's doing for all the brilliance. Goethe and even old Shaw were better models — striving and striving until you break up — the new Dante who will bring off the synthesis won't do it in his twenties or his thirties — if done at all it will be done in somebody's eighties or nineties — so much more now to learn and digest and so little time. This is putting my own pretensions pretty high maybe, but never mind. Even such incredible stupidities and cruelties as the trial of the Beaulieu man on the 2nd lot of charges doesn't worry me overmuch these days. I can even look forward to my own and the good earth's vapourization with the belief that there's a meaning and purpose in it somewhere. Probably I'm talking balls. [. . .]

Best to all the family,

F.S.

['the talk on the book of stories': an abbreviated version of FS's address at the Wellington launch of the Oxford New Zealand Short Stories *appeared in* Landfall *in March 1954. The full text appears as 'One Hundred Years of Story-Telling' in* Conversation in a Train, *pp. 71-77. The trials of Edward Douglas-Scott-Montagu, Lord Montagu of Beaulieu, which resulted in his imprisonment in 1954 for 'homosexual offences', became a pivotal event in the eventual decriminalization of homosexuality in Britain.]*

To C.K. Stead, *Auckland*

Alexander Turnbull Library

[In early May C.K. Stead had invited FS to read to the Auckland University College students' Literary Society.]

14 May 1954

Dear Stead,

Many thanks — for fee & your notes. Formal receipt enclosed in case of audit-trouble.

I'm always interested in the new names — when they're attached to what *has* something. My version of the Second Coming is a sort of Ibsen who will be big enough to force recognition from our provincial public, besides discerning fellow writers — prove to it that a poet with his pencil & paper can be as good as & better than Hillary with his oxygen & nylon rope. Poetry in our set-up is a lonely business — all wrong no doubt, but there it is. I wonder that such as [Geoff] Fuller & yourself spring up so accomplished — technically, but in other ways too. All quite different from what my own experience was. But that's what we need — precocious fertile talents forcing their way up — & even though much may be owed to the pioneering work it doesn't matter if the pioneers get no thanks. Let's have the poetry — but I do hanker after the long poems & plays (Ibsen called all his plays poems). It's up to some young poet to take a hint from Curnow & Cresswell — I mean *not* wait until the first fine careless rupture is all over, before getting round to what they should have been attempting in the hay days. We older people perhaps had to start little & work up big — or attempt to. I'm always looking for the young who will start where others left off — not start all over again. The social condition may be all against it, & I don't know the recipe myself, but surely it's worth having a shot at. Good luck to the pair of you anyway.

I don't know how much money the Literary Club has available — but if I may make a suggestion. Otago has a guest speaker once a year — Fairburn Baxter Glover myself — we have had our fares paid, & quite a show put on. The press invited etc. All to the good, I think — & a much better idea than having poets & writers permanently on the premises — probably bad for them, & bad for pupils who show signs of brilliance & *originality* in excess of their masters'. If your Club has the funds I'd suggest you try something similar. If you invited people like Glover Brasch Vogt Baxter Johnson it would be a challenge to them to produce something worth hearing — & in most instances you'd certainly get something worth hearing. AUC has always been backward in this sort of thing — for no good reason it seems to me. The aim in all these matters should be to try to close the gap between the poet & the public.

Yours,

F.S.

[C.K. Stead later recalled that Geoff Fuller was probably the first of his student cohort to have poetry accepted by an editor outside the university — 'unless I was, with a poem in the Jindyworobak Anthology *in Australia'. Fuller graduated with degrees in English and Law, and, according to Stead, 'moved to Hamilton, and fell silent'.* South-West of Eden *pp. 224–225.]*

To Dennis McEldowney, *Upper Hutt*

Alexander Turnbull Library

[McEldowney wrote to FS on 19 May 1954 to say he had acquired a set of Tomorrow *and had 'been enjoying the yesterdays of my elders & betters. [. . .] There was an abundance of F.S. in* Tomorrow *but I gather from the style & other internal evidence that much of it wasn't you. One letter which* was *you I enjoyed. Do you remember suggesting that a correspondent had several cousins answering to the name of Pollyanna?' ATL MS-Papers-0432-173.]*

27 May 1954

Dear Dennis,

Your remarks about *Tomorrow* made me go hot & cold all over. My copies seem to have gradually disappeared, & I'd be hard put to it I fancy to turn up a single one. I think the Devil himself must have inspired you — apparently he wasn't knocked out of you when you were (no doubt) baptized into the Presbyterian heresy. As I suppose a good orthodox person such as myself would expect. But you sent me off into a reverie — I seem to have forgotten about *Tomorrow* for so long, & there is so much connected with those days worth remembering for various complicated personal reasons. You are right about the other F.S. — that was Professor [Frederick] Sinclaire, who was extremely annoyed that my initials were the same as his own. But I seem to remember so many of us had so many disguises — sometimes, particularly near the beginning, they seemed to be necessary to fill up the paper. I simply cannot remember about the letter you mention (the Pollyanna one), but I can remember a letter I wrote about 'Vulcan' — who I didn't know was D'Arcy Cresswell, at that time living at Castor Bay. I think Glover wrote a letter about Vulcan too, & *he* didn't know it was D'Arcy. I remember I did a thing called *This Charming Country* for what seems ages now, also some wicked parodies, particularly one on Mulgan. I wonder if you ever knew the editor, Kennaway Henderson, in Christchurch. I looked him up again at the time of the Writers' Conference — he must have been over 70, but he was baching in a little house, & painting away as ever. He had a strange dry sense of humour. *Tomorrow* was only possible through him — he had a sick wife at the time, & was either on relief work or sustenance, I forget which — anyhow he had no money, but he had time, & he used it all up on *Tomorrow*. In spite of his poverty he was always very neat & well-dressed, with just that touch of something different, the artist in him. Without his humour he would have been impossible perhaps, but with it he was a delight. And incidentally, the best of his water-colours are really something, a particular sort of lyricism very special to himself, & sometimes it used to come off.

P.K. I remember was Denis Glover (Peter Kettle), & Julian was Curnow. There were many others, but I forget them. W.N. Pharazyn, a name I never see now, was a tower of strength, & so was W.B. Sutch. I expect the history of it all will be written someday, but the thought of it rather makes me go all hot & cold again.

My reverie extended on beyond *Tomorrow* — (which, incidentally, was suppressed by the Labour Govt. in a rather roundabout semi-intentional way, with some Catholic influence assisting) to the Auckland *Observer*. Fairburn did an enormous big page of Radio criticism under the name of Ben Bolt — for a pound an issue (each week). He threw it up & I took over under the same name. But I hadn't a radio. I used to visit some friends who had a live-in shop [Gladys and Len Salter], but usually their daughter would permit nothing but ZB. So mainly I used to stop & listen to radios whenever I heard them in the street day or night. I even continued to write the page when I was in Hospital. But all this is just my babble — I had forgotten how much of all this I used to flog out of myself — for either no pay, or the pittance one got from Observer, Star, Chch Press etc. Not of course that I could ever come near the quantity Fairburn turned out. But all in all you are a Bad Boy for distracting my thoughts from my play (perhaps not so Bad, though — I'm reminded the difficulties I'm having are no worse than what I encountered on some of those bits of journalism).

I shall be faithful to *By the Lake* until the day I die. I tried it the other day on Brian Bell — know him? a Wellington bohemian who teeters perpetually on becoming quite impossible. It actually sobered him for quite 5 minutes — he saw the point: his own stories are of the same kind, but none so good as B.T.L. I think you should try to dragoon Jock [Dennis McEldowney's brother] into showering the avant-garde periodicals on you. You never know when you may hit on the very kind of writing which makes you feel sure of your own talent without any doubt at all.

Isn't it curious? — I've fallen for Katherine Mansfield at last. What I mean is that by some strange oversight I had never read *An Indiscreet Journey* until the other evening. I was fascinated — it seems the best thing she ever wrote.

James Courage says he had his new novel turned down by Constable, but Cape has taken it. What a lot of N.Z. books published & unpublished there must be now. But babble again.

All my best,

F.S.

Perhaps I am wrong about not rivaling Fairburn's quantity. Before I wrote in *Tomorrow* I had written a novel, a 3 act play, & great numbers of longish short stories — I must try to find some of this old stuff & look at it. [. . .]

To Dan Davin, *Oxford*

Alexander Turnbull Library

[On 20 April Davin told FS that the National Book League had arranged an exhibition of books published by the New Zealand Literary Fund — 'Ian Gordon may be the instigator' — and that Davin had been invited to give a talk on new writing in New Zealand. ATL MS-Papers-0432-155. Davin's edition of Mansfield's stories was published in 1953.]

8 June 1954

Dear Dan,

The cable news appeared to be silent about your talk, but we received the benefit of a few more slaps from Gordon. I hope his pose as an Angel of Light doesn't deceive you. I think of him as very nearly as dangerous as the worst of them — point is he would like things to remain just as they are so he can remain what he is — petty provincial tycoon in the realm of letters. I expect he's quite genuine in his belief that there never can be any literature here worth mentioning (where would he be if there was?), and one doesn't object to beliefs sincerely held — but when he singled out Baxter and myself as a pair of crybaby boobs for decent sturdy suburban Philistines to heave their rocks at, he didn't attack in Landfall — he much preferred the Listener where he could be sure of the support of 99 per cent of his readers. I'm afraid he's a sort of symbol — one that blocks up the road we've been trying to cut through the flax swamp so that we can sweeten the soil after draining off the bog-water — all so that something might grow which would give our country real distinction. But it's a shame to waste so much vitriol on a midget among the tight-sitting oblivion-destined mediocrities, the ignorant dead-headed heavy-gutted provincial morons whose putrefying Public Bodies litter and pollute the entire social landscape. [. . .]

I got round to reading carefully your Mansfield introduction and then the stories. By some strange oversight I had never read before An Indiscreet [Journey], which seemed to me extraordinarily good apart from the Karori prejudice against the hat. A really outstanding story, and I should say among the best she wrote. I went on and read everything else in the Collected Vol., and found it all a bigger challenge than I had imagined previously. Isn't the fairytale influence extremely strong — Hans Andersen, Wilde's fairy stories? First England is fairyland and at last NZ. There are very few 'truthful' ones, and they are devastating when they appear. I know an old bloke whose brother married Beauchamp's sister — he won't read KM because he's been told she wrote about her family, and to have to put up with them on paper as well as in life is something he's pleased to do without. Anyhow, your introduction is quite a good piece of work it seems to me. I see Antony's [Alpers] book [*Katherine Mansfield: A Biography*] has been getting rather a rough spin. I haven't read it yet. [. . .]

Cheers,

F.S.

[Davin to FS, 24 June: 'Sorry Gordon gets your goat so much. I found him pleasant enough but then I would since he has no power over me and the academic tycoon is a thing I meet in one form or another every day — as why wouldn't I being a kind of tiny tycoon myself'. ATL MS-Papers-0432-155.]

To John Reece Cole, *Wellington*

Alexander Turnbull Library

24 June 1954

Dear Reece,

[. . .] It has been all upset here. Harry went finally cold on the bach, & it's still as it was — available anytime you like. Though I don't exactly recommend it in the dead of winter — it hasn't been cold, but wickedly moist, & I have catarrh & a bad throat — all the usual troubles & complaints. I expect the frantic burst of writing I had in the autumn couldn't last, but then the sickening impasses I've had since shouldn't have lasted either — this 2nd Act of the play has such damn good stuff in it I just can't abandon it — but I can't get it to come right nohow despite all the slogging & the shocking waste of paper. [. . .]

I worked Alpers book [about Katherine Mansfield] into my wide & strangely mixed reading lately. I don't know. It's rather like a very good documentary film — never becomes a work of art as I imagine biographies should be because of my devotion to the amazing Boswell. I was reminded of a remark you made about an early article of Lou Johnson's — about how he didn't dare to look right or left himself. There are a few touches where Antony catches fire, but mainly he's too keen on saying nothing if he hasn't seen the documents. I don't get a feeling of life, though it does seem to me he quite cleverly in the end brings off a moving conclusion. Anyhow, I was stimulated to read right through the Coll. Vol. of stories — & got more than ever previously. Strikes me the Hans Andersen influence has been overlooked, also Wilde's fairy stories — perhaps it was that side of Wilde that influenced her more than she was aware of. Anyhow there are endless fairly tale passages, & particularly the food is always fairy tale — & no wonder she got phthisis if she tried to live on it, which isn't altogether unlikely. Also Maeterlinck is important — the Blue Bird. It was always fairyland happiness she was after, & eventually it was identified with the place she'd come from. This view explains Murry too — the Fairy Prince: also Carco, & that very good fairy tale — *An Indiscreet Journey*, which somehow I had always missed previously: it *should* be called *The Little Corporal*.

Charles was up, & I was awfully upset about the 2 nights he slept in the hut — a strange sort of snobbery on my part, perhaps. I got to *The Wild Duck*, & didn't think Ibsen was butchered, as some did. Also John Rhodes is around again, which worries me as my simple, but equally neurotic & trying waifs, such as my friend Jack, get more & more tossed out of their jobs because of incapacity & high wages. [Brian] Bell is still about, but I must say he's most considerate (though less so to Maurice). He's on the point of leaving Ring-a-Mop because they insist on sending him out on the road, with their latest creation called The Little Beaut. Bell feels he can't go to a hundred housewives a day, with a request to be allowed to show them his Little Beaut. And as you know he claims the description is a misnomer anyhow.

What a lovely murder in Chch! Just shows how far astray we writers are when Life insists on copying the Greek playwrights — instead of the creations we provide for it. But it isn't clear yet whether the brick was in the stocking or employed separately. Surely Baxter can rise to something as distinguished as 'Lizzie Borden took an axe. . . .'

I am away to hell behind with letters — so if you see Phil [Wilson] or Lou [Johnson] do say I shall write — particularly Lou whom I've never yet thanked for his Year-book.

Hope all your personal & family garden is cultivated & lovely.

My fondest,

F.S.

Barbara's baby due in a few weeks.

P.S. PEN should wake up. It's Election Year & you can insult the bloody politicians with some impunity.

[The Parker-Hulme murder had taken place two days previously, on 22 June 1954.]

To Keith Sinclair, *Auckland*

Private collection

[FS met 'old B' — William Levenet Bakewell (1879–1962) — in 1948. Bake grew up in and around Karangahape Road and Symonds Street, became a bank manager in Taumarunui (where FS fancied meeting him some twenty years previously) and had retired to Castor Bay. FS relished Bake's bawdy stories and polysyllabic vocabulary; in Never Enough *he describes him as 'the man who was to turn out a most extraordinarily fruitful influence upon the difficult and complex business of my being a professional writer', and the founding impulse for* Memoirs of a Peon, *pp. 82–83.]*

8 July 1954

Dear Keith,

I was out seeing my elderly cobber the other night — old B. he had better be for the purposes of this note, and with very little persuasion he gave me a 2 hour talk about Brothels and such at the beginning of the century. Do understand that I set down all this distasteful matter solely in the interests of your historical research — you must be careful not to attribute any salacious motives. According to B. there were very few amateurs — nice girls fell, but only because of love or violence. Never from the desire to experience a disgusting animal pleasure. (B. rather contradicts himself though when he speaks of his love-child — the finest of all his children he says: the lad was the product of violence). B's favourite house was one in the blind street off Upper Queen Street before you get to City Road. It was run by Black Julia — a magnificent Junoesque creature. Apparently the taste of young men did not run to the pert piece in those days. B. insists that a mature age and generous proportions were what everyone was after — and I heard several touching anecdotes about motherly solicitude for his inexperience, and an understanding touch for a temporarily inhibited member. Indeed, I gathered that there was a deep concern — a yearning as it were to provide young men with pleasures that would be in every way good for them and necessary to their health well-being and character-development. (Though health requires some qualification — but luckily B's father was a doctor). This concern for healthy pleasure was a marked characteristic of solo operators as well as the inhabitants of houses. And from both B. can remember hearing complaints about gentlemen from the Northern Club who demanded fancy variations — one of them so revolting that it brings the blush to my cheek. (You see, I am coming to the point — there just might be something in the story about the subject of your biography [of William Pember Reeves]). B. had an engaging story about one solo operator who lived behind a shop just above the Town Hall. A nice room, a good fire, a double bed — but a yawning gap in the floor in one corner with a ladder descending into the depths. B. used to be worried about the noises that went on below, until he discovered the husband was a cabby who kept his horse down there. Incidentally some solo operators were not to be trusted — husband or lover was liable to appear and demand money and possibly crack you as well, but B. usually came out quite well from such an affair, as he only just escaped being included among the forwards of the 1905 All Blacks. Solo operators charged 10/- for a short time, 15/- for a longer time, and 25/- for the night — all a lot of money in those days. A brief time at a house was 10/-, but for a longer time the price might be very high. And incidentally again (puritanism raising its ugly head perhaps), the young men preferred to separate drink and sex on the ground that one pleasure tended to interfere with the other. I've forgotten to say that one famous solo operator kept a lolly shop in Symonds Street and was known as the Lollypop Queen. B. brought out a lot of ancient Football and Swimming and Rowing photos so that I could inspect the features and demeanour of the young men who indulged in all this licentious behaviour. The bowler hats moustaches etc made them look round about 40 in most cases, but B. insisted that very few would be more than 25. Such a galaxy of frank open clear-eyed nothing-to-hide young Pig Island manhood! I pointed to the captain of one Football Team, and suggested he probably taught Sunday School. B. didn't know about that, but soon after the photo he got syphilis, and staggers round to this day with a stick to assist him against his disability of locomotor ataxia. B. says though there wasn't much syphilis, but plenty of gonorrhoea — and he had 3 doses, always from the solo operators (one was the Lollypop Queen), never from house inhabitants. He's now 73 and very vigorous strong and healthy, so apparently it never affected his heart as it's supposed to — and his old man cured him each time with concoctions brewed from the bark of pine trees (probably the trees are still at the top end of Myers Park).

To think that the amateur has ruined all this! Without alas, acquiring either professional skill, or an understanding of the needs of the human male. And who can wonder at the growth of nameless vices from which the stricken imagination reels in horror! I feel that if I could establish a decent house before I die I should have done something to re-establish our not so ancient virtue and glory.

F.S.

B. told me quite a lot about Ettie Rout whom he knew quite well in Paris 1914–18. I expect you know about Lady Stout and her campaign.

A Slogan for my Banner:

Up the Wine and Women! Down with Soda-water and Sodomy!

To Dan Davin, *Oxford*

Alexander Turnbull Library

12 July 1954

Dear Dan,

I shouldn't be writing. I take up your own time and my own. But Maurice came in last night very excited to tell me about your *Crete*. I shall certainly disobey your instructions and read it now. But how it all seems to relate to your letter! New Zealanders, and your feelings about them. [. . .] What I can't work out is the contradiction between NZ virtues in a very narrow context (Crete — though I cannot rid myself of a very basic conviction that all that sort of thing is all balls these days — something did happen in the world in 1917, and it's no advantage not to know that it did), and the dismal showing of those virtues in the suburban and provincial context — a very wide context indeed, because outside a few places like Oxford and London the whole damn world is going to be suburban and provincial. One thinks of Tolstoy's remark about the brave soldier defeated in the marriage bed. What I would like to make you understand is that something really disastrous has happened out here since the present Government took the lid off: the old morality was suspended in the air God knows, but nobody in power has had any notion about how to replace it except to issue open licenses for go-getting, and as fear and anxiety increases about butter and meat there's an iron clamping down on everything marginal that doesn't bring in cash returns. We've got it coming to us in some way analogous to the thirties shortly now I imagine, and your brave soldiers are going to find themselves with unpaid for tasty suburban homes provided with a few streamlined utilities also unpaid for besides the usual priceless collections of fantastic junk and rubbish. That's NZ for you in her great moment of crisis, and I'm damned if I'll give in and say that the virtues of Crete are a consolation. I don't doubt that you did find Gordon pleasant enough, but what gets me is that all this sort of thing is not altogether uncongenial to him — a hard thing to say, but I believe it's true. It suits him. Worse, he's by no means the worst of the bunch — indeed, many would be very severe with me for saying this, on the ground that if we don't pin our faith to the Gordons we'll have them replaced by the very worst. Please understand I don't want to be interpreted as getting at you. Oxford Cambridge London — they're going to be very much cut off eventually, but meanwhile they are *the* places, and I don't need to assure you of my admiration for your energy and the work you've put out from where you are. But outside, in the provinces and suburbs, you've got to decide on which side you are on, and it's Gordon's ludicrous and painful delusion that he can cut quite a satisfactory figure walking the tightrope.

Despair is very much in the air all around. I leave Maurice to mention his own if he feels like it. Middleton will shortly be blind, and no help from the SLF. Glover turned down by SLF and now writing ads for some agency in Wellington. Lilburn's first symphony played once by the National Orchestra, and I don't know that anybody has had the opportunity to hear his second. The most valuable person *to* the arts in NZ is Cole. He does a great job at the Turnbull, and works persistently behind the scenes trying to break down the official apathy, and with some very good minor results. [. . .] Those in a position to exercise effective power ensure that none of us exercises any effective influence. There are a few exceptions, but of no great importance. I must jot down a few notes about the fairytale influence on KM — I think I could make out quite a case.

Good summer to you and good holidays,

F.S. [. . .]

To Charles Brasch, *Dunedin*

Hocken Library

[Brasch to FS, 14 October: 'I don't think that the press can be attacked for their reporting of the Parker-Hulme trial — not the main N.Z. Dailies. They were quite restrained and didn't report all [Crown Prosecutor] Brown's dirt; I spent a morning in court and feel that I know something about it all [. . .]'. ATL MS-Papers-0432-147. George Cecil Horry was convicted of murder in 1951.]

16 October 1954

Dear Charles,

[. . .] Oh, but I disagree about the press and Parker-Hulme. The Star published the big wonderful photograph of the two girls before they were convicted — and surely this is against the law unless it has recently been altered. (Truth was fined about £500 for publishing Horry's picture before conviction). And so damaging to the girls — the one all elegance etc. — calculated to produce feelings of disgust that such aplomb could conceal such 'depravity'. MacVincent had in his Gossip column chatty pars about Brown and his career during the trial. And after the conviction the Star wouldn't leave it alone — 'girl killers' etc. Also the devilish touched up photographs taken through the bars — and the Herald's photo when it came to light with it was a nasty one too. You know that Hulme and his son left the boat in Marseilles because of press persecution — the Standard had a front page article begging the press to lay off. And what about Mrs Hulme changing her name? And then it was all tied up with the prurient prying into children's behaviour. It was marvellous Curnow got his sizzling Whim-Wham into the Herald — and I hope

Press too. I had been to see him previously, and we agreed on everything. Point about Hulme-Parker is the universal nerve is touched. Getting rid of a parent — what everybody has thought of — the foundation of every religion — Freud, the anthropologists. Only real point of interest in the case is just why the strongest taboo of all broke down in two intelligent schoolgirls. Nearest parallel I know of is Lizzie Borden, and she accounted for both:

Lizzie Borden took an axe,
And gave her mother forty whacks.
When she saw what she had done
She gave her father forty one!

Amazing that about 40 blows should operate in Christchurch just as in New England. [. . .]

No more — flying out to Greenlane to see Maurice.

F.S.

All the parent-child business is in my play — it's my one & only subject. [. . .]

[In a letter to Brasch of 3 November FS clarifies that the 'Whim Wham' poem he refers to above is about the Mazengarb Report rather than the Parker-Hulme trial. See 'Modesty's a Good Thing Too', September 1954, Whim Wham's New Zealand, *pp. 108–109.]*

To Denis Glover, *Wellington*

Alexander Turnbull Library

19 October 1954

Dear Glover,

[. . .] I had been thinking of writing you about a play I'm doing. Full length and 2 thirds done. But in the third Act (or Scene as I prefer to call it) the characters are all dead, and seem to call for more overt poetry than I can do. I see them all huddled together under some of Campion's dim and coloured lights with *three* bright objects in the sky (the third is the burning world). Obviously a case for poesy, but if I ask any of the younger poets to help I'll no doubt be supplied with plenty of lines, but what the hell they will mean will keep everybody guessing far too much. I'm just about to work on this last part now, and if I find I can't do it I shall type out a fair copy of what's gone before and let you see it in case it appeals to you. But I may be able to bring it off by pinching a certain amount from the end of Fairburn's Dominion. The play by the way begins in 1880 or thereabouts, and is quite Ibsenian; but then it jumps to present-day and becomes more 'unreal' (the scene is the lounge of a passenger plane nose on to the audience with the pilots up on top reading Comics etc). The entire thing has I think the chance of turning out a very lively piece of pastiche (and who among us can do anything much more than that?) Anyhow the dialogue so far is lively and funny (probably too overloaded, and too many laughs good and bad). Anyhow we shall see. It's all been hard work — the resolution should be easier, but it's not because of the need for poetry.

I gape everytime I see fresh things of yours. The incredible Denis!

If you come up and call well and good. Unfortunately I don't have much liquor these days — very poor at present costs, but a pretty healthy mixed in door out door life, and a reasonably happy one. No complaints.

Maybe anon,

F.S.

To John Reece Cole, *Wellington*

Alexander Turnbull Library

21 October 1954

Dear Reece,

The Duggans do have bad luck. Barbara was carted off to Private Hosp. on Saturday for urgent belly operation — apparently appendicitis. The baby had to be weaned. Of course women friends flocked around, so I gave up & sat back & read the Zola [*Earth*]. I'm not terribly shook on Angus Wilson's Preface — I don't know whether it's Z's masterpiece, but it's a marvellous piece of work, a sort of nineteenth century Pastoral. (My eyes popped out of my head when I looked up the map on finding the country scene strangely familiar. In 1927 I skirted that plain to the north-east. For 3 or 4 days the country was exactly as described — the strips, the harvest (it was July or August), a thunderstorm, the very few farm-houses, the villages, the carts going out in the morning & returning evenings, (some of the louts were pretty rude & aggressive, but there were pleasant ones like Jean). Not a fence anywhere, cows tethered, & sheep in hurdles. I never saw any actual fucking, but the Buteaus would drop their scythes a few yards off the road, & then drop their pants & squat. I expect I was lucky I wasn't bumped off when I put up for the night in the villages. The peasants would discuss me in a cafe, & then one would offer to find me a room — upstairs in a kind of Buteau establishment. I always had to pay twice, though I must say not very much. Anyhow, there it all was, exactly. I think it's Zola's particular genius to tie everything up, so you can scarcely draw lines of distinction between animal vegetable mineral & human (this is what Faulkner does too, doesn't he?). That wonderful scene where Buteau & Francoise are thrashing — sweating & straining over forcing the seed out of its husk. It could be the man's seed of course. I remember Z does much the same sort of thing in

L'Assommoir, only with machinery. Isn't it some Frenchman who says 19th cent. mechanical developments aped the human — every engine consisted essentially of a steel Romeo that went on working indefinitely in a cast-iron Juliet? (How bloody intelligent the French are!) If only this book could be put in the hands of every school child — what mountains of nonsense could be swept away with the turning of the pages. It's surely cleansing to be forced to face up to the basic conditions of life on the earth. But I see there has been trouble in Australia, & I don't suppose the book has a ghost of a chance if the sex-spotters do their stuff around here. Anyhow, damn nice to have the text on one's shelves, thanks to you. No doubt the thing's a tremendous lyric pastoral saturated right through with Zola's super-sense of love wonder & compassion. His didacticism only amounts to saying, Here are the honest facts, go on now & make your brave new world. And how little real progress we've made! [. . .]

All my best,

F.S. [. . .]

To Keith Sinclair, *London*

Private collection

23 November 1954

Dear Keith,

I'm writing you this between books — that's to say, at about 1.30 Sunday morning I finished revising and retyping my play. It's turned out a comedy thank God, and so far I call it *The Cradle and the Egg*. The egg in the last part is probably the most amusing invention my poor brains have ever laboured over. Anyhow, as I begin the plaguey business of pestering Rodney [Kennedy] [Richard] Campion and whoever, I naturally begin my new book. You humiliate me with your account of your mastery of historical detail. (For my play — the first part — I looked at the map and picked on Waiuku as the possible scene of violent dispute over a branch railway last century, and when I had read Carlyle's essay on Chartism I felt I had done enough research on the possible thinking of a sturdy NZ conservative radical coachbuilder). But I await your book very eagerly. Don't write it in rhymed couplets — it's stimulation I'm wanting for my next play, not art. For similar reasons I'm anxiously awaiting Burdon's *Seddon* which I'm told is finished now.

There was an excellent poem of yours in the Listener, *Summer Son*, I think. It went beautifully until the last 2 lines where some rather high-falutin cliché suddenly appeared. Of course I sent off the order card for your poems [*Strangers or Beasts*], but I don't know how many they got in.

Maurice came out of hospital, fled out, for a week, but he's back there now. I don't know what to think. Sputum negative for weeks etc. — in the old days nobody would have been worried, and the Doc Smiths would have told him to get on and enjoy his life. But Xrays reveal cavities. He can write that very lovely prose of *Voyages III*, but he seems to have so little of the abominable egotism and show-off-ishness of the artist which helps so much to keep him going. In short, he's too fine a person to be just an artist. Perhaps he's a genius — but what will be the good of a dead one? And that's what will happen if his appetite for life isn't crude and hearty enough. His fastidiousness was always apparent, but I now feel it goes deeper than I ever supposed.

But speaking of your research, how on earth do you manage to sit still in libraries for so many hours? What genius on the part of your genes to choose Mary for a wife! I don't so much mean crossing Pt Chev with Oriental Bay (if that's the place), but the neurotic steering clear of another of the same kind. Neurotics should choose non-neurotics of either sex, and if necessary animals. Conversely the non-neurotic needs the neurotic — for antic-entertainment. But perhaps your library-pose is something I know nothing about. After all, in the old days of the bach I used to sit in the corner writing and at the same time take part in conversation with visitors. And I've read somewhere that Bernard Shaw used to sit like a Buddha in hotel lounges and write brilliant articles.

Actually I don't think you should bring the 'art' business to the surface of your mind while writing the Reeves. You have the distinction of being a poet, and what makes you a poet will provide the art for your history provided you don't aim at it. I am wagging my sage old head about this, so you had better take notice. It's something like my present situation. What is my next book to be? (Though I have my Roof expanded by 30,000 words, and I expect I should work on it). Provided I don't consciously think about it an idea will pop into my head. Then comes the doubt about all the detail, a set of people and circumstances, all incredibly lively and witty, something that doesn't exist yet — and how can it? But the reservoir down in the sub-conscious is inexhaustible. Strictly speaking the only problems for the artist are how to tap it, and technique. All the rest is always there. If you don't believe me, ask somebody like Somerset Maugham. [. . .]

I envy you the theatre — but who knows? My Egg may get me there too, eventually.

My love to all,

F.S.

To Helen Shaw, *Remuera*

Alexander Turnbull Library

9 December 1954

Dear Hella,

Just a line to say what a beautifully-done story ['The Orange Tree'] in *Landfall*. My congratulations. The women are showing the way — that was a very nicely done one by Jacquie Baxter in *Numbers*. Yours there didn't altogether satisfy me — but others might very well think differently. Anyhow you should have no worries — it must be all adding up to a solid achievement.

My kind regards all round,

F.S.

I finished my 3 act comedy, & am now fantastically busy cajoling & arguing with the few people in N.Z. who know what's what in these matters. Afraid I'm in for some stiff work on revision.

[Shaw's 'The Three Strange Miss Vinings' and J.C. Sturm's 'Where To, Lady' appeared in Numbers 2, *Nov 1954.]*

To Dan Davin, *Oxford*

Alexander Turnbull Library

[Davin to FS, 2 Dec: 'You will have seen Winston Rhodes [review of Davin's edition of Mansfield] in the September Landfall. *Curious stuff, like an intelligent blind man talking about pictures. It seems to me that he is incapable of an innocent, direct response to a story.' Davin told FS that he had enjoyed FS's 'The Undertaker's Story' in* Landfall: *'I get the impression from this & your other recent writing that I've read that you are busily widening your range. Of course, your earlier stuff was experimental since no-one had done it before but we tend to take that side of it for granted now & so to be impressed by what seems to us at any rate to be a new experimental vigour'. ATL MS-Papers-0432-155. Davin's novel* The Sullen Bell *was published in London in 1956.]*

10 December [1954]

Dear Dan,

Strange how I always seem to hear from you when I have a moment to spare. Nothing more uncivilised than to bung back a letter I know, but this December I have the feeling I've done a tolerably decent year's work, visitors will arrive, the work in the garden in the heat will exhaust me. In theory I wouldn't feel like writing until next March.

But what I want to urge with all my heart is that you glue yourself to that novel, and let us have it as soon as you can. I value more and more everything creative, made, not to mention honest, literal — and of course *against*! I expect everything we do may eventually be rated as having negative value only, but unless we stick at it there won't be any society with intelligence enough to do any sort of valuing. That gutter-report on children's behaviour! [The Mazengarb Report] And gentility getting mixed up with quotes from the gutter-press! Note how they don't mention masturbation. But even so, God preserve us from a more intelligent investigation within the present context of society. But be assured we're doing what we can, and I think I told you last time Curnow has been quite valuable.

Anyhow, I for one am depending on you for the novel, and no punches pulled. The Courage novel [*The Young Have Secrets*] has its points. I think he attempts more. Not too satisfying as a work of art, but he's quite good at handling the child world. By the way, I think *Lucky Jim* could have been considerably better, but it too has its agreeable points.

Maurice has been out of Hospital, but is in again now. Still, a rather elaborate lung collapse has been done this week, and he should be out again next week — for good this time we hope. I shall urge him to write you. The best parts of that *Voyages* were simply superb. You know his trouble — words. But he's finally mastering them now, and I don't imagine they'll be getting the chance to get him under in the future. He's pretty cheerful, the boy is indeed lovely and the place looks like heaven — except for the drought which is a thorn all round.

Take no notice of Rhodes. I have a sympathy for him — his quite courageous Marxist views out of fashion just now, and I expect his personal frustrations are pretty severe. I can't imagine a more unhappy combination than a belief in social realism, creative inability, and having to lecture at Canterbury college. [. . .]

I appreciate your kind remarks about my story. I have had the feeling that I'm never supposed to do anything but what's expected from me. Probably it was a feeling connected with the play. I was badly stuck in the middle in mid-year, but Cole stayed with me for a few weeks, and a remark of his set me off again. Anyhow, all finished now, a comedy thank God, pastiche I'm afraid — but a lively range from a 'real' opening to a very 'unreal' ending. It will need a fireworks production, I imagine. First reports from the few people who know quite encouraging, and it goes to Campion now. My fingers crossed. His NZ Players productions by the way are enormously improved, though depending much too much for my taste on modern technics. Just now he's touring with the lady who felt it was better to marry than to burn. Not my kind of play, I can appreciate the language, but growing up on Ibsen and Shaw I do like a few ideas — and after Molière and Congreve who can be funny on the stage without having learnt the lessons of the masters. I expect this sounds pretentious nonsense. But the Players stand a good chance of surviving (Campion is married to Edith Hannah — on whom the entire fortunes of Hannah's Shoes descended, and the story is she's put £25,000 into the company. Just now they've imported Barbara Jefford and Keith Michell from the Stratford company for the Fry), so for God's sake let us all write plays. Come on, how about it? No doubt I'll get turned down, but while I lick my wounds I shall reassure myself with the thought that I've written something too good for either the country or the company.

It seems as though Eric McCormick has three books out simultaneously, though I haven't seen any of them yet. Do you see Keith Sinclair who is somewhere around Chatham House at work on his *Reeves*? I'm very fond of him. His proletarian bounce enables one to say such insulting things to him, and when I'm in the mood I find his nervousness entertaining. Smithyman has written a curious thing in the *Landfall* just out — about *Goblin Market*. The Bowras et al. will have to pull up their socks.

May I hope to see a story you mentioned before in *Landfall* soon? Charles has another of mine ['The Colonel's Daughter'] which I pray he may use so that I can finish paying the rates. I must send you a copy of Lou Johnson's *Numbers*, with quite a remarkable story by Jim Baxter's wife, Jacquie. I still don't know quite what to make of *London Mag*, but I enjoyed Tennessee Williams and the *Tomato Patch*.

But afraid I'm burbling, dear Dan. Write this letter off as something between books — but what the next is to be I haven't an idea. Probably I'll return to the endless old *Roof*. Or can I tempt you into writing a play aimed at Campion, by promising to write another myself?

Sorry about your dim summer and winter storms. Love to W[inifred].

F.S.

PS This didn't get posted and I've now finished the Amis and feel inclined to take back my remark. Too wordy, but good comedy, I don't know whether any critics have noticed, but it strikes me as pretty close to Henry Green of Party Going in its kind of comic attitude. In the current Landfall there's really a beautifully done story by La Shaw. An impossible person, but it looks as though she may eventually write something dazzling enough to blind the reader.

To E.P. Dawson, *Mt Maunganui*

Hocken Library

18 January [1955]

Dear Peter,

We seem to have a genius for writing letters that cross. I was determined last time either to write immediately or wait — so now I hope I'm getting in first again and perhaps somehow setting some sort of ball rolling.

But first, [. . .] about only being unhappy when you think of your self as a writer. I don't know the full range of touchstones — but happiness is certainly one of them. I should be very unhappy if I didn't think of myself as a writer, and how well after all these years do I know some of my moods of irritation in the afternoon — I've either shirked the morning's work, or else made a hash of it. When no hash and no shirking I always at least *tend* to bubble. So there you are. Happiness is such an important touchstone to me, I'm pretty sure I'd give up writing if it didn't make me happy (not publication or success — just the page where something, something very tiny maybe, seems to have been created). But if it made me persistently unhappy, surely I'd plump for something else that did — and quite a variety of forms of creativeness would. But don't reckon me quite the knowall in this or any other matter. It's sad sometimes that there seems nothing else to do, except leave the matter in hand to the person concerned. [. . .]

Not such a bad Christmas. I've tried to choke visitors off while I've pushed on with the [play about Thomas] Kendall [*A Time for Sowing*] — and I've pushed on a surprising lot. I suppose it's the writing to a ready-made situation. I think my first experience. Anyhow, it's cunningly designed to ease the disappointment I'll feel if I can't get anybody to take up the other play. Charles was impressed in quite a different way from Rodney — and I've had a very short note from Campion. He's quite impressed too, but he wants time before he says anything. No doubt he's a bit frantically going round his theatrical friends, saying Look what this bastard Sargeson has challenged me with — what the hell do I do? The fact is of course that nobody has ever been able to tell beforehand whether any given play will play or not — no matter how lively (or awful) it may read. I have my fingers crossed. One of my fantasies by the way is that I may be invited to stay with the Campions at the luxury villa I think they have at Rotorua to talk things over. (Edith Campion was Edith Hannah and it's said she inherited the entire Shoe fortune. Anyhow, I knew her deceased uncle Bobby, and he had the villa). Tell you more when my fingers are uncrossed — Rotorua's near enough to the Mount for a run over if it comes off.

The phenomenal December rain has sent all the vegetation on the section sky high. The benefits over now, but the tomatoes are early, and I start the rather tiresome bottling business tomorrow. Everything else promises well, and there's a lot of it as now that Harry is living on the pension he likes me to garden for him as well. Only trouble is I'm taking more out of the soil than a few years back, and the few bags of cowshit (the boy on the farm next to the Duggans always asks if I want cowshit or bullshit — and I always say the former as I can produce any amount of the latter myself) I put on is only tinkering with the problem.

If you come across a book called *Lucky Jim* by Kingsley Amis, do read it. For years the Musgroves J.C. Reids etc have been clamouring for something gay and funny — and now they've got it, only it's gay and funny about people like them. I hope they appreciate the joke.

I got shouted to a Saturday afternoon ballet, and it wasn't bad — Swan Lake and Petrushka, and an amusing piece of mime called Graduation Ball. The Marx Bros. in Monkey Business, a marvellous old film, at the local tomorrow night.

I don't hope the next Test is close — I hope the Englishmen knock the daylights out of the Aussies — but I was sorry they had them knocked out by the American tennis team. I'm also in favour of its being compulsory for all Rugby players to attend the ballet regularly — to learn a little about the grace of movement and stop bullocking — the curse of NZ sport.

I read nothing except what's round and about Kendall. Just now it's the entire Bronte family. I also have to read all the known plays by Greek dramatists — for technical and other tips. After all the scene and sunlight in the Bay of Islands is very close to what you get in one of Sophocles' plays.

Must stop. Read no more of Symposium, and haven't written Hella yet, but hope to soon.

All best,

F.S.

Listened to *Milk Wood*. Well done, but unsatisfactory. A kind of Hymn to Life — but that sort of thing takes a lot of getting away with. Anyhow, as a jealous so far unproduced play writer I don't feel obliged to say a single word about any of my contemporaries.

[FS had read about the Anglican missionary Thomas Kendall (?1778–1832) in the third volume of R.M. Burdon's New Zealand Notables, *1950.]*

To James K. Baxter, *Wellington*

Hocken Library

[In an undated letter, probably early January 1955, Baxter told FS that he had been re-reading I Saw in My Dream *and* That Summer *and thanked FS for a remark which had 'helped him over some rough going'. Baxter suggested the comment ('Why do you have to write about the hellish setup one is often in, instead of the green myth which is mankind's constant dream of Eden?') was in line with Wilde's essay 'The Decay of Lying', and mentioned that he has stopped drinking. He asked FS's permission to dedicate his Macmillan Brown lectures (*The Fire and the Anvil*) to him 'not because they are about literature, but because they are mostly about sex, religion and politics'. ATL MS-Papers-0432-144.]*

29 January 1955

Dear Jim,

You paraphrase much better than I write, so I hope you won't mind if I pinch your remark [. . .] for something I'm writing.

I had only skimmed through the collection of essays [*The Puritan and the Waif*] (except for Davin — I read him twice with immense interest), but Maurice Duggan has several times remarked on the brilliance of your contribution, so I have just read it carefully. It is pretty good indeed. Naturally I haven't read That Summer since I finished the typescript, but at this distance I seem to remember that irony was behind Maggie and her getting the narrator into quod. All the pompous paraphernalia of the law was brought into action upon a set of 'facts' which were quite different from the 'reality'. Also, I think I wanted the 'reality' to be revealed to the narrator without his making a single comment upon it, and without its influencing in any way his relationship with his cobber. But that distance I can't be sure.

I was very interested in [John] Rhodes' marriage, and I wonder whether it was prompted by despair. If I'm not mistaken, and not too clinical, I'd say his psychogenetic complications make him a presby- or geronto-phile (would this make him a concealed Presbyterian?), and he always too uncomfortably reminds me of somebody much nearer home not to excite my rather horrified sympathy. But there are so many of them, and the clinical names are so various — not to mention probably all balls anyway.

Ah yes, the drink — I wish I had the time and money for it. As it is I must make do with smoking, and even that is getting too expensive. In my wage-earning days I think I was always too conscious of personal problems, and my personal puritanism would never have been satisfied by temporary solutions. But I wonder if I can get you to help me with a different kind of problem. Last November I finished a play, full-length and a comedy — now I'm well into something much grimmer, a play about the missionary Kendall. In Act II I want a chorus of drunken whaling sailors with a bunch of native girls. They will probably be presented as a dream of Kendall's — he will be asleep in a chair, and groan and fling himself about over erotic action and verses. I think a terrific old soak of a bosun will chant the verses, while the rest dance. Anyhow, will you let this roll about in your mind. At the rate I'm writing (for the first time to a set situation) I shouldn't be long in getting the thing finished, and when I do I'll let you see the draft and provide the verses if you will.

The other play [*The Cradle and the Egg*] is quite different — plays hell with the unities, and has very complicated symbolism — Charles thinks I beat the poets at their own game, but I must say I don't want to beat anyone. Just give a lead. You should all be unloading plays in the gorgeous dress of verse on Campion at the rate of at least one every six months. Campion hasn't said his say about my play yet, but he's said enough to indicate that he knows I have challenged him. Put him on the spot, indeed. But I shall be surprised if he has a shot at it.

Yes, The Decay of Lying. I must go through all [Wilde's] dialogues again. And The Soul of Man under Socialism — from that I always remember the crack about journalists — how they used to have their ears nailed to the village pump, but now they nail their own ears to the keyhole.

I have never had anything dedicated to me, and I am quite moved. Sex religion politics — there should be economics too, they're coming back, and soon now the heat has been turned on through the banks from Wellington. I have grown a grey beard to help me terrify the mortgagee. So much is coming back — Goethe for example. Have you ever read the Eckermann Conversations — a noble book, and particularly absorbing to anyone with presby-geronto-philic characteristics. Down with sin and evil and all that crap. Up Plato (before he got crabbed in The Laws) and Buddha. Let's agree to call sin and evil by their proper names — stupidity and ignorance, so that the possibility of solutions may be immediately apprehended. And let all of us agree never to give up striving for the solutions, right to our ninetieth and hundredth year.

I wish I had something to let you have for Numbers. I must write [Arnold] Wall [Jnr] in Christchurch to find out if he has used what I had to say about — something. I forget what it was now, but it might be worth printing.

I have been very much a propagandist for Jacquie's story, and nobody disagrees.

From yours most truly,

F.S.

If you ever feel like a quiet holiday in my Army hut it is there. Autumn or late spring is best — the right temperature, and I can feed visitors best then.

Of course the Shanty sort of thing suggests itself for the sailor verses, but you will need to see the text for your points of reference.

The trouble with the Christian theology is that it is so childish. It must be held largely responsible for keeping so many of us children. The ethic is valuable for several reasons, and it is extremely beautiful, but it is native to other religions. I think that Graves and his friend Podro have done a good job in re-emphasizing the Jewishness of Christian beginnings. It is now up to Western man, particularly in this part of the world, to ask whether a colossal mistake may not have been made. It is monstrously fantastic that a prejudiced Oriental tribe, suffering from a poisonous inferiority complex, should have imposed its cruel and childish fantasies on Western man.

To Charles Brasch, *Dunedin*

Hocken Library

[FS had heard Brasch hoped to marry: '[. . .] I hope you insist on a wife who can type, proof-read, bully the Caxton Press, cook, house-keep and shop. A large guilt-edged income is also essential. I've always understood there are other desirable qualities but I'm such a dumb cluck I can't recollect what they are'. And on 31 January 1955: 'Rumours of your impending marriage are very persistent'. Hocken MS-0996-002/344. Brasch replied on 11 February: 'Talking of marriage and all that, how would you regard a request to act as godfather? or do you get asked too often, and have you godfathered too many little monkeys?' ATL MS-Papers-0432-147.]

16 February 1955

Dear Charles,

[. . .] Godfather? The idea disturbs me. That's already what I'm supposed to be to Miles, Bob Gilbert's son — and the thought of the lad's leaning on such a broken reed in the hour of his distress isn't very pleasant. I turned down Phil Wilson last year, and he seemed so upset I said he must just please himself. I heard nothing more — but for all I know some poor young woman twenty years hence who has put a bullet through her lover's kidney may be asking me to pay her counsel's fee. I am enormously flattered, Charles, but I do think these things should be taken with some seriousness which I'm not capable of for a variety of reasons. Perhaps you had better ask me again when you are on the way to the Font. Though the thought that you may now be on the way back from the Font is, to say the least of it, just a little perplexing.

Campion and all that. He hasn't written — and how could he when he's been busy cutting up Shakespeare and hunting out sound effects for Petruchio's horse? (Is it Petruchio's? — I'm not sure.) I'm thinking up various cunning schemes for both production and publication. Perhaps I'd better keep them to myself, as I am bound to make a mess of them — and let it be my own mess. The Caxton is certainly trying, but there again I'd better just go ahead and cook my own goose. What does it all matter when I'm rushing through the 2nd Act of Kendall. At the end of Act One it is plain to the audience that Kendall is doomed — in other words so Greek that my chemist's brew may prove to have some quality.

Please give no thought to my adventures with my bank manager (my very hairy beard did terrify him a little anyway). It is all such a dull complicated story. I'll promise to let you know if I'm still in a tangle as I approach my day of reckoning, the 31st March. Of course if the *Landfall* fee, however much it is, did arrive a few days before that day, it would be a great help. Pressure on people or at any rate certain people with overdrafts was turned on about last August, but since the election it has become more severe. Apparently the banks are furious with Holland. What it all presages is a matter for wiseacres a little less fanciful than I am. But at the moment I am not so preoccupied with the fate of my country as that of my 82 year old 20 stone widowed aunt who had a stroke the other day. I did the housekeeping for her for two days, and feel very virtuous because I only lightly powdered the roast with arsenic, and put a mere sprinkling of prussic acid in the gravy. Admittedly the custard I made for dessert was a confection composed of the purest ground glass, but I was very light with a dusting of iron filings. Naturally enough I returned after four hours to find her sitting up in bed, eager to congratulate me on my cooking, and the most delicious meal she had ever tasted. She was also feeling ever so much better. However, if I inherit her unspeakable beach mansion I intend to turn it into a Home for Poets — on condition they live with all the junk, and undertake to use it as a subject for a succession of surrealist poems.

Glad about The Colonel's D. I daren't read it myself after such a time.

All best, Charles, and 3 guesses I could tell you the solution of the marriage mystery?

F.S.

[Brasch's friend Margaret Scott recalls that although Brasch was sexually attracted only to men, he longed to be 'conventional, married, a father'. The engagement alluded to above may have been to Rose Archdall, whom Brasch had met on the ship returning to New Zealand after the war. '[Rose] was a war-widow with a small child, and Charles did seriously think about marrying her over a period of several years, until he woke up and came down to earth'. Margaret Scott, personal correspondence, 9 May 2011.]

To William Plomer, *Sussex*

Alexander Turnbull Library

19 March 1955

Dear Plomer,

[. . .] About the play: I was enormously glad to finish it with gusto and stingo and suchlike last November. It's comedy mainly, pastiche I'm afraid, but it looks as though it might go on this coming winter. There is quite a good company here — the NZ Players. Unfortunately the man who runs it [Richard Campion] was trained at the Old Vic not long back, so what he mainly gives us is a lot of (as a friend of mine puts it) Sweet Nell of Old Vickery. But we must be grateful even though it's hardly going to lead to the writing of first-rate plays out here. I'm very conscious I'm writing to somebody who has had a Covent Garden production, but sweet Fanny Adams to too many batteries of coloured lights and all that. Let playwrights pack their lines, and let actors learn to speak them, and all's pretty well with a few simple properties. This NZ Players man recently had here 2 Stratford Players who fled from the aftereffects of the English summer — Keith Michell and Barbara Jefford. Both have quite a way to go yet, but they made Fry's Non-Burning Lady quite interesting even though it's one hell of a muddle as a play. Unfortunately I'm considered rather too advanced for a commercial production by this company, so it will be a bit hole in corner — but I don't mind a great deal. I'm more interested in seeing whether we have actors intelligent enough to know what I'm up to. I hope when there are a few more typescript copies of the thing about I can send you one — you will giggle over the dialogue anyhow. Also, I got stuck right into another play — about Kendall, the first NZ missionary at the beginning of last century. He saw the natives weren't just superstitious savages, and so to his undoing became the first NZ anthropologist — a role which led him under the Maori women's mats. His wife meantime consoled herself with her husband's ex-convict servant. It's all a gift dramatically speaking, and I'm annoyed that none of our many able poets has taken it up. Here I am doing it in my poor old prose, when it really demands much splendid poetry. [. . .]

And your own work? I do hope it's going nicely. I must send you another Landfall. There's a period story I've written in it, the first time I've tried to depict a kind of aristocratic woman — and such a contrast to the superb way you do such things, with your wealth of visual detail. I find I have to rely almost wholly on the ear. On a short holiday recently some of us were reading some of your ballads aloud. How I love those bits about Neptune loving the breast-stroke, and about how the King on the Queen won't go. Will they be giggled over centuries hence? I think they may well be.

From ever yours,

F.S.

To Dennis McEldowney, *Upper Hutt*

Alexander Turnbull Library

27 March 1955

Dear Dennis,

[. . .] Oh yes, Dr [G.M.] Smith's suburban [Waikanae] corner! Mrs S. lives, or did live, in a curious tiled kind of outhouse. Somewhere else, down passages &1 across paths live matron (inherited from Rawene), the sempstress (also inherited from R. & what she sews or sempts I don't know, & Mrs S didn't either) — other oddments. An incredible set-up, but I expect G.M.S rules the lot. [. . .]

Some people turned up lately with Janet Frame in the back of a car. Too shy to say anything at all, but as she appears to be living not far away I have offered her my army hut to work in.

My summer labours of so many sorts brought on neurotic ailments, & I was lucky to get away for a week at Kawhia, which is a very Maori place — the Tainui allegedly sank there, & the pohutukawa which it tied up to still surviving after 800 years or so.

I have had assorted adventures with my play. Everybody including Campion impressed, but I am regarded as too advanced for a commercial production. [. . .] [A]t the moment my nose is rather put out of joint owing to my listening the other evening to young Stead, the poet, while he read me his 5 act play in verse [based on Racine's *Andromaque*]. All plays, with the exception of Congreve's comedies, & possibly the Importance of Being Ernest, should be in verse, & this very intelligent & promising young man has really written, I think, something new for N.Z. All very clear & logical too, & I don't mean the interior belly-logic which has become the mode, & sometimes the bore, of N.Z. verse. [. . .]

My wireless still doesn't go, & I'm delighted to leave off paying the fee. But I regret the music I miss. Still, it means I do more reading for my Kendall — not research, which is too embarrassing for one's imagination, but Melville's novels for example — they stimulate one into wanting to go even better, though at his best he can't be beaten.

Well, I'm being dull. I do hope it's cooled down in the Hutt Valley, & you don't suffer from mosquitoes as I do just now. [. . .]

More good luck to all.

F.S. [. . .]

To Helen Shaw, *Remuera*

Alexander Turnbull Library

[Helen Hofmann [Shaw] had written on 29 March to say she had been asked to write a brief memoir of Karl Wolfskehl for the Poetry Yearbook: 'Margot Selwyn (Reuben) [Wolfskehl's companion] is supplying the facts etc. but it occurred to me that you knew the old man and I thought you might have even a sentence in mind concerning him which would help me put a little life into the account'. ATL MS-Papers-0432-113.]

30 March 1955

Dear Hella,

Karl Wolfskehl is a rather painful subject with me, mainly because I withdrew myself from him over the last few years. He was a very great man (I think Thomas Mann in an essay described him as 'the last man') with an overwhelming amount to give, but his genius was such he didn't understand how much he took from people who couldn't come within a thousand miles of his own manifold riches. (Perhaps he did understand and felt he had the right to what anybody else had: if so, he was probably quite right in claiming the right — but it meant deadlock between him and me, and I can only put forward my probably poor and miserable work as an excuse). What I mainly remember now is his amazing awareness of what it was like to be living in New Zealand, despite the fact that he had virtually one sense missing — I mean his eyesight. I remember mentioning broad beans to him, and he was at sea until he identified them as horse beans from my description. Margot was with us and said we didn't have horse beans in New Zealand, and she was immediately contradicted and told not so, he had seen them. He was so sensitive he seemed literally to miss nothing, and there seemed to be no limits to the range of his humanism. He could establish contact with any kind of New Zealander whatsoever — that is to say, provided they were capable of going a fraction of an inch towards him, in return for the miles he was capable of travelling towards them. From this point of view he was civilized far beyond anything New Zealand has to show. It was an enormous privilege to know him — and here I must correct an impression that seems to be getting about: namely, that he was quite unappreciated in New Zealand. Glover was never in any doubt about him from the moment of their meeting, nor was I. I think there were one or two others — Curnow, I think, and Fairburn. But although we tried we could never get the scholarly (so-called) and academic people to take much interest. (There were exceptions — I think Olssen was one). Either they thought his English wasn't good enough for conversation, or else they knew virtually nothing about Stephan George and the Munich group. Karl was deeply hurt. He also suffered particularly badly at the time he and Margot were pushed out of the house they rented in Mt Eden — indeed from that time everything seemed to go wrong. Gladys Salter and I got him lodging with a friend of mine who lives not far from here. It was all very sad indeed. Sometimes of a rainy evening I would find him sitting huddled in a bus shelter, and perhaps he had wandered out very upset over having experienced a heart attack. I remember one wet winter night he called out to me from half way up the path to my hut — and I found him off the path and up to his ankles in mud. He had found Esmond road by coming along the main road, and where each road turned off he had stood patiently looking up where he supposed the sign would be until a passing car or bus gave him enough light to give him his bearings. That was during the time of blackout and gas shortages. If I dried his shoes over the gas ring the light went out. With low gas pressure there was no means of heating the hut. But he was happy to sit huddled in his overcoat while I read him poetry by candlelight. The point of all this is that he was one of the world's most distinguished philologists, perhaps a great German poet, and certainly a rare example of a super-civilized man. And speaking of philology, I can never remember his being in doubt over a word. Syntax might occasionally hold him up for a second, but never a word. I remember reading him the line 'her undinal vast belly moonward bends' — and then pausing to say 'Undinal, do you get it?' He answered of course, and asked me to continue.

Well, there you are. There are anecdotes by the score. (When he went swimming during a visit to Ian Hamilton's at Torbay, Fairburn said he looked like an intellectual porpoise). But if you want something 100 per cent authentic you could probably get it from Paul Hoffmann (his address is Runciman, near Drury) who was closer to him than anyone else, and whose humanity and high gifts were a greater boon to Karl in NZ than anything any NZder had. Another close friend was [the Austrian-born conductor Georg] Tintner. But if you approach these people don't mention my name because it would hardly make you popular with them. They were faithful to the end — and if it is their view that I turned out a heartless renegade I don't imagine I have any excuses to offer that wouldn't sound very hollow indeed. Also for God's sake don't mention my name in anything you write — but if anything I have said helps you to enhance Karl's greatness well and good. Perhaps some of his friends might be charitable enough to think I did my best for him according to my lights — but if they should go on to think my lights weren't very bright I just haven't got an answer.

F.S.

Bruce Mason is interested in my play, and there seems some chance of a rather hole in corner [Unity Theatre] production in Wellington this winter. I read a paper up at the university literary society the other evening, and discovered among the audience Robin Hyde's son.

[The Austrian-born Germanist Paul Hoffmann, whose family were also refugees, met Wolfskehl in Auckland in 1940. He returned to Vienna in 1951 and began a distinguished academic career with a PhD on the poet.]

To John Reece Cole, *Wellington*

Alexander Turnbull Library

1 April 1955

Dear Reece,

Many thanks for your letter. I felt very worried after I'd posted my letter. I felt you must feel I remain quite unimpressed by what you say about library problems and the pressures that never let up on you. [. . .] My own upset is connected with autumn feelings plus some chance meetings that have profoundly disturbed me. I read a paper at the College Literary society the other evening, and spent about 2 hours during the discussion trying to place a well-set-up handsome young man with a head of fluffy brownish hair and a look of the Navy about him, who had quite a lot to say that was intelligent and to the point. He turned out to be Robin Hyde's son. I last saw him at Jess Whitworth's when he was about 8 or 9. He lives in a bach where Gloria Rawlinson lives in Ellerslie. He's coming over soon, and obviously wants to know whatever I can tell him — which is a difficulty as so much I know was told me by Iris herself, and there are so many discrepancies about her stories when you get other people's versions of them. For example, she told me she had her first child in Sydney, called it Robin Hyde, and when it died took the name for her writing. I'm inclined to believe this, but whether it's true or not I don't know. Derek is the young man's name, and I remember that all right, but I always thought he was Derek Wilkinson, but he calls himself Derek Challis (my God!) which he says is the name Iris registered him under. I have a fancy he has no information about his father, but I could put him on to the man from whom Iris used to get maintenance — but whether I do or not is another question.

But all this wouldn't disturb me quite so much if it hadn't got tangled up with Janet Frame, who is living at Northcote. She came to have lunch with me, and impressed me almost more than anybody I have ever met. In colouring and looks there is a marked resemblance to Robin Hyde, but there is a masculine touch which gives her an apparent balance which one didn't find in Iris. She says she has a great pile of writing done, and it's no trouble to her — writes in her mind at night, and types it out in the morning. But she doesn't want to show it to anybody. I tried to lead her on by telling about your and Lou's proposals for the Fellowship, and her eyes lit up at the prospect of being able to get out of NZ for a while. I said that with so much material she should have an excellent chance, but she dismissed it as just a dream and repeated about being unwilling to let anyone see her writing. She doesn't possess a copy of her own book [*The Lagoon and Other Stories*], and had never seen the Oxford book — but I bought her a copy down at the corner before I put her on the bus. She's not out on parole, she is discharged on the understanding she goes in again voluntarily when she feels she has to take herself in hand. How she's classified I don't know, but I got out of her that she likes very much Blake's visionary poems, the Book of Revelations Dylan Thomas etc. And re-reading her book I can see the tie-up. My own stuff for example I would say is a re-arrangement of a reality which is accessible to everyone, but what she writes is dreamlike and visionary and she's more concerned with using mundane reality as a springboard than re-arranging it. Here again she resembles Robin Hyde, but it seems to me she's more intelligent and a much surer writer in spite of her fluency. She is in fact enormously intelligent, and I can see the point about her reluctance to speak. Whatever one begins to say she understands immediately, and there's no need to say it. (In this, she seems to me to have reached somewhere about the point you yourself have reached in more recent years: I don't want to depreciate myself stupidly by saying I haven't reached it — the real point is I think that I am an essentially different kettle of fish). I also noticed that she is enormously observant, taking in everything — and Iris wasn't: she just picked on points here and there, very much as Greville used to. Nor can I imagine her getting angry and violent as Iris used to, yet I expect at times she must because I have been told that in the mental hospital she sometimes behaves very badly. The crowning piece of information I extracted from her was about her mother, whose maiden name was Godfrey, and who was apparently at one time maid to the Beauchamp family. I asked did that mean she knew Katherine, and was told yes. But I couldn't get anything more — except that she (Janet) had never read Mansfield with much warm interest because as a child she had got tired of hearing her mother talk about the Beauchamps.

It all goes round and round in my head. I feel very strongly that I have met one of the most remarkable people NZ has produced, but how it all adds up and what is going to happen I haven't a clue. (She professed to forget what poems she had sent to the *Listener*, and what had appeared there. And when I asked about the story, *Lolly Legs* she said she had merely sent that in — apparently one of many she has — as a celebration to mark the occasion of her last release from the mental hospital). She is living with her sister (nowhere near up to her mark so far as one can detect) and rather pitiful snag of a husband: also 3 noisy children. Apparently she gets some kind of benefit temporarily (Health Department or Soc Sec) but will have to take a job — perhaps in a hotel. She says she likes that kind of work and company. Meantime I have suggested that she might care to bus over here and back each day and use my hut for working in, coming and going without paying any attention to me, which I think she would prefer. All in all I don't know that her visit did her any good — except perhaps that I presented her with my copy of *The Story of An African Farm* which she had never read. And if there's any book that might give her a momentous and thundering leg-up, I think perhaps it might be that one.

I am bucked by your remarks about my play. Bruce [Mason] wrote me a letter of excellent criticism, and I could admit much that he said, and put him right as I thought on one or two points. I am desperately keen on getting the Kendall moving again, and there's hope because I've left off the pheno-barb and the damn nerves seem to be quietening. My main worry is mosquitos at night (but I've rigged up a net over the window) and green shield beetles infesting the garden day and night. Are the insects about to take over — or the plants? (I got a thrill of real horror over reading *The Day of the Triffids* — and look suspiciously at my six Chinese pawpaws: they have a disturbing triffid look about them: incidentally, now they are beginning to flower they seem to be all males. Would this be a judgment on me?)

[. . .] No more, dear Reece — and dear Chris too. My love to the kids,

F.S.

To Dan Davin, *Oxford*

Alexander Turnbull Library

17 April 1955

Dear Dan,

I seem to be snatching a moment to write to you — was I last time? Reading Sty of an Afcn Fm for about the 10th time and as wonderful as ever — Schreiner was born in 1855, and I am after a few guineas. Also, I began that second play in December and now I am just about to go with a rush into the third act.

Great good news about the novel [*The Sullen Bell*]. May your doubts be airy nothings, and the book another lovely brick for the House Beautiful of Literature we're all so bent over, building. [. . .]

I lost the run of my copy of the Symposium before I had read it. The Library was having an exhibition of NZ books so I lent it — they had of course never heard of it. I skipped the interpretative articles except Baxter's, and I read yours first and twice with fascinated interest. I would rather all the rest were people who had never met me, and people living 100 years hence. But I am always ready to pick up technical points. My God, was I worth all that! And you are dead right on everything except about the perfect ear — was it 'perfect?' I wish I had. If there is anyone who has it's Curnow, who has as good an ear as any living English or American poet. I am (I hope) humbly grateful for such attention and perception. You even encourage me to hope you may look forward to seeing my plays with some anticipation — because of course the necessities of the dialogue stimulate me into delving right to the bottom of my technical bag.

But about the play: Campion, the cunt, wrote me over three months ago that he was immensely interested, and since then not a word. I rightly guessed I was considered too advanced for a commercial production, so I began the new play — I mean I really began it after some weeks of stimulating my imagination with titbits about Kendall, the first missionary. Within a few weeks I shall have two complete plays in my hands, and with that bright spark Bruce Mason quite interested it looks as though something will happen — probably this winter. Though I have a fantasy about having two plays running together next winter. Campion, I have heard indirectly, feels guilty, so I intend to forgive him on condition he lends us his best players, whom I hope we will return to him disinfected of the Sweet Smell of Old Vickery. Well boy, if it comes off you must be in on it. If I am to be the new Ibsen of the South, would you care to be the new Strindberg? — though I am afraid I shall have to appropriate both, as Kendall is very Strindberg with his booze and native women, and his wife with her boy lover. Here's to a success of esteem plus scandal!

I was quite absorbed by Eric McCormick's two books [about Frances Hodgkins], but it is the Expatriate which I think is the masterpiece. A few prejudices perhaps get in the way in the latter half, but his dramatic handling of his material, rising to a climax when he prints in full Fanny's letter to her mother about the Technical college teaching job, reveals him to me in something of a new light. Needless to say both volumes monuments to patience and integrity, and new standards set for all NZ writers. I hope he is relaxing a little after his labours — he's probably having some fascinating Scrutiny conversations with D.W. Harding anyhow. He has by the way suffered cruelly from an unhappy love-affair over the last year or two. There's surely no suffering so severe when it happens to such a person at such a time of life. I have been profoundly moved and disturbed myself over what I know about it.

Poor Maurice is so unlucky that the luck of a Duggan will soon be a standard expression for bad luck. His lung, air-collapsed, still worries him. He is working on a final polishing of the best of his stories over the past ten years, and then a superhuman effort all round has to be made to get them into print. Middleton has apparently been persuaded to accept £200 from the SLF, without any degrading tags attached to it, so our efforts weren't quite fruitless. Also Cole and Johnson are working hard on a travel bursary scheme. I had a wonderful week with Maurice and Barbara and the baby (who is a monster in size and energy) at Kawhia — a great Maori place, and still comparatively unspoiled by trippers Dew Drop Inns and suchlike abominations. I gave a most repulsive display of elderly energy zest for life and all that crap by never stopping talking cooking washing the nappies and general chores — but something has to be done to persuade Maurice that life is earnest and real and bloody heads are buggered but unbowed even though scrotums are sadly fallen arches — and a lot more crap.

Nuff sed. Too wrapped up in what I'm doing to really write,

F.S.

PS. I have recently been delighted by a young poet who has taken my plea for verse play instead of poems stiff with belly-logic seriously. His five act play, beautifully clear, sounded to me like an astonishing tour de force when he read it to me.

To E.P. Dawson, *Mt Maunganui*

Hocken Library

10 May 1955

Dear Peter,

Just a line. All at sixes & sevens with headaches, neurosis, & trouble with my waterworks.

If you are not visiting Akld before too long, I think Janet Fame would be glad of an invitation to visit you if you felt like it. She is 100 p.c. thoroughly nice. Very shy & silent, but a good listener, & amazingly quick & intelligent. She wants to see more of N.Z. & has never been your way. She gets Invalidity at present, but it won't, it seems, be very long, & then she will probably take some factory job or something of the sort. Anyhow I just leave it to you, but I am pretty sure she would go if you asked her. Every chance of mutual understanding & no sparks. She is fresh-complexioned Scottish type with reddish hair of Renate's type, & quite athletic. [. . .]

Campion I'm sure will never write now. But still something goes on with other people in Wellington. I can't worry until I've puzzled out the final act of my *Kendall*. Then perhaps I had better take a job as a plain cook in a quiet country hotel, & do sewing jobs as a sideline.

All best from

F.S.

To Rodney Kennedy, *Dunedin*

Hocken Library

[FS to Brasch, 18 March: 'I must mention to you my delight that young Stead has written a five act play. I and his young wife listened while he read [. . .]. He is devoted to Racine — hence he has produced something very lucid and logical. [. . .] I couldn't help thinking of almost any novel by Ivy Compton-Burnett. Classicism, I suppose'. Hocken MS-0996-

002/344. Brasch delivered his own 'irremediably negative' verdict sometime later (C.K. Stead, Book Self, *p. 30); Brasch's friend Rodney Kennedy, who had read the play with a theatre producer's eye, wrote to FS on 18 May: 'I am sorry Stead thought the criticism of his play too harsh but really it was more suited to Radio than the stage. It had a distinct echo of Ivy Compton-Burnett in Wanganui. Still he can write'. ATL MS-Papers-0432-071.]*
23 May 1955

Honey,

I have a horrid feeling I have caught you out in 'Ivy Compton-Burnett in Wanganui'. Are you prepared to lay your hand on your heart and swear you didn't get that out of a phony novel by John Gillies (from Gore), called *Voyages in Aspic*? (Not that it's completely phony — he has a genuine comic talent). But let it pass. I meant that Stead's characters being concerned with achieving their own ends without regard to opposition, do suggest the way I C-B goes about things. But let that pass too. I still hold that the play deserves to be put on, and if there was the intelligence and the will among theatre people in NZ, NZ plays could be tried out each week in some derelict warehouse — or better on a few square feet of dais in one or other of the fabulously expensive restaurants that spring up overnight all over the place. All over this town anyhow. I know the expense and all that of setups such as Campion's, but I am in such a rage about the lack of imagination you mustn't be surprised if you come home to find I have set up in effective opposition. Still, if I haven't it's nice to think you will have the choice of several of my plays to produce. The *Kendall* not far off completion, and a much tighter piece of work. But again — where in NZ does one find actors whose energetic egos are supplemented by brains and imagination let alone an ability to make themselves heard? Not to mention the deficiencies of producers. [. . .]

I am extremely happy to have Janet Frame living in my army hut, and I grow more devoted to her each day. Her plight is infinitely moving. A brilliantly intelligent and sensitive mind inaccessible to all other minds — and accessible to herself only through painfully vivid and quite indecipherable images. The confidence that she has in me plunges me into abysses of humility, and it is more than infinitely moving to realize that she talks to me more than she has talked to anyone over ten years. I am getting to the point of praying daily for the miracle that will cast out her devils and save her. Say a little prayer for both of us sometimes if you don't find yourself too deeply embedded in European fleshpots to remember.

Well, a fond goodbye, and do try not to get yourself murdered in Naples or any such place. I had a narrow escape in Genoa. Winckelmann you will remember was not so fortunate.

Fx

To James K. Baxter, *Wellington*

Hocken Library

[Baxter to FS, 20 May: 'Good to know that Janet Frame is with you. You may help her considerably — in schizophrenia the person is fully aware of environment & people, though not able to communicate; or so they say. Have met her. She has I believe been smashed (in the socially intelligent aspect only) by the dead, inadequate climate of a middle-class N.Z. family. Have met her relatives. They make adjustment by dying. Her psychosis strikes me as in a sense an enormous catastrophic protest of a mind & heart too much alive to bear what we in our brutalized selves learn to bear. Get some of her 'private' work if you can do it gently — it may not be as private as it looks. Give her my warm regards if you communicate to that extent'. ATL MS-Papers-0432-144.]

28 May 1955

Dear Baxter,

[. . .] Your diagnosis of the La Frame plight is probably dead right. I wish I could do more for her. I strung together the enclosed lines from some prose I persuaded her to read me — though 'read me' is a misdescription; it took about 3 hours to get out of her some disjointed whispered fragments. Don't you agree the lines make a pure & lovely poem — quite unique? But she won't at present put her name to them, or agree to publication, at any rate in N.Z. — so meantime they are strictly for your private delight. Jacquie's also. But if I do my stuff I may get more — & I have at least half-succeeded in extracting from her a promise not to destroy her work — which she has an unfortunate habit of doing from time to time. It is a tremendous paradox that her intelligence has so far saved her from complete insanity in the conventional sense, but it stands as a barrier against 'externalisation' — because it enables her to decipher many of the images & makes her fear that other people may do the same. That is unbearable to her. Whatever it is that she is defending must on no account be brought out naked into the light of day. And considering the sort of society we're living in, who can blame her? I taught her to play chess, & it's most revealing that she quickly learned to play an excellent defensive game, but it never occurs to her to try to attack.

Faced with your verses in the *Listener* ['Song for the Middle Years'] I don't know what to say — except to admit the poetry & deny everything else. I'm all in favour of people who have been forced at an early age into deciding whether they will live or die. If the decision is an affirmative one, it follows that the middle years afford one excellent opportunities for re-affirmations. I am sorry to have missed your IYC versions of the MacM.-B. lectures — my radio broke down last year, & Bob Gilbert doesn't turn up to mend it.

With all best wishes,

F.S.

Unfortunately you may not write to Janet about her lines if you are deeply moved by them. They apparently belong to a different part of her personality, not the one known as Janet Frame. My sending them cuts right across what confidence she has in me so far, & it would be very bad if I were found out. But I should be interested to know if you agree with me that they are superbly beautiful & what else.
[The 'enclosed lines' do not survive. Frame offers a different view of the origins of the 'Santie Cross' poems, which derive from the opening section of Owls Do Cry, *in* An Autobiography, *p. 260. FS's letter to Brasch of 18 August 1955 also includes 'Santie Cross' material. 'Your diagnosis': Frame's doctors later concluded that she was neither schizophrenic nor psychotic and as* An Autobiography *shows her background was working class.]*

To Dennis McEldowney, *Upper Hutt*

Alexander Turnbull Library

[McEldowney had written to FS on 8 June saying he was reading Proust, but could have 'no faith at all' in the artistic integrity of a translator named Frederick A. Blossom. 'The relation of names to works is quite a study. Could you have written as you have if your name were Rupert Waring? (I didn't make that up. It belongs to a friend of my father's, who was brought up in a Methodist Home & has spent most of his time since in gaol'. ATL MS-Papers-0432-173.]

27 June 1955

Dear Dennis,

At last I seem able to write you a note that might turn out not to be my usual hurried bit of gossip. I have, you see, just the other day finished the first draft of the Kendall, and I must let it all lie a week or so before I begin on the revision and the retyping. Oh, I have hopes it may turn out as it should, then I shall have 2 plays in my hands, and can concentrate on pushing for productions of some kind. One idea is to put on plays in a fabulously expensive restaurant recently opened alongside the Mon Desir [Hotel], and run by Felix Millar the violinist. Young Karl Stead the poet has his verse play too, and I think his, which would be easy to produce, would make a good opening number. The idea would be to whip plays on and off, very exclusive performances which would tantalise play-producing professors and other deadheads, whose ideas stick somewhere between Ben Jonson and Noel Coward. Anyhow, we shall see, but I feel faint at the thought of the organising work that will be required. The supply of intelligence and imagination available in NZ when it is a question of original works of art is so very limited.

My congratulations on you 44,000 words [of *The World Regained*] which don't sound so very meagre — very slightly less than my 2 plays put together. It doesn't sound such a big publishing job, so I hope you dump it on one or other of the presses very soon, with the suggestion that they apply to the SLF for support.

I should like very much to write under the name of Rupert Waring. After all, I could cash in on the literary association with Browning's Waring. Was it a Methodist Home or just a Methodist home? — in any case either would be likely enough to land one in gaol eventually. I notice a young man along the street heading in that direction, though in his case a mental hospital may be more likely. And talking of mental hospitals, Renate has had a number of temporary successors in the hut, of one sex or the other and occasionally of both, but a remarkable person who seems more permanent is Janet Frame. A striking thought — after ten years of mental hospitals she establishes herself in my garden. But a most remarkable girl, marvellously intelligent, and a very pure person in the best sense of the word. She is visually hallucinated, but manages to keep a balance between the spectres and something more solid by writing continuously. But she won't allow what she writes to be communicated to anyone — and after much thought and exercise of intuition, Dr Sargeson has at last got it all worked out. She can deal with the menace of the imaginary landscape and its figures by putting it all down on paper — that is to say, she asserts her power over these severed parts of herself by fixing them on paper. But if anyone reads what she writes she fears she may be letting them all loose again, and all my arguments about her having on paper created moral and aesthetic orders which can never slip back into the chaos she has wrestled with and defeated, are of no avail. How like Bunyan and Pilgrim's Progress it all is, but how very much more terrible! Bunyan could feel himself backed by the Christian tradition, so was not entirely alone in his wrestlings with Apollyon and what have you. But poor Janet stands for the solitary modern soul depending entirely upon personal resources when confronted by chaos. What miracle could save her, or indeed any of us, I don't know, but at least while her typewriter taps, one knows that she is swimming instead of sinking. What is very remarkable is her family background. Her father was a railway engine driver, and the large family, growing up at the time of the depression was very poorly off. Her father by the way is technically a Presbyterian, and her mother a sincere Christadelphian. Anyhow she is welcome to the hut, and my main worry is not the spectres but the meagre meals she eats — and yet she is a neat athletic type with a Scottish fresh complexion and a fuzz of reddish hair. Do you think I should, in the interests of our literature, buy a photostat machine, and pick the locks of the boxes where she keeps her typescripts? Of course I should be murdered if I were caught, but I'm sure all of you would give me a gorgeous funeral as a literary martyr. [. . .]

It's good news about Baxter's radio play [*Jack Winter's Dream*], which is supposed to be put on pretty soon. And young Stead has received a 100 dollar poetry award for his poem in Landfall called Night Watch in the Tararuas. I wish somebody would give me a prize for just having read The Three Musketeers — a wonderfully absorbing amusing really immoral and sinister book. It is scandalous that I should recommend Proust to you, and then read Dumas, but I needed a holiday from the Bhagavadgita and the Sayings of the Buddha. Somewhere at the back of my mind I am troubled to think what my next literary work will be, and Buddha and Dumas might make a good mixture for something that might be a worthy successor to The Robe or The Razor's Edge. The few people who said anything about my Landfall story ['The Colonel's Daughter'] found it amusing, and I hoped people would. Many thanks for your comments.

Good news that I shall see you in October, and Janet of course will turn you into a spectre within 3 seconds after she has set eyes on you.

If only you hadn't changed your residence, I could take leave of you with some such phrase, as Dear Brother in Christchurch — but Hutt Valley doesn't sound quite right. I can however imagine a pleasant limerick beginning:

There was a young man of Hutt Valley
Who corrupted a Sunday School rally,
He said to the judge, sir,
This is all fudge, sir . . . .
But I leave you to finish,
F.S.

[C.K. Stead's 'Night Watch in the Tararuas' won first prize in the undergraduate poetry section of the Borestone Mountain Poetry Awards for poems published in 1954.]

To James K. Baxter, *Wellington*

Hocken Library

[On 22 July Baxter sent FS a cable of congratulations on the script of A Time for Sowing.*]*

24 July 1955

Dear Baxter,

Very generous of you to send the telegram. You make me feel a little rueful — I didn't send you one about your radio script [*Jack Winter's Dream*]. I must apologise for being so choked up with my own matters. I have a sense of life running out, and so much still to do. I have been so fortunate in some ways — the TB toxins-cum-psyche-troubles don't exhaust me as they used to, and my time is for me to use as I choose instead of as chosen for me. All very fortunate — but another set of pressures is substituted, and if it wasn't my heart wouldn't begin its knocking like a ferry-boat engine pump when it's not in order. (It doesn't even amuse me to recall the bit about a steel Romeo working in a cast-iron Juliet — even the toughest metal wears out.)

Have since carefully re-read your script, which is superb as poetry — I mean it's all poetry. Only poets can write prose like that, and perhaps it's just as well. The language I try to write is intended to be the thinnest of veils — without which, paradoxically, reality can't be discerned. At least not on paper. But in your prose you thicken language so that it becomes part of the reality one is searching for. Probably I explain very badly. I cling to my notion that there should be more drama at the level which is accessible to the more hick-minded. But it is for you to decide in years to come whether or not you can make that concession. Jack Winter is I think a superb name, and both name and man are to me rich symbols. The time-trick which puts him inside the wall is a very clever invention, and beautifully worked out. How goes production? I do hope, well.

It worries me very much to think of Numbers collapsing after reaching the standard of the last number. Surely some patron could be found. Maurice [Duggan]'s story ['Towards the Mountains'] reads wonderfully well, much better than when he read it to me — but it may have been altered. I don't get the full weight of your Landfall poem ['Letter to the World'] yet. You are more fortunate than I was when I first got the impact of Wilde. No such article could have been published. Does this closed world you speak of exist in NZ at the highest levels? I mean cultural levels — if so I should be glad of an introduction. I know it does at the highest social levels, but all that is too boring. I don't know what your thesis really amounts to. Old Mother Nature like the Catholic church can include everything. (I imagine that both have quite a fondness for the unnatural by nature). What on earth would present day society do for really efficient waiters hairdressers dress designers actors ballet dancers etc etc if there wasn't that permanent component? But I admit to being frivolous. Your thesis amounts to a very great deal, and you propound a very difficult problem.

I will put your script in the post in a day or two. And here's to your capping off the play with Baxter at his ballady best!

From yours,

F.S.

['Your radio script': Jack Winter's Dream *was published in* Landfall *in September 1956, and first broadcast on 26 September 1958. 'the impact of Wilde': Baxter's essay 'Over the Tin Fence: A Consideration of the life and Work of Oscar Wilde' appeared in* Numbers *3 (June 1955).* Numbers *survived until 1959. The day of his cable, Baxter also sent FS his 'bo's'n's song' with a careful gloss of its imagery (ATL MS-Papers-0432-144). The poem survives only in manuscript in Baxter's papers as 'The Bo's'n's Song (for Frank Sargeson's play on Kendall)', Book XVIII, MS-0704/018, Hocken Library.]*

To Charles Brasch, *Dunedin*

Hocken Library

[Brasch to FS, 25 July: 'Has Janet any money to live on, or are you supporting her entirely? If you are, may I be allowed to help? only it would have to be without her knowledge, for the sake of both sides, you will understand.' He congratulated FS on finishing the Kendall play, and told him he was 'all agog' to read it: 'I hope Baxter gives you some good sea shanties; what an admirable collaboration'. ATL MS-Papers-0432-147.]

27 July 1955

Dear Charles,

What a kind letter, particularly about Janet. She has some very bad spells, but I think it is good for her in the hut all round. I am hoping something can be done to get her a travel grant of some sort. So long as she can be continually typing away she seems to be able to pin the nightmare down on paper, and thus assert her power over it. I find her a tremendously civilized person. With the help of an understanding doctor who signs social security certificates each month, she gets £3-10/- per week. But this may not go on indefinitely — the S.S. department raises its queries, and it is all so stupid, because if she is forced back into a Hospital, I believe the cost to the country per week runs out at about £14. When the crisis comes, as I expect it will eventually, I shall see whether Cole can put the matter to the Minister. The gravest difficulties are with the so-called mental experts, such as [Geoffrey] Blake-Palmer — although he has done her kindnesses it seems he would be not unwilling to force her back into Hospital. The man is a preposterous egotist. If pressure is brought on Janet to return to Hospital at this stage I think she will suicide — but luckily things haven't reached that stage yet. Thanks tremendously for your offer of financial help — I won't forget, but it's not necessary at the moment. [. . .]

Here's the play Charles. Baxter is very complimentary about it. Do you think his verses are all right? He sent me a long exegesis on them, but what virginal impact do they make on you? I must apologise for an inadequate carbon copy — my typewriter is wearing out after 30 years. [. . .] I will be pushing The Cradle and Egg now I have 2 plays to bargain with. [. . .]

All my best,

F.S.

[On 15 August Brasch wrote FS a warm appreciation of A Time for Sowing*: 'What a nicely complex character you've made your Kendall, how full of contradictions, & lovable, & frustrating — self-frustrating too. I don't feel like I've seen more than part of him; he seems very solidly there; it ought to be a rewarding role for a good actor. All the chief people come across very well: one knows them — even though Maubey is somewhat enigmatic in manner [. . .]. It's a new myth for us to pasture on, which*

is what we so badly want.' He told him he liked Baxter's shanty, which he felt owed 'a hint or two to Sinclair's Half Moon Bay, and is none the worse for that'. ATL MS-Papers-0432-147.]

To Charles Brasch, *Dunedin*

Hocken Library

18 August 1955

Dear Charles,

Immensely grateful to you. Your remarks are just what I need. It's a curious situation — the more one keeps on, the less people there are of one's own age, more or less, to turn to for advice and encouragement. Those whose mature judgment should be of value have lost interest, and the young are naturally most interested in their own affairs. Yes, very grateful. I've never before worked at something that seemed so detached from myself (not really of course), and nothing has ever before so completely drained me out. I've been trying for weeks to write some radio talks on Olive Schreiner, and I can't write a single line. But I felt the energy returning as I read your letter.

With Kendall it is very much as you discern, but theatrically speaking, I am afraid it is going to be very difficult to prevent Mrs K from stealing too much from him. Maubey was at first intended to be just a convenience, but I saw the possibility of making him take the weight of a point of view of some value. The Kendalls between them plus Richard are supposed to anticipate much of the New Zealand pattern — Richard as it were, the first Bohemian. Yes, I felt often I was dealing in dynamite. But the factual basis is pretty clear. I avoided all research once I had the stimulation I was after, but Burdon kindly copied out this letter [for] me — from William Hall to Josiah Pratt April 1822 '. . . and about the same time R. Stockwell, the convict that Mr Kendall brought out to New Zealand with him, was cohabiting with Mrs Kendall, well known to all the settlement except to Mr Kendall's self, and she actually brought forth a son by Stockwell, nothing like any other part of Mr Kendall's family, and when she was charged with it she confessed the whole of her shameful conduct and the child remains a spurious brood in Mr Kendall's family to this day.'

Will you Charles, mention the play to Rodney when you are writing? I have already mentioned it myself, but what you say will carry more weight. I feel I can't go on writing plays in the meantime — I mean two years work on material which hasn't nearly such a chance of being brought out into public light as what I have written previously, and no more chance of bringing me in a little money.

I expect I will try a novel again, and probably some stories. But I don't despair. Bruce Mason is naturally preoccupied with his own plays, but no doubt I'll hear what he thinks of the Kendall eventually, and apart from him I have several other schemes up my sleeve. We shall see, and I must try not to be impatient.

And what can I do for you?

I hope to refer to your notes in last Landfall as a very convenient peg to hang my Schreiner talks on. What a masterly story Maurice wrote in Numbers — the last section of it surely provides some ground for a feeling of hope in all young people.

Janet surprised me by suddenly going off to Oamaru, but I fancy she will be back before long.

Stead sent his play to Broadcasting months ago. No reply, not even an acknowledgement, and when he inquired they just put him off with something about its receiving attention.

But *is* there some service I can do you? Is the Caxton sitting on your poems?

F.S.

I risk sending you the enclosed lines because they are such a delight. I strung them together from what I could remember from some prose I persuaded Janet to read me (but never again, she suffered too severely afterwards from letting herself be persuaded into communicating). For your eyes alone, and they mustn't be mentioned to anyone — particularly J. herself.

Buy a caterpillar that is wound up
and crawls with rippling back
across your day and night
    the wind breathed a blow away spell
The wind is warm, was warm
the days above burst unheeded
explode their atoms of snow-black bean flower,
and white rose,
mock the last intuitive whodunnit whodunnit of the summer thrush
    it said to plant
The sun pinned in the pocket of my land
taking underground green all willowed
and white rose
and bean flower
and morning mist picnic of song in pepper-pot breast of thrush.

[The phrase 'particularly J. herself' is a handwritten addition; the typed lines are pinned to the letter. An identical version, which includes the typed pseudonym 'SANTIE CROSS' and the handwritten identification 'Janet', is preserved in ATL MS-Papers-0432-165. This 'Santie Cross' poem is derived from the opening paragraphs of Owls Do Cry. *See FS to James K Baxter, 28 May 1955. Frame and FS offered it to*

John Lehmann, who declined to publish it. Michael King provides an account of the collaborative origins of this material in Wrestling with the Angel, *pp. 129-130, and relates Frame's reluctance to share work in progress to FS's criticism of an earlier story. Brasch replied to FS on 23 August: 'Two things you could do for me, Frank. One is to offer me something for next year (LF's tenth); the other is to hint that Janet might offer me something. The last stories she sent me I had to turn down; they were too terrible — very well done, but appalling passive suffering of an intolerable kind, I felt. And Janet may have been hurt, though I tried to explain; she's a bit frightened of me anyway, I fear. Those stories were ones she had to get out of her system, clearly; in a collection they might be bearable, but not isolated in a magazine. Do you see what she is writing? if you do, perhaps you could make suggestions. I'll keep her extraordinary lines to myself — thank you'. ATL MS-Papers-0432-147. Brasch also said he'd been considering* A Time For Sowing *for* Landfall *but felt Caxton should publish FS's two plays in a single volume, and had suggested this idea to Leo Bensemann. He also wrote that Margaret Garland was writing about Olive Schreiner for* Landfall, *and suggested it might carry both Garland's work and the Schreiner talks FS was planning. ATL MS-Papers-0432-147.]*

To Charles Brasch, *Dunedin*

Hocken Library

29 August 1955

Dear Charles,

That might turn out quite well — about Olive Schreiner. I expect Margaret would emphasise social ideas about Africa, black and white etc. While I shall be concerned almost entirely with the fiction, the intensity of feeling about a limited Bible background. Yes, I shall go ahead feeling much better because of aiming at either Landfall or the air or both. Only trouble, Charles, is that I am still very dazed and scattered. I read Tolstoy one moment and eighteenth century plays the next and stare at the garden without doing what is needful — I suppose what I am trying to decide is whether to write another play or a novel. So very difficult — dialogue is so attractive to me.

Thanks very much for putting that idea to Leo. Again so difficult. One should not publish the text of a play without a stage tryout, and it all means endless delay argument and waste of energy — not to mention that the author's need to rake in a little money for his work is the last thing 9 people out of 10 are going to think about. If nobody will take up one or other of the plays for production next winter, then early next year I had better write off the theatre people, and go ahead with publishing the texts *as literature*. I could write an introductory note. In spite of my publicising the fact that I had written 2 plays in the elaborate catalogue Wynne Colgan prepared for the display of Auckland writing some weeks back, I don't get one inquiry from the local theatre people — and I would be very sceptical if I did, as local people of that kind seem to be entirely concerned with technical tricks of lighting etc. This must sound like bitter complaining, but it's not quite. I realise very well that these people just don't think in terms of work from their own country, and it's up to the author to force recognition. But this costs so much in time and energy, it well might be as well to think in terms of literature instead of the theatre. However, once I am launched upon fresh work I shall forget about my impatience, and the entire matter may be put aside until early next year.

Yes, I had realised about the 10th year. It should be marked in some way apart from what Landfall can print to mark it — I mean I have discussed with various people how best we can express our congratulations, and I hope, our gratitude. And about something to offer — I long to write something quite first-rate for you. And Janet? If she communicates what she writes she lets loose the nightmare she has asserted her power over — but some of her numerous personalities don't mind communicating quite so much — in other words, it may be possible to get something from her provided it appears over an invented name. Those lines I sent you by the way were by Santie Cross — a half Polynesian girl I invented for her who has since I believe written quite a batch of Santie Cross poems. If I can get some of these for you I will, but it's very difficult. Her reaction plunges her into the lower depths of insanity, and it's of course very disturbing to me. She mentioned the stories she sent you, and felt you were quite right in turning them down.

We are having an early spring. Plum and peach out, potatoes well up, peas a foot high. Etc. The most wonderful season for grapefruit I have ever had, and my first Chinese pawpaws are nearly ripe.

I was most interested to see John Wain, a very young man, saying in the London Mag. what the future is to be. I suppose my curious mixture of a kind of peasant cum intellectual life has been based on similar assumptions. Yet I don't know. This age may be unique in that technology may carry over one civilization into another without centuries of complete breakdown — in which case we must look to America and Russia where the seed of the future may be germinating.

Best wishes, Charles.

F.S.

This business of numerous personalities has its curious side. In theory Janet and I have a secretary called Aphrodite Taillefer Thickpenny who is supposed to write all our letters for us.

[A Time For Sowing was performed in Auckland in 1961 and *The Cradle and the Egg* in 1962. Caxton published them as *Wrestling with The Angel: Two Plays* in 1964.]*

To Charles Brasch, *Dunedin*

Hocken Library

30 October 1955

Dear Charles,

Just to say I'll let you see the Schreiner talks as soon as I've got the recording off my mind — 3 talks, 21 pages in all. The trouble is I had to write them so as to make absolutely sure if I could, that Broadcasting would have them on. Luckily they haven't turned me down — but only extracts would be printable in their present form. If you think the various points I make are worth while, you can decide whether you would care to print extracts, or whether you'd prefer me to rewrite — which wouldn't cost me more than about a week's work with such a handy draft to work from.

I am really enormously pleased about Janet's long typescript [*Owls Do Cry*] that Pegasus say they will bring out. Of course there is the upset with the Caxton Press, but J acted entirely on her own impulse and I had nothing at all to do with the matter. It's all extremely awkward, because in J's present state I daren't even tell her about Caxton's complaints. The work is a strange mixture of what is crazy absurd touching tragic and funny. The hut has at least enabled her to get it down on paper, and she apparently feels a sufficient degree of security there to enable her to stay at large.

I hope you are still coming up,

F.S. [. . .]

[FS's three radio talks on Schreiner were broadcast in 1956. They were published for the first time in Conversation in a Train, *pp. 99–112. 'the upset with the Caxton Press': on 10 September 1955 Frame had written to Albion Wright at the Pegasus Press asking if he would read her manuscript. On 30 September, Dennis Donovan, the director of the Caxton Press, wrote to FS to say that he had learned 'confidentially of course, via the grape vine' that Frame had submitted work elsewhere: 'She is, of course, quite entitled to do so as she had no agreement with us. [. . .] However, what makes us mad when authors do this sort of thing is that we bring out the first work — handsomely and at a loss — while our competitors now will stand on our shoulders and approach the Literary Fund for a nice fat grant.' ATL MS-Papers-0432-190.]*

To Charles Brasch, *Dunedin*

Hocken Library

26 November 1955

Dear Charles,

[. . .] I [. . .] have in mind *An Open Letter to Richard Campion and Other Theatrical Producers*. Pocock's letter in the Listener should be followed up. It's monstrous that we should have our beginnings in prose and poetry, while theatrical 'editors' fall far short of Hoggard and his Arena. If I get this done I shall certainly try it on you. [. . .] [I]n the meantime Janet is a great problem. She can stay 'out' and write apparently, but not publish. She says now she is returning to hospital, but I have little idea what she will do. Nor do *I* know what to do. She depends on me a lot, but really I have little idea just how to deal with her. Her core obsessions become extremely trying, and they breed minor obsessions like rabbits in spring. The plain fact of the matter is that she is insane beyond all hope of recovery — terribly perplexing when most of the people walking the streets are worse cases than she is. [. . .]

Stead is in a most excited state. Apparently he has done brilliant papers which have completely rattled the faculty. His association with me did him no good during the year (as I warned him it wouldn't), and he has been so disliked that [Prof. Sydney] Musgrove neglected to advise him to apply for an Oxford scholarship, and now it is, or may be, too late. Now his extraordinary papers can't be got round, and there's the entire staff all aflutter wondering what can be done to make amends. And yet it may mean his being popped into the living tomb of the university at an early age.

Too dithery with work and worry for more,

F.S.

[The historian J.G.A. Pocock had written to the Listener *(18 November) decrying a production of* Virtue in Danger *directed by Richard Campion. 'It is time the [New Zealand] Players were spanked. They have fallen into a style which habitually [. . .] sets the display of theatrical cleverness above the performance of comedy and tragedy'.]*

To David Ballantyne, *London*

Alexander Turnbull Library

11 February 1956

Dear Dave,

Cucumber salad the other night troubled my belly, which must be either closely connected or identical with my conscience because I was thinking all the time of the the letters I haven't written you. [. . .] I expect you have been told that Janet Frame has been living since early last year in my army hut. A very intelligent girl, but quite crackers. Unfortunately her mental state causes her almost constant and I imagine quite acute suffering, so all in all not too pleasant for me. However she knocked off quite a long typescript last year which the Pegasus are bringing out — a very strange mixture of the absurd crazy funny pathetic and tragic. Her father was a railway engineer driver, and the family background Presbyterian plus Christadelphian. Two sisters drowned and her brother an epileptic. It's very strange that she can be so funny on paper, in patches at any rate. But at its best what she writes is extraordinarily beautiful. If she can only get launched on fresh work I'm in hopes she can be dissuaded from either suiciding or putting herself into the position of being returned to Hospital.

I haven't had much literary luck myself. Two plays, and I exhaust myself struggling with theatrical morons. However the missionary play (about Kendall) may go on with the help of Arthur Jackson Thomas this winter in a small way. If I can get the texts published I'll certainly send you a copy. For the rest it's just hack work to pay rates etc — but I have hopes of another play this year despite the low-grade intelligence of the theatrical types. Big compensation at moment is the garden and the summer. Also my widowed childless 17 stone 84 year old aunt has just had her third stroke in 12 months. I have paid her assiduous attention with garden produce and loving care during her periods of being laid aside. (It's worse for others — John Weeks' father has just had his 100th birthday. He looks like a garden gnome with rosy cheeks white hair and whiskers, and shoes that turn up at the toes. Wouldn't you think it would occur to John to spray him with liquid cement, trim and colour it when dry and put him in the garden?) [. . .]

Two to Looe,

F.S. [. . .]

[The political activist and editor Arthur Jackson-Thomas managed Auckland's Progressive Bookshop. Sargeson revisits the 'garden gnome' motif in 'Making Father Pay', 1975.]

To Charles Brasch, *Dunedin*

Hocken Library

[On 19 February Brasch had apologised for a 'long silence' following the death of his father, and sympathised with FS: 'It must be a great strain having Janet with you all the time, as well as a drain on your resources. [. . .] I send the enclosed to help with any necessities or emergencies. Please use it and forget it.' ATL MS-Papers-0432-147. Karl Stead had recently accepted a lectureship in English at the University of New England in Armidale, NSW.]

24 February 1956

Dear Charles,

Many thanks for your note. I knew nothing about your father, & do hope you aren't feeling it too severely — one's feelings about the death of a parent are enormously complicated.

I am tremendously worried about your kind help, but grateful too — everything is behind, even my Landfall subscription, & as I understand more & more about Janet I feel a blank despair. For a time I couldn't understand how she had escaped from the Hospital (that is, how she could be at large, *discharged*, though with certain reservations). The truth has emerged that her very remarkable intelligence prompted her to simulate sanity in order to get free — to give herself one last chance. But it is all turning out quite badly. She has literally no-one — except perhaps myself, but the emotional complications, closely tied up with her type of insanity, are at this present stage just no good for her at all. She has no where to go, except back to Hospital. The only possible alternative is to see if getting out of N.Z. will be of any benefit. I have encouraged her to save every penny she can, & I've been waiting to hear from [Louis] Johnson about the travelling fellowship proposed — but I think a straightout application for at least £200 should be made to the Lit. Com. immediately. I think Janet has about £30 saved up (I can bring myself to take only a pound from her each week, but she buys me all sorts of queer gifts continuously: she received £15 advance from Pegasus on her book), but her savings are liable to be dissipated at any moment on back-to-childhood frivolities (tied up with her mental condition). I reluctantly see now that for most of the time Hospital is the only answer — but the Hospitals as at present run are such abominations! I also see that anyone mentally ill needs the full-time attention of at least one other person — or rather a continuous stream of other people. There are times when one just can't listen any more — to fantastic misinterpretations, accounts of nightmares, & unceasing talk of death. The compensation is contact with a brilliant talent & intelligence — & how deceiving (but ominous to me now) an assumed facade can sometimes be! We went the other afternoon on a farewell expedition with the Steads, swimming under the cliffs away up the coast, on a perfect day, with nobody else about. But Janet, apparently enjoying herself, was collecting misinterpretations & minor traumas to last her for several days afterwards. There is nothing I can do — except push along an application to the Lit. Fund. If the money came to light, I think Janet would go off with at least temporary feelings of renewed hope — & a miracle might happen. If it didn't, & she met her death, or surrendered herself finally to those who are officially in charge of the incurably insane, at least she would have known for herself that the pain of living, somewhere in southern France, say, is not quite so severe as it can be too often in N.Z.

I spent weeks over the Schreiner, & got a good opening, but I can't get beyond that. You said, 'What journalism has to answer for!' — in connection with Robin Hyde. Well, my trouble is what radio journalism has to answer for in this instance. I'm afraid it is just no go — I dug a mental channel for myself, & all the best things got lost in side-pockets. I may take it up sometime in the future, but for the present you must rule it out. As alternatives I tried 2 short stories, but so far I'm not very hopeful of either — and my mind keeps on being taken up with ideas of another play — about the touring companies that used to come round with *Uncle Tom's Cabin* etc. Bruce Mason when he at last wrote thought I hadn't conceived of Kendall dramatically enough — but at present I'm not worrying as some people up here have been toying with the idea of having a shot at it.

Thanks for sending me the *Observers*. And excellent news about your galley proofs. I re-checked Maurice's for him, & the book [*Immanuel's Land: Stories*] will be quite a splendid & individual achievement, I think. There is no solution to their problem, yet they somehow manage: Barbara's mother is taking the Stead's flat, & since she is good at looking after the little boy, B. will perhaps be able to take up earning again. M. is reading his Voyages on the air & although I shudder to think what radio talking may do to him, I think I may be able to get him reviews to do on ZB — I am popular with them, as they always push work on to me at short notice, & always get what I hope is a competent script on deadline. If you are writing Courage do send him my best wishes — I intend to write him as soon as I have a moment.

Well, many thanks Charles — I was so constricted I felt I couldn't breathe — now I feel I've had a dose of oxygen.

F.S. [. . .]

To Denis Glover, *Wellington*

Alexander Turnbull Library

[Janet Frame had been contemplating leaving Esmonde Road at least since September 1955. FS encouraged her desire to travel. Glover was a member of the State Literary Fund advisory committee.]

25 February 1956

Dear Glover,

[. . .] In case I can persuade Janet to apply to the Literary Fund for money to get overseas, I want to set out for your private information something about her. To get out of New Zealand seems her last possible chance. She simulated sanity in order to get out of Hospital, but it's not working out. She can't bear to go on staying in the hut, but she has nowhere to go except that she would go overseas if the money was available. Lately she has been so hopelessly insane as to be quite unbearable. I never have a let-up — I have poured over me interminable accounts of the never-ending nightmare, including an infinite number of variations on her main theme, death, and its necessity for her. Everything I do or say is misinterpreted, and the misinterpretations go to feed her fantasy. An hour or so of apparent calm is a facade behind which is concealed the possibility of suicide at any moment. She could be put back in Hospital, but if this happens she will go deep in and never emerge again — and in any case she's so intuitive she could see it coming and avoid it by suicide. I don't believe anything would come of her going overseas except that in some way she would meet her death — but at least she might get one further considerable work written, and in addition understand for herself that, somewhere in the south of France, say, the pain of living is not at all times so severe as it frequently is in NZ — at least for her. Anyhow, there it is. If an application goes in, you can take my word for it, the Committee can give her one last chance to stretch her wings. The alternatives are incurable and very severe (and at last completely acknowledged) insanity — or suicide. [. . .]

F.S. [. . .]

[Glover's reply of 28 February, ATL MS-Papers-0432-167, provides the context for FS's letter of 3 March]:

Dear Sarge,

A most disturbing letter. It has worried me all day. After much thinking, I do not see any solution through the SLF. We all tend to lean too heavily on the Welfare State, while knowing very well that it is quite incapable, even with the best designed machinery, of dealing with any problem that is really real. £sd is its only, if its clumsiest answer.

Are you suggesting that J should be given a lot of money in order to jump overboard from a ship? That she should, like Robin Hyde, have enough of a pittance to afford a rented gas oven? That she should fetch up in Auvergne (with one or two ears) and do herself in where van Gogh once painted? And all this on the grounds that if the SLF doesn't make a grant it will happen sooner rather than later! I tell you, the machinery isn't designed for that sort of call on it — otherwise we would have every Louis K, and James K, and Ted K saying 'You gimme a grant or I'll jump off the wharf'.

I could show your letter to that grandly sympathetic little Sassenach IAG [Ian Gordon] if you hadn't been silly enough to have a poke at him on your own behalf, just above your signature. As it is, the grant for the novel [*Owls Do Cry*] comes up next meeting. Between ourselves (as all this *must* be) I got myself appointed reader, and have made my recommendation. There is no question of the publisher not getting what he asked for [. . .].

You must remember that I have only met J once, for five minutes, when she fled. I know little about her, though she has my anxious, sympathetic interest. Here are some of the things I should know further, if she is to merit my curiosity or your answer:

Apart from the intransigent sister in Ak, what is her family up to?

If she can be sane enough to bluff all the white-coated monsters of the Welfare Mental Homes, why can't she be sane enough to keep it up for a while with herself?

Does she get enough Social Security, or somesuch, to exist on?

Having found your monastic garden the ideal refuge, with all that personal freedom so sadly lacking in her life, why should she wish to quit it, unless to confide in others, while shunning them, the nightmares of her life?

Has she ever thought that an easy job (two of which she has had, to my knowledge) might pre-occupy her enough to keep her unhappy in a *tired* way?

If she is so unpredictable to you, why is it that [Glover's partner] Khura should find her so more than pleasantly rational, and that, while fleeing me like the devil, she should sally forth to the more than curmudgeonly Curnow's?

Have *you* perhaps been guilty of encouraging her in the notion that her writing is in some way of the most tremendous importance when in fact she has always preferred to tear it up, as she tells me she did her extraordinary poems?

Is she as selfishly egocentric as the rest of us, while looking for an emotional Gibraltar to shelter beneath?

I know too well that I am making a silly attempt at rationalizing the irrational, something only dimly within my ken [. . .]. And I wonder if in the goodness of your own heart (and your own belief in your own infallibility) you haven't involved yourself in something that is as terrifyingly large as J's introspections.

Jesus, once I was a simple sailor, with no problems but to stay awake and stay alive. And here were all these terrible things all the time.

I am just not capable of seeing an immediate solution. But I shall continue to worry at the problem. Meantime the great planets roll on in their courses, Venus veiled in mist, bloodshot Mars in apogee or perigee, Jupiter, far from jovial, hurling through the dark with small, pale moons. Sorry about the poetic conceit: let me know as much as you think I am capable of hoisting in.

D.G.

A silly letter, but I send it after all.

Poor girl: has she never had real & understanding love?

To Denis Glover, *Wellington*

Alexander Turnbull Library

3 March 1956

Dear Glover,

I have to write this immediately in reply to yours, because J. has sent off an application to the Secretary of the [SLF] Committee. I don't know exactly what was in it, but she had her own draft letter and my emendations to go on, and I expect what she would say is that she feels the need of widening her experience in order to develope her writing. I'm sure the request will be quite reasonable (actors musicians painters get travel grants on the same grounds). The only real point is whether the Fund Advisory committee can recommend that money be used in this way — needless to point out it has been so used in the past. On general grounds of talent and achievement J obviously has a good case. The special grounds are her desperate need of the miracle that might enable her to turn in the direction of sweetness and light, so far as any such thing is to be found within present social frameworks. I have absolutely no grounds for believing that any such miracle can happen in New Zealand, and only faint grounds that it might happen elsewhere. I should be very much against your showing any letter on the matter that I wrote to Ian Gordon. The Committee should know the exterior facts — ten years approximately in Mental Hospitals, and if necessary, have one or two medical certificates setting out present exterior facts, with a few observations — such as, that a complete change of environment would be very desirable. (I think with luck I could manage both certificates, though preferably, just one). For the rest, the Committee would have to take your word for it — and practically speaking, that means taking mine.

I don't know about my goodness of heart, and I am not infallible, but I will admit that when I first had a talk with J just a year ago, I was misled by the fact that she was discharged — with only the reservation that she undertook to return voluntarily if suicide again loomed as her only solution. (She has had four goes at suicide, one by hanging — and if you suppose I have only her information to go on, you are right. But you can if you like read two Pelicans — *To Define True Madness*, by a man called Yellowlees, and *Psychiatry Today*, by Derek Stanford-Clark, who also writes poetry. They confirm my observations that people afflicted as J is are truthful and reliable, and don't break promises if they can be induced to make them). But the suicide question is a side-issue. This girl according to the text-books is suffering from acute schizophrenia with paranoid and manic complications. Her morbid depression is a constant, with frequent dips into a state in which the hallucinations get quite out of bounds (I feel pretty sure that she is hallucinated aurally as well as visually — but she won't admit to the aural ones, mainly because she is well aware that they are the more serious. The aurally hallucinated receive commands which they must obey — and in the present instance, if J received a command that she was to bump me off she would have to obey — and I should have nothing and no one to blame except my goodness of heart and infallibility). A part of what I call her constant, however, is that she is never quite certain who she is or where she is. The reason for her avoiding people is that she can assume a personality, but it is a tremendous strain and impossible to maintain for more than a short time. The reaction can be devastating, but the assumed personality can deceive doctors and people such as Khura. You were misled by her being with me at Curnow's — in a year I have been able to persuade her to accompany me on a walk, with someone to visit in view, on only four occasions. The stay has to be short or she just disappears.

An easy job? — that's been tried. She has to assume a personality even to dry the dishes, and the result of the strain is exhaustion and an increase in depression. The suffering involved in being all in pieces is severe enough, the strain of having to pretend to gather yourself together can only be endured over very short stretches.

Her writing? It is the only therapeutic activity she has. I could give you dozens of instances of my observations. She temporarily rids herself of the nightmare by pinning it on paper. Completed sheets of paper have to be turned face down so the nightmare doesn't get up and walk again. Sheets of paper bound up or pinned together have to open cautiously and briefly, or the thing will get loose. A final burning is a few moments of delight — *that's* something dangerous and menacing which she has asserted her power over by sending up in smoke.

Her writing? She's undone by her brilliant intelligence combined with her frightening clarity of perception. If she was an intellectually mediocre zany scribbling away to amuse herself I should be sympathetic but only faintly interested. But she's so brilliantly acute she sees through every illusion until she becomes, paradoxically, the ultimate in blasphemy and heresy. She's a walking example of what happens when there are no gods to bear the burdens which human beings can't bear. She won't accept the illusions, and finds herself obliged to face up to emptiness and disorder. The problems the gods should be solving she attempts to solve herself. She's mad, as she must be — but the rest of us are blind if we don't see the intimations of love harmony order meaning and all the rest of it which she gets on to paper.

Practical points? Her family with the exception of her sister understand nothing about her. Her father is entirely convinced there isn't a thing wrong with her — but he consented to the Hospital's doing a brain operation — one of the main reasons for her deceiving the doctors and getting out. (I met some weeks ago the daughter of a lecturer in Dunedin Training College, who has had the operation: the result, reduced to the mental age of about 12, and the emotional age of about 4 — when out visiting she removes her false teeth to toy with them, and masturbates at the same time if she feels like it). J gets Social Security Sickness benefit of £3-15/- a week, and I'm not happy about the pound I take from her, but in present circumstances I'm compelled to. There is a sense in which it is true to say that J is a monster of egotism (I would suppose that all schizophrenics are) — the reason being that although the ego contracts, it also secretes layer upon layer of protective material, and the final effect is that the two things can't be distinguished from each other. This is only a guess of my own, but I imagine it gives a better idea of 'fragmentation' than one gets from the text books. Your 'emotional Gibraltar' implies something that is on the level of Birdlime Villa — which is just not the case. The last thing this girl is going to tell anyone is her 'soul-secrets'. Schizophrenics can communicate nothing which is of any importance to them, and emotional relationships are completely ruled out. J. indicates her awareness of her dependence on me for her food and shelter in various ways (mainly by buying me endless little, and often absurdly childish, gifts) but any feeling of security she may have is just another illusion which has to be destroyed. Her endless talk of her dreams and her obsessions is rather like having pushed under one's nose page after page of the most obscure and difficult modern poetry, with the demand that one should read it but make no attempt to discover its meaning. There is a wry comedy in the fact that in some of her worst states she can soundly defeat me in three games of chess one after the other.

Am I aiming at getting rid of this girl? She talked of getting out of NZ right from the start. She saved money from her Dunedin hotel job, but handed most of it over to her father who was apparently in some jam. I think she has at the moment somewhere about £30. The aim of getting out of NZ is the only aim which she has ever revealed which hasn't been 'insane'. She has on several occasions been packed up to go off somewhere within NZ, first assuming another name and without the faintest indication of location or direction. She knows that she has literally had NZ — there is nowhere to go, and nobody. There is Hospital — but she has had over one hundred shock treatments (which have destroyed large areas of her memory without any compensating benefit so far as one can tell), she has had one insulin treatment — and apart from treatment she has been confined for months at a time in refractory wards with people quite out of their minds, sometimes solitarily in a room of her own. She knows the whole business — 'punishment' violence (she has been dragged the length of the ward by her hair, and tried to scale walls studded with spikes). She has been described as the worst patient they have ever had to deal with in Seacliff. In theory she could go on living in the hut. I have stood a lot, and am prepared to stand a lot more. But she can't and won't stay. Why should the Committee dither over a few hundred pounds which would enable her to pull herself together, and make a more valid decision than she has any show of making in NZ? In addition, there would be the very good chance of another astonishing and beautiful book.

But here at last, and to wind up with, is my strongest card. You mention 'a lot of money'. What do you suppose is the average cost to the country of a Mental Hospital patient? — I believe the figure is somewhere about £14 a week — say £700 a year. Let's be conservative, and say that J. has already cost the country more than £5000. These people have a tough physical life — say she returns to Hospital and survives there until she's 70. That's going to cost the country a lot more than £20,000. Say she did manage to continue as things are — that's costing the country about £180 a year. So what in the name of hell or heaven is wrong with the Committee if they dither over doing a little simple book keeping on the country's behalf? One doesn't expect that any of them will remember their Karl Marx even if they have ever read it — but one at least expects them to be capable of simple arithmetic. Perhaps that was the secret of Joe Heenan's genius — he was capable of doing simple arithmetic.

Will you do your best? Be as plain downright and practical as you can — you can leave all the suffering to J, and a part of it, by proxy, to me.

F.S.

If you help Janet to survive you will eventually experience the exquisite delight of finding out (on paper) what she thinks of me!!!!

[On 7 March Glover told FS that his letter had given him 'a lot more knowledge, & therefore, I hope, insight'. He reported that the Committee had received Frame's application for £250 and that it was 'consistent with [his] own notion of the cmte's function, & with [his] own inclination' to support it. ATL MS-Papers-0432-167. The March meeting approved Albion Wright's request for £300 to support the publication of Owls Do Cry, *and deferred consideration of Frame's personal application until May.]*

To Charles Brasch, *Dunedin*

Hocken Library

[On 27 March Brasch told FS that he had seen Denis Glover in Wellington — '[he] talked to me about Janet & had hopes of a grant for her' — and expressed his own horror of hospitals and asylums in foreign countries: 'the language barrier can be so absolute'. ATL MS-Papers-0432-147.]

31 March 1956

Dear Charles,

Your note. Glover has been most helpful. A decision has been put off until the next meeting in May. Meantime Janet has to somehow stand up to an interview with Miss Loudon (ex Grammar School mistress, and a perfectly reasonable intelligent woman so Glover says). I think Janet can put up an excellent front with luck. She is very buoyed up at present over her prospects of getting away, and has even paid a deposit on a fare. The idea is to get her to Ibiza (where my friends the Goldwaters were for six months last year, and where she would be close to Keith Patterson and his wife). Living is very cheap in Spain, and if she liked the place she could stay long enough to get the run of the ropes in a totally different environment — God knows, a miracle might happen, and I pray that it may.

Meantime there are several tricky problems to be got round. Pegasus got the full sum asked for for her book, but since it was coming up at the same meeting, we thought it as well to keep the amount asked for personally on the low side — £250. Glover thinks more than this amount can be granted, and of course a considerable amount more is pretty necessary, what with fares up and costs generally. J. will probably amend her application to cover a larger sum before the meeting. Also, there's the need to bamboozle the passport people shipping agents etc. — besides, I'm afraid, Miss L. (The monthly medical certificate necessary to enable her to draw Sickness Benefit says she is suffering from 'schizophrenia', and the name may mean damnall, but I am unfortunately in a position to know that it covers a situation of appalling pain distress and uncertainty). However, I am trying to steer J through all the reefs. It may be necessary for her to drop the Benefit and take a hotel job — but I'd much rather she didn't have to screw herself up to the sticking point until she's on the point of embarking. She well knows she must maintain it until she's off the ship at the other end, otherwise she would no doubt be returned.

I agree about overseas institutions, but in the meantime she wants to have her fling. (I want her to have it too — which no doubt places me under the suspicion of wanting to rid myself of a burden — and something in it, too. But what else? And out of it may well come at least one more astonishing and beautiful book, perhaps of a somewhat different kind). If she breaks down it should be possible to get her back to New Zealand if she wants to come. [. . .]

I have been a little undone by the opening of a local National Library sponsored library — but I have requested all the plays of Claude Evans. I should know more about Kendall very shortly, also I'm trying to do a line with Allen Lane on the matter of reprints. I've had to abandon the attempts at the two stories as the new play seems to be opening out with some promise. I avidly tore into the new Landfall as usual. All *interesting*, and very grateful for Finlayson's fine story ['The Bulls']. How can I judge Lincoln Lee? — I used to know him so well 20 years ago. And the Lowry daughter's boy friend — [Alan] Roddick, can he really be so promising? Karl Stead writes me long letters from Armidale, very puzzled and uncertain. I shall send a note to Rodney on the boat — I could put him up if he cared to stay. The entire Coles are dividing themselves between here and the Duggans the coming week on the way to Indonesia.

Thanks for the interested and kind help with Janet, Charles,

F.S.

['my friends the Goldwaters': the Auckland architect John Goldwater and his wife Hinda. 'The new play': probably 'The Ugly Head' (aka 'Bacchae'), a play in 3 acts (1955–56), apparently abandoned. See ATL MS-Papers-0432-350.]

To William Plomer, *Sussex*

Alexander Turnbull Library

5 June 1956

Dear Plomer,

I have left your February letter so long I expect you are away in South Africa now. I do hope that at least you have a lot of sunshine and feel yourself thoroughly renewed by the break. I hope very much I may read somewhere, in the London Magazine perhaps, much about how SA struck you these days. My reading is very scrappy these troubling middle-aged days I'm passing through, but I have much admired a good deal of Doris Lessing. A New Zealander must, I think, besides admiring her verve and fluency, envy her hold upon a perpetual subject. Here we have our perpetual wowserism, but it is a very difficult and complicated subject to get a firm grasp on, and so much that is more obvious, such as what is called juvenile delinquency is just a lot of nonsense for the main part, and no true subject at all. Also, of course, Schreiner really started something in SA, and one can't say that Mansfield did anything like the same thing in NZ.

You asked about my plays, but nothing much has happened so far, and instead of bothering too much I'm plugging along with a third one. The details are much too boring — you would have a good idea of the bickering lack of intelligence and all the rest of it one meets in a small and scattered community. In any case for the past year I have been much preoccupied with looking after a schizophrenic girl who lives in my army hut. She has worn me down very severely, and at the moment I am trying to pick myself up on a diet of phenobarb and benzedrine while she is away for a short time — but she has written what I think is a remarkable book down my garden path, and there has been no difficulty in coaxing £300 out of the State Literary Fund in order to assist with its publication. You shall see it later on — uneven perhaps, but on the whole remarkably beautiful touching crazy, and (most remarkably of all) funny. Still, I can't go on looking after her indefinitely, and unless another sum can be coaxed to enable her to take a chance overseas, there seems nothing but the awful thought of her returning to Mental Hospital — and she has already had 10 years of that. But I have great hopes that the money may be granted.

Most interested in the visit you had from Isherwood. I did not greatly admire his World in the Evening — in fact I was disappointed, because what he was attempting seemed to me enormous but even so I expected he might have done better. Perhaps though I should take that back — the difficulties for all are so great, and we should be grateful for every brave honest attempt.

I have the notion that poetry may be a little on the upsurge in England — poets such as Larkin for example. When next you write I wonder if you would say whether Cape will look sympathetically at poetry. I have a young friend who recently won some American award (called the Borestone, I think) for undergraduate poetry from all English-speaking universities. He is no longer an undergraduate, having in fact a well-paid job at the University of New England (sounds most improbable, doesn't it?) at Armidale New South Wales, and the development in the poems he sends over to me I find quite a delight. Of course we both think you should call his collection Thorns in My Flesh, by Christian K. Stead (or perhaps C. Kristos Stead) and send to Faber and Faber. But he is in no hurry, and it would be kind if you would give some indication about the poetry publishing front.

A short time ago I tried Allen Lane with the suggestion he use my That Summer and I for One in a Penguin fiction book, but it appears they are very crowded — and indeed I can well understand they are under such pressure from authors agents and so on on the spot, one wouldn't have much show with a singlehanded shot from this distance. I don't worry much. How can I? — when an excellent young Lancashire bloke I have recently met, a new New Zealander, a very sincere Catholic and a promising carver and mural painter [probably Anthony Stones] has met with the most ignorant and bigoted refusals when he has suggested to the priests he do some decent work for the local churches.

I hope the English summer when you get back is a good one. Such inches of rain fall on my garden this winter a nice light shower of atomic dust would be a welcome change.

All my best as always,

F.S.

To Charles Brasch, *Dunedin*

Hocken Library

[Brasch wrote on 31 May asking for news of Frame's grant application, and offering financial help.]

13 June 1956

Dear Charles,

I should have answered your note. Yes, Glover sent me private word and now Janet has been notified of a grant of £300 — very good of course, and enough to enable her to set out but not nearly enough when money is so devalued. (A single fare £125, on one-class boat is monstrously high. That is six berth cabin too.) I don't know what to say about your kind offer. You might feel you could subsidize with whatever sum you could spare, and I fancy this is what Janet would prefer — yet I can't rid myself of the feeling that friendly helpful people should be kept in reserve perhaps, to help her out of the difficulties I am desperately fearful she will meet with. (How on earth she is going to hold herself together in one piece for the time of the boat journey is something I just can't imagine — and that's to mention only one of my fears). I really don't know what to say — I expect apart from all other points it's desperately stupid of me to allow myself to have been so completely worn down by my endeavours to cope with a situation which I've found much too difficult to explain. (In point of fact, I've had my first relaxation over the last fortnight since long before Christmas — I managed to get her off to my friend Miss Dawson in Mt Maunganui. But tension suddenly taken off was worse than tension continually on, and my inside must be rather like a chemist's lab with the modern drugs I've taken to try to pull myself round).

I must leave it to you I'm afraid. God knows how many you have helped (though I'm in no doubt about myself — what you have done for me). It's so difficult to know what is in Janet's mind — what she hopes for from this journey (she says she is leaving just before the end of July by the way) I haven't an inkling. But there's no doubt she needs help — sometimes I think of her as the hand coming out of the sea in one of Blake's drawings.

Of course I have done very little work, and got myself into an awkward situation over an invitation to speak at the school for playwrights recently held at Lower Hutt. I was in no mood to speak of the incidentals they insisted on, and they didn't want to hear me on the realities as I conceived them. The matter would have ended there if by some mistake they hadn't publicised me in the press as a lecturer quite a time after I had turned them down. To ease my smart over this I have arranged with [Radio] Talks to allow me to do two or three talks about indigenous theatre — and I'm hoping I can get quite a lot of my own back.

Have you heard that Dennis McEldowney's book about his return to the world [*The World Regained*] has been accepted by Chapman and Hall. Very splendid for him, and I am delighted.

I cling tenaciously to the notion I am really on to something big in my new play if I can only rise to it. But apart from the Janet business I can't work at it at the moment because I get terribly depressed by the notion that my ideas about trying to do something for NZ theatre were entirely mistaken. Karl Stead's lively and brilliant letters from Armidale cheer me almost more than anything — such a lively display of intelligence and grasp surely indicates that he is about to astonish us with really big things. (He mentioned by the way that Vance Palmer has noticed Hella Hofmann's Symposium in Meanjin — apparently the first mention. A review copy sent to Holcroft ages ago was not even listed in his acknowledgements).

Hope very much we see your Poems out soon — and soon I shall be forgetting my troubles while I welcome another Landfall.

Cheers,

F.S. [. . .]

To Charles Brasch, *Dunedin*

Hocken Library

[On 18 June Brasch told FS he was prepared to guarantee Janet Frame's return fare at any time, and also to be called on 'in an emergency'. 'I am enclosing two tenners for necessities before J. sets out and can send same again in about a fortnight; or does she need more?' ATL MS-Papers-0432-147.]

24 June 1956

Dear Charles,

Your letter with enclosures turned up — many thanks — and the money has been handed over to Janet as a gift from a well-wisher. She is naturally very grateful.

I will write again and let you know whether any more is really needed at this stage. And of course your offer to guarantee the return fare is infinitely kind.

Actually Charles I haven't a hope of expressing what I feel about the entire thing now it looks certain she will get away. I am caught in a cleft stick — the two incredibly old and primal factors of guilt and necessity have me by the knackers. I am in the grip of Original Sin as firmly as the first Son who bumped off the first Old Man. Her getting away is a necessity, but the guilt is chiefly mine if she doesn't survive — and I don't think she will. I can argue with her, but I haven't a hope in the world of breaking down the fantasy which controls her. She won't admit that anyone is responsible for her — hence she won't admit that much could be solved if she could find a few people in New Zealand in addition to myself, each of whom would take the responsibility of caring for her for say three months each year. I would gladly do my share — but she won't agree to accept my share, nor anyone else's.

There seems to me only one possibility. If her forthcoming book makes an impact, confirming that she has a brilliant talent — then the writers of New Zealand must try to do as much for her as has been done for such people as Ezra Pound and Kenneth Patchen. Nobody with a personal interest will ever persuade her to return to the prison which she conceives New Zealand to be — but it is just possible that an impersonal interest on the grounds of appreciation of craft might persuade her to accept the care she can't do without, but which she won't accept. Her notion that once she gets away from NZ she will at last become an entirely free and private individual is just madness — but it is a very necessary madness within the surrounding circumstances, and I am left to put up with my guilt as best I can.

Yes, I hear that [Blackwood] Paul is to publish the Pocock-Mason book and I should be glad of an opportunity to review. [*Theatre in danger: a correspondence between Bruce Mason and John Pocock.*] Bruce has recently sent me a lot of material of his — and it is all quite lively and interesting even though I think many of his ideas are mistaken. The texts of three short plays he sent me are a somewhat different matter — I would expect to find them rather embarrassing on the stage, but I may be quite wrong about this. There is no doubt he is lively and promising, but I can't decide whether he is writing down to a NZ audience, or whether he is genuinely writing at the level which comes naturally to him — and it is a little disturbing either way. But I do wish him all the best of good fortune, and great strides of development with fresh work.

I have got a ZB script off my mind, and am now starting on my theatre talks — and once they are done I shall return to my play in the hope that it may rebut one or two of Bruce's ideas if I can show myself good enough.

More before too long, Charles,

F.S.

Most interested to see your unpublished work in the Chapman-Bennett Anthology [*An Anthology of New Zealand Verse*, OUP 1956]. But what a pity the poems aren't numbered on the pages — one has to refer back to the index before looking up the sources. A very useful book, I think, but in talking about it I am not going to attempt to *review* it.

To Charles Brasch, *Dunedin*

Hocken Library

28 June 1956

Dear Charles,

Yes, it does seem that J. could do with the same again to set her up as well as can be hoped for for sailing. So far as I can make out, she won't have a great deal more than £200 by the time she is all ready. My position in it all grows more and more hopeless. She doesn't admit that I have any responsibility for her, or that her concerns concern me one scrap — but she makes a rather bad bargain in selling her radio, and now she is in bed with a most alarming reaction from being vaccinated for smallpox — this latter, I imagine, is related to the constant struggle I have always had to induce her to eat nourishing food in adequate quantities: she will readily eat fruit, but apart from that I fancy she would prefer to live on sweet and highly-coloured trash — probably part of her 'trouble': vilely attractive sticky stuff behind glass was out of her reach during childhood. (Something very New Zealand here perhaps: the NZ child with an imagination has no visual wonders of art — architecture carvings paintings — to feed on — and the visual imagination, not to be denied, fastens on all that is most highly coloured and fanciful in cakeshop windows).

It seems extraordinary that the Pegasus Press with its £300 grant to help with her book, can apparently only afford to advance her £20 on possible royalties. (This is private, of course). I have at last got under way with my theatre talks, and I intend to touch on what seems to me the heart of the problem — when there was private patronage, the patron was in no doubt as to the person to whom his help should be given. But now that patronage is transferred to the State, it is the executant rather than the creator who gets most of the benefit. For example, it is undreamed of that the potentially good playwright might need wider experience than the country has to offer, but it is granted that the actor and the producer should go overseas. (I don't mean this to refer to myself by the way — age and much else tells too heavily against me, but it is just blind thick-headed folly to suppose we can ever see the theatre we want to see develope, unless the emphasis can be shifted).

Well Charles, again I just have to leave it to you. I don't imagine you will be called upon once she is overseas — except perhaps for an advance in a case of hurry. Glover has indicated that if she will only keep in touch with the Committee and report progress, there is every chance of further help. It is the devil's own job to get promises out of her, but she is good at keeping promises if she can be induced to make them. In this case she has promised — and I don't think she's unaware of what the promise means: that the thread that holds her to NZ is not cut: that she will be enabled to come back to NZ if she wants to.

Tell Rodney I will write soon,

F.S.

[FS's two 'theatre talks', 'The Play and the Playwright', were broadcast in 1957. ATL MS-Papers-0432-408 and 409.]

To C.K. Stead, *Armidale, NSW*

Alexander Turnbull Library

30 June 1956

Dear Karl,

[. . .]The other night very late I walked down to the bus stop with Jowsey [Kevin Ireland], and on the way back got myself accosted by a police patrol car. Very severe cross-examination believe me — had I any explanation why I was out so late? They were finally a little dashed when I said I owned my own property and had lived on it for thirty years — so there was no need to play my Coronation Medal as a trump card. But the dossier will no doubt mention my beard ragged appearance etc (and no doubt fail to mention that during the cross-examination numerous thieves and perpetrators of violence were dashing by in fast and expensive cars). [. . .]

Janet is very much in a dither with her sailing date at the end of July. She should have about £250 in addition to her single fare. She has sold her radio, and on the whole it's a relief. I got the Penguin Matthew Arnold the other day, and want to take it in steadily without distraction. Also, some of the latest plays are really remarkable — Waiting for Godot, Cat On a Hot Tin Roof (no good play can be without the 'unorthodox' element apparently nowadays — but in this one it's handled not as a theme, but as one of many elements which go to the making of a theme — in other words, it's handled as it should be). Angus Wilson's The Mulberry Bush is interesting, but a novelist's play I think — hence has some warnings for myself.

Immediately I had the rejection from Lane the Caxton at last came to light with I For One — it looks surprisingly well in the small Landfall type, but has the absurdity of 1954 as date of publication in large type. The stupid bastards should know themselves well enough to be more cautious. I'm sending you over a copy — it's old hat, but it pleases me to send. A little gift from heaven dropped in the other day from Denmark — offer of £7 for An Affair of the Heart in Danish language anthology. Oh yes, one has one's little blessings descending on one! (Bastard — shut up talking crap!) [. . .]

Janet has had a most alarming reaction from smallpox vaccination — in bed with fever and *very* delirious. [. . .]

Really tender good thoughts about Kay, and best wishes,

F.S. [. . .]

[For Kevin Ireland's version of the late-night encounter with the police, see Speaking Frankly: The Frank Sargeson Memorial Lectures 2003–2010, *pp. 54–56.]*

To Charles Brasch, *Dunedin*

Hocken Library

[On 6 July Brasch had written saying he felt 'sad and rather bitter' about the Chapman-Bennett anthology. Where Curnow's 1945 A Book of New Zealand Verse *was one of 'real distinction — immeasurably the best anthology to have come from any British colony except the States' he felt the two recent Oxford anthologies had been 'blatantly commonplace and [. . .] ill-conceived'. ATL MS-Papers-0432-147.]*

9 July 1956

Dear Charles,

Thanks for your note, and the enclosures have again been handed on to Janet as an anonymous gift. She *does* seem quite embarrassed, but how much she knows or guesses I wouldn't like to say. I'm afraid one neither knows what goes on in her mind, nor what factual knowledge she has. It sounds a dreadful thing to say about anyone, but I have had to take extreme precautions with my papers, since she is compulsively impelled to investigate any piece of paper on which she suspects her name might appear. (The other morning I nearly died of bottled-up rage. I had broken open a letter from Stead and then gone to the bathroom — and when I returned after a minute or two I found she had glanced through the letter before I had read it myself. And yet I maintain despite such impossible conduct she is a very sweet girl, very civilized, and psychosis must be blamed for imperatives which can't be resisted and which are tied up with her generally hallucinated condition.) Yes, I'll tell you if she reveals that you have written to her personally.

Did you know that John Money is visiting NZ — I think in September.

I am surprised that you should feel that way about the Poetry book. What we need is a talk. I have felt mainly irritated by technical matters — the poems should be numbered — as it is one has to look back to the index first before referring to Sources. I hope indeed you didn't hear me talk about it on ZB — I let nobody know I was to, and I imagine very few people who might be interested were listening. (I know I was heard in Mt Eden gaol, since a friend of mine who was visiting a friend of his there told me that I was). But I am afraid I don't understand the basis of your approach to either the Poetry book or [Dan Davin's] book of stories. Landfall is one thing, and you can't possibly be in any doubt about my admiration for it and you — and what you have done. But it is only one possible approach to the future. The rough edges and rawness etc of say Arena is another, and I read it with great interest. I don't agree when I hear the very youngest people speak with distain of what they call the Landfall kind of poetry or story, but because the future can't be foreknown, and vitality is the basis of all we hope for, I try not to be unresponsive to vitality wherever it seems to be present. So on this basis, it seems I can't agree with you. For example, I believe very firmly that no finer poetry has been written by a New Zealander than R.A.K. Mason's best — and Chapman and Bennett have provided quite a good selection. But I should understand your point of view better if we had a talk.

No more just now — and all inadequate to say how helpful you have been,

F.S.

To Christine Cole and family, *Indonesia*

Alexander Turnbull Library

10 July 1956

Dearest Chris Sarah Jane and Martin,

I've been so long in writing, but thanks to Chris for her long and lively letter. It is strange how I seem to have been reading bits about Java since you have been there — I suppose I overlooked them before, not having the Cole family to attract my attention to the strange and distant place. Anyhow, after you had told me of vegetables like Jack's beanstalk, I read the other day that if you are a gardener you plant any old time, because there is so little difference between spring summer autumn and winter. Well, how different from Takapuna! I am trying to get the digging done for my potatoes. If I don't get them in by the end of this month it will be too hot and dry for them later on — but it is so difficult at present because the ground is stone cold, and wetter than I have ever known it. A miserable winter indeed, and poor Janet has to go off to her hut through a quagmire.

It will be a wonderful release for me when Janet goes to Wellington in about another ten days to begin her voyage, but with the tension suddenly taken off I expect I shall need about a fortnight to recover. Professor Gordon has come to light with an invitation to do three lectures at Victoria for an inclusive fee of £50 — but I have countered with the suggestion he pay £50 for just one — just good old fashioned Dada. And I am offering him a very cheap rate as I shall have to share with an assistant whom I shall need to take charge of the rabbits or whatever else I decide on to make the thing really go. I shall appear as the Wizard of the Esmond, in long white beard and my little woollen cap. I shall wear the enormous pullover Janet has knitted for me and have my trousers tucked inside my socks. I shall wear my gardening boots. I shall have with me a number of pictures objects etc taken from about the house, and from time to time will leave off talking to arrange and re-arrange these into some very obscene juxtapositions. Most of the talk will consist of quotation from the Medical section of Pears Encyclopaedia, particularly the one under the heading, 'Exercise' — if you have never struck that gem I highly recommend it. Alternatively, I've proposed that I should be paid £150 for three lectures to be delivered in 1958, and they can pay me the £50 on account now. Oh, well, well! And alas, I hardly expect to see the colour of their money.

Very remiss of me, but I haven't yet sent you off a bundle of books etc. Davin's new novel [*The Sullen Bell*] has turned up, and I have read it with absorbed attention and interest whoever else has. Also, Thomas Mann's Confessions of Felix Krull is good fun in spite of a few Germanic longeurs. But mainly I have had to be a general factotum nursemaid etc. to all and sundry. Dear old Jim next door got bad with his chest five weeks ago and looked obviously as though dying. A damned puppy of a doctor came regularly and looked at him from the neck up and pumped him full of antibotics. I used to sit on his bed and ask him about his bowels etc, but he was so uninterested it seemed better to let him be if he had decided to die. But last weekend I discerned a spark of interest and persuaded him to let me investigate his bed. Dear oh dear — I found I had a very dirty job on my hands. He'd done very little in five weeks, but what he'd done he'd done just there. So I set to work with an improvised enema first using my finger as a hook to get things started. And what I finally got would surprise you. Within 12 hours of the clean-up he had definitely decided to live and was taking beef tea and everything else I feed him. Today I have walked him up and down his room and he'll shortly be right and in his best nick. I could ring that damned doctor's neck. Maybe his antibotics did help, but it was what we call life that decided it wasn't defeated and played the winning card that did the trick. And why the hell should the doctor do his stuff and completely ignore the fact that the complementary nursing stuff was completely absent?

I wonder, considering that dear daddy Cole and me have our perpetual seesaw about the merits of the American way of life — I wonder whether he has seen about a book called The Power Elite, by C. Wright Mills, said to be the angriest attack on the American set-up since Veblen's Theory of the Leisure Class. Lately too there has been some extraordinary stuff about the French worker priest movement. But what I thought really funny was the report by the Church of England Moral Welfare Committee on sexual affairs. The Committee (chaired by a bishop) suggests the age of consent in hs [homosexual] matters be 17! Well, maybe, and perhaps I am surprised only because adolescents of either sex don't happen to be my cup of tea. But could that Bishop be say 65 — could he be reckoning say on still having a few shots in the locker in another five years — and could he at the moment have his eye on a cherub aged 12? But there you are, I have a deplorably horrid mind.

No more dear Chris. Of course *all* this letter is supposed to be read aloud to your children. I expect Edward in Children of the NF [*New Forest*] is very vieux jeu with Sarah now. I do really hope to post off some books and papers soon, but if I don't forgive me. Like you I need a secretary and housekeeper.

With love,

Frank

To E.P. Dawson, *Mt Maunganui*

Hocken Library

18 July 1956

Dear Peter,

I have been meaning to write as usual. I have to say officially that Janet had no foundation for saying that Charles had helped financially — so will you please if possible just forget that she ever said any such thing. Apart from that though, it is extremely kind of you to help her, particularly as I am positive you have helped far beyond what you can really afford. Charles sent on your fiver and added £7 of his own bringing the cheque up to £12. Janet was a little embarrassed, but I think she wrote him off a polite note. Apparently he didn't feel like writing her again, so he sent me your second fiver which I have handed on to her as an anonymous donation. You have only my good faith to depend on for that, but I have had a few other sums to hand on, and although it is a little embarrassing to be trusted so completely — well, it would be like robbing the church poor box wouldn't it? Please don't let your generosity run away with you any further, at least not just now, because I have a notion that it would be very bad to have too many contributors doing their bit at the start, when the testing time will come in the future.

Yes, I expect a lot of the worry is my own creation, and I agree that she has a great deal of wisdom — a very great deal. But that doesn't alter the fact that insanity is terrifying to anyone who is not afflicted the same way (one of the certainties I have got out of the past year is that no matter how neurotic I am, I am nevertheless not psychotic), and no layman can be expected to cope with it except in short doses from time to time. Part of the trouble is that I am one of the very few people (apart from the white-coated Mental Hospital guardians of the welfare State) who fully knows J's appalling situation — I expect she needs possibly just one or two. But the result is she feels a perfect ambivalence of love and hate towards me. I wish I could agree with you about convalescing etc., but when I remember last Christmas I shiver. (The Christmas season is a notoriously bad time for schizophrenics, emotional memories of family security etc.) Right back in January I used to sit and tell myself I couldn't stand things one more minute, and Pat Hitchings the doctor, although he can be very tiresome, is no fool. He argued that there are times when the Hospital is literally the only answer and although I was forced to agree with him I did keep on reiterating a NO! And what was my position in the matter? Most ambiguous, and yet the whole of the responsibility was mine. I could not have conceived then that I could last out until now — and yet I am still going. Until the last day I must endure the nightmares the screamings the threats the fantastic misinterpretations (which can sometimes be so uncannily right on the nail). I must try to accept the communication which indicates that the fantasy, temporarily checked at one point, is blossoming like some poisonous flower at another. (But of course it occurs to me that you know all this from your experience of your sister — and I don't know what stops you from sitting down and cursing any possible Creator any more than I know what stops myself). [. . .] However, Janet now says she leaves for Wellington on Friday — I don't know whether this date will be stuck to. [. . .]

Well, Peter, this is a moan and groan. I expect I'm just complaining about what turns up in life willy-nilly. However. And I hope eventually to be feeling better as no doubt everybody does when balled-up.

Salud,

F.S.

To E.P. Dawson, *Mt Maunganui*

Hocken Library

26 July 1956

Dear Peter,

Your second letter today and I must try to cope. Last weekend was a nightmare. Janet couldn't eat anything Thursday evening and began vomiting. On Friday she was very ill with high temperature (I thought — psychosomatic — she doesn't really want to go) — and the doctor I had to get was a stranger (Pat Hitchings never turns up now no matter how often he's rung) who suspected from the setup and J's symptoms that she and I had been up to one of those backstreet jobs. He said gastric flu — which meant soup and barley water which she wouldn't take (at least only in mouthfuls) endless hot water bottles and codeine tablets (which she was fully prepared to eat in handfuls like lollies). Saturday it flooded and I was up and down to the hut ankle deep in mud and water — until she finally established herself in the living room. By Sunday I had become hysterical so had to get drunk and go out and leave her. On Monday she got up though obviously still very sick and weak. I went down to Devonport for her sleeper ticket, but she wouldn't go unless she had a bottom berth, which luckily she had. I haven't heard since. I expect she's still alive, but with the meeting with her father coming on top if it all the chances of catching the boat suicide or Porirua [psychiatric hospital] are I should say somewhere about even.

Write me off in the meantime Peter. I had thought of getting Una to take a trip down in the car and take me too. But Una would be much too great a strain at the moment. I haven't relaxed yet — that would be too dangerous meantime. Instead I've cleaned out the house (a kind of purging of all the filth that strain has made me much too conscious of in my soul) and soon I start on the hut. I hope eventually to drift into getting started on my theatre talks and thinking of myself as a writer again. On top of all has come news that my mother has had a stroke. Also I'm still faced with the task of doing my share towards straightening out J's proofs [of *Owls Do Cry*].

I expect by the end of next week I'll be feeling better and I'll write then.

Yours,

F.S.

To Charles Brasch, *Dunedin*

Hocken Library

4 August 1956

Dear Charles,

[. . .] I can't so far pick myself up from the last shattering weekend that Janet was here. She collapsed (with flu, so the doctor said, but my head was in a whirl with imaginings of dark psychosomatic symptoms) and couldn't make the trip to Wellington that she had booked for. Luckily she was allowing herself plenty of time, and she was got into a sleeper still ill and very weak a few days later. I know she reached Wellington, but I have no definite evidence that she was on the boat last Tuesday.

Left behind with me I have a copy of her typescript novel (the galley proofs are all done now), a few poems (one of which I think she may have sent you) which I managed to hedge over when she demanded them back from me — also a few odds and ends of prose which I also managed to keep. I think she had completed another long work (about 30,000 words I think), but I was never allowed to catch sight of it and I have no idea what she has done with it. Also I have a few photographs of her and the family when she was a child, and one 'studio' portrait which is the usual awful NZ thing (taken I think about 2 years ago), but if cut to the shoulders and head it at least provides some record of her (interestingly enough, it catches the more masculine side of her, and something of the 'madness' too). In my present mood I can't believe that NZ will ever see her again, but I am still wrung by torment over what she suffers — not to mention the torment over my own failures too often to cope and do my best for her, even though superhuman qualities which I don't possess were obviously required. [. . .]

Best wishes, Charles,

F.S.

['another long work': probably 'Uncle Pylades', referred to in the next letter.]

To Janet Frame, *London*

Private collection

7 September 1956

Dear Janet,

Very good to hear from you from Panama, and now again (today) from London. I was very upset over your illness — but who knows what that Psyche of yours was up to? If I had been a Cynic, which of course I am not, I would have said to myself, Well, one should never worry about our Janet, because she will always contrive to fall on her back. (But of course such a thought never occurred to me).

I'm reckoning on your finding a lot in London worth nosing out — and provided the money doesn't go too fast, you'll enjoy yourself more if you don't worry about spending it even at the rate it goes — because, well, because I have lately finished off the page proofs (what a job it was before I had finally decided I had done everything I could do) and I should think Albion Wright won't be too long in getting it out, (though I believe there *is* a horrid bottleneck in binding at present) and with luck then it won't be long before more money is due to you. But what I really want to say is this — if at the distance you are, you can get over your reluctance to let your stuff out, then if the present book is what is known as a success, you should think seriously soon of putting your next typescript to Albion, because it with luck will mean more money for you. What is your new typescript called — Uncle Pylades — well, don't allow yourself to judge of its merits — pile it on to Albion pretty soon, or me at any rate. Where is it located by the way? I mean have you the text with you, or have you left it behind?

I am just posting off to Wellington my two theatre talks, and the first silkworms have hatched — luckily I set some young mulberry trees, and they have budded in time to give them a start. Your father turned up one Sunday morning with June when Nigel Cook was here. A crowd of us, and your father did nearly all the talking — Nigel and I fed him railway questions, and poor June had to sit bored while N. and I listened with much interest to the language of the biscuit. You never got mentioned (come now, aren't you disappointed?)

No word from John Money yet. My mother has recovered from her stroke, but is more difficult than ever. As against that some wretched quack over in town has told Harry that he seems to be suffering from cancer of the spine.

I shall be looking forward to any little notes you send me, and wonderful if everything works out. Your story not in Listener yet — and if you can bear to let it out, remember a great deal you might write without too much strain would be likely to get you money. Don't on any account tell the Pegasus Press you want any sort of acknowledgements to me, because to some readers there will be already some relation between the book and some of my own work (we must have been in touch with the same Arch-types).

Now that's all dearie this time — I'm tired out. Chin up and cheers as Harry always says (though he's taken his doctor's news rather sorely, I'm afraid).

From,

Aunt Sannie

Good God, do those dray horses still clump around London? They used to be driven by muffled up old men with beards — very like me now.

[Aunt Sannie: the owner of the farm in Olive Schreiner's Story of an African Farm. *Frame worked on 'Uncle Pylades' in Ibiza and later in London, but in March 1958 she told Albion Wright that the novel was 'not satisfactory enough for publication'. It remained unpublished in her lifetime. King,* Wrestling with the Angel, *p. 190.]*

To Dan Davin, *Oxford*

Alexander Turnbull Library

9 September 1956

Dear Dan,

[. . .] Janet is now in London, and got there by going all the way in the ship's hospital. Christ knows whether she'll survive, but Providence looks after its own, and she couldn't be so profoundly wise if she wasn't one of God's children specially in favour. She knows perfectly well where you and Winnie are, but it's probably very unlikely she'll get in touch. But if she does, she's one of the rarest people — a South Island railway enginedriver's daughter by the way. A fuzz of reddish hair fresh Scottish complexion if you ever see her approaching over the horizon. As soon as a copy of her book is available I'll send you a copy — it's just possible it may be taken up in England, I don't know, I've been much too close to it to assess it accurately. There's genius in it but whether too thinly spread I wouldn't know. [. . .]

Well, spring thank God, the silkworms have hatched with the first mulberry leaves — my fifty fourth spring — I feel old and cranky, my beard is snow white, and I can't get the nicotine off my moustache — just a dirty old man, and some quack has told my best friend he has cancer of the spine. I reach for St Thomas, The Little Flowers, the Sayings of the Buddha, and the Gitas. [. . .]

Nevertheless blessings,

F.S.

To Denis Glover, *Wellington*

Alexander Turnbull Library

[On 11 September Glover reported the silkworms FS had sent him had hatched, and were feeding happily on lettuce. 'The healthiest of the dear wee wrigglers is of course called Frank. The one that seems to spurn lettuce and sets off madly to get out of the box, somehow, anyhow, is naturally Janet'. ATL MS-Papers-0432-167.]

21 September 1956

Dear D,

Down on the farm there was an old faggot nearby who got hauled up in the police court because she presented a loaded gun at a neighbour — and all because that neighbour had had the cheek to name a cow after her. So be careful — but I hope you are more of a sericulturist than I am. Most of the young caterpillars die. It may be the foliage, or it may be the pebrine disease, or something more mysterious. However, I am now bringing my biggest and best batch of eggs out from my neighbour's fridg — so I can let you have replacements if you have had no luck.

J now has a young negro boyfriend — a law student from the West Indies. Possibly his roving hand is licensed — I wouldn't know. But her letters are remarkable, because she apparently has no trouble in making them read just like her Works. When writing from Petone, before she sailed, after hoping that I had cleaned from my memory's teeth the unpalatable meal of her once served daily, she went on, 'a witch lives in this house — my aunt who has a cruel weapon used in secret or openly by all people, an instrument to snip and kill each blade of grass which dares to stray from the green conformity called lawn or Average'. Just before Panama, she 'passed the Galapagos with Brown dying on Resolution, and the sea was a Blakeian waste ridged and grey like the face of the moon, and white with the raised arms of the nearly drowned'. But by the time she had reached London, she had to 'confess that if the voyage had lasted a few days longer, I'd have been confined to some dim psychiatric ward, in a permanent delirium of rock and roll. Pacific Caribbean Atlantic were all very calm, but any fool knows that they are not the Real Seas'.

Truly a brilliant young woman!

[. . .] Maurice [Duggan]'s book [*Immanuel's Land: Stories*] is quite an achievement — his sun is definitely rising, and more of the public adore the sun rising than the sun setting. Let's note that, take heart, and make our twilight gracious. But M has also written a remarkable thing in the last School Journal — a kind of fairy story (really about death) called Falter Tom and the Water Boy. (I suggested Merboy, but this was coldly received.) Take a look at this if you can lay your hands on it — it's quite unique in this country, and would probably stand up to anything like it anywhere.

I expect you have sent your burnous to be dry-cleaned, and have inquired from the Admiralty whether ships of the desert will be manned for the forthcoming [Suez] campaign. And by the way — prithee tell me why you referred to Professor Gordon as a Sassanach in a note some time back. I am reminded, because I note from De Quincey that the Welsh also called an Englishman a Sassanach (a Saxon), in his day. Could you possibly mean that G is a lowland Scot and therefore Anglo-Saxon? No, it is too puzzling. But since you once dispatched a telegram in Old English you should be scholar enough to clear the matter up. How is your Greek these days? Mine is coming along.

F.S.

To Kay and Karl Stead, *Armidale, NSW*

Alexander Turnbull Library

11 November 1956

Dear K-K,

I've been a long time getting round to a note after your excellent letter. (Various little troubles — and while lying on my back I have listened to the amazing rain destroying my early tomatoes. But the rain-loving crops such as peas have been marvellous. I've also got away with an excellent crop of spuds). [. . .]

For quite a time I was more puzzled than anything else about your poem ['Whether the Will is Free'.] I tried it for sound, and could agree with you (with the exception of slug-blood, which I'm still doubtful about), then meaning and struck more difficulties there. Then one evening Jowsey asked what it was lying on my bench and I showed it to him. Read on and you'll pardon me — he thought it terrific. I asked him about the girl's doved hand which had worried me, and he said that was one of the best bits. 'Of course,' he said, looking at me as one who grew up last century, 'it's very modern'. All this interested me no end. And by the way I've seen the second of the two poems you sent for their under thirties — very good, I had no trouble with that. They also showed me all the material for the under thirties — and it looks as though it might turn out a remarkable collection. A monstrously long story by Shadbolt — with crap in it, besides patches of very fruity prose, yet demonstrating a formidable talent which hasn't yet completely found itself. Two interesting stories by Maurice Gee (they brought him over, and I was surprised and disturbed — obviously balled up in difficult neurotic problems. A very different kettle of fish from Jowsey, who may eventually turn out to be psychotic, but is not neurotic — but write this off as just balls if you like) also some interesting verse. (Also, I forgot, a very good story by Jacquie Baxter). One or two pieces of the verse had quite a 'camp' flavour — particularly a few stanzas by [Conrad] Bollinger.

Have you heard the gossip about Fairburn? He was suddenly shot into hospital to have a kidney removed with a hulking great malignant tumour attached. I find this truly awful. I mean after all these years of being Fairburnius Arbiter and bashing people for the unhealthy colour of their hair etc etc. One should not be a giant of health and righteousness and be caught out in this way. He's been having some sort of ray treatment after the operation — naturally one hopes for the best, but it's difficult to conceive the size of the psychological shock he must have had.

The Chinese opera is worth seeing — I mean the best of it, some of it is I fear flossied up for Western audiences and rather Hollywood. But the mime and the acrobatics are wonderful. They gave a wow of a party on stage the final night — packed with poets musicians painters leftists trade unionists Maoris and the Chinese community. Quite a change from the usual Remuera-Chamber of Commerce-Rotary Club turn-out. I was there with Una Platts who refused to drive round the harbour, so we had to catch the last vehicle ferry and leave much sucking pig etc unconsumed (but even so I had the worst headache next day for years). The girls and the young men by the way were just as good to look at at close quarters as in the show — what uncouth barbarians we are by contrast (except of course the beautiful K2 or K1 — I don't know the order you place yourselves in within the family). [. . .]

Janet's book will be out before Christmas, and I will send a copy as promised. In her last letter she enclosed a lively photograph and said she was just off to Ibiza. She has dropped her negro boyfriend because he had 'wicked hands', and she didn't want curly-headed pickaninnies bobbing up right and left.

I expect you are all balled up with exam papers — bad for writing no doubt. [. . .] The first silkworm has spun — and my play inches forward — but what I am trying to make it do is so vast I feel quite overpowered and unable to rise to the occasion. Still, I watch a drab-looking caterpillar manage its cocoon — and I am encouraged. [. . .]

Broodily but affectionately,

F.S. [. . .]

[The 'under thirties' anthology was the working title of an ill-fated collection planned by Maurice Shadbolt and Kevin Ireland, 'hatched in Somerville's coffee bar, with the approval and enthusiastic support of a penniless and heavily indebted Bob Lowry'. It was to have included work by Fleur Adcock, Conrad Bollinger, Jacquie Baxter, Marilyn Duckworth, Maurice Gee, Philip Mincher, C.K. Stead and others. 'It was to be a kind of 1950s echo of Speaking for Ourselves, *a kind of* New Directions. *However, the Lowry factor undid everything, Maurice S took off for England in 1958, and I followed a year later'. Kevin Ireland, personal correspondence, 7 May 2011.]*

To Janet Frame, *Ibiza*

Private collection

[Janet Frame left London on 31 October but lost most of her luggage, including her typewriter, in transit through Paris. Cristina Droescher and Keith ('Spud') Patterson met her at the railway station in Barcelona, and she caught the ferry for Ibiza the

following day. Greville Texidor, Werner Droesher, Cristina and Keith were all living in or near Barcelona at the time.]

27 November 1956

Dear J,

Your second letter from Ibiza this morning — I hesitated to reply to the first as I wasn't sure if mail should still go through the London Bank. Please be always sure about addresses.

Well, love, too bad about the luggage. Have you appealed to Spud to help you try to recover it — or Greville and Werner? Greville is just as nice as Cristina, and Werner is always very efficient organisational and helpful — being a German. Main thing though is not to worry if you can help it. I am beginning right away to rustle up some more money for you. Albion Wright [at the Pegasus Press] can probably be touched again now, and I shall be getting in touch with Glover about the £500 annual scholarship which has just been added to the State Literary Fund. I can think of three people who should be the first three to have it, you Maurice [Shadbolt] and Karl Stead. Also it eases my mind that Charles Brasch will be leaving for England at the end of February for a six months visit to England. And I have already asked him to act as a kind of clearing house to help with any arrangements that can be made on your behalf. One last point — you say you have £50 worth of pesetas, but if you do your stuff (Werner again would be a great help) I don't imagine you would have much difficulty in getting more. If you don't recover your luggage I should think the best for you to do would be to renew your clothes etc. and try to get a second hand typewriter — and not worry about the money you spend, as some more money can almost certainly be rustled up for you early next year at the latest.

Now, do you feel a little reassured? And I do hope at the distance the apparitions don't attach themselves to me and turn me into a monster. (Pity a camera hasn't been invented that would catch that appearance of me — I should be most interested).

Do you want your six presentation copies [of *Owls Do Cry*] sent on to you? If not, how many? To save you postage I could send off to the friends you wanted to give them to on your behalf. Albion is giving me 6 copies too as a reward for my assistance — and these I will send to such figures as Plomer Lehmann Davin Merrill Moore etc. in the hope there may be offers, and hence an income for you, from English and American publishers. I assume the airmail letter cards don't operate in Spain — so writing is costly. But a good excuse for you to lay off letters.

If you can bring yourself to the point of handing over to me such things as *Uncle Pylades* and just forgetting about them yourself, that would be very good. Nobody is questioning your good taste and sense on literary matters, but I see no harm in your admitting that you are not the one to decide about what you write yourself — apart from the squalid truth that money-spinners might be just lying idle.

Nice to hear about Caterina etc. Surely it makes you feel almost for the first time that you are accepted and at home.

The sensation here is that the preposterously healthy gigantic basher of all 'unhealthy' people — namely Fairburn, has been rushed into hospital to have a wickedly cancerized kidney removed. Unless a miracle happens he's got from one to three years more. It's awful to think what a shock it must have been to him. Some of us dimly feel we are subject to the universal death sentence — but I doubt whether F has ever really felt so, except perhaps on paper. I have myself lately been inhibited from walking and Una had to drive me over to hospital to have one knee and both feet Xrayed. However it turns out to be merely 'early degenerative lipping and bilateral Hallux Valgus' — and I am no wiser as Pears' Cyclopaedia is not at all helpful. But I infer that in 20 years time I shall inhabit a bath chair.

But (oh joy) my play goes, and is now half done. I think I told you I came 6th in the Invercargill Competition — the rest all writing club women except one man who hires theatrical wigs in Wellington. It's my plays or nothing — I think of the Roof with horror. June and Wilson [Frame's sister and her husband] brought George [Frame's brother] to see me — quite impressive poor fellow with his strong-cut features, and J. and W. were obviously giving him hell. Sorry he's tracking you up, but I don't imagine you'll have much difficulty in keeping out of his reach. Your appreciation of oil and olives marks the difference between then and now. But you don't say anything about the vino, and you should be drinking at least a quart of that a day.

All my love, ducky,

F.S.

['Caterina etc': one of the two peasant women (Catalina and Francesca) who made Frame welcome in Ibiza. 'bilateral Hallux Valgus': bunions.]

To Karl and Kay Stead, *Armidale, NSW*

Alexander Turnbull Library

22 January 1957

Dear Karl and Kay,

[. . .] Janet's mishap has been largely cleared up. She had to pay £15 in freight agents' charges etc on recovery of her luggage, but more pesetas have been got to her, and with luck she'll be at Ibiza until end of April. She says that before that she will have a new long book finished ['Uncle Pylades'], and it sounds very promising from what she says. (It's about a member of parliament with a stain inside his hat — I hope a very shocking and deplorable one; and people who shop with cardboard boxes and buy blood). It's amazing how well she contrives to fall on her feet (her back of course, when that brings better results). Her landlord is apparently a positive angel — called Fermin. (That name sounded Moorish, and prompted me into hurrying on with Gibbon, and it's been hard to unglue my eyes from the marvellous chapters about the Arab conquests over the last few weeks — I mean the last few weeks of reading, not Nasser). Fermin is a middle-aged fairy (if you and Kay giggle over that I don't mind) who plays his violin in cafes and at weddings, and when not practising or cleaning his bicycle shows J photos of his *amigos* and teaches her Spanish (since she's spoken to no English-speaking people since she's been there she's now no doubt Spanish speaking, though probably in the Mallorquin dialect). There's also Jose, Fermin's nephew, (nepotism?) who is a law student at Valencia university, and he must be quite bright, because when J asked him why he never learned English at school, he asked why didn't she learn Japanese at her school. Anyhow, although she insists she is not in good shape mentally (all this means is that the schizophrenic country of lit-upness is too vivid and glaring and shadowless and menacing to be easily endured very often), she feels herself at home among intelligently human Latins. Two elderly servants, Catalina and Francesca, bed-sisters, because their husbands are dead, are devoted to her. Out on the hills she sometimes meets an elderly bearded unbuttoner, but as she says, where else would you find an old unbuttoner sitting in the sun and reading *Los Quartos Evangelios*? — that's to say, not just as an alibi while waiting for a seducee to turn up. Unfortunately Pegasus won't have her book out until the end of March, but it doesn't matter much if she's hard at work, with eating lodging and privacy costing only £2 a week. You two must think over all this. It might be the alternative to Oxford, and Janet can no doubt tell you a lot about the ropes if you get in touch with her over there.

I read a few pages of the Patrick White [*The Tree of Man*] just before Christmas. Could easily see it was something new for the Aussies, but couldn't see how he was going to keep it up — then Jess Whitworth who is mad on all things Australian borrowed it. It has just been returned, and I am impatient to begin again. Thanks very much, I'll let you know later.

Shadbolt came during the holidays with his wife — she is Aussie, and I think a little dissatisfied with S's marital performances. (She had some rather severe cracks at him before company). Apparently he saves nearly everything for his writing. He wants praise, but I could only say I felt he has a massive potential talent about which I would prefer to say nothing at this stage. I think you are pretty right. He must develope all round — but this crude stage promises much for the future. He's better at set scenes than narrative. He must learn how to write — avoid borrowed expressions and make every sentence tell — I suggested he read Defoe and Swift. But of course if he does big books clumsiness mightn't matter — it doesn't with Dostoevsky, or Thomas Wolfe even. He's something to be reckoned with (as I thought from very near the beginning), but I don't imagine he'll ever be very much my cup of tea. Jowsey is quite a different proposition. He stayed in my hut over the holidays. He's much more developed than Shadbolt and much more complex — but he definitely has something of Janet's trouble about him. With a beard he has grown he is extraordinarily good-looking (apparently without the beard he has for years been pestered by pederasts), but so far (as he is acutely conscious) he has found himself inhibited from all emotional relationships, and fear of not being able to achieve a climax in his sensual relationships (with women) is a great worry to him. I shouldn't be telling you this — but I have been very touched by his delicacy and his extraordinary generosity towards many people. (Fortunately he doesn't stir my senses — at least only a very little). Like Janet he doesn't like anybody to see the things he writes in a large MS book — verse and prose poems. I persuaded him to read out before company a short prose poem — and Shadbolt didn't like my remarking 'Clever Kevin, perhaps you will save us from the blight of Sargesonian naturalism'. These prose poems are rather like that one you published in Arena (about the man and the girl) ['Girl Under the Plane Trees'] — that's to say a step removed from pure naturalism, sometimes a big step, but so far he's not nearly as good as you, because he's nowhere near achieving word and sentence perfection (you saw that from his lines in the Listener). I don't think he and Shadbolt will be going to England this year — S because he hopes to get the £500 award and write a novel on it here at home, and J because he's donkey's deep in financial help to Bob Lowry, and also has to try to get back the money he has put into *Mate* and the under thirties anthology. [. . .]

I mentioned *Portrait of a Lady* to Kevin and in a day or two was presented with it in the World's Classics. A really good James — did you read together the sentence: 'she made no secret of the fact that the fount of passion, thanks to having been rather violently tapped at one period, didn't flow quite so freely as of yore'. I couldn't focus my attention on [Angus Wilson's novel] *Anglo-Saxon Attitudes* — and see now I was wrong in thinking pretty highly of *Hemlock and After*. As you say or imply you can get the universal out of any subject if you are good enough — James holds me even though it is all so remote from personal experience on the naturalistic level, but Wilson eventually doesn't even though (at least in Hemlock and After) I know only too well much he is talking about. [. . .]

[. . .] I don't see Fairburn, but I am told he looks like the walking image of death. But he is still having deep ray treatment, and that would make him look that way quite apart from the chance that morbid cells may be taking charge in God knows what parts of his anatomy. The cellular dance of death — it may be going on in any of us, and the younger you are the quicker it is over since the morbid cell growth keeps pace with the normal rate for one's age.

Now no more. Although I haven't said so I am transfixed by conscience that I didn't give you full details about the £500 award when I saw it mentioned in a PEN bulletin. Very glad you liked *Kangaroo* some parts of which I shall never ever forget.

My quite aching love to both of you,

F.S.

I broke off a front tooth the other evening eating a corn cob and have a horrid gap — which surprisingly worries me much less than I would have supposed. What does it matter now? — if Janet will only 'make good' I should be the happiest person in the world to be a retired writer and act as her secretary and editor (on a reasonable yet modest commission).

To John Reece Cole, *Indonesia*

Alexander Turnbull Library

16 February 1957

Dear Reece,

[. . .] Spud Cristina and child have arrived back, but I haven't seen them yet. I am anxious to though as they saw Janet for a short time in Barcelona when J was making for Ibiza. Cristina is reported to be willing to stay only a short time, but I expect she may change her mind. Janet has sent me some really insane letters lately, and although I have managed to push more funds in her direction it's all a great worry as she says she is leaving her cheap-living hangout in April — but by that time she will have a new book well finished. It annoys me that Pegasus brings her out according to her place in the queue of careerists hobbyists academics who expect only pocket-money from their writings — there's apparently no preference for a vocational writer. Albion Wright says end of March, but I'm not hopeful.

Jowsey Shadbolt and company have shown much energy and devotion over the two publications that Bob Lowry is printing for them [*Mate* and the 'under thirties' anthology], but of course the trouble is Bob. And lately I have discovered an additional reason for living in John Graham. He had a story in Numbers, and all I noted about it then was that he knew how to write. But I've now discovered that he can write good plays, and I've been trying to jack something up over one of them with Unity and a Wellington woman called Margaret McLuskie whom you or Chris would probably know. Graham is a Birkdale strawberry and tomato grower who rents 16 acres at £6 a week and doesn't make much of a do of it even though he's a damned good gardener and worker. (The trouble perhaps is an unsatisfactory wife and very nearly four children.) I've been toying with the notion of selling out here and buying the 16 acres, and the pair of us would establish a Little Theatre which would be run in conjunction with the garden. The plays would be put on in a rather special kind of packing shed by a group which would have to be ruthlessly screened to exclude people not fundamentally serious, and prepared to work (at the tomatoes as well as in the theatre). Actually it's not quite all a pipe dream. I can't carry on here much longer on a low income, and I may shortly have a little money to handle apart from what I could get from the property. (My two aunts are quite cuckoo, and my mother has just had a devastating stroke from which she has miraculously recovered in part — but she's in her 88th year). Anyhow we shall see. I've struck an awful snag in the last few pages of my third play, but I'll fix it eventually. And Graham has one excellent play (about a Dally winegrower), and another (based on Chesney) which isn't satisfactory yet, but I think the two of us can salvage it quite effectively. The idea would be to lay the foundations for real NZ theatre — and defy the producer-actor setup which is holding things up. [. . .]

Jacquie and Jim [Baxter] stayed with me two nights lately, and Jim is very much a reformed character (alcoholically speaking anyhow). Also Pat Hitchings has reformed — I think among other things Fairburn's calamity shook him up very severely. I don't see Rex, but I am told he looks a very sick man — but that may be on account of the deep ray treatment. (The cobalt bomb business isn't established yet, and I'm told some patients just curl up and die under it).

Well, all for now. But fondest love all round,

F.S.

To E.P. Dawson, *Mt Maunganui*

Hocken Library

7 April 1957

Dear Peter,

I am so sorry I haven't written, also sorry I missed you. As perhaps you have heard I tied myself up in a rather strange adventure at the end of February — growing 4000 tomatoes with a man called John Graham who has a rented place (very beautiful) at Birkdale. Unfortunately he also has a rather unfortunate wife and four children, but on the whole the violent (and probably temporary) breaking of the pattern of my life has been very good for me. I have had only Sundays off and one other day in six weeks, and the work has been from soon after daylight to dark all other days. (A few weeks back in dry weather I was out watering until nearly midnight). The pay-off is very doubtful, but the crop at the moment looks very beautiful, and we are now sending in our first cases to the market. If all goes well we should get over a thousand cases, but bad weather could ruin everything in two or three days. A fantastic gamble, and besides my labour I have gone a bit into debt over it. But I love the long hours of work (at least as a change), the only thing I don't like is the nauseating business of spraying — very unhealthy too with DDT.

A part of the idea has been that if the crop paid off Graham and myself might be able to acquire the property (it would probably involve selling Esmond Road), and besides cropping would try to run a little theatre in the packing shed — an attempt at what might eventually be reckoned as the first truly indigenous theatre in NZ. Besides my own plays (yours too if they are possibilities) there are Graham's plays which are rather extraordinary (he is a kind of literary primitive, and such people are very rare), and it is heartening that Unity in Wellington is daring to put one on very shortly. Also any other plays we can get.

Anyhow, there it is, and so much hinges on the next few weeks and the weather. I can do the work (I have lost a lot of weight), but the anxiety is terrible.

Thanks very much for the eggs.

When it is all over I shall be getting out of Auckland for a break, and think very strongly I shall be seeing you then.

Janet's book is out at last, but my copies haven't arrived yet. Will send you one the coming week for certain, I think. I hardly dare think of her situation. She has left Ibiza and gone to Andorra where she can get a better rate of exchange for what money she has left. I believe she is waiting for the snow to melt and then walking down into France. But I am shuddering over what will happen when all funds are exhausted. If only Albion Wright had hurried up a copy of her book would be in Plomer's hands by now, and Jonathan Cape for whom P. is reader might have made her an offer. It is awful to think that everything might be too late.

It is said that Fairburn did not know he was going to die so soon (he was under morphine for some weeks, and I'm told it gives you a feeling of euphoria). It struck me as quite horrible that he stuck to the last to attitudes which have distressed so many of us over the last few years. I never saw him — at least I never saw him since last June. Fortunately that last meeting was reasonably friendly. I hear people say that his death marks the end of an epoch. I wish it marked the beginning of a better one, but the outlook for all that you and I believe in appears to me distressingly gloomy and hopeless.

Hope to write again soon,
From yours,
F.S.

[A.R.D. Fairburn died on 25 March 1957. 'That last meeting' took place on the Devonport ferry. See Kevin Ireland, 'A Few Simple Words' in Dinah Holman and Christine Cole Catley (eds.), Fairburn and Friends, *pp. 69-73.]*

To Janet Frame, *Andorra*

Private collection

7 April 1957

Dear Janet,

I am worried over not having written you, particularly as I have had three letters from you. I ran into June and Wilson [Gordon] the other night at the Onewa Players (*Lace on Her Petticoat* — a charming but trivial play, and they returned me my Kendall — not enough plot in it! the Committee thinks), and was told you had written from Andorra. I do hope things are going pretty well. [. . .]

One of the six copies [of *Owls Do Cry*] I am airmailing immediately to Plomer (who is Jonathan Cape's reader) with a request that he get Cape to make an offer for English publication if he likes the work and thinks he can put it across in England. I am hoping and praying and keeping my fingers crossed about all this. Will let you know as soon as I have news. June and Wilson have kindly provided the money for the airmail.

Your letters most interesting. I do hope you have benefited marvellously from the *affaire* — also that there won't be any tiresomely substantial results. (My God John Graham has three children, and another almost due, and all are completely buggered up by the bad marital setup.)

I was too busy to go to Fairburn's funeral about ten days ago. Apparently, being under morphine for weeks, he didn't know he was going to die so soon and was looking forward to two years before the success or otherwise of the treatment would become manifest. A sad business. But now it's all over one can't help a sort of envy. He's finished with all the sorry business — out of the cactus once and for all, and here are the rest of us plagued with all the worries. I think whether the tomatoes pay off or not I shall sell Esmond Road and try something else somewhere. The overhead here is getting too costly, and I can't meet expenses unless I can increase income, and I can only do that effectively by cutting into my writing — which I would like to be done with anyway. It's all so complicated. Tell you more later.

Let me know how your finances are going, and I will do my utmost. What American publishing firm might be interested in your book? If you tell me I could airmail them a copy, also mention fresh work and get Albion to agree to first publication in America if you submitted there.

No more this time (I have to get up at 5.30 and catch bus) but soon more I hope,

Love,

F.S.

['The affaire': Frame's relationship with the American accountant and poet manqué George Parlette — the 'Bernard' of her autobiography. She become pregnant and miscarried in Andorra in April. See An Autobiography, *pp. 343–358 and Frame's letter to FS of April 1957, in King,* Wrestling with the Angel, *p. 169, fns 66 and 68.]*

To E.P. Dawson, *Mt Maunganui*

Hocken Library

12 May 1957

Dear Peter,

I am suddenly struck by your remark about 5 acres not being used at Kumeu, and the possibility of your building. It strikes me you and I might build a place big enough for both of us. Nor do I exclude the possibility of Graham going to garden there too. Admittedly he has his rather ordinary and largely wrong sort of Cockney wife, not to mention 4 altogether too lively children, but he is an astonishing character. The best and fastest garden worker I have ever struck, and really very intelligent and devoted. [. . .]

Alternatively, there is much about the Birkdale property to recommend it to anyone who appreciates a really lovely and very handy property. A huge old pear orchard, also apples citrus walnuts persimmons and quinces. Belts of great macrocarpas and pines. All in all 16 acres — and this week George Haydn (who built my house) has offered to pay £3000 for 2 acres of frontage for building sections. The landlord would sell us the sixteen acres for £6000, but it may be possible to keep him down to £5000 — that would mean we would be getting 14 acres for £2000, and at the price, for such a beautiful property so handy to the city when the bridge is over, it seems almost criminal not to buy. Anyhow Haydn's offer will hold for six weeks, there are various details I have to find out, rates etc., so I can tell you all about it when I see you. Even at £6000 it would be good, but much better if one or two more people would come in on it. (I'm told I can't expect to get more than about £1500–£1600 for Esmond Road, and there's about £170 owing to the bloody Bank). The chief difficulty would be accommodation. The old farmhouse is occupied by the Graham family, and nobody could share it with such a fantastic family. I have thought of shifting my house here onto the property, and it might be possible.

We are a little more cheerful about the crop as the prices have at last gone up. And so much depends upon the crop — I mean mainly that Graham is completely without resources if the crop fails. (You would like him by the way — very thin with colouring like Janet's and a long red beard. Rather like D.H. Lawrence — & in character too. Anyhow, from now on we should be getting not less than 25/-. Yesterday we worked into the evening and got fifty cases done — quite an undertaking when we do such quality packing to fit our quality product. We don't have time to spray any more, so may the gods hold their thunder in the shape of blight etc.

I believe J's book got a good review on Bookshop, but I didn't hear it as I was on the way home. I'm glad you thought there was something to it. [Marginal note: The book, I mean.] I'm damned if I really know what to think of it.

Well, here's to thoughts of a possible solution of the problem where to live and what to do with the rest of one's life. Theatre plus gardening seems to me the answer. So you think it over too. (I am reminded how years ago you had that idea of starting up a community). I have the notion that the crop, if the weather stays reasonably mild, may come to a peak of colouring in the next fortnight, then rapidly collapse under winter rain and cold temperatures. But it still means that hundreds of cases may fetch glasshouse prices. Immediately Graham can cope with what work is left I'll let you know and come your way.

Meantime, good wishes,

F.S.

To Karl and Kay Stead, *Armidale, NSW*

Alexander Turnbull Library

28 May 1957

Dear K and K,

I feel a bit desolate when I look at your last letter and see the date (March 27). Since then I have managed to get off to you a copy of Janet's book, but no letter. Do understand though you aren't the only ones I've neglected.

The tomato affair is virtually over — I won't say disastrously over, but very near to something like that. In other words The Playwright's Theatre is no nearer, and I have lost money instead of making it — not a very great deal, but enough to make me wonder how I am going to hang on at Esmond Road and get by on a very inadequate income. (It wasn't mark you the tomatoes that failed — we produced one of the most wonderful late crops ever known in the district, it was the damned set-up of debts and no capital that dished us). I am now buzzing round trying to find my solution which is very complicated, but may be reduced to something like this — do I just sell out for what I can get, and establish myself elsewhere, or do I first shift the house in one piece onto the cheapest suitable section I can find, and then sell the blank section? (It seems I should do a better deal the second way.) Other alternatives are to let the house, find somebody who will help me to reduce the overdraft to satisfy the Bank Manager, take in a boarder etc etc. I wouldn't feel quite so gloomy if it wasn't that the outlook for everybody engaged with the arts in a creative way couldn't be more depressing. These days I get offered no Broadcasting at all, and I haven't yet recovered enough energy to push for some. (You would by the way be quite entranced by my sylph-like figure — I feel pretty fit physically, and the hard work hasn't knocked me so far as I can tell, but I am going on for two stone lighter than I was).

Perhaps the reason for or key to the entire affair is to be found in Janet and the strain and worry she meant for me. Who knows, perhaps I have suffered what I have seen described as a brain-storm. The relief I experienced when she at last got away last year seemed very real for a time, but always I knew that getting her away was no real solution. There were her letters, much of them very wonderful — but what happened eventually? And now, with the money nearly run out, after moving from Ibiza to Andorra (where by the way you get the best rate of exchange for your money anywhere in Europe), she is now back in London. Her last letter, a few days ago was terrible — the cost of living eating up her meagre bit of remaining money, and a job as a cinema usher (the job fills me with the gravest apprehensions — I know for a positive fact she can't do any job except writing for more than a fortnight at the outside without going completely to pieces). My friend Miss Dawson has most generously sent her £30, but presumably it can only delay for a while a very evil day. (Sorry to trouble you with my anxieties in this way). She has some new work completed, but I can't find out much information about it. I got off a copy of her book airmail to Plomer, asking him to put it to Cape, but now he has written that although it has its definite points it doesn't appeal enough to common appetites, isn't sensational topical sexy etc. Better write you no more about this — everything adds up for all of us eventually. And the contradiction is that although none of us can really take it we all have to nevertheless. [. . .]

Very glad that you will be making the break [to the UK] in August — I mean on the whole I am very glad. I expect money will be enough though not exactly princely. I expect you will manage to enjoy yourselves, and it makes me very glad to think that you will.

I am very probably off to Tauranga to stay with my friend Miss Dawson early next week. Who knows, licking my wounds down there while strolling on the ocean beach may provide me with the very balm I'm sorely in need of at the moment.

All my love to both,

F.S.

To Janet Frame, *London*

Private collection

24 June 1957

Dear J,

Not long back from a very pleasant stay with Peter. She got your letter, and we were both bucked to know you are managing to hang on — do hope you continue somehow to manage, and without cinema jobs if possible. Your book continues to be discussed in Listener, so the Pegasus should be pleased even if you are not. (I wonder if Albion Wright is sending people fivers, saying I'm sure you will agree this is worth a letter to the editor — if so, I can't see myself getting one, though I suppose I could sign myself Interested Reader or A Grandfather — or even Harold Peel). Also somebody sent me a cutting from the Otago Times, and you got a very good notice there. (I am in two minds about sending you notices — think it best to leave it to Peter to send you a selection).

With luck the copy of Owls shouldn't be too far off getting to NY now, so I shall send a short explanatory airmail to [the book-promoting agency] Sussman and Sugar. Will ask them to write you in London if they are interested.

If you can bring yourself to, just post off any fresh material you have completed — just post it off in a zombie fashion and forget about it as soon as it's in the post. Send it to me John Money Albion Wright — or anyone who you know (with a part of yourself at least) will do his best to help you. Don't think over this. Just do it. And then forget it. Also, do try a line with a London literary agent with Owls — do it in a roundabout way if you don't feel like doing directly. If you can't bring yourself to, let me know and I'll do it for you. [. . .]

There's another thing for you to think over. My working for John Graham on his tomatoes turned out pretty badly. A good crop until a disastrously early frost destroyed much of it. He was too overloaded with debt anyway and is now bankrupt. I got very little in the way of wages, which didn't compensate for the help I felt obliged to give the family when they had no income at all. (The poverty was very like Owls). I'm not worrying overmuch as I feel I've had Takapuna now, and Peter and I have been discussing the possibilities of setting up a joint establishment at Mt Maunganui. To begin with, I may let my place and go and share with Peter — but it's also quite likely I'll sell and then buy a share in Peter's place so that the two of us can build an additional room and veranda onto the house. I'm mentioning all this, because I would like to know how you would feel if Peter and I suggested that sooner or later you returned to NZ and established yourself in a permanent niche with us at Mt Maunganui. In the meantime this is only a suggestion. Peter's and my arrangement, rather proposed arrangement, mightn't come off. But if it does she would be as glad as I would be if you felt you could be at home with us. When writing to Peter don't mention the matter in the meantime. She will send you her own invitation when (and if) our proposed arrangements begin to work out. But I think at this stage it's important to let you know the idea, so that you may feel that NZ needn't necessarily be ruled out when you are thinking of the future.

No more just now. Very strange, but when I was with Peter I heard that both the Victoria University Drama Society and the similar Auckland group are thinking of putting on my Kendall play. (Did I tell you that Wilson and June fell for Graham's three-acter, Beyond the Limit — 'the most refreshing thing I've read for years', Wilson said.)

Salud,

F.S.

['Harold Peel': a pseudonym Frame and her sister June used in series of 'hoax' letters to the NZ Herald *in Feb/March1956. See* Janet Frame in Her Own Words, *pp. 166-168.]*

To William Plomer, *Sussex*

Alexander Turnbull Library

[Plomer had written to FS on 21 May saying he had read Owls Do Cry *'with a kind of fascination. It is so real and so sad, like the sadness of the moon & the night sky above the mountains & housetops in the picture on the jacket. I think it owes a good deal to your own example. [. . .] I find the book very feminine, and the work of a caged spirit, and I am glad to have had the chance of reading it. But I am sorry to say that the feeling at 30 Bedford Square is that it is not a book which would have good prospects in this country. [. . .] I think it would be difficult, if not impossible, to find a publisher here now for this particular book, though I may be wrong. I suppose the reason is that it doesn't appeal enough to common appetites & is not sensational, topical, sexy &c &c'. ATL MS-Papers-0432-177.]*

15 September 1957

Dear Plomer,

[. . .] Very kind of you to do what you could about Owls Do Cry. My attitude to the book is a bit complicated by personal interest, plus what is called here these days 'the double standard' — that's to say a work of art may have regional value which affects one's judgment when trying to look at it from some more distant stand-point. I think it's a real problem for a New Zealander in literary matters, largely because of the reputation Katherine Mansfield has overseas for what appear to him the wrong reasons. I by no means like all of Janet Frame's book, and I regret that her particular type of mental illness makes it necessary for her to borrow somebody else's form. But what I admire no end are her brilliant verbal associations — and they're not merely verbal or literary. I find them more truly rooted in what is actual than in any writer I know with a related talent. Of course I realise quite well it might be very difficult in present circumstances to find an overseas publisher for such a book. Thanks again for what you tried to do. The girl herself is now in a London mental hospital [the Maudsley]. I'm hoping it will be only temporary, but it is a great worry to me trying to be helpful in every way I can. I'm hoping I may soon arrange for her to return to Ibiza, where she was happy most of the time if I can judge by the brilliantly wonderful letters she wrote me from there. [. . .]

From yours,

F.S.

I have abandoned theatre in the meantime to write what I think may turn out a kind of picaresque novel [*Memoirs of Peon*].

To Charles Brasch, *Dunedin*

Hocken Library

[Brasch wrote to FS on 4 October thanking him for Owls Do Cry*. 'The writing is almost terrifyingly vivid; and the control over what seems entirely spontaneous and uncontrollable is astonishing. It's an extraordinary and penetrating and poignant book, which goes very deep. The image of the house upon the rubbish dump gave me a physical pang; how can one ever forget it now? [. . .] And how much do we owe it to you, as its midwife? You must have felt you were giving birth to it too, with Janet producing it on your doorstep'. ATL MS-Papers-0432-148.]*

7 October 1957

Dear Charles,

[. . .] Don't for heavens sake think I had any interfering hand in Janet's novel. The various forms she uses are all borrowed. Her mental illness prevents her from achieving any form of her own, and the writing she hides which gives her the feeling that she has been loyal to her daemon is I believe entirely formless. This is a question I have often touched on with her. I have begged her to compromise — to take down any novel off a library shelf, plot the shape of it and then pour her own riches into the mould. She knows that something of this nature is necessary to enable her to write publishable work, but her resistance is for the most part adamant and sets up an awful tension. Her last letter was very encouraging. She is apparently being looked after in an enlightened way [in the Maudsley], she feels she is where she is voluntarily, and hopes to be out before too long. In the meantime there are no financial worries. I'll let you know more later. [. . .]

Bruce Mason's play [*The Pohutukawa Tree*] didn't get much of a notice in the Listener, but he tells me that Jim Bertram wrote a handsome radio review of it. I am very glad if it is a good play, and it seems there may be a chance of seeing it up here shortly. [. . .] I find it hard to forgive Campion and Mason for holding a rehearsal of The Pohutukawa Tree the night John Graham's play was tried out by Unity. Are NZ playwrights so two a penny they need to clash with each other? Nothing though will stop Graham (except gaol insanity or death — any one within the next five years I would estimate). He arrived from the Bay of Plenty lately in a car which was nothing more than old scrap iron tied together with wire. He stayed two days and wrote another 3 act play — in a sense the same play, but he improves each time he writes it. [. . .]

F.S.

To Dan Davin, *Oxford*

Alexander Turnbull Library

16 October 1957

Dear Dan,

Maurice [Shadbolt] has told me you thought there was much to Janet's book, and very glad about that — I believe I have a reputation for seeing a swan every time there's a goose about. Janet has had your address ever since she went over, but quite characteristic that she shouldn't make any contact. That sad fact of the matter at present is that she's in the Maudsley hospital at Denmark Hill Camberwell. She says voluntarily, and that she will be out again soon. It's naturally been a very great worry to me as she was getting along not too badly, though nobody has so far succeeded in getting her to part with fresh work* (she has a stack of it in typescript). She's pretty OK for finance for a few months ahead, so no pressing worry on that score. Now I know you and probably Winnie are all balled up with this and that, with quite a full belly of psychopaths, and I'm not asking you to do anything whatsoever. All I say is that her official address is c/o Bank of New South Wales, Berkeley Square. [. . .] One of my difficulties has been that I can get no report on her*, because she's careful (or I imagine she is) to avoid anyone who might send me one. I think I've said before (and as you can easily judge from her book) she's an extraordinary girl and a very intelligent one — the long letters she wrote me from Ibiza, where she was a tremendous success with her landlord (who played the violin in a cafe) and others, including a few Americans, are the most marvellous letters I have ever received from anyone. As for the mental affliction I have to admit it's severe, though she doesn't wear it as a decoration and it passes unnoticed by most people. As a matter of fact I'm not unduly perturbed about getting no reports of her as Karl Stead and his wife recently went over to Bristol university. They were among the few people Janet would take while she was living here, she wants to see them again, and eventually I'll hear from them. [. . .]

[. . .] I have given up the local theatrical tycoons as far too unintelligent, and after recovering my energy after the upset managed to get into a kind of picaresque novel which thank God seems to go. It and the chores keep me so occupied I've had to knock off the paper in the mornings in order to read Gibbon for the third time. [. . .]

Best to all,

F.S. [. . .]

*These points important, as I hope with Glover's help to squeeze some money out of the Lit Fund for her.

To John Graham, *Whakatane*

Alexander Turnbull Library

10 November 1957

Dear Johnnie,

I got to [Bruce] Mason's play [*The Pohutukawa Tree*] which has its points, but just didn't focus. It's a concoction, very synthetic, with some bright patches and some very dull, not to mention embarrassing ones. Mason had written in a part for himself (there was his egotism even in the name of the character — Lomas, which will nearly make Mason and I should say that's why he chose it) which he over-hammed. Well, there you are. I was afflicted with such longeurs I doubt whether I would have sat it out if I hadn't been with Una Platts.

He's the reverse of you as a playwright — your intensity and focus is never in doubt to my mind in your best work.

We came home with Curnow who as usual made some deadly precise comments. He liked the play better than I did, but chiefly because he regarded it as useful pioneering work, like Gorboduc or Gammer Gurton's Needle for example — nobody else will have to do that sort of thing now, so the ground is cleared for the Marlowes Kyds Shakespeares and all the better boys. (C no doubt reserves the more outstanding names for himself). There was one very outstanding Maori woman among the cast, but the rest white and brown were so so. [. . .]

Love to all. How's Betty?

F.S.

*[*The Pohutukawa Tree*, produced by Richard Campion and Bruce Mason, was performed in Auckland and Wellington by the New Zealand Players Theatre Workshop with Mary Nimmo as Queenie Mataira and Hira Tauwhare as Aroha Mataira.]*

To Charles Brasch, *Dunedin*

Hocken Library

[Brasch to FS, 22 November 1957: 'Could you get Janet to offer me a story — or better, let me see several if there are several? That was a good one in Mate*' ['Face Downwards in the Grass']. ATL MS-Papers-0432-148.]*

4 December 1957

Dear Charles,

[. . .] You make me throw up my hands over a story from Janet. There is a pile of stuff if she hasn't destroyed it (in London after Ibiza she wrote about criminal writing waste there — but the hints she had previously given were very attractive — a long story about an M.P. with a stain inside his hat for example. (I think I have told you, most of her long letters have been wonderful, and will make wonderful publishing some day). If I could get stuff out of her Charles, I would, but I've had no success. The Mate story she tried on Monte [Holcroft], and when he turned it down she was putting it in the fire when young Jowsey called in (it was remarkable she took to him almost as well as she did the Steads) and coaxed it out of her. The only news of her at present is from her epileptic brother, who says Janie is in a bad way. I don't think anything can be done. John Money was emphatic when he called last year that no advances in curing the disease once it has such a hold have been made. Apparently the way she is treated in the Maudsley is a great improvement on NZ. Nobody can have any idea of what is going on in her mind, but her remarkable intelligence has saved her previously and may again. At least worry about finance can be shelved in the meantime — and who knows? she may with some deliberation be giving everybody some respite. [. . .]

Cheers,

F.S.

To John Reece Cole, *Indonesia*

Alexander Turnbull Library

[FS's mother Rachel Davey died on 10 December 1957.]

22 December 1957

Dear Reece,

[. . .] My delay with [. . .] new gossip is the upset over the death of my mother — the remains disposed of at the new Super-Incinerator at Purewa by my brother's arrangement. All very tasty Hollywood, and no doubt a whacking bill. I had to meet people and relatives I'd hoped never to see again. I have been left a one-sixth share in the estate, but I don't know the details yet. If I get enough to pay off an old debt to my brother I may have about £50 to £100 left. I'm rather glad about the one sixth in fact, since it clears away my last doubt about leaving my own property away from the family. Females should never be entrusted with the disposition of property, I mean family property. In the old days my sisters would have had their dowry when they married and that would have been that. As it is they get two sixths each, when they have successful tradesmen husbands to support them, who presumably were willing to take them without dowry. My brother gets the remaining sixth. However, my parents did a certain amount for me — I got this section off them for one thing. Nevertheless it always puzzled me that my mother wasn't sweetened up a bit when they were amply over-compensated by the windfall from my uncle's farm — £1500 to £2000 I think. If only the sour old wowserism could have been disposed of along with the remains. (Old Bake by the way has disposed of his cadaver to Otago university).

I still have the aunt-string to my bow, and I got a quick glance at some papers the other day she had left lying about. I judge her property to be between £15,000 and £20,000, but I don't know how it is disposed of, and some might be only life-estate. Still, worth heaping the vegetables on her (I could even chuck a few pumpkins at her, hoping) — probably a better bet than Tatts. The last stroke, very luckily for her, hit her in the eye. She has to wear a frosted lens, and the other day said the sight was improving, *but it might take years*. Still, the old thing shows signs of mellowing — she pressed a fiver on me lately for the vegetables, and now has given me another for Christmas (actually I think she thought the one sixth was a little unfair, since I seem to have some good points after all. Also, over the years I've persistently though delicately hinted that *her* accepting £1500 to £2000 from my uncle's farm was a monstrous piece of avarice. I hate avarice in other people, much preferring to exhibit it myself).

Well, well. Hoping to see you before too long now. I make real yoghurt now out of bulgarian bug, and much superior to the simple curd. Garden is superb, and I'm surprisingly full of energy, perhaps because summer is so far not too hot. Over 15,000 words of my novel [*Memoirs of a Peon*] done now, and I chuckle over my intellectual rogue's adventures. Also typing out Graham's third play. Janet still in a bad way in the Maudsley, and Peter Dawson doesn't seem to be taking her English trip. Faber and Faber want to publish Maurice [Duggan]'s *Falter Tom*, and he has two other children's stories of the same length just as good. All best to all [. . .].

F.S

To Charles Brasch, *Dunedin*

Hocken Library

[Brasch to FS, 22 November 1957: 'Is the autobiography then proceeding steadily? is there any more of it that you would think suitable for LF? The novel must almost be writing itself, from what you say. It's magnificent, Frank, that you continue to burst out like this'. ATL MS-Papers-0432-148.]

22 January 1958

Dear Charles,

I am sorry I have never gone through the Roof typescript to see if there is anything I could find for you; but instead I will shortly send you a section of what I am working on now [*Memoirs of a Peon*] — it amuses me and may amuse you, and in any case I should be interested to know what reactions you would have to the style persona etc. I have doggedly stuck at the work and 25,000 words are done. (I would send now, but the particular section is the latest which I haven't quite completed yet).

But oh oh oh how heartless I have to appear to get my work done. Everything seems to fall on top of me. A telegram from Bob Gilbert to say his son Miles was accidentally killed a short time ago. No details, and I am not even sure where to write to (the telegram came from Lincoln). Miles was my godson. And Rodney who came to see me one afternoon thought that was Tristram Hall killed in the Alps. Another long-drawn-out affair has come to end with the death of my mother in her 89th year. [. . .] But all the disorder goes on — I had some excruciatingly tiring visits from Janet's epileptic brother George just back from England and the

Continent after incredible adventures which it seems a miracle he has survived. Not much news of Janet except that she's apparently in bad shape mentally. She still doesn't answer my letters, but I hope to get information from Davin and Stead. John Graham left his wife and four children in Whakatane and for a time lived in a room in Wellington with Baxter (who is apparently being judicially separated from his wife, and has become a Catholic) until his wife went down and recaptured him. I really fear it may end up in one of those affairs where the entire family is done in. [. . .]

A pleasant summer to you, Charles. The garden which is splendidly prolific this year with animal manure is my great soother. And I will let you see the typescript pages before the end of next week.

F.S.

To Dan Davin, *Oxford*

Alexander Turnbull Library

[Davin had written on 19 February to say that he had tried to see Janet Frame in hospital, but she had left before he could arrange a visit. He did, however, meet her physician: 'He is very interested in her case & obviously perplexed. He says she needs a great deal of reassurance & although she claims not to be a writer & to intend to write no more she is now talking of buying a new typewriter. While she needs all this reassurance she at the same time doesn't want to be bossed & so tends to dodge people who want to help her. New Zealand house people, friends of mine, are also anxious about her & wd like to help. She may give us all the slip but I hope I can at least meet her & so form an impression of how best to help her in the least obtrusive way'. ATL MS-Papers-0432-155.]

16 March 1958

Dear Dan,

Good of you to trouble about J, I know what a damn pest these things can be. She has come to light with a letter after many months, not too re-assuring, but better than it might have been. I give you the address which I think is a very recent one (Durham House, Flat 3, 20 Fortress Road, Kentish Town NW5), but I don't recommend you write her there except upon some emergency. I may possibly be the only one she has given the address to. If writing I'd say write to the Bank of NSW in Berkeley Square — otherwise she might put herself to all the bother of upping and offing to escape. Apparently just previously she was living in some hell-hole — this place is better. And another point: NZ House would no doubt be marvellous in an emergency, but short of an emergency they might scare the lights out of her — capture, repatriation out here etc. It's nice to know you're there to assist, but even apart from the thousand calls on your time I'd say take it lightly — as I do. I have to, I've had such experience of it now, and the frustrations and dead-ends can be killing. The two crucial points are finance, and fresh work. But the first is OK at present as Pegasus has just squared with £75 on her book (they are now going ahead with a re-issue) — it's the second that's more urgent, but she seems adamant. And the danger is that piles of excellent stuff may be burnt. (The bloody witch-dances she used to have in my garden around a pile of stuff nobody had ever seen except herself used to be like something out of the Golden Bough). One of the things I've worked out is this: the stuff she really wants to write she burns (she knows, probably quite rightly, that it will be thought insane): the straighter stuff she will occasionally part with, but she thinks poorly of it, considers it betrays her daemon etc (Owls D.C. is in this category). The solution would be to hit on a compromise, but schizophrenics don't compromise do they? or rather, they can't. But pardon me for attempting to teach grandpa to suck eggs.

[. . .] Courage says he has finished his new novel, a Wolfenden one apparently [*A Way of Love*], which has sent *him* in and out of hospitals, but Cape after some surprise are bringing it out in November. He sounds ill, poor fellow, and I tend to throw up my hands on the theory that one can't stand too much.

I spend much time planting exotic fruit trees in my garden (the latest is an avocado pear, the seed brought from Gauguin's old garden in Tahiti — there's arty sentimentality for you!), but I've never worked to a stricter timetable than I do at present on the picaresque novel. A chunk of it will probably appear in the June Landfall. Not a good idea perhaps, but I can't write anything else at present while I am doing my 300 words a day excluding Sundays. What those 300 cost me! but damn me if they don't surprise me by appearing lively — unless I'm now an adept at self-deception senile variety. [. . .]

Reece Cole and family return from Indonesia next month, and he and I are going to the King Country in a car they've diplomatically got cheap. Chris has been ABC correspondent and Reece has apparently done nice work for Unesco. The financial benefits if they've managed to save will be excellent, and possibly Reece may be able to write again. We plan to have a damn good holiday anyhow. [. . .]

F.S.

[The Report of the Departmental Committee on Homosexual Offences and Prostitution, better known as the Wolfenden Report, was published in Britain on 4 September 1957. It recommended that homosexual behaviour between consenting adults in private should no longer be a criminal offence. Excerpts from Memoirs of a Peon *were published in* Landfall *in June and November 1958 as 'The Problem of Pocket Money' and 'A Ponsonby Wake'.]*

To William Plomer, *Sussex*

Alexander Turnbull Library

11 May 1958

Dear Plomer,

[. . .] Lately [. . .] I've been reading your introduction to [Joseph Conrad's] Victory. The Oxford Press is crazily dilatory in responding to orders for books but this one turned up at last. I've never been able to make up my mind about Conrad, and am in no better case after this one which I had omitted previously. I'm worried that the careful plausibility of the beginning goes down the drain as the melodrama begins to go really into action. C's old-school-tie borrowings from the English worry me (like Ngaio Marsh pretending to be more English than the English), and where he is, or pretends to be obtuse he's like a man who insists on having frosted lenses in his glasses. Do *you* believe that the truly feral member of the trio wouldn't have had a better line on the spectre? But of course such objections are rendered of no account by your cunning epigram about thrillers and moralities. I expect it's just my colonial puritanism which rendered my enjoyment of the story an envious shade less than your own. How excellent those little WC books! If this country eventually has its major trade tie-up with the USA (and so-called living standards, logic and such point in that direction), it will grieve me in my old age to have to handle the plastic abominations which will still be going by the name of books unless some new name is invented.

My dear sweet good and crazy Janet Frame is still in darkest Kentish Town, and such odd things turn up in the post from her. Last time it was a little bottle of most pansily-scented snuff (perhaps I can offer it to the local waitresses — and barmen, seeing that barmaids in this country have so rigorously devoured their young that they don't exist any more) wrapped up in a copy of the Wolfenden report! Her humour always bobbing up despite the most atrocious mental suffering is one of the most remarkable things about her, and I could wish rather more of it had got into that novel of hers. But who takes snuff these days? [. . .]

I wonder if I have mentioned that my mother died at last at 89. A strange stubborn (I shouldn't complain there) woman who persisted to the last in trying to destroy the love that any of us had for her. May the angels have received her, though with a good-natured reprimand for having left her bit of money tied up in Government stock which doesn't mature until 1965. [. . .]

Good wishes and many hopes for more books.

F.S. [. . .]

To Dan Davin, *Oxford*

Alexander Turnbull Library

22 July 1958

Dear Dan,

The Eve of Armageddon, so do interpret my last thoughts as kind ones — though you may have private arrangements to tow the Scilly Islands underneath the Arctic Ice until the geiger shows a more propitious count for some forms of life in advance of ants and wood lice. [. . .] And by the way, if the Oxford Press is atomised it would be much nicer during the short time remaining to one *not* to think a damn good thing too — & the reason for that tart remark is that I lately had an Oxford Shorter Dictionary sent out to me. I overlook the worn out type and stinginess with ink, but the binding is an unpleasant hoax. What particularly narks me is that although it should be rejected after one minute's examination, this particular example was broken-backed before it left the Press. I can just imagine some bastard saying 'the cunt in N.Z. won't send it back, so let him have it'. This cunt isn't sending it back — it would be very vulgar to hurl a Shorter Oxford into Armageddon anyway — it might injure some Angel on Horseback — but honestly, a few tears over the decay of craftsmanship, not to mention lack of commonsense etc. would be far from unmanly. [. . .]

I have been terribly worried about Janet, who seems to be suffering a prolonged bout of her worst in Kentish Town. The break with Cole was very good. A super car (M.G. Magnette — 5 seater) — we had movie cameras & did documentaries for Aust. Television — of ruined Hawkes Bay, & stinking aerial top-dressing. But best of all were the thermal spout baths — all along the road. Very immoral, by controlling the water you can have everything from a barmaid's hand to an angel's kiss. [. . .]

Best,

F.S.

['The Eve of Armageddon': FS's sense of imminent catastrophe may have been fuelled by the accelerating arms race, by feverish British and American thermonuclear testing in the Pacific in advance of a moratorium set for October 1958, and by the widely held fear that instability in the Middle East and Taiwan might trigger world war.]

To James Courage, *London*

Hocken Library

[On 11 May Courage told FS that the British Government was waiting on 'public opinion' before taking action on the Wolfenden Report — 'and, of course, the public

is notably mute [. . .] on the whole matter. I'm very afraid that we'll all have to remain felons — or dishonest boyos — in our lifetime'. Courage had recently attended an exhibition at New Zealand House of Katherine Mansfield letters and papers, purchased by the Turnbull Library from John Middleton Murry's estate. ATL MS-Papers-0432-152.]

23 July 1958

Dear Jim,

I expect since you wrote in May you have done your proofs [for *A Way of Love*]. I do hope the novel is not worrying you too much. Surely if you have made it a good work of art that is all that concerns you. Self-exhibition is irrelevant — one's only concern should be no exhibition as a bad artist.

Strangely enough, Holcroft has just come to light with some prominent comments on Wolfenden in the Listener. I think though the most we can hope for here is that the worst persecution may be made impossible in England, then there would be some chance of analogous legislation in N.Z. But too big a subject, & legalistic changes can only be a sort of patchwork. (Can you envisage an age of consent put low enough to satisfy the paederasts?) The real problems remain, & I hope your book throws some light on them — I doubt whether alteration in the law would result in a greater proportion of homosexuals showing greater capacity for pulling themselves up by their bootstraps — I have found many of these people awful nuisances — boring one to death by the narrowness & shallowness of their desires & interests on the one hand, & by their pretensions on the other — the latter particularly infuriating when they imagine themselves competent to meddle with the arts. But living in London I'm sure you would know much more of these people than I do. What moves me is to see unpretentious people caring for & tending each other, each with an unwavering core of loyalty. But they are pretty rare, I'm afraid. [. . .]

[. . .] I am afraid I can't take the Mansfield racket at all. It seems strange that after all the harm Murry did to her real (though small) reputation & talent, N.Z. should officially take over. And why doesn't the money go to the living Frames instead? But then I've always believed that apart from the geniuses, the work of other people when dead deserves only a slender volume with very rare exceptions.

From yours,

F.S.

To E.P. Dawson, *Mt Maunganui*

Hocken Library

30 July 1958

Dear Peter,

Thanks for your July 15 letter, & I take it that Janet hasn't written you. Which is a little strange though perhaps it's stranger that one should think it strange. I don't agree with you that her letters impress one as more stable than anything she had to show for herself in N.Z. One can only guess, but I imagine that she's constantly very mentally ill indeed, & whatever show she puts up (& sometimes puts across) is just so much camouflage which costs her a tremendous amount of strain. I don't think any letter she writes is written to express herself or as a relief for feelings — instead she writes out of a compulsive duty to bury herself deeper & deeper inside the protective cocoon which she never ceases working at. Frankly, I find it all extremely hopeless, & none of us can ever be sure that his or her decisions concerning her are the right ones. I don't of course question for one moment your LSD [pounds, shillings and pence] decision, particularly when you have been generous far beyond what even over-generous people would consider generosity. The bright spot lately is that I have heard from Jess [Whitworth] (who is homesick & mad to get a boat home very quickly), & she says that she has seen J, & found her bright & communicative. According to Jess J now has her Benefit, which is £4 a week. (But Jess so easily gets things muddled, & J would be in no doubt that Jess is the right sort of person to be *apparently* communicative with). Anyhow, if I hear anything more I'll let you know — I have in fact rung the sister in Northcote, but from her I got such a different picture, & so muddled, that I don't propose to muddle you with it in the meantime. As for myself, I shall wait until September when with luck I may be able to contribute something more myself; but quite frankly, like yourself, I'm hoping that if the Maudsley is as good a sort of place as can be found when everything is balanced up, it will be over to the people there with the faint hope that improvement rather than deterioration may eventually be the result. One can't bear to think of it any more in terms of human suffering: it is much too much.

I have found that some strange people tend to identify the 'I' in my [*Landfall*] extract [from *Memoirs of a Peon*] with myself, & interpret as an attack on Remuera. Very strange — & as for identification, if there's anything, it should be with the young workman in the football jersey. I can't be worried — & literally because I have temporarily finished with the 'rich' part & am busy on the 'poor' which, although it doesn't have to be nearly so much invented, I am finding monstrously difficult to do.

Did I tell you I was re-reading Shakespeare — before breakfast, as a change from Gibbon. Nearly through, & now have a much clearer grasp on many good plays, & a few very tiresome ones (among the Comedies). I had never known previously however how very charming *L's L's L [Love's Labour's Lost]* is. I've also been struck with how marvellous *The Blithedale Romance* is on a re-reading.

The weather cold & wet, & trying to get all my potatoes in a dismal muddy job. But nothing seems to matter much if we are on the eve of Armageddon (Will the Angels appear on horseback or in Jaguar cars?) It is monstrous to think that the ants & wood-lice which are plaguing me so much will survive radiation sickness & take over the house — & they are so cocky it almost seems as though they know in advance. [. . .]

Well, must say goodnight. From yours,

F.S.

I took a bag of vegetables down to my aunts today, & they flourish so rudely that I see nothing is to be done except for me to acquire a blunt instrument & practise with it several hours a day.

I think what I conclude from my Janet experience is that how to come to grips with insanity is an insoluble problem. A few outstanding professionals may know how, but I'm doubtful. Refuge in the old-fashioned Bedlam idea is out of the question, but it becomes painfully understandable.

To C.K. Stead, *Bristol*

Alexander Turnbull Library

10 August 1958

Dear Karl,

I'm appalled to see the date-stamp on yours — June 3. But I think I got you off a quick note as I was on the point of my trip with Cole. That long past now — & very good, but too non-stop neurotic. The car a wow — 85 miles p.h & smooth as milk, but poor Reece lives on drugs & could not bear to be in one place for more than a minute at a time. Thank God I could induce him to stop for a number of those very immoral thermal spout baths now & then.

It's been very difficult to settle since I got back. A bleak wet winter, & all my friends seem to be in trouble. I just can't get anything out of Janet, though it's heartening to believe she may now be in receipt of some sickness benefit. But I seem to put a foot wrong every time I write her — all told, everything her friends do for her seems only to make her more guilt-ridden & miserable.

I have been catching up on N.Z. Lit. I can't read [M.K.] Joseph [*I'll Soldier No*

More] either, at least beyond the opening chapter — it appalls me to think that after taking that in one has to go in an enormous presumably monstrously dull circle back to it again. I managed [Ian Cross's] *The God Boy* though — a bit hard to swallow the convention, but a remarkable portrait of a boy *does* emerge. His next book will be his test. [Sylvia Ashton-Warner's] *Spinster* — everyone seems to think this is good, but the writing seems to me wooden & rhythmless, & I can't read it. I conclude one shouldn't read contemporary work at my age — I mean unless it is written by friends for whom one has a special affection (& even then one's blundering expressions of appreciation & attempts at assessment are suspiciously received!!) What I am an expert on at the moment is Shaks. Persisting with him as my pre-breakfast reading I've knocked off all the Trags. & Coms. & am now on the Hists. I had to buy a Shorter Oxford Dict. to help out. But what joy (again at my age) to read for the first time *The Compleat Angler* (with Cotton's part II). And re-reading Hawthorne's *Blithedale Romance* prompts me to re-affirm that's one of the most remarkable most teasing & most profound novels in the language — & particularly good as colonial work.

I've read your last letter many times — absolutely crammed with so much. What happened to Smith in Empire Games? I never sighted him among the results. [. . .]

[. . .] Young Kevin [Jowsey] [. . .] is now guiding at Waitomo, & told me very amusing stories of his dealings with tourists — the Americans refuse to believe the glowworms are not an hydro-electric job. [. . .]

No more for now, but hope summer hols. have been marvellous for you,

F.S.

P.S. All my love to Kay. Also by the way, Cole & I did all the new industry places — Kinleith, Murapara [sic], Kawarau [sic] etc & stayed at their tasty hotels — it was like touring round a circle of the Inferno — the living dead, or the dead living — hard to say which.

P.P.S. Faber & Faber are bringing out Maurice Duggan's *Falter Tom and the Water Boy* — *not* Merboy — a very good children's story.

[Stead's friend Don Smith, then studying at Oxford, represented New Zealand in the 800m at the 1958 Empire Games and the 1960 Rome Olympics.]

To C.K. Stead, *Bristol*

Alexander Turnbull Library

Monday [August 1958]

Dear K,

[...] There's been a curious upset over Curnow's Penguin vol. Apparently Alistair Campbell got to know of a set of galley proofs with the Penguin agent in Wellington, and representing himself as Mr Campbell of the Education Department, and hinting at an enormous order, got a look at the proofs. The story is that Curnow had not included poems of his which he had got consent for, but had included one poem which Campbell hadn't consented to. In some way Baxter and Johnson came into the dispute, and letters flew all over the place, with Campbell threatening to sue Penguins etc. I'm told it has cost Curnow in cables the £25 he got for Jessie Mackay Memorial prize. (Incidentally too the anthology was supposed to consist of Curnow and the rest — one-third Curnow, but C denies this and says it is only one-fourth Curnow). Anyhow the present situation is said to be that Penguins will continue to back their horse Curnow, and the also-rans can kick up their heels in whatever way they please. I've no idea how all this would affect you, but I should think not at all, as C would be bound to include you among his very latest poets. I've no idea when the Anthology is to appear — though I think not until next year. I think Sinclair's Hist of NZ is due at the end of this year. (His Origins of the Maori Wars by the way is a very substantial piece of work, but he has made it virtually unreadable with his footnotes. I know that Gibbon isn't a historian at all to these modern historians, but at least he had the cunning to make a tremendous virtue out of his footnotes. Great lists of Sinclair's read like this GbPP, 1860 HC/2719 etc.).

I think that's about all, honi soit,

F.S.

[Keith Sinclair's A History of New Zealand *appeared in 1959 and* The Penguin Book of New Zealand Verse, *selected and introduced by Allen Curnow, in 1960.]*

To William Plomer, *Sussex*

Alexander Turnbull Library

21 September 1958

Dear Plomer,

This just a note. I've been trying to get round to it ever since your good letter turned up. Don't for Pete's sake ever write unless you feel like it and have a moment — and of course you would feel like it oftener than you would have the moment. I tell you I understand these things. And the same about Janet Frame. I might plague you if she came to light with what looked like a masterpiece, but the personal situation is up to a few of us who have got our lines tangled with hers. (Incidentally she has been fished out of the Thames lately by the water-police. Not a nice experience as you can imagine). Perish the thought that I would ever want to entangle you personally. [. . .]

[. . .] I manage to slog along with my own novel, and I hope you raised a chuckle over the bit in *Landfall*. My prosy old man narrator gets a bit tiresome at times, but I like to think of him as quite as wicked in his own way as somebody like say [the sometime diplomat, writer and reprobate] Norman Douglas. I am much too conceited not to think he is not too bad, and if he for the most part entertains people that is what I am aiming at.

What an international situation! Armageddon on one's doorstep with the strontium clouds passing overhead. I daren't eat anything out of my garden without first testing it with my geiger gadget — and to think that those 65,000,000 gals. of nuclear waste in the USA might leak from their tanks and start of sort of Kon-tiki across the Pacific. I am thinking of constructing my own private submarine which I hope to lodge beneath the Great Ice Barrier until the planet is a fit place again for something in advance of the pismire or the wood louse. When will you be retiring from Capes? — you must spend a long old age writing books.

All my best to you,

F.S

[An elided version of Frame's letter to FS of 11 September 1958 appears in King, Wrestling with the Angel, *p. 194. It confirms that a suicide threat was made, but says nothing either way about any actual attempt.]*

To Charles Brasch, *Dunedin*

Hocken Library

25 December 1958

Dear Charles,

I have been so harassed one way & another (7½ inches of rain in December on my 6 doz tomatoes — from that number you get an awful lot if all goes well — and apart from the danger of their complete destruction, every damn fungus & virus ever thought of attacks melons pumpkins beans etc. Only garlic & leeks as always take any sort of weather. But it has all meant much work & worry), I haven't yet completely got the hang of *Landfall*. [. . .]

I have just read *A Room in Chelsea Square*, & hope it is *not* by Courage. It has its points, but is soft & limp when it should be quite hard [. . .]. But a much more remarkable book is Jack Kerouac's *On the Road* — a wonderfully illuminating & moving novel about the American bodgies. It irks me that with a little more luck somebody such as Kevin Ireland might have written this story in a N.Z. setting (the 'beat' generation here resembles exactly that in America). And before I forget, Cole on the trail of *Lolita* got 2 copies (Paris edition) & gave me one. It's very sad, very funny, not terribly good perhaps (mainly on the score of language), but worth reading, & very interesting to read alongside Kerouac. I'd be awfully glad to lend you *Lolita* if it doesn't happen to come your way.

I agree that the *Catcher in the Rye* is in part the source of *The God Boy*. But Salinger is phony, & Cross, although thin as a story, is superior in presenting a more faithful portrait of a boy. I must try [Ruth France's] *The Race* again, but in my present mood I find myself slightly insulted by being expected to take average lives so very exactly as they are without any imaginative transformation. Let the dull bastards be heightened a few cubits or let them be satirized, even brutally; but don't let them be photographed — my God, look at the photographs in the *Weekly News*.

But I invite you to ignore write off or skip all comments in this note. Working feverishly as I am at my own creation I'm no person to provide reliable comments on anybody else's work. My heart symptoms have mended thank heaven, but my stomach is wrecked, & I have a mouth so sore that I think every fungus & virus in the garden has got into it to destroy every bit of membrane. And *no hope* of being free from these nervous troubles until the entire thing is on paper — within 6 months I hope, or I shall be dead. [. . .]

My road is left in mud & chaos for the holidays. I go out at night & hit the giant machines with a padded hammer. A futile gesture — a genuine Titan would tie himself like a Titan or a suffragette to the road in front of them when they are working. [. . .]

Very good holidays to you. (My own day today has been marvellous. I have seen nobody. [. . .]). And I recommend reading Milton at 6 o'clock in the morning — my most enchanting habit each day.

From yours,

F.S.

[Michael Nelson's A Room in Chelsea Square *was published anonymously in 1958.]*

To Janet Frame, *London*

Private collection

25 May 1959

Dear Janet,

I'm so sorry I've been so long sending you a note. I seem to be continually in a mess, even though I've found myself very isolated for various reasons lately. But over-isolation will shortly I'm afraid be transformed into the reverse (whatever it may be), as the bridge opens at the end of the week. It means I will be about 15 mins. from town by car or bus. The road outside has been frigged around with for about 8 months, but it's about finished; widened, & a super-motorway. I expect far too many people from town will find themselves passing me & stop & call in. Of course I'm put in a bit of a quandary. Rates about to be terrific, & the inflation generally continues. I wouldn't mind so much if I had managed to finish my book, but although the typescript is at p. 260, (about as long as O.D.C.) it has to be about 150 pp. longer. Very hard going lately, but if I can't make it funny I pile on the indecency — or vice versa. I expect I shall have to publish it privately with my aunts' money — if there is any after estate duties, but in any case those 2 old faggots thrive better than I do, & think I'm joking if I tell them I'm only about 3½ years off the Old Age Pension.

I believe the Steads will reach Wellington about June 9, so I am hoping to have news (of a good sort) of you. [. . .] Did you hear at all that Sylvia Ashton-Warner sold [the film rights for] that novel of hers (*Spinster*) to M.G.M. for £10,000? I managed to read it after several attempts. She has some points of contact with your own work, & I decided her novel was a freak affair of strange but genuine distinction. Also *The God Boy* is to be a play in New York. [. . .]

Two things at least I remain — a persistent gardener, & (same adjective) early-morning reader. Have lately been fascinated by Byron's plays or dramas or whatever one should call them. Still, I wish it wasn't turning out such a cold wet winter. I have too much vegetation round my boundaries, & the hut is now shrouded by the pawpaws & very dark inside. But if I manage the digging I have to let the hacking down over-growth slide. All my very best to you, & will be very glad to hear if you can write.

All my love,

F.S.

To Janet Frame, *London*

Private collection

[Frame wrote to FS on 4 June telling him that she was leaving hospital and planned to 'write like hell'. 'I'm sure that what I'm writing is utter nonsense, indeed it is *nonsense,' she added, 'but my doctor has assured me [. . .] that I must stop deciding what is and is not nonsense — that I must throw away [that] label.' Cited in King,* Wrestling with the Angel, *p. 199.]*

11 July 1959

Dear Janet,

I am sorry to be so long writing: all must be blamed on to my book which torments me — so near & so far — such a lot down on paper but so much more required, & then a very exacting job of revision & manipulating of material until all is as good as I am capable of making it.

Very interested in your June letter. I felt a little wry over your doctor's saying you 'must stop deciding what is & what is not nonsense'. Now that's one of the key points that I hit on long ago: & how sore I have been that none of my pleas has ever persuaded you. How golden if you would be persuaded now! How truly marvellous if this lump of grit that has oh so seldom been absent from the works could be removed from them once more, even if again only temporarily! Don't, my dear, grin to yourself & say 'Ah! he doesn't get round me that way!' That's all the plea I am making this time. I know you will co-operate if you can. Nor need I remind you of how much benefit to all of us (including yourself) might accrue.

Do write again soon. Tell me how fast your finances are leaking away. I have been expecting to see something of the Steads. They didn't write, but I believe their boat is due at Wellington soon.

The bridge, or rather the road outside, is a great trial, but most seriously in the weekends: sometimes there has been a traffic jam from here to the city. I resent the fumes & diesel soot more than the noise, & look for the soot on my lettuces & peppers, & am almost disgusted over not discovering it there: the hedge has been my great blessing, I think. I have by the way been across only once since the opening at the end of May — to see Curnow's play called *Moon Section*. Dramatically speaking I found it a boring flop. The Old School Ties (Courage, Davin, Curnow) have let the Old School down in their latest works; & I fear it would need only a no-good lump of Sargeson for the O. S. to be written off for ever. It's all over now to the Frames, Crosses, Ashton-Warners, Duckworths (have you seen hers? — *A Gap in the Spectrum* — about a N.Z. girl losing her memory in London & getting herself into hospital? but I'm told it is no great shakes).

The toll plaza at the Bridge by the way is like a Luna Park; but you pay & drive in & nothing happens, you just drive on: night in Takapuna is very much the same — masses of coloured lights over concrete & nobody there — as though all designed as a signal to Mars by people who have long since ceased to live. I think sometimes I am the only remaining inhabitant with only the best English poets & prose writers for company. No more this time, but write soon if you can,

Love,

F.S.

To Kevin Ireland, *London*

Alexander Turnbull Library

23 July 1959

Dear Kevin,

[. . .] My trouble at moment is I haven't an ounce of energy to spare — it all goes into the damn book, which is my task & my despair. I haven't an idea whether it's any good, but with 300 pages of typescript I have to plug on to the 400 which should finish it. Meantime besides the exhaustion I suffer from every neurosis ever invented, & daily fancy myself a cot case with a brand-new fatal disease every few hours. I got Stead to read your *Shirt of Nessus* in *Mate*, & he was impressed, as indeed he should be as it's probably the best work you have done. *Maproom* more lightweight, though very pleasant — but I can't remember how much it's been altered since you wrote it in the hut. In same number there's a story by [John] Graham ['Somewhere to Stay'], so black & pessimistic it seems to transcend itself & become a modern prose Inferno in miniature. But the prize story lately is one by Maurice Gee in *Landfall* ['The Losers'] — about racing & people connected with it: it can be faulted, but it's devastatingly authentic, & very surely written at a level he has never previously achieved to my knowledge. In fact, a milestone story. In same number there's a very derivative & literary poem sequence by Stead ['Pictures in a Gallery Undersea'] — but a remarkable achievement, & one that makes me feel very gloomy about the mistake he has made in returning here. Curnow's play *Moon Section* has been put on — a bore, a ragbag, quite hopeless as theatre, & very harmful to the chances of anyone else who might write a play: C made an ass of himself by being very prominent at every performance — horribly embarrassing. [. . .]

I've lately [. . .] read Kerouac's *The Subterraneans*, & my God he's slipped badly since *On The Road*. But damn modern stuff when there's (hold your breath) Hooker's *Laws of Ecclesiastical Polity* to read: and Byron — he's my poet since I knocked off dear old Mr Wordsworth & bright young angel Shelley. Returning to NZders though — I find it a great pleasure to think of retiring to sit back & enjoy watching the Shadbolts, Gees, Ashton-Warners, Crosses, Irelands, Grahams, Duggans, Duckworths ..... fight it out among themselves. [. . .]

All best,

F.S. [. . .]

P.S. The 2 bodgies down the road have taught me to call Takapuna people who drive about in cars, peons. I'd previously only known them as zombies.

To William Plomer, *Sussex*

Alexander Turnbull Library

[On 18 August Plomer wrote to say he had been in Germany with his 'friend & house-sharer' Charles Erdmann. 'So many busy, healthy bodies in new clothes, going from new houses in new cars to new shops to buy new things — all gained by too much work-for-work's-sake: and so many uneasy natures & deep wells & streams of self-pity and self-deception and resentments looking for a way out'. ATL MS-Papers-0432-177.]

23 October 1959

Dear Plomer,

[. . .] [T]he same disease, raging hell-for-leather, plagues us here too. Those few glimpses of old N.Z. which writers such as Roderick Finlayson & myself provided a few years ago are now curiosities like moa bones. And I'm damned if the Maori too isn't going neurotic. Perhaps the current rumpus over the non-inclusion of Maoris in the rugby touring team for South Africa next year may have achieved some mention in the English press. What is distressing is the *way* in which the Maoris themselves are protesting. I'm all pro-Maori, anti-apartheid, but I feel uneasy when I seem to recognize much that is neurotically based according to the approved European pattern. One's never happy about the high proportion of Maoris in gaol, but how awful if they edge the rest of us out of the mental hospitals as well. Still, racialism such a minor question in this country compared to our all being hell-bent on going American, my poor remarks will probably sound to you intolerably provincial. (What does it matter anyway, when the Indonesians Chinese or Japs will be here within the next 50 years — they may empty out the gaols, but they won't hand the Maori his land back).

That word provincial: a young friend of mine [Kevin Ireland] (a few years ago he used to deliver my newspaper) has just married a Bulgarian girl in Sofia, where he's bent on staying. What astonishes me though, is that he is reported to be living on translations of his poetry, & living comfortably. I can't wait for more information. It seems there must be some vital difference between a provincial outpost of Communism, & ditto of Capitalism. And unless you are a Betjamin wicked centres like London are no improvement.

I am excited over the 100,000 words of my book, & seem to be within striking distance of making it. I find it tedious searching for loose ends to tie up. My title will be *Memoirs of a Peon* (my young bodgie friends call people who drive about in cars, particularly cars with fins, peons: very good, I think, because they work harder, need tranquillizers instead of lime water for their rheumatism, & don't have nearly as much fun), & with luck all should be done by early next year. But it will have taken me 2½ years, & although I've housekept & gardened as well, I've not had to read for a publisher; & I've written nothing else. But speaking of books, the one that has held me most closely lately has been the *Laws of Ecclesiastical Polity*. I was fascinated by both prose & thought, both much superior to the 2 great 1920 volumes of letters by Henry James which for some reason I followed up with, & which made me think of you whenever he was writing from Rye. (I hope I am not too far out in my distances). A baffling person! How *could* he have such a dislike for vulgarity, yet call one of his characters Mrs Cundrip? And with his superb intelligence, how could he fail to see that people like Wilde & Shaw were at least smashing a few windows, & letting in a breath of fresh air? [. . .]

From yours,

F.S.

The Letters 1960–1969

To Janet Frame, *London*

Private collection

15 January 1960

Dear Janet,

I had intended to get off a Christmas note to you, but I was very occupied getting my novel finished. It finally ran out at about 110,000 words, but a heart-breaking job of revision & re-typing is still ahead of me. Then a producing-woman [Edna Harris] became interested in my *Kendall* play, & I have spent the holidays revising & re-typing it for her. She has some reputation from the productions of *The Crucible* & *Under Milk Wood* over in town last year; but I must say I am rapidly reaching the point of exasperation with her. I don't need to tell you that theatrical people exceed writers for vanity illiteracy & a few other execrable vices. But if I can put up with having my darling work generally hacked up, I daresay the public will have a chance of turning thumbs up or down the coming winter.

Albion Wright is feeding the Press with nice pieces of praise for you from your American publisher. He also says he is negotiating publication in England & France. So may you soon benefit financially — & the world be better for the light which shines on its naughtiness from the wonderful little candle which you so inextinguishably ignite for all of us who examine your pages.

I had the other day a visit from Sylvia Ashton-Warner. She has just completed her contract with Metro-Goldwyn-Mayer for *Spinster* (£10,000 down!). S A-W quite fascinating — ravaged with age & the trials of teaching Maori children, but repaired with make-up ½ an inch thick. She is the Anna of the book: i.e. a woman of attractive dottiness touched with just the right amount of dotty genius — very engaging, & moving. [. . .]

I rather too obviously told June & Wilson [Gordon] about the interest in my play, & their come-back is to take up one of John Graham's & push it through their committee. [. . .]

Don't be cross with me, & write sometime soon. And if you can't hang out financially until you have dollars & francs to distribute about the London streets I can get Somebody to accommodate you — I think 'accommodate' is the word. All best you sweet best of writers,

F.S. [. . .]

To Janet Frame, *London*

Private collection

16 July 1960

Dear Janet,

Your excellent letter is dated 10 June, and I am so sorry I have been so long in writing. Getting my novel finally out of the way was a tiresome business, and my reaction was stomach trouble tachycardia and a horrid thing on my arm which 3 surgeons looked at before doing an excision. I was at my wits' end to know what to do with the novel, but finally sent it airmail to London. Your line is with Patience Ross [of A.M. Heath Ltd.], and mine is with Sheila Watson [of Pearn, Pollinger & Higham] (I suspect of course that when literary agents with masculine names hand you over to female offsiders they consider you either no good or else good but virtually unsaleable). I'll tell you more about my literary agent when I know more, i.e. when they turn me down, although Lord knows a few of my pages make Lolita look like a Sunday school prize, and surely all that sort of thing can't have gone out of fashion.

As for my play, my troubles there haven't been good for my illnesses either, particularly my tachycardia. The insolent theatrical non-entities I am dealing with now want me to provide a sufficient number of copies of the text, and as it would kill me to do the job myself just at present the cost would be a mere £25. *And* after 6 to 8 rehearsals the end product would probably be merely a reading before an invited audience. Fortunately I've had to apply myself to doing a memorial note on D'Arcy Cresswell for Landfall, and the job stops (I use language which you will readily understand) my troubles from preying on my mind.

I sent off Landfall 54 a short time ago, and you will *love* Karl's long story in it ['A Race Apart']. Amazing, stupid people can't see anything to it, and how wrong they are!

In a roundabout way I discovered that the Pegasus has about £300 to your credit. Have you received this yet? If not you should ask for it, or what you want from it immediately. Let me know if there is any hold-up. But your best news is about parting with fresh work. Marvellous! And do tell me more next time. Of course if you have spare copies I should be delighted to be accorded the privilege of a peep. (If Karl had never let me peep his story would never have seen the light of day — he had tried to force it all into the diary form and it wouldn't go. It was very easy to tell him to make it mainly a narrative and he adjusted it marvellously).

Am afraid I am feeling my years, and the three year strain of the novel cost me too much. I have been trying to substitute fruit trees for vegetables in the garden, and now what with the high hedges as well I am cramped and hemmed in. Neighbours complain on all sides. Also I neglected to repair the roof of the hut and now until I get to it it is uninhabitable. My aunts defeat me by flourishing abominably. If it wasn't for the Divine Comedy I would be a sad case indeed. I have the whole of The Faery Queene to read, but I started on the Commedia (with an excellent page by page crib) and couldn't leave it off. The Purgatorio is much the best from several points of view (we all know what hell is like, what we want to know is how to get out) except for Beatrice at the end of it (she is presented as an impossible bitch). The Paradiso is the most difficult, but I have enjoyed going from heaven to heaven and nearly am now to the empyrean. (All not true of course, but a wonderful Metaphor).

My old friend Bake and I get the Spectator, and I see *Ross* (about T.E. Lawrence) at the Haymarket is getting good notices. If finances permit you a visit, do tell me whether the rape of the hero takes place on or off stage.

Nothing much to this letter, but do write soon if you can,

Love,

F.S.

[D'Arcy Cresswell died in London on 21 February 1960.]

To W.H. Henderson, *Takapuna Borough Council*

Alexander Turnbull Library

[On 1 August 1960 Takapuna ratepayers received a circular letter from the Borough Council justifying a recent rate increase, and outlining how revenue would be spent. In addition to normal servicing and maintenance, priority would be given to re-sealing streets, kerbing and channelling, stormwater provision and concrete footpaths. ATL MS-Papers-0432-140.]

[August 1960]

Mr Mayor,

This is all very well, and if drainage improvements rid the beach of french letters well and good — but when are those of us who don't own cars going to have proper transport? And when is the Bus Company going to be prevented from polluting the atmosphere with diesel soot? When is the Council going to wake up about the fumes problem generally? When are we going to see the Library enlarged to ten times its size to provide for us adequately? And when is the Council going to see beyond the mechanics of kerbing and channelling and take a lead in endeavouring to establish a proper COMMUNITY instead of the tasty dormitory suburb it is committed to?

Frank Sargeson

To E.P. Dawson, *Mt Maunganui*

Hocken Library

[A rehearsed reading of A Time For Sowing, *presented by Edna Harris and the W.E.A. Dramatic Club players, took place on 20 October 1960.]*

31 October 1960

Dear Peter,

Since you were one of the few people who knew something of what was in my play before performance, perhaps I should give you some account of what has happened. I am myself mainly reminded of what has happened by a row of little bottles — assorted vitamins, phenol-barb, tranquillizers, colloidal aluminium, anti-spasm pills, migraine-disperser. I think that's about the lot, but not nearly enough — I mean when one is engaged with the presentation of one's own play. After the mad and exhausting rehearsals it went on a week ago last Thursday in a derelict Presbyterian church not far from the Zoo. (Formerly St Mungo's, apparently). There was no publicity except in the Star on the night, and whether or not that produced an effect quite a crowd turned up. Standing room only. There was a scratch setting, scratch costuming, and scratch lighting, and each character endeavoured to act with script in hand (it was officially a reading). And yet, strangely, 2 of the five principal figures came off beautifully, and 2 did well enough — but the fifth, alas, Kendall himself, was an unspeakable travesty of the part which still makes me blush. Edna Harris played Mrs Kendall herself — quite successfully. But of course she had to struggle with the double task of her part and her heroic endeavour to hold the thing together in the face of K's atrocious bumbling and banalities. The audience behaved like a collective angel — no titters or laughs in the wrong places. Interesting though the evening was however, I very much doubt whether I have any chance of seeing it as [an Auckland] Festival play for next year. The theatrical crowd are now presuming to judge it on the evidence of the evening's Kendall — and that is ridiculous. His part has so far been neither seen nor heard, and until he is properly presented no valid judgment is possible. The root of the trouble is that alone among the five principals he is a round character — all the rest are flat, and of course theatrical people are at home with flat characters, and much resent anyone who does not behave according to their preconceived notions.

Any how I am a wreck. I have a great pile of script that was used and out of it I have somehow to extract what should be the final text of the play. But at the moment it appears to me a task far beyond my powers.

My novel [*Memoirs of a Peon*] went off to begin its adventures in June — but in 4 to 5 months it has succeeded only in getting itself rejected by a firm of agents [Pearn, Pollinger and Higham], and being silently sat upon for six weeks by Weidenfeld and Nicholson (I thought I would try them as they published Lolita — hence should have a little money in hand.) I am informed however that publishing is in a state of chaos in London at present owing to the continuing inflation and rising costs. Janet has greatly assisted me by receiving and posting off the typescript as I direct, and after reading the thing she wrote me letters which encourage me to believe the whole thing is not altogether a waste of time. I hope she is right. Perhaps you have heard from her, and know that she has signed a contract with Pegasus for another book [*Faces in the Water*]. She insists on its demerits, but I hope on that point she is wrong.

And you? I hope very much you have been getting along. I have managed to keep the garden going in this worst of all miserable springs, but everything is slow (the potatoes I dig are distressingly small for mature plants.)

No more just now, but all my best wishes,

F.S.

[The Scottish meat inspector-cum-theatre director Christopher Cathcart and the artist Colin McCahon, then working for the Auckland Art Gallery, were present at the reading of A Time for Sowing. *They agreed the play had potential if a suitable Kendall could be found, and began to discuss plans for a production at the Gallery. Cathcart would direct; McCahon would provide the venue and set.]*

To William Plomer, *Sussex*

Alexander Turnbull Library

[On 12 April 1960 Plomer had told FS he was a co-editor of the annual PEN anthology for 1961: 'Barrow-loads of poems arrive at my hide-out. All are interesting, very few indeed worth thinking twice about'. ATL MS-Papers-0432-177. The following letter replies to one of 27 November 1960.]

3 February 1961

Dear Plomer,

I was so sorry about your weather last year, but it was here too; atomic weather I think — the sort of rainwater that leaks into the Thames at Harwell (is it?) & should really confine itself to the USSR, US & the Sahara (& if that word has any relation to Abraham's wife, it's a pity it didn't leak onto her too, & dish the O.T. What a loss that wouldn't have been!) But we have reached the age when we know there is no justice in this world.

Still, a wonderful summer season. For you, I'm glad the sun is going your way again; but full of pity for myself. Each year when I gather the summer & autumn fruits I'm sure it's for the last time.

About your barrowloads of verse last year, I meant to mention Merrill Moore who was about these parts in the war years — he had at that time written 40,000 sonnets; but he more than doubled the number before he died a few years ago: he kept them, I believe, in a sonnetarium — which I always imagine as a kind of strong-box summerhouse, built on the front lawn of his place in Boston. The point is, you must admit, that your reading task could not compare with his creative giantism. But a really extraordinary person — I can still remember how to mimic his doing a talk up at the university college — & yet he was more incomprehensible to me than any improbable Kurd who might have wandered into the college from darkest Kurdistan. [. . .]

Since I wrote last a scratch reading-performance of my play about the first missionary has been put on. But now I am busy helping with plans for an arena-ed performance in a huge room at the Art Gallery in the winter. My producer this time is a little Scotsman improbably (to me) named Cathcart, who has been only 4 years in the country. He is the 1st theatrical person to understand my play — I mean what it's about. I asked him how come? and he replied well, he was brought up in Scotland — in other words, he finds the decayed puritanism, guilt etc. pretty much the same. The trouble is, perhaps, I have to handle my material with such discretion — the Church of England got off to such an unpropitious start at the beginning of last century. My missionary, Kendall, brought his Maori concubines into the house to live, & his wife produced a child by their ex-convict servant. He was replaced by a man who also had trouble — & then came the Rev. Yate who earned himself the distinction of being the 1st N.Z. homosexual to be officially found out. (Interesting that after returning to England he ran a home for seamen in Plymouth).

It is very kind of you to ask after my novel. I'm afraid I am better at asking for help on behalf of other people (the Frames & the Steads), than I am to push along my own interests. In fact I have tried 2 English publishers — a 'quality' firm took 3½ months to say no, & the same answer came from one of the big big shows in 3 weeks. What I more or less expected. I sometimes think of you as *The Last Publisher's Reader*. (We've already had *The Last Romantic*, & I remember an article by Thomas Mann in which dear old Karl Wolfskehl was called *The Last Man*). I mean publishers' clerks will flick over the pages of typescripts to see how many tits & crotches can be put on the plastic cover — & that will be all. I find I can't be seriously bothered — I read so much poetry these days, prose becomes tedious. Yes, I can guess how difficult publishing is — costs catching up on prices, & fear of increasing the latter. [. . .] And when you get round to your next letter, just jot down for me the names of a few firms with whom there might be a chance. (I may be wrong, but despite even severer costs in America, I have the notion American publishers are somewhat more adventurous — also I imagine that despite appearances to the contrary they sometimes connect liveliness with good writing). [. . .]

Did you hear the story of the American woman who had Kennedy's face tattooed on the top of one thigh, & Nixon's on the other? but she still couldn't make up her mind how to vote & returned to the tattooist to have the faces removed: he said he could do that; but definitely, he couldn't do anything about Fidel Castro's in the middle.

Happy Spring for you,

F.S.

To Charles Brasch, *Dunedin*

Hocken Library

[The build-up to the six-night season of A Time for Sowing *was stressful. In March FS suffered a haemorrhage in his right eye and learned that yet another publisher (Putnam) had rejected* Memoirs of a Peon*; two weeks before the play opened on 31 May the actor cast in the crucial role of Kendall walked out, and Chris Cathcart stepped into the breach. FS medicated himself with 'a terrible new drug "Librium" — I really poisoned myself, but some obscure instinct prompted me to sip lots of honey in hot water, and I came to'. To John Reece Cole, 27 May. ATL MS-Papers-4648-14. Brasch and Cole travelled to Auckland especially for the production; FS travelled back to Wellington with Cole — via Tokaanu — for a much-needed break.]*

Tokaanu
Friday [June 1961]

Dear Charles,

It was all so infinitely kind of you — the trip to Auckland, everything. I do hope you got home safely.

Here I am just out of the thermal water [. . .] — here thanks to John Cole. We reach Wellington tomorrow & I expect I shall be back in Takapuna by the end of the next week.

The play built up & built up — next to no advertising but the audience became more & more overflowing. The last night was said to be the best — Roberta [Elliott in the role of Mrs Kendall] by that time had become quite marvellous & the others did nobly — Chris never missing a cue. I looked in only at the end. The cast nearly wept at its being all over — but the strain was becoming too much for Colin & the Gallery people. A performance may however be given in Hamilton in a week or a fortnight — an urgent invitation, & the cast has held its tears meantime.

It's all really been wonderful — much too exciting for me. Tell you more when I'm home again. [. . .]

My ever-renewed thanks to you for so much

from Frank

To Janet Frame, *London*

Private collection

18 August 1961

My dear Janet,

[. . .] I haven't [seen the] good Steads for ages, I've fallen out with Karl who finds me malicious (which of course I am: I on my part am inclined to find him brutal), and apparently doesn't understand that one should never dislike people for their vices, (which can be charming), only for the virtues (which can be nauseating: I'm inclined to think it's really on account of my virtues that Karl dislikes me). The root of the matter is that it pains me very much to see Karl sucked into the University (I really am malicious in mentioning all the poetry and prose he hasn't read and which he certainly should have if he is going to take the University seriously).

I think these days my obsession with reading is connected with my obsession that it may not be long before I am unable to read at all. Meantime I gobble up God knows what — Chaucer, Trollope (one great political novel after another), I adored *Geoffry Hamlyn* (Henry Kingsley) — but it is Chaucer who has topped the lot lately (you can by the way get a slightly modernised *Troilus* in Everyman, and also a magnificent volume of the *Tales* which gives you the real text).

So Peter sent you some of the notices of the play. Nobody saw we produced it as a passion play (did I tell you this before?), but never mind, it hit the crowd in the solar plexus and the great moment each night was when Chris Cathcart threw the big Bible on the floor (the Art Gallery floor is tiled and it went a terrific slap, and finally he knocked the cover off it, and it was a prize last century copy borrowed from some collection). Strangely, although I swore never to endure the strain of another play, we are now beginning to try to repeat our success by preparing for a shot at my other play [*The Cradle and the Egg*] next year.

Do I pain you by saying I was very pleased to see the prominence of the ODC review in the N[ew] S[tatesman]? Not a wholly dumb notice, and no matter how *you* feel it thrills *me* to think of your getting a pretty good hearing. I only hope and pray some money has come in. I must confess I find myself in somewhat straitened circumstances at present, but hope the situation may be somewhat remedied before too long. At any rate I must find pocket money for you if I have to employ you as literary agent again. [Rupert] Hart-Davis is now threatening me that if I leave the *Peon* there any longer it will probably get lost. I am awaiting a decision from [the publisher and bookseller] Blackwood Paul in Hamilton who has shilly-shallied for months (he's apparently scared of offering to take 3000 or so copies from H-D and then finding they get held up by the Customs). I'm afraid, more about this anon.

I have to have labour in now to top my hedges and rotary hoe the soil if I'm to get my vegetables. I have to plant without stooping which is supposed to be dangerous to my eyesight, so I remember by remembering that I'm largely a woman anyhow, and going down as though about to do a female widdle. [. . .]

Bye-bye for now. I hope the Indian summer is on you and lovely (remember bathing in a lukewarm sea in Devon in mid-September, with Lundy Island — where Ngaio Marsh's ancestors lived, I think — pirates — very appropriate — off the coast like a battleship as Curnow says in one of his poems).

All best love,

F.S.

['I have fallen out with Karl': around this time Brasch invited Stead to succeed him as editor of Landfall. *To FS's disappointment Stead declined the offer, citing the financial insecurity of the position. Stead confirmed that the cause of friction was FS's feeling that he should not be in the university, but 'out writing, living on air as he did'. Personal correspondence, 24 May 2011.]*

To Janet Frame, *London*

Private collection

[In 1958 Janet Frame had changed her name by deed poll to Janet Clutha. The review of Owls Do Cry *in* Time *blew this carefully constructed cover: 'Author Frame has herself been in and out of mental hospitals as a voluntary patient. Shy and wary of publicity, she has recently changed her name to Janet Clutha (after a New Zealand river).' FS blamed Albion Wright for the indiscretion. [FS to Christine Cole, 28 September, ATL MS-Papers-4648-14.] A performance of* A Time for Sowing *had been videotaped in September for television broadcast.]*

4 October 1961

Dear Janet,

I have just lately seen TIME for 22 Sept. Of course I'm enormously pleased the book has attracted this attention because my dear it may well mean you will have a little more than pocket money to handle. But equally of course I am enormously worried over the upset the introduction of the personal matter may cause you. I think we can both guess who has supplied the personal detail, and I find it unforgivable. I can only emphatically say, Never mind! It's a kind of occupational risk we all run. I will say no more, but believe me, you have all my deepest sympathy — very genuine when I can imagine so vividly the pain it may well cause you. [. . .]

Incidentally, I too grow more and more shy of publicity, and I fear now I must face some over the television. I haven't seen the preview yet, but I'm told it is so impressive (mainly on account of the work of Cathcart who plays Kendall — Cathcart is one of the good fortunes of my life. When you read the text of the play here he was far away in Scotland, a working-class-lower-middle-class young man who had no schooling after about 14. But he has the tenacity and respect for learning of the Scot, and with his flair for acting and producing, not to mention understanding, he has done more for the play than I ever dreamed possible despite my resistance to the dim opinions of the local theatrical illiterati), that they are thinking of trying to do a more technically perfect remake with a view to sending it over to Australia. Who knows? — it might continue to snowball. Who knows? — it might even penetrate the parlours of Camberwell. It won't of course be the play I wrote, but my guess is that Cathcart and his team will be worth watching — and may it bring a little money to us all! [. . .]

I'm sorry about your coming winter but glad over our spring. Unfortunately I haunt a medical laboratory — no kidney disease, no diabetes, but no nearer to discovering why the retinal veins should break.

Did I tell you one aunt died? — the blind one — she had about a thousand pounds but she has left all to my widowed sister who two years ago did so well out of her deceased husband that one can only assume she could hardly have done better if she had been a call-girl.

No more, but fondest love,

Fx

[In late October 1961, Cathcart, Sargeson and McCahon formed the New Independant Theatre, complete with letterhead, 'with view to prizing money out of the Arts Council for Cradle and Egg *next year. If we clinch the success of Kendall we would want to go on producing NZ plays'. FS to John Reece Cole, 25 October 1961. ATL MS-Papers-4648-14.]*

To Janet Frame, *London*

Private collection

25 October 1961

Dearest Janet,

[. . .] Very kind of you with Patience [Ross] — I too shall be Patience sitting on my own private monument here until I am told (as I probably will be) that I am no good to Patience in London no matter how mutually patient (or impatiently patient) we may be.

My dear, this should be an airmail *letter* with a little pocket money for you — for heaven's sake don't suppose that I suppose you are in the money now and not in need of a teeny-tiny kind thought. Simple truth is until I am over the delay of the television contract I am just a teeny bit financially embarrassed. (Did I tell you the blind aunt died and never left me a penny — all to my widowed sister, who I'm afraid will share a tiny fraction only with reluctance. However it's the fat 88 year old aunt who has all the money, and it's my last chance).

So glad about the [funds received for stories published in the] *New Yorker*, but of course I worry about your being in the hands of rapacious literary hangers-on like agents and publishers.

I read [marginal note: present tense] the long and prominent review of *Faces* with much interest indeed — I mean in the local papers. My ordered copy turned up, and although I shall *never* agree with you in your estimates of your own work, I am just a teeny-tiny bit inclined to suppose, being the luminously intelligent young woman you are, you may be partly right in supposing yourself not to be too satisfied with this book. The opening chapter is one of the most brilliant passages of modern writing I know of — but afterwards, *perhaps*, you *may* fall between the two stools of your imaginative genius and the necessity of reporting. However my dear, you have told me that you wrote it for the doctor, so why not just sit back and let the public take it — it's nothing to do with you now, and if anyone of us has the right to a little public support you have. Do I upset you? I do hope not.

Oh, I wish my nervousness would abate a bit. My eyesight is all the time very chancey, but the general nervousness is the more upsetting. I simply go on reaching for the barbitone bottle.

Now no more this time, as I'm not too bad this morning and am trying to knock off a necessary letter or two. I expect vapourization impending is a common topic of conversation in London, and special umbrellas in the shops to keep off a rain of copper needles. As for me, I try to memorize all the best verses of the poets.

All my best,
Lyndall

[The USSR resumed nuclear testing in September 1961. Lyndall: one of the three main characters, with Em and Waldo, of Olive Schreiner's Story of an African Farm.*]*

To Charles Brasch, *Dunedin*

Hocken Library

[Blackwood Paul wrote to FS in April 1961 suggesting a NZ reprint of That Summer and Other Stories, *and approached Bill Pearson to write an introduction.]*

28 November 1961

Dear Charles,

Can *you* understand the kind of world which surrounds us in our near old age? For 3 weeks that video tape [of *A Time for Sowing*] was lost — it was thought in the post, but eventually it turned out somebody had posted it to Christchurch instead of Wellington. The preview here was at last jacked up for last Thursday, and quite a crowd (many I invited myself as I think I had a premonition of calamity). I won't say it was surprisingly good, but it was at least surprising. Telecasting date was 18 December, but in the Star last Friday it was announced that the tape had been irreparably damaged during preview and would never be telecast. Sabotage? Or what? Anyhow the contract cunningly said I would be paid (the original £60 had been reduced to £30 as it had been decided that it would be used on Channel 2 only to test reactions) when telecast. So no money (the cast haven't been paid yet either, but I expect they will be) no plans for a re-make so far as I know and indeed no official news at all.

Blackwood Paul still dithers most irritatingly over the reprint of *That Summer*, and Lawson at Whitcombes is taking as long to decide about the *Peon* as Blackwood did. Janet most kindly tried to get her London agent to help with the *Peon*, and now they say they regret very much not taking it up as the book has 'distinct quality'. However they say Day Lewis is now with Chatto and most kindly offered to send it on in a plain wrapper if I would write him. So this is my current shot. [. . .]

And you? I still feel guilty over my neglect of the last *Landfall* (I turned to the poetry and for some reason it drove me to *Don Juan* which I now find becomes more profound towards the end as it becomes less lively than in its beginnings — I find myself with the crazy notion of devoting a year or so to putting my *Peon* into verse — it's the kind of thing which should be in verse anyhow).

Alas, more eye trouble, but the young specialist thinks I am still quite a way from losing my sight — though I suspect he conceals from me that the good eye may show 'sympathetic' reactions. But alas, alas, Dennis McEldowney who came to Greenlane for another heart operation has now had a stroke and is in bad shape poor fellow. [. . .] [Only one page survives.]

To Janet Frame, *London*

Private collection

[FS to Frame, 5 December 1961: 'My dear, I am entranced by your success — I am continuously coming across snippets and long notices [. . .]. My dear, take it all in your stride. You know Trollope, who said success should only be taken late in life and even then in small doses — but he took his in large doses fairly early on. Of course it can kill — vide Dickens — but I've lately read for the first time The Mystery of Edwin Drood, *and what genius!' Janet Frame Literary Trust.]*

18 January 1962

Dear Janet,

Many thanks for yours, and I am so sorry I was foolish enough to talk of your 'success' — I expect I was partly taken in by Albion Wright's propaganda which appears everywhere. Believe me, it has worried me very much that he would without doubt be sticking to the letter of his contract, and thus soaking you far too heavily for his over-share of income. Of course I have my reservations about all middlemen and suchlike, but if Patience can bring off better arrangements for you that will be very good. Anyhow I see now that a re-issue of *The Lagoon* has lately come from the Caxton — and surely by no legerdemain can the Pegasus claim any share from *that*.

Instead of congratulating you upon your 'success' may I instead speak my little tribute to your wonderful energy-cum-very-wonderful-literary-quality. (How 'success' can come to any of us I don't know — what is one to think when people who should know better ask if they may borrow from me my copy of *Faces*?) Let's leave it at that.

Do accept the enclosed poor few shillings — Holyoake's Government in sad trouble has reduced the pound limit to five shillings, and I could hit on only one acquaintance to help when I was along at the post office. And so nice of you to send me the snuff — I am so interested to go out smelling like a man of a certain type. And no tobacco smell to cover it up now — I've left off smoking to see if this non-indulgence may perhaps give my eyes a chance — I have about six pairs of glasses and sometimes put them all on at once (ha ha fourteen eyes!), but nothing is going to be much good when the clever technique I've developed enables me to sit back and watch the haemorrhages oozing inside my eyes until I flick them about to get the blood to mix with the vitreous humour. Horrid though this sounds, it's much horrider when a different type of bleeding makes horrid patches on the retina. Strangely, I expect to go some time yet before things get impossibly worse — they may even take a turn for the better.

Peter as perhaps you know has sold up at Mt Maunganui, and speaks of getting off to England. What on earth she is searching for at her age I don't know — I mean a 'what' that implies a geographical change.

I have decided not to trouble any more with the *Peon* in England, so the typescript is now on the way back to me. Whitcombe and Ts have been considering the work here for the last 4 months. Many thanks for all you did on its behalf. At the moment heat and drought and the entire section and garden is all tinder — I should be paying attention to last revisions of the play we hope to put on this year, but instead I dream & read poetry and forgotten out of the way novels. When your *Landfall* reaches you for December you will find Maurice [Duggan]'s *Riley's Handbook* interesting — a kind of anti-epic, a real creation against odds. [. . .]

Well, must fly. Am sorry about the chairs facing the same way — but at your age something *does* turn up again — you'll see. Not for me though — now. I don't mind (if I can give up tobacco, I can give up *any*thing.)

All so much of the best,

Love,

Fx.

To Charles Brasch, *Dunedin*

Hocken Library

*[Brasch to FS, 6 March: 'I am reeling through Patrick White's new novel [*Riders in the Chariot*], now and then hardly able to go on, it is so terrible and powerful; some of the pages abt life in Australia are the most withering satire I think I've ever read and turn me to jelly with terror for the future of the world. [. . .]' ATL MS-Papers-0432-148.]*

12 March 1962

Dear Charles,

[. . .] Theatre plans are one minute off and the next on — on at present — but much theatre in Auckland has suddenly become uncertain as [the Adult Education/Community Arts Service theatre producer Ronald] Barker has created a sensation by staging a brief episode from his private life under the eye of the law in a public convenience. So grotesque as to be madly funny if one for a moment forgets the suffering (which one can't). But just to indicate how determined I am to cope (and putting on a play is always I think a prolonged headache), let me say that from the beginning of the year I have given up smoking — I find I can't go on working in several directions and have that indulgence as well.

I have lately concluded my correspondence with Stringer of the NZBS over the damaged video tape. He never got round to one word of apology or regret, and I think chances of their doing the play again are very slight. I was paid £30 — but I *had* to resist the suggestion that this was their compassion instead of my right. They were incompetent and bungling, but of course I couldn't reveal how I came by my certain knowledge that they were when Stringer would admit only to 'a simple mechanical failure'. But how much of one's energy is wasted in nonsense of this kind!

I believe Bill Pearson has been busy during vacation and hasn't got very far with my stories. Whitcombes believe it or not have been deciding about my *Peon* novel since the beginning of October and haven't decided yet. Bob Chapman kindly arranged for me a meeting with 2 Heinemann directors lately, and they have taken the typescript with them to London — but I shall be very surprised if this move leads to anything. [. . .]

Must fly, Charles. Others have told me I should give Patrick White another chance now. [. . .]

F.S.

Actually Charles I gave up the smoking because I had more bleeding in my bad eye, and commonsense told me I would have a better chance without cigarettes. My doctor is very elated — how rarely can he persuade his human guinea pigs to cooperate when such austerity is required! He is just frothing to discover what will happen now. [. . .]

To John Reece Cole, *Wellington*

Alexander Turnbull Library

28 April 1962

Dear Reece,

[. . .] [W]e are well into rehearsals [of *The Cradle and the Egg*], and damn me, the thing comes to life quicker than Kendall. Colin and Chris do wonders, but we have severe casting problems, and by the time we go on Colin and I will probably have put up £50 or more each. Any one of a dozen slips, and it's all down the drain. However the adventure of the thing is stimulating, and surely it's a real achievement if something can be brought off two years running.

I suggested a collection among the University people of money for Barker, and we managed to collect about £50. The axe in the form of dismissal has fallen, but in a sense he's behaving badly as he continues to kick against a stroke of fate which none of us can see put into reverse. (Yet nothing ads up — after all Johnnie Ray is here now, and Claudio Arrau and Liberace are to follow, and the Herald after featuring nauseating attacks on B will be carrying ads for these others).

I came across *The Voyage of the Beagle* in the new Everyman paper backs lately. What a marvellous book! And how ever has one missed it! (And I have always been such an admirer of Darwin's momentous book). Anyhow the wonders of the Beagle have even knocked my poetry-reading. (His distaste for New Zealand, people and scenery, I find refreshing — I expect all of us who make a prolonged effort to do something in this country eventually get a kick out of discovering that notable people also felt themselves up against it.)

Should I send you on Mike Joseph's *A Pound of Saffron*? The play-producing professor is suspiciously like Musgrove. But oh God, Mike, he's the Square of Squares — he becomes Cube. (Where he refers to his children as 'riotous offshoots' I couldn't resist altering it to 'chips off the old blockhead'.)

Whitcombes say they would put the *Peon* to the Lit Fund, but would like the first fifty pages and the last ten re-written. I don't mind this, but I just can't take their sending me a summary of God knows how many anonymous reviews. (Prepublication reviews by Square reviewers — what preposterous publishing!) [. . .]

F.S.

[The American pop singer Johnnie Ray was arrested twice for homosexual activity; the Chilean concert pianist Claudio Arrau had been charged with 'offensive behaviour' in Sydney in 1957.]

To Charles Brasch, *[London]*

Hocken Library

3 July 1962

Dear Charles,

[. . .] Just a word about the play [*The Cradle and the Egg*]. We got very bad press notices — the *Herald* really vicious, and Harold Carter on the air ridiculously stupid. Nonetheless we had three good nights out of six, and built up again to a really splendid final with cheers and everything (all the students came at last and caught on). And now Musgrove has surprisingly (to me) reviewed us appreciatively and intelligently in the *Listener*. Not the 'success' of last year, but Colin and I are very gratified at recovering every penny we laid out (indeed, we show a profit of one pound). Discriminating people such as [Art Gallery director Peter] Tomory were not in doubt, and now the New Independent Theatre has been invited to put on a play for his November Season of the Arts (this is his answer to the big Festival falseness which gets worse each year). Expenses thank heaven guaranteed by the City Council, and Colin and I are letting Chris put on a Graham play — Chris wants to do it, and if anyone can get something out of it he can. (He insists that he is leaving us all next June — a tragedy, his producing and acting in the *Cradle* was a marvel when he carried such a burden). [. . .]

But WHY should you read this when it must be like a lump of tough raw meat tossed into a nice European dish just ready to be served?

I do hope you are having the best of times, Charles,

From yours,

F.S. [. . .]

To William Plomer, *Sussex*

Alexander Turnbull Library

24 December 1962

Dear Plomer,

[. . .] Well well, Cuba etc. what a world, and how much longer! Yet tiny personal things nag and nag (I remember for example that a few Christmas's ago I wrote a note to E.M. Forster — that wonder among men and writers! — and what should I address him as — I think as *Foster*. The reason being that for many years I was fond of an old lady who spelt herself that way. Anyhow, for years I have intended to apologise, and never have — apart of course from renewing my regards for him — before it is too late!).

I have lately sent you a very substantial and really quite handsome volume, an Anthology picked from Charles Brasch's *Landfall* over fifteen years or so [*Landfall Country*]. Of course you don't have to read it, a glance will be sufficient. And all probably that is deserved by many of the embalmed fossils between its covers. But what devoted work Charles Brasch has done for literature in this country.

I wonder if you get on with Patrick White these days. I still find I just can't read him at all, but remain undecided whether this is to his disadvantage or my own. I rejoice in Janet Frame's success. She writes me many curious letters — and curiously they come now from a somewhat expensive flat in Kensington. I get very irritated over her limitations as a writer, but for a sentence or two she can break from them, and when she is at her best she is very good indeed. The most curious blend of what is both amusing and pathetic, and verbal brilliance of remarkable quality. Of course she is far more desperately insane than she will ever permit anyone to discern.

My sixtieth birthday is coming up — and so is yours too I think. May you be finding life bearable and perhaps a little more (I don't see how any of us can expect more than a little more). I worry a bit about my damned varicosed retina, but I continue with the garden (wonderful this year — no drought so far), and our New Independent Theatre, although very time-consuming is a wonderful addition to more usual literary work. (We have lately finished playing a work by another New Zealander [John Graham's *Lest We Resemble*] — not much intellectual substance, but tolerably good theatre).

[. . .] I greatly offended a Zen Buddhist the other day by referring to his latest piece of Scripture as *Let's Go* instead of *Let Go*.

I wonder sometimes too how you manage with old friends — mine tend to be somewhat older than I am. So they suddenly die, or become breathless with leaky valves, and so on. One must be loyal, but what is one to think of any possible Creator? I judge myself pretty much convinced of one thing — human life is a mistake which we have to put up with. I don't mind putting up once, but that will be quite enough. Thank nobody very much.

However, and if only I could send you today's sunlight from my garden!

F.S.

To Janet Frame, *London*

Private collection

7 January 1963

Dearest J,

[. . .] I want to say I finished the *Alphabet* shouting mental cheers (I shall not cease from mental cheers). A very excellent performance. Apart from all else, there's nobody who excels you for verbal brilliance. But the 'all else' is tremendous too. Let's take the excellences and all that is tremendous for granted, and get down to a point of criticism. There may be the tiniest grain of lack of sophistication in your insistence on death. Can't we, (I mean you and I and some others) take it for granted that everything worth reading is about death — I mean fundamentally. Then why plug it overmuch? Let me put it in a more practical way. I hope and hope that in your next you will be delighting all of us with much drawn from your Spanish experience. The death will be very much there very naturally — but surely there of all places is where you may safely allow it to be taken for granted, mainly.

Perhaps though I am all wrong about this. If so, just ignore what I say.

Incidentally, did I ever tell you, or do you know independently, one of George [Frame]'s best anecdotes? Somewhere round Notthing Hill some kind of actor type first shouted him a few drinks before getting him to his flat. It became a question of staying all night. George made quite a point about how he wouldn't stay even though he was offered a fiver. At this point Mr Mischief Sargeson inquired whether his decision would have been the same if the sum had been £50. George's brow was a bit furrowed with thought but he was definite. No. So I kept raising it until I got to £5000. The furrows disappeared, and the thinker triumphantly announced, 'Ah, but he wouldn't have offered that'.

A trifle enclosed. (Incidentally I sent a similar trifle to Roberta Elliott — leading lady in both my plays, but now doing it hard in London — though now gone to Finland to teach in Berlitz School. Anyhow, according to her it virtually saved her from freezing, at 6d in the gasmeter at a time).

All best,

F.S. (*Lyndall-Waldo*)

[Frame's third novel, The Edge of the Alphabet, *was published in the US in September 1962 and in the UK in November. The NZ edition was released in March 1963. Lyndall-Waldo: See* The Story of An African Farm.*]*

To John Reece Cole, *Wellington*

Alexander Turnbull Library

3 May 1963

[The Arts Advisory Council commissioned a bronze bust of FS from the Auckland sculptor Alison Duff in December 1962. FS initially prevaricated on the grounds that the Arts Council had turned down the New Independent Theatre's request for funding — 'I am reluctant to believe that a responsible body would want to see the achievement of our Theatre, and its significance for our country, wiped out: and at the same time commission you [. . .]', FS to Alison Duff, 22 December (ATL MS-Papers-0432-140), but he had relented by February 1963.]

Dear Reece,

[. . .]Your remarks have triggered me off for a paper on private and state patronage which I will read if there is a function when AD's bust is handed over to the Library. The core of the matter is that these state servants suppose that wealth is a matter of bits of paper issued by the treasury — that's to say they part with wealth to satisfy pests who want to have fun and games. The Duke of Rutland on the contrary was in no uncertainty when he supported Crabbe — he parted with something which he knew was nothing unless it could be put to use in assisting Crabbe to produce real wealth. But damn it all, it isn't only Fairway Malcolm and who else who have let me down (I don't mean *me* personally, I mean what I stand for) it's (sad to say) the whole lot of you. When is just one of you going to stand up to your Minister boss or whatever and say 'The job I am doing demands that I be a person of cultivated mind and sensibilities, and that's only possible if I devote most of my time to achieving that end — that's to say, 9 to 5 is OUT, but 2 to 4 would be reasonable'. And you! who know how these things are done in more enlightened communities too!

Nor will economics and demand solve anything. For about 3 days at the hypertension clinic I stared across the valley at a fresh abomination below St Paul's church — asking myself why in heaven a new cinema or perhaps a super milk bar had to be built down there — until I woke up and realized I was looking at the new Elam School [of Fine Arts].

And the final blow! (really wrapped round with cotton wool). I always remember how Bake would repeat, 'No NZder can delegate authority and responsibility'. This ties up with 'do it yourself' — anybody can produce plays for example, (even people like John Thompson), so why bother with anyone with every skill at his fingertips like Chris Cathcart?

Well! Well!

Best,

F.S.

To James Laughlin, *New York*

Houghton Library

24 July 1963

Dear Laughlin,

God knows how many times I have intended sending you a line, particularly when I have found myself jolted by events on one's personal horizon as horrid as that bloodstain that spread over my rooftop from the rainbow bomb too damn close to this hideout country. Merrill Moore was a shock — I wonder if you heard of Fairburn. One of the most extraordinary people ever to come to light in the southern hemisphere, a ball of health and all, and he goes and folds up on us at the age of 52.

I have so much to thank you for too — all those *Perspectives*, many of your books which I contrive to get hold of, and your catalogues are always a reminder of some things I've put off for far too long.

Meantime, this note goes to you with a typescript called MEMOIRS OF A PEON which I've been getting Curtis Brown to look at in New York. They don't think I'm salable, and probably they are right. But you or some reader might care to have a look at the thing. If so I'd be grateful for a line with suggestions if any occur to you. A line anyhow, and I will then supply you with postal coupons for returning the typescript to me if you think that's what should be done with it.

Incidentally, the thing is supposed to be mainly *funny*. But I would agree that this may not be blindingly obvious to the reader until he gets beyond page 50.

All my regards to you,

Frank Sargeson [. . .]

To William Harrison [Bill] Pearson, *Auckland*

Alexander Turnbull Library

[Pearson's novel Coal Flat *was published by Blackwood and Janet Paul in April 1963.]*

26 July 1963

Dear Bill,

My final attack on CF was successful, and I have also managed to read quite a lot of it again.

I don't know what Glover meant by your not finishing it, but I suppose he may have wanted some word about what happened to the boy. (Not important in my view — insofar as the boy may be taken as, in part anyhow, one of your own self-identifications, the answer is obvious).

It's a very remarkable book — I thought it was no longer possible to write a novel of that kind (perhaps it is, one must remember how long it has taken to achieve print). There's no denying you build up sentence by sentence and have solved the problem how to make these strike the reader as containing a tremendous force. I can instance the 10 line paragraph on p 94 as a wonderfully handled passage in a novel of this kind. (Also there's the one beginning at the bottom of p 322 — but perhaps this echoes a little too closely reflections in many novels. But it fits wonderfully the context, and only the literary reader would have reservations).

But while I am speaking of set passages, there is also the wonderful journey and 'pastoral' — chap. 22.

Of course there is already praise for you for the wrong reasons — [H. Winston] Rhodes [cartoonist Max] Bollinger and such. The achievement of this novel in my view is that it so very worthily takes its place in one great branch of novel-writing. *Germinal* of course, but nearer to home I think, *Sister Carrie*. (I think some of your sentences are very clumsy, like very many of Dreiser's, but it doesn't matter). The core of the achievement is I think the creation of the three Palmers — Mum first, of course, then Don, then Dad. Somewhat lesser creations are along the same lines, Seldoms and Herlihys. But there has to be the context, and your sentences bring the entire town into view — a view one won't ever forget.

The limitations? — oh yes. The device of Paul Rogers works very well, and it is right that he should as it were plump for Coal Flat. But this is at the same time a disadvantage. Where, one asks, is his measuring-rod? Take for example the business of the boy and what it implies — Rogers never indicates anything about other times other places other people, that the entire business is largely nonsense anyhow (again you are right in the context since R's preoccupation is with the immediate suffering involved). How far is he prepared to submit to Coal Flat edicts on human nature? This proposition can be reduced by extension to absurdity if you consider that the reader would never have known about Coal Flat if it hadn't been for the literary artist. And no literary artist has succeeded in creating what we think of as plausible and significant fictions without employing the bisexual elements of the human nature. The last word on this matter can never be with Coal Flat.

But all right, limitations? *All* limited in this world. I understand Curnow has admired the work. I hope this is true — I would expect it of him anyhow.

Sometime I expect I would like to write upon the novel for publication. I would welcome a talk to make a note of relevant details. When actually written — and who exactly has knocked you back about it.

Also I have a short list of literals you might like to have for future resettings — and one piece of dubious grammar which doesn't seem right in context. Your terminating 'buts' (in places) interest me. They were in the King Country about 1930.

Renewed congratulations and gratitude,

F.S.

You make me remember I am a lawyer — perhaps it's different on the West Coast, but anywhere else Rogers would have to be charged in l[ower] court.

['I would like to write upon the novel': See 'Conversation in a Train: or, What Happened to Michael's Boots', Landfall, *December 1967. The school teacher Paul Rogers, falsely accused of indecent assault, is charged in the Supreme Court. See* Coal Flat, *Ch 16 section 4, and Ch 19.]*

To Charles Brasch, *Dunedin*

Hocken Library

29 July 1963

Dear Charles,

[. . .] I wonder if you feel as I do about Pearson's book — I began it and was surprised to find myself rapidly hooked. I put it aside while in Wellington but resumed when I saw bad notices. I can only say I find it one of the most extraordinary things ever to come out of this country. I didn't think it possible any more to write a novel of that kind. It belongs with things of very great clumsy force such as *Sister Carrie*, and more remotely, *Germinal*. Of course the stupid cross-fire that is going on is all for wrong reasons. (Shadbolt for example would be quite unable to understand that whatever its faults it is entirely lacking in the literary nonsense which is such a disconcerting element in his own work). I have heard by the way that Curnow thinks exactly the same as I do, but I'm not totally sure of this.

I have my very wide literary interests however and Karl's little novel is entirely different. I think the question is whether what he is doing is viable or not — whether he's ahead of what's to come or up a blind street. I can understand people not cottoning on — I think those who didn't care for *A Race Apart* would very probably care for this less. In a way I can agree that it would be better for it not to appear in *Landfall*. But I can't get away from the fact that it just might be streets ahead of most work that is being done in its anticipation of the kind of writing which will be read in the future. I would of course agree that some unsatisfactory features really stick out — I think the young man who transmits everything doesn't raise quite enough interest in the reader, and should be both funnier and a figure for deeper compassion.

Oh yes, I must write and write. No luck in New York yet. Curtis Brown nearly had me on, and I have now appealed to Laughlin at New Directions for his advice and suggestions. As for being one-eyed at least Greenlane has come to light with the notion that my trouble just might be a rare case of tuberculosis in the eye. I have consented to take the dreadful drugs in addition to what I am told to keep on with. I suppose I must give it a go — though with such drugs it's difficult to say whether one is half-dead with them, or too many common troubles.

After demolishing her first torso Alison Duff has now produced one which obliges me to admire — her work much more than myself. But she says it *must* be in bronze — and she goes to the waist and has arms and hands. I foresee that bronze would cost a packet, and who could do it anyway?

But to work,

F.S.

May you somehow flourish — despite Landfall, despite the cold — and how the cold is killing me this winter.

My aunt has had a stroke, paralysed in one arm — and I can't get her to see a doctor. 'My arm will get better, but it might take years'!! Age 90!!!

['Karl's little novel': 'a novella I wrote and which Charles rejected for Landfall, *about a rather effete but brilliant concert pianist. I think it was called 'Finch among the shadows'. Finch was the pianist. The only thing I clearly remember from it is that a woman puts her pearls into the Wastemaster in a fit of rage. When Charles turned it down I went on to other things and it was never published'. C.K. Stead, personal correspondence, 23 August 2011.]*

To Bill Pearson, *Auckland*

Alexander Turnbull Library

[Although Blackwood Paul's initial intention had been a photographic reprint of That Summer and Other Stories, *the poor state of the Lehmann edition instead prompted a fresh and updated selection. This became the* Collected Stories, *edited and introduced by Bill Pearson.]*

10 August 1963

Dear Bill,

Points as I went through [a draft of Pearson's introduction]:

p. 1. Could you rather *suggest* something of nature of [Gogol's] Overcoat instead of laying it down. (Our authors, if I know them, just don't make claims of that kind). And a point is that it was very generous of Rod Finlayson to sign the Landfall letter when with Brown Man's Burden (1938) he was in hard covers before I was — and needless to say BM'sB contains The Totara Tree and work of very high order.

p. 2. Again suggestion instead of the 'it had stimulated'. Incidentally I can't remember when Man Alone appeared — I doubt whether I in any way influenced John Mulgan.

p. 3. Is F.S. Anthony self-conscious? Perhaps occasionally, but I noticed only occasional lapses into cliché when the Hawera-printed-and-published Me and Gus came to me in 1938. I loved the new fresh voice in it. Bottom line, 'his' for 'her'.

pp. 5–7 I have no memory of saying what you say I said, but I take your word for it.

p. 10 I can't turn up a copy of Park Seat, but so far as I can remember my interpretation of the sketch is that the old man gets so far, and then the *narrator* starts to remember. The two are old acquaintances so to speak — and it's probably characteristic of my kind of work that the narrator presumably doesn't reveal his identity. But if you interpret differently you are perfectly entitled to.

p. 13 If you are referring to something strikingly specific in Beckett why not use as footnote? If just general, I agree, cut.

p. 14 The earth has a skin; that skin is infested by a louse; that louse is man — is I think something like something that Schopenhauer said.

p. 15 'transvest*ist*'?

I suggest you cut from 'In his later work' to 'new country'.

Well. You know you make it all sound very grim — as though before you came along I had put in a claim to the Seldoms — I feel like saying if you put in a property claim I shall be glad to let you have judgement by default.

No, actually I think you have done a very good job — but still I am a little disconcerted. Such attention gets close to scholarship, Eng. Lit. and all I resist. Reading is for pleasure, that's to say prose — poetry is for delight, and who falls for pleasure if delight is around? But I mean that what you have written is far from a blurb. If Blackwood resists I would understand even though I don't agree with his turning our sacred words into objects of commercial profit. Anyhow you must fight it out with Blackwood if necessary. I have no overt objections — my resistance is just another of my private vices.

I am not too happy about taking so much time from your own work & interests.

My best,

F.S.

In return for my being adamant about Aunt Clara and the Landlady I will compromise with you over Granma. She turned up lately somewhere in my papers, and I thought the thing was damn badly written. I'll try to turn it up again and if necessary revise. Perhaps it could be used last in the book, called *A Personal Memory*, and placed just in advance of your biographical paragraph.

'Characters' spelt wrongly page 11

If ever I get another chance I am plumping for a country with a nice name, like *Ruanda Urundi*, & people with nice natures, like the Tutsies.

To C.K. Stead, *Auckland*

Alexander Turnbull Library

[Re: Stead's review of A Small Room with Large Windows, Landfall, *March 1963.]*

12 August 1963

Dear Karl,

Have gone through your Curnow carefully, and see what work you have put into it.

I would agree — real experience is behind every poem — but surely what one expects. What troubles me — too many remains of the struggle for the poem remain and show. You approve of the density, I want the final talent or genius which makes clarity out of the density.

How damaging (it seems to me) that bit of Auden you quote — he charmingly and effortlessly (apparently) makes it — what one longs for in C and only gets very rarely when he is at his best.

Also, is C's developement organic? — Why the constant changeover from Yeats to Thomas to Williams etc? Does Auden comparably do this?

I must hope you will concentrate on your own work — your best patches are not inferior to Curnow's best, and a higher proportion for your bulk.

Oh of *course*, Curnow is *terrific*, but *bugger* him!

F.S.

To James Laughlin, *New York*

Houghton Library

[Laughlin to FS, 13 August: 'It was good of you to send along your "Memoirs of a Peon", but, while I find it personally very interesting because of my connection with you and the country, I'm afraid I can't hold out any very great hope that it will be easy to find a publisher for it here in this country. The report from our reader, who is very good in judging things, was pretty discouraging, at least as far as suitability for this market here is concerned'. ATL MS-Papers-0432-192.]

20 August 1963

Dear Laughlin,

Very good of you to write me about that *Peon* book. I am sure you would be dead right about its chances in New York, so just kindly when you have a moment put it in the post back to me. Surface mail and second class I should say — I do hope a few postal coupons enclosed will help.

Never mind — Heinemann in London dickered with the damn thing for a year, and annoyed me over lost time — a consideration at the age of 60. Also at my age I'm beginning to come round again to notions of regional literature which I thought I had tossed in for good many years ago. Still, I'm interested in NZders who make it overseas — 8 years ago a girl turned up to see me one afternoon, and as I still have an army hut down at the bottom of my section she stayed for 18 months and wrote a book. Her name, Janet Frame — her American publisher gets her reviewed in *Time*, though I think she does better in England — though her best work is still I think to be found in a little book of sketches she wrote during the ten years she was a mental patient before she visited me. One thing I learned is that one may be able to look after somebody who is insane (so called) for perhaps three months, but 18 months was very definitely too long. And the pair of us were too poor to buy shoelaces anyhow.

Another occasional visitor is Sylvia Ashton-Warner, but she is only a good writer in very tiny patches — but she had the gumption to say in the newspaper she hoped nobody would go to the film Hollywood made of her first book. (Now MGM is doing one of another — a terrible book this second one).

It always astonishes me how often I come across your books in some of the bookshops, and many of the Libraries. You mustn't dream of sending me anything. I owe you such a lot, and a thousand times I've been going to bundle up quite a few bits and pieces of tolerably good writing to send you. Now after your latest kindness in bothering with the *Peon* I shall really get round to it. AND I mean it this time.

[. . .] Incidentally, the only way Janet Frame could be saved from being returned to MH was to get her to England. She has pushed along surprisingly well there on her own.

All my good wishes meantime,

Frank Sargeson

[The reader's report on Memoirs of a Peon, *signed 'May' and dated 12 August 1963, survives in Laughlin's papers: '[. . .] I've scanned the manuscript, which is written in a very old-fashioned, drawn out, boring style. Author says in letter that it's supposed to be funny — I guess he means his hero's attempts at various affairs with women — but the style keeps it from being anything but tiresome'. Houghton Library.]*

To Bill Pearson, *Auckland*

Alexander Turnbull Library

[Louis Johnson's hostile review of Coal Flat *on IYC's 'Perspective' programme in late August disparaged both the novel and Pearson's essay 'Fretful Sleepers: A Sketch of New Zealand Behaviour and Its Implications for the Artist' (1952). Pearson to FS,*

30 August: 'I suppose you heard Johnson's venom the other night. But he did himself more harm than me'. Pearson also addressed FS's earlier query about legal process in Coal Flat*: 'As for bail, a legal friend tells me a policeman can at discretion allow bail till the hearing, and it is likely in a country town when the policeman already knows the accused, that he would do this'. ATL MS-Papers-4261-143.]*

1 September 1963

Dear Bill,

It was curious the way Johnson tried to connect Fretful S and Coal F. Logic doesn't work in that way with works of art — Fretful S appears to be deflating all of us, but in fact it is just you getting rid of a lot of wind. Coal F on the other hand is the kind of miracle which can happen if your personal daemon familiar (or if you like a stray Muse) happens to be hanging around just to see nothing goes wrong. My experience (I mean *now*) prompts me to say just forget about it, but of course I'm forgetting about all the upset I used to experience.

I daresay your legal friends are right, but you remind me of my 81 pc for Procedure, and Jurisprudence at 65 wasn't so bad — to me it is contrary to all science of law that a police officer has any such power with bail — in my day it would have *had* to be at the very lowest a J. P. Remember too crimes law has lately been codified (I mean re-codified), and before that there have been a number of years of gradual modifications to relieve the S[upreme] C[ourt] by increasing jurisdiction of magistrates. I wouldn't be quite sure where the time you cover in C.F. fits into all this. Not that it matters much, though I think you are safer if you indicate something about a police court charge.

Incidentally, coal mining being up against it (and lately I listened to a documentary about how the entire West C has virtually had it short of some brainwave), it interests me no end that C.F. should do what so many kind of key fiction writers have done. Twain catches Huck F and the America that could have been just as it was about to be over to Sawyer the bore and Hemingway. Lawson catches Australia just as that kind if A is on the point of disappearing — and now C.F. [. . .] [Only one page survives.]

To Charles Brasch, *Dunedin*

Hocken Library

[Brasch to FS, 30 August: 'I think of writing a note for December Lf *commenting on the refusal of the Lit. Fund to make a grant towards the publication of* Coal Flat*. Since it is now no secret that the committee refused a grant for your novel too, I shd like to mention it as well, so long as this would not embarrass you'. ATL MS-Papers-0432-148.]*

2 September 1963

Dear Charles,

Your note just to hand — so far as I know my *Memoirs of a Peon* has never been put to the Lit Fund. Who has told you differently? All I know is from Blackwood — he and one of his readers were against it, and two others in favour. He said nothing of any application to the Fund.

Then a young man, David Lawson, of Whitcombes persuaded me to let him see it. He said *he* liked it very much, but he would let me know later. After a long delay he wrote indicating it had been round God knows how many readers of all sorts of opinions. In a very offhand kind of manner he indicated Whitcombes would go ahead probably if I considered revisions and if the Literary Fund would help. But I was infuriated by his indicating he had gathered in long kind of pre-publication reviews and told him I could not stand the thought of its being pawed over by more readers for the Lit Fund. No correspondence since.

Years ago the Lit Fund turned down the Caxton's application for help with a volume of Collected Work — Holcroft I was told. Also Hella Shaw's Symposium was refused help — again Holcroft I was told.

Tell me if there is some authentic information I know nothing of. [. . .]

I can only get the enclosed ['Shakespeare and the Kiwi'] off my mind by sending you now. Raise all the objections you like in your own good time. I send carbon because it is darker.

Suburban Uglification, Impossibility of Roads and Traffic. Radio, Parliament and Politics (Ldfl should instruct Winston Rhodes how not to be as dull in his MR) Athletics, Football. Etc. Try me on anything if you are short of Notes.

Anticipating Ldfl,

F.S.

I wonder if anything happened with Lit. Fund when Heinemann had my novel for a year? [Marginal note: last year] Bob Chapman would perhaps know, as he read it (favourably), for H.

[Brasch to FS, 5 September: 'I thought you'd told me that the Lit. Fund had refused a grant for Peon. *If not, I must have dreamed (nightmare!) it, or heard it from some other source [. . .].' ATL MS-Papers-0432-148.]*

To Bill Pearson, *Auckland*

Alexander Turnbull Library

3 September 1963

Dear Bill,

I have no objections to the Glossary [for the *Collected Stories*] if you can get it past Blackwood — a long face over expense I should imagine.

Here are some comments — one or two are corrections, the rest suggestions. It's damn difficult in NZ sometimes — usage varies from district to district.

back-chat	I can't see definition is necessary, and anyhow another colloquialism now in fashion strikes me as wrong method of defining.
back-pedal	Isn't it to be more discreet?
balloon	This is a very difficult one. I don't know the practice now, but use of the balloon was different sometimes on different courses. Perhaps it was used above the Tote — the ones I knew were above the number board out on the course. It was primarily for use of starter, only incidentally for public. I'd suggest you use something slightly vague like this 'a small balloon at race meetings may be used to indicate that the totalisator has closed, and a race is about to begin'.
billy	tin with lid and swinging handle used mainly for milk?
cabinet	I've forgotten but it wasn't quite what you say. Why not, Cold steamed pudding?
cowpats	rounds of cow dung? (pudding strikes me too coprophilic)
dingbats	disturbed?
double	shouldn't there be passing reference that off-course betting was illegal?
kauri gum	A slight shock that this has to be defined. In the 1870's Trollope in *The Prime Minister* headed a chapter 'Kauri gum'.
pub-stiff	I don't know about now, but to us in those days a pub-stiff was definitely a hotel worker.
riggers	here again, a rigger to us was a large bottle of beer
sea-eggs	fluid I seem to remember after being stirred up by somebody's finger (a Maori's usually) — then tossed off like a cocktail (I could never quite manage that one)
taipo	I've heard a Maori call a weta a taipo (he may have been copying the European).
weta	I don't know about being pretty well harmless. A male

> (slightly smaller than the female) really provoked, with his hind legs over his shoulders and his frighteningly large mandibles raised and opened ready for biting has never looked harmless to me. Also to strike an enormous colony in the bush (hundreds and hundreds) will give you bad dreams. I'll admit I've never yet been bitten (touch wood — there's plenty on my section). My experience is that although it's terribly alarming to discover them on you you won't get bitten unless you injure them by accident. But then I've never had a male on me, and this is something I never want to experience.

[Marginal note: A strapper is not necessarily an apprentice, so I've altered to 'stable-boy'.]

Incidentally, I discovered the bookseller at my corner had one last copy of C.F. tucked away. I bought it to send to Bruce Beaver — but if you are in need of a copy yourself I'd gladly present it to you, and leave Bruce (in Australia now) until the new printing arrives.

Did I say how glad I was Gaskell had written? — he would know, very exactly how very authentic it all is. Is Gaskell's address still Hamilton by the way?

best,

F.S.

I expect you know how much Charles (Brasch) admires C.F. I've mislaid his letter, something about the 'richest of its kind, & probably the last' — he seems to agree with me exactly. He said it seems to be writers & other plain people who enjoy — teachers of English who fasten on what is weak & overlook all the strength. Professional envy in part, perhaps.

To Bill Pearson, *Auckland*

Alexander Turnbull Library

9 September 1963

Dear Bill,

Many thanks.

It seems to me the didactic tone of your opening paragraph is in the writing. The brief blunt sentences might take on more of a tentative air if you could get them to flow a bit more. It is really a question of tact — I must leave it to you.

p10 Why not just mention the Beckett coincidence (which I myself find quite interesting) and leave it at that?

p11 Ditch Schopenhauer. Just another coincidence — the quotation came up years after I had written the story from Karl Wolfskehl when we were talking together.

p13 It is my annoyance that I can't put my hands on the Landfall with the last section of the Roof in it. The point I was making, surely, was that the tree was a magnificent specimen of *native* honeysuckle (a different proposition from the domesticated affair of the cottage garden mentioned earlier). My uncle hadn't planted it — it was just there in the bush (such trees usually grow on the tops of ridges and show up like plumes — I think I mentioned that).

I must apologise for failing to pick this up in the first text — not a good omen for my proof-reading.

Very glad C.F. will be available again pretty soon. I decided to buy Shadbolt's new book [*Summer Fires and Winter Country*], and am pleased that in his opening story he seems to have improved somewhat — (but damn it he slumps away with slick words in the next). A curious and probably fatal talent — I mean fatal to himself and all of us. Very disconcerting.

I can't remember my taipo footnote, but of course it should come out. A Maori was supposed to run for the lick of his life if you said munga-munga taipo to him — that was our story as kids.

Thanks for the Glossary which I'll keep a few days as some points seem to require checking with some of my friends of the early thirties. (Incidentally I meant to mention before the irony that the last I heard of the transvestist Maggie and cobber was they had set up house together on the West Coast where cobber had a job in the mines — irony is that unknown to you or me the pair of them might have got into C.F. The joke though would be that Maggie was such a hand at adultery she probably has a successful career as a concealed Ganymede up and down the Coast.

I get this off pronto to you as a poke in a new direction among my papers has assisted with your labours.

In the Department appeared in Auckland Weekly News 9 June '37

A Pair of Socks appeared in World Digest probably in January 1947 (Press Cutting Agency clipping is so dated anyhow, but of course the actual number of the W.D. may well have been December 1946

A Great Day, Bulletin Nov 17 1937 (I suspect also that A Man of Goodwill also appeared in Bulletin, but can find no record

A Man of Goodwill was in New Writing and Daylight for Winter 1943–44

I confirm Near and Far (Last Adventure) Auckland Weekly News Dec 8 1937

I've Lost My Pal would be in Man about 1941–2–3, I should think.

Incidentally, when I see your list I can confirm exactly about New Directions and Penguin New Writing also hard cover New Writing, but not so sure about Folios of New Writing.

I can find no reference and think Old Man's Story never appeared in any periodical — I think I wrote it just in time to go into Glover's 1st printing of A man and his W.

Terribly sorry I could have saved you much trouble. [. . .] I won't be long with the Gloss.

To Bill Pearson, *Auckland*

Alexander Turnbull Library

[Pearson to FS, 18 September: 'The misreading of the honeysuckle passage made me feel ashamed and it would have been unforgivable of me if it had got as far as print', and enclosed the revised glossary and opening of his introduction: '[. . .] but I am not completely happy about the phrase from Baxter ['a pioneer and vital power']. I could easily say the same thing in effect without having to cite anyone. And I'm not sure that as it stands I'm not playing politics, anticipating as it were (by citing one of his friends) the Johnsonian efflatus that will descend on publication . . . "fatuous introduction" . . . overblown reputation . . . etc. (I see incidentally in Critic *[. . .] that Maurice Shadbolt on the N.Z Short Story says that you and Gaskell failed to fulfil your "most striking promise". It was sent to Noel Hilliard [. . .] and he sent it to me with the comment that S. was setting himself up as a potential Grand Old Man of New Zealand letters.)' ATL MS-Papers-4261-143.]*

21 September 1963

Dear Bill,

Cheer up about the honeysuckle, nobody expects you to be Housman doing his job on Manilius — M wasn't worth it, probably, and probably the same goes for youknowwhom.

Yes, I think the Gloss with shorter definitions is much improved. (But worried about such re-typing — in all my journalism I've learned from that juvenile gentleman with the scissors in Martin Chuz. who terrorized the Court of Saint J).

But you've thrown up a nice piece of surrealism — which would be all right if we were doing that sort of book. Your definition of the balloon contradicts my use of it in *That Summer* (which is my *only* use of it so far as I know). That was Ellerslie, and I think what happened was this. So long as the tote was open there was no balloon. When the tote closed the balloon was raised (this was an indication to the starter to be on his toes). When the tote was balanced the balloon came down (this indicated to starter he could go ahead). Anyhow, if I'm not mistaken, when I hear from Ellerslie on racedays now, the commentator says 'the balloon is down', to mean the race is about to begin. Most certainly I can never remember his saying 'the balloon is up'. But as I said before, I seem to recollect that in the thirties there was some variation among race clubs.

Yes, revised pages of Introduction OK. I shouldn't worry about the quote from Baxter. My extreme feeling about all writing is that it should be so good it doesn't need any name to it at all (writers who say they despise fame still attach their names to their work, alas), and should most certainly not be an object of commerce. But what would you? — exigencies demand I hand the cadaver over to Alison Duff, and spiritus corporis to you. I don't mind the politics. Nor about Shadbolt — he's so naive I can almost love the bastard. (I remember before he went to England he made sure I saw something derogatory he wrote about *That Summer* in a Wellington paper. But he seemed to overlook that not long before he'd told me of the difficulties of getting a copy to read — the librarian at Wellington had been so long producing the work he had only *15 minutes* to read it before closing time). [. . .]

From yours

F.S.

To Bill Pearson, *Auckland*

Alexander Turnbull Library

9 October 1963

Dear Bill,

[. . .] I forgot to supply you with a note on *transvestist*. Instead of this word you could say *Eonist* or *crossed-dressed*. The non-mandarin *cross-dressed* might indeed be the answer. Eonist is from Eonism (Havelock Ellis — the Chevalier d'Eon a cross-dressed woman became an officer in the French army. And incidentally, Gibbon has a marvellous footnote about a cross-dressed Pope who was accouched during a Papal procession through the Roman streets — he doesn't blame you if you don't believe it).

Transvestist can be a bit difficult to say but I prefer it to transvestite. If the archaeologists renovate Sodom and I get myself appointed *vice-consul* there (just an interesting job for my old age), I will send to Wellington reports on the Sodomist citizens not Sodomite — though in fact I shall say they are just exactly like the Wellington citizens.

I think transvestism originates from Hirschfeld — too fine a point perhaps that it doesn't necessarily imply homosexuality. In Bert and Maggie's case, as much as anything else, it was to try and help Bert to cover up his tracks after deserting from the Navy.

However you must decide.

F.S.

Ellis seems not to object to transvestist, & as you know he was not without taste in high literary matters. But cross-dressed is factually accurate, with all overtones left floating.

To Charles Brasch, *Dunedin*

Hocken Library

24 October 1963

Dear Charles,

About Janet: if she doesn't get in touch with you in the next fortnight I suggest you write her c/o Mrs Gordon, 61, Gladstone Road, Northcote, Akld N.4. I think she will agree to writing in your ['How I Began'] series. She will try to get in touch next week (in Chch): if not, later in Dunedin (where, I think, she will be hiding in some bed & breakfast place).

She says (& probably it is so) that she is just as ill: but it's evident she *can* now manage a few contacts. (Apparently the improvement must be credited to the doctor she dedicates her books to [RHC; Robert Hugh Cawley] — not George Orwell's brother-in-law after all). Anyhow she's just as wonderful as ever — her secret where she gets the strength from to present the appearance of something so rare to the world, when (I think I agree with her) there's nobody there. A profound mystery, & no wonder no one can solve it.

Her 'success' can hardly be reckoned a financial one, but thank heaven there is enough money to enable her to get by very modestly. She has bought herself a caravan, & can return to it on my friend Miss Dawson's place in Norfolk. (I expect I forgot to tell you — she uprooted herself from Mt Maunganui & returned to England last year — a village cottage near the North Coast of N). It greatly moves me that so many people recognise her quality & feel impelled to lend a hand. [. . .]

[. . .] Bill Pearson's scholarship & the final text of my stories has now been put to Blackwood P. (but angina! the poor man — how can we dare to trouble him)

Enough,

F.

To Martin Green, *MacGibbon and Kee, London*

Alexander Turnbull Library

[Green to FS, 28 November: 'I should very much like to see the typescript of your novel [. . .]'. ATL MS-Papers-4261-112.]

7 December 1963

Dear Mr Green,

Many thanks for your note 28 November.

I am putting the *Peon* in the post (2nd class airmail, so it should reach you quickly).

I haven't yet quite completed my arrangement with Paul for the collected and edited Stories. I shall let you know more later. I am sorry I haven't in the meantime a copy of the material.

Let me know about Peon at your leisure. If not wanted I will send you a swag of postal coupons and the typescript can come back to me surface mail.

Many thanks,

Frank Sargeson

I am reluctant to say one word about the Peon. What I have mainly attempted to do is twofold — sum up a period in European settlement of this country — and write something entertaining (but perhaps this latter may not be so blindingly obvious until a reader reaches approx page 50.) No need to pull any punches — I am very accustomed to knockbacks.

[On 26 January 1964 Kevin Ireland explained to FS: 'A friend of mine — Neil Perrett, a North Shore doctor now over here — ran into Martin Green at a party. [Green] knew of your writing from Penguin N.W. days and wondered what you were up to. I had only just been talking to Neil about your book, and shown him the bits in Mate, *so he said he thought it worth while writing to you. Ray Grover (who works with J.R. Cole) and I brainwashed Neil even further, and gave him your address to give to Green. I saw [Green] a couple of nights ago — and he is living in the world of your book. He thinks it is a masterpiece — "a great comic novel. One of the best books of our times. . ." all that stuff. Marvellous'. ATL MS-Papers-0432-170.]*

To Charles Brasch, *Dunedin*

Hocken Library

18 December 1963

Dear Charles,

I find I have to get this away from me so I can be free to try my hand again —

up at the Hospital though I am warned not to get *too* excited.

Thanks for pulling me up — I remember lecturing you about points years ago, and I demonstrate how I have slipped. I use 3 points when a thought is interrupted and then continues. I use 4 when a thought tails right off. 3 points are followed by a word beginning in lower case, 4 by word beginning with a cap. I count in a question mark as *part* of this system.

I don't think my title was satisfactory. What about the enclosed? Pretentious? Does it give away too much before the story is even started? I will go on trying if you think I should. [. . .]

May you have the pleasantest of breaks! And may no garden of yours be suffering our cruel drought. [Brasch's poetry collection] *Ambulando* in NYear — another Building Stone for our House. Paul and Caxton really moving now, and I await MacGibbon and Kee's decision on *Peon*.

From

F.S.

If you feel my story really requires retyping now I'll do this for you.

['I have to get this away from me': a list of corrections for a story provisionally entitled 'Et Satyri fratres'. Brasch replied on 22 December: 'I'm not sure abt a Latin quote for title. An English one, yes; but . . . . Would it be tolerable to translate et Satyri fratres? [. . .]'. On 2 January FS offered 'Perhaps a Greek Encounter', citing Ovid's Metamorphoses. *Brasch to FS, 19 January: '[I]sn't this too literary a title?' ATL MS-Papers-0432-148.]*

To Charles Brasch, *Dunedin*

Hocken Library

[Brasch to FS, 19 January: 'In her last letter Janet wrote sadly abt being unable to live in N.Z. because to live away from it is a means of ensuring physical safety and security. I hardly like to question her about this, but does she mean that she depends on the Maudsley, both for psychological help and for enabling her to get a pension. If it were a matter of a pension solely, I think we might be able to get her one here, don't you? And if she wants to remain, we ought to do everything we can to make it possible. Perhaps you can sound her — ?' ATL MS-Papers-0432-148.]

26 January 1964

Dear Charles,

[. . .] I confess with humility you're dead right about my title. How about

JUST TRESPASSING, THANKS

It does point to the young people, and also expresses pretty well much in the attitudes of the young people I was working from.

I'll write you again about Janet. It's very complicated. She has been very close to disappearing back to England overnight, but now she at last has a secluded room in Devonport where she is confident she can be uninterrupted and work. I've talked all round what you say with her, but it's difficult to be sure of any stable attitude in her mind. Yes, she depends on the Maudsley — but more properly on some who work there and also some who have worked there and are now elsewhere (the RHC of her books is now at Birmingham University, and she relies on him enormously). The question of finance very important too but remote at present — her biggest gain came from the *New Yorker*, and they chase her for more but at present she won't. I was lately despairing about my efforts to coax her into sending you the script ['How I Began'] she has written according to your suggestion. She won't let me see it and as usual she says it's hopelessly bad — but yesterday she surprised me by saying she was determined to make a few amendments and let you have it immediately. I can only pray. (Lately she sent a script to broadcasting they had asked for, and it has seemed highly unlikely she would for months).

Fortunately I was interested in Phillip Wilson's countryside [in *Beneath the Thunder*, 1963] which was roughly mine too. Also I felt I could genuinely say he had succeeded in rendering much suffering which seems to me peculiar to those Waikato parts. Ah yes, a Huck Finn etc? But it is more likely to be another version of that little bore Tom Sawyer. And how right you are to doubt whether any of us would recognise it!

Let your dreams be of more poems, and even turgid mss could have their uses in nourishing them. I hope Leo-Alpers a very busy composite midwife to you.

[. . .] I've plugged away at a new story which holiday intruders too much interrupt. I haggle with Blackwood Paul and await news from MacGibbon and Kee. Has news about poor Cole reached you? We were very alarmed 2 weeks ago when he returned from a visit to the Duggans to Wellington with something very wrong in a kidney. Since then he has had a stroke while riding his daughter's scooter, and added a broken collar-bone and skull to other woes. He seems to be inviting so much — I feel very sorry for his wife. And yet his chances are said to be quite hopeful.

F.S.

Janet did let fall the important information that she was strongly advised by her doctors *not* to return to this country. From my knowledge of the entire business I can only say I agree.

Encourage me to go on trying if title still not good enough. [. . .]

To Rhondda Coleman, *Christchurch*

Alexander Turnbull Library

Monday [February 1964]

Dear Rhonda,

Oh, you lucky girl! — a man coming home covered with sweat and cement, with a raging thirst in his throat only outdone by a mad mad love in his heart, and . . . well, what have you somewhere elsewhere. But all my best wishes for the (ad)venture. (Say you were to become the couple to end all the nonsense of the age — the honest labourer worthy of his hire, turning and earning his honest penny, and knocking off an honest Whitmanist poem every evening by candlelight — that same light catching the gold of the little woman's hair as she sews yet another heartthrob into yet another little garment. . . Oh no, I shall be converted myself in a moment and be sending my letter wet with tears).

But to cease jesting, my best wishes, and it's a sad commentary on my own situation (*sub specie aeternitatis*) to say that I sadly miss the pair of you.

Peppers and tomatoes are two flavours which go very much together. But of course both should come out of one's own garden. Cook tomatoes (stew with a little oil or butter, pepper, salt and quite a surprisingly lot of sugar (for bringing out the flavour) and put in the cut-up peppers towards the end). What heating have you got? If cheap (coal stove), soups (thick) are the cheapest nourishing things. Boil up bones then put practically anything you can think of into the stock, making your own experiments. I am sorry you are out of reach of your own garden and mine at the moment. I have never had a season quite like it for apples peaches pawpaws tomatoes and peppers. Also the buttercup pumpkins are simply ravishing. [. . .]

I have been strangely busy with literary affairs over holidays. I have my signed contract with Paul for *Collected Stories* now, and all is under weigh with a printer in England. But according to a letter from Kevin Ireland (I hope what he said is not part of a drunken and very cruel hoax) the editor of the London publisher I sent the *Peon* to thinks the book is a masterpiece 'a great comic novel, one of the best books of our times' (I really shouldn't repeat such stuff). But he is waiting until he sees Paul (who has left for England before writing me. My fingers are so doubly crossed and joined to wood that typing is very difficult.

Incidentally, I finally called the beatnik story, JUST TRESPASSING, THANKS.

Janet was wandering about Auckland with a cheque for a thousand pounds in her hand [the Literary Fund Scholarship in Letters for 1964], and couldn't get any Bank to accept it as a deposit, not even Auckland Savings Bank. They all thought it some sort of hoax by a lunatic — told her to go elsewhere. (But there's quite a story there — how dumb NZders can be beyond the range of their football wall to wall carpets etc!!)

Pardon all this, But much love,

Fx

To Garth Powell, *Ophthalmologist, Auckland*

Alexander Turnbull Library

20 February 1964

Dear Mr Powell,

After leaving you yesterday I paid a duty visit of a mildly compassionate nature, and arrived finally very tired at the outdoor Shakespeare staged in the university grounds. It was probably on account of fatigue that my visual experience there was somewhat unique, and in view of the unique nature of my ocular pathology I feel you should not be deprived of it.

The play was *The Merchant*, and it had no sooner begun than I was aware I was going to (with one eye) see a duplicated (laterally) performance of it. (This of course had its satisfactory aspect as I had paid admission for only one performance). With my profound knowledge of Greco-Latin terminology I informed myself that this was owing to my diplopia. But shortly it occurred to me that I must by no means underestimate my own uniqueness — stage lighting was very good, and I became aware of a third performance!! (In passing I mention that I promptly discarded diplopia, and plumped for triplopia). This was a very ghostly affair indeed, airy figures floated about the stage and in and out among the audience. But (*and here's the pay-off*) what was being played seemed not to be *The Merchant*!!! At first I thought it was *The Tempest*. (Ariel up the oak tree centre stage — but with a little care I could discern that it was Portia (again in passing I would say that on her performance she deserved more to be permanently fixed up a gum tree); and in any case it was soon clear to me that this third play was not The Tempest as it very definitely had more than one woman in it. So I finally settled for *The Midsummer Night's Dream*. The performance of Puck was very charming despite the fact that he did indeed seem to be tenuously related to Launcelot Gobbo in the play that was on the programme and which I had paid to see.

But there you are, three plays, one of them a different play from the other two, and all for the price of admission to one. It has all reminded me of a passage in Bernard Shaw who was complimented by his oculist, (though such was the superstition of medical science in those days that some care was required before these people could be distinguished from occultists), who informed him that he was virtually unique in having perfectly normal eyesight. Now could I be in the Shaw tradition? Am I to be the unrecognised pioneer of unique visual experience? Three plays instead of one — extend the principle and what do you get? three (anything you like to name) instead of one. . . .

Or am I to be just a new name (Greco-Latin) in a textbook. If you insisted I would no doubt have to agree to *myasthenia gravissimis*.

But to cease jesting — I don't wholly exaggerate. I was of course very tired, I had woken yesterday morning with a migraine headache which was transformed shortly before I visited you into a nasty bout of palpitation, for which I took some phenol-barb. In addition there is the open shutter in the right eye. But possibly the recurring bouts of double vision in the other eye should be investigated further. I shall be most interested to find out what happens from discarding the atropine — but must keep my fingers crossed in case of fresh bleedings. (And incidentally, your remarks about a very peculiar interior to my eye do somewhat contradict a previous remark you comforted me with — that essentially what was practically most evident was a half teaspoonful, say, of blood in front of the retina).

May I emphasize that I have no complaints about what you have done and are doing for me. I am indeed very very grateful — so much so that I would ask you not to let me off so cheaply on these monthly visits. I would take it as a compliment to my sincerity in this matter if you would increase your half guinea fee to at least a guinea.

From yours,

I do not at all suppose that this note calls for any reply from you,

F.S.

To Rhondda Coleman, *Christchurch*

Alexander Turnbull Library

2 March 1964

Dear Rhonda,

I was hoping to reply to your letter, but am choked up with chores.

So instead I copy from my dear Gibbon a passage which I am trying to bring nicely into my story ['City and Suburban'] about the finger found on the beach (tell Andy I'm still writing it).

> 'The inclination of the Roman husband discharged or withheld the conjugal debt, so scrupulously exacted by the Athenian and Jewish laws: but, as polygamy was unknown, he could never admit to his bed a fairer or more favoured partner.'

> 'Solon requires three payments a month. By the Misna (a section of the Talmud — FS) a daily debt was imposed on an idle, vigorous, young husband; twice a week on a citizen; once on a peasant; once in thirty days on a camel-driver; once in six months on a seaman. But the student or doctor was free from tribute; and *no* wife, if she received a *weekly* sustenance, could sue for a divorce; for once a week a vow of abstinence was allowed. Polygamy divided, without multiplying, the duties of the husband'.

So you see. But who would you say sends in the bill in a modern suburb — wives or husbands? Janet thinks her sister would send in the bill, and frequently.

Love,

Fx

To Rhondda Coleman, *Christchurch*

Alexander Turnbull Library

Thursday [1964]

Dear Rhonda,

This is Sargeson Garden Service Clinic — quick hints for Busy Housewives on Seed Control, Propagation, Cross-Fertilization, Nurture etc. (The Pen is Mightier than the Sword).

(1) Beans & Peas do *very well in New Soil* — if you can get strips of lawn dug up you will have good crops *without Manure. Greenfeast* peas, *probably*, & *Scarlet Runner* (or *Derivative*) Beans — the beans will come from roots again next year. If old Soil you will need a *Mixed* Manure (mainly Chemical).

(2) Tomatoes are easy. *Don't* plant — that's to say, buy your plants & plant out *not before* mid-October. *No manure* — this is not put on until fruit has set.

(3) Pumkins need *very rich* soil. You need Mixed (mainly Chemical) manure, plus if you can get it compost & animal manure. *Don't* plant your seed (Queensland Blue, Crown, Triamble, Butter*cup*) until near mid-October. Also you should have Butter*nuts*. *Vegetable Marrows* (bush — non-running) are much hardier, quicker — you can plant your seed about beginning October. [Marginal note: *Use your compost for the Pumpkins*]

I was sorry about your predicament the Friday you called — very troubled indeed, as I had only a few shillings myself, & now old Jim next door is dead I can't borrow readily in an emergency. Anyhow I'm glad you seem to have survived (without eating your son, I hope — but not being a barmaid no doubt you wouldn't anyhow). Also, hope somehow the intolerable money-situation is solved for you someway.

I hope your virtue is proving insurmountable,

Love,

F.S.

To Glaister Ennor and Kiff, *Solicitors, Auckland*

Alexander Turnbull Library

30 March 1964

Dear Mr Ennor,

You will I think remember you advised me away back in 1957 about payments which would reach me from an anonymous well-wisher [probably Charles Brasch] whose aim was to ensure that I continued writing.

The payments have of course reached me regularly right to December 1963. I should, long before now (I mean years ago), have re-expressed my thanks through you. I must apologize for my neglect to do so.

Will you kindly convey to your client my renewed thanks to your client for the generous assistance which I have so greatly benefited by.

Perhaps your client will find some interest in this brief summary of what the benefit has enabled me to do. (To save you trouble I am enclosing a copy of this letter which you may forward to your client if you will)

1. During the latter part of 1957 (when theatre plans were temporarily laid aside), I was engaged in writing a long picaresque novel which is at present called *The Memoirs of a Peon*. This work continued through 1958, and was completed by the end of 1959 except for final revisions which extended the work to mid-1960.
2. In the latter part of 1960 theatre plans were taken up again, and my three act play *A Time for Sowing*, (a play concerning the tragedy of the first missionary to New Zealand, Thomas Kendall) was tried out in a rehearsed reading by Miss Edna Harris. This proved to be something of a failure. But fortunately early the following year I joined with Mr Colin McCahon and Mr Christopher Cathcart to produce the play again in the Auckland Art Gallery. And the result was an outstanding success.

3. My energies were then devoted to developing our group into what finally emerged as the New Independent Theatre. In 1962 we produced my play called *The Cradle and the Egg*. But this did not meet with the same success. The following year we produced *Lest We Resemble* by John Graham (again, not with any marked success — but the play was seen by the film producer John O'Shea, who as a result, is making a film based on another play by Mr Graham [*Runaway*, 1964]). In 1963 we produced *The Forest*, by D'Arcy Cresswell. During the present year we are in recess as our producer, Mr Cathcart, has been awarded an Arts Council bursary and is at present in England.
4. Since mid-1963 I have been able to channel my activities back to my own writing, and have been glad to achieve two contributions for *Landfall* — a Shakespeare essay, and a longish (for me) short story. My financial prospects at the moment are reasonably bright. I still retain a small Arts Council pension of £4 which provides a very handy basis for my activities, and with a little luck I will be making a London contract for my *Memoirs of a Peon* pretty soon this year. Towards the end of this year a large volume of my *Collected Stories* will be published by Paul's Book Arcade (and again with luck this book will also be issued in England), and I am upon publication to be paid £100 advance (less £25 as my contribution to the fee for Dr W. H. Pearson's skilful editing of the book). Once again with luck my *Two Plays* will be issued by the Caxton Press in Christchurch.
5. It may perhaps also interest your client to know that a great deal of my energy is consumed in attending to the needs of a widowed aunt who is very well provided for but not given to expending a penny (and particularly upon myself) more than can be extracted from her (and which, beyond meagre household needs, is precisely nothing). She is however in her 91st year, and I have been informed by her prospective executor that I have my share in her estate according to her will. I mention this matter for the reason that I would hope quite strongly that I may eventually be in the position of being able to repay your client (or some of the amount he — or she — has provided at least).
6. I mention an Arts Council commission to provide a bronze head of me for the Art Gallery only to indicate my satisfaction that your client's confidence in my abilities can hardly be judged to have been wholly mistaken.

I can only reiterate my thanks, and say that a great part of my activities has been made possible by your client's (to me — enormous and moving) generosity.

Yours sincerely,

Frank Sargeson

P.S. I have lately begun my 62nd year.

To Charles Brasch, *Dunedin*

Hocken Library

11 April 1964

Dear Charles,

Yes, Janet would accept a pension, but as you say unconditionally, which is only right and proper. For your information I tell you something of what I gather about her affairs. She has lately had a six-monthly royalty statement from her London agent — the cheque amounts to £8 odd [Marginal note: this is on all her published books — & Eng. & American editions], though there might be some small separate amount to come from Albion Wright. What she really got back here on was payment by the *New Yorker* for two stories (an editor there wants more, but she insists *no* unless she gets hard up — she doesn't think they were very good — of course she's unreliable as judge of her own work). One thing about her — she is thoroughly professional, that is, she writes incessantly and becomes disturbed and upset if any obstacle gets in her way. I forget whether I told you that lately I had to assist her with arrangements for a breast operation — after much anxiety (and I suppose mainly because the thought of any approach to an operating table and what they might be planning to do about her brain, was sufficient to send her as nuts as she has ever been — but she came through wonderfully) it has turned out to be a benign tumour. And of course with her scholarship money there has been no worry over paying bills.

Ask me anything else you think I may be able to help with, Charles — one question, obviously, is what sized pension could be obtained. Perhaps it may be of some help if I refer to my own experience. I remember when I was taken off Invalidity Benefit by Jo Heenan (the IB then was about £2/10/- a week) I insisted that I had no objection to being helped, but I thought dangers could result if I was helped too much — I thought £4 a week would do very nicely indeed (although this was only £3 for the first 4 years as I had to pay off £200 allowed in advance to help me get my house). But of course I reckoned, like everyone else, without any idea of how severe inflation was to become. My point is this, that if pensions are granted they should err on the generous side, as inflation is bound to continue into the foreseeable future, and Powers-that-be just cannot be reckoned upon to provide cost of living bonuses no matter how urgently necessary they may prove to be.

Anyhow, I haven't much idea of exactly what move you have in mind, but so glad to assist you if I can.

Janet's copy of *Landfall* has turned up though not my own yet — and I must congratulate you on the poets this number — some young people have seemed to me to derive a certain amount of false authority by having their verses nicely set out in Lfl — but there is no chaff mixed in with the grain with your two this time — in fact pure gold, and most delightful wit lightness and skill. It seems the two non-academics on Shakespeare don't come off so badly. Ngaio [Marsh] will usually irritate me, but not (much) this time — of course I can always read anything Jim Bertram writes, but [Don] McKenzie forbidding? — I must try again. The concentration of your own note demands not two readings but several. [. . .]

I won't forget to fix about Winston and get to you *About How I Began* before too long. I have in W. another supporter for the *Peon* (Alpers found it extremely difficult to read — shame! — after his expensive schooling I thought he might appreciate Olde Port on Mahogany Furniture with a Gamey Smell of Venison around).

No more — blessings, and special ones for *Ambulando*,

F.S. [. . .]

To Charles Brasch, *Dunedin*

Hocken Library

28 April [1964]

My dear Charles,

I do want you to have the news before anyone — MacGibbon and Kee will do the *Peon*, though I am asked to agree to some pruning in the opening section (no great moment I think). Advance to be £150.

Oh dear I am nearly in tears — I am sure you will understand. In these later years we need these shreds of consolation. I can face the doctors better now, and cope with whatever they say about eyesight hospital and all.

All my fondest regards and gratitude for endless encouragement,

F.

To Christine Cole, *Wellington*

Private collection

9 May 1964

Dear Chris,

[. . .] Now we must hope [about John Reece Cole's health], but I must raise a matter with you. You probably know I have a will in Reece's favour (it's with Paul von Sturmer a Takapuna lawyer along at the corner). Whatever happens about Reece I had better have a new will made in your favour. Let me say apart from all else I can think of no-one I would prefer to have as my literary executor (my untidy papers! — but you would cope, and of course apart from the property here, and what I may get from my aunt if I am lucky, my literary copyrights might really be of some value — I expect Ray Grover has told you about MacGibbon and Kee and the *Peon* novel, and there's the *Collected Stories* from Paul, and my *two* plays from Caxton). It's not unlikely MacG. & K. will do the *Collected Stories* too.

Anyhow, none of this means any immediate benefit to you — but I do want you to know I don't forget you and Reece have been kind to me in my own troubles, and I *don't* forget.

Not a word to Reece, I would think — except if he should express doubts about Frank's reliability, you could just say you feel he can have confidence in F.

Doctors talk about my being immobile in hospital for six months, then 'Laser' ray. But of course I am far too busy with all this tidying up of my literary work to pay attention to them.

Love for now,

Fx

It goes without saying you won't allow this to be seen by R.

To H. Winston Rhodes, *Christchurch*

Alexander Turnbull Library

[In January 1964 Rhodes was invited to write a volume on FS for the Twayne 'World Authors' series. FS to Rhodes, 30 January: 'I don't particularly relish its being done by anyone in my lifetime, and I'm afraid I will be uncooperative with biographical detail'. ATL MS-Papers-0424-23. He did however lend Rhodes typescripts of his radio journalism, fiction and autobiographical writing.]

1 June 1964

Dear Winston,

I am most grateful for the radio script, (how astonishing! — like that it just doesn't seem to be what I wrote at all, and of course in some parts it's not. But quite a revelation to me of the difference between the written and the spoken word — I never heard it when broadcast). Anyhow it greatly assists me in jacking up an article for Charles ['How I Began']. [. . .]

Thanks also for the pages of the *Roof* which are what I want. And about the *Peon* — my contract with MacGibbon and Kee called for two copies of the script, but that still leaves me with a thin-paper copy (quite legible, but uncorrected in the main, I think), which I can let you have if you want it — with the reservation that I will have to hang on to it until I know whether MacGibbon and Kee will be returning any script with their proofs. (They seem mad keen to publish sell and profit, and I anticipate all will move very swiftly. From what I hear through the grape vine the book is thought to have chances of becoming one of the outstanding comic novels this century — something to reckon comparable to [Jaroslav Hašek's] *Good Soldier Schweik*. This of course is flattering, but I must confess a publishing success would be welcome consolation quite apart from merits which will no doubt be unknown in my lifetime). [Marginal note: I have told them about your contract with Twayne.]

Anyhow, if I don't hear from you on this point I will send you the script when uncertainty about copy to use with proofs is cleared up.

Performances of the plays depended upon Cathcart McCahon and myself all working together. We thought this a most fruitful cooperation. Cathcart is a little nuggety Scot with only elementary education. (A few years ago after coming to NZ he managed to become qualified as a meat inspector — and during the six nights of success with *Kendall* he used to have to hurry in from Westfield, make up the cast, & be responsible for their playing besides playing his own gruelling part of Kendall. It was the same with the *Cradle* in which he had to play two parts. The secret of it all is that he had been in the amateur Scottish theatre and also touched the fringes of professional work — but most importantly, he is rooted in Scottish folk theatre. Hence the wonderful simple moving humanity which he gets into his productions. Until the three of us cooperated he had known a little success in Auckland, but mainly indifference and hostility. The latter persists — Colin and I had to fight like the devil against it to get him the bursary which has taken him to England and the better experience which he has always been after. The local theatre set-up and people are truly impossible — and I suspect it's the same throughout NZ. The hostility extends to Colin and myself. We had our great success with *Kendall* at the time of the Festival, but the Festival Drama Committee refused to have us in the Festival, and condemned the script as hopelessly bad from every point of view. And the decision was unanimous.

And they learned nothing from the reception we got from public and press — the following year when we announced our intentions with the *Cradle and the Egg* we aroused no interest, were not invited to submit the script — and no doubt all were pleased when we failed that time with the press, though not wholly with the public (we had a most splendid concluding night — we thought the news had at last got round that the press notices were to be disregarded).

Anyhow, the script of the plays as they stand is very much *post-production*. For instance, in *Kendall* we only discovered the bit about Kendall throwing the Bible on the floor in production; also Mrs Kendall blowing out the candle at end of that Act. And I can say here that Act II of Kendall can be the most superb piece of theatre if anyone can be found to do it. We found Act I *very* difficult, and the difficulty with Act III is that in our experience it is difficult to get the players to understand they are engaged in a duel, not a debate. But Act II — I am sorry to be so emphatic, but what an experience! (What a potent symbol the Bible is shown still to be, for example!)

Of course the Cradle hasn't the same unity, but the comedy at its best, and when the players put it across was most agreeable — as Musgrove at any rate discerned in his *Listener* review. Indeed, some people think (apparently like yourself) that it is the *Cradle* that could be taken up and given a much wider currency than *Kendall*. Anyhow, all this to kind of warn you about any 'prodding' — the hostility is something not to be believed until it is encountered. Print may carry some authority — I don't know.

We are all much harrowed by the sad situation of John Reece Cole. He is up here having the powerful x ray treatment for cancer, & it all seems quite hopeless. His brain seems to be afflicted & we can only hope for euphoria & a swift & reasonably painless decline.

F.S.

To Janet Frame, *Waiheke*

Private collection

[FS's dislike of Blackwood Paul was longstanding but becomes a regular note in the correspondence from around this time. Paul had rejected Memoirs of a Peon, *and arrangements regarding the publication of the* Collected Stories *became increasingly fraught.]*

10 June 1964

Dear Janet,

I intended to write, but was caught up in something for C.B. [Charles

Brasch] (his *How I began* series); then that horrid Blackwood Paul in London told MacGibbon & Kee it would be a very *bad thing* if *their* Novel coincided with *his* Stories. I had to make some hasty inquiries & send off a cable flatly contradicting. And indeed, just for once in a poor little lifetime, it is thought if *Wrestling With the Angel* (the plays) coincides too, such a unique event will be worth more than a ton of conventional publicity.

But enough of this me — over to that *other* me — *you*. I am a teeny bit worried over what you say, but remember Kay Stead was just the same, & it was eventually diagnosed as an inflammatory bladder condition — not serious, I think. Anyhow, we shall see, & such awful things would be found in my waters, I really think they had better have your own — which will probably prove to be the Purest Maidenswater ever tested. (If only nurserymen could get it, it's supposed to be the most marvellous thing for growing luxury crops like pineapples, adding a flavour which nobody can ever quite be sure about, really je ne sais quoi — or the final word may be quoint (though I don't guarantee my Middle English spellings — but you will be in no doubt about such a trivial piece of scholarship. Also, remember dear Peter had the same — & Maidenswater there without a shadow of a doubt Etc. Etc.

Anyhow, of course come Monday for dinner, come Sunday too if you like, and don't bring anything as I am still saving asparagus etc you brought last time. [Marginal note: Next Sunday Harry doesn't come over.]

Poor Karl described in *Star* by rival poet as having *no Blood*. Oh dear! And poor Cole, more & more cuckoo — quite delighted with that lovely lovely Machine at the Hospital, doing him such a *Lot of Good*. He still talks of impending announcements of the [Hubert] Church Award, so keep on hoping.

Well, I finish my *How I Began* tomorrow, so will be kind of holidaying at weekend.

May you be having good Birmingham, London New York Hamburg etc etc letters.

Your Broadcast very very masterly indeed. And Maurice [Duggan], particularly, also asked me to send you his *most admiring congratulations* on a splendid piece of radio work.

Clever girl. And, this
from xFx

To Bill Pearson, *London*

Alexander Turnbull Library

12 June 1964

Dear Bill,

Phoebe Meikle [Blackwood Paul's editor] called in and left me the proof copy [of the *Collected Stories*] read by Curnow for literals. I don't know whether you are expecting me to go through this — I think not, but in glancing at a few pages I've hit on C's query about 'the very Reverend Dean Doyle'. It should be left like that — I don't know whether the title is still used but it was when I was a boy. I've checked with two Catholics older than myself and they ridicule the notion that it *wasn't* used.

For yourself alone — Blackwood told Martin Green his *Novel* shouldn't coincide with B's *Stories*. But this is not the view of Arthur Jackson-Thomas plus librarians plus quite a few odd people. A unique event, just once in a lifetime — and we all hope *Wrestling with the Angel* (the plays) might join in too. With your splendid editing introduction etc. Blackwood has nothing to worry about. The *Stories* will sell and go on selling, particularly as the price will be very reasonable — a LF grant is to be made.

I don't think MacGibbon and Kee will do the *Stories* — I think they would prefer a good blurb, or somebody in England to introduce if that was thought necessary. And this is fair enough — all your work is a lead and a lesson for NZders. However we shall see, I don't hear from Blackwood, and am not sure what he may be up to now proof copies can be passed round.

And now I have some unpleasant news. I hear through the grapevine that Janet will receive the Hubert Church prize. As you can very much imagine my hands are very much tied from making any public statement. [Marginal note: Oh, mixed metaphor!] But I have written to Charles pointing out this means a grave injustice to *Coal Flat* — just one more on top of the injustice of the 10 year wait etc. The point is that Janet has *already* been recognised — and now there will be the disgrace of no official recognition of CF. I dare not breathe a word of my views to Janet as she is very unstable just now. I think Bertram is the judge, and I shall, I think, send him a line, though I will wait until I see what Charles says.

Poor John Cole seems to be rapidly dying, but his state with his brain sadly afflicted is a great grief to all of us.

If in a hurry for anything concerning the job send me a cable and I will pay.

Best

F.S.

To Bill Pearson, *London*

Alexander Turnbull Library

15 June 1964

Dearest Bill,

Your sheaf of cards 8–11 June arrived today.

You are the most marvellous editor of all time anywhere.

Unfortunately I can't get under weigh on what you ask — a really nasty attack of virus influenza has got me — the whole population has gone down to it.

But note — are you allowing for fact that my literary convention is presupposing nearly all these stories are written each time by a different narrator? Aren't minor inconsistencies part of the technique? If my sickness stops me from replying for too long use your own judgment. But don't be too puritanical (I've just read that marvellous book *The Last Puritan* by Santayana anyhow). What didn't worry Curnow shouldn't worry you — it wouldn't me anyhow.

It's no disrespect to you to say that I can see MacG and K's point of view. I mentioned this in letter to you Friday.

Did I tell you Dennis McEldowney, a *close friend of Shadbolt*, read C.F on my strong recommendation and found it best first & everything else of NZ novels ever.

Never been so groggy for years,

Love,

F.S.

['Your sheaf of cards': editorial queries, including questions about apparent inconsistencies in spelling and punctuation. Sargeson's annotations suggest his vehement defence of idiosyncrasies.]

To Bill Pearson, *London*

Alexander Turnbull Library

[On 12 June Pearson told FS that MacGibbon and Kee's proposed English edition of the Collected Stories *would only proceed on the condition that his editorial material was dropped: 'I find it a bit disheartening. It looks as if they don't even want the glossary. [. . .] However, the editor can be allowed to indulge his wounded pride, but I don't think you should let this influence your decision on the matter'. ATL MS-Papers-4343-041.]*

in bed Wednesday
[17 June 1964]

My good Bill,

You must pardon the flashes of bad temper — coinciding with waves of nausea

— thank God, I have laughed too (But this is a damned awful virus).

Listen, the job you have done is what is usually done after the author is dead — I've never had any wish to be *edited* to death. You must remember you were brought in on what was to be a straight reprinting job of the Lehmann vol. (photographic) — you were brought in solely to ensure that the book sold & B didn't lose money. He doesn't care a damn for your scholarship — & if there had been an alternative safe (& cheap) way of getting in his dough he would have used that.

I appreciate your scholarship very much. But I think in many ways you are undone by your N.Z. desire to be pure. You mention pride & I shudder — because I know when a N.Zder uses the word it will never be backed by the knowledge that it is (I mean, the thing) the deadliest of all sins. It should go without saying I wrote those stories hoping they would each carry their own message without the need of any interfering agency. I was glad to accept you when I saw what a painstaking job you would do — but don't push it too far. Nothing I have ever written was intended to be done over with a comb or examined through a microscope — at least not while I'm alive.

Please finish with me AND WRITE THE BOOKS WE EXPECT OF YOU NOW WE KNOW ABOUT *COAL FLAT*.

Until we knew about CF we expected nothing of you except that dire academic stuff from up the hill here. [Marginal note: And how many square feet a Maori house is supposed to have is an irrelevancy as far as I'm concerned.] Don't finally have it said of you, 'Sargeson had to lie cadge twist etc etc his way through life, but he got his books written; Pearson wanted at least to *appear* respectable, but he managed *Coal Flat* — leaving us for ever to wonder what else there might have been if he hadn't shied off the notion that a NZder can ever endure to let people know there are the marks of crap on his psyche'.

I love you Bill, & as much for your weakness as your strength

F.S.

['how many square feet a Maori house is supposed to have': a detail mentioned in 'New Zealand Since the War: The Maori People', Pearson's indictment of the systemic disenfranchisement of Maori, which had appeared in Landfall *in June 1962.]*

To Charles Brasch, *Dunedin*

Hocken Library

28 June 1964

Dear Charles,

[. . .] It is not *finally* certain yet that MacG and K will do the stories as well as the novel — though it is that they won't want Bill's editing. But Bill has been so scrupulously exact in doing all this tidying up of this part of my work, and is now suffering so acutely from what seems to him a rebuff, that I find he engages my heart very powerfully. I would like to be useful to him in return — and the best I could do, I think, would be to persuade him into, and support him with encouragement through, the opening pages of a new novel. After all, he must have known untold agonies since he used up the material in *Coal Flat* — and this kind of work is the only real anodyne for so much suffering. Let him keep his Maoris and the number of square feet they are supposed to have in their houses as a sideline. [. . .]

Poor Janet persecuted on Waiheke — a rock smashed her window — but fortunately she wasn't hurt. A worse worry is that she has been having tests and the lab people are finding things that shouldn't be there in her urine. I think she is in control of her apprehensions and will face up to decisions.

Oh dear, *life*, but of course books of poetry turn up etc.

F. [. . .]

['Janet persecuted on Waiheke': see A State of Siege, *1966.]*

To Bill Pearson, *London*

Alexander Turnbull Library

12 July 1964

Dear Bill,

I was no end grateful to get your letter on Friday — a fine dignity and charity about it, Bill. All these sore and tender matters may be put aside in the meantime, but I must remark that of course it was inevitable this storm would blow up from the moment Blackwood told me he had engaged you to attend to the book. Nobody lays a finger anywhere near at least half a dozen stories in the book except at great peril to themselves and me — I expect it's for this reason I have never done more than glance at such things as Helen Shaw's symposium, and Joan Stevens [*The New Zealand Novel, 1860–1960*] for example I have never even seen. All right, bless you Bill, things may now be left to cool down — though again, bless you.

Now for comments:

1. Joan Stevens — this entirely for you [to decide about including in a select bibliography of writing about FS], see above.

2. I don't know how the dots got into [Dan Davin's OUP anthology version of] the *Making of a New Zealander*, but your insertion of them has my entire approval.

3. I can't find text of *The Colonel's Daughter* (when I consulted Phoebe about the proof copy I had she wanted it back immediately for some reason — I think she is making a story anthology for schools), but the underlining of *was* would certainly be right — hence I approve of your italics.

4. I *sent* [marginal note: strictly, 'I am sending'] the cable because the plaguey exclamation suddenly became one of the most important of your queries. It is so far as I know impossible to render fully on paper what I am after. I thought two exclamations were right, but when I thought how Cathcart would do it on stage I realized I was risking a kind of vulgarity in using two. Yes, you are dead right. Any solution must be *faute de mieux*, but Jock! my Jock. it should be — at least then I don't appear to be trying to bludgeon the reader into sharing the emotion. Thanks a lot for this one.

5. The change in your remarks about the prose style in your Introduction — yes, I think that is an improvement. But I would say please *please* do not think *I* think it a matter of importance when I draw your attention to the very few stories written in the third person. (*Just Trespassing, Thanks* is a late and another rare example). As the book is in one aspect a test of your scholarship, I would suggest this matter could be the subject of a pendant article which you could publish in *Landfall* if you thought the matter worth investigating — an article which led off with the remark that you had not touched on this matter in your introduction could be in the best scholarly tradition.

6. I am with you on part up and toi-toi for glossary.

And now for a different set of comments, but brief I hope, and don't be alarmed.

1. I'm too damned probing, I know. And you might well say why when I'm so scared of much of my own work being touched should I poke away at CF? I have no answer (except that CF hasn't perhaps the same concentration, and I may miss causing you the worst pain). But if I have any excuse it is perhaps that when one has been so profoundly moved as I was by CF, and then involved with the author too, one longs to help, to be useful — also, being a writer one may sometimes (and sometimes often) see how the variety of masks has been devized and manipulated. The sad conclusion I draw is that other writers are not perhaps our best readers.

2. The anti-academy business is one of my obsessions (all valuable for writers). There it pops up again in *Just Trespassing, Thanks*, and in a piece I've just done for Charles, and it's very strong in the *Peon*. And about the *Peon* — I think I see now it was probably not a good idea to ask you to help with the proofs. I don't want any more storms blowing round you and me — and this might well be. I've been concealing from you that although Martin Green would like to publish the 120,000 words in toto, this is not the view of other important readers, who have thought the opening 15,000 words tend to drag here and there, and want pruning done. I have agreed to this (because in fact I have never been happy about those pages even though their substance must be somehow retained) — I have even agreed that Green will do the pruning 'to increase the pace' (what they think is lacking there). And I even doubt whether I will see what he has done until I see the proofs. I don't really mind this — after all if one is a genius (unlikely), the text can be restored in a hundred years. What the firm thinks it can successfully market is a comic novel of a kind related to *The Good Soldier Schweik* (again unlikely — but that's something you may omit telling Green if you meet him). I'll somehow manage the proofs with the help of Maurice Duggan, and perhaps I can get help from Curnow too.
3. All matters relating to your own work past present and to come I lay off just now (though assuring you I have them as much in my heart as you do). [. . .] [D]on't bother to return the photograph [of Harry Doyle] — I live with all that and don't have to look at it on paper — I live with it with all the pain and delight (still) until the pair of us are (I would hope) in the one grave.

More than enough for this time,

F.

I never got a degree Bill, though I did manage the solicitor's part — at Property Part I it took me four goes, climbing up through 8 per cent 22, 46, to the required 50 percent. But for Procedure I got 81 percent. [Marginal note: Or was it 86? I may have told you this previously.] What relation does this have to my literary work? And I wanted to be 'well-read', literate, more than to write myself. My first attempts were so hopeless. [Marginal note: My remarks on the square feet in Maori houses just a piece of nastiness. I apologize.]

['things may now be left to cool down': tempers had become frayed over the mounting costs of corrections to page proofs. 'Jock! my Jock.' 'The Undertaker's Story' ends with a young Scottish farmer burying his son under a tree in the backyard, while his wife

holds a lantern. Neither speaks a word, but before returning to the house the farmer stands for a moment and utters his three words of lament. Pearson found 'Jock! my Jock.' in the Landfall *edition of the story, but 'Jock! my Jock!' in the typescript. cf letter to Max Harris of 1 May 1946. 'the cable': FS to Pearson 14 July: 'THANKS ALTER TO STOP LETTER POSTED SUNDAY'. ATL MS-Papers-4343-041.]*

To William Plomer, *Sussex*

Alexander Turnbull Library

30 July 1964

Dear Plomer,

Your letter today, and thank heaven letters won't be crossing this time — I've been putting off writing since yours of a month ago — depression, things going wrong, not a cold but an incredibly wet winter. [. . .]

[M]y depression — what lately went wrong was that somebody I'm not sure who it was, told Martin Green at MacGibbon and Kee that Forster had admired my work. So Green writes off to F asking him whether he would contribute a Note for the *Collected Stories*. He (Green) tells me about this *afterwards*, and I hastily write back and say I hope he has made it clear that he asked quite independently of myself. I still don't know whether he did — but I do know that EMF has had the great kindness to comply. At his age! I am really floored — and each time I try to get up again I sink back with the thought I may be thought to have angled for this. (Quite the contrary indeed — do I insult you by saying I several times mentioned to Green that a Foreword by you would be very nice?) Anyhow, I give up, the ways of publishers etc. And of course I know they have to sell their books somehow.

I must write and thank dear EMF when I know the exact details. I'm not sure of his address and will send through you if you will be so kind as to forward on.

But now that MacG and K are doing the *Collected* I expect the *Novel* will be deferred until early next year. I have heard they seem to think they may have got hold of a kind of comic novel of some (distant, I should say), relation to *The Good Soldier Schweik*. This is flattering, but quite untrue — though if they can persuade the public I shall at least keep my own counsel. [. . .]

From yours (ever),

F.S.

[Plomer to FS, 8 August: 'So glad about the Forster introduction. I have ventured to tell him that you're pleased, that you would hate him to think that you pushed for it, & that you will be writing to him yourself'. ATL MS-Papers-0432-177. E.M. Forster to Plomer,

11 August 1964: 'Frank Sargeson is quite correct in thinking he did not ask me to preface his collection. The suggestion was entirely the publisher's and I wrote a few words with much pleasure, and the introduction of your name!' Durham University Library, Plomer MSS 66/312.]

To E.M. Forster, *King's College, Cambridge*

Alexander Turnbull Library

23 August 1964

Dear E.M. Forster,

I think sometimes when I've typed letters to friends I have excused myself by saying it's quicker that way — you see, get one's friends done with rapidly. Ah well, human nature! But in fact this time I have such a hand — some infection from my garden I think — and the thought crosses my mind that if it's tetanus this may be the last letter I ever write.

Such a long time since I have written — yet I can give you at least one convincing proof that you have been in my thoughts. I was re-reading Gray's Letters which I have always found such a consolation when things have gone wrong with some friend or other. In my colonial way it's such a wonder for me that you get round the streets G got round — know no doubt the very same places and rooms that he knew.

But to your little *Note* — may I jest a little? — you made me blush. You are so perceptive that you made me feel you knew exactly what I was up to at the moment you were writing it. (Oh, nothing unusual — just writing a friend some perhaps over-affectionate letters — if that is possible)

You must allow what I call my modesty (but for which the French have a somewhat better name, I think) to say I don't deserve your kindness. I'll appeal to Gray though — he comes in very handy. 'I am proud of your approbation, having no relish for any other fame than what is conferred by the few real judges, that are so thinly scattered over the face of the earth'.

I didn't know that man at MacGibbon and Kee would write you — I think you know that. I expect he sent you a proof with a great deal of material in it of not much relevancy except to New Zealanders. But I have an affection for the man who wrote it, Bill Pearson. I don't go along with him too far in his being tangled up with social sciences and such, but he wrote a very long kind of Victorian novel called Coal Flat about the remotest part of NZ. Nobody would publish it for many years, but at last Mr Paul did. I think I will send a copy to William Plomer who may be kind enough to look into it and then only send it on to you if he thought it something you might be interested in.

It often strikes me as such an anomaly that with my place done wrong to by being now on a motorway, I go on reading poetry — ah, but then I get up early in the morning to read [. . .] [Only one page survives.]

To Charles Brasch, *Dunedin*

Hocken Library

29 August 1964

Dear Charles,

Every time I sit down to try to discover what you are up to in your Landfall and Mate poems some damn thing or person interrupts me. Still, anon.

Bruce Beaver did his usual workmanlike notice [of *Ambulando*] in the Herald on your behalf — but Doyle in the Star! — I don't know what to make of anyone so thoroughly balled up. I hope nobody sent you that crap.

This is the Forster Note [enclosed], and as you see the wording lends itself to jests I wouldn't relish if they were repeated to me. Apart from that though, sharp perception. But oh heavens! — just not compatible with the heavy-handed Bill. Really, it is quite impossible of Blackwood to insert it into the book without consulting me. As a blurb yes. I am as cross as I can be about this.

Yes, I knew Pip [Ardern] meant a lot to his bright students — but for me he was quite different (he was the basis of my old gentleman engaged on street adventures in Up Onto the Roof — at least he and another old cuss who was so like Pip that it was difficult to tell them apart — because we met in quite a different way he appeared never to be able to accept me as a person with serious literary interests and aims. I was a joke, perhaps even a bad joke, belonging to a different time and different part of his life. It was infuriating — but whether the fault was mainly in him or me I wouldn't know.

I am very doubtful whether Bill Pearson will oblige with anything [for 'How I Began'], Charles. He says he gets tight-lipped so long as there is even one enemy around. What with Janet (who is pretty unstable just at present), I get really knocked to leg by all this sort of thing these days — as though I can stand no more of it for one moment. I am very fond of Bill — but one begins to ask, Where is Bill? — often I think he is simply distributed round his various personae — Paul Rogers, the Herlihy boy and the rest. His greatest danger is that Paul Rogers will before long kill him off, stone dead — it's a kind of love affair of the most destroying kind.

I hope the Minister isn't too long with some sort of answer about Janet —

she is such a bundle of worries and troubles at the moment.

Sorry for letting off so much steam. Will feel better tomorrow.

Best,

F.S.

I think I should like to do a Note on Forster — though somehow with *him* it's awful to anticipate & talk of it now. [. . .]

[Associate Professor of English Philip Sydney Ardern d. 1964 aged 83.]

To H. Winston Rhodes, *Christchurch*

Alexander Turnbull Library

[FS to Rhodes, 19 August: '[. . .] MacG and K are dropping all Bill's materials and substituting a short prefatory note by E.M. Forster. Of course when he knew of the note Paul grabbed it and got it — and it goes in after *Bill's introduction in the NZ edition. Tough on Bill — I had at least hoped that although the English edition might be said to be Forster's, the NZ could remain definitely Bill's'. ATL MS-Papers-0424-23.]*

21 September 1964

Dear Winston,

I have seen an advance copy of the Collected Stories, and Paul's blatant commercial grabbing at the Forster note has had most unfortunate results. It just doesn't go with poor Bill's earnest Eng Lit approach. The whole thing reeks of all the crap I thought we had done with years ago.

To make matters worse, I didn't see a blurb re-written by Curnow, and God damn me if he hasn't dragged in Mansfield.

I knew nothing of these matters until it was too late, and the baby I'm still carrying — making my apologies to Forster, is pretty monstrous.

I am not recommending this book to anyone or sending out any copies to anyone — so take this as an intimation I won't be presenting you with a copy. I am still considering what remedy I might have against Paul — 'the Work' in my contract would in my view be stories plus Bill's editing, certainly not anything by Mr E.M. Forster — it looks to me like a job for [FS's lawyer] Frank Haigh. Of course MacGibbon and Kee look on Paul's overloading as just laughable. Their edition should be OK (except for possibly Mansfield) [marginal note: I *might* have been in time to have her *removed*] — but of course it's all very tough on Bill and all his painstaking work.

I have been precipitated into beginning a new novel [*The Hangover*], but first I finished off a third story ['Beau'] which Dudding is using in *Mate* — before the end of the year he hopes. If so you will see it — I'd send you the carbon but it's damnably faint, though say if you want it. [. . .]

From yours,

F.S.

I still don't know when I'll be handling Peon proofs.

To William Plomer, *Sussex*

Alexander Turnbull Library

1 October 1964

Dear Plomer,

That business of Forster's Note has had its incredible extensions. My tit of a NZ publisher, a man called Blackwood Paul, managed to get hold of it, and without consulting me (and I believe without waiting for Forster's consent) inserted it into the NZ edition of the Stories. That quite impossibly bad enough — but I have now seen an advance copy of the book and it has gone in *after* the introductory matter done by the young fellow Paul employed to edit the book.

My expletives are all very obscene. I don't know what can be done about it — I mean effectively done about it. But I have been busy with one of my lawyer friends [Frank Haigh] and Paul has been threatened with Court action plus an order which would restrain him from publishing the book.

It is made ten thousand times more difficult owing to Paul's being at present in London where he has gone to try and save himself from the cancer which has doubled up on the angina he was already suffering from.

I don't even ask you to convey my apologies to F — I have nothing to say and can only go on blushing for my country and my countrymen.

Before I knew the fuller details of this horror I posted off to you a weighty novel called *Coal Flat*, written by this young editor of mine. I wanted to send EMF something very much NZ — but am doubtful whether he should at his age be troubled by this great clumsy book. After the 1st 50 pages I found myself hooked and was reminded of Dreiser at his earliest (and best). Anyhow, you I am sure see much too much of this sort of thing, but you may have a friend who might look at the book and decide whether it could be passed on to EMF or not. (What I will send to him direct will be a copy of my two plays which should be out from the Caxton Press any day now).

Glover has just had a virtually complete collection of his Poems brought out, and they add up to such an achievement I think a copy should be on your shelves — so one will go to you.

Glover as a person still shows incredible vitality, but in appearance he is these days so purple that I never see him without being reminded of the emperor Porphyrogenitus. Yet he is never ill — while the rest of us drop off at a rate which constantly accelerates. [. . .]

[unsigned]

Paul is of course about the most successful and richest bookseller in the country — a formidable little tit indeed. (The kindest thing to suppose is that his brain has been afflicted by his sickness).

[Sargeson's fussing tried the patience of all concerned. Plomer to FS, 12 October: 'I can understand your worry about the way the note by Forster has been used by B. Paul — but don't worry, *Forster* won't mind *& will value your minding that he might. Perhaps I'll say nothing to him'. ATL MS-Papers-0432-177.*

FS to Plomer, 19 October: 'Thanks so much — I don't feel quite so bad now. But you might have *to say a word to Forster — Paul [in reality Janet not Blackwood as FS suggests] has sent him a copy of the book, & accompanied it by a pitifully horrid letter, of which he has (as the last turn of the screw) sent me a copy. I would gladly have suffered more in life, to have been spared this. Pardon my fuss'. ATL MS-Papers-0432-187.*

'a pitifully horrid letter': Janet Paul to E.M. Forster, 9 October: 'It is a great pleasure to be able to send you a copy of the New Zealand edition of Frank Sargeon's Collected Stories *and to thank you for allowing us to use the warm commendation which you wrote for them. [. . .] We were so pleased to support the work of one admired writer with the understanding praise of another that we decided to use it, not only on the expendable dustwrapper, but inside as well. Page proofs had already been passed but printing was held up by negotiations with MacGibbon and Kee. We found that we could use your introduction without resetting (and consequent delay and expense) only in one place — opposite the first page of the text and following Bill Pearson's introduction. I am adding this tedious detail because Mr Sargeson, while not objecting to the use of your prefatory note on the dust-wrapper, is very annoyed that we have placed your note inside the book* after *Pearson's introduction. He thinks this shows disrespect to you. This letter is to assure you that no disrespect was intended and that the decision to use the note was made entirely by us. There was no time to consult Mr Sargeson without holding up the book further and delaying its already late arrival in New Zealand. We would, of course, not have used your note in this way if we had known of Mr Sargeson's feelings'. ATL MS-Papers-0432-189.*

Forster to Plomer, 19 October: 'Frank Sargeson is a bloody nuisance. I wrote those few words with pleasure and in the hope of pleasing him, and I have tried to make this plain to him. If he still has to go on fussing he must fuss. What does concern me is your tiresome knee [. . .]'. Durham University Library, Plomer MSS 66/313.

Plomer to FS, 31 October: 'I told [Forster] you were worried, & perhaps you told him too. 'Pardon my fuss', you said in your letter to me. His view was rather that if you must fuss, you would fuss, so I hope all will simmer down'. ATL MS-Papers-0432-177.]

To C.K. Stead, *Auckland*

Alexander Turnbull Library

7 October 1964

Dear Karl,

That's splendid about the story ['A Fitting Tribute'], and as the K[enyon] R[eview] is something unlikely to be seen by me I do hope I may see your own copy sometime (or if you can tell me how I might obtain that particular number I would be pleased.)

Oh, I don't think Dudding is right at all — strange though I thought of *Beau* as simply a character study of no very special merit. I see now it is a sort of parable of the fall of an Empire. Very strange — I don't think this saves it in any way — but my theory is supported that it's always the symbolism you're never aware of when working that's most effective.

Somebody (I don't think Charles) has jacked up the Burns Fellowship for next year for Janet. [Marginal note: This is probably still a bit private.] This has coincided with an offer from John Money, the eminent sexologist of Baltimore to pay her air fare there for a visit. (He is so wealthy and eminent now he has bought and done up an old house on the waterfront and entertains some of the negro population). Anyhow I think she will go, then on to England to clear up her affairs there and back here to go into residence at end of January. She has written 150,000 words since last October — two novels, though the second will take a fortnight to finish. To what degree I may find myself figuring in this work I don't know — but if I am there and you are not, please try not to be jealous.

She has now no top to either Charlie (a candidate for wearing topless dresses without conflicting with the Law would you think?). She is still very worried by the mess she has landed herself in with you — I hope myself you will eventually write it all off as the insanity which it is.

Yes, I would like to have you for a dinner. If you would care to name a suitable day I will confirm. Not Mondays or Tuesdays (I find myself on those nights doing a reading aloud for Middleton of *Coal F* — I find this quite interesting — though we have the disadvantage of only one eye where 4 should be) [Marginal note: I haven't checked yet on how knackers number out.] But virtually any other night I can very probably make do.

Middleton has an advance copy of his book [*A Walk on the Beach*] (Michael

Joseph) from London. It looks quite well done and you will of course have to see it.

Again congratulations on story. I expect you saw review of you in London Mag. Frank Haigh and I may be taking very drastic action against Blackwood Paul. If he breaks the contract by introducing unbargained for matter into the text at least he is not going to take his 50 pc on overseas publications — we hope. [. . .]

Best love,

F.S.

['please try not to be jealous'/ 'the mess she has landed herself in with you': FS had recently drawn Frame's story 'The Triumph of Poetry' to Stead's attention. This appeared to derive much detail from the Steads' life in Takapuna, and seemed to them 'so blackly targeted it felt like a malediction'. (C.K. Stead, South-west of Eden, *p. 342). FS to Stead 20 September: 'Janet is sadly rocked [by the consternation she has caused you]. [. . .] It seems that I figured in another one called* The Silkworms *which she withdrew. I asked was it worse than your one, and she said she thought I might find it so. Of course nothing can be repaired I'm afraid, bad luck. But it is undoubtedly her insanity. As she says neither you nor I is her 'enemy' — yet she goes ahead and produces a situation in which we appear to be. Apparently it's all hopelessly compulsive'. ATL MS-Papers-8220-01. 'The Silkworms': see* Granta *105, Spring 2009.]*

To Charles Brasch, *Dunedin*

Hocken Library

18 October 1964

Dear C,

[. . .] I have been lending a hand with Janet — she got away by plane Thursday, & will stop with John Money in Baltimore before going on to England where she tidies up her affairs (150,000 words in 12 months she has written! — to my poor 15,000).

J.M. is helping her with this excursion.

What to do about the Pension now? — could the Minister, surely well primed-up by this time, just hold it all in suspension meantime?

I have enough troubles these days without the nagging suspicion that something has gone wrong at Caxton — almost as though Alpers has faded out. In mid-August all seemed set for my plays for N.Z. Authors week — but since then dead silence. And I note *no* Caxton book ad. in *Landfl*. Oh well, it doesn't matter, though the thought of a return to mad former days is distressing.

Frank Haigh (whose views on my affairs I *must* listen to — we have known each other for 40 years now) has convinced me it is time for a showdown with Blackwood Paul. Among other things we find a letter he has written to E.M. Forster so terribly disgraceful (I don't wonder there is a complete silence for me from the direction of both F. & William Plomer). Anyhow, our terms are quite reasonable — Blackwood *must* surrender all his rights in the book beyond N.Z. (so that we may confine his misdeeds to N.Z), & that means he must also surrender his right to 50 p.c. of all my overseas net earnings, taking instead only a commission which should not exceed 10 p.c. (although to settle the sorry affair I would agree to 20 p.c.). But Blackwood squeals like a stuck pig, & his local harem runs in circles uttering screams which suggest a bunch of fairies doing a daisy-chain at a drag party. If no settlement we must move for an Injunction — & then the book will go into deep freeze for I should say at least a year. If this happens MacGibbon & K's English edition may be held up too (they plan for March — with the *Peon* to follow in English autumn. As the strain of working on my new book is a daily strain which seems almost to drag the guts out of me, I think I shall be mildly surprised if I am still alive then).

Incidentally, there is no doubt whatsoever that Blackwood has broken the contract by introducing Forster into the text without consulting me — & yet he clings to the absurd notion he acted for the best! for me!! And he's incapable of understanding that if the contract is broken he can't expect to collect that iniquitous 50 p.c.

Charles, my sympathy for you on what that insensitive bitch wrote about your poems in the *Listener*. Believe me, I have learned a lot from Janet in these matters — *I am not going to read one single line of any thing anyone publishes about any book of mine*. It is the only way if one wants to continue with one's work. Incidentally, Janet is the worst seller ever — her sales are virtually nil. No more, I'm distressed & under far too much strain.

F.

['that insensitive bitch': Joan Stevens had reviewed Brasch's Ambulando *in the* Listener, *16 October 1964.]*

To Charles Brasch, *Dunedin*

Hocken Library

24 October 1964

Dear Charles,

[. . .] Yes, well it is quite a task for you over Janet. Do ask me to help if there is anything I can *do* to help. (Incidentally, I don't think my name should be brought forward too openly. I have had confidential information that I have lately been kept off the air 'on political grounds'. This probably goes back to the letters I used to write Odo Strewe while he was on Soames Island during the war, and now in the Russian Book of NZ stories I am credited with having sent MSS to Moscow (if I did I did so in my sleep)). I think what has happened is that *Truth* in defending itself against the action Middleton and Frank Haigh are taking against it, has got a complete translation of all the matter surrounding the stories in the Russian book, and a copy of this is very likely in the hands of Brigadier Gilbert [the director of the New Zealand Security Intelligence Service]. Of course I simply don't care a damn, it is such crazy nonsense, but it could harm Janet if I was presented as very closely associated with her).

Yes, it is quite splendid that J accepted the Burns. It is just that I get a little irritated by people who seem to want to jump on the bandwagon (I wonder how they would react if they knew her sales are virtually nil — we had better keep that to ourselves. I think Janet has been perhaps just a little worried by the warmth and enthusiasm of Margaret Dalziel's letters, and by her having jacked the whole thing up for her — however, we have had a word or two on the matter, and she will be able to manage anything that comes up — many years in a MH can be a wonderful training for much in life). [. . .]

The Paul situation has altered a little owing to the good office of Plomer — his tender consideration for Forster, and also myself in the matter has been most welcome (how coarse-grained and crude NZ attitudes seem to me by contrast!) It seems Forster may have minded *very much* what has been done in the book, but Plomer has assured me he won't mind so much when I have suffered so much over his minding. I feel an enormous relief, and look forward to a settlement — particularly as at the back of mind is the notion (supported by reliable evidence) that Blackwood is suffering a mortal illness. (I have the most shattering reports about Cole). [. . .]

I do not expect you to write when you will be so rushed. [. . .] But send me a coloured postcard depicting the gorgeous East with all the stage properties,

A thousand good wishes,

F.S.

[Margaret Dalziel was acting head of English at the University of Otago at the time Frame was awarded the Burns Fellowship for 1965.]

To William Plomer, *Sussex*

Alexander Turnbull Library

15 November 1964

Dear Plomer,

Thank you so much for your note 31 October, and you have been the Very Personification of Kindness Itself (or something of that kind) in this matter. Yes, let things simmer down — and indeed there is No Other Way (I must sound as though I have joined the Zen people). But a thousand blessings on you — I don't feel nearly so bad. Do though excuse me from sending you a copy of this book — you shall have the MacG and K edition instead (which incidentally has a lovely bit in the blurb about my tiny little sketches being rather like Japanese haiku verses — I must say I had never thought of that), which should look a much better job — with of course E.M.F. in his right and proper place right at the beginning. But this won't be until March.

Of course with so much upset there was nothing else for it but glue myself to my new book — a short novel, I think, and going (for me at this stage) surprisingly well — to be at last able to handle things one has tried for over a lifetime! — but all my fingers crossed (and typing made difficult).

Your [gouty] knee! — I am hoping I remember you once said at our age we must often expect to feel like porcupines with all the spines growing in instead of out. A list of the pains I feel at this moment would take up all the remaining space on this page.

My poor Harry — he can't expect to be much better, but at least I can crown all my pain by the last sweet agony of doing for him all that can be done. Alas he is Irish and stubborn, but I always relish his last answers.

How right you are that Pearson's book is not for Forster. It is a rather curious piece of regional work — people who scratch and bite at each other like Neanderthals (a few alas, quite phoney Piltdowns) — you don't perhaps get much beyond the region out of it — but people in that part of NZ are still that kind of creature. It's like taking a stroll through a Zoo.

Oh no, you were very good on the air, and don't worry about my listening. I still listen to learn — I know the air is a kind of acting, and I feel I don't do so bad myself when I have a script in my hand, but I have never learned to act even passably without a script. I wouldn't say this about you, even though your scripted talks far back (crossing Siberia eg) were some of the most beautifully done I have ever heard.

Quinces in Auckland don't do well (I envy you, a beautiful tree and the smell, and the rest!) but I have two loquats, one of which is for the first time bearing lovely clean fruit. My most irritating tree at the moment is a custard apple — it will bear again this season I think, but its habit of branching is quite absurd. The slightest wind and even the oldest wood is likely to split. [. . .]

Ever, & again thanks,

F.S.

Awake at 6am the other morning and hearing the first news I learned you are to be wildly extravagant with £500 — thanks to that fairytale figure James Bond. May your debauchery be everything short of disaster!

[Ian Fleming (died 12 August 1964) and Plomer had been friends since the 1930s. Fleming was Plomer's most valuable discovery as a reader for Jonathan Cape.]

To Rhondda Coleman, *Christchurch*

Alexander Turnbull Library

15 November 1964

Dear Rhonda,

[. . .] I haven't written because I had so much upset over Blackwood Paul's vulgarity in grabbing and inserting Forster's note into the NZ edition of my Stories (Frank Haigh and I have been threatening him with a big Action), and the Caxton Press delay with my plays, that I tried to forget it all by plunging into writing another book — and damn me if it isn't going surprisingly well — no nostalgic memories — right up to date — I have young men in it called Solly Jasper Whacko Finny, a girl called Raewyn — I read a chapter to the Steads the other night, and they were surprised moved and entertained — I am dying to have Andy's verdict and his reactions to his own mirror image — but it will have to wait until January — by which time I will have a lot more done anyhow.

Karl Stead and his wife go off to England soon on a Nuffield Fellowship for a year (£5000 I think), and K is now an Associate Professor. How Curnow hasn't liked that! For consolation he was made a D. Litt — but he's not consoled. If I am offered any such thing I will immediately hand over the letter of offer to Frank Haigh for a big Libel action. [. . .]

I am really longing to see Justin — anything that is part of you and Andy is (I won't say, my meat — too vulgar).

Did you see John Graham's film [*Runaway*]? — he had a story, but O'Shea didn't make it. Brian Wood, who at last goes off to be a missionary climb the Eiger (Ogre) or something in December, took me to see Tom Jones. I didn't like it because of my love of Fielding and his great novel — but afterwards I said to B that had I been aged 26 and a virgin I wouldn't have liked to go home and sleep by myself. He was a little embarrassed — I expect having to get himself fit for climbing the Ogre (or Eiger) would deter him from making too too passionate love to himself.

Did you hear the story of the pope coming down the aisle of St Peter's during Oecumenical Council swinging a smoking censer? — an eager young Bishop reached out his hand to pluck his sleeve, and say, 'My dear, I think your drag is absolutely *marvellous*, but your *handbag* is on fire!'

Best love, see you in January,

F.

I am thrilled by your Art School success.

To C.K. Stead, *Auckland*

Alexander Turnbull Library

[Stead to FS, 16 November: 'You should stop worrying about me. I chose my situation, and with only slight and occasional reservations about the university I'm very happy in it'. He cites his fiction to date, the three critical essays 'which may last in N.Z. as long as Dr Johnson's have in England', and his faith that at least four of his poems 'will prove truly durable'. 'I'm not boasting. [. . .] I just believe it to be true. Well I'm 32. Could you say you had done better at that age?' ATL MS-Papers-0432-179.]

21 November 1964

Dear Karl,

[. . .] My dear man, I thought I was talking about the present and future not the past — your achievements are stupendous — what concerned me was your poor heart worry overwork and all that.

And done better at your age! — perish the thought — I had to learn by do it yourself — when . . . . Well, let me tell you a little story. I meant to keep this secret but I have been so curious about how you came by your natural gifts that I have been having secret interviews with your mother. And it all transpires as I had suspected. I don't expect she will ever get round to telling you this story so I will.

Once upon a time (32 years ago in fact) your mama was pining to have a little baby boy of her own and she cried and cried (we can skip all this, it was just that despite much trying nothing happened). Well, one day being moved by a beautiful morning to take a walk beneath the pine trees on Mt Eden, imagine her surprise when the most beautiful of young men came bounding across the pasture. She has described this young man as being the living spit of Apollo in Perugino's beautiful picture of Apollo and Marsyas. (As you know she is and was a woman of culture).

Now she immediately supposed her prayers had been answered and the gods had sent her the young man as a potent lover. (Though she has confessed to some doubt as to this thought — despite the young man's golden nudity (see Perugino's picture) he showed by no exterior sign any urgent wish to become the lover of anyone — which of course included your mother).

And here's the payoff (you'll be surprised)! To the unabounded surprise and everlasting delight of your parent as the young man came within a yard of her his side suddenly opened right down its entire length as though the unseen hand of Zeus had operated a zip fastener — and who should emerge, clasping a portable Olivetti against his embryonic bosom but YOU!!

It *was* Apollo! Now!!! (though I am sorry, I think your mother must have been mistaken about the brand of typewriter — it was more likely a baby Underwood).

Well, that's how it all happened.

And you can understand, knowing the facts as I do I sometimes worry because your career does not proceed wholly according to plans which I, with my inside information, have made for it. And you will understand that occasionally this is as annoying to me as it would be to you if the new poetry on full arrival proved to be something rather different from *your* plans.

Oh, well well. And nice of Press — but I thought he was a member of that weight-lifting family, John Snatch, John Jerk and John Press.

Well, I'll be seeing you. [. . .]

F.S.

Actually the long narrative poem I have had in mind for you for years is entitled *Emily on Eden*.

And it goes without saying I love you all, even your mother, and although I may have been myself on Mt Eden at the time I make no claim to have actually been that young man.

To E.P. Dawson, *Itteringham, Norwich*

Hocken Library

30 January 1965

Dear Peter,

I am so sorry the line went dead just like that. I expect it was that I simply couldn't cope as I had so much upset with Blackwood Paul and the Caxton Press. I took refuge in plunging into the writing of a new lengthy fiction — everything, friends chores garden obligations, went overboard. Anyhow I feel a little better now that I have knocked off a sheaf of pages — and the best of them aren't too bad, particularly for my time of life.

MacGibbon and Kee have instructions to send you a copy of the *Collected Stories* with the little introduction by E.M. Forster. Publication will be March 29. For the English edition all the Bill Pearson material, Introduction, Bibliography, Glossary, has been dropped. (I expect though all this might have some interest for you, and I will think about sending you a copy). [Marginal note: Actually he has done a most painstaking job.]

As for the *Peon* — it is dedicated FOR PETER — I hope you don't mind — I wanted it to be like that — just a few people aware of the person I am paying my regards to. Publication is English autumn, so I expect I shall be doing the proofs pretty soon now. As for the Plays, they are still held up at Caxton even though advertised as available. (This very bad, as Cathcart had the Glasgow Peoples' Theatre virtually jacked up for the Commonwealth Festival, and a few other contacts have failed because of the delay).

Vernon Brown has just died — and how they add up! Fairburn, my brother in law Frank Gadd, Bob Lowry, Cresswell, now Vernon. Poor Harry is so very ill with valvular heart disease and a great anxiety to me as he won't go into hospital, and lives in a very pinched way in a flat which is really a converted toolshed. [. . .]

How sick I am of Churchill!

A curious summer, Peter — rain, and the pumpkins have rioted everywhere — but blighty tomatoes. The whole place hopelessly overgrown now — the eye doctor says he washes his hands of me if I do sharp muscular jerks particularly with my head down — so I can't slash at the greenery.

And you? I read of ice and snow.

Janet seems to thrive in Dunedin — I hope it lasts.

No more just now, but all my best to you, dear Peter,

From

F.S.

[The architect Vernon Brown (born 23 March 1905) died 28 January 1965; Winston Churchill died 24 January 1965.]

To Charles Brasch, *Dunedin*

Hocken Library

30 January 1965

Dear Charles,

[. . .] And you? I hope you are refreshed by some revivifying break anyhow. Janet seems to like Dunedin. It shouldn't be long now before I am doing my *Peon* proofs, and the English edition of the *Stories* appears at the end of March (a different jacket, and a marvellous blurb — the Paul blurb was done by Curnow, and I could have strangled him for dragging in Mansfield).

Better (less egotistic) letter next time [. . .].

From F.S.

Vernon Brown dead. I remember 1935 — Rex F, Vernon, my brother-in-law Frank Gadd, my friend Harry Doyle, & myself all in the Hot Baths at Helensville — I remember I thought all those bodies were stronger & better put together than my own. Harry was 10 years older than any of us. He lives even though grievously sick with valvular heart trouble, & so do I — the other 3 all dead. I even remember a bit of comedy driving home. Frank Gadd & Rex in front seat, & the car went slower & slower as they discussed Douglas Credit, & E.M. Forster — I remember Rex sent a silence through the car when he said 'he had been told' that E.M.F. was a very 'unhealthy' man. Alas, alas, 'unhealth' is unconnected with longevity, it seems.

To Charles Brasch, *Dunedin*

Hocken Library

3 April 1965

Dear Charles,

Yes, I hope too about Janet. I think you would know that a Medical Benefit would be utterly the wrong thing — she would feel classified as a lunatic officially, and lose promptly the confidence so necessary for her work.

Anyhow, some strange things seem to have been happening in Wellington. My own little assistance of £4 a week has not been paid since 26 January (don't let this alarm you, I now have Cole and his wife on the job), and it wasn't such a long time ago I received a confidential wire from somebody in Broadcasting that I had been kept off the air. I think much derives from that Russian book — I am credited in the biographical Notes with sending MSS direct to Moscow (not true unless I did so sleepwalking). There seems to be a pretty tie-up between 'Truth', Mr G.G.G.Watson who used to be Truth's lawyer, and Brigadier Gilbert. Also Stringer of Broadcasting. I hate to say it, but I think one must conclude that Shadbolt has much to answer for — from Middleton's account of what has happened in his case against Truth so far, it seems there was only one typescript of Rhodes' translation of the introduction to the Russian book. It came to me via Middleton, and I handed it to Shadbolt to return to Middleton. It never reached Middleton for many months, & reached him from Shadbolt, with the excuse that he had been busy. Now Truth, forced to declare what papers it has, admits to a copy of this document. How did they get it? Shadbolt of course indignantly denies — but the evidence of a nasty bit of clerical treason is pretty strong. Anyhow, unless Truth settle out of Court the case should be aired pretty soon — Frank Haigh is very hopeful.

My *Stories* were published in London beginning of week (without BP's editing — alas, poor Bill, I think he's still sore about it. Incidentally I saw him, and he looks very well), and *Peon* has been brought forward from October to September to fit in with Commonwealth Festival, I think. (There is some suggestion one of my plays might be put on in NZ House, with the bust exhibited on loan — casting difficulties aren't solved yet — and London-published books by NZders on exhibition. I am afraid I can't be very interested, with fresh work on hand).

And your own work, Charles? I pray you may be left some time for it.

About Texidor when you are ready,

F.

['I hope too about Janet': Brasch was working on a literary pension scheme for Frame. Greville Texidor committed suicide in Australia in September 1964. FS wrote a memorial note for Landfall, *June 1965.]*

To Janet Frame, *Dunedin*

Private collection

17 April 1965

Dear Janet,

Yes, I am very very sorry about Birmingham, and don't know the answers. If it's any help — not a word [from Bill Pearson] since that fatal *whetting* evening. I must admit though that I have been a little tempted to be unfaithful — a meeting was arranged for me with E.H. Audley who wrote *No Boots for Mr Moehau*. He is as charming as his book, 69, retired schoolteacher. We had some very pleasant conversation, and I think both of us could have done with more — but then his wife was there too — very nice indeed, very intelligent — but oh, very watchful (I couldn't decide whether some reputation of my own might have preceded me, or whether so far as his wife is concerned *he* has one). Anyhow, I fancy more may come of this — anyhow a spare, most lively bright-eyed man for 69 — and he has two books written since Mr Moehau, one to come out soon. [. . .]

I really did think Beginnings [*Landfall,* March 1965] a most marvellous piece of writing. The march to the scaffold even better than in Berlioz's Symphony indeed. I've read out that part to several people already. My story ['City and

Suburban'] I looked on as just a kind of squib, but I see now it is very precisely written (yet manages to contain double and contradictory notions which I suppose do throw some light on what is 'going on in the man's mind') — what do you suppose happened? My private idea is (don't tell anyone) — no, too unrefined.

I am reading *Castle Rackrent*, and quite an experience — I had no idea — nothing Fanny Burney or even Jane A about Miss Edgeworth — she could be Mr Edgeworth if one didn't know she wasn't.

Now you must promise no more fivers unless I say. It's true Wellington hasn't paid since 26 January — but my bank account still holds out, and in any case I would worry only if Harry had to go short. But that won't happen. [. . .]

I shall pray about Birmingham. And just go on writing, I am too.

Best love,

Fx [. . .]

['Birmingham': a codeword for Frame's Maudsley consultant, R.H. Cawley, who had been based at the University of Birmingham since 1962.]

To Janet Frame, *Dunedin*

Private collection

8 May 1965

Dear J,

Are you suffering, my dear?

Same here.

Did you listen to Joan Stevens? — oh, how I could have torn that woman to pieces! How could the poor soul know she was inviting murder by 1) Claiming our dear dear Janet as her own precious property 2) Being sub-adequate in inadequate time on another dear one. Oh, just let me meet that woman someday, I'll please your own Margaret D[alziel] by tearing her up into little pieces.

Actually she has persuaded me into another investigation of SGFB [*Scented Gardens for the Blind*] and congratulations, you give me pleasure.

In Wellington they suddenly pulled their socks up with a great show of doing me justice — trouble was the accountant could count, but apparently not calculate. He counted up 7 fortnights in arrear, and then paid me at the rate of £2 a week instead of 4 — exactly half the arrears. I have explained the matter to him, but of course I retained the cheque.

No worrying, sweetheart, you see everything works out eventually — now that's something you *never* knew did you?

Somebody sent me out a horrid clipping from Observer — Simon Raven reviewing me, Maurice Duggan, and the terrible Shadbolt. My name was mentioned *six* times, D's *four*, and S's *3* [Marginal note: which is all that matters] — but said of S 'oh how mixed up and whimsical the hero is, how sensitive and misunderstood. And oh how I wished he'd trip over a Coca-cola bottle and break his cute little neck'. S stands for Shad. In the Spectator I was greatly preferred to John Cheever and Pirandello. Oh, how I feel I tremble on the edge of Frame — sorry, Fame.

My bronze is done — very heavy — I managed to tilt it, and it's HOLLOW. After all it might have been Hollow — sorry, Holy-oake, or Nash, or Marsh, so I'm told. Look in Spring number of Kenyon Review (if not available I will send later on) story by Karl — very funny — you could congratulate him and all would be well.

All my love (no, not *quite* all — teeny tiny bit withheld just in case)

From Fx

[Joan Stevens (1908–1990) grew up in Hamilton, studied at Oxford, and lectured in English at Dunedin Teachers' College, where she met Frame. She later taught New Zealand literature at Victoria University.]

To Mr Read, *Internal Affairs, Wellington*

Alexander Turnbull Library

5 June 1965

Dear Mr Read,

Thank you for your letter of 1 June, and I don't doubt that your account of what happened about the literary pension is quite accurate from your point of view.

But you must pardon me for supposing there may well be more to this sorry matter. I haven't failed to notice that trouble seemed to date from the time of the publication of the Russian book of New Zealand Short Stories last year. I knew nothing of this book until it was published, and I have since seen a copy only for a few moments. But I have learned that it contains false information concerning me: namely, that I sent MS copies of two of my stories used to Moscow. It has also lately come to my knowledge that besides falling for this piece of nonsense, the paper Truth has invented a further piece of its own: namely, that these two stories have never been published elsewhere than in Russia. (Publishing history of the two stories is recorded in Dr Pearson's Bibliography at the end of my Collected Stories: besides New Zealand publications extending back thirty or so years, there has also been a publication in the English Listener, and one of the stories has just lately been highly praised by the highly Tory English Spectator).

It must have been about the time of the publication of the Russian book that the Council refused to accept the obligation of the pension. Also, about that time, I received confidential information that I had been excluded from the air on political grounds.

It is possible that these matters may receive an airing however shortly, as my friend, O. E. Middleton, has now a near date set down in Auckland for the hearing of his libel action against Truth.

I have no information yet whether or not the Age Benefit will be granted. It is kind of you to arrange for those few pounds, but I must point out that they could be an embarrassment to me — added to my literary earnings for a period of one year, they might only further reduce the Age Benefit for the ensuing year. But I appreciate your kind endeavours.

To Janet Frame, *Dunedin*

Private collection

12 June 1965

Dear J,

I feel quite like a scoutmaster — grit your teeth, dig your toes in, never say die, be British, remember the yellow peril, Faintheart never won Fairboy, etc.

In fact I am hopeful, Charles will be up here end of next week, and we will talk about pension after he has seen Wellington people on way up.

If you can get a photograph of an orgasm from J[ohn] M[oney] I will take a copy at any cost. When you were up had I done my researches into the missionary William Yate? I have now discovered from [J.S.] Polack [*New Zealand*] that the Maoris up north had a deity called Niturehu who lived on the top of a hill, and simply lived for collecting young Maoris of either sex. But the one sine qua non was that they just *had* to be red-haired. If you ever see a red-haired Maori you can test his culture by telling him your name is Niturehu.

Yes, miserable too, with cold & wet (the blanket still a marvel), though my stomach has improved — the doctor examined my rectum and didn't use a glove — I informed him he had violated a public monument and threatened to call on the police. He said he preferred to wash his finger to save the bother of cleaning a glove. I told him what worried me was where his finger had been that day until I got the benefit of it. Did he make a habit of this sort of thing? We even got a little acrimonious — I expect I was disappointed that he failed to give me even the suggestion of the thrill I might have reasonably expected — after I had paid him five shillings too.

To cheer up do think you could now take a fourth husband?

But much love,

Fx

To Kevin Ireland, *London*

Alexander Turnbull Library

26 June 1965

Dear Kevin,

It seems to me Stead wrote that middle. Not Davin, I feel sure. Possibly Basil Dowling, perhaps Dave B[allantyne], or Kevin. Well then, I don't know except Stead.

May it help with launching the novel! — and I shall ask Martin Green to send you a copy.

Middleton collects £4570 out of his action against Truth. Strangely, I've been the one to suffer most over Truth's untruths. My little literary pension was withdrawn (I've applied for Age Benefit), and I was confidentially told I had been kept off Air on political grounds.

I just can't be bothered about this bullshit as I am more than 30,000 words on in my new book, but have struck a rock. Have tried bulldozing etc. NBG. Am worried sick at moment, but still hoping.

[. . .] I will be sending Green soon huge photo of Torso to exhibit in NZ House in September.

Janet and I worked round the clock doing proofs of Peon in hurry. We thought it stands up as a comic novel. She has her own new novel coming — good title, *The Adaptable Man*.

Much love,

Fx

I like all the poems you write. And thanks for Guardian.

['that middle': an anonymous review of the Collected Stories *and* Wrestling with the Angel, *under the title 'A Sad and Savage World', appeared in the* Times Literary Supplement, *17 June 1965. FS later found it was by Davin.]*

To Janet Frame, *Dunedin*

Private collection

10 July 1965

Dear Janet,

I am so sorry I never got round to writing last weekend — you know how it is. [. . .] (Incidentally, how does one keep a check on publishers? In the reference library the other day I was curiously prompted to turn over the pages of a copy of QUEEN — you know British glossy — perhaps the name attracted me. Anyhow this number was April 7, and there bang in the middle was A Man and His Wife with a note about me and a whole page illustration. First I knew of it, and I suppose I must make sure when Pauls account to me that MacGibbon and Kee have accounted to them for this. But how much of this sort of thing goes on? I expect in such matters you are better off than I am with your agent). [. . .]

Mumps? I do hope all goes well. My guts keep getting bad again, but my doctor still isn't alarmed. Nerves — and my God lately I have been rocked. Shadbolt wrote a nasty patronising page about me in [the Sydney] Bulletin [19 June 1965]. I need have known nothing about it, but Pearson remedied that. Copied out all the worst bits omitted the compensating passages and thought I'd be pleased. I could have rung his neck. (No, on second thoughts I think if I had got that close I would probably have changed my mind).

I tell you this because we are the same kind of bibliophiles in many ways — I now and then came across references to Barry Lyndon (Thackeray) — I simply *had* to read it but could get hold of it only by buying a £2 copy from England. Isn't one's nose curious — it's picaresque, rather like my Peon, I don't regret the £2, I think very good. Also about one's nose, I have worried myself sick at page 103 of my typescript trying to get all the suspended elements to crystalize out — and suddenly I pick up Dostoevsky's Dream of a Queer Fellow. There it all is just as I wanted it. I may have to abandon the book or else pinch.

What news of Adaptable Man? And fresh work? Thanks for telling me about the Shadbolt. No more this time, forgive me if I should have answered questions. And best love,

Fx [. . .]

To Janet Frame, *Dunedin*

Private collection

1 August 1965

Dearest J,

Are you suffering? — I hope not too much.

My God, what would I be doing without your blanket? — it's probably age, but I don't remember such cold weather here before. But perhaps it's just the chill round my heart — I've lately woken to the fact that I should have somehow contrived to introduce you to Bill Pearson — for your expert diagnosis. I realize now he's one of those people who has gone on wrapping himself in protective layers (within which the ego has thinned itself out) until there's no core left at all. There's nobody at home. The layers are useless anyhow as the ego has come to the surface and all that keeps him ticking is agonised reactions to raw stimuli. His latest agony is over Horsman — of course he is mainly wrong and Horsman is mainly right but he's not concerned with this, only his agony — rapped over the knuckles by an academic senior, patronised, slighted. I'm terribly sorry of course but this doesn't bring me any closer to him (there's nobody to go closer to anyhow), oh no, I'm to be kept at a distance and he puts it into letters.

All this is my agony. And what do I do to help? (I caught a glimpse of him from a bus the other day and he looks ghastly).

But not really co-opting you.

And your agony?

Well!

I have read Thackeray's *Barry Lyndon*, am now on Conrad and I have a complete Chaucer which makes me as happy as a sandboy just to look at.

Be good (in your work anyhow)

with
this X from
Frank

[University of Otago Professor of English Alan Horsman reviewed FS's Collected Stories *in* Landfall, *June 1965.]*

To Bill Pearson, *Auckland*

Alexander Turnbull Library

[Pearson sent FS a draft of a letter he had written to Landfall *taking issue with Alan Horsman's 'indirect and peevish' comments about the* Collected Stories. *ATL MS-Papers-4261-143.]*

3 August 1965

Dear Bill,

You will understand the yearnings I feel when you are hurt, and the Landfall letter is very difficult — I kick against damaging myself with you by adding to the hurt.

Your protest is dignified in a dour kind of way, but it seems to give away too much. I think I would have been good-humoured and rueful. Horsman was peevish (I would prefer to think of him as much too offhand and patronising), so you seem to repay him in kind. Is that good, Bill? — think of the wonderful things in literature we've had from the imperturbably good-humoured Shaw and Wilde.

Wouldn't it be better to limit your reply to the fact that Horsman diminished you (and that, surely, is where the hurt is) — if only he hadn't done that, differences of critical opinion would be welcomed all round.

I don't think you should go into any details about the differences — there you gain on dignity if you don't. If you aren't a worthy opponent how can you reply? (And unless you want to open up the question of differences you are perhaps inviting Horsman to say all right, fetch out your guns and we'll see who is going to demolish whom. This of course might be a good thing — though I am doubtful. Remember I said on the phone about the dangers of your critical approach (that it may finally resolve itself into a question whether artist and critic agree on 'humanity and understanding'). Horsman would reply that he is only concerned with the self-contained work of art and it wouldn't be worth investigating if humanity and understanding weren't taken for granted. But of course there's a final difficulty here too — for example, H's perception of what is going on in the Undertaker's Story is very acute, but he can't know (as I know, and you too, now, know) that behind it all is a consistently worked out scheme of drama which is intended to remain private. The clue here is [the farmer] Duncan, the man with a conviction rejected by society and rejected by the individual at his own level with the sole exception of the undertaker. From there you can go on to the meaning of the child the wife etc etal).

But perhaps Bill the worst hurt I am inflicting is to question your use of the word 'capable'. That to me suggests being active, and I know a work of art can be active — but perhaps not quite in the way suggested by that word. I think I would have said 'that his stories should lend themselves to more than one interpretation'.

Now forgive me for these questionings. And forgive me for saying let us put away letters now for a while, let us meet and be civilized and talk (and not talk about Shadbolt), and let this meeting satisfy for a time my over-active heart, and let it, if even for a moment, call a halt to the windings of these never-ending wrappings round yourself. Believe me Bill this is something I *know*, finally they don't protect, and finally they destroy the self that they are intended to protect.

Be seeing you, Bill,

F.

You protect by loving — and how can you protect when you protect yourself against love? — I mean *over*-protect, some protection is sometimes necessary, I agree.

No Bulletin in Takapuna — I hope to look in town.

[On 8 August Brasch told FS that Pearson had withdrawn his letter to Landfall. *ATL MS-Papers-0432-149. 'No Bulletin in Takapuna': The Sydney* Bulletin *had published Pearson's response to Maurice Shabolt's review of the* Collected Stories *on 31 July, and carried letters between Pearson and Shadbolt until 4 September.]*

To Bill Pearson, *Auckland*

Alexander Turnbull Library

7 August 1965

Dear Bill,

All my literary skill doesn't enable me to say how deeply you touch me. All I can do is use a sheet of white paper instead. May it stand for something that is or could be good sweet and clean!

Don't pull on too many overcoats — one maybe when the need is desperate, but not ten or more. Strange that one pair of encircling arms can do the job of ten overcoats, they communicate their own strength too (and even when they remain only metaphors), when the overcoats only weaken.

And talking of strength — it is strength in you not weakness to withdraw the Landfall letter, but that's not to say one doesn't feel sorry for the soreness you feel.

And again talking of strength, I know I have shown my own strengths as a person and a writer — but since the impact of CF I have never really wavered in believing you have shown a greater degree in both capacities. Don't think this is a piece of mock humility on my part. If it would ensure that pilot-light gains in strength I would tear up my work of the moment and never write another line so long as all my energies were going towards your own support. You could see me do the tearing-up if you liked.

It was strange that your own splendidly written letter should appear with Lou's modest verses — great strength there too, though of course *very* clumsy and rough (how I *don't* agree with your Mr Jackson!). [. . .]

(I am faced with a problem about Winston's book. Similar to what I had with you, but not really the same. The Roof extensions I let him see break off just before that which I still can't face up to on the printed page. All I can do with Winston is (a) see that he makes it clear to the reader that since his subject is still alive and writing all is tentative, not definitive, and full of gaps. (a) see that he doesn't put his foot in it owing to the gaps which I'm not prepared to fill in for him. You don't have to comment on these propositions, but you can if you like).

From,

Fx [. . .]

['your Mr Jackson': MacD.P. Jackson, a colleague of Pearson's in the English Department at the University of Auckland, reviewed Hone Tuwhare's No Ordinary Sun *and Richard Parker's* Prince of the Plague Country *in* Landfall, *June 1965.]*

To Martin Green, *London*

Alexander Turnbull Library

15 August 1965

Dear Martin,

[. . .] As there appears no hurry I am posting I Saw in My Dream and I for One surface mail. I have been looking through the first for literals and surprised it appears to retain so much life. It was this book first brought me in contact with E.M. Forster — he was kind enough to write, quite out of the blue. (Forster by the way is a very ill man now according to Plomer. Send a Peon by all means, but it's doubtful whether it will penetrate the shield of his devoted admirers). I must say I find his age and illness quite a grief to me — that spontaneous letter was very kind and appreciative and encouraged me very much.

Don't breathe a word, I've never read Casanova. (I think when I was young somebody who I thought would do a Fijian fire-walking act if it would end up in something lecherous told me it was dull). I think the Newhouse idea first occurred to me when I saw many years ago a tasty modern villa labelled Casanova. If you remember sometime tell me which paper-back people and I'll get myself a copy. But it grieves me about your finances — my own have a habit of being so thin I never notice now after so many years. Surely one of your rich authors can leave you something — after all Ian Fleming did that with Plomer — and as Cape's reader P is a sort of publisher. [. . .]

Good luck,

To Bill Pearson, *Auckland*

Alexander Turnbull Library

[24 August 1965]

Lines for Mr W(illiam) H(arrison)

I gave my love, and gave my all:
Forgive my grief that kind regards
Were given only to recall.

To accompany the gift of a book [*Memoirs of a Peon*].
Helpful notes:
1) the epigraph is invented
2) the person the book is dedicated to is a woman.
3) the only begetter was 'Bake' (of the dedication in my *Plays*)
4) I suspect many literals (I have discovered some, & cannot bear to look further)
5) I do not expect or want you to comment on the book. I hope you may receive pleasure.
That is all.

To Bill Pearson, *Auckland*

Alexander Turnbull Library

[5 September 1965]

Dear Bill,

There are the usual thousand things to say to you, but what you sounded so badly in need of was re-assurance. Will you accept that from me, with everything else thrown in I don't have to specify?

I have put Kevin right on that point, and I am sorry I yielded to telling you of his eulogy on my book — but in truth what excited me was that he didn't question the prolonged womanising, I mean it apparently went over with him with conviction. Needless to say to you perhaps, it all had to be done out of my imagination. So forgive me the more than touch of vanity I feel.

But I have also told Kevin that it is all very kind of him, but a much stronger book, the sort of sort of book I would like to do because of its solid and comprehensive architecture, is C.F. And indeed, dear Bill, I think all your problems in life could be reduced to one — why did the daemon at one time take hold of you and make you write that book? If you could discover why you might know whether it can happen again and plan accordingly. (I mean plan in the sense of being ready when the miracle happens).

Do keep in mind always my rejoicing over Karl's using the Egyptian story.

I realize now my Yate Dialogue is to be more a kind of *Imaginary Conversation*. Yate in old age, and Samuel Butler in middle age. I have lately gone again into all that appalling Pauli business that afflicted Butler. How odd that he should have had to come to NZ to meet Pauli, and there is no doubt their relationship started off with ecstatic happiness for Butler; but by the time Pauli had died he had relieved B of virtually his entire fortune — and it seems B never wavered in his passionate adoration and worship even though pretty early on P had detached himself. There is no suggestion of blackmail in the crude sense — my notion is that only by paying up could B alleviate his own intolerable suffering. Anyhow if the daemon will play ball I know I could make something quite powerful out of bringing these two together.

I have to look for Chris [probably Cathcart] in the Kiwi [tavern] on Thursday evening and we are to eat in town. If you are about it will be a pleasure to see you and of course if you cared to join us for eating that would be too. But that is entirely as it pleases you.

I send you a great packet of love, use what you can of it,

F.

['the Egyptian story': Pearson's 'At the Leicesters'', first published in 1949, was reprinted in New Zealand Short Stories *ed. by C.K. Stead, OUP, 1965.]*

To William Plomer, *Sussex*

Alexander Turnbull Library

5 September 1965

Dear Plomer,

Do pardon me bunging a letter right back at you — so uncivilized! But I know how you must feel with all that literary matter. Of course my dear man you don't have to write me any 'proper' letter about my *Peon*. If you get round to it some time and find pleasure and some laughs that's all I ask. As you say it will be interesting to discover whether the reviewers are prepared to follow all that involved prose — I am vain enough to suppose they will be missing something if not.

I was indeed very glad to get yours as I supposed you might be unwell. My friend is a great worry — I think I probably told you — he is ten years older, and the emotional strain is as you say. He used to train and ride horses, and in those days he was as wonderfully composed physically as any of his thoroughbreds. Now he is a bag of bones. I know you understand these things. I love him more now than ever I did then — it must be that favourite goddess of mine hanging around. Agape.

I can't resist sending the enclosed photograph. Note the hands and see them repeated in your T.W. [*Turbott Wolfe*] page 22 — do you think this means we must be complementary Platonic halves? [. . .]

The damned chores this Saturday morning — and don't be amazed about my being forward with another book — it goes so damned badly at present,

From yours as ever,

F.S.

Don't die before you have a look at Hawthorne's *Blithedale Romance*.

Yes, those plays of mine, thanks. *Not* avant-garde, but we found they seemed to work in production.

To Bill Pearson, *Auckland*

Alexander Turnbull Library

26 September 1965

Dear Bill,

Yes, I do bring so much emotion to the story, though perhaps it's just another instance of what Janet calls my 'reverence for what seems to be literature'.

First though I must note that you create another memorable image [in 'At the Leicesters"] in the bedding that droops like lolling tongues. This for me goes alongside 3 others, which I'm not likely to forget (the lyre frame cattle-horns, the postman's whistle chimney ((perhaps the finest)) and the yo-yos of dangling spit.) This is a high percentage of what can't be forgotten for any writer — I remember only four others which persistently recur: the lady in What Maisie Knew whose eye-brows were arched like skipping ropes; Mr Wemmick's post-box mouth in which he posted biscuits; and two from Meredith — the rogue in porcelain, and Sir Willoughby Patterne's leg.

Also what seems remarkable about the story is that you create the narrator so memorably without ever describing him — gruff-shy, self-conscious, awkward, touching, and (though here I am definitely bringing something) a *little* soldier (forgive me) the wisp of a man it must have broken the hearts of those who cared for you to see flung into the brutal bloody army. (It would have killed me, and it didn't you — there's the strength.) [. . .]

There's true creative magic in the story, and it's something I could never have got within miles of achieving soon after my mid-twenties. It's very good that the shift to Miss Leicester comes last, a strong conclusion. Do you know, too, I find in it the melancholy which is in everything you write? — it is strangely and powerfully attractive (at its finest perhaps in the passage you give to Heath in CF, anyhow a fresh reading of CF is coming up again for me soon I can see).

Anyhow I have been absorbed in the pleasure the piece has given me, and my grateful thanks — and do you mind if I finish by nagging (though with deep humility I hope)? There must be many stories you have long intended to write. Of course they won't come with an easy confidence now, one doesn't work nearly so much by intuition in later years — but the compensations can be rewarding, that's what touched me when Horsman showed he understood the struggle with the material. All this sort of thing has kept me alive and with a heart that's alive too. Dear Bill (allow me the emotion) — here am I man, now's your time/ Send me now, and I shall go...

Poor Karl is going to have trouble with Janet over their quarrel — she has refused him permission with her story he has chosen ['The Reservoir'], and knowing only too well *her* strength I'm not sure I can talk her round.

For hours the other day Ron Holloway and I continued our Great Debate which has been going on for more than 30 years. The question? — how can one sanctify one's personal and private life in these times of religious breakdown? Ronald said only by adhering to the Church, and I said only by a private invocation of Charity. Many things have kept this Debate going, many things in common, such as periods of grotesque poverty — and we still go our different ways. For Ronald when we continue to debate it is like the relief of a holiday off from heaven — my hell is very attractive to him still — and so is his heaven to me. It is strange that we both recognise clearly how certainly we both in a sense missed our vocations — we should have been priests. Anyhow he went off back to a wife and six surviving children (out of 8) holiday-happy on a bottle and half of wine. Incidentally he spoke most warmly of you, greatly appreciated your remarks on his memorial of Bob L[owry] — he hasn't though read Coal Flat, though intending to, and I think I shall send him a copy.

Call me, I shall hear your call...

Over to you,

F.S.

Your health Bill — dare I be priggish & say Vitamins aren't going to be any good without healthy food? — that, & creativity with love.

[Bob Lowry had committed suicide on 6 or 7 December 1963.]

To Janet Frame, *Dunedin*

Private collection

9 October 1965

Dear Janet,

My appetite for *Adaptable Man* is getting hotter and hotter — good reports, very readable, etc — from so many sources. Peter, CB. I ordered along at the corner but not in yet. But all this very nice to hear.

I didn't like to mention Karl's story ['A Fitting Tribute'] to you — but so nice don't you think?

And what a *horrifying* story in Landfall!! [Frame's 'The Bath'] — C [Brasch] told me it would be good and he's probably right — but how can I know when I've been trying to get my aunt out of the bath only this week — fortunately she had been there only about half an hour when discovered. But the next night she spent on the floor, though fortunately found about mid-morning only 15 hours later. I now report she is in good rude (very rude) health — all a tonic.

Incidentally, I immediately sent that Landfall on airmail to CKS [Stead]. Perhaps he will like your story.

Oh dear, I'm busy trying to get off to Wellington where I receive the Mansfield from Ngaio on a silver salver. How will I survive all this? Already I have had to get off Harry to Palmerston North where his only remaining brother dropped dead (hold your breath, believe it or not, the *theatrical* brother — he stage-managed for J.C. Williamson and in old age (ie my age) was managing the Opera House in PN [Palmerston North] — he used to get H and I backstage in the thirties when the J.C.W. shows came over from Australia — that was when I met so many theatrical 'girls'.)

Anyhow, H not really fit for travel 10 yards, but he got to P.N.

Well love dear, yes Gosse's book — I'm so disgustingly literary — isn't there a bit about God creating all the fossils readymade just to try your faith?

I can't possibly cope — this Wellington trip, and the blank sheet of paper which is my *life* my *raison d'etre* is curling up and dying round the edges.

Fx

Broadcasting terms aren't bad, £15 a story. Write them. They are interested in my plays too — & suggest a fee of £196!!!!

To C.K. Stead, *London*

Alexander Turnbull Library

19 October 1965

Dear Karl,

Your two notes, and here goes a hasty reply. (I'm just back from Wellington — the Mansfield Award for *Just Trespassing, Thanks*).

Yes, *do* write to Janet (Frame or Clutha — I think better the latter — 116, Saint David Street, Dunedin). She should be in a good mood as, although Baxter has got the Burns for 1966, some sort of arrangement has been jacked up for Janet, and she stays in Dunedin another year. This year she has completed 3 full length books plus her new book of short stories. I on my part will do my best to induce her to send you what she considers the best of her late work. I don't much myself care for *The Bath*.

Charles warned me about McKenzie's notice and asked me not to read it — and I haven't — I am worrying at my current work so I can't be bothered (except to think up things like, a university is an institution inhabited by impotent spinsters of both sexes, or, another of those bastards who has been doctored — I think Glover's comment on Curnow's D. Litt. was, I thought that bloke had been doctored years ago.

The Wellington do a luncheon, very VIP Mrs Holyoake, also Director of Education, also Sir Walter [Nash] — about 160 guests — about three times the 100 guineas [prize] must have been spent on it all. Ngaio presented, judge was R.A. Copland (Dr), and he spoke too. I cracked back at money and banking, tell you when you return — it was KM's birthday so I said I hoped we all understood how much she had honoured Sir Harold Beauchamp by having him for her father. But I hated it all — I've done no work for a fortnight, and once forget the blank sheet of paper which is at the centre of our lives and we're buggered.

If you can bear to let me know sometime your Oxford list. Yes, I thoroughly agree about Pearson's piece, but I suspect from my point of view there will be many surprising inclusions and omissions.

I'm glad about all your pleasure and the joy of the year. Perhaps just once in a lifetime. Again thanks for remarks on *Peon*, and I'll send you *Listener* cutting. Of course always hoping to write at leisure and more elegantly. Love to Kay and the boy.

from, F

[D.F. McKenzie reviewed Wrestling with the Angel *in* Landfall, *September 1965. 'Pearson's piece': Stead to FS, 12 October: 'I was glad you thought the Pearson story worthwhile. I feel sure it's his best'. ATL MS-Papers-0432-179.]*

To Bruce Rennie, *Christchurch*

Alexander Turnbull Library

[Bruce Rennie wrote to FS requesting information about his writing habits and style for a high school English project.]

[October 1965]

Dear Bruce Rennie,

I am afraid I can only say I am a very *professional* writer — that's to say, writing is the central thing I *work* at, every day, for many years. I can't say whether I would have continued if I had never been published — but I'm pretty certain I continue now, whether I continue to be published or not.

A writer I imagine uses everything in his experience for writing that seems to lend itself as material to work on. Always remember to credit him with imagination. Life is one thing, what gets down on paper is something else — in my kind of writing it has, I hope, the *appearance* of life. Essentially though I think it is something other than life.

My work is written slowly with great difficulty. Everything & particularly the language, is painstakingly considered & calculated. Short stories are different from novels — some people think some of mine border on poetry. It pleases me to think some of them perhaps do. I think it not unfair to make a short story 'difficult' — after all it doesn't retain the reader for very long. But a novel has to 'hold' over perhaps many hours — therefore it should be primarily interesting & entertaining. I hope that what I write may 'entertain' people, also move them & make them laugh. I also dare to hope that some things I write may enlarge a little other people's experience. I hope this may be of some use to you — it is, I'm afraid, the best a busy man can do at the moment.

From yours sincerely,

Frank Sargeson

To Janet Frame, *Dunedin*

Private collection

31 October 1965

Dearest J,

First about your being written off, that's not quite what I hear. Listen to Plomer, just the other day. 'I see a new novel by Janet Frame conspicuously reviewed here and there. Her view of life (if that is what the novel gives) is made to sound rather beyond the reviewer's understanding, but not beyond their respect. I should think she is more rewarding to read than some of the contemporary novelists of her own sex who are made much of in this country. I did see that one of them was said the other day to have revealed that she "had nothing but sawdust up her sleeve".'

Anyhow almost worthwhile being written off when you can come to light with such lines — no, I don't mean that, but my God if I am written off (and I *was* by the New S), I can only *try* to keep writing — hoping for a chance to rehabilitate myself in about ten years. My dear, if I have any envy of you it is because of your fluency — my eye tooth (the remaining one) would be a slight gift compared to that gift which is yours.

But cheer up, I know how awful it is, but with all up your sleeve, and not sawdust, you needn't be too worried. (Pegasus is awfully slow with the copy of AM I ordered. Do you remember Jean Watson who sat with you over the fire one evening while I went out to see Bake? Her book about her life with Crump is slight [*Stand in the Rain*], but honest and not malicious — that's to say as much of it as I've read. I suspect it is much too easy to get published now — where is the art of writing going to? And even though words are honestly used they're still no good unless they carry all that we can load on to them when we're at our best).

Before I forget I read a volume of Kipling's Stories, a very early vol. *Life's Handicap*. He was an astonishing story-teller right from the beginning — I've found this book a most deep and complex experience.

Look, that sounds fun about the house. I wish I could say right now I would pay you a visit immediately. Hold on, though, my summer garden is in, and the potatoes I'm eating now are simply marvellous. And I am slowly getting back into my stride after Mansfield (No, *not* stride*s*) — I do so much want to knock off this new horrible book, and Lord help me, I think it may be coming right.

Of course you are quite right about Karl. But the hard logic (or these days is it logistics?) about these things!! If you don't oblige him he will take his opportunity in his introduction to put you in the wrong, 'I deeply regret that New Zealand should be unrepresented in this book by perhaps her finest short story writer, but for that omission the public must blame Miss Frame who refused permission'. Do you know Karl's address? — 8, Prince Albert Road, London N.W.1. Anyhow, I think he is writing you, and I am sure, as nice as pie.

I got a plaintive letter from Holcroft — at *Listener* office in Wellington I shot off my mouth for about 2 hours, shocking lot of crap much of it defamatory — but Holcroft says machine wasn't working and nothing on tape. So the gods can be kind.

Does Birmingham bake? I gave Auckland [i.e. Pearson] a copy of *Peon* in August saying no hurry, but it would be nice to have a list of literals. Now I inquire but he 'hasn't had time to read it yet'. Incidentally *he* is to be in the Oxford book — to some degree owing to my efforts — a story in Canterbury mag about 1945 or 6 about Cairo — not bad at all, in fact really good, though why the hell young people don't wake up to the fact that writing means *writing* — I mean respecting words and language and demonstrating what you can do with both — I don't know. This gentleman's fatal error I suspect is to suppose that it means having sound humane notions and allowing their communication to take care of itself.

I am glad of your remark about Middleton — perhaps the purest writer we've got — and being so impure myself I'm always reproaching myself for being wishful that he'd come to light with a bit of dirt.

Spare a prayer that I may be done with my story by Christmas — overhopeful, I'm afraid.

from,

Fx

with l x

Do you still use your blanket? I do most nights.

To Janet Frame, *Dunedin*

Private collection

6 November 1965

Dear Janet,

I want to put off writing as my copy of AM turned up in bookshop yesterday and I began it last night. Enchanted my dear, I am holding my breath to see if you can keep it up (oh, such a risk, starting off so beautifully — such a standard to live up to!)

But in my rushed life Saturday is virtually the only decent time I can find for letters. My God, how tired I always am in the evenings! [. . .]

Oh Charles' lecture was most noble — beautifully written and well spoken. A kind of expression of faith, uncompromising orotund. A good test was a Maori I know sitting next to me — Buster, a neurotic unsuccessful Maori (I think I don't like successful Maoris any more than the same kind of Europeans) — he loved it — it was oratory, the sort of thing he would know from the marae. Of course some Aucklands were sniffy — 'Dunedin' etc.

My worst splash with Mansfield dough was 3 huge volumes of Henry Lawson. I was cross with loved Bill in the Listener — I thought he subtly condescended, pretended he could interpret Lawson's experience better than the man could himself. I think I will write something contradictory in Landfall (after all it was very unwise of Bill to describe Lawson to me some time back as a neurotic bumpkin) — yes, I think I have to defend poor old drunken loving Henry — a very great literary artist at his best (and why draw attention to his worst?).

My book may be coming right — such a struggle with it though. — I'd be in despair if the spring wasn't here at last, and the garden stuff cheers me,

Back to *AM*

This, with love,

Fx [. . .]

[Pearson's 'The Reluctant Bushman', a review of a new 3-volume edition of The Stories of Henry Lawson *ed. by Cecil Mann, appeared in the* Listener *on 1 October 1965.]*

To Janet Frame, *Dunedin*

Private collection

13 November 1965

Dearest J,

Unless I delay my letters until the weekend I never get ahead of myself (query: is it a 'good thing' to get ahead of oneself? Perhaps I'd better be more ordinary and say, *even* with myself).

Anyhow the pleasure of complimenting you a little more fully on the novel has been delayed. I feel immensely proud to know you. That you have created all that is a wonder. I am filled with awe and reverence. I won't say I found sheer delight on every page, but it did recur again and again on many pages. Best of all I admire and envy your power to organise sentences that carry a great weight of thought and suggestion. All of which goes to say that I think you are unique and so is your book.

It's been strange about the incest in the garden shed — I've lately been to see Bergman's *The Silence*. I didn't like it much, too much like the end of the world with not too many compensations. But certainly as a wee boy when I began with Charlie Chaplin I had no idea I would live to see a frustrated Lesbian depicted masturbating on the screen in the plainest possible manner. It wasn't that though that worried me — just that there was no Charity in the film, and no Fun — and both C and F are markedly present in the A.M.

Anyhow, my congratulations again — I don't know how good it is — I only know I read with attention and immense admiration. It's obvious with the reviewers I think — you don't give them what they expect and want and they're too disconcerted to take you on your own terms.

But what a marvellous and charming book you have up your sleeve — I mean the one about Botti Julio — about his life before his journey Alwyn-wise.

Tell me sometime — what did Birmingham [Cawley] say about this book?

Did I tell you my runner-up in the Mansfield was Karl Stead with his *A Fitting Tribute*. The judge's report made thrilling reading — we ran neck and neck.

I never will and never can forget that Dunedin cemetery — the most sinister jagged graveyard in the world I should think. [. . .] I have to be off to my aunt's 92nd birthday party with a big box of dates, so sorry this is short — but I had to go to town about your book. Thanks for the copy.

Best love for now,

Fx

['incest in the garden shed': see The Adaptable Man, *Chapters 23 and 24.]*

To Janet Frame, *Dunedin*

Private collection

27 November 1965

Dearest J,

Two letters, lucky me. And about Yate — I should have made clearer that what I am after is some little concrete detail — and apparently there is none. I don't know whether I told you I had Karl looking in London too, and apparently nothing there either. The depositions seem to have vanished. Anyhow I have told one or two historians they must cease their off-hand references to Yate as a 'guilty' man — I'm sure many a nice Maori boy was very pleased to be in bed with him — but plain unquestionable evidence that this was so just can't be brought to light.

But many thanks for your [Yate] material, one or two points I didn't know and of course your own observations very good and amusing. When you are up at Christmas I will tell you about what I found here and there — but I think I've got enough now, it only remains to set Yate and Samuel Butler talking (alas, *only* the *very* operational word).

You do my poor Michael N[ewhouse] too much honour — the critics seem to think it is very much a one character book and I suppose it is. But how I could have got M N to stand out if I had brought the others too far forward I don't know — though I will admit some of the other characters I just couldn't do anything with. Incidentally, some critics think I was *aiming* at writing an eighteenth century novel — I never thought of that — I had only one idea to see to it that the narration was right for the narrator. Anyhow we can talk — though more about your book if I can persuade you — and just one technical point now p. 89 — prone. Should that be supine? It's a splendid book, such strength, it enlarges East Anglia literature and you.

Auckland University is as silent as apparently Birmingham is — but lucky you, if silence is too prolonged you can always select a several 100 page MS from among your many and send it on and raise a reply for certain. Alas I have nothing except my current faltering work.

Your house sounds delightful. [. . .]

Thanks for such work on Yate. And hoping you will be up pretty soon.

M.L., from Fx

To Ray Copland, *Christchurch*

Private collection

27 November 1965

Dear Ray Copland,

Your note, many thanks — and kind of you about *Peon*. I know it sounds like affectation — I get very apprehensive about notices. I think it's because past work is so remote (perhaps the ideal would be that it would be alive for everybody except the author — for whom it couldn't be deader. [Marginal note: I think I probably mean by this, when he is still working — more accurately perhaps *until* he has *finished* working. Then perhaps it might all come to life again.] — I think it *has* to be remote so one can be engaged with quite different work. Janet Frame has taught me a lot about detaching one's self in order to continue.

Yes, you probably couldn't be more right — I don't imagine I aimed at writing an 18th c. novel. My concern was to see that the narration fitted the narrator, but it greatly suited me that he was so literary. I don't remember where I used 'my charmer', but I do remember that 'lovely culprit' was a straight crib from Peacock. I think at that time I was reacting from the 'raw' — it was comic effect I was after, an *elegant* effect — after all, for me the most utterly sure & beautiful sentences in the language have been written by Congreve. To get the one supreme character to stand out I had to push all the others back — I remember I could do very little with some of the others anyhow, e.g. Margaret, the schoolteacher. But as I say it's all past — even my theatrical adventures which followed seem very much past.

Incidentally, I should hate a sympathetic reviewer to be sucked in by the epigraph — that's invented. And I must apologise for misprints — Janet F. helped me in a rush job last May, but the time my publishers allowed made it hopeless.

I expect that Karl Stead might resist my saying that my young people got into his own story ['A Fitting Tribute']. I seem to remember though one evening when one of them produced his poem, only to have it dismissed with the remark that it was Wallace Stevens — I think that was the evening when this was afterwards produced:

All right, critics,
Let's call it evens,
The poet I copied
Was Wallace Stevens.

But C.K. Stead
And the learned few
Know that Allen Curnow
Copied him too.

In my defence
Let this be said:
The habit's catching —
See K. Stead.

May I send my good wishes for your own work. I was not being insincere when I appreciated those comic pieces — even though I seem not to have noticed or followed them since the *Many* . . . (I can't remember the parody, nor find the *Listener* page among my untidy papers — shades of de Quincey, & the several paper-stuffed lodgings discovered after his death)!!

And my good wishes to your wife,

From yours:

Frank Sargeson [. . .]

To Bill Pearson, *Auckland*

Alexander Turnbull Library

28 November 1965

Dear Bill,

[. . .] I am semi-committed to write on Lawson, but I don't look forward to the task; & feel if only I could have had an enlarging discussion with you on what you wrote [in the *Listener*] I could have (for myself anyhow) resolved our differences. What interests me about the *Fragment* [*of Autobiography*] is how far L goes — I mean in relation to his notion of what might be printed (crimson sheol[?] etc). For example, he tells you about holding his father's hand, & as he puts it it is revealing & moving; but he stops short of what would be the actual situation — probably; that's to say, that after a quarrel between the parents his mother would be in the cot & he in bed with his father. This looks to me very important for any study of his character. I am doubtful about the 'loneliness' — a kind of contingency, where 'isolation' would be more of an absolute. I interpret his situation in being driven to the dog as not so much 'loneliness' — simply the agony of his love for his father — I would think the most powerful love of his life, & all the root of the mateship business — again probably.

Very briefly, as I see it, his best work is an odd kind of pastoral celebration of life.

I don't think there's much to any suggestion that he was naive — all that time he spent in Sydney, & Sydney streets would be pretty much as today — his silence about what is often the end-logic of mateship isn't naivety — the reverse (that's to say *if* he is silent — I haven't read all 3 volumes yet).

It's evident to me I couldn't write the kind of study you are engaged on [*Henry Lawson Among Maoris,* 1968]. Too much emotion. I'm reminded so much of my uncle — & I think I've always forgotten to tell you a little of Jim Miller, he lives near me, a very lively & intelligent 73 — he was in Mallacoota when Lawson was there (perhaps about 1912 — perhaps it was once when L's friends had got him out of Sydney because of the booze — if so, it didn't work, as Jim saw him suffering an attack of dt's). Jim however can tell little more than just that, & I don't imagine he would be any use to you. He has a job as an attendant at the Museum though, & you could talk to him there sometime if you liked. He's German-Australian, & very intelligent.

But also of course there's Harry, who was all round Lawson's country as a child; & later with his horses used to go as far as Bourke.

I'm unkind enough to say one thing is clear — the man was no 'neurotic bumpkin' — at his best a very great artist. His cranky views don't matter — look at Kipling, many of his stories are powerful terrifying & moving beyond description — 'time that with this strange excuse/Pardoned Kipling & his views . . .' And who cares that Beethoven wrote his absurd Battle Symphony! We all have our aberrations.

I think I never thanked you for the Yate references. I know about the Hocken material, but had been told I wouldn't find what I wanted there. Janet made sure for me — nothing, but she sent her own penetrating & highly comic observations.

My love to you, Bill — I wish I knew what to do with my wealth of tender anxiety for your well-being — a mystery, no matter how far that kind of wealth is stretched, nobody who is willing to receive ever goes short.

From,

Frank

['I am semi-committed to write on Lawson': FS's 'Henry Lawson: some notes after re-reading' appeared in Landfall, *June 1966.]*

To Bill Pearson, *Auckland*

Alexander Turnbull Library

4 December 1965

Dear Bill,

[. . .] The thought of writing about L[awson] plagues me, and also I feel like a trespasser on your own ground. On the other hand your studies have directed me back to the texts and they absorb me very much. I believe there is something in my Theocritus idea, and there is some connection with your remarks in Fretful Sleepers (p 370 *Landfall Country*) about Latin colonial writers. (One writer you would be meaning was Sidonius Apollinaris, and I can remember Karl Wolfskehl one evening insisting that S.A. was a better poet than Virgil — I remember too asking Eric Schwimmer what he thought of this idea and he said he thought there might be something in it — anyhow two people with oceans more scholarship than I can pretend to).

Point about Theocritus is that as a Sicilian Greek he was a colonial poet — well, kind of anyhow. Point too is that he set a line of literature in motion (whatever that bad metaphor may mean). Like all innovators he was let down by those who followed — Virgil dressed up handsome slave-boys and put them into his Bucolics as shepherds (this is not to say his Pastorals aren't extremely beautiful — and I should know as I can manage the Latin up to a point, and have lately completed a complete reading of Virgil translated by Dryden. Such was my ignorance that I didn't know previously that one of our major English poets wrote much, very much, of his most superb poetry in his translations — surely unique in our literature. Anyhow I shall be able to discuss it with Horsman who is a Dryden man); and Milton and such as Matthew Arnold people the countryside with their bookish friends, Arnold making it all very sad because they had lost their faith. But listen to Theocritus (by courtesy of Andrew Lang), 'a goatherd was he, nor could any that saw him have taken him for other than he was. Stripped from the roughest of he-goats was the tawny skin he wore on his shoulders, the smell of rennet clinging to it still, and about his breast an old cloak was buckled with a plaited belt, and in his right hand he carried a crooked staff of wild olive; and quietly he accosted me with a smile, a twinkling eye, and a laugh still on his lips'.

Well, put in a cabbage-tree hat and make him a bit dour and he comes right out of Lawson. (It's much closer to Lawson than Virgil — for whom the whiff of rennet would have been quite *quite* too much)!

Did you see the notice of the 3 Lawson vols? — in TLS 16 September (Plomer's poem in the same number is worth reading too). Anyhow, there was something to it — the Victorianism, that's obvious, but like all writers who produce such a sharp atmosphere of actuality Lawson has been too much thought of as national.

The thing is to determine what he was essentially up to — and for me Theocritus is helpful.

I am touched every now and then to note your perception and how much I agree with you. [Lawson's] The [Bush] Undertaker story is simply superb. And 'It's all over now . . .' doesn't suffer no matter what comparisons are used. In a different sense the vignettes in A Wild Irishman are close to what you find in the Greek Anthology.

But I expect I am to be envied, following my bent in this way — when so much of your energy and time goes in set studies.

Bill, that's quite an idea, sending 25 guineas to Haigh. Yes, high-handed or light-headed or whatsoever — but if you won't have it just tell me sometime what cause would deservedly benefit from 50 guineas (because I will bring it up to that before too long. It really is a problem with me. I'm I think allowed to earn £200 a year under Means Test, and every pound over is deducted from Age Benefit in succeeding year. Well £196 from NZBC for my two plays is the biggest blow so far — and incidentally all this business lends itself to a lot of comedy — MacGibbon and Kee were very late squaring up for the English edition of the *Collected* — so late indeed that their payment was too late to be included in Paul's yearly accounting. Well, what with Broadcasting paying for a number of stories as well they began to get a bit conscience-smitten about withholding from me so much money until next October — but to their surprise when they tried to pay me I insisted NO! — you must stick to the letter of the contract I have with you. Of course I do rather hope they won't go into liquidation until I can accept payment).

Anyhow what it all amounts to is I want to be able next year to say to the Tax and S.S. people that I have paid my editor 50 guineas which they will see he richly deserves if they take a look at the work he has done. I have other means of politely diddling them too which I won't go into — I aim at keeping the Age Benefit *alive*, no matter how much *reduced* — I know all these things so well — it's difficult enough to get a Benefit, but it's ten times more difficult to revive one if it lapses. The publicity I get does me a disservice — these people can't believe that anybody who gets into the news hasn't got tons of money tucked away somewhere.

Sometime, no hurry, just say where you would like to contribute 50 guineas — could be a Maori-people thing if you liked, probably anonymous, but just as you wish. And I will direct Frank Haigh. [Marginal note: Let me know as soon as you like — I find I can run to the final 25 guineas right now.]

I should tell you that some time back I destroyed all my letters to you, and also the carbon copies. I'm not sure I wasn't committing a clerical treason — think (perhaps) how much you, as a N.Z. scholar would have treasured all that inscribed paper if only it had been written to somebody else by somebody else.

Never mind — I'll be careful not to leave anything behind me that could embarrass you. Will say no more — it all rather does move me,

All best, Bill,

F.

['I destroyed all my letters to you': Pearson returned FS's letters on the assumption that Sargeson would not want his homosexuality revealed to posterity, and left FS to decide their fate. See Pearson, 'Frank Sargeson and Me: Afterthoughts', ATL MS-Papers-6419. Pearson's biographer Paul Millar suggests that FS probably destroyed no more than five letters. No Fretful Sleeper, *p. 271.]*

To Bill Pearson, *Auckland*

Alexander Turnbull Library

11 December 1965

Dear Bill,

I'd probably better tell you the little I got from Jim Miller. He has some old postcard photographs of Mallacoota. His being there himself is a kind of Henry Lawson story — he had been apprenticed to a surveyor and their camp was burnt out, instruments etc destroyed. So he got a job as rouseabout at an accommodation house with license (shown in one photograph). He was nineteen at the time. He remembers Mutch, and that he afterwards became a Government minister. He only faintly remembers Brady. Lawson he remembers as 'a skeleton' he didn't see much of — only to take him drinks in the hut he occupied. That's where he saw him suffering his dt's. Apparently the Mutch-Brady-Lawson party occupied huts attached to the establishment (it was run by a man called Dollon) for some weeks at least. Jim does remember clearly there was no attempt by L's companions to deny him his liquor, in fact they indicated he was to have what he wanted. Jim found Lawson morose reserved and unpleasant. Jim's colouring is very much what Lawson's father's must have been — I asked if this seemed to excite any interest in L. He has no recollection.

Well, virtually nothing of any value I'm afraid. Pity.

I have virtually only the 3rd L vol. to investigate now. I must say the two first are rewarding — such a high percentage of good work — he must have been short of good material for the last pages of Over the Sliprails — several pieces there (including The Selector's Daughter) are I should think of anthropological interest only.

I must disagree with you about *The Hero of Redclay*. The inset story is Bret Harte true, but the way it has been used in relation to the triangular situation of

Drew Mitchell and Joe makes the entire piece one of Lawson's best. First there's the out-west setting, then the jealousy. It is marvellously well hinted that Mitchell is aware of Joe's jealousy, and tries to put it right by squatting down and telling the story. The smoke-oh half-time bit is wonderful, and about the pup (one is by now thoroughly aware that this story is about relations between people — & people and animals). The finish lifts the whole thing into universal experience. The feeling of reconciliation. Ah, but not quite! Mitchell sleeps, but Joe wakes and watches his face, remembers that terrible dream.

I think Bill, that here L is touching something very profound that all of us have experienced. Is there anything in the world quite like watching over somebody you love when asleep? — and the moment of waking, the smile of recognition and trust, and the kiss that is the sweetest and best that we ever give or get — no desire, gratitude that separation (death) is not yet to be. But there is the terrible memory of the dream of jealousy (death).

There are others I would like to talk to you about but not on paper because of the risk of misunderstanding and hurt. Particularly Daughter of Maoriland.

I would beg you to re-consider 'cult'. I notice Mann uses the more or less neutral 'creed'. Cult implies a judgement I think, so one naturally wants to inquire what criteria you invoke in order to judge. And if you can't or don't do this satisfactorily, then you leave the reader with the unfortunate impression that you have condescended. I'm not making a personal criticism of you, and certainly don't wish to hurt you — I am thinking in terms of strict literary criticism.

I must have my fun — it has occurred to me that one way of saving my letters from destruction might have been a simple amusing stratagem. Each one should have been addressed, Dear Doc, or say (now and then) Dear Mus. And they should have been signed Morrie, or Shadders.

From yours, Bill,

Frank.

I look forward to discovering what Mann has dredged up in vol 3 — though I assume anthropological value here will be dominant.

A psychotic boy who lives in the next street was around Western NSW & Queensland last year. He wrote me some intelligent but horrible letters. He worked for a travelling go-kart outfit — & they got as far as Mt Isa. His descriptions of men from out back lying drunk for a fortnight on beds soaked with piss were just Lawson's 'shanty' stories brought up to date. Anyhow, it was all more than this kid could take — he's now an Avondale patient.

My God, notice Shadbolt wooing me in *Listener*!! Buy a 50 guinea camera Bill, & I'll do the repulsive good deed of allowing you to snap us *in flagrante*. That ought to fix S — & at my age it won't matter if it fixes me as well.

To H. Winston Rhodes, *Christchurch*

Alexander Turnbull Library

19 February 1966

Dear Winston,

Oh yes, I see your comments on the Peon now. By chance I heard [J.C.] Reid going to town about the book on the air, I expect what he said was one way of dealing with a book in which one finds one's self figuring. But one thing did interest me — he was on to the Caliban-Ariel-Island business. I must say I never worked out anything consistently (it is up to anyone to say who Prospero is for example), but at some stage it did occur to me that quite a complex of symbolism had got going, and to some slight extent I began manipulating it. I expect it is rooted in my being involved in tentative plans for a Tempest soon after I came to Auckland (I wasn't Caliban though, I was Ariel — or would have been if the play had ever gone on. Caliban was a contemporary from my Hamilton school, born on that farm not far from town, he was at first a theological student, then training college — he is now dead, as is the other Peon original, dear old Bake — who figures in my dedication to my Plays — he really did have a squire-ish ancestor who is very important in the history of sheep-breeding — he was 20 years my senior).

Pardon the spiel.

[. . .]

from

F.S.

When you return the material, and there is no hurry at all, would you enclose a note of Twayne's NY address (if it is NY?) I sometime soon want to try to induce Rod Finlayson to think seriously about doing the Cresswell book.

To Alan Horsman, *Dunedin*

Hocken Library

[Horsman to FS, 6 May: 'We are just finishing a term in which your Collected Stories *were on our programme and I can't resist writing to tell you how* quickly *the students have responded to them. [. . .] Have you ever been much of a reader of Conrad?' ATL MS-Papers-0432-063.]*

21 May 1966

Dear Alan,

It's strange you should mention Conrad. I return to him frequently, but we don't get along. I think it's because for me he combines so little sound with his pictorial effects. When young people show me their work it's always sound I look (indeed! — I mean listen) for first — if there's no aural base I'm usually inclined to be a little discouraging. Music has always been my second interest, away ahead of visual art, and the relationship between music and writing seems to me much closer. It's the *flow* of writing that makes it readable — if one is confronted by a series of pictures reading difficulties can be very severe. (A good example which I think is probably unknown to you is almost any novel by Norman Lindsay — pictorial qualities can be astonishing, and there is simply nothing for the ear at all).

Also too, a sound base fits in much more readily with what I am up to on paper. Sometimes when beginning fresh work I think directly of music. A theme has to be announced, then it's dropped, a sub-theme appears, then echoes of the first are heard. Very much etc. I've always been conscious of this sort of thing right from the beginning. (Little technical refinements are such as these: 'a lean middle-aged man' 'I was horrified by the sight of his hook and his mutilated hand yet fascinated by the way he managed'.)

I've always thought my thirty years of correspondence with William Plomer has been very helpful to me. He is one of the best visual writers this century, and by reading him I've been encouraged to try to improve my visual abilities. I wouldn't dare to say that he has learned anything from me, but he knows well how much I rely on sound and pays me the compliment of being my reader.

But I'm doubtful about being a subject for university studies. One's readers should be conscious that there is something agreeable to the ear, and through the ear to the mind, in a writer they find they can read — but I doubt much whether they are any better off for having the donkey-work explained to them.

I remember you surprised me a little by wondering that I should be so attracted to writing plays. A play seems to me the tightest of all forms, and lends itself admirably to all this tossing the sound ball backwards and around. And the visual part solves itself, because there it is with no verbal trouble. (Perhaps I should remark that my own plays were written some time before the stage went non-literary — I see Shaw is back now — good, and may Congreve never be out).

Thank you for your mention of the *Peon* — a work of the imagination if ever there was one. It is a somewhat special entertainment for literate people, and I can't see any critic need say anything other than that about it. But how can I ever keep up with Janet? How can anyone else? Bless the girl anyhow.

I have been occupied with a story and my Yate-Butler *Conversation*. But soon back to the unfinished novel — a severe struggle there, I'm afraid.

With my kind thoughts,

Frank S.

And to your wife.

['lean middle-aged man': see FS, Once is Enough *p. 45.]*

To Dennis McEldowney, *Remuera*

Alexander Turnbull Library

29 May 1966

Dear Dennis,

Nice to have your address again (not that I've lost your letters, but they're playing hide-and-seek among the incredible chaos of my papers), and I know it looks like a Mutual Admiration Society in full operation, but I must say how splendidly you have done Donald [Anderson]'s biography. Donald — yes, I met him once and had a little correspondence — I don't think we ever quite hit it off — I once sent a rather elaborate recommendation for him off into a Void, and I wanted to spank him across my knee when he was so superior and patronising and I think wrong about D'Arcy's Forest in the Listener. I didn't think of him as a very promising subject for a biography — but that was to reckon without his biographer — when the Johnson-Boswell partnership was there as a warning, too.

It's a very good book, Dennis, as Charles says, 'compulsively' readable. It's like Proust, taking all those musty people and applying his creative magic. I think your book is *very* 'creative'. To make those denominational waverings so interesting *now*! Yes, my hat is off to you.

By the way have you ever thought of the word:

interdenominationalisationism

Do you think either you or I should try to use it one day?

But the other side of our Society. My Peon is very much a work of the imagination, I think. In 1957 I was a bit down — nobody interested in my plays and false starts with all new work I attempted. Then I flung myself for about 3 months into an attempt to save John Graham from bankruptcy on his tomato plantation. Such work! — but he went bankrupt — then he was separated from his wife and children. He was miserable and would call on me pretty miserable nearly every evening. I was fiddling with fresh work, and thought I would try to cheer John up by having one amusing page to read to him each evening. It worked — it became the Peon — by the time John was on the way to new matrimonial arrangements I didn't need this stimulus as I was about 80 pages in. I had always promised John I would at some point drop him into the book — but I only just managed it a few pages from the conclusion.

Of course this is by no means the 'truth' about the Peon, but it's one tiny particle of it. [. . .]

The years are catching up on me fast. I read Dante in the morning, Montaigne in the evening, and once a week I read Gibbon to Ted Middleton — we are just about to begin the famous (notorious?) Chap. XV. And yet it does astonish me that this year I have contrived to write my Lawson re-appraisal, a story ['Charity

Begins at Home'], and a William Yate-Samuel Butler Imaginary Conversation. Now it's back to something that may be a long novel.

My thanks for all your kind words, and if you are up you will let me know, won't you?

And again thanks for the book — I imagine Rod Finlayson is going to be thankful too, he is about to begin work on a book about D'Arcy.

From yours,

Frank

Please remember me kindly to your mother.

[Donald Anderson (died 1961): New Zealand-born literary scholar and academic who suffered from cerebral palsy. 'Interdenominationalisationism': see Joy of the Worm, *p. 30.]*

To Charles Brasch, *Dunedin*

Hocken Library

[Brasch to FS, 2 June 1966: 'Your [Yate-Butler] dialogue is fascinating at first reading: it carries one irresistibly. [. . .] Which wise Frenchman does Butler quote on p. 7 — Montaigne?' ATL MS-Papers-4261-099.]

8 June 1966

Dear Charles,

Quite frankly I'm not much of a reader of Butler — I expect in a sense I've lived with him spiritually a long number of years — I should say the dialogue has come out of this spiritual living together. Too much attention to his texts would have been inhibiting. No doubt I make him say things a Butler scholar might question — it's the Butler-Ernest of The Way of All Flesh I'm trying to present — that was the unfinished book. It was never published in his life-time. I should think it most unlikely he ever met Yate, but he might well have read his book. As for Yate — it's a kind of rehabilitation I'm attempting — the historians owe him that. The depositions that would show exactly what there was on him can't be found — in the Hocken, the Mitchell or in London at the missionary societies. I've had some cooperation from Judith Binney about this — she agrees that the depositions are not to be found.

Incidentally to have them sit and talk and mention what they do it would be necessary for Yate to be a very old man (all I know is that he lived to 'an advanced age'). There was a bit of scandal concerning him which I have completely left out — this concerned the third mate of the ship he returned from England on about 1835 (He had been to England to get published his book, An Account of New Zealand). When Butler speaks of a conspiracy black as hell I am making him refer to a semi-official report on this part of the Yate scandal. [Marginal note: The scandal broke very soon after he was back in N.S.W — Marsden (whose condemnation of him is violent) wouldn't allow him to go on to the Bay of Islands. His only answer to the allegations was that he had been 'indiscreet'.]

I say all this, because obviously one is taking on a great responsibility in presenting people who have actually lived in this undisguised way. It is all 'imaginary' of course — I would never have tried any such thing unless I aimed at moving people to understanding and compassion.

Yes, let Janet see the piece by all means. And would you like me to get an independent opinion here — I could get one from Ron Mason — I am seeing a lot of him just now, it is almost certain the Gallery Associates are sponsoring his play [*Strait is the Gate*] for November — but we await a letter from them. [. . .]

From F.S.

I hope the faint touch of irony comes through — the Maoris were Y's downfall, not the reverse.

To C. K. Stead, *Auckland*

Alexander Turnbull Library

26 June 1966

Dear Karl,

This business of getting [R.A.K.] Mason's play started is like one of the labours of Herakles. Also I'm about to approach the Ombudsman about Soc Sec's action in cancelling my Age pension owing to Katherine Mansfield and some other monetary assistance. Incidentally, you once spoke of the Oxford Press as 'that idiot organisation'. I assure you they have nothing on Pauls — who were asked by Soc Sec for details of payments to me over a twelve month period — the incredible bastards included the advance of £100 paid many months before (which by the way Soc Sec accepted as correct without reference to me), and this bloody muck-up I think tipped the scales against me in Wellington. But forget it — it's what I've been up to my neck in all my life.

About the New Poetic. My praise without reservations would be tedious, so if I seem all reservations don't believe it — the praise is there all right — the book is away out ahead of anything anyone else at present can or could do. But that of course doesn't mean I totally go along with you. So —

p 11 I've spoken of a point being an area — this is a little troubling to my notions of geometry.

The 3 omissions which spring most to my mind are Hardy Housman and Bridges. Also Hopkins.

p 107 Shouldn't last word of footnote be dispensable ?

p158 It interests me that homosexuals who appear about the streets and beats from time to time are often called trade.

p 83 top of page. One of the most ify bits in the book. The comeback (equally futile) would be that Mr Stead was a poor boy very limited etc. . . .

I think somewhere you refer to Prufrock as 'difficult'. I must say I've never thought it that at all. Also I think it odd you don't draw attention to the lines beginning we have lingered in the chambers etc. Surely along with the concluding line of Byzantium these are as good as can be found in poetry this century. I imagine the reason you *don't* draw attention to the lines is that you are not concerned with good great poetry as such (and by such, I mean without any concern for whether it's Image Discursive or anything else) — all you are concerned with is your theory and the necessities of putting it over. In the largest sense this is of course bad — though no doubt necessary to the making of your brilliant book.

(By the way, speaking of Byzantium, do you remember I pointed out Coleridge, Remorse Act IV Sc III — I stood in unimaginable trance/ And agony that cannot be remembered, as possibly connected with Dying into a dance/ An agony of trance etc. It now strikes me that although the obvious connection of the Coleridge is with Yeats, the Coleridge *tone* is surprisingly like Eliot).

If I had been reviewing The New Poetic I think I would have had only trifling reservations about its brilliance, the work put into it, the logic of its argument — all that. But that what it finally amounts to is a most curious endeavour at limitation. Kubla Khan — okay, who would want to disagree? But how many K K's can there be? One must be grateful for the Image when it turns up in Yeats and Eliot — and Stead. But surely only a very young man would want virtually to say let's wipe most of the rest. [Marginal note: Is it the same old Puritanism?] I can only say that you simply cannot do that. Also it is far far better that you should be yourself a poet who holds our attention (whether your poetry conforms to your theories or not) than that you should write the concluding half-page of your book. Too clever. No definition. A belief, a faith — well and good, but you must risk eventual defeat by somebody who may turn up with a belief and faith in the Discursive — Lucretius, and I can't explain the thrill I get even with my poor Latin. Or Milton, and you know how I admire there. Or.

Anyhow, let me be tedious with more congratulations — and particularly that one watches for another book of poetry from you with breathless anticipation

Best love,

F.S.

I went to a C.N.D. [Campaign for Nuclear Disarmament] meeting & disturbed

Dr Whittlestone by asking if he couldn't as a dairy scientist keep the DDT & Christ knows what poison out of the milk & meat how did he suppose he was going to keep out the Strontium 90.

To Ray Copland, *Christchurch*

Private collection

4 December 1966

Dear Ray Copland,

[. . .] [Y]our Smollett reference interests me a great deal & I have been greatly stimulated in thinking about it. I rather hope what you say about his 18th cent. position isn't true. Well, yes, it's been my pleasure to read *Random* & *Clinker* (I could never get on with *Pickle*, & *Greaves* & *The Atom* have remained many years unread — on my shelves, too). No, for me it has always been Fielding (like Shaw I am devoted to *Tom Thumb*), & Richardson. Fielding of course a towering figure, & Smollett such small beer by comparison it becomes a very subtle kind of smack-compliment to be credited with imitating him. The interest is mainly on the surface, & that's the reverse of what I was after — plenty of surface interest true, but it's the underneath part I'm trying to put across. With Fielding it's the superb intelligence that clinches it all. Like Montaigne — the incredibly wonderful combination of observation & principle. Mr Maugham, I believe, comes along & cuts the marvellous chapter-prefaces — plagues on his Shade! Even the invention of humour-names. Miss Straddle — my Ramswell comes nowhere near to that — even though he is a Yorkshireman, & Ramswell is the name of a place in Yorkshire. Richardson too is infinitely superior to Smollett — can knock-about richness compensate for a lack of psychological knowledge (even though without much psychological understanding)? What that man opened the door to! — like Charlotte Bronte, I'm saying all this from the originals, not from what I've read in books — or rather from the books I don't read. The other day on the phone talking to Karl Stead I mentioned how clear it was becoming to me that Eliot's work can be clearly divided into 3 sections corresponding to the Inferno, the Purg. & the Paradiso. He said, oh yes, that's well-known — it wasn't well-known to me until I discovered it for myself, & it's well-known no doubt to most at second-hand. (Ironically I forget whether I've ever mentioned to anyone that I know where (il) miglior fabbro comes from — another of my own discoveries: another, I know what translation Eliot had in mind when he wrote about death undoing so many).

So what I am probably saying is if I reminded you of Smollett that might well be so, but there was never to my memory a single moment of conscious modelling. Model. There were 2 models for my peon — a boy I went to school with & greatly cared for: he had all the physical-strength-confidence-determination etc, which I lacked. He came up to Auckland from the Waikato about the same time that I did, & was first a theological student, then he became a teacher (about 3 years ago he was drowned in a boating accident not far up the coast from here: he had just retired as a primary school headmaster). But this boyhood friend was only the book's kick-off. The more important model was a friend 20 years older than myself, a retired bank-manager who I met 25 years ago; & until he died suddenly in 1963 I very rarely missed spending an evening with him once a week. I give a physical description of him on pp 106–107 of the *Peon*, & at the same time use a lot of detail (such as dropsical Prinny) which I picked up from the delights of his conversation & the pieces he delighted to read to me from the books he read. He actually *was* descended from the famous English squire (Robert Bakewell), who made that important sheep-cross. His own name was Bakewell, & he had a father a physician who practised in Auckland until the end of last cent. He had a brother who was chief inspector of Schools (for the whole of N.Z, I think). Well, that was it — I have lost a wonderful friend, but if I've managed to get across on a fraction of his vitality I've done pretty well. He never read the book. He said he preferred to wait until it was printed, & since nobody for years wanted to print it, it got forgotten. In any case he wasn't all that interested — I was grateful that he liked me personally, but I suspect he thought I had no great literary talent as he conceived it. I also suspect he had no idea I could adopt my talent to create a language that near enough fitted him.

Well, I've run on, but have got it off my chest. I think I see why you should speak of a literary model — because of the nature of your own talents. Those lively parodies! But a truly creative talent is different — the model is to be found in the material — despite the problem of trying to separate material from language. [. . .]

From

F.S.

To Charles Brasch, *Dunedin*

Hocken Library

[The December 1966 issue of Landfall *marked Brasch's retirement. FS and Stead organised a surprise tribute page signed by* Landfall *contributors.]*

12 [December] 1966

Dear C,

Crazy life! But so nice to see the *Landfall*. I hope you didn't find the page tasteless. [. . .]

[William] Austin has made a [radio] contract now for Mason's play — he thinks it 'like granite' — splendid play, and so it is. It will help us rehabilitate the text and get a cast the next time we try. (Chris [Cathcart] at the moment is a *very* successful Cuddles in the pantomime — do imagine! Cuddles! and by day he has to go and be a Meat Inspector at Westfield).

MacGibbon and Kee were not only smart with *The Hangover* but increased the advance this time to £200. I now ask myself when this wave I'm on will topple me. I'm getting more news of my aunt's estate now, and it looks as though my days of money-worries are over. I'll know for certain pretty soon. [Marginal note: My brother thinks 4 of us will have £4000–£5000 each — yes, demoralising for me, I think — though I hope I can be 'sensible'.]

No more just now, but soon again,

F.

Yours arrives just as I go out to the post. So relieved & pleased you can take it. Yes, Karl & I began it. Phillip Wilson & Jim Bertram helped in Wn. & Ruth [Dallas] in Dunedin. Middleton wanted to tear Karl to pieces for getting Reid, & me for Shadbolt — but I never approached S — I heard he *wanted* to sign, so the sheet went to a party where S & also Crump seized the opportunity to plant themselves large & centre-page. No novelist could *ever* elucidate the characters of some people. Of course Leo was good in co-operating. So glad, Charles, a fine tribute, I think. And also in this post I see you in *Monthly Review*. I must read — & now must fly.

[FS's aunt Dinah Runciman died on 18 November aged 93.]

To Christine Cole, *Wellington*

Private collection

22 December 1966

Dear Chris,

[. . .] MacGibbon and Kee have now exchanged copies of the contract [for *The Hangover*], so all sewn up, and half the advance shouldn't be long. [. . .] I feared melodrama, but if it seems to read all right to tough London publishers I expect it may be. The entire thing is also here and there quite funny. Oh, I dunno, but we may see — they say August for publication at present. What they are doing about re-printing *Peon* and *Stories* they don't say (both now out of print). Anyhow, if I do pop off, all this will be for you to manage, and I daresay you could find it all quite interesting, even profitable, and I'm sure you'd handle it better and make better bargains than I do.

Meanwhile, believe or not, I couldn't snap out of the reaction from frantic typing and rapid results, so thought it best to continue — I'm well started on a longish story about a strange doctor ['A Final Cure'], another in my *Beau, Charity Begins at Home*, series.

My brother and sisters have been around and nothing much will be done about selling the beach house until next year — probably auction first, with a reserve of about £15000 I should say. I daresay each of the four shares will eventually work out at not less than £4000.

Touching of you about small justices — mainly Harry. If he gets another attack of 'flu' on top of his heart trouble as he did in winter he won't survive. I'm trying to persuade him to either go with me into, or have on his own, better lodgings — but he wants things to remain as they are at present — at 34 Burleigh Street, Mt Eden. The only others are promising and struggling writers I've liked to help if possible. Peter Dawson was trying to wish money onto me earlier this year, so she can't be hard up. And the family! Two tips. When my father made this section over to me in 1946 or 7 its unimproved value was only £200, I may well have said I regarded it as a sort of family trust — but as against that my father and mother not long afterwards got their share from my uncle's farm (I should think about £1500) which neither of them had ever seen. I got a smallish legacy which had to go in repaying to the estate money my uncle had helped me with for this house.

Being the sort of person I am I forget what rash promises I must have made to various people when under the influence of alcohol love admiration or what have you — but you and John are the ones who have remained permanent, and you particularly I want to do your best for what I've written. (My God, the irritations — Pauls' new printing of the *Stories* has 'slab where' for 'slab whare' —

That Summer, beginning — when according to my memory I had warned Bill Pearson and a Paul executive this might happen — it was so in the MacGibbon and Kee printing). And of course I want too to help with Martin Jane and Sarah.

Anyhow, let's leave it at that. I may *well* pop off — and nice to have the comfort of having provided in the way I think best.

I am so glad the burden will be lifted a little the coming year. And of course I've been talking of myself, when I'm writing to somebody in many ways much more able (as I see it somebody touched by a quite brilliant genius) than I am. How you manage all those books in the Listener I don't know. How incredible that you seem to have read them, how cunning to make it seem that way if you haven't. You have such a grasp of the world you live in — and I haven't (at bottom The Hangover is I think the strangest fantasy). [. . .]

No more dear Chris, but if you are short of ready cash tell me — I can send you ten, twenty pounds immediately if need be,

From,

Fx [. . .]

To Janet Frame, *Dunedin*

Private collection

28 December 1966

Dear Janet,

I am so sorry — I got all muddled up, what with *nobody* being anymore where one expected them to be — Charles done with Landfall Dennis McEd. in a Remuera flat — and expecting to discover you in Northcote. Anyhow. And many thanks for the very handsome book [*A State of Siege*]. I see you have hold of a seducing idea and look forward to discovering what you have made of it. Malfred, that could be Wicked Fred, not even Wicked Freda — and Wicked Fred with his Signal — up or down? Really, I just can't wait.

But I'll have to wait. Damn visitors — though one with a van took me down to make a raid on the aunt's house — spoil, the fridge, a great set of bookshelves — you wouldn't recognise the old place now. And I am already demoralised, counting my thousands, and converting them into dollars. Also Harry and I now have three eiderdowns between us.

And this trip to NY! Oh, lucky lucky G[eorge] B[raziller] — at least at this stage I'm sure that's how he will be thinking of himself.

I expect you have heard about my poor little book (45,000 words — 150 pages — *The Hangover*) but at least MacGibbon and Kee quite jumped at it and increased the advance to £200. They talk to me about Ian Brady and Myra Hindley, so I suppose they are thinking in terms of an intellectual-horror-thriller — I hope they may be right, but how very likely they're not! [Marginal note: after all, 5 murders in the last 3 pages!] (Have you read of the Auckland young man who set his mother on fire? And there was another, a married man who set fire to the marital bed — when asked if he knew his wife was in it he said he wouldn't have wasted the match if the bed had been empty).

I must tell you — the hotel manager was short of staff for Christmas, but when he rang the Bureau they said they had only one man, and he was a thief an alcoholic and a queer into the bargain. The manager said send him along, rushed him into his office and closed the door. 'Now look here, do you want the job? All right, but if I catch you with your fingers in the till I'll cut your hands off, and if I catch you getting into the booze I'll boot you round the hotel — is that clear? Okay, well give us a kiss and go and get cracking on the job'.

Hoping very much to see you before too long,

With love,

Fx

To H. Winston Rhodes, *Christchurch*

Alexander Turnbull Library

15 January 1967

Dear Winston,

I sympathise with you over the optical engineering. Pardon the egotism — the engineers are talking about the same sort of thing for me so I am most interested. My trouble fundamentally different I think — hemorrhage, but very little this year and fortunately one eye still relatively unaffected. I have (to me) the most fantastic pain at times and this is connected with the condition which has produced a cataract. My doubt about an operation is I'm uncertain whether a troublesome wandering image I get from that eye will be improved or made worse — after all the bad eye used to be the boss and now the other one has taken over. To try to make things as they were could make the good eye say, okay, I give up. Anyhow, the hem. has destroyed the retina except for the macula — my visual conceptions are strictly maculate. [. . .]

[. . .] [Janet Frame] has just sent me the American edition of *A State of Siege*, and I must say she more and more worries me. Her obsession, okay, most writers are I daresay better off for having one, but the test is what they can contrive to wrap around it. I more and more get the feeling as I used to with Kafka that I can't identify. We all have to die and we are all more or less frustrated, but nine-tenths of the time it is best to forget about it. It all rather reminds me of St Teresa when somebody complained they were visited with carnal thoughts while saying their prayers. She said she had noticed the same thing herself but found it best to take *no* notice. However, no doubt it's best for Janet to be left alone to work it all out for herself — she's damn lucky in her American publisher who seems not to mind bringing out virtually unsellable books. [. . .]

Oh yes, I will feel bound to throw away some of my aunt's money on Mason's play, but meantime several of us are about to go into a huddle with Austin about it first week in February. [. . .]

F.S.

To E.P. Dawson, *Itteringham, Norwich*

Hocken Library

19 February 1967

Dear Peter,

I feel like starting off with a plea to pardon my fatigue. Well, all the past week Broadcasting was making a sound tape of A Time for Sowing. Austin seemed to want me there and it was nine to five, virtually, virtually every day. The only satisfaction — I think we got it. Like so much else it will be submitted to BBC — but I don't think they take much offered from here. But well acted and closely knit — I think no melodrama, and not staginess — but a surprising amount of genuine emotion generated if I am not mistaken. Later on this year they do the Cradle and Egg. And in between I am helping to get R.A.K. Mason's Strait is the Gate (about Dunedin in 60's last century) similarly launched — afterwards Chris Colin and I hope to put it on as a stage performance.

All through the hot weather I have sat here to try to prove to myself that the prospect of some affluence (following my aunt's departure) is not going to make me change my way of life — I knocked off, I think, my longest short story (about 4500 words), about a strange doctor — called A Final Cure (sinister!). Anyhow perhaps later on you will see it in Landfall. My brother who is from time to time seemingly at the point of departure himself (aren't we all?) does very little about the estate, and I still don't know much about my prospects. By the greatest of good fortune MacGibbon and Kee are talking about, in addition to The Hangover, a book of Collected pieces — containing I think I For One, the Roof, about six short pieces, etc. But I would think not until next year.

[. . .] Of course we have suffered a visit of the [Premier of South Vietnam Air]

Marshal [Ky] and La Ky (the latter very beautiful — I saw her close to while a policeman had me gripped by the shirt front. The gossip is that she was a call girl — one the American officers can't have any more presumably). All a very shocking and depressing business.

About the letters. I think the test would be — are they interesting? If you think they are (and I can't conceive now what may be in them) yes, hand them over by all means to whomsoever might take care of them.

I think you probably know the law — copyright in them remains mine, and physical ownership of them yours. So why not allow access to them after my unrestricted copyright ends. (My unrestricted copyright will I think last for 25, or it may be 30, years after my death, then there would be a further period (some years, I forget how long) of restricted copyright until all copyright lapsed).

God knows who I've gossiped about, but doing it that way everybody I've libelled should by that time be well dead.

Well, no more this morning Peter dear. I've said goodbye to Janet and she flies tomorrow. She takes with me all my best love and for you too. (I am clearing up letters as invalid Harry who would usually be here today is in Palmerston North — and what a gargantuan task getting him off — he can only move ten yards without a ten minute rest).

From,

F.S.

To H. Winston Rhodes, *Christchurch*

Alexander Turnbull Library

26 March 1967

Dear Winston,

[. . .] Dudding seems to be under great strain with his first Landfall, and doesn't let me know about (for me) a longish short story I sent him some weeks ago. Since then I've worked on a kind of exploration of the possibilities and limitations of naturalism in novel-writing, with very special reference to Coal Flat. But I have tried to make it lively by putting it all into dialogue form — this enables me to take up all I hear said against CF and try to provide the answers. Some of it I don't expect Pearson will like (I don't think I have seen him since I saw you, and have had almost no communication — I expect he finds me difficult, but it very much cuts both ways), but it's far better to bring up all that can be said against and then answer, than leave it to somebody who will rake up the bad and just leave it at that. Anyhow, the intention is to show that CF is, for anyone who will take the time to read it repeatedly, as I have done, a very remarkable piece of work indeed. I'm not sure where I would like to see this dialogue printed, so will keep in mind M[onthly] R[eview]. More perhaps, later.

I was interested in the examination papers — but it is mortifying that I would clearly fail miserably if required to answer questions about my own work, Yes, properly done and marketed, Gaskell Cole Finlayson and others would be very good in paperbacks.

Janet took off by plane, touched down in Tahiti, then in Mexico city, and finished in Baltimore (she's liable to faint and vomit in buses round Auckland). The first evening she met dos Passos, wife, daughter; and editor of Washington Post — with a pair of dark glasses and the standard NZ florals she wears she can get away with simply anything. A marvellous girl and companion.

My brother as executor of my aunt's estate is too decrepit to do much, so affluence (temporary) eludes me.

My good regards to Sophie, & I hope the boys thrive.

F.S.

[FS's 'dialogue': 'Conversation in a Train: Or What Happened to Michael's Boots', Landfall, *December 1967.]*

To William Plomer, *Sussex*

Alexander Turnbull Library

10 April 1967

Dear Plomer,

Of course you can't help the name of your street. I'm reminded of my radical days when I helped to compose & distribute a pamphlet addressed to the Grammar School boys of Takapuna. The School's motto is Per Angusta ad Augusta. We said the only Great Things the boys would attain to would be Highways where they would mattock up the weeds on relief work paid for at 14/- per week. I remember though that affair taught me something — we had distributed many pamphlets — but we had the demons [police] after us only when we tried to influence schoolchildren. I've always assumed since nothing much is to be hoped for from Social Democracy as it will never dare teach its principles in the only place where they may have some effect — in the schools.

But I rather like to think of you in Adastra Avenue — we do eventually get put in exactly the place where the kind of world we live in thinks we belong. The stars for you — that's because there's some remnant of civilisation in England. But a motorway for me. [. . .]

Do you notice a poem Letter to the Enemy in L[ondon] M[agazine] February — by Karl Stead — he is such a *clever* poet — it's impossible to fault his ear, & the unique & beautiful image *will* turn up in everything he writes. He is young, ambitious, & will go a long long way. He wrote *The New Poetic* which I don't admire as he is plumping for non-mainstream poetry. But it too is very clever. Baxter I can no longer take — although his Pyrrha poems aren't quite usual. He lets you know usually that he is a Catholic & such a bad bad boy, but bad in a good way — not like the unbelievers who are good in a bad way, & will not go to heaven for their reward.

Oh yes, I have written a story (about a doctor) with a most appropriate name — *A Final Cure*. And I see *The Hangover* is announced for July though I've seen no proofs yet. Perhaps it's not terribly good — I know I feel a little doubtful about sending you a copy, though I expect I will — perhaps I'm a little worried that I couldn't resist stealing one of your jokes from At Home. (There now, I'll *have* to send you a copy, & you will *have* to read it to find out which one. I gratefully acknowledge — privately!! — anyhow). The book is only 45,000 words, anyhow.

I'm being scrappy — I'm light headed with a bad cold at peak. I dread the coming winter for my friend's sake. And I'm not sure I have any more books of any kind to write.

E.M. Forster is surely to be immortal — & Woolf, & Russell! Oh but wouldn't they have devoted slaves? With my housekeeping in a mess & my garden a wreck & any one of half a dozen waifs likely to appear at my door at any moment I feel like signing myself

A. Slave

May spring be gladdening you!

F.S.

To Dennis McEldowney, *Auckland*

Alexander Turnbull Library

7 May 1967

Dear Dennis,

After reading you again in the Listener I almost feel like snapping up your invitation — so that I can become very garrulous and tell you all my Royalty gossip. You see, I knew Dr Campbell Duncan who was in charge of the Spa at Rotorua, and Cam knew — well, the list would be far too long, but of course the Prince of Wales (as he was then), Mountbatten, Prince Erik of Denmark, not to mention lesser figures (Siegfried Wagner) and indefinable figures (Hector

Bolitho) et many many als. (Incidentally Duncan was very much the prototype of my Duncannon of the Peon — and you can see how I can go on — his long-jawed wife was a Joynson-Hicks. Also I have it on his reliable (?) information that the man who put Hector on his feet in England was not the Prince — it was Mountbatten. When Hector was caught out in contradicting himself at the time of the abdication, I remember Fairburn came out in his Farmers' Union paper with a headline, Profit without Honour — which brought into his office Hector's father, a nice old man, a Devonport tobacconist who spent his life feeling himself knocked sideways by having fathered Hector and his brother, not to mention by having married Mrs Bolitho previous to that).

Anyhow your reviews are most interesting. Yes, I dutifully bought the Thoughts of Mao (but somebody else can read them).

Look, yes, it would be nice to visit you sometime. But best make it distant. Meantime it would be nice to see you a few times more when you come past here. So I will be getting in touch before too long, and that phone number next door is pretty often a good communicating instrument, if you care to try it.

My best (a dull life persuading the novel [*Joy of the Worm*] to get up and stroll around — better still, trot). A little social life with your mother would be very pleasant,

from,

F.S.

To E.P. Dawson, *Itteringham, Norwich*

Hocken Library

9 July 1967

Dear Peter,

I have been chewing your letter over, also the ones from Michael H[itchings, Hocken Librarian]. I could go on thinking indefinitely — so instead, just this brief note to say I think that an embargo of 25 years would be quite sufficient, & after that all would be at the discretion of the Librarian. If you act on this, it frees you from any more worry, & best then forget about the letters — I'm sure a load for anyone in several senses of the word. Let the load be taken by somebody of the future — I won't be worried & I most sincerely hope you cease to be. Okay? Then just go ahead. [. . .]

I've had proof of *The Hangover* & cover — which is good, though I wouldn't think a popular kind of thing. Publication scheduled for 11 Sept, & I will have a copy sent you. [. . .] Oh dear, I'm afraid it is a horrifying story. But to compensate I work steadily at my new long comic novel [*Joy of the Worm*] about!! clergy-men!!!! I think 2 of them, but there may be 3. [. . .] I haven't heard from Janet, but I believe she has been at Saratoga Springs. She sent me copy of *The Pocket Mirror* — poems, but I have only just got round to the *Reservoir* stories, & am astonished how good they are at their best. Surely the one about the 2 sheep is a superb fable — of the standard of Aesop, La Fontaine, or anyone who may be named. Our Janet is certainly the Goods — & incidentally in the *Landfall* there is a strange over-written, but on the whole good story by a girl called Narena [Randal] ['And So I Sing'] who seems greatly to have been influenced by J.

No more tonight, Peter, but I wanted to give you a firm decision smartly so the plaguey thing may rest. Kind thoughts & best love to you

from

F.S.

To H. Winston Rhodes, *Christchurch*

Alexander Turnbull Library

[On 9 June 1967 Rhodes accepted 'Breakfast with the Reverend' (an extract from Joy of the Worm*) for the* Monthly Review*, and mentioned his own colourful 'parsonic background': a Methodist great grandfather had the 'secret vice' of playing the flute in his attic; an uncle was an Anglican missionary in New Guinea. Rhodes's paternal grandmother married four times. ATL MS-Papers-0432-178.]*

18 July 1967

Dear Winston,

You told me about the many marriages when you visited, but I don't remember about the background clergy. The flute reminds me of a time when Greville Texidor and I were visiting our friend Miss Dawson (to us, always Peter Dawson) at Mt Maunganui. Somebody called, wanting instruments for a school orchestra, and Peter went and rummaged to bring out a dozen or so recorders — surprising, but some of them (and some were plastic) must have at times been left in the sun, and the shapes they had taken were hardly to be believed either. Peter gave away the lot, telling us wryly that she had decided at long last to surrender her masculinity (she was a product of Rodean — or is it Rhodean? — which she loved, and from which she derived her strongest ambition in life — to become a professional cricketer. Texidor was Cheltenham Ladies College and hated it — and would have hated Rodean still more. Incidentally, contemporary with Peter at school were the young women who afterwards became Princess Hohenlohe (I think famous for espionage), and Lady Vansittart — Peter sadly informed us that neither were at all good at hockey or cricket).

I can see great literary possibilities in your parsonic family saga, but I knew so many Methodist parsons as a boy, falling in and out of love with several — but best of all, my King Country uncle when he began his farm had a remote and more or less financial partner in Taranaki, and his father was the Methodist parson I derive my Reverend Cooper from — he often coincided with me on a visit to the farm, and it was trying, but amusing and instructive. Also he was an Australian —Victorian originally, and I am hoping to introduce something of this. [. . .]

Did I ever tell you I lately heard from Marcel Aurousseau after 40 years? He is living in Balgowlah, and has spent the last 30 years on Leichhardt and his disappearance — and all to be published soon by the Hakluyt Society. His letter seemed almost to hint that he had solved the mystery.

From yours,

F.S.

To Christine Cole, *Wellington*

Private collection

18 July 1967

Dear Chris,

I've thought literally thousands of times of writing, to the children too, what stops me is the thought of a letter lying around and seen by Reece (his so often up and down trips to Wellington have also worried me). Yet here's me — only the other day after hastily reading your letter I had to go out and forgot to put it away, and when I came back found my note on my step had been noted and initialled by Reece. (Not of course that I'm suggesting he would pry into letters, but it is all part of the heart-breaking business of his breakdown).

Well, a kind letter from you. Most heartening about my *Peon*. And I am vain enough to think it will eventually make its way — as a comic novel, I should think. Trouble is now, it takes reading, and only those who are at leisure and in the mood will discover what they get out of it. But also dear Chris, nice of you to keep up with my stuff — because if I suddenly fade out, as my literary and other kind of executor you will have all at your fingertips to do your best with publishers etc. I've lately returned the proofs of *The Hangover* to London and publication is scheduled (in London) for 11 September. But hang me if I didn't nearly 2 months ago start work on another — it sounds impossible, about 3 clergymen (I think) — anyhow, it's comic again, and Winston Rhodes seems pleased to be publishing an extract in his Monthly Review for August. I have a story in the coming Landfall ['A Final Cure'], and later this year Landfall will use *Conversation in a Train*, subtitle, *What Happened to Michael's Boots?* — an inquiry into the limitations and possibilities of naturalist fiction, with special (and mainly commendatory) reference to *Coal Flat*. Incidentally my relations with Bill Pearson became so difficult (he is for three years in Canberra now), that when he brought his Bibliography up to date for the second printing of *Collected Stories* he omitted mention of stories I had written since, without referring to me. These total now 5, and of course it's senseless having the Bibliography otherwise pretty exhaustive if there's going to be any repetition of such an omission. A small point you may think, but I expect at my time of life one wants to see one's work tidied up as well as may be.

[. . .] Did Reece tell you I was quite a surprise on television (On Camera), the garden especially came out as a tropical jungle? [. . .]

It's wonderful to hear you say you enjoy the lecturing — really heartening to me, work that absorbs one isn't a curse (although we all know the inertia so often when it's contemplated — even Janet suffers from this, so she says). It comforts me to think of you at work, and how solacing I find those 2–3 hours in my chair and how I try to ensure them every day.

Harry has his winter bronchitis on top of his heart trouble as he did last year, but I think he will recover. Anyhow, there are strong signs now that The Estate is about to pay out a thousand or two, so I will have to consider plans for enlarging this place a little or going elsewhere. I am in confab with Nigel Cook. Also, if you have some damn thing nagging at you, something that requires say £50, don't hesitate one second to let me know.

All for now, dear Chris, and tell Martin Jane and Sarah I think of them often and with much love,

From,

Fx

To Janet Frame, *New York*

Private collection

22 July 1967

Dearest J,

I've looked into the verse [*The Pocket Mirror*], & see much I will give more time to.

This really just to acknowledge yours, & wish you well in England, Yaddo etc.

I am rather driven mad by enlargements to house to accommodate Harry (the cost? — not far short of $2000 I imagine). Anyhow if he survives that long he will be well provided for — very necessary, he's completely invalid now.

Also I paid $60 to 2 university students to clean out 20 years rubbish from section — they demolished & burnt the hut & everything in it, including many dead rats.

I sent off June *Landfall* to Peter lately, so you will see it in England I imagine.

I'm sorry about Birmingham [Cawley] — & hope you don't feel it too severely — I note Letter — Dear Friend in the book. With me the same thing has metaphorically happened for more than a year — an endless yawning hole, & silence.

Oh, never mind. I had to support my cousin at the funeral of my last (& 90 year old) uncle the other day.

All best love, & may work go well!

From Fx

To Christine Cole, *Wellington*

Private collection

30 July 1967

Dearest Chris,

I am sorry that I may have spoken a little too soon about up to $100 to spare. What has happened is this. My aunt had her other Takapuna house let to some Greek people who have indeed lived there for nearly 20 years. It was my unpleasant task as my brother's representative to go and tell them the Estate was being offered $9000 cash, and unless they could equal this they would have to go. I found them extremely nice people, and it was impossible to behave to them in this inhuman way. Although the cash offer was increased to $10,000 my sisters and brother behaved nicely and agreed that I might take the place over at the $9000 — so that I could pass it on to the Greeks at the same figure, giving them time to pay up.

What it has meant is that my own share of the Estate (roughly $11,000) is largely taken up by the Greek deal, and what I have in cash at the moment is largely earmarked for additions to 14, Esmond Road (an almost detached comfortable room with all the doings for Harry in his remaining months or years — that's to say if he will cease to be temperamental and go into residence when it is ready. Though if not, I have more accommodation, and the present structure, already painted up, with the section in process of being tidied of 30 years rubbish, already looks quite an agreeable place. Nigel Cook has designed the addition).

But the Greeks make me their first payment ($1000) by the end of September, their next, the same at end of November, so it won't be long before I can be confident of redeeming my offer and promise to you.

I've continued a lot of work on the new long book through all the bother and upset.

I saw Reece a week ago for a few moments, and he spoke of your being up next month — it will be wonderful to see you, and I can tell you lots more then.

My kindest to all for the present,

from,

Fx

To H. Winston Rhodes, *Christchurch*

Alexander Turnbull Library

20 August 1967

Dear Winston,

I have been interested in your remarks on Janet's book in [*Landfall*] 81 ['The Short Story in New Zealand']. The American copy she gave me lay around unread far too long then somebody borrowed it. I at last got it back, began to read and now it's borrowed again. To compensate I at last got round to The Reservoir and felt very cross with Karl Stead for not indicating in his Oxford book that we have a writer who can write fables of a quiet unique sort, and occasionally one very good indeed. Unfortunately the pair of them have a personal quarrel, but that's no excuse for Stead.

Anyhow, I was getting very interested in the Siege when it the second time disappeared — I thought the prose was coming off more surely than some things lately. But my God, the material and the coincidences! In the house she rented for a time on Waiheke she got a stone through the window and the lights were switched off from outside. Also, shortly before she rented the place there had died in it a Miss Rowlandson, very old, who had taught me at secondary school in Hamilton. She was my favourite teacher, and the one I mainly drew my teacher from at the beginning of the Peon. I had been rather out of touch the last few years and didn't know she had died. Janet found in the house a copy of my A Man and His Wife inscribed to her, also snaps, among them a soldier brother killed in the 1914 war whom she must have been very fond of as she used to tell us such a lot about him. (Miss R was in her day a Tinline scholar, and she had some family connection with the famous caricaturist [Thomas Rowlandson].)

I am looking forward to getting the book back and finishing, and probably everything you say is dead right. (J and I have had our jokes about the heroine

— Malfred, Wicked Fred, but I believe it's never revealed whether Wicked Fred's Signal is up or down).

It's completely marvellous the way she has Braziller eating out of her hand. She sent me lately The Pocket Mirror, a most elaborately brought out book of verse — very much her own kind, and a hell of a lot of it. Unfortunately it's borrowed. And the extraordinary person herself — she has been at the Yaddo Foundation at Saratoga Springs (the Welties, the Capotes etal have all benefited there in their time), but at moment she has use of an apartment in New York formerly occupied by Ethel Barrymore. You see, ghosts stalk round her day and night wherever she goes, and she laps them up as others would the scenery — although she doesn't miss much of that either. An astonishing, a very dear girl.

[. . .]

Kind wishes, [. . .]

To William Plomer, *Sussex*

Alexander Turnbull Library

5 November 1967

Dear Plomer,

I repay you for your calligraphic excellence (a tautology, I think) with my blundering typing — and how blundering one gets without binocular vision! Just put a patch on and try it (no, don't!)

And I always forget to inquire — does your knee improve or stay good, is blood pressure down (I have the most fabulously expensive pellets at present for stopping palpitation rapid pulse etc. — if no side-effects I feel saved) has pocket or have pockets of diverticulosis been turned inside out? Ah yes, indeed, it is all old age.

You should not be so kind with comments on my book [*The Hangover*]. You, a poet, and you can waste time on prose. That book was just to put away on your shelves and look at someday. But yes of course you are all so right, that's all just how it is, and particularly about the puritan time-lag. We still have murders that are relatively nice, you get along (helped of course by your own ballads) with such things as the Moors Murders. And here it's so cut-across by so much that nobody could have reckoned on. This city is the largest Polynesian city in the world — the ghetto is with us, more than one too, the Islanders arrange their own groupings and all consider themselves superior to our own Maoris. They drink fight and rob and from time to time murder — with a pakeha getting in the way occasionally. There is apartheid but not in the African sense. If it wasn't that I can stay detached from young people I would find myself involved — as it is I am so soon bored, a few guitars and much pop music with its own slant will go a long way. But nobody seems to mind mixed marriage, and matings of various descriptions don't put people right in the cactus. [. . .]

Kind of you too not to rap me on the knuckles for your stolen joke. And I don't know what NZ thinks of the book. Not reached here — a package deal with the big literary grocers, Whitcombes and Tombs (Titcombes), they will think up some kind of kiss of death to administer to me — suppression (they could afford it), forget to send out review copies, deliver the whole edition to the Sunday School union for Bible Class prizes. But you present me with a nice idea, a very NZ half-baked pair, myself divided perhaps, another B[ouvard] and Pecuchet. As for disguises, do any of us ever really know for sure what particular mask we happen to be wearing? I know if my friend Harry read the Hangover (unlikely, he's too busy with the racehorses he bets on) he might comment upon my shoving myself into the book as Dottie.

I am fortunate with some enlargement to my house finished, hence Harry secluded in his nearly detached room, very slick and new, a kind of pocket palace (for the hoi polloi). Anyhow he can win or lose his doubles in there without my having to listen to the radio commentator.

You were interested in my writing something about Melville. It has been quite wonderful doing the reading, but alas I have too often been side-tracked. Somehow Henry James got tied in, and although I will never read again a number of the novels, I am fascinated to take the stories again and again from so many different angles. Was there ever such a monumental innocent? — with literary genius. (I suspect it would be the immense amount of buried stuff just beyond the reaches of his consciousness which would make him the incredibly fluent genius he was). But another to tie in is Hawthorne — strange, Melville so much admired Hawthorne, but influence didn't work out very happily. H does some sketches that are quite freezing, but Melville's shots at the same sort of thing don't come off. I imagine I might have to live a long while to get what I am after written. [. . .]

No more this beautiful sunny Sunday morning 7.30. I have been out in a pair of underpants improvised into a G string while I have watered my peppers.

From yours as ever,

F.S.

To Bruce and Brenda Beaver, *Sydney*

Alexander Turnbull Library

3 March 1968

Dear Bruce, and Brenda,

[. . .] Janet has just returned after being away since May — mostly in America. She says a great movement among young Americans to turn queer — they won't have you in the Army. And no certificate needed — you just say you are. But how glad the Yanks are so stupid — inevitably they must run out of generals eventually and have to call wars off. The *Thoughts of President Lyndon B Johnson* are published at last, I believe. And [Australian Prime Minister Harold] Holt? I never thought one shark would eat another. Naturally some of us have sent Mr Holyoake a pair of rubber flippers.

Janet doesn't read notices, but I do, and you were in Herald Saturday [reviewing *The Pocket Mirror*]. Nice of you. I don't think you knew what to say for Herald readers, and very understandable. I'm sorry she published (her American publishers were crazy keen), a bit too private regional etc. [. . .]

Frank

To William Plomer, *Sussex*

Alexander Turnbull Library

14 April 1968

Dear Plomer,

I would have been writing after your so good letter of January — I mean I would have been writing a few days ago, if the Wahine (which is Maori for wife or woman) hadn't been tipping 700 people into the Wellington harbour during the most awful gale ever known to hit this country, and one was transfixed by the wireless reports which made it clear that nobody was able (or even willing — in time), to do anything about it.

Why does it come into my mind? — Maori names, I wonder if I have ever told you the anecdote — a European is a pakeha to a Maori, but this is thought not to be a true Maori word — it is supposed to be the Maori version of the most common expression heard from the lips of the first Englishmen they ever saw. A most valuable and richly suggestive anecdote — you can take your pick from bugger you or fuck you — a marvellous way of explaining to a stranger the right pronunciation of pakeha — and even though I am such a bookworm I have never discovered from the printed page that such phrases were in fact common during the 18th century.

Indeed yes, I very much remember [the author and *NY Times* book reviewer] James Stern (not to mention the lift he gave to Patrick White — but sotto voce a book which I tried to read [*The Tree of Man*] and found the very quintessence of boredom — but I'm aiming no dart at you, you presented PW with the Prize after Voss which was an advance — although how they have turned out since is an investigation I am reserving for my octogenarian years), remember about the visit he and his wife paid to you not too many years ago (after the years in America), and best of all his lively stories in New Writing. Good wishes to his book [*The Stories of James Stern*].

This is probably all light-hearted or even perhaps light-headed as the end of my new book is in sight, and almost a year since I began it — I think probably a record for me. A very different affair from The Hangover — I think. Anyhow keep a spare little finger crossed for me over the next few weeks of the first draft. I expect hard-cover books by now are impossible to sell and off the market — but I nonetheless relish the thought of dumping the typescript on MacGibbon and Kee [. . .].

My own boring exercises are limited to sit-ups — could I endure to live with a non-flat belly or one that has slipped? (The answer is that exercises or not there will shortly be no choice in the matter).

A book about the Sitwells from J[ohn]. L[ehmann] [*A Nest of Tigers*], the Wilde book you mentioned [by Philippe Jullian], and Poems from the Africaans — what things to read in my retirement (or will I be like my poor brother, four years older than I am? He stares fixedly at the television screen for six hours every day — until transmission begins — *then he completely loses interest*).

As I teased Harry this morning, our Lord is risen today, and I looked out at daylight and saw him going up like a shot off a shovel (he is a Catholic and corrected me for being a little too previous) — but what I mean for you is it's Easter and spring and hope and anything can happen — with us autumn and melancholy and God only knows. I feel blasphemous:

> The Holy Ghost
> frequently used to boast
> to the Reverend Mr Spurgeon
> that he'd — *once* — seduced a Virgin!

Best always,

F.S.

To Charles Brasch, *Dunedin*

Hocken Library

14 April 1968

Dear Charles,

[. . .] I look forward to another play by Baxter in print (I have been fearing the current Landfall for the North Island has gone in the Wahine). Baxter did very agreeably poetry-reading in the Festival (indeed so did we all, and I think I put over Janet's Two Sheep quite successfully — mainly by reading it as though reading to children, which is how that sort of story should be read), but the fees we were paid were simply shocking — really enraging when John Reid with his Theatre is about to throw about 100,000 dollars and more away — all paranoid nonsense that completely ignores the beginnings that came from Colin Chris and myself, which could have developed if only we had got even moderate support. Oh well, theatre is the most difficult of all to try to do anything with.

My house and all in a mess as I started my current book 19 April last and hoped to finish by same date this year — not quite, but end is in sight. A very different affair from The Hangover. It has been an advantage having Harry with me — the discipline is valuable — I have to get up so early but it's good for me and the daily page has been knocked off more consistently than ever before (Of course my readers might not go along with my optimism, but we shall see). [. . .]

Good luck and best wishes,

F.

[J.C. Reid had established the Auckland Theatre Trust in 1966. This was the administrative and funding umbrella for the Mercury Theatre, opened in 1968.]

To C.K. Stead, *Auckland*

Alexander Turnbull Library

[Stead to FS, 12 June: 'I've just finished reading The Hangover. *[. . .] It's a rare book — high art — an object of admiration for the many perhaps but a delight to the few. [. . .] [S]ome of the puzzlement you have caused recently is because the substance or "subject matter" of your early stories led people to think of you as a 'social realist'. [. . .] You were never that, but the mistake prevails. [. . .]' ATL MS-Papers-4261-163.]*

16 June 1968

Dear Karl,

Very kind of you to write, the more especially when you are absorbed in work of your own.

Well of course. To write fiction one must have a certain understanding of the way people behave (if this can't be taken for granted, nbg); then one chooses the most convenient 'subject matter' (of course it will have a leftist slant if one inclines that way); & what one hopes will entertain (literate people) is handling of words, & sentences, keeping the thing in focus, themes taken up, dropped, taken up again & developed (like music), the surprise of juxtapositions based on a sense of irony allied to a sense of comedy. Etc. It all has to be arranged, apparently innocently, really with endless cunning (ars celare artem), highlights, lowlights, crises. Etc. One hopes the finished article will give pleasure. How remarkable that in this society one can have the capacity for all this, & unless the final balance is all there (like tightrope walkers) who cares? — & next to nobody will have an inkling of what one is up to, or care a damn anyhow.

Anyhow, although I probably should strike you a cruel blow across the cheek with my fan for flattery, your letter pleases me; & I need bit of pleasing at the moment because of what I'm encountering in (hold your breath) *Joy of the Worm* (probably won't do, but it's tempting), over a third of which is finally typed now. But Harry in his dissolution is very querulous & childish (how old men & children go together!), & some days, I have the sensation of spinning round like a ballerina.

I hope you solve all your own problems, major (literary), & ancillary (domestic), & sub-ancillary (university). Anyhow, looking forward — I expect to be freer for a week or two towards end of next month.

No more just now,

Fx

Timon of Athens. Nobody should ever miss the poet & painter discussing their own work in Act I Sc.I. They re-appear in Act V Sc I, & are even more instructive & entertaining.

To H. Winston Rhodes, *Christchurch*

Alexander Turnbull Library

21 August 1968

Dear Winston,

A short respite before the tyranny of another damned book clamps down on me. I've never acknowledged the copy of Meanjin, and what a stodgy-looking object typographically speaking! Landfall can be bad enough, but this looks as though it has deliberately aimed at winning the Stodgy Stakes at Randwick! And the mélange of material — is it possible to be as 'successful' as [the Australian playwright Alan] Seymour and at the same time so naive? But I don't want to single out names. How define or come to any kind of grips that would make sense with that great raw chunk of matter known as Australia and the people who live there? Perhaps the best I can do is drop Meanjin and tell you of an encounter prolonged over about 25 years with Aussie casualness.

About that time ago I had a story in Coast to Coast, and ever since, I think roughly every two years, I get from Angus and Robertson an invitation to submit a contribution. From time to time I have responded, but nothing sent has ever been used. I don't know the reasons — and that is the point. It may be that editors, or most of them, are against stories beyond Australia, but on each occasion my work comes back without any comment beyond A and R's stereo'd slip to say my story was not among those accepted for publication. For instance, Henrietta Drake-Brockman was the editor just after she and Murdoch had been editing the Oxford Book of Australian Stories, and Davin McCormick and I had been doing the companion NZ volume. The story I sent was The Undertaker's Story, which some people think one of my best, but it came back without comment. The latest instance was the other day — Arthur Phillips editor, and A Final Cure (they say on their invitation that previous publication is no disadvantage) was returned in the usual way. There have been only 2 exceptions — one, many years ago, was a note from Douglas Stewart with his regrets but he thought what I had sent was too slight (I forget what it was); and the other two years ago was from editor Clement Semmler (I expect you are in no doubt who *he* is). I had sent in Beau, but instead of cutting it out of Mate I sent the entire number with a note saying I wished to draw the editor's attention to Drift by O.E. Middleton which seemed to me a fine piece of writing. After months, Semmler wrote me on super ABC embossed notepaper saying he wasn't taking my story, but he was using Middleton's. He also said he wished to compliment me on my generosity, and added that after long experience of writers this was something he had found quite unique. But he didn't say anything about his experience of editors, and I never thought it worth my time to tell him my own. I did tell him however I was very glad on Middleton's behalf, supplied his address, and asked him to write (Middleton, to whom an appearance in Coast to Coast appeared very good fortune, would not believe his story would appear until he had been advised). Semmler did not write, and Middleton being fussy and anxious I had to write Angus and Robertson twice before they formally advised him.

Well. Perhaps nothing. Perhaps everything. I expect it's an exaggeration, but I never read Australians writing about their own writing without being suspicious they have very little idea what they are talking about. Incidentally, I've never found I can read Patrick White. I soon gave up the Tree one, and Voss even sooner (though I have been much chided about this). That's all I have tried. But Plomer just the other day remarked that I should have Riders in the Chariot on my reading list. (Again incidentally, if you ever get round to reading the Stories of James Stern you may perhaps, as I certainly do, infer the reason why he was so extravagantly lavish with his praise of the Tree — contributing greatly to bringing W[hite] out into the limelight).

This too long. May your affair with Twayne be approaching its conclusion.

From yours,

F.S.

To Mr Byran, *Senior Health Inspector, [Takapuna]*

Alexander Turnbull Library

27 October 1968

Dear Mr Bryan,

I am glad to cooperate with you in the matter of my hedge.

In return I should be glad of your cooperation in the following related matters.

But first, I shall be obliged if you will supply me with name and address of the person complaining. From my inquiries it appears that the person I supposed had complained, did not in fact do so. If there is a bone fide complaint I would like to offer compensation for damage which may have been suffered. At the same time I must draw your attention to the enclosed newspaper page. The hedge photograph would be taken on 10 October, and from appearances it hardly appears to be suggested there is obstructed access for the passer-by.

Speaking of passers-by however, I must inform you that my hedge is much used by the public as shelter from the weather while waiting for buses, or in between buses. (One man this winter has even made himself a hole shown in photograph where he huddles from bad weather).

It is of course no admirable matter that no bus-stop shelter is provided immediately across the road. And I have seen many unpleasant sights, drenched elderly people and that sort of thing. If you meet me with the objection that some property-holder will not consent to a shelter, it is my answer that the objection is unreal. In default of all else a bus shelter could be constructed beneath either roadway or footway.

But further, you speak of privacy, and that is important; but the main function of my hedge is to afford me with some protection from petrol fumes and diesel soot. The latter is particularly bad on account of the bus stop. I am informed that much of the trouble derives from buses which are badly driven, quite apart from servicing. One I think very evidently shortens one's life by living in such a neighbourhood, but a thick hedge and vegetation generally do help; and I am especially affected as I work where I live and am thus more continuously exposed to this pollution. [. . .] [One page only survives.]

To Mr Fisher, *[Takapuna]*

Alexander Turnbull Library

6 November 1968

Dear Mr Fisher,

I am very sorry to learn that you suffered a fall on the footpath outside my property.

It puzzles me a little to know how my hedge may have contributed to this misfortune, but if you would care to try to convince me, I shall most gladly offer you any compensation which we might agree would be reasonable.

Be assured that I am quite sincere in this matter, and if you have been harmed by any fault of my own I am indeed very sorry about it.

I am yours sincerely,
Frank Sargeson

To Charles Brasch, *Dunedin*

Hocken Library

24 November 1968

Dear Charles,

I am wondering what you would think of the enclosed. I care little for either Hone or Una as shown, but they come out better on the wall — indeed I think Hone outstandingly (the colours glow, I think of Diego Rivera). On the other hand I almost like myself better than on the wall.

The Barry Lett people persuaded me into this, and I have rather fallen for the painter [Alan Thornton], I find him an exceedingly nice Australian living with his young wife and two children in the most squalid poverty in Parnell. I would much like to help him as I think the show has been pretty much of a failure, and New Zealanders seem so dumb. For example I have never been painted before, and surely I would only have to die, and there would be no difficulty in securing the 200$ asked for me. For anyone who bought it now it would surely be something of a safe investment. I am very far from suggesting you buy it yourself (I have a notion you wouldn't think too well of it, but I do myself think it is not too bad, surely worthwhile for the National Gallery, the Hocken if they have Funds, or whatsoever Institution.)

If you have the time and inclination to help, please do, I don't know how other sitters felt, but I found I could not sit without leaving a few dollars behind me, I don't think anything was staged, and there was almost nothing for anyone including the two young children to eat. [. . .]

Your poems? And prose? The autobiography we would all so much like to have?

No more just now,

from Frank.

I forget how far I got telling you the fortunes of Joy of the Worm — MacG and K seemed pleased to get it but I don't know when it's scheduled for.

Frank

To H. Winston Rhodes, *Christchurch*

Alexander Turnbull Library

1 December 1968

Dear Winston,

[. . .] There's not very much the very brilliant Karl Stead and Bill Pearson coincide on I think — except about Shadbolt. Stead says he can't take anybody seriously who takes Shadbolt seriously; and it was interesting that in last night's Star Gilmore really carved Shadbolt up over his Shell guide book — meaningless adjectives, lush descriptions etc. It is extraordinary how Shadbolt has persuaded so many people to take him at his own valuation, but just occasionally somebody rebels — though not often journalists in NZ (overseas Simon Raven did a cruel notice of Among the Cinders). I myself don't know about Shadbolt for the good reason I can't read him. He seems not to focus, so that from the little I've tried him he seems no improvement on what is to me the windy nonsense of The Tree of Man.

But of course these remarks are of no account. For all I know Shadbolt may be rated eventually the best writer of his day, all I do very much know is that I must myself go on trying to make every sentence I write look and sound right, and carry the meaning I am aiming at.

I wouldn't understand if intelligent interested people don't find your remarks [in *New Zealand Fiction Since 1945: A Critical Survey of Recent Novels and Short Stories*] very stimulating. One doesn't have to agree. Some of the people I care for very much personally, hence I was glad you did the hard work and saw what is good in Phillip Wilson, and he has taken some severe bashings from several directions. It was curious you seemed to miss the point of Ballantyne's extraordinary little potted epic And the Glory (I am sure he lifts from the Lord's Prayer, but very cunning, because the little man's epic struggle is with the Power Board). The whole of Ballantyne seems to me to be contained within this little story, and it seems extraordinary to me that all his other books seem extensions of this particular core he has — a fantastic kind of thinning out of material which makes him very difficult for me to read. But there again I am so fond of him personally I cannot see him as I should.

It has been Ballantyne who has spoken to me of some of your omissions. Crump for example. Again difficult for me. Crump is quite as formidable a person in his own direction as D'Arcy Cresswell was. Also he has a very tender quite feminine side to him, which makes him think it an enormous joke that he is the very type of NZ he-masculinity. I think he and I have always respected each other very much — well, I don't know much about from his side, but I am in no doubt about my own feelings. I hope I may live long enough to see what critics of the future see in him.

Within its own frame of reference I thought Copland's essay ['The Goodly Roof'] very good. But an author preoccupied as he may be with how he is to present his people and his story, would never (I imagine) think like that. I don't know the truth of the matter, but I think Ray Copland's approach, interesting though it may be to a handful of people, is what one would expect Shakespeare to find so appalling if he revisited the planet — I mean if he glanced at what has been written about him. I think no matter how strenuously one thinks *how*, it is *what* one each time hopes to put over that is closest to the core of the matter.

However excuse this all dashed off. [. . .]

I sent Davin a copy of your little book, and no doubt he will comment eventually, and I would think he would be interesting from his remote point of view.

Three beautiful boxed volumes, Hakluyt Society, the Leichhardt letters, the German originals with Marcel's translations and his Introduction turned up some weeks ago. I've hardly looked at them except to read the Intro — much shorter than I anticipated, but very clearly written. All 17$ worth (but Aurousseau was the first writer I ever knew, and it will give me a lot of pleasure to write and tell him how glad I am to have this work of so many years). Incidentally sometime, probably late next year I shall be looking for somebody to present these volumes to, as they will be too much wasted on me. I had thought of Eric McCormick, but if you would like them (as an Aussie, more entitled to them), I'd be glad to make a gift of them to you.

My poor old Harry is more and more in a bad way, but with a lot of discipline I can cope, and have even knocked off quite a lot of a new work.

From yours,

F.S.

To David Ballantyne, *Auckland*

Alexander Turnbull Library

28 December 1968

Dear Dave,

Very glad the Star did have a good word for you this time. Reading the notice pushed me into finding the time, and you gathered me in up & all & I finished with an immense (though still maybe a little puzzled) feeling of admiration for the book [*Sydney Bridge Upside Down*] & you. (I believe Stead greatly admired too, good on him).

I'm not writing any kind of critical exegesis or what have you. I expect it's all still Dave, but different nonetheless, perhaps the best thing you've done, I don't know. It's a very brilliant idea using the meat works ruin as a kind of Mrs Radcliffe castle, & I think probably what you are up to does give you a let-out from neatly tying up *all* the loose ends (the pistol e.g. or am I dumb?) I think why it took me some time to settle in was it didn't in a hurry come clear to me exactly the sort of fiction you had written — I agree that in the end one can accept that the Dibs boy can disappear over a perilous cliff without the reader feeling cheated; but for me reading-time was a necessary ingredient to assist me in seeing.

I noted the Star made the point of the risk of monotony with it all handed over to the boy — but I found it a matter of reconciling myself to the angle, then I was willing to go along.

How well it comes off like everything contemporary is for the future to say — but I'm in no doubt about all the immediate necessaries — everything in focus, & all got sentence by sentence with a skill that very few except a few of your [journalist] colleagues will understand. And the result for the reader an experience not quite like anything previously experienced.

My regards to Viv & Stephen, & may you be full of good spirits (no joke) for fresh work from the achievement of SBUD.

From yours

F.S.

To Charles Brasch, *Dunedin*

Hocken Library

19 January 1969

Dear Charles,

I heard from the Barry Lett people that the Hocken completed the purchase of the one picture but returned the McCormick. Well, I have to agree, apparently he, I mean Thornton, couldn't produce much head of steam there. (I have heard people say he painted me as a businessman, but this I think fatuous, he painted one of my masks and also got something of what — I hope — is behind it). Anyhow, I am very grateful particularly for Thornton's sake, the sale should help him out of the red, though so much red I fear. (Incidentally, in a new popular weekly called THURSDAY, for Jan 9th, there are a number of interesting shots round Thornton's studio — if you can't readily see these I'll send you the cut out pages).

Do forgive me for not taking up points from your letter. I am working so hard and have been right through holidaytime — I began my new book in October and now astonishingly have 20,000 words done [*A Game of Hide and Seek*]. (I note that MacGibbon and Kee have just announced Joy of the Worm — did I tell you that like the Peon it aims at being a comic book, though not nearly so drawn out as the P?)

Sunday, choreday, I must get Harry some dinner. [. . .]

from F.S. [. . .]

[Brasch was the anonymous donor of the Thornton portrait.]

To Phillip Wilson, *Wellington*

Alexander Turnbull Library

9 March 1969

Dear Phil,

[. . .] [A]bout Janet. At Waiheke she curiously inhabited a bach formerly owned by my favourite teacher at high school — the one I tried to turn into Margaret in the Peon, but admit I couldn't do much with. When she finally retired to Waiheke I had rather lost touch with her and didn't know she had died — which she did rather in the manner of Emily Bronte (I think), refusing to give in and staying on her feet. Janet found in the place snapshots which tied up with Hamilton high school before I left in 1920, also some that went back to Dunedin where she had in her day won the Tinline. Also there was a paperback edition of A Man and his

Wife which I had inscribed to her early 1940's. She was tall thin high-and-square-shouldered, never married, and told me her name, Rowlandson, really *was* a link with *the* Rowlandson. I was in touch with her off and on through the thirties and forties when she was living in rooms (illegally living I imagine) in high buildings round about Queen Street where she tried to make a living teaching the fiddle — she was determined never to resume schoolteaching. She had a very very thin time. But, again curiously, as an artistic endeavour, it had its links with *the* Rowlandson. I've never been able to read A State of Siege as I want to keep my own memories and fantasies, and I suspect Janet has made some use, perhaps only slight, of what I told her.

I'm just getting the Rainbirds to read now, and glad Sarah Campion has given it a good notice in the Star. As for J, she made the Bahamas again alright, and is now at Yaddo, Saratoga Springs, until April.

May your own work turn out well! We all go through the whole damn business of despair doubt what have you. For myself I've never doubted so much for years over what I have kept working at since last October. It's well advanced now, but a book as odd as they come and I just don't know. It seems MacGibbon and Kee may be trying Spring (English) publishing for me for the first time with Joy of the Worm. I finished off the proofs about a fortnight ago, a very odd book too perhaps, but I mean for me — perhaps I never thought I could make a randy old clergyman so rounded and funny — and I hope a good deal more. But I must wait and see. [. . .]

Did you hear of the poor old couple who won an Art Union? After a few days she said, 'What will we do about all these begging letters?' And after considering he shouted back at her, 'Keep on writing them!'

All best, hope the family thrives,

F.S.

To William Plomer, *Sussex*

Alexander Turnbull Library

30 March 1969

Dear Plomer,

My life has been made miserable by a mystery. How could I have missed the lines by you in a London Magazine! — you mentioned them in your letter. Now cleared up, one must blame the ridiculous surface mails — *that* copy of the LM posted early in January has only just reached me. And very nicely done, but heavens are you still alive after the septic bites that must have been inflicted on you?

Oh dear oh dear, one wishes only to plug along with one's job, and there is so much. Friends long ago established overseas have been coming back on visits — among them the darling little German-Jewish girl [Renate Prince] who preceded Janet Frame in my army hut in the early fifties when she was 'doing' architecture at the university. Since then it has been Stuttgart where she wanted to get some diploma, and now along with her constant boy-friend (snapped up while in Auckland), she is established in Hampstead. An architect? Perish that thought! An architectural engineer. She has become the most beautiful elegant woman in the world, the rarest kind of blonde, luminous intelligence, and of course she consorts with all the student leaders, and even suffers battery in Trafalgar Square (though how anyone could wish to injure her rocks the imagination). The pair of them left here by plane for home via Cuba.

But more soberly, I asked her how she could bother when it is all so hopeless, and particularly with students where there is always a breakdown in continuity (apart from students so often being square at heart, at any rate becoming so); and her answer was that one must make at least some gesture of stopping the Americans.

All whatsoever, I shall love her devouringly until I die.

For a change there has been a visit from John Money, a New Zealander a little nearer my own age, who did not do very brilliantly at his studies here, but worked his way to America and got a very good Harvard degree. He is now an associate-professor at the Johns Hopkins, a specialist in idiopathic sexual precocity and other and kindred tasty subjects. He greatly embarrasses me (at the Customs) by sending me copies of Drum and the Adventures of Harry Chess (a comic strip in which there are no women, only men with huge codpieces and other exaggerations); and he seems to be forever organizing world conferences of 'sexologists' (the conference town seems always to be Bangkok). Still, his industry and his publications are prodigious (and again I am embarrassed by de luxe photographs of operations for priapism, in books which may be entitled Sex Errors of the Human Body). In fact he is in some ways a kind of modern intellectual (and American) idiot. But I can't withhold my admiration of his energy. All has been done on a financial shoestring under his own steam. He was determined not to be caught in this petty potty little dump, and I have no answer for those who take that view and mean it and act.

Now, how remiss of me! Renate and Dick, the two architects, were enraptured by Curlew River, did not care quite so much for the next one [*The Burning Fiery Furnace*], and were sore that they had missed The Prodigal Son [Plomer's librettos for Benjamin Britten]. By everything, Britten, you, and production. I've always believed every word Renate says about any of the arts, naturally the dear creature has impeccable taste.

Alas, I must do the chores. May your Festival appearance have gratified everyone. And up the Poetry Society! (although personally I begin with Chaucer, and have now given up reading everyone later than Auden).

I've had the page proofs for Joy of the Worm, so apparently MacG and Kee are this time trying Spring publishing. I must remember to have a copy sent to you. And my God I haven't mentioned the Forster birthday book (also turned up a few days ago, and not looked at yet). Many thanks. I've finished my new story, but it's turned out a bit short, about 35,000 words, and until I can get to it for final retyping I'm suffering the usual agonies of doubt. My good wishes to you and your Charles. I have got my Harry off to his nieces for Easter. I hope they persuade him to do his duty and so return with a clean soul full of hope (no Spoonerisms). A good Spring for you!

From

F.S.

To Charles Brasch, *Dunedin*

Hocken Library

18 June 1969

Dear Charles,

[. . .] Perhaps it was a mistake to begin another book immediately after I'd signed up for Joy of the Worm last September. I sailed in, and now thank God have sailed out. The result is 35,000 words called A Game of Hide and Seek not yet sent off to London. More anon (the story *could* make a good companion to I For One reprinted).

But I have a stomach virus, (since beginning of March), I lose weight, I have to cope with housekeeping which I can't any longer. It suddenly hits me that it is nonsense to be sitting on this bit of land when I could have a much smaller bit, which even then I wouldn't have to cope with as I would try for a pretty small house which I would let some honest retired workman and his wife living on a pension for nothing in return for their lodging me in a room I would build on. No intellectuals, of course. It all might come true. It had better, I can't see myself writing another book unless. As for poor Harry, he is either a hospital job now or else for his nephews and nieces (who are willing although he isn't — not quite). Oh dear oh dear, one should not live on, but if one does I am sure a room is the thing not a house. Somewhere, I think perhaps in I For One, I wrote something about life's territory becoming limited as we age, our enclosures becoming smaller and smaller. I expect I sound morbid.

Because of the struggle to finish the book I've been out of touch with so many lately, Janet, most unfortunately. I hope I may have endless things straightened out by Christmas, which I am allowing myself to recover. Who knows, by next year if I've survived and pressures are reduced I may be pushing myself as a candidate for the Burns in 1971 (I had to stick by Harry as he was last year, but he rapidly passes any help I can give now except constant nursing).

I expect you are digging your way out of the snow,

from yours as ever,

F.S.

To William Plomer, *Sussex*

Alexander Turnbull Library

8 July 1969

Dear Plomer,

To take you up about having 'nothing to complain of' I believe you, and yet I have a complaint on your behalf. I can't remember telling you this anecdote, but about 18 months ago I was turning the pages of the latest edition of The Oxford Companion in a bookshop and came on Kilvert. There was your name [as editor of Kilvert's diary] of course. So I turned on to see your own entry. Nothing. Remember this is NZ, think of your SA days, and think of my astonishment at discovering my own entry (a note clearly written many years previously and never brought up to date). Do believe me when I say I had never thought of myself in any such terms. But you! I don't exaggerate, a man who has done things miles beyond anything I could hope for. What a world for ironies and nonsense!

The months since summer have slid by, and I brought myself very close to a breakdown by finishing my new novel. I called it A Game of Hide and Seek, and after only a fortnight Martin Green at MacGibbon and Kee says he has enjoyed it. Alas though, it is on the short side, so some bits and pieces, or perhaps another short novel will have to go in with it (there was one called I For One and perhaps that will do). As for Joy of the Worm it appears 5 August and I have asked for a copy to be sent you. I suffered from severe temporary melancholia on seeing the pop art jacket wrapped around it — I expect it's bound to happen when one's publishers become part of a vast television-publishing complex with its target the great floss-sugar heart of the television public.

But oh dear oh dear I really have been down. A little unbalanced too, I'm afraid. So I try to put a lot of emotional data through my own private computer. Can I look after my Harry (very nearly a full time job now), and write another book? (The answer is no, but that's not to say I take Computer answers for Gospel).

Also, am I sick of housekeeping (even for myself)! Why should I not clear away from here, finding a house which I could let very cheaply to some honest retired working man and his wife (ahem! — but they are still occasionally to be found) in return for their taking me as a lodger and slipping me an occasional plate of sausage and mash (and here's me a cook who can do all sorts of undreamt things given minimum ingredients and maximum encouragement).

Well, I have a notion that seeing I must take at least six months off writing anyhow, something of several possible sorts is going to happen — though may it NOT be the stroke which some days seems so imminent.

What a strange note to my goodest of good Plomers! But then I said about my being unbalanced.

Oh yes, there's a Twayne book, but a New Zealand professor [Winston Rhodes]. I saw some of it and thought it very good. I believe there have been proofs. At least I won't be credited with swopping stories with Captain Cook, or being a Social Welfare Officer among the convicts at Botany Bay. [. . .]

The mood will pass. I regret it, and don't. And whatever, I send my dearest Plomer all the good wishes in the world (that's to say I would if I could command them).

My greetings and good wishes too to your Charles,

F.S.

A French professor from Toulouse [Victor Dupont] has been travelling about NZ lecturing on Janet Frame, whom he describes as one of the world's great authors. Somebody gave him a telephone number that would get me, but I didn't hear, and infer I don't make the grade. I must write & tell Janet, who sends me most interesting letters on Americans & Americana — from Yaddo. Though now she's gone on to the MacDowell colony. It's very nice that she's moved far & fast from my army hut.

To Janet Frame, *Norwich*

Private collection

13 August 1969

Dearest J,

Am so sorry to have fallen by wayside and bedside. It was all connected with aiming at getting some piece of work knocked off in case I'm out of writing action for six months or more while I try to get myself better accommodated. The idea is to sell and buy — less land larger house where I can have pensioner tenant and wife and in return for cheap rent get some looking after. Harry terribly exhausting now. Anyhow, I must try to blunder my way through it all. [. . .]

Give Peter my love and say I hope to write again soon. Nice the Barkers don't mistake her quality.

French professors and visiting Australian impresarios continue to proclaim your genius (I am embarrassed when they especially mention Owls Do Cry — it will be extra sacrilege to sell the piece of ground it was written on when I've already burned the habitation. It probably means I can only sell provided the flat-dwellers on the exact spot agree to a perpetual plaque). But it enormously pleases me to think it might even mean a little extra money in your purse. Perhaps even a lot.

Everybody praises John Money's Riot Report — and then produces excuses for not using it. I shall know you are around again when I hear you coming up the path singing To a Wild Rose. Ever my favourite MacDowell.

Best love, and forgive this, I am disintegrating,

x F x

To William Plomer, *Sussex*

Alexander Turnbull Library

24 August 1969

Dear Plomer,

I agree with you that no letter about one's book is ever adequate; but who could expect anything nicer than you have written [about *Joy of the Worm*]!

But to your former most kind & comforting letter in July. Indeed alas, alas, no part of my problem is solved, age with its monstrous exaggerations of our less admirable quirks crotchets etc seems to me a cruel monstrosity in Harry. I just can't think of what will happen — except what of course *will* happen; and unfortunately that is part of the problem, my poor Harry knows quite well we will all die, but even now he cannot see it as a fact of life for *him*. No more about it to say. It is for the forces of nature, in me & elsewhere, to solve; and perhaps to slightly paraphrase Forster, nothing will have been done wrong eventually (I say that to balance up your mother's equally true 'whatever one does is wrong'.) We shall see. [. . .]

Oh, and your mention of Janet Frame reminds me I probably never told you my English friend, Elizabeth Dawson (I think I made something of a figure of her in that seaside piece printed in the big vol. *Landfall Country*) a few years ago returned to England & settled in a hamlet in Norfolk, where her neighbours have lately been George Barker & his wife (presumably a 2nd wife) & their 3 young children. Elizabeth as a propagandist for N.Z. Lit. tries our work on Barker, but he won't have it on. His wife however falls for Janet Frame whom she considers (I think) 'by far the most powerful woman writer at present writing in English'. Of course she knows Janet, who stays with my friend (she is there now); & Janet is one of the rarest persons to know anywhere on earth. By her sheer rarity she gets about everywhere. Some Americans paid her jet air fare to Bermuda for Christmas last, and since she has written in the seclusion of the Yaddo Foundation at Saratoga Springs (as she wrote, 'listening to the brilliant conversation of Philip Roth' (for me I think she can have it: I haven't read *Portnoy*, but from picking it up in shops, I suspect R. to be a young man who supposes you can take short cuts in works of literary art)); besides the MacDowell Colony (shades of Edward Arlington Robinson!) and now she's in Norfolk, Itteringham. And yet it's not much more than a decade since she was incarcerated in Mental Hospital (14 years!) with the brain operation impending! A modern miracle story — as though some great person like Simone Weil having left us, Nature or Whatsoever had to raise somebody much the same as a replacement.

Yes, your appreciation of *Joy of the Worm* all I could wish for, most perfectly expressed (remember how I was too fulsome about *At Home* & you suspected me. And yet I meant it all (what price objectivity when we are creatures of mood!), & could tell you of the misprints. *J of the W* appears to have something of a success of esteem by the way. The New Statesman announced a masterpiece, even though the reviewer (Jonathan Raban), made me feel he had somehow read a book which wasn't the one I wrote. Also I was again in your company & Forster's (Who is this dangerously knowledgeable person who goes about telling reviewers, 'Yes, those 3 always go together'?) in the Observer.

What interested me enormously in your July letter was your 'sweat blood over . . . poem etc'. How wrong one can be! All my life, writing has been so difficult & slow; but to you I have always attributed a marvellously ready fluency, a teeming number of lively visual images to choose from. I have been wrongly envying you. My admiration & respect increases. How *can* you have done so much, & such a variety! I just don't listen when you say you weren't cut out to be a novelist. What then is *Turbott Wolfe*, *Museum Pieces* & the others in between? Who cares whether it's women or what? Cheers for Henry Fielding & Charles Dickens — & my voice will always cheer too for W.P.

No more. Chores.

F.S.

To Jim Shaw, *Takapuna City Council Workman*

Alexander Turnbull Library

[30 September 1969]

[Marginal note: In a sense this is the $500 which I would have contributed as my share of gift to Miss Hayward if she hadn't behaved so outrageously. Conscience money. I picked on Jim Shaw as somebody near to hand & so very worthy of a lift unlikely ever to be afforded him by anyone else. F.S.]

Jim/

I have known you so long, and have such a regard for you. And I know how difficult it is for you, living in a costly rented flat, to decide about giving up your tough job, even though you are now in your 68th year.

Because of these circumstances I am very glad to be able to afford some help. The $500 which is enclosed is a gift to you.

May it help to make your problems a little less difficult to solve.

F.S.

Sgd 30 Sept '69

Witness/P. von Sturmer

Solicitor

Takapuna

[Marginal note: Jim born 9 April '02]

The Letters 1970–1981

To Michael Beveridge, *Christchurch*

Alexander Turnbull Library

[Beveridge recorded interviews with FS in December 1969 and January 1970, subsequently published in Landfall, *March and June 1970.]*

3 February 1970

Dear Michael,

When you end up with that PhD I shall expect you to go halves with it.

Copland on the air. He sounded like Lord Weary himself, you know that character out of a book of poems called Lord Weary's Parcel.

I'm priming you. Copland detective work in discovering from the Dictionary of National Biography a Rev Bohun, apparently one of *the* Bohuns, (and so it is 'pretty obvious' where Sargeson picked up that character) is nothing short of marvellous. I feel that his suspense must have been nearly impossible to endure. Anyhow, first I've heard, all I know of the Bohuns I got from a note on the family out of Everyman Enc. As for the all too real life grandsons of my fictional-real life Bohun [Bert and Nigel Cook], *they're* in no doubt where I got him from — and I'm not wholly popular with them at the moment. [Reverend Bohun and his son Jeremy are the protagonists of *Joy of the Worm*.]

But irresponsible Copland — irresponsible because he's the typical academic showing himself off to a popular audience — the erotic worm, he got that, the intellectual worm and he got that — but is he worth his 3000 or so university dollars a year when he falls down on the worm of death — 'joy of the worm' Cleopatra and the peasant at the end of Antony and C. Irresponsible with his talk of Sterne and Smollett, I see myself with their works propped open all around me, lifting this character lifting that, that notion, that phrase. Irresponsible, because he's the thickest head if he doesn't see I'm trying to write a NZ novel that's intellectually acceptable, and all he can do is be su-superior at the same time as he tells his pop audience, I mean pop-square, they'll be bored to death and probably give the thing up as hopeless.

I don't write poetry, I mean not as good as this, so I'll quote,

Yeats to those who hated Synge's Play.

> Once, when midnight smote the air,
> Eunuchs ran through Hell and met
> On every crowded street to stare
> Upon great Juan riding by:
> Even like these to rail and sweat
> Staring upon his sinewy thigh.

No great Juan I, but the rest of it will fit the Coplands. This all to help with PhD for you and nobody else.

To William Plomer, *Sussex*

Alexander Turnbull Library

29 March 1970

Dear Plomer,

No, I'm the one who should have written (excuse that 'should'). I think I mentioned sending you a Landfall with something of mine in it illustrated ['An International Occasion']. The next Landfall [March 1970] with a cover depicting me in four of my stages from 8 years on is due very soon so I'll send both copies together. Meantime I've been all mucked about with the Queen coming to Esmond Road (you went to the Palace to see her, but you must admit it's rather different her coming to see) . . . well, all a fuss, because from Harry's view she is Betty Guelph (alias Windsor), one of a family with a record of wrongs to old Ireland — but it turned out he *did* want me to help him to the gap in the hedge where I sat him on a tall stool (he turned down my offer to hold him up while I shouted out that he suffered from the King's Evil). BW didn't see him but bless me I think the Duke did, also one of the two royal brats. Afterwards I said oh well, once a NZ Irish Catholic always a NZ ditto. And he lived up to his Irish reputation with 'All right, but what you don't understand is once a NZ Methodist always a NZ ditto' — as you no doubt know there are always advantages in having to endure the company of an Irishman.

The Queen surprised us all by awarding an OM [Order of Merit] (I suppose Russell died opportunely) to one of our scholars, a man called John Beaglehole. I don't care for him personally although I've never seen much of him, but he's a fine scholar and has lately settled the text that records Cook's three voyages (handsomely brought out by the Hakluyt Soc.) He should have had some sort of acknowledgement of his scholarship ages ago, but our vulgar and embarrassing Holyoake would never approve of his name because of Leftist activities in the thirties. (We have here a snooping Security Department, ridiculously amateur but also dangerous — my own name went onto the files during the war when I consistently wrote to a German friend [Odo Strewe], interned (for really no other reason than that he was non-Jewish) on an Island in Wellington harbour). Well this is a gratifying minor triumph for liberals — the Queen's going over the Prime Minster's head.

Talking of scholars though, when I lived at 27 Little Russell Street for nearly a year in 1927–28 (*Pension Binyon* as it were, there was Denis Binyon on his way to becoming a classical scholar, his father a brother of Laurence — he was a solicitor, retired, I somehow think he had put a foot wrong, hence his retirement, and the necessity for his wife to run the lodging house) anyhow up on the top floor lived an Australian who had been a captain with Aussie infantry in the war and had a small pension for 'shell-shock' as it was then. He was trying to become a writer and I'm afraid I did not think very highly of the sketches and stories he was trying to place. I had quite an affection for him and when I left I wrote him but he never replied — but through the decades I would occasionally see his name, signed to [letters] in the Times Lit S. for example — from which I learned he was quite a figure and an official in the Geographical Society. Well, from time to time I went on writing and at last after just on 40 years he replied. He is across in Sydney, married, and of course over 70, well over, but there has now appeared from the Hakluyt Society the results of 30 years research and work — Leichhardt's Letters, in three volumes. I nearly cried when I opened his letter. He had followed my own 'career' — well, a little. His name is a striking one, he is Marcel Aurousseau, and besides this massive work of scholarship one typescript he showed me in 1927 did get published sometime a few years later — I always forget its title, but it was about Marcel's walk with a young American friend from Paris to Madrid. (One of the things we had in common in a way — I about the same time had walked solo from Paris to Milan via Strasbourg Bern the Gemmi and the Simplon). [. . .]

All very best,

F.S.

Now it's *not* your turn to write. Wait until I do again. Among other things I want to tell you about how Glover has sold a packet of my letters for (NZ dollar approx 10/-) $550. [. . .]

To William Plomer, *Sussex*

Alexander Turnbull Library

6 June 1970

Dear Plomer,

Yes, I run later and later (soon I won't be running at all). [. . .]

And oh dear, in case I forget and run short of space, my dear and dearest Janet turned up the other day after keeping herself afloat in America (with a few weeks in England) for well over a year. Her gift for people, for knowing (now) they will love her, her gift for not abusing that love — it is all so remarkable, perhaps unique. In Boston she stays with the Marquands, and returns to TAKAPUNA to find their relatives the Rothschilds (the real ones from France, the Baroness here for a heart operation for which a local doctor is more (genuinely) famous than Dr Barnard). Before I say so, you can take it for granted she stayed with two painters in California, 'Bill and Paul', and it would be quite impossible for 'Christopher' not to drop in. Now she's back in Dunedin. I notice her new book called *Intensive Care*, apparently a 'Dystopia', gets quite a notice in *Time*. Nobody who knows Janet would ever for one second grudge her whatever success she might have, and in money terms she doesn't have much.

But about those letters that Glover sold. It's very sad, poor Denis is on the downfall with Booze. He's very sick and sad (his mistress or second wife [Khura Skelton], I've never been sure which, died and he's lost). Also he needs money. When he asked me if he might pass on a packet of my letters to Wellington's quite noted Turnbull Library (that's where Beaglehole did a lot of the work that brought him the OM), I suspected he might get a few dollars for them, but I never reckoned on $550 (our dollar is about 10/- sterling). But it seems California (and for some reason Texas) are both mad to buy up 'cultural documents' all round the Pacific. The story is the Turnbull had to pay $550 since Texas would have paid $500. Anyhow blow me down, if Turnbull hasn't since written suggesting perhaps a deal which would be aiming at my 'complete archive'. Depending on what I could let them have the figure could be between 4 and 5 thousand dollars. Well! Of course I have all my longhand stuff, and being a compulsive saver vast quantities of paper all in I should imagine a state of chaotic disorder scarcely equalled by all those abandoned lodgings stuffed with paper which De Quincey left behind him. If you have inferred from this that somewhere I have all the letters you have written me (I pray forgiveness for not keeping them in sequence and where I can put my hand on them), you are quite right. I put Turnbull off, saying I must first finish a 'novella' [*Man of England Now*] (which thank God is at last at least drafted), then I would try to put my papers in order (rough) and let them have some idea of what I have. Now your letters, pieces of solid gold (I mean true worth, not money), extracted from the dross, will be lovingly packeted to await your wishes concerning them. After all this problem *must* come up eventually. Perhaps the time is now. Will you let me know what you think? It goes without saying that whatever happens about my 'archive' nothing will happen about your letters except according to your wishes. Also, only mortality suggests there should be any hurry in the matter. When you get round to writing again you can if you like tell me about my own letters.

Before I forget, MacGibbon and Kee sent on the Penguin letter about the Pen NW reprint by surface mail — to reach me only a few weeks ago. You and I must have been among the largest contributors, anyhow my figure came to £32 for which I was very grateful (but I do hope John Lehmann wasn't forgotten). As for my publishing affairs, I think I have put MacG and K on the spot. They must make up their minds whether they want me on their list or not, if not I demand my rights back and begin a fresh career as my own literary agent. [. . .]

But about L[ondon] M[agazine], I we and quite a few of us were interested about Anna Kavan and could have made one or two corrections. She came out here with a friend of mine (I hesitate to say his name is Ian Hamilton, when that name must be one of the most over-occupational names in letters for all time), at the beginning of the war and stayed for about a year. She was always very nice to me, and yet I have never cared much for what she wrote except the pieces in Asylum Piece — until now, that is; Julia and the Bazooka (the title-piece) mysteriously transcends the tiresome egotism, and it moves me to think she apparently at last arrived at writing that when so close to death. [. . .]

Chores, and Harry clamours for his Saturday mid-day dinner, we are very plebian.

F.S.

I type so badly (yet with speed), it's because I have no binocular vision.

To Janet Frame, *Dunedin*

Private collection

14 June 1970

Dearest J,

I loved the last of the letters you don't write. Write me lots and lots of the ones you don't write me, I adore them. I also adore you on radio. As perhaps you know (or don't know) this stupid YC station failed to put on what appeared to be the last two of your stories. I indignantly rung them, and they said Wellington hadn't sent up the tape. But they never apologised nor nothing, and I never got round to writing to Wellington.

But what a radio personality! I heard you on Fem View. I don't know whether it's the result of staying in California (or other places), but you handle things so beautifully. A lovely touch indeed, one that nicely knows just how much attention to give this, and cut down a little on what may be due to those. Anyhow, a beautiful job, and of course the last word, and probably the only one listeners will remember was 'Sargeson'. Let's agree always to push our mutual admiration society, let's agree never to read each other's books but have the most exclusive MA society in the whole world.

Anyhow, oh clever girl!

(Oh, and it's lovely to have littorals in one's books — in my next I'm going to have starfish rockpools sea anemones, the lot, too).

I'm deeply sorry it has to be Dunedin for you at the moment, but hang on, cheer up. If I sell my archive we can join forces (!) and shout Paul [Wonner] and

Bill [Brown] over for a holiday.

And talking about selling, money etc. I've finished, at least it's done in longhand and in the first typescript, MAN OF ENGLAND NOW (25,000). Before the final typing I'm taking a few weeks off to get the papers in rough order so the archive-selling can be more a reality. [. . .]

Love,

Fx

To E.H. McCormick, *Green Bay, Auckland*

Alexander Turnbull Library

4 July 1970

Dear Eric,

In case it's my misfortune to survive longer than I care to, I'm putting in an application for the Burns Fellowship (once I've exhausted capital resources I owe to my aunt I can see myself on the breadline — that's to say if I don't succeed in straightening out my present publishing difficulties).

Would you do me the kindness of allowing me to send forward your name as a reference? But please say immediately if you would rather not (I've had the same request put to me far too many times for my comfort — and in any case you too might well feel troubled by breadlines, and be contemplating an application on your own behalf. In which case I would withdraw, and be much pleased to provide *you* with a reference).

I am only taking this daring step because they did offer me the Fellowship a few years back, but I couldn't see my way clear to drop my obligations to Harry (who God save us, is much better since then, even though feebler, perhaps because he's much better fed etc). Anyhow, nearly 70 and they prefer applicants to be under 40. And I am suggesting to them if they have me on they allow me to 'commute'. Three weeks perhaps in first and last term? Cheek no doubt. But truth is, having lately finished something which is a curious return to the earliest period of my writing (before I could get published), I meditate plans whereby I embed Up Onto the Roof etc into some kind of Autobiography. It is going to be very difficult, because a good deal of the stuff I intended using went into the Peon and other things, and now I have to conceive it all over again. It will mean hunting through an immense chaos of papers and how can I do that in Dunedin? Hence if I explain they may make me this concession.

And speaking of papers, my papers, I have been trying to put them into some sort of order. Perhaps I told you the Turnbull are interested, and now I feel they are quite right to be. I am amazed to find novels plays and Lord knows what, running into many thousands of words, abandoned in the third act etc, all put aside and since completely forgotten — I am astonished to see them, decipher a few pages and even then have only dim notions of what I was up to.

I think if I am lucky enough to get some kind of a curious very unusual kind of autobiography done, it's about the last thing anyone, including myself, can expect of me.

If you can manage a ring (496,999) in somewhere about a fortnight I would be much obliged.

Good wishes, and to Myra,

From yours

F.S.

To William Plomer, *Sussex*

Alexander Turnbull Library

25 August 1970

Dear Plomer,

I haven't been sitting here waiting to hear what you might say about the letters — indeed no, to sort out my papers, and roughly at that, has taken me quite two months. I've fumed (fumes are very common these days, the damned motorway), such waste of time when I have things to write.

But all done now. The 'archive' sits waiting to be inspected and appraised — a man from the Turnbull will arrive next month (I feel I am acting so impossibly out of character).

Your letters altogether in a folder, I think about 76 (I was wrong in my last, I've lost a good many, and it must have been many years ago. My papers were shifted twice — once from the old hut into the army job, and when that was too decayed, a refuge for rats, I roughly salvaged before we burnt the hut down as the most practical solution). What I have begin 17 November 1945, and I think very few lost since then. *And* a most agreeable collection. Last night I was held into the morning hours. I was moved too, and mainly I think because of an extraordinary *generosity* (I do compliment you). The liveliness and the humanity can be taken for granted.

Well, I have no wish to re-read my own letters, but I'm sure the Turnbull would be glad of them, and I have little doubt I can sell them for you. The double collection could really be something, and I imagine it has to be here — in England yours would be something very definitely, but mine, well, I would doubt it. Out here (and especially keeping in mind South Africa) all could be fascinating materials for hopeful Ph.Ds.

But if you have different views please tell me. If not, take your time — what would be handy reasonably soon would be to let me know how many you have, and soon I would hope to tell you the sum that would be paid. [. . .]

Those Twayne books are devilish hard to get hold of out here. Apparently in New York small orders go into the wastepaper basket. So all I have seen of yours so far is its listing. I enclose an assessment of my own by James Bertram, and it interested me because along with J.A.W. Bennett (now a hair-raising Medievalist at Oxford or Cambridge — I think he stepped into C.S. Lewis's chair — or should that be onto —) he was a clever university boy ten years after me here in Auckland, and although he had quite a career as a journalist in China, until captured by the Japs who luckily failed to recognize him for the man he was, he has always kept in touch with my work even though I haven't seen him in 20 years. As you see he doesn't care for my plays, but some of his remarks are, I would think, pretty right.

On dear, as usual I'm talking too much of my own affairs. And here I go on. I don't know about 'lifelike' applied to An International Occasion. I had completely drafted it before I saw that I had made central a carpenter called Chris, who is attended by an angel. There is a kind of Last Supper followed by a kind of Crucifixion, and I even used the word 'petrified' before I saw what I was doing. Often I have noticed this sort of thing in my work, yet I *never* think of it before I start. The house etc might look like 'slumming' on my part. But I don't think so — the connection with myself is the man I call Lionel, and he figures remarkably in another Mrs Hinchinghorn story which someday I must let you see. He also figures as far back as I Saw in My Dream — can you believe it, his name is John Unsworth Whewell, and who besides myself has ever thought Whewell, the famous Cambridge Platonist last century? And Unsworth? — it interested me immensely when John Lehmann spoke of a clergyman in the Thames valley, a classical scholar, of that name. The combination of the two names in Johnny's case looks pretty clinching. He is as I say short of the full pound, and for some reason was shipped out here in the twenties, but he is full of an extraordinary delicacy and courtesy, writes me hundreds of fluent misspelt letters full of accounts of his doings (when he sees a film he writes a ten page account of it, remembering every detail). He is aged and broken (he has the most dreadful hernia I have ever seen, and a dreadful discharge from the bowel which should be cancer but which the doctors I take him to say isn't — but none has ever told him how to keep his clothes clean — I had to think up that one, I have bought him a packed of women's monthly pads once a week for the last ten years). But I love him for his incredible courage, and his good humour when he meets with kindness and consideration. [. . .]

With the 'archive' out of my hair I can now set to work. MacGibbon and Kee not playing ball yet. But signs. But I expect all will be undone with all hardcovers going off the market (except the coffee table ones), nothing but paperbacks that display weapons for copulation and slaying.

No need to bustle, when you are ready,

From yours,

F.S.

To William Plomer, *Sussex*

Alexander Turnbull Library

16 September 1970

Dear Plomer,

It has been as though one of those up-to-date Hurricanes called Flossie or Maybelle, a fancy female name anyhow, has swept into my house.

First I found myself turned down by the best University (Otago) in this country on an application to become for a year a kind of Honorary Fellow (on a rather Handsome Honorarium, I think about $4000), so I might have some hopes of what I might dare to call an Autobiography (with things not quite so tight while I did the work). Oh well — but foolish Academic Dumb Clucks or Boobies or whatsoever! I would have split up my papers somewhat and presented some of them to Otago. And all no go. So I made my big decision for a package deal with the Turnbull, and up came the Chief Librarian all hot on the scent and a very pleasant very efficient man to deal with. The place is now clear of vast untidy heaps of MSS TSS Documents Letters, great cartons of them accompanying him in his taxi.

Well, I went straight to the point of Item Plomer-Sargeson, and after he had told me the True Glover Story (alas poor Denis, hopelessly sick and alcoholic, fed my letters not too many at a time to an agent who threatened Turnbull with Texas, hence the final total of $550 was quite a strain on resources), he went on to say that our Government is niggardly with funds despite the cultural denudation threatened by America (as though they can't be satisfied with their own Dust Bowl)!

I didn't know before, the Library derives its funds from a Society of Friends and Well-Wishers (I mean for purchases of the kind), also from sales of prints made from its own priceless material, drawings and paintings made by draughtsmen and painters who accompanied Cook and early explorers (one early painter I am very fond of, Augustus Earle, he was on board the Beagle with Fitzroy and Darwin as far as South America, but afterwards he did visit NZ and some of his paintings are wonderfully charming).

To be shorter, the Turnbull taking our Item apart from the rest would be pleased to pay $400. Well, half is $200, and for sterling you halve again, £100. Do you feel you are being exploited? If so I think I could argue them into some increase, although not a great deal. But if you think, oh well, a hundred nickers is a hundred nickers I think Turnbull will pay pretty promptly (it's far easier for them to send money out of the country than for me).

As for the rest of my 'archive' they may eventually decide to pay me as much as $5000, but this will have to be spread over a number of years (although I'm hoping they may show me the colour of their money up to $2000, and that will include my share of our Item. All in all I will be satisfied, I care enough about my country to want to keep *some* natural assets out of the hands of the Americans. Also I'm temperamentally not the sort of person into whose hands a too goodish sum of money should ever be put.

Send a line when convenient. [. . .]

Many cheers and good cheer,

F.S.

[. . .] I've been trying to re-construct a limerick somebody told me in a pub 40 years ago, & said was by Aldous Huxley. My version, (if you know the true one, please tell me)

> Said a man to a pretty maid, please,
> If you must explore to my knees,
> In return for a kiss
> Wrap your hand round *this* —
> And pay *less* attention to these!

To Michael Beveridge, *Christchurch*

Alexander Turnbull Library

2 October 1970

Dear Michael,

Naturally I've tried to think of a way of accommodating you but I don't think there is one.

The matter is out of my hands strictly speaking. I'll explain.

When you went off with the material last year my papers weren't in my head as a means of remedying lack of income. All my hopes were on the Burns, and I had good grounds for belief that if I applied they'd have me on — in the event they did have me on in another sense, alas!

About last March I got the word about Glover with my letters and the deal he did. After that I discovered the Turnbull had funds and would be interested in what I had, and the more particularly if I could provide a complete archive.

It was then I sent you a sort of warning. But my thoughts were still on the Burns. Also I'd begun to think (not wanting to spend a damn winter in Dunedin), I might bargain with them over my papers if they'd ease up on their requirements about residence in Dunedin.

I thought since they'd previously offered me the Burns when it suited them (a personal approach), they'd personally approach me again if I indicated I was interested. Nothing doing, run of the mill, and formal notice application unsuccessful. Very bad manners.

Meantime, to be ready for whatever happened I'd fumingly wasted weeks and weeks (time off from Man of England Now) roughly sorting my papers. An immense heap of valuable rubbish, novels plays God knows what I'd *absolutely* forgotten about, nothing finished but a surprisingly great distance into several items. Then too great bundles of letters, most of the writers still alive so there must be an embargo on them meantime.

So my reaction to Otago's behaviour was promptly to do a package deal with the Turnbull, including, naturally, the items you have. And Turnbull has all except those items. Frankly I'm a little nervous about them and so am I. They are covered (inadequately) by insurance, but in the event of calamity insurance wouldn't remedy matters as total price is based on purchase of my *complete* archive — with an option on items created in the future.

So now do you see? The nature of the thesis you are engaged upon is your own affair, but it seems to me your wish to retain items is based on a fallacy — because surely you must work at the Turnbull on items greatly in excess of what you have and haven't seen and haven't a hope of borrowing.

I don't think I have treated unfairly. It has turned out that what you have can be reckoned to be worth at least $2000, and there's no hope that my deal can be finally clinched with certainty of full payment until Turnbull has possession of all that it is buying.

Of course I wish you all the luck in the world with the thesis, but theses on living authors always have their difficulties. Before you I'd turned down several pleas for cooperation, and no doubt it was the Landfall sideline which turned you into a special case (and I've much enjoyed the contact), but you see my two points. So far as possible I want to be left alone to plug along with my work, and I want to ensure I'm financially secure enough (at my age) to reduce the strain of that work.

No panicky hurry Michael, but I can't see a way out your *way*. Country Library Service will be fine. Be careful to say it's all according to Mr Bagnall's wishes, and hold on to the carton until you have my advice that the Transit Insurance is on.

Thanks for the Press cutting. But oh wicked man! I can read what was said about Barry Crump only in a *half* column.

I can't see you forgiving me, yet I hope you do (I don't forget that golden fiver you sent when I was broke),

Good wishes, [. . .]

[Beveridge did not complete his doctorate.]

To Margaret Scott, *Alexander Turnbull Library, Wellington*

Alexander Turnbull Library

21 October 1970

Dear Margaret Scott,

Alas my personal note has to be typed (an arthritic finger which typing strangely doesn't worry so much).

I have so much to thank you for, the one who set the paper business in motion. You encouraged me no end when you said I shouldn't worry too much over the chaos. I did my best in the time I allotted for the job, but results still make me go hot and cold. It seemed impossible so often to get the right sequence for two page letters, and I hope you don't hunt too long and too fruitlessly for sequences which mightn't be there anyway. People are still astonished by the appearance of my place now, a compulsive saver I'd simply tossed everything anything anywhere, nobody unless they had seen it could have any idea.

You make me blush too over my hasty annotations. Well, I can only hope there *may* be something which the future could be interested in.

I have retained some Robin Hyde material which I forgot I had and which I think came to me through her son Derek Challis. I *must* ask Gloria [Rawlinson] about it first and see what she says. She most probably knows it and has it all in typing, but I'll see, and later let you know. (It was interesting that I lately helped Gloria to discover the score of a Waltz de Thierry wrote).

Anyhow, let me know if there is anything I can do to help about Robin Hyde. [. . .]

I will look forward to writing again when I feel more recovered,

Meantime, with good and grateful wishes,

F.S. [. . .]

To William Plomer, *Sussex*

Alexander Turnbull Library

27 October 1970

Dear Plomer,

Alas I should have acknowledged yours weeks ago. But very kind of you to agree to the Turnbull transaction [. . .].

Yes, I shall be glad of the Turnbull money, glad it's to be spread too. Granada's hatchet men have just been paying me attention and it seems I'm finished with M and K (it looks as though *they* are finished too — it seems that the Big Power Boss decided some time ago to reserve Hart-Davis for cultural books — Papillon and Colin Wilson — and use M and K for the vulgar rubbish — Kavanagh, George Barker, Flann O'Brien, E.E. Cummings, Colin MacInnes, Lessing, Sargeson et al. Well, Sargeson's now chopped and who's next? I rather like the idea of a Giant Publishing Complex without any authors at all. Panther Books raging and howling for palatable authors and going unsatisfied). All this is not to say I'm not sympathetic to publishers, even tycoon ones, over the dilemma they're in with imaginative literature. But seeing it's not going to be solved in my time I anticipate being as happy as may be returning to New Zealand publishing.

Indeed I'm having a little rest at the moment as I've knocked off at last my *Man of England Now*, about 28,000 words, and a curious kind of return to the sort of thing I began with (and never had published) in the 1920's.

Oh, Otago. It's all very Presbyterian down there. Trams and buses run only about church time on Sunday. They offered me the Burns Fellowship worth about $4000 a year some years ago, but I couldn't take it because of Harry — in two senses (he wouldn't have been willing to go to Dunedin, and he wouldn't have been acceptable if he had). This time the idea was for him to spend part of the year in a Returned Soldiers' Home, and for me not to be stuck the entire year in Dunedin if I made over to the University my papers as a gift. But I must be under Suspicion. When they offered they made a personal approach, when I was willing to accept I was put through formally and run of mill. It's not worth thinking about — very Otago, worse, quite New Zealand.

Curiously though, the English professor, Alan Horsman, would I think almost certainly have been at Durham when they bestowed upon you the laurel. He's a New Zealander, an ex-Plymouth Brother, and I can almost forgive him for everything because he beautifully wrote a book about Alfred Domett, you know, Browning's 'Waring'. Domett became prime minister of NZ before he returned to England, (where in his old age he bestowed upon Browning many tips concerning the shortcomings of his versification).

A curious thing too, Horsman, a Plymouth Brother, and also Jack Bennett (yes, it is C.S. Lewis's Chair he occupies now at Cambridge). In my *Hangover* I have the boy's father intending to accompany him to university lectures in case he hears anything improper — and in Jack Bennett's young life this actually happened (I don't suppose he would ever forgive me for reviving it publicly). But my point is how *can* a person launched in this way become one of the most distinguished scholars of his day, I mean in medieval studies?

I haven't seen the American book of limericks you mention. I always thought it curious that the only copy of Norman Douglas's book [*Some Limericks*] I ever saw had been printed (I expect pirated) in Boston. I used to get thoroughly 'dirty' stories and limericks from GIs I sat next to on trams and buses during the war. And curiously, now I get the same sort of thing sent on to me from John Money at the Johns Hopkins. (Money has been very active on the American Pornography Report and threatens to send me a lot of material despite my pleas for him not to. He is a very special kind of American Lunatic).

But I like good limericks very much, and although I can't come within a mile of you in your Ballads, I do manage usually to round my own off quite neatly.

A clever young surgeon called Robb
Never stalled when required on the job.
He replied if you wrote him
I'll slit open your scrotum
And nip out a ball for a bob.

For those with cardiac wimble-wambles
No touch is so soothing as Dr Campbell's,
He prescribed methyl dopa
For the Bull of Europa —
Until he was all shame and She was a shambles.

An episcopal old party called Liston
While confessing a Convent was kissed on
His Episcopal ring: a permissive nun:
She episcopally said, I adore you my son —
And for penance she was episcopally pissed on.

A giggle? Oh well.

May your Indian summer (unknown in these parts) be elongating itself,

F.S.

To E.P. Dawson, *Itteringham, Norwich*

Alexander Turnbull Library

11 November 1970

Dear Peter,

It's a blazing shame I never got round to this pretty soon after I got your excellent September letter. Really one of the best you have ever written me, all so nicely expressed, and quite splendidly typed too.

Let's see if I can take you up on all the points you raise.

Only first, a bit of my own news. I am typing this mid-morning as it seems for the first time in years I am forced into taking a kind of holiday. This year I was determined to get a further little novel finished. I call it *Man of England Now*, and I think it's somehow related to a remark of yours — when you said once you hoped I wasn't going to abandon my typical Sargeson characters. Anyhow this is a kind of potted life-history of a little immigrant of the twenties, a bowlegged Lancashire man, a dustman. I hope I have made him as charming as I've always found his real-life model [Jim Shaw]. But of course publishing for me couldn't at present be worse. I've been axed by MacGibbon and Kee, Granada hatchet-men I imagine, and one can well imagine that pretty nearly all imaginative work presents great difficulties for all publishers, not to mention authors. I wonder how George Barker gets on. I noticed his new book from MacG and K lately, and there was a clever (too clever, perhaps I mean for his age now), extract from it in the *London Magazine*. I read it with very great interest indeed, and particularly relished his right on the ball observation about McLuhan. Anyhow here I am with two short novels in hand, and God knows how I'm going to face up to touting them round the publishers at my age. Very curious isn't it, when one finds one's name entered in the Oxford Companion (along with such as Dame Ngaio, Patrick White, and George Barker — although he gets more lines than any of us —) without a hint of a publisher standing on one's doorstep. [. . .]

You make me envy you and England and the summer. And that's not to mention the garden. Mine is limited now to peppers, which I breed very large without a hint of heat in them. A few tomatoes. But I have a good many fruits, paw-paws apples peaches loquats and now at last I'm hoping a few avocado pears will show up. My lovely custard apple alas, had to make way for the room I built on for Harry (who incidentally should now go into the Ranfurly Home but won't, he takes one hell of a lot of looking after). [. . .]

And Pearson's book, do please keep it. That book has become a kind of NZ background novel, and has lately been issued by Pauls in a limp cover. I am delighted about this. Such novels mean we less than heavy-weight people can do our literary ballets in front of a mise-en-scene instead of a vacuum. [. . .]

I made pumpkin rum once when I was in the hut, hung it up in a net after packing with sugar, under corrugated iron roof where it was pretty warm. It turned out very well, although I thought the pumpkin shell would leak and piped off a little too soon.

Now no more this time, dear Peter, but clearly, if I don't get stuck into another of my damn 'Works' I will much hope to write again before too long. I expect you have heard that Janet thinks of getting off again to America.

From yours with much love,

F.S.

To William Plomer, *Sussex*

Alexander Turnbull Library

15 November 1970

Dear Plomer,

Clearly I must write, because clearly I overlooked telling you it was arranged with Turnbull that 'the letters must be out of bounds for writers still living without consent'. I thought that should fix it, putting it that way, with of course the copyright as a clear protection. [. . .]

How nice too about the medal, I rather hope it is not the size of a tea-tray so you can wear it instead of keeping it about the house. And yes, galloping inflation, we have it too. But fortunately among the Social Security benefits there is something called Universal Superannuation — for everybody as it says, no means test, and it has lately been raised to just above $18 a week. It's available for all at the age of 65, and 'all' it seems takes it, even the millionaires. And even then how 'all' gets by I'm sure I don't know. There's a little bow-legged Lancashire friend of mine [Jim Shaw] (migrating here in the twenties), he's one of the dustmen, but of course they are not dustmen now, they are Zone Caretakers. Anyhow he pays more than $750 a year for rent of his flat (and freeholders who must pay $100 a year for their rates cry about being bled to death). I expect I tell you this because my friend is the Man of England Now, a title deriving from Shelley's poem, which I'm never able to read without emotion. I expect because it has always hooked on to the strange brand of Anarchist-Marxist belief which has always been with me some kind of peg to swing around. [. . .]

Sorry about your winter, the peppers in my garden thrive in near-tropical weather,

From

F.S.

['the medal': in 1970 Plomer received a gold medal from the Poetry Society of the Phillipines. 'What nonsense!' he wrote to his brother. William Plomer: A Biography, *p. 318. Shelley's poem: 'Song to the Men of England', 1819: 'Men of England, wherefore plough/ For the lords who lay ye low?/ Wherefore weave with toil and care/ The rich robes your tyrants wear?']*

To Catherine Styles-McLeod, *London*

Alexander Turnbull Library

[The Mercury Theatre mounted a production of Jenny McLeod's opera Earth and Sky *(1968) for the Auckland Festival of 1970. At the end of the same year, at the age of 29, McLeod was appointed professor of music at Victoria University of Wellington. Styles-McLeod's husband Ronald and Jenny McLeod were cousins.]*

8 January 1971

Dear Catherine,

[. . .] I can manage only little notes these days. I missed Earth and Sky — I was told it was terribly noisy for the Mercury, and as I can't stand very noisy music now I didn't go. Most people who've seen it (in various parts of New Zealand) thought it was very good (except a few here agreed the noise was too much).

Had no idea of Ronald's relationship. I thought Jenny's appointment to the Music Chair at Victoria astonishing. I discovered Lilburn didn't want it anyhow. But it is said [David] Farquhar may have been a bit indignant. Anyhow Jenny certainly trails her coat. Wiping Beethoven in what seems to me an uncivilised impertinent manner. However no doubt it is all over to her and the younger people.

It is thrilling what you say about plays. You deserve success — you know how much I admire your looks your talents and perhaps most of all your wonderful intelligence.

MacGibbon and Kee seem to be hesitating a little now I've put them on the spot. Let me go, or else!

Best wishes to all,

['what you say about plays': Catherine Styles-McLeod's Mister King Hongi *(music by Tony Baker; directed by Tony Richardson) was produced at the Mercury Theatre in 1973.]*

To H. Winston Rhodes, *Christchurch*

Alexander Turnbull Library

18 January 1971

Dear Winston,

I did get my copy of [James McNeish's] *Mackenzie*, so just for what they are worth, probably not much, here are some comments.

Perhaps I put myself at a disadvantage by knowing so little about what's in Patrick White, and after a few glances at *Voss* and the *Tree* I tend to see McNeish working with these propped open in front of him. But I think all in all I am baffled, and should much hate to be asked for any sort of assessment.

Is it all a kind of return to Mrs Radcliffe? Gothic horror etc? Or even if you like Mrs Behn, the noble savage — and the ghost of Rousseau hanging around? Yet what kept coming into my mind as more apt was *The Swiss Family Robinson*, fauna and flora gratefully collected from anywhere and labelled Canterbury, and all presided over by a knowall father-artist-philosopher figure. I think McEldowney's remark about a kit-set was pretty apt, you catch the author out in a mistake over assembling his cathedral, and immediately you regret being probably bamboozled over scores of other 'constructions'.

As for the writing it ranges from 'She stiffened.', to sentences paragraphs and pages which really do appear fresh and beautiful.

Who is going to fall for all this? And who is going to say whether or not it is good to fall for it. Hope called the *Tree* verbal sludge, but I think McCauley was probably fairer when he said (I think), 'this is not a novel it's a meta-novel'.

I suppose it's all the old problem about a possible work of art in one's lifetime. (Does Ulysses wear well after the years? It's my impression it doesn't, yet it is in part an engenderer of *Mackenzie*.)

I found I left off reading about a hundred pages from the end. Too fatiguing, too fruity. Yet like McEldowney I would think it ungenerous not to admire the immense energy of imagination and writing which has gone into the book. I don't imagine I'd be much interested in what reviewers might say about it, I'd prefer to put it aside for 20 years and then try again (but of course too late, I won't be here). Anyhow I've done my duty in the *Kingdom* of Letters, I've bought the book and had a serious crack at reading it, I hope all my colleagues do as much. [Marginal note: Oh well, Republic (of letters) if you like.]

It now seems MacGibbon and Kee won't let me go — they are making a decision about reprints and a campaign to put my books over — curious they seem only now to have thought up this bright idea.

Good wishes,

F.S.

To David Hill, *Takapuna*

Alexander Turnbull Library

[Hill had written to FS to tell him his 6th form class at Takapuna Grammar School had been reading FS and A.P. Gaskell, and invited him to talk to the class.]

14 February 1971

Dear Mr Hill,

I am sympathetic, but I'm afraid I must disappoint you.

I do go up to the University very occasionally, and it's been interesting to see how the students change and yet remain the same over 30 years and more. But up there one can take a good deal more for granted. I just don't see it's my function to talk about relevance — I know it's difficult for you with television journalism, and God only knows what other varieties of the same thing, putting themselves over so speciously these days; and perhaps some simple test should be devised, a sort of either/or affair which might ensure less wear and tear for the teacher. After all there's a good deal any kid must discover for himself, and I would imagine any attempt at teaching isn't going to improve matters, on the contrary make them worse.

Why not a test of this kind? Is there the thing we call literature and is it relevant? OK give them the first forty pages or so of *Great Expectations* to read — and if they're not interested, or resist by saying yes, but it's not relevant, then OUT, FINISH. They must be left to their own boredom, and with luck that might remedy matters 40 or so years later on. But meantime I don't see that either you or I should act as drudges to this kind of person no matter how prevalent (I think temporarily prevalent), in our present world.

So with apologies and good wishes,

From yours sincerely,

Frank Sargeson

I expect you know Gaskell is himself a teacher, name Pickard — and pity when he wrote some of our loveliest of all stories he seemed to dry up.

To R.H. Morrieson, *Hawera*

Alexander Turnbull Library

20 February 1971

Dear Mr Morrieson,

May I send you a line or two to compliment you on The Scarecrow?

It has been my loss that for years I have passed it by, now I see you have written what will be surely reckoned a masterpiece of a work when it is eventually seen within the context of a good number of years.

It's not often that at my age I get so much pleasure from a new work. I hope I am suitably humble confronted with such sureness of touch in every particular. A very splendid piece of literary artistry indeed.

With every good wish to you,

It of course greatly interests me that my last surviving uncle lived in Regent street, and my Sargeson grandfather was elected a member of the Hawera Council 3 years before I was born, that's to say, in 1900.

To Murray Edmond, *Auckland*

Private collection

[The literary magazine Freed, *edited by Murray Edmond and others, ran under various titles from July 1969 to July 1972.]*

20 February 1971

Dear Murray Edmond,

Thanks for the copy of Freed which I've been intending to acknowledge for God knows how long. I haven't had much of a crack at it — I usually manage to pretend the Season doesn't exist by sticking to work, and this time for G's sake if I don't seem to have got close to the end of another book.

But good luck, a trifle enclosed, and I did read [Russell] Haley rather closely after seeing he got a good pass.

What do you younger people think of The Scarecrow? (R.H. Morrieson). I passed it by for years, now I suspect it's an extraordinary masterpiece (I expect I mean it will readily be rated as such within the context of a few more years.)

Best of luck for your own high pass this year,

Frank Sargeson

To David Hill, *Takapuna*

Alexander Turnbull Library

[Hill to Jim Traue, ATL Librarian, 9 April 1982: 'I wrote again to F.S. thanking him for his comments and making some very callow observations on how I felt it was worthwhile persevering with literature teaching in spite of the lack of response from many of the kids. FS replied immediately [. . .]'. ATL MS-Papers-4216.]

22 February 1971

Dear Mr Hill,

You make me want to cry *touché, touché*, with pain too. Yes, yes, I understand (I get some of these kids too — a few years later on, when they've had a touch of Oakley or Kingseat or Waikeria: and at my age! my God! their hopelessness & their boredom, and both can be infectious!)

Let me say I am perhaps mainly touched because I see you love them. So do I (also when I was at school I greatly loved some of my teachers). But now I cannot — what would be the word? — partake. I am too exhausted. A professional writer doing his daily stint at my age. The effort, the discipline, I find literally killing: and that's not to mention the financial worry: on top of it all I have a sick bedridden friend 10 years older than myself to look after. There I think you have the inner final reason why I cannot help you. I am at full stretch, I can't cope any more, with not one single thing extra, I mean.

But my deep & genuine good wishes to you.

A few years ago Alec Pickard was teaching in Hamilton, but I noted only lately his name no longer appears in Telephone Directory. His writing came out of his graduating about 1934 (he was a contemporary of Davin), yet because of slump having to go primary-school-teaching in country. Then he married, in Invercargill, & we seemed to get out of touch, & with a family his writing ceased.

Incidentally, speaking of N.Z. literature, do you know The Scarecrow (1963, republished in Angus and R paperback 1967), by Ronald Hugh Morrieson? A book about schoolchildren with a difference. Melodramatically horrible beyond belief, yet an extraordinary masterpiece, astonishing language, & psychological insights which have probably never been equalled in N.Z. except perhaps by Janet Frame. I couldn't be more keen in putting you onto this book if you have missed it.

From yours with I hope a good dose of humility,

Frank Sargeson

To William Plomer, *Sussex*

Alexander Turnbull Library

14 March 1971

Dear Plomer,

[. . .] Frustration (supposed to be very prevalent anyhow I'm told despite the permissive society)!

All I could do was forget my sorrows [with MacGibbon and Kee] in work, and lo, I follow a long way behind you with your double life at home and abroad.

My own is called *Once Is Enough*, composed of two sections, Up Onto the Roof and Down Again, and Third Class Country. And blow me down if I'm not just finishing the revised typescript, rather more than 50,000 words I should think, that's to say 'viable' as a publishing venture. Of course some sections have already appeared (in for example that Landfall Country volume I sent you,) but by far the most of it has never yet seen the light of day. Anyhow as you know a writer's work is a great preserver of sanity.

You terrify me with your story of Forster's knitting needle (it couldn't be Gammer Gurton's turned up again perhaps?) — you remind me of a man who lived near my uncle's farm who slipped on a hillside where he was cutting manuka scrub and died when he sat suddenly on a spike of manuka he'd left behind him. The doctor told us it had penetrated six inches into his rectum.

Oh the poets! They swarm here too, but don't thrive. And the same sort of sorting out — the Wellington wallop, the Picton sound, the Waikikamoukau bellow. But some of them I like as temporary phenomena, and some I suspect may be a good deal more permanent — indeed one [R.A.K. Mason] I'm doing my best to help right now.

And Patrick White? I shall have to read him first. And the other day I was pecking at *Voss*. A NZ novelist called James McNeish (he's part Maori) has lately done a huge Voss imitation called *Mackenzie* (published by Hodder). It has its points but floundering about in verbiage by the ton I looked to Voss to see how much he owed there. Meantime I keep my conclusions to myself. But P W? I just don't know. It's said he'll be Nobel-prized soon. I think with such a writer the question comes up much the same as it does with Dostoevsky — how much is Vision, and how much is Inflated Language? Without a doubt with Dostoevsky the Vision is there, so what matter the language so long as it manages to carry it? (I find the Russian critics who slate him for his poor style and melodrama tiresome). But of course if there is no Vision, or very little, and all is depending on the language, blown up? Well! But as I say I don't know. What I do know is that I much prefer Tolstoy — how marvellous to be so great and so modest (but of course I don't mean as a person, simply as a writer judged from his own printed page.) But what nonsense I'm probably talking, I have no Russian. [. . .]

May your household flourish! My poor Harry grows more and more helpless, I'll be feeding him with a spoon before long. But he remains very bouncey.

I can happily kiss goodbye to a golden summer now that it's promising to move off in your direction.

Good wishes,

F.S. [. . .]

['Forster's knitting needle': E.M. Forster died in June 1970, and Plomer had kept his 'easy chair' as a memento. 'The springs are broken, but it's remarkably easy, even soporific,

all the same — & likely they can be mended. It is covered with a faded Wm Morris material [. . .]. And there was one knitting-needle, which had slipped down in the folds. I thought this highly characteristic of Forster'. Plomer to FS, 17 Jan 1971. ATL MS-Papers-4247.]

To Janet Frame, *New York*

Private collection

4 April 1971

Dear Janet,

I'm worried because I seem to have become *a real* non-letter-writer. I have an awful problem with Harry. At last the Ranfurly Home is ready to admit him. But he doesn't want to go. This is not unexpected — but say I crack-up? Then he's really on the rocks. In the Ranfurly he would have company good quarters and good food. He will have a room to himself if he is prepared to pay up somewhat more out of his pension — and his is now $65 every four weeks. And he will be looked after. What it means is that he wants me to go on being his drudge, and seeing he pays me only $15 every four weeks he has plenty of money left for his betting. It all looks like extraordinary built-in determination to have his own way, and built up over about 40 years. He won't discuss anything rationally with me (for instance I have suggested he go as though for a holiday, and his room will remain exactly as it is, that's to say chockfull of very good clothing he will never need, and he can come back from time to time, or for good if he is absolutely sure after a trial he wants to, but he just gets angry tells me he's not going and it's none of my business. Whatever else this is it's a kind of madness — how would one classify it?) Of course it all rather rocks me that probably the key to it all is that the Ranfurly would take about $40 every four weeks from him, and besides thinking that's too much (which for present times it isn't), he also thinks it would leave him too little for betting. I must say I can't solve this one — but I foresee a nice story about somebody in the situation (I mean *my* situation) who goes on being the drudge and then takes a terrible revenge by suiciding.

Oh well, just regard that paragraph as non-existing, a non-paragraph.

[. . .] Poor dear Jack (and at least Harry so long as he remains is a protection *there*) got me to address one of his letters to you.

No, I'm as dead as a doornail with my problem, so no more this time.

Good luck for now,

xFx

To Janet Frame, *New York*

Private collection

28 April 1971

Dearest J,

Two notes from you. Yes, thanks about Braziller, and I'm doing my best to get stuff to him.

As for other New Zealand writers, Karl and I have just written appreciations of an extraordinary overlooked New Zealander, Ronald Hugh Morrieson (*The Scarecrow*, and *Came A Hot Friday*) which we hope may be published in next Landfall (a month or two off yet). He's published by Angus and Robertson.

This very brief as I have a dreadful cold, yet must appear in Art Gallery tomorrow for 12 minutes reading for 12 dollars (such space rates!)

But much concerned about your friend Sue, and possible repercussions for you. You can depend on me to help in an emergency — in which I could help for sure up to $500, and probably go higher than that without any great difficulty.

So let that be for sure.

No more as the cold is murder quite — the only thing will be for me to make a virtue of it.

F.S.

Harry at last saw the point when I showed him a note I had from the doctor sending me to hospital, a lump on my left testis — they think it not carcinoma, a cyst (I suggested to them a neoplasm, in which case metastasis would be slow — they seemed mystified — all the top Auckland experts, but after all if *you* could make 500$ a week at 'surgery' would you bother over words like metastasis). Anyhow I'm to have more Xrays and no hurry about surgery. If I become a case what happens to Harry? — astonishingly he saw the point, and is now making not such a bad job out of the Ranfurly Home.

['your friend Sue': in March/April Frame's New York benefactor Sue Marquand had been mugged, then taken ill, then confided to Frame that she was about to leave her husband. Frame told FS that this, plus noise in the apartment Sue had leased for her, seemed to promise 'battalions of misfortune'. Cited in King, Wrestling with the Angel, *pp. 361–362.]*

To Janet Frame, *New York*

Private collection

18 May 1971

Dearest J,

Thanks for the one telling me about coming change of address. But meantime I'm jealous you can so readily learn idiomatic German simply by putting your ear to the wall.

I hope MacGibbon & Kee send Braziller my books promptly. Also I've now completed my Memoir (Once is Enough), but it will take time getting a copy of the text to New York. As soon as I can recover the copy I was in honour bound obliged to let Caxton see. I'll let them have it — & really shouldn't be long.

But oh am I smacked to leg! Harry died. And right in the middle of me down with Asian 'flu — I failed to get it 2 years ago, hence had no anti-bodies. I wouldn't wish it on my worst enemy.

Anyhow, suddenly, after little more than a fortnight in Ranfurly. It appears he left no will, hence tribes of nieces nephews etc, & 2 sisters will collect — & really in a way from me, because he left the amazing sum of about $2600 — part betting no doubt, but after 4 years, much I imagine because for nearly a year I charged nothing, then it's been little more than nominal (never more than $15 a month) & his veteran's pension had lately been $65. Of course I loved him, and I even admire him for his cunning — the sort of thing I would love to be capable of, but feel I could never make it. [. . .]

May you be getting by without too much worry, & of course getting your work done.

Much love,

Fx

[Harry Doyle died on 10 May 1971.]

To Charles Brasch, *Dunedin*

Hocken Library

22 May 1971

Dear Charles,

[. . .] I should tell you it looks much as though my publishing fortunes have improved. Martin Green with two others has created a new firm, and at moment he wants to make his first two books Patrick Kavanagh's autobiography, and my three little novels. Also it looks as though Caxton will cooperate.

Though all up in the air yet. [. . .]

I forgot to say I finished my Memoir (sort of), Once is Enough (two parts, I the Roof and 2 Third Class Country; and I seem to have ended with an opening for another volume).

But all has been a bit difficult. I had bad flu, the first in forty years (hence I had no antibodies it seems), and while I was down Harry went and died in the Ranfurly Home where he had been for less than a fortnight. Oh dear, how I miss him! And of course the depression which follows flu doesn't improve matters at all.

A great consolation this year has been my belated discovery of the two novels of Ronald Hugh Morrieson (The Scarecrow and Came a Hot Friday). These are so remarkable I checked with Karl, then we both did our Appreciations for Landfall without showing each other what we had written. I am happy to know Bob Dudding is delighted (and he knows we speak very sincerely our own truth, because he somehow failed to let me know that he too discovered the novels several years ago). The two are published by Angus and Robertson and The Scarecrow appeared also in Pacific Books (same firm, paperback). And dates are 1963, 64, and 67. Morrieson lives in Hawera, and I have been cautiously in touch. Anyhow you can take if from me there is little doubt about his quality at its best, and his 'thing' is an extraordinary variety of the macabre, sometimes extreme almost beyond belief.

And again, Dunedin? and you?

All my kindest thoughts anyhow,

F.S.

['my three little novels': Martin, Brian and O'Keeffe, Green's new firm, published Man of England Now, I for One . . . *and* A Game of Hide and Seek *under the title* Man of England Now *in 1972. Caxton published the NZ edition.]*

To Harold *[Harry Doyle's nephew]*

Alexander Turnbull Library

25 May 1971

Dear Harold,

There's not a great deal to tell you about uncle Harry that you don't already know.

It seemed to me extraordinarily bad luck that he seemed to pick up some pulmonary infection in the Ranfurly Home. I think they did all they could for him, but there has been the risk for years that his heart would just stop beating — and in my experience he just *would not* take the digitalis or digoxin tablets which were the only things that might have helped him, particularly if he had taken them regularly over a good long period. [. . .]

As for any will, as you might expect I've urged him for years to make one just in case (certainly not thinking of myself, I knew that was definitely out), but just to leave things a little tidier if anything happened. Of course he listened and said almost nothing. So I'm sorry it's going to be quite a job for the lawyer.

I had an idea he had a fair bit of money in the PO Bank. I know that when he went on the pension nearly 18 years ago he had saved £500. I think that amount had sunk a good bit when he came here going on for four years ago. But he's had sometimes astonishing luck with the horses, and you must pardon me for saying I charged him so very little he must have had a fair bit of pension to put away.

Now I very definitely don't want any of you to think for one moment of rewarding me in any way. That's definitely out. I was fond of him and for many years, and although he could be very difficult I think I managed to keep him clean and pretty well fed, and his room was comfortable and those were the main things. Far from any kind of recompense I would like instead if there is any sort of plaque put where he is buried I would like to make my contribution to any cost involved. Please remember this.

Your cousin Jocelyn and your aunt Grace cleared his belongings apart from a few items which you might feel like picking up sometime when somebody in the family is passing. There's for instance those very sacred objects, two jockeys' caps, a jockey's jacket with colour, and his riding whip. Also a few Turf publications. Nothing much else except shoes a potty and sundry personal gadgets which I doubt could be of much interest to anyone. Anyhow what there is will be kept meantime.

Of course I miss the Old Terror very much.

And how are you? Well, I hope. Also the family.

Please give my best wishes to your brothers and sisters, and of course your mother,

From yours sincerely,

To Christine Cole, *Wellington*

Alexander Turnbull Library

30 May 1971

Dearest Chris,

Seeing your picture at the wedding reminded me I should have written ages ago.

The will remains the same, except that I made a slight adjustment after the death of Harry (10 May, and how I miss him! I'm recovering with my own private jests — it was always understood that he would leave this world with a note in his hand from me to the Almighty, Nobodaddy, or whohaveyou saying that if he was given horses to play with, particularly winners he'd give no trouble and would be very happy. Of course it was understood that if either of us died we'd never see each other again, Protestants don't go to the same place as Catholics, no madam, very definitely).

Anyhow I've managed over about 12 months to keep the capital amount of the Estate much the same, (between $10 and $11 thousand dollars), but naturally it grows difficult — I've had very little literary income, and U.S. [universal superannuation]. plus interest doesn't leave much to come and go on. Nonetheless I've managed. And astonishingly, things seem all set now for a fresh burst of publishing in London and perhaps too, owing to good offices of Janet, in New York as well. Anyhow two books — three little novels, and a Memoir called Once is Enough. All this as you can guess is necessary encouragement for me in my age and other troubles.

(Incidentally I've been offered an O.B.E. But I wired smartly back to the GG saying not acceptable — I'm damned if I'd run along with the white slavers, Watties and the rest. How nice though when the list comes out — I'll know that everybody on it has wired back, 'Acceptable'.) [. . .]

My researches on Pukekawa have come up with the result that not only was Demler much suspected, he was grilled by the demons over long periods — it is said until he was reduced to wringing his hands and a ghastly smile. 'Yes, but you've still got to find the bodies haven't you?'

If this is true, then for weeks he was under strong pressure to jack up a few leads in another direction. He knew that Thomas in his daughter's view was a bit of a pest. He had been round the district a long long time and may have known where the axle was — why not heave it into the river where he'd already disposed of a body? And the unwrapped parcel — if that's how his daughter felt would she have taken it along with her when she married? More likely she left it behind — for Demler to put in the wardrobe of the room from which one of the bedspreads was taken.

It's to be hoped Temm does his stuff before the Appeal judges — and after all

he was hamstrung by a jury — he could only *strongly* point in Demler's direction at the risk of antagonising a probable moralising bunch of mediocrities. With luck the judges could say, Look, on the evidence nobody can be convicted.
['Pukekawa': the so-called 'Crewe murders' of 1970, which resulted in the wrongful conviction of Arthur Allan Thomas. Jeanette Crewe's father Lenard Demler was also a suspect.]

To Father John Weir, *English Department, University of Canterbury*

Alexander Turnbull Library

13 June 1971

Dear John Weir,

I was sorry to hear about the depression, but felt I could say nothing that might help. [. . .]

Perhaps it may be a trifle of help if I say I have lately suffered the loss of my friend of nearly forty years. He was ten years older and for the last seven or eight years it has been clear he could die any moment. Now he's just not there any more. (And how curious, two days afterwards a stray black cat turned up at the porch and door at his side of the house. Very stray. I'm still not able to get near it, but it now takes for granted the food I provide it with. I expect apart from 'superstition' the broad generalisation would be that nothing goes out the window without something coming in at the door). [. . .]

I have seen your little Baxter book [*The Poetry of James K. Baxter*] noticed in Herald and Star by people who have had very little to say. I shall buy it. I don't much go along with these Celtic talents which throw off masterpieces between pub-crawls — (later to become Jerusalem-retreats — but were the Essenes quite like that, I expect the Scrolls of the Master will be deposited in Maori burial-caves). I don't expect you to pardon me — there is and always has been something dismayingly *provincial* about Baxter. I should hate to tell him about the death of my friend, even tell him about my friend. There is something so awful about *provincial* caritas! And that thought leaves me with nothing more to say.

Good wishes to you anyhow,

To Dorothy Sutherland, *Oamaru*

Alexander Turnbull Library

[Sutherland had come across an allusion to FS's Wellington friend Don Doran in Winston Rhodes's Twayne biography, and on 23 June wrote to FS to ask 'what sort of man he was. I believe he was exceptional, but perhaps that is because he was my father'. ATL MS-Papers-4261-166.]

27 June 1971

Dear Mrs Sutherland,

Thank you for your note, and indeed I do remember your father (I called him Don, but I also remember that his name was Dominic).

I looked up the reference to him in Rhodes' biography, and see it is very brief. So how strange that you should write when I have lately put into order a kind of memoir which I drafted out about twenty years ago, but have since done nothing about [Marginal note: I mean until now]. (I lent much of the material to Rhodes to write his Biography, and that's how he comes to make that reference to your father).

Well, before too long I think a publisher, either in NZ or in London, will be bringing out this memoir (which I call, *Once is Enough*) — and in the final version I have written about 2000 words (roughly six or seven pages) about your father, telling of my affection for him, and giving a sketch of some of his philosophy of life as I understood it at the time. I so much agree with what you say about him — wisdom humour intelligence, and I think he had a wonderful sense of values, although I think it would sound to me just a little too conventional if I described it in terms of high or low. He meant so much to me at that time of my life, that he determined a good deal of my later activities and development. And if I have in fact achieved anything, as some people say, then I can never cease to be grateful to your father.

In those days in the late twenties I would have much liked to know the family, but I think it was part of Don's philosophy (as I explain it in my account) not to introduce me. And yet I saw some of you once. It was in the depression years and I was on a short visit to Wellington. I was determined to see something of your father and was on my way to calling at your home, when there he was — attending to some plots of cultivated land up the hillside (sustenance-men's gardens I think they were, vegetables). Anyhow we had talked our heads off, and I was saying goodbye when he pointed down to the roadway and said there was his wife on her way home — and I can't remember how many children, girls, but tagging behind was the little boy, his only son I think I am right in saying.

We never wrote letters to each other, but each time he was in Auckland (visiting I think a married daughter — was it you?) he came to see me, and by some miracle never failed to find me at home. The last time I saw him would be in 1948 or 1949, very soon after I had been fortunate enough to build this little house. Yet because he never seemed to want me to write to him, I had to rely on another Wellington friend for news of his death (he saw the notice in the paper). I was much disturbed, and I think it was then, or soon after, that I began to write the memoir I have mentioned.

Well, this must be all for now as I find myself rather over-loaded with chores, including the endless writing. But if you would like to write again there is a little thing that would help me very much. In my memoir I have said that your father belonged to and grew up in Taranaki — and that must have been my memory when I was writing. But now I remember that sometimes in the last twenty years when I have thought of Don I have somehow connected him with Hawkes Bay. I have a strong notion one of these localities is the right one. Could *you* do me the great kindness to put me right.

And one last thing for the moment — again it was part of his philosophy, he either never had or would never let *me* have a photograph, snapshot, anything. Is there anything that could be spared? To reward you I am sending you a rather nice picture of myself, taken lately when some Takapuna people and a sculptor friend put a bronze head of me into the local library.

With all my kind wishes, and please do not trouble yourself too much on my behalf, but one or two little snippets would gratify me — I expect there would be a good number of grandchildren, even great etc. now?

From,

Frank Sargeson

I envy all who are descended from him. I think I would have been very very happy to have had him for my father.

I remember too he told me of a daughter who won at the Convent School a gold medal for Irish history. Were you the one? And your mother — does she still live?

To R.H. Morrieson, *Hawera*

Alexander Turnbull Library

11 July 1971

Dear Ron Morrieson,

May you have continued to be busy! For myself I've doubled up on my business — I find that nothing else will enable me to forget that my dear Harry is just not there any more. (He was always very good at variations on a theme — you too, as your work shows. Once when I said we couldn't keep the wolf from the door he said well, we'd just have to keep the door shut. And I made use of that in a story. But the other day I heard the best wolf-door story yet. One must be careful to keep the wolf from the door — in case it should get out).

It seems to me probable that Robinson told you I read your Pallet for him. I put in a much-recommending report and lend him the text of my Landfall piece in case it might help too. I hope you have had some results by now. I *very* much hope so, but more than that I won't say at the moment. Try to pardon me for my presumption in looking at your unpublished work — I felt on balance it might possibly help if I did the job.

I hope your present muddle is at least not worse than mine. If not, may you be a little cheered by Stead's comments. I think what he has written is very good.

Do let me hear sometime if you can spare a moment between musick and whatnot,

From yours constantly,

To Phillip Wilson, *Wellington*

Alexander Turnbull Library

13 July 1971

Dear Phil,

[. . .] I have to write this morning as Ron Mason died last night. I sent a wire to Charles Brasch, but thought I would write you. A news item not too readily picked up perhaps. I worked away at Seath, also Gair, on Ron's behalf and of course got nowhere. I can't help feeling a little vindictively pleased the bastards may feel a slight pang at least, now.

Yes, Taranaki, is it specially like that? — I daresay it is. Did I tell you that Morrieson lives (and has lived all his life, and I think he is 47, is it? — in Regent Street Hawera — the street where lived until a few years ago my last surviving Sargeson uncle. My Sargeson grandfather was elected to Hawera Council in 1900, three years before I was born. I believe Morrie- has been much rocked and sent to the booze lately by the death of his mother. Apparently he leaves himself out of his books — he teaches music and travels round the country with dance bands. Anyhow no doubt he convinces you he knows one hell of a lot about the Taranaki Kiwi. (I am not suggesting by the above he is fairy-like, I'm told the reverse, he is big, and popular in pubs). Anyhow I've seen he's been at least invited to the P.N. Writers' Conference — which I shan't be attending, I agree with you.

Thanks for comments on my Note — I thought Karl, young and clever did very well, being y and c he's surer of himself than I am, I'd rather be sure of Morrieson.

No more now (Ron's funeral is Thursday), and we're getting Curnow to be spokesman,

All best,

F.S.

To Phillip Wilson, *Wellington*

Alexander Turnbull Library

12 September [1971]

Dear Phil,

I've fallen down on responding to a previous note of yours, so here's rightaway to your last.

It seems you weren't at Palmstn N, and I seem to remember I saw a list with your name on it. I'd hoped you might have been able to give me some account of Morrieson (I believe he had beer for breakfast, and was generally shot and incoherent). As for Jim B, the story is he is now cuckoo beyond recall — faints with horror at the sight of a contraceptive of any description and insists that prayer and trust in the Lord will fix everything, even a string of pregnancies. I sound gossipy and malicious — which I am as I've had the backwash from some of the boring pieces who have made the pilgrimage to the Holy City to throw themselves into the arms of the Master (the Lord save me from young women I've been rash enough to give my telephone number to — mainly as a piece of risky strategy for removing them off the doorstep in the direction of the street). But seriously, far from leading young people into the Light I would think Our Poet is a good deal more a Prize Buggerer up. But I may be MOST UNJUST.

I'm glad if you find things tolerable. For myself I find myself singularly unable to adjust to Harry's not being there any more.

Of course work is the Anodyne. I wrote a note on Mason and quite a piece on the reissue of Yate's Account for Bob, and have lately finished a kind of fable, (I call it The Power of Thought — to be taken ironically), but Bob doesn't yet say whether it's acceptable. I expect I envy you the fee, these days, you must get for your Listener pieces. Poor Janet is a great worry at the moment as this American go doesn't seem to be working out too well — though I expect she'll finish some long piece of fresh work and things will come right again. She's been very kind getting Braziller interested in my work, but my God, what with dealing with Martin Brian and O'Keeffe in London and also the Caxton, I now find myself able to provide texts only by laying out I should say about $80 to $100 for photocopying.

It seems I now have a contract with M B and O'K, but there are so many hold-ups I wouldn't be surprised if they never get off the ground. Hard cover novels are simply a non-commodity. I got the wireless Current Affairs man to do a telly feature which turned out quite well, Jack Lee, Dave B. Shadders and myself — but it won't be seen down South (Wellington arrogance somebody said).

I got round to [Solzhenitsyn's] Cancer Ward and thought it most agreeably humanist and not morbid, a most worthy novel. What will I do? I think [. . .] perhaps another Memoir, Vol 2. [. . .]

No more this time,

['Yate's Account for Bob': a review of William Yate's An Account of New Zealand, *introduced by Judith Binney, for* Landfall, *September 1971.]*

To Dorothy Sutherland, *Oamaru*

Alexander Turnbull Library

3 October 1971

Dear Dorothy Sutherland,

Just a note — and more compliments. It is immensely nice of you to suggest that what I have written [about Don Doran] should be left as it is. I have been thinking and thinking and wondering if there is a real problem. Your letters have helped me. I have of course written of Don as I saw him, and recorded what I seem to remember he told me. There are no sensational revelations — I have tried to write this entire memoir so that the only one who might in the view of some people be shown up in a harmful way is myself. I think readers nowadays would be interested and amused to read his views on how to establish a happy and stable marriage — with the one possible exception, your mother. But who knows? As well all know women in a good many ways are more perceptive than men, and it is quite possible there is nothing I record, no matter how imperfectly, which would be news to her. Anyhow there is such a time still to go (a hard-cover book is rapidly becoming a non-commodity), publishers are in such difficulty, and I expect I am among the lucky ones with prospects of being published at all, let alone questions of profit and loss.

And the compliment? You remind me again you are your intelligent father's intelligent daughter.

By the way the title of this memoir is *Once is Enough*, as I think I have told you. And it is divided into two parts, *Up onto the Roof and Down Again*, and *Third Class Country* (this latter referring to King Country land classification). The *Roof* part has already appeared many years ago in Landfall in four parts, of which I have photocopies. I will hunt out a set and let you see them shortly — they will show you the tone of the thing, but I don't there get round to bringing in your father (who, I may not have told you, I never mention by name anyhow).

The new section of my memoir which is far from being written yet I am calling (I think), *More Than Enough*. Here and there I intend to refer again to Don (after all, it was interesting that although for nearly a year and a half we rarely went twenty four hours without seeing each other, we went another twenty years with very rare meetings indeed; and although during that time I — if I don't sound too immodest when I say so — had advanced somewhat from being a nobody to a somebody, we never ever exchanged one single letter so far as I can remember). [. . .]

All good wishes, [. . .]

Frank Sargeson

You know, it is perhaps a bold request (one which might prompt your husband to say, 'Look this bloke is getting a bit too up-and-coming') — but you don't happen to have a snap of yourself to spare do you? I know what you looked like as a baby-in-arms, & as a little girl — but for some reason my imagination fails to picture you in any of your maturities. I hope I don't sound too insulting when I say I'm interested because it seems clear to me that you were your father's most intelligent, also favourite, daughter.

After all, I have to put up with the visual exposures of me which from time to time get themselves printed.

Just ignore this if it doesn't attract you one scrap.

F.S.

To Phillip Wilson, *Wellington*

Alexander Turnbull Library

24 October 1971

Dear Phil,

I very much hope to God things do come right for you and your work eventually. I'm all held up again at moment, dispute between Green in London and Caxton Press over who's to pay what in cooperative publishing. I plug away at work and keep out of it. But Karl yes, his Smith's Dream is out at last. Very readable. He's kinda followed Graham Greene and kinda written a B.O.P. [Boys' Own Paper] adventure story, making the hero from the Left instead of Right, tying it all up with the [Viet] Cong etc. Intelligent stuff, it could be popular and DO GOOD. I hope so, though perhaps better if Muldoon perhaps read it by accident and found something had got under his skin. You'll get pleasure from this book.

Oh shite it's too kind of you to tell me about Melville's row with the Missionary Societies. I'm as ignorant as hell though I pretend not to be and took a wild shot in the dark about not being congenial to Christians. I've read some letters of Melville in the Portable Melville, and they are very damn good (Of course you know the Americans didn't hesitate over doing a Portable Poe).

Don Binney is the husband of Judith Binney (or was, I think she has been divorcing him). J.B. is Musgrove's daughter. Ian Hamilton took her excellently to pieces for her Kendall in the Polynesian Journal. I should say she's about the sloppiest writer we've produced, and the irritating thing is she hasn't a notion that she is.

I thought the Landfall one of the most interesting Bob has produced. Lively new poets, Don Binney very good indeed, but I thought that piece by Hilliard ['Encounter'] the most *readable* thing he's ever done (I'm not certain about the actual working out of the story though — I expect it somehow reached me because I so well remember when I was under twenty finding myself in railway carriages full of only Maoris going down to Okahukura, and some of them — the more intellectual looking ones — would now and then scowl in my direction and draw their hands across their throats. I used to look out the window mildly terrified). But Beveridge (Davin-cum-Duggan?) looks as though set for a career if he can stand being penniless and impose the discipline (perhaps switch over to something slicker and perhaps profitable?) Well, I was interested anyhow.

You are too kind. I speeded with the Mason and committed two tautologies plus no doubt much else. [. . .]

Karl gets off to Menton soon (strictly speaking he shouldn't have it, but he gets no envy from me — though I'm sorry for one or two others). Janet is my headache — she's caught in America this time, and it would take $500 I think to tide her over. My thinking and shrinking cap is fitting so tight I have a headache.

Fond wishes

F.S.

To the Mayor of Auckland

Alexander Turnbull Library

6 November 1971

Memorandum for the Mayor of Auckland [Dove-Myer Robinson]

The enclosed invitation seems to have reached me by mistake. I have lately been active in the matter of Public Lending rights for New Zealand authors.

My views have been publicised in the Listener and on television. On sound radio I have explained my reasons for declining the honour of becoming an O.B.E.

But sir, none of these matters seem to have penetrated very far in your direction.

I have no intention of being present at the opening of an expensive Library when our country's most distinguished poet, R.A.K. Mason, has lately died while living very close to the breadline despite all the endeavours of his friends and colleagues to win even a gesture of support from public figures who should know better but clearly do not.

Frank Sargeson

To Charles Brasch, *Dunedin*

Hocken Library

14 November 1971

Dear Charles,

I have several times been on the point of writing you.

I have been kept quite busy (the Caxton and Green in London continue to dispute over terms for a joint do, first of the three little novels, to be followed by *Once is Enough* — so 2nd part of autobiography *More Than Enough* seems appropriately named — I worry at it daily).

But oh dear, the worries we all have. I am a little too close to Dorothea Mason [R.A.K. Mason's widow] for my comfort. I am most sorry for her, but she gets terribly muddled. Then there's Janet, in a sense stranded in America for the time being. She has shelter at Yaddo until about 10 December, then I think she goes again to the Bahamas with her Marquand friends (who — who can measure American madness? — are separating, yet going on their winter holiday for the last time: and according to Janet the Inflation has cost them half their income). Anyhow Janet seems to have been penniless literally (and among her items of information was the harrowing one that her black ((as you know there are no negroes or negresses now, and how sex is indicated I'm not sure)) friend [Elnora Coleman] has drowned herself in the East River. This did rather send me up the wall as Janet has such a thing about water, her two sisters, and perhaps you know the story that in London at one stage she went off London Bridge and got beaten up by the most formidable lesbian policewomen determined to teach her a useful lesson). Anyhow, I think with new work nearly ready for Braziller it's mainly a matter of tiding her over, and I have been able to get $50 through to her for pocket money (sending through her sister in Northcote to get round the bureaucracy, relatives may help with $100 in one year, and as the husband is judged a relative too, this will enable me to get another $150 through before Christmas. Fortunately I can afford this little bit of help without any difficulty).

Of course I have been a bit on edge about this present American venture of Janet's all along. I don't know whether you know about the two Californian painters, Paul Wonner and Bill Brown (Isherwood stays with them sometimes) — it was on account of Bill that she was set on going. I felt very helpless but said almost nothing as she is of course so intelligent. Anyhow it seems to be now all finished and surely it is probably remarkable that she still survives. Anyhow none of this is intended to worry you or suggest any obligation — I've a notion the worst is over, and emotionally and financially she'll come as right again as she ever is.

I tend not to read her books nowadays (though I buy them), so I haven't much idea what is in Intensive Care (though I rather intend to find out).

I was touched that you used your lines about me in Father Mackay's book (another one bought but little read so far. Karl's novel is of course like a Boys' Own Paper story with a Left hero instead of a Right and a sort of dolce vita touch thrown in (adultery with one's own wife) to bring all up to date. I thought it all most agreeable and refreshing reading. If K's not careful he'll become known as the NZ Graham Greene.

I was much interested in your linking Mason with Ursula Bethell — I hadn't thought of that, but of course it is dead right. I felt a little sorry for you though about your note because I know you never greatly cared for Mason's work, and who can be sure? — events may prove you right. [. . .]

And Yate? In 1948, just the once, Musgrove called on me, bringing with him his perhaps 7 or 8 year old daughter — I shouldn't say it, but a distinctly trying aggressive female brat! Dudding has sent me the photocopy of a long letter from her ticking me off for scholarship which 'falls short of his prejudices'. I suggest you don't miss this in next Landfall together with my brief answer. You could be amused.

You raise with me a smile over *MacKenzie* — it seems to me that anybody who could read the last 100 or so pages could read anything, say a thick volume of speeches by Sir Keith Holyoake.

Best wishes Charles, I think often of you,

F.S. [. . .]

[. . .] And oh oh oh! I received from publishers two little vols of Czech verse, trans. I and J Milner. All very nice, but how can I *judge*. I must think more about this problem.

[Judith Binney's letter and FS's reply appear in Landfall, *December 1971.]*

To Dorothy Sutherland, *Oamaru*

Alexander Turnbull Library

14 November 1971

Dear Dorothy Sutherland,

[. . .] I nearly overlooked your trip which must have been wonderful. I have thought that perhaps with a little luck I might be able to shout a pensioner couple I am fond of some sort of trip as far as the Haast early next year. It would mean blowing in a good lump of my resources, I'll have to see. But Arrowtown — I stayed for a few days once with my writer friend G.R. Gilbert (alas, he doesn't write any more — his books were *Free to Laugh and Dance*, and *Glass Sharp and Poisonous* [Marginal note: Also a light one called *Love in a Lighthouse*] — he went all Buddhist and carried out a sort of 'burying' of himself by going back into the Airforce) his wife Joy, and two children — the boy, Miles, was my godson. But the Buddhism didn't seem to work too well, one day when the two children were playing together they played at hanging, and Miles was hanged, a very shocking affair. Anyhow Bob and Joy went to Arrowtown after the war intending to build their own *pisé* house (which they did), introduce all sorts of exotic plants into Central (which they did, but whether they survive or not I don't know). Lately I've rather lost touch with them (I've never got over a feeling of being such a washout as a godfather, there was a replacement for Miles, but I wasn't asked to sponsor, and indeed I would have had to refuse if I had been asked. I expect their house still stands in Arrowtown, and indeed it was such a fine specimen of its kind I would think it could stand almost to the end of time. To be at Arrowtown was as though to be on another planet, and I mean the people as well as the terrain. It was early winter, I am sure you would know it all exactly.

I think I will try to catch the mail with this.

Yes, there is one photograph (you holding the child) in which you most strongly recall to me your father. I expect there must have been times when your husband has felt he married your father as well as yourself. Or perhaps you have for the most part kept it all close within yourself. Personal magnetism (for want of a better expression), can be a very real, not to mention very devastating, affair.

To R.H. Morrieson, *Hawera*

Alexander Turnbull Library

12 December 1971

Dear Ron,

Believe me I haven't been wholly idle over shots at trying to lend you a hand. What I am trying to say is that something more is required than writing an appreciative note on your work. I do confess though I'm wary these days about helping people — I've got myself into some pretty messes in my time.

Quite sometime back I wrote my new London publishers (my old ones were eaten up by Granada and dumped me) and said I knew a writer here who was a master of the macabre etc, and they only had to say the word and I'd see they saw something. They have never yet replied. But nothing surprising, they were three blokes who were sackees from MacGibbon and Kee after the Granada act of cannibalism. They seem to have launched themselves now with a book by the dead Irish poet Patrick Kavanagh called Green Fool, and it is my undeserved good luck to be their second shot with a book in February and another in April-May. But their capital consists of bank over draft ('we seem to have convinced our bank manager we know what we are doing'). Later on I shall remind them I mentioned you, and what do they think? (Of course I'd get on much better if I could buy up half a dozen paperback copies of The Scarecrow, but no luck despite all my enquiries).

I think you must have sent your new typescript on to Rutherford as you mentioned, as I met a R traveller in a bookshop the other day who seemed to think a typescript had come in from you. I took the liberty of inquiring about what they would do with it, and he mentioned W.H. Allen — which rather pleased me as WHA publish Janet Frame in England, and Janet is due back from USA early in January (like all of us at present she too is broke), I'll get her to read The Scarecrow and see if she could recommend you to W.H.A. So you see. But I'm very conscious I'm poking my nose in, and that's sometimes disastrous. Anyhow Janet will almost certain be staying with me a few days, so at least I can thoroughly acquaint her with your masterpiece.

If you are in a jam for a few dollars I can always help. Until 1966 (that was til I was 63) I was never too far removed from the breadline. But then my 94 year old aunt widowed without children died and God knows why she disapproved of me as much as anyone hadn't let me out of her will. Since then what with Universal Superannuation I get by and so do a few people I'm fond of.

Strange, I envy you your music. I've had no real chances of access to a piano since 1925. I wouldn't say I love writing. But I've learned an awful lot about discipline and all the rest of it. If anything of mine is any good it's come from the hardest work of all the work jobs I've done.

Pardon this garrulity, and all good wishes,

To Marcel Aurousseau, *Sydney*

Alexander Turnbull Library

18 December 1971

Dear Marcel,

So soon again it seems. May you survive (if you wish to)! May you too be well taken care of, and I say this last because how clear this need becomes for all of us. This year two of my cousins have died, one younger than myself. But what I have felt most has been the loss of my friend for many many years. Ten years older than I am, I was never able to do all I wanted to for him until about four years ago, when I was fortunate enough to stand the expense of enlarging a little this cottage house. So he did have those years in a comfortable room which is now devastatingly empty — and all the worse on a day like this when the peppers and tomatoes outside his little verandah are coming along nicely and the sun is so bright I have to screen it out. Forty years ago he was much in Australia — with his horses, his own and those he trained for other people. In his time he did quite well at the gallops in NSW and Vict — until alas, a horse that should have won didn't (according to the Inquiry Committee) and that was the finish of his career both here and there. An Irishman, impossible at times (like myself), but there you are we did manage to get along over about 4 decades.

And for a moment I continue along this line — communication is so bad between us and you may not have heard that Beaglehole died suddenly not a great many weeks ago. So there goes our one and only OM (living), and although I knew remarkably little about him and met him only once about 15 years ago, I am sorry for the gap it leaves in the line of the older literary gang.

May your own year be fruitful! Mine hasn't been too bad. [. . .] 3 little novels of mine come next in February (so they say, and they have paid me half the advance) under the somewhat catchpenny title of *Man of England Now*. Then in April? May? they say they will follow with *Once is Enough*, the first half of my autobiography (kinda, and there have been so many delays I'm at present calling the second half, *More than Enough*, but there's much to write yet, and the list of my ills, from hypertension rheumatism and the rest at present add up to a rather frightening total). Anyhow, we all fling our bread upon the waters don't we — and it's not for any of the flingers to know what exactly may happen then is it?

All my kind thoughts go to you. And to your wife too. And I nearly forgot — in the latest number of Landfall there is a most beautifully written biographical note on Beaglehole by E.H. McCormick, (our best critic), and with luck I will be remembering to send you a copy of the number.

No more for now, but many cheers,

To William Plomer, *Sussex*

Alexander Turnbull Library

[E.M. Forster's Maurice *(1913–14) was published posthumously in 1971.]*

9 January 1972

Dear Plomer,

I must send you a note to say how interested I was in Forster's Maurice. How it renewed all my admiration for the man as a novelist! I expect you have been familiar with this work for perhaps forty years — I expect you learned something of your own skill as a novelist from it, I know I certainly have even at my age now.

But of course there is his subject to be taken into account, and what reserves of knowledge he had about it. I found his [terminal] note [to *Maurice*] about Edward Carpenter extraordinary, I had no idea despite my having discovered Love's Coming of Age about the time I left school — I think for a time I used to sleep with it under my pillow. Also I remember an anecdote Cresswell told me about Carpenter. It must have been in the twenties not long before C died. D'Arcy got to see him (living at the time if I remember right somewhere around Guildford), and he was sitting in a garden shelter with room for two but only just. I think he had had a stroke and was partly paralysed. Anyhow he asked D'Arcy to sit beside him and the position of his hand suggested he would welcome a handshake. But apparently he hadn't the power to withdraw his hand, and D'Arcy, not understanding, went on holding it — until at last he tumbled. Paralysis and embarrassment had robbed Carpenter of speech as he made pitiful endeavours to free his hand. Well, maybe — but (I expect I am displaying my ignorance) I don't remember F's making any reference elsewhere to C in his writings.

Anyhow I still much deplore the Sunday Times pages which I think gave a very false idea of the whole work (but perhaps the Estate was trying to make a bit of money). And particularly unfortunate when the novel, worked out over so many years, finally turns out to be perhaps the most beautifully balanced piece of work the man achieved.

And of course I've been sent back to Aspects of Forster which you so kindly sent me. I don't appreciate Malcolm Bradbury any more now than I did then, but I have got rather more from it this time (besides finding out about Jack Sprott).

The weather too hot and humid, but my peppers and tomatoes this season are splendid: and I anticipate proofs from my madcap publishers (God bless them) any moment.

With all good greetings, and to Charles.

Byebye for now,

F.S.

To Robert Buckingham, *[UK]*

Alexander Turnbull Library

[To E.M. Forster's 'friend and protector', who was planning to visit New Zealand with his wife May.]

10 February 1972

Dear Robert Buckingham,

[. . .] I remember (and it must be almost exactly 20 years ago) your kindness in writing to me when E.M. Forster had become a temporary cot case nursed by your wife.

Well 20 years!

Yes, I would much enjoy a chat. The trouble is my little house is not really a house although no New Zder understands that. It is a writer's workshop where I happen also to eat and sleep. It has also these days become much run down. I think I am about the age Morgan Forster was at the time we were writing, I have become a bit exhausted from four years of nursing a friend who not so very long ago died. I am sure you will understand about the place a writer much wants always to defend so that he can press on with the one thing left to him, his work.

I think I would suggest some place in Milford perhaps where we could have coffee or whatever, where I could meet too your wife, and of course Miss Evans whom I do not know, but once very nearly met through a schoolteaching friend of mine.

Anyhow I am making it over to you. I have a telephone no. but do not have it listed. 496,999. Perhaps you have a better idea, and I shall be glad to hear.

I hope your health is good. Also, do not believe people who tell you this country is beautiful. It resembles other parts of the earth's surface, nothing more than that.

Yours sincerely,
Frank Sargeson

To Dorothy Sutherland, *Oamaru*

Alexander Turnbull Library

12 February 1972

Dear Dorothy Sutherland,

I thought your Christmas Card very nice, most kind of you. And now your letter, and Janet — yes, she was more or less rescued (making her sound like an oldtime fallen woman), and arrived early January. Boats send her nuts so she always has to fly. Anyhow a delightful few days before she went on to Dunedin (she is always the most marvellous companion if only she can be got to accept you, such sweetness, and I always find it comforting to communicate in monosyllables — she always knows what you have to say before you say it. I expect I sound fulsome, whatever that might mean, but J is so unique like her books — although I wish they were unique in *her* way, not the way they are).

It is a mark of her extraordinary humour that at the time of that unspeakable tragedy which you mention she wrote and told me what had happened, and Donald being a cricketer, she ended up by saying at least there was one thing to be thankful for — he had finally hit his own wicket.

Anyhow she is back in her own little tumble-down house in Ohopo in Dunedin, not too happy because of grieving about American ties, but there's one thing we share absolutely — the capacity to forget our griefs over long stretches because we become so absorbed in projecting it all onto paper. Writing apart from all else can be the most therapeutic thing.

But nice to hear about your holiday. My two little pensioners wouldn't hear of my bankrupting myself with a threesome as far as the Haast, although they have compromised by going off to a motel in Tauranga (I am glad for them to have it without me, a horrid place stinking of money worse than my own home town of Hamilton where they use dollar notes for wallpaper and spray them with odeur de butter-fat).

How wise you are about your husband not marrying your father! And I expect even your mother at some bad times may wish that she hadn't either. It's sad for all of us isn't it? — no absolutes, only relatives (and that word works in rather well there doesn't it?) The only love that lasts is the Divine Love (if it so much as exists), but some of us are perhaps conscious sometimes (and I know I have been several times in my life) that we have been fortunate enough beyond measure to have received a touch of it. I expect it's the Christian doctrine of Grace — one may receive or one may not, one can't do much about it, and one mustn't ever complain.

I must sound almost like St Thomas (Aquinas). [Marginal note: Ahem! Ahem! Meaning a cough of apology] Never mind. No more this time, but many good wishes,

F.S.

['that unspeakable tragedy': in February 1962 Frame's cousin the Otago cricketer 'Big Bill' Frame shot his lover and her parents and then turned the rifle on himself, leaving a pregnant wife and two children. See King, Wrestling with the Angel, *pp. 287–8.]*

To Janet Frame, *Dunedin*

Alexander Turnbull Library

13 February 1972

Dear J,

[. . .] Meantime though to keep you afloat. Please tell me poor pauper girl that you are how thin your resources are being stretched, and if now paper-thin I will send you $50 for stopgap immediately. [. . .]

I think I forgot to thank you for postcards, particularly the cat. I have shown it to my Blackie-Harry who now looks more than ever slant-eyed at me. He suspects I am going to have his ears pierced for large-sized earrings, though I suspect he won't mind so much a bead necklace.

I forgot too to say I managed to buy a copy of Commonwealth Short Stories — quite interesting collection except for a few lapses, and the editors stick a note in front of each story telling you what to think of it. They think you are the bee's knees and everything of that kind, you are the only one with two, Two Sheep, and A Boy's Will. Some of the black writers are very attractive, notably I thought Chinua Achebe.

By the way Mrs (Oamaru) Sutherland wrote again, and mentioned that [Bill] (Hit-wicket) Frame's wife was a friend of her husband's family. Mrs S is pretty bright, what she says in her letter shows she has read The Pocket Mirror and also Intensive Care — which reminds me, sometime, I must get that virgin plastic flask of that precious fluid posted off to you.

Pardon my gaucheries jokes that don't come off etc. BUT JUST TELL ME STRAIGHT ABOUT FINANCES,

To Janet Frame, *Dunedin*

Alexander Turnbull Library

20 February 1972

Dear J,

[. . .] Never such an impossible week. The cat bit me (full length of top and bottom canine cat teeth. Infection in 3 hours, my arm swelled up past the elbow and a thick red streak was heading for armpit. Worse thing of the kind I've ever had. Round the bend now antitoxin and antibotic every four hours for a week). But all through it I had to be busy with proofs besides trying to collate with what Caxton had sent up. Gave up and posted all the stuff back to London Saturday morning not nearly half done.

Have you seen E.M. Forster's *Maurice*? Of course name should be changed to Maurice Chatterley's Lover, and brought out as paperback pornography (by the way did you see the Truth poster

SWINDLED
AND
SEDUCED
EX-NUN'S DOWNFALL but bad luck not Patricia Bartlett.)

But About *Maurice* — Forster's friend, one of his closest [. . .], Robert Buckingham, came to see me. And his wife. Both very very nice people. It can't be true and yet it is — when he met Forster he was a policeman. Maurice's lover in the novel is a gamekeeper — yet it was written long before Lawrence, and long before the meeting with the cop. So — if you want things to happen you first write about them.

No more my dear (another immersion of my arm in boiling water) but I hope Dunedin and all is not too intolerable. [. . .]

Bye-bye for now,

To William Plomer, *Sussex*

Alexander Turnbull Library

25 March 1972

Dear Plomer,

Your letter is dated 31 January, so a reproach to me now, and my usual muddle is not really the excuse I could like it to be. [. . .] (and I put behind me proof stage of the three little novels weeks ago — and what a poor job, my black tom cat, a wild one who turned up two days after Harry died, was having a confrontation with the neighbouring neuter, and I interfered with a bare hand instead of booted foot — result, he bit me, an arm swollen to my shoulder, and I daresay my life might well have hinged on antibiotics and antitoxins. But what poor proofreading I did during that time!)

But a more striking event about the same time was a visit from Robert Buckingham and his wife — and indeed, I think the pair are still in NZ, though a thousand miles off among mountains and fjords. He had written me away back about 1949 when Forster was in trouble with his prostate. Anyhow, very nice and pleasant people and we spent an agreeable time. I even dared to remark that when Furbank had been directed to alter the name of a character in Maurice, what a pity it didn't occur to him to make a pile of money for the estate by re-naming the book *Maurice Chatterley's Lover*. Of course I rather drew my breath on the sudden thought that Buckingham had been perhaps the original of the gamekeeper — and then remembered dates and things, and they didn't work out. Anyhow this joke (?) appeared to go over very well. But a policeman for friend and protector — what noble instinct for self-preservation! I wish I could claim equal sagacity — I have had to make do with racing trainers (and I do remember one nasty pub scene during the thirties when I was very grateful), plus — but alas, sometimes it is best to draw the veil.

And I have little to tell that might interest you. You go to a party at a new university while I sit and read (wait for it!) Robert Elsmere; which I did not nearly so much enjoy as The Marriage of William Ashe (but that was so long ago so how can I be sure?) And *Hair* has visited us and been prosecuted and been found not guilty. And Germaine Greer has come and gone too without bra or briefs, but for a four letter word she has been fined. What crap! And you tell me about the books that will interest me and I so seldom get round to them! This week I set out to get into my hands a copy of [Harold Owen's] Aftermath, and this time I *will* tell you how right you were, I mean I will before too long.

The 2nd half of my autobiog. is proving devilish hard to write, More Than Enough — I should damn well think so. And the summer has been tropical, humidity up to 100 day after day yet the ground parched so I hardly dare put a foot along the street in case a match is put to my vegetation — 'and that would be all' as you nearly say in one if your ballads. (Yet when I investigated the recesses of my junble [Marginal note: jungle, but really too good to alter] on the back boundary I found several boxes of marijuana some with seedlings a foot high — and an absolute responsibility according to law!) More Than Enough! [. . .]

From,

F.S.

To Karl and Kay Stead, *Menton, France*

Alexander Turnbull Library

8 April 1972

Dear Karl and Kay,

Many thanks for the letter, and I daresay you are quite right — if you ever got round to Texidor's These Dark Glasses you would remember that the underpaid hairdresser was very bourgeois. T's Calanques was Cassis, a good long way from Menton, and all *I* saw of Provence was when the ship put in a few hours at Toulon, and from that I remember only that an old old market woman when I asked her how much said 'carter' — just like that. But what I really did see was the Zola

(Earth) country between Fontainebleau and Troyes and beyond, then it was more perhaps a lower-middleclass France right to Strasbourg (which was German). Switzerland was what you would expect, but beneath the Alps on the Italian side some of the villages were nice and the inhabitants not so dangerous-seeming as in the Zola country. I expect I must have been about the last walker. I would be surprised to hear of anyone walking my way these days.

Anyway nice to hear, and March Landfall isn't out yet, but when it is I will get the review of *S's D [Smith's Dream]* photocopied and let you have it.

Charles is just going off to read poetry in Rotterdam and seems mildly excited about it. He will be away until August. I wonder if you have heard that Paul's (bookselling, not publishing) have gone into liquidation. I don't wonder, all those hundreds of university students who stole books (or if they didn't didn't pay their bills), together with lecturers and professors (ditto in part, and I leave you to guess which part). But something of a tragedy for all of us I imagine, and particularly unfortunate when there have been rumours of the tide turning — people browned off with the telly and turning to reading again. Lately Bill Austin exchanged some letters with me and I told him that Television was in my view the Biggest Disaster to hit the Planet since the Ice Age. As for Section 7 (moralizing, alleged to be entertainment, a series centring round the probation officer ((Ewen Solon)) and his helpers, scripts by Hamish Keith and David Ballantyne ((toughies reclaimed from converting motor vehicles, fallen girls set up again only to be knocked down by bosses keen to get a slice off a cut loaf))), I told BA it was just the old-fashioned Religious Tract Society little book all over again, Jessica's First Prayer brought up to date. I also pointed out that English telly doesn't by any means fall for the trendy right up to the minute line — instead it mines Somerset Maugham. Of course it was all leading up to my point that what crap it all was when if they liked to take a look at my stories they'd find a few marvellous half-hour telly features almost written for them (A Great Day for example.) And no reply yet.

When I send the photostats I'll enclose a little cutting from Star about a certain university professor driving on the Southern Motorway fined $131 for 161mgm of alcohol per ml. Aged 55. I am told quite unrepentant, quite oblivious of perhaps moral questions (and strange when he has lately been spending rather more time than usual publicly rocking it into fellow-delinquents). Anyhow, guess who? And I forgot to mention, defended by QC.

Prevailing local winds have lately been thick with bullshit and other ordure. Germaine Greer prosecuted for four and eight letter words (convicted), 'Hair' prosecuted and acquitted, the Mayor falling into a state of coma upon looking into the Little Red School Book.

Well well well. No more for now, how's the Sirocco? Mistral? There's no tide in the Med and I understand you wade in for a swim through hair and body oil, other assorted cosmetics, and a great range of ingenious contraceptives. Do you mind if I remind you that somewhere along the Cote d'Azur there's a chapel decorated by Cocteau?

All the best, and to bunch of bi-tri-quatro-lingual kids,

xFx

I forgot — a close & especial friend of EM Forster over many years came to see me accompanied by his wife — both going on for my age, & very nice people. Not literary — he is a retired policeman. [. . .]

To Karl Stead, *Menton, France*

Alexander Turnbull Library

[Brasch had picked Robin Dudding as his successor at Landfall *in 1966. Caxton dismissed Dudding in 1972 reputedly for the late delivery of* Landfall *101 (March 1972), and he immediately set up* Islands *magazine. The first issue of* Islands *appeared in Spring 1972.]*

30 April 1972

Dear Karl,

A few lines. I expect you have heard of what looks like the collapse of Landfall. My present news is that it's doubtful whether the March number will appear, although it must be virtually all ready to. Dudding sacked, and Donovan behaving like a lunatic, and of course I am involved, because it *may be* that Caxton generally is in deep financial water, and I'm not going to be popular with my London publisher if he doesn't get paid for the 1500 copies he may for all I know have by this time despatched from London.

What is so curious is that in No. 101 there was to appear the virtually unknown Mansfield story unearthed by Margaret Scott ['Brave Love']. Surely a scoop. But it seems Donovan (perhaps personally) owns Landfall, and if he wants to incinerate this number nobody can stop him.

When Dudding is a little less harrassed I might be able to get from him a photocopy of [W.H.] Oliver's review [of *Smith's Dream* for *Islands*.]

Other news which no doubt you know, is that J.C. Reid had a daisy of a coronary attack in Albert Park (I think perhaps he had been reading Zealandia — about Father Donnolly's loving support for queer people — all quite natural, the hearties should be learning from them and the Church should help by putting them in touch with one another). Bulletins appear in the paper frequently and it looks as though JC may be spared for another period of being wedded to his car and his booze (no doubt the angels of heaven who were to turn out en masse to greet him will be wiping away their tears of frustrated joy) — the gentleman was of course the motorway drunk I told you about last time.

Except for a bit of eye-bleeding at moment I am surviving and have now more than 20,000 words of More Than Enough, all that is left for me to do except for — well perhaps never mind.

With luck I will keep you posted, and of course 'you' includes the brave little woman. Really *must* tuck up my skirts and run like a faun about my chores,

> There was an old woman who lived in a shoe —
> She had so many children
> It was clear that nobody had ever told her what to do.

Am *adoring* the reading of *Robert Elsmere* & Lockhart's *Life of Scott*.

To Karl Stead, *Menton, France*

Alexander Turnbull Library

21 May 1972

Dear Karl,

Literally a line. I've seen Dudding, and despite a bit of nagging he couldn't get Oliver to turn in a review in time. [. . .]

Oh but how can it be a line — your letter, stones of Venice, Ruskin Byron (wrong order) Baron Corvo, Proust . . . No, I never got there. I came down from Simplon through Domodossola, Lago Maggiore, Stresa, on the plain it got terribly hot walking and I took train to Milan, and afterwards got down to Genoa, then Florence, where I got dysentery and went sort of goodstrainy via Modane [Modena] to Paris Dieppe Newhaven London. Goethe went Brenner and Garda way. What I always remember about the peasants before one was out of the foothills to the mountains is that every woman had a wedding ring and a goitre.

Anyhow that trip must have been very nice, mine was very solitary, although several times I had my morals ruined, which I thought neither difficult nor dangerous (despite the sad fate of Winckelmann) in Italy.

Robert Elsmere — Mrs Humphrey Ward, Matthew Arnold's Tasmanian-born niece. She was very clever and is relevant for today — plugging for social Christianity nearly 100 years before it's become à la mode.

Man of England Now has had 3 extraordinary lead reviews — New Statesman Guardian Listener (although the Listener man didn't like me, but he still put me first [Marginal note: above Bernard Fergusson! John Hersey et al.] — photo in

Guardian. Martin Green would like to top it off with *Once is Enough*, so I have to work like the devil fighting free of moronic Donovan and Caxton — blank blank instead (must be secret meantime)

So back to literally a line. But much love to all, especially the trilinguallers,

xFx

xx

x

To Charles Brasch, *London*

Hocken Library

31 May 1972

Dear Charles,

Kind of you to write and enclose the notices (and how nice they printed my name so often and spelt it rightly, also my book and my publishers — it's all what one hopes for most from reviewers).

In fact what I've worried a little over is the little Manhire-Hotere book you sent me [*The Elaboration: Poems*] — it worries me that I seem to fail to appreciate as I perhaps should. I know very little about Manhire (is he a Maori too?), I've not been much hooked on the few bits of his verse I've seen, and remember once I questioned his worth to Stead and he rebuked me, asserting he was very good indeed (that's as I remember it). Really I think I will be very humble and ask you to instruct me sometime when you can spare me your attention.

Useless to speak of the calamities, Pauls, Landfall, and what next? But I would agree Ldfl may have had its day — 101 numbers and 80 were from you. Very remarkable! There's really only one recurring trouble I have with the younger people who clearly are not going to write in the sense that we did (and still do). So often I can't find any point of focus in their work — and so I don't find they catch my interest as I'd like it to be caught.

And Caxton, well of course they haven't got Man of Eng. etc out, their edition is still on the water and God only knows when it will arrive (that hasn't deterred the stupid Star from lifting from the Guardian *now*). Nor have I noticed any promotion going on. I don't mind this really, I want only that they pay Martin Brian and O'Keeffe, and so put me in the position of politely being able to tell them to go and get stuffed. I swore never to go back to them after Alpers (whose final bad manners I found atrocious); and I went back only because of Dudding. And incidentally, Janet is very bucked to be out of the hands of Pegasus and into those of Reeds — who are pleased to have her besides being pleased with the number of copies they can sell. Let's face it, neither Pegasus nor Caxton ever woke up to the fact they could do quite well if they only tried out of one or two writers rather more than average. They remain as publishers (I don't say printers), parish pump and provincial in all the worst senses, as for the booze the paranoia the bombast the shocking manners it all remains the tedious bore it always was.

Well, that's got something off my chest, but don't put it too much around, not yet.

Good wishes, Charles,

F.S.

As I came out wireless announced the death of J.C. Reid

To Dorothy Sutherland, *Oamaru*

Alexander Turnbull Library

2 June 1972

Dear Dorothy Sutherland,

Alas alas I don't know whether it has been my plaguey busyness or my plain cunning which has delayed my writing. I felt troubled when I read your letters, but you know sometimes when people feel their troubles too severely and write, and one delays replying — well, by that time all or most has cleared up — as indeed it must or we do in truth find life intolerable. But I sound as though I am handing out encouraging home truths supplied by the man on the wireless (and probably collected by him from the Readers Digest).

Well, never mind, I do very much hope things seem brighter. Outright downright pain is something I never can bear, yet I sometimes think it is to be preferred to that prolonged ache which comes from our having been born (without being consulted first) and willy-nilly having to live our little lives. Of course no doubt the big trouble comes from our being so solitary through it all. Nobody can really help — much, and I think at heart even the *simplist** of us knows it. [Marginal note: *I'm not sure there is such a word]

But about being busy. One of my Ponsonby (that means Auckland ghetto) friends moves steadily towards disintegration (that's a polite name for death), which one sees could be for him the great comforter, as in truth there's nothing left for him in this world. But he finds it all difficult to accept and so I do my best (feeling as false as they come) with all sorts of assorted comforts (except that I won't have him here, as he would like, because I looked after my Irish friend Harry for nearly four years and he could do nothing for himself, and this meant feeding washing everything, and now, still false, I tell myself I have done my share

— that's to say if I'm to continue writing). Anyhow all a horrid moral dilemma which I am determined NOT to take too seriously. After all think of Vietnam, think of Mr Nixon and his napalm. But that's enough.

Oh, and about being locked up to read my books in Hamilton — I think it's another form of shoplifting. Pauls, one of the biggest and best bookshops in NZ has just gone broke, and more than anything else shoplifting has done it. I know students who have their rooms lined with books, often very expensive coffee-table ones, and not one paid for. All on principle, you see — not like poor Don Clarke who so they say stole ice creams and sticking plaster and suchlike on non-principle escaped conviction and remains the (perhaps a little tarnished) Idol of a former generation of schoolchildren.

The World the World indeed, and we're all guilty!

How nice that you benefited from your stepfather. These little comforts! (as I explain to Ponsonby Jack, I can be your alleviation, I can't be your remedy — but he doesn't believe me). And comforts — my old widowed aunt who never had any children lived near me here for nearly 25 years on her own, and I was the only one of her blood in Auckland. My God the tie and drag it became, she weighed about 17 stone, went blind and lived until 93. Her house was large but much out of date and right on the beach, the land very valuable. I resolutely tried (though never very successfully) to put any HOPES out of my mind — I had heard she had said it was a blessing to have me living so close, but look what X (my brother) or Y and Z (my sisters) would have done to help if only *they* had been near. The one fibre of comfort I clung to was that she would when it came to the point show a sense of fairness. And she did, she treated the four of us equally in her will (but it goes without saying I immediately began to think *that* was unfair — I should have got more). Anyhow without this lift in 1966 I would have remained as impoverished as I'd long got used to being.

But I must finish. [. . .]

All my good wishes to you

from: Frank Sargeson

[. . .] Oh Janet Frame: a quarry has opened next to her in Dunedin so she says she is coming to live near me here. It will be very nice if she does. And Germaine Greer, a gale of fresh air no doubt, but I get bored with those lines now — *Playboy* & now imitation de luxe Playboy, the local product, *HIS*. [. . .]

NO MORE But *very* good wishes.

['locked up to read my books': Sutherland to FS, 28 April: 'My sister wrote from Hamilton yesterday & she mentioned she'd asked for some of your books at the Hamilton Library, but was not allowed to take any out. She was locked in a room full of books by N.Z. authors & had to leave her bag outside!! I'd never heard of such a thing.

It looks as if the people at Hamilton have been stealing books. Of course so many would be out of print & irreplaceable'. ATL MS-Papers-4261-166.]

To Oxford University Press, *Wellington*

Alexander Turnbull Library

9 July 1972

Dear Sirs,

It seems you are not willing to despatch a single copy of *Crossing the Bar*, a book of poems by C.K. Stead, distributed by you on behalf of Auckland University Press, and ordered on my behalf by my Takapuna bookseller, Mr Lowery.

I would like to point out that if it is your aim to lose the goodwill of the few remaining private buyers of books you are rapidly achieving that aim.

I can suggest several remedies to you. Why don't you together with other publishers and agents establish a Book Centre from which all despatches of books would be made, and which would be indifferent to the size of the order? Surely time for such a scheme is overdue. Alternatively I would suggest to you personally that you bung on a few extra cents to the illimitable quantities of that perpetual best-seller of yours the Bible (I am told that God is so confident about his continuing sales that he never so much as bothers to enquire from you how his book is doing), and use the extra profit to employ somebody whose sole duty it would be to attend promptly to single orders.

I would say I don't want to hear from you in reply to this letter (one gets very tired of crappy letters from people who want to sell you things you don't want, or who won't sell you things you do want), but it might be helpful if you were to say (in not more than a dozen words if possible) how I am to obtain a copy of Mr Stead's book — after all the author impatiently awaits from me word that I have at last obtained a copy, and am in a position to discuss with him the contents.

Without any good wishes to you at all,

Sgd F.S.

Frank Sargeson

To C.K. Stead, *London*

Alexander Turnbull Library

[Stead to FS, 28 July 1972: 'Charles Brasch turned up here one night (with a Dutchman called Rob Wendholt — or something like that) [. . .]. We took them to a restaurant here one night and Kay and I agreed that we hadn't, after all, been unfair to Charles. He really is a thoroughly mean-minded and self-protective shy little Kiwi *— not at all the civilized European you always insist he is. Of course he can't help being what he is — but for meanness of spirit, lack of generosity, spontaneity, he takes a lot of beating. You will think this rave comes out of some particular wound or bone of contention but I swear it doesn't. In fact we had quite a pleasant evening and I'm being pretty unkind in saying this without even the excuse of some particular grudge. It's just that in a different setting I was freshly struck by the qualities that have annoyed me in the past and left wondering why everyone (esp in the Sth) is so pious about such a precious old spoof whose nearest approach to gaiety is a giggle behind a coyly clenched right knee and whose jealousies and grudges are dressed up as Good Taste and paraded as Critical Judgements'. ATL MS-Papers-8220-02.]*

13 August 1972

Dear Karl,

Again it has to be short. I simply can't catch up.

Look, you simply can't write things like that (last part of your letter) to me. God knows what happens to my correspondence sometimes and provided it isn't lost eventually it will be sold. I am doing you a service, returning your text and sending copy of photocopy just to assure you I took from it only what wouldn't ever do you harm. There's nothing nasty about this, I'm simply trying to protect you.

Yes, I believe you about my book [*Man of England Now*] and you are assured you can believe me about your own [*Crossing the Bar*]. I rather like Beaver's 'lapidary' but had I been writing the notice I would have said something about the incredibly cultivated ear which (apart from all else) is behind all the work in the book. And anyhow I should know as I do a lot of the same sort of thing myself, usually finding I have done it unconsciously when I revise (and of course fiddling then to improve it). But you have raised what I am getting at to a degree in which anyone would be lucky to surpass you. Meantime I go on reading the poems and hope to have them fixed in myself for keeps before too long.

Nice of you about my stories. I hope time confirms you. And very sorry about what must have been a frightening [car] accident [in France] (I know photos of the bridge at Nimes by the way). Poor Smithyman is having a terrible time — Mary has gangrenous extremes and has lost several fingers besides being constantly in pain. I expect too you know that Sinclair has left home for somebody, I think a student, thank God I'm a gerontophile. Sorry this must be all, but much love,

F. [. . .]

[Stead to FS, 14 October: 'You know I write to you, not to the Turnbull Library or the Future. Am I, every time "I take up my pen", to visualise carefully edited published versions? [. . .] Anyway if anything I write is too shocking for the Turnbull & the Future don't please send it back to me (I will only put it on file for the same Turnbull & the same Future) — burn it'. ATL MS-Papers-4261-163.]

To Charles Brasch, *Dunedin*

Hocken Library

11 September 1972

Dear Charles,

How nice that you are safely home again (I feel unsafe if I am a few feet off the ground, but you quite clearly are not worried by many thousands). How I loved something on the air about the lost astronauts. Something had gone wrong. 'But', the announcer said, 'the astronauts are not in any danger'. [. . .]

And about that contribution I sent Leo ['The Power of Thought']. I felt very sorry to see such a sad thin number [of *Landfall*, June 1972] (but you know, the story by Patricia Grace ['A Way of Talking'] is very good, I have been interested in some of the poetry, and of course Winston — I know so little so often what to think of Janet I read avidly what other people think (provided they are not half-witted reviewers naturally)). Anyhow I look on my contribution as just something by a professional writer trying to sell where he can — in fact the piece was written for (asked for by) Dudding. But he thought it wasn't quite me and turned it down. I tried Alan Ross [*London Magazine*] under pseudonym, and he wrote on his slip, 'not quite, we felt'. So then I tried a new NZ deluxe pornographic affair called HIS. Regretfully refused. Thursday did the same, quite a letter from the woman editor [Marcia Russell] very worried (apparently about her public's probable reluctance to take something above average and unusual). Then I tried Leo [Bensemann] and he seemed quite pleased. We shall see. You will recognise it immediately, but I don't expect you to think much of it.

Strange, I lately finished the Shak histories also, they deserve a lifetime's reading on their own. I see the patches of straight Marlowe more clearly now. I've gone on to the Trags, but rather sorry not to be beginning immediately again on the Hists.

My continuing regrets over M of EN. I know it has appeared in shops in Wellington and Christchurch. I know of no shop copy here, and when I rang the wholesaler Caxton deals with he said he had heard of the book by accident a few days ago. By agreement I was to have 6 copies. But nothing.

I apply myself very rigorously to More than Enough. And I expect you do the same with your work — what else? (let me into the secret if there is another answer).

F.S.

To Janet Frame, *Whangaparaoa*

Alexander Turnbull Library

23 September 1972

My dear,

Glad to hear. June told me you had been sick before they brought you. Psychological? Viral? Anyhow if nothing has developed very good. Well, I tire quickly and very deadily these days — I can't pretend I can keep going all the time as it now seems I used to.

I hope very much the place works out, the whole business of frequent changes is something outside my experience. I seem to remember I couldn't take my home town and I wanted a look around before I settled anywhere else. I suppose I am a settling type because it seems to me one can't establish personal relationships unless one *is* settled. I don't imagine there would ever have been Harry for so many years (with a few sidekicks) if not. And all that seemed to make once is enough possible. Every uprooting is a kind of death, and maybe that is why or partly why you have that perennially in fashion subject to write about. Cunning girl. But naturally I'll get round to your subject eventually, and what a marvellous tustle, with its getting round to me!

Anyhow I hope you solve all the problems, water supply garden shelter neighbours heat cold and the rest.

I found under your bed a most extraordinary object in a great plastic bag. I have put it away in a drawer, but I have been thinking of sending it to Miss Bartlett. Also under a pillow your nightie. I hope to wash it this weekend, and if urgent I'll post it.

Caxton still don't send me the M of ENs I want to give away. When it finally gets your way I don't think you need bother with it much except for A Game of Hide and Seek which isn't bad. Of course I was grateful if there was what you appeared to find in Once is Enough. I shall get hold of Daughter Buffalo as soon as Reeds are offering it, and you must not give me a copy. (These free copies — I got a wire from Cole in Wellington asking for a copy of M of EN to be sent to his ex-wife at Wellington Hospital — he might as well have asked for the $4.50 plus postage it cost me in a shop in Milford to have one posted).

I ran into Baxter the other day, and he looked much healthier than I've seen him for many years — apparently he's eating better. I pushed a couple of dollars on to him. Token resistance. Then he informed me he had posted in to Listener his review of M of EN. I made him promise he'd say in his autobiog I gave him $2 before I knew he had the book to review.

To H. Winston Rhodes, *Christchurch*

Alexander Turnbull Library

7 October 1972

Dear Winston,

I've been meaning to write to say that Colin Roderick's *Henry Lawson Criticism* (1894–1971) at last appeared. I haven't had a good crack at it yet (a big book), but it enters my mind I had better eventually toss a coin to decide whether I hand my copy over to you or Bill Pearson. I daresay I'll find a good deal of dead wood (from my viewpoint), but I have at least so far been interested to discover that apparently the first to see that Lawson's landscape existed more inside himself than outside was a Continental called Emile Saillens (away back in 1909 and 1910). Also it seems that although some of the Australian critics sniff doubtfully around the question of the Aussie masculinity-virility myth, I seem to be the only one to say that so far as Lawson goes it really is a myth.

An eleven dollar book, so perhaps the coin will come down in your favour. [. . .]

It seems to me quite a joke — M of EN made the bestseller list in the Sunday Herald last weekend, Davin too with *Brides of Peace* (and right at the top), and along with Irving Wallace and such. May there be something in it! (I think the title could be catchy — no reviewer has breathed a word about any connection with Shelley's poem — also the man in the local Herald was I imagine mistaken in supposing he was writing the book off by describing it as boring, while at the same time mentioning 'the fading love of a professional-class aging man for a Samoan bulldozer driver' or words to that effect.

It seems *Once is Enough* will appear in London in Jan and out here next March. I've only lately realised I have some interesting stuff to tell about Cresswell, also Karl Wolfskehl, in *More Than Enough* — so I work on it very closely.

Janet's *Daughter Buffalo* will be out here soon. I took the risk of asking if she had read your essay and she was surprisingly vocal — appreciative. She mentioned she might write you to say the notion of a room two inches behind the eyes (or whatever it was) is not her own invention — she derived it from a book (I think) on Wagner which she discovered in the Waiheke bach she inhabited for a few months. I think I told you something of this before — my favourite high school teacher Rebie Eleanor Rowlandson, one time Tinline scholar and related to the famous painting Rowlandson, died there some few years previously. She gave up school teaching while comparatively young to devote herself to the violin and music generally, and suffered terribly from poverty. I kept in touch with her spasmodically over the decades until she went off to Waiheke and I did not know when she died. She was much in my mind for the woman teacher near the beginning of the *Peon*, and it was remarkable that she influenced the creation of the teacher in *A State of Siege*. [. . .]

This too long, I hope not too (like M of EN) boring,

Good wishes to family.

F.S. [. . .]

To Janet Frame, *Whangaparaoa*

Private collection

12 October 1972

Dear J,

Thanks for letter phone call obscene arsehole etc. Also thanks for offer of D. Buffalo — but I am at present engaged in persuading the local booksellers to redeem promises to get heaven knows how many NZ books already, and it may even do them good to add your own to track down.

I find myself unseemily preoccupied — what I try to write seems impossibly difficult, and if it were not for spells of reading The Bostonians by H. James, I would fling myself from Takapuna beach (thereby pre-empting your own theme or one of them) and land on more Takapuna beach not more than 2 yards distant.

Hella Hofmann sent me lately a heap of photocopied pages out of Salient whereby it appears from J Bertram (Violence in NZ Lit) that you are wearing these days the mantle of K. Mansfield (alias Beauchamp), the pair of you so far out ahead of the rest of us also runners that we need no longer even try to keep up. Good. (Did I tell you I found in Robert Elsmere a mysterious character called Evershed (for reference see K. Mansfield's Brave Love (Landfall 101 first publication)?

I hope you get by etc. In spare time I go to see my doctor in expensive hospital, taking him from Health Shop expensive health items to do him good. After all his stomach broke away from his gullet and before sewn back again he required 3 galls of blood — just think bringing all that in from front gate along with milk in morning.

Just dashed off trying to be friendly note,

Best l,

F

Oh I see that hand is at my little Mister's . . . . . I keep whispering Neg [Frame's white cat] to him (but if I listen I can only make out not aneg aniceslice of topside.)

To H. Winston Rhodes, *Christchurch*

Alexander Turnbull Library

4 November 1972

Dear Winston,

I am deep in chores — but I find it comic that Leo should have used that jeu d'esprit of mine à la Voltaire-cum-Ronald Firbank (though very probably with little of the quality of either) in the same number as your notice [of *Man of England Now*]. Find the author indeed — I am almost conceited enough to suggest an opinion poll to find out how many can. Anyhow I have nothing to say on behalf of the story — except suggest that perhaps it could have been written by the young man in A Game of H and S.

And that young man — I've not thought of him as insufferable. He's intelligent (and how many of that kind do you find?), he's kindly (he goes to a lot of trouble over the young woman in the phone box), and surely his views on Vietnam and their pungent expression are beyond reproach — he's the sort of person in whose company I from time to time like to find myself — the sort of person I would like to see write his own story (and after all J.R. Ackerley in My Father and Myself actually did this), but who far too often is afflicted by failure of will (which might not matter so much, but it is often accompanied by chronic bitchiness instead of the same thing in patches.)

But you provide me with a number of insights (it can of course be argued that they are ones the author can do without to his advantage, but I would think this is not the case when the writer is past a certain age and keeps on writing). Also from the writer's own viewpoint it can be very interesting the way contrasting views tend to cancel each other out. I leave out Joan Stevens (I always knew about her stupidity, we were at school together in Hamilton), but Bertram almost writes I For One off (and on the strangest, phoniest grounds — that it should be written by a woman), while you and Baxter tempt me to agree with you by being ever so much more intelligent about it. And so on. And about M of EN, I think that it came out of a long affection for a particular person plus irritation over hearing so many people complain about their *rates* — around these parts there are not many workmen of the old-fashioned kind left, and it rocks me sometimes to discover what they pay in *rent* for somewhere to live. From $600 up to nearly a thousand. And the ratepayers are indignant at anything above a hundred. So I think the story is a sort of composite thing, falling perhaps between the two very different stools of an idea and a person.

On one point I am right with you. I have never aimed at any kind of map-making and I find it laughable that anybody should suppose I come anywhere near being that kind of writer.

Have I time for an anecdote? — I think writers, perhaps some of them, trigger off incidents. The other day a very middle-class woman of my street asked me in the butchers' if I would like to put my meat into her trundle. There was so much to take in, with a shop full of people, and the two butchers especially turning their backs to hide their grins. I think I said quite simply well no thank you, I would manage. But of course the simple polite answer wouldn't have done, not for me, if I had been writing — and it soon occurred to me the answer would have been, well no thank you very much madam if you don't mind — I see the size of your trundle. An indecency, but I think it does illustrate the sort of thing that is pretty regularly a part of the inner and outer life of anyone who writes fiction.

Oh yes, A.H. and A.W. Reed do Janet now and they are very pleased to have her. She has so far had one large royalty cheque, something that had never before happened.

I bought the new Maurice Gee [*In My Father's Den*], I much admire his quiet devotion to what he does — and it's all handled with great assurance. The suspense is very good. A book that greatly pleased me (except that perhaps he had an insoluble problem on his hands over the last dozen pages or so. Some of young Witi [Ihimaera]'s stories appeared in the Star, and they seemed to aim at printing the ones most overwritten, but I agree fresh and breezy and it will be interesting to see his novel.

Alas, I've run on and Janet is coming to share dinner which I haven't yet got started.

Good wishes,

F.S. [. . .]

To C.K. Stead, *London*

Alexander Turnbull Library

[James K. Baxter, 'the patriarch of Jerusalem', died in Auckland on 22 October 1972.]

9 November 1972

Dear Karl,

Poor dear Jim that former pink gnome but latterly Greek patriarch swinging pectoral crosses etc has rapidly passed through all preliminary stages, and I would expect final canonisation to be announced any day now. I am expecting that Curnow will probably be invited by the Church to function as Honorary Pope.

But this is really just to say that la comédie humaine catches up with all of us. After my defending Charles what happens? He sent me the latest Square and Circle book, *The Loners* by Ted Middleton, but I am such a pusher for public lending rights these days (I have withheld part of my rates on the grounds that portion goes to support a library that makes my professional work available to the public free with no thought of what is owing to me: also I have begun agitating against Awards — Janet has just got her annual ((Jessie Buckland this time)) — on grounds that they are the hall mark of a provincial society — a pat on the head for the local boy as compensation for refusal to recognise professional status; Frank Haigh is keen to come over to Takapuna Mag Court when I am prosecuted), that I wrote and said I could not bear the thought of reading for nothing a book by Middleton, so he must permit me to pay. My money returned with sharp bitchy note.

Still, I think you may have got it all wrong in Menton. Are you allowing for cachet (and euphoria) from Prix Mansfield, and money in pocket. I remember one golden afternoon walking into Stresa (de luxe resort on Maggiore) very tired dusty and hot yet overwhelmed by the beauty of everything and wanting to stay somewhere overnight. But money, money! I had the sensation of being led by the ear back to the threshold wherever I tried, with a boot in the backside to send me on my way. I had to retreat a few hot miles to a village albergo. But despite the stinking arrogance of affluence I thoroughly enjoyed the following day in Stresa (Bernard Shaw was sitting under a beach umbrella with ((as one would expect)) a book. I would like to say it was a copy of The Intelligent Woman's Guide to Socialism, but although I tried to see the title I couldn't, and anyhow he hadn't at the time written TIWG to S)

No more. Landfall 103 (September) is out and there is most amusing kind of Voltairean-Ronald Firbank story in it by somebody called R.M. Shaw. You must tell me what you think of it. Also the patriarch of Jerusalem had been writing Sestinas and five of them are in the Landfall — oh dear oh dear the great Simplicities of Love conjoined with the most artificial verse form. However superior to some pieces by Smithyman — jolting junk.

If you see Eric McCormick see if he has heard John Pascoe died same day as J.B. But I expect he knows. (Did you by the way tell EHM the *exact words* you wrote about Charles Brasch?)

All for now and lover [Marginal note: I leave that as too good to correct] to all,

F.S.

To Dora Somerville, *Secretary of PEN (NZ), Wellington*

Alexander Turnbull Library

3 December 1972

My dear excellent DS,

An invitation to eat and drink all day! Oh dear oh dear I must have got the Seven Deadly Sins all wrong after all. How fortunate for my virtue I am separated from the residence of Mr I. Cross by a long line of railway (for me flying's out on med. grds.)

But to be very sober it LOOKS as though Pub. Ld. Rts. [Public Lending Rights] may turn out not to be fantasy after all. We must all press Mr Kirk mustn't we? [. . .]

Lately I have dreamed up my own tactics — I've paid my rates but withheld $5 on the grounds that I'm rated to support the local library which makes my professional work available to readers free, and of course the point is I agree about the 'free' but the authors have been forgotten overlooked dished diddled and so on. I have a barrister friend who will appear with me if we can get the Takapuna City Council to sue. And if it works out that way I'll have to check up on all the documentation available. Frank Haigh my lawyer says PEN should have by now issued a pamphlet. I wonder if you would inquire from Ian Cross whether, if it comes to the point, he would lend me what file of papers he has — we would then blind the Magistrate with profound knowledge, and as we won't have any trouble in getting press cover, a good and witty PA'd story should get about the country with luck. All this, other things being equal (which means unless Kirk can be pressurized into going into action — I'm suspicious though of his 'we're not a one man band' it could be a convenient excuse that it's no good because too many Cabinet Minsters have never opened a book and have no idea anyone writes them), won't come to Court until sometime after the end of February when balance on rates becomes overdue.

I still think a set day for our removing our books from Library shelves should be kept in mind.

Meantime I enclose my more or less anonymous donation to PEN and send you my good wishes. May you be writing as I am (in my old age now it's about the only thing I haven't forgotten how to do),

from,

F.S.

To Dora Somerville, *Wellington*

Alexander Turnbull Library

[Somerville had written to FS asking him not to refuse the Hubert Church Award.]

[10 December 1972]

Dear Dora Somerville,

Thanks for your note about the Hubert Church.

I don't want to appear ungrateful, but it does seem to me a little difficult — it's even difficult for anyone in my situation to refuse money. But you know I've had it twice already, and for that and other reasons, it may well look like my filching money from widow Jacquie (and my God I've already got another widow on my conscience, Ron Mason's).

The point is (I think) I am a professional writer, I dislike the whole idea of Awards, the pat on the hand for the local (but Amateur) boy. You yourself know how keen I am that professional people should have their professional rights, that's to say their Public Lending Rights. And my God, I've already turned down that O.B.E. thing on more or less these grounds (and perhaps I had better be honest and say that was easier — no money to be had there).

Look my dear DS, please don't, if you haven't so far, announce the thing just yet — give me time to think. And I'd much appreciate any news about chances of rapid progress with PLR — no doubt you got my letter which must have crossed yours.

It really is difficult — I expect it would have been most improper for Dudding to be in touch with me, but if he had been I think at that stage he would have got a firm NO. Now I'm not keen to knock him back in anyway — on top of his Caxton-Landfall troubles.

From yours,

F.S.

Frank Sargeson

PS And pray, why hasn't one or other of your delightful plays been so honoured? Oh, those secret tears when one was overlooked as a child — but it is just as bad grown up.

[In the end FS accepted the Hubert Church award for 1971. This was for 'The Drive', 'a longish extract from his forthcoming autobiographical work Once Is Enough *published in Landfall 100, December 1971'. Memo from Bob Dudding in ATL MS-Papers-4261-082.]*

To C.K. Stead, *London*

Alexander Turnbull Library

17 December 1972

Dear Karl,

A few kind Christmas words. I was on the point of writing not long ago, but then I looked in the Listener and saw what Roddick had said about *S's D [Smith's Dream]* — and I thought to hell, somebody else can send you that. Not that it should be taken seriously or that it writes you off. It's just that I'm worried about R and all these New Zealanders who make a point of refusing to be entertained. One might say a jeu d'esprit is just that — but not for a New Zealander. One said to me about *S's D* 'it's not that Karl wrote it, but that he should have thought it worth writing'. I nearly hit him (yes, it was a him/he).

Of course all this is assuming somebody sent you the notice.

In fact my consolations are very genuine. I have lately been up against exactly the same sort of thing. Instead of teasing you, let me say I wrote a thing in *Landfall* 103 called *The Power of Thought* by R.M. Shaw. It dates back over a year when Dudding asked me for a story then turned it down on the grounds it wasn't me. (What irony! In *Ldfl* 103 Rhodes reviews *Man of England Now*, and says the question about me is where does one find the author. And there on another page was the author and who found him? My piece too is a *jeu d'esprit*, nicely and elegantly written and very entertaining. Pommie and other foreign Enzeders love it, but the true Kiwi is sour. Nuff sed — you'll be entertained exactly as I was with *S's D.* Both *jeux d'esprit* — and why on earth not?)

Nice election — I partially picked it, after all I think it's going to cost me nearly $500 to help my little friend (Mof EN) have his hip attended to with plastic ball and steel pin — in private hospital, public is out because of motor casualties (but my friend paid all his social security tax over a lifetime). Lots and lots of people were wake-ups to what the Nats have been up to — trying to create a new kind of poor, *affluent* poor (one Nat had the impertinence to say on air that 'our Government believes that people prefer to make private arrangements for illness' — like hell they do.) Also the prices. Also not just hospitals, *everything* run down. (It lately took a book I ordered, a paperback, indeed *Wilhelm Meister*, to get from the warehouse in Northcote to the Progressive Shop in Darby Street *eight days*, and the Post Office had the impudence to say this was reasonable when I confronted it with the facts.)

No more just now. When are you returning? Love to Kay and kids,

xFx

x x

x

To Bill Pearson, *Auckland*

Alexander Turnbull Library

19 December 1972

Dear Bill,

How clever of you! Yes, Voltaire, with a touch of Firbank perhaps — maybe the sort of story the *type* in A Game of Hide and Seek might have written. Anyhow written to entertain which I think it does — but Enzeders can absolutely refuse to be entertained. Anyhow, many thanks.

And Lawson — I'm genuinely very sorry the coin didn't come down in your favour, you and Rhodes both have done so much for me.

I too 'found merit' in your Lawson book — I mean up to page somewhere. In the last four years I have in one bus and two taxis left three umbrellas (none recovered) and one book (I infer somebody else found merit). I am told I should borrow it now from the local Library. Yes, I think so. I remember you almost literally stunned me with your scholarship, and I suspect you intended that effect. It's very difficult to refuse to be stunned, you mustn't blame me — but I do blame those who refuse to be entertained.

Good wishes, [. . .]

To Lawrence Jones, *Dunedin*

Alexander Turnbull Library

[Jones reviewed Man of England Now *for the first issue of* Islands.*]*

24 December 1972

Dear Lawrence Jones,

I daresay it's a bad business — writing to a reviewer (making it awkward for him for the next occasion and so on). If I ever wrote to one before I have forgotten (thought I might well have when I was young).

However, pretty much aging one can't be worried.

I've noted your remarks previously, and now I want to say it's pleasant that you pick up the threads as nicely as anyone could wish for. I probably have seen most of your comments on my work, but you haven't seen I am sure anything but a small fraction of other people's — one knows there are lots of illiterates, but how can they so readily get into print!

Just a friendly remark — nobody it seems connects my title (M of EN) with Shelley's poem, Song for the Men of England (after nearly fifty years I can never read it without emotion). I wrote that story mainly out of a personal affection, but without doubt my mention of rent on the first page and again on the last derives from Shelley.

It is a great compliment when one's work is comprehensively read — so may I identify with myself a kind of Voltairean jeu d'esprit I wrote in Landfall 103, The Power of Thought. I wanted to entertain besides play a game of find the author — after all, one clue, I made the opening line almost a copy of M of EN's opening.

My good wishes to you,

To Robin Dudding, *Christchurch*

Alexander Turnbull Library

[R.H. Morrieson died on 26 December 1972]

14 January 1973

Dear Bob,

I must be as brief as I can (too much work on hand).

First, Morrieson — yes, indeed, there was a short piece in Star 29 December '72 about his having died in his home in Hawera (famous in south Taranaki as a novelist — there was nearly a contract with Disney people — philosopher and musician, aged 50). I haven't written yet, but I will now you've reminded me — there was an aunt, address, same as M's, 1 Regent Street, I think; or I may write to Executor and ask for letter to be handed on. I feel I can't write any formal piece about him at present, I mean so soon after the Landfall piece. But I'll tell you what I'll do — I'll write you a letter for ISLANDS, drawing attention to the death, and expressing hope unpublished works (and I've read one, the same one as you, about the freezing workers [*Pallet on the Floor*]) will be preserved and that an editor and publisher will eventually be found. A damned awful business really, as it could be he'd still be alive if he'd had better publishing fortunes. And these damned young people — I lent Michael Volkerling The Scarecrow about last April, and he doesn't return it despite repeated promisings — I suspect the young hound may have lost it. [. . .]

To Mr Smith, *Health Inspector, [Takapuna]*

Alexander Turnbull Library

1 March 1973

Dear Mr Smith

I have your note about my front hedge which I agree hangs too low above the footway and I hope to remedy the matter very shortly.

But you know, you have had a complaint; but I have had thanks from people who have been grateful for shelter from the weather — and especially so when the Council has failed to provide shelter at the bus stop immediately opposite. It doesn't please me as I am sure it wouldn't you to see bunches of school children exposed to drenching rain on their way to school.

Then too you speak of 'the lawful use of the public thoroughfare', and this seems to me an unfortunate expression when a great variety of motor vehicles are making unlawful uses of the roadway at all hours day and night. What has been done about this? I don't relish diesel soot or fumes or noise or speeds up to I would say 60–70 miles an hour. I have complained, but I have no evidence that anything has been done. Did you write to Bus people or private lorry owners? Have motorists been prosecuted? Is it unreasonable that I should use my hedge as some barrier against these modern horrors? After all you sign yourself 'Health Inspector'. Is my health not to be taken into account? — and the more particular when I am tied to this spot inasmuch as I work at home and so live for too many hours of the day right bang in the middle of this modern hell.

I hope to attend to the hedge matter over the coming weekend. I think I would be optimistic to suppose you have taken action on the matters I mention by that time. Nonetheless I will be greatly pleased if I see some indication that at least you are doing your best.

Yours sincerely,

Frank Sargeson

To Ngahuia Volkerling, *Auckland*

Alexander Turnbull Library

[At the time Volkerling [Ngahuia Te Awekotuku] was writing an MA thesis on Janet Frame at the University of Auckland.]

25 March 1973

Dear Ngahuia Volkerling,

Kind of you to ask me, and most interested to have a note from you, but I can't see I could be of any use to you. I'm the sort of person who gets choked up with his own work (if you will forgive me for mentioning it age is the very devil), and I really haven't much idea what Janet has been up to in her books since about The Adaptable Man — yes, that one. I'd gladly switch you over to her if that were possible, but nothing could be plainer that she won't be switched by me or anyone (just this week I begged her to be photographed either on her own or along with me. No go.)

I'm quite sorry about all this — but pardon me for saying you have the text in front of you. What else really can you want? The work of art is one thing, the artist another — I don't think it's very good to get the two mixed up and confused.

My good wishes for all your works — from literary works to the reformation of society and the regeneration of man-woman-kind,

Yours sincerely

To Kevin Ryan, *Auckland*

Alexander Turnbull Library

[Arthur Allan Thomas's lawyer.]

11 April 1973

Dear Mr Ryan,

Pardon my butting in, and I know the case only from what I pick up from the newspaper — but since one can readily suppose that Crewe may have hit his wife during a row that evening, followed by her going off down the road to her father (and surely a good deal falls into place if this is what happened) — then surely what she was wearing on her feet becomes very important. I can recall no evidence whether or not the body had footwear, nor whether a pair of shoes remains unaccounted for.

Good wishes for the verdict so many I am sure would like to see,

from yours

Frank Sargeson

No doubt the various corollaries of this view will have occurred to you — no dogs barking and Crewe remaining in the armchair when his wife and father returned. And of course a *partly* consumed meal would indicate when the row began.

To William Plomer, *Sussex*

Alexander Turnbull Library

30 April 1973

Dear Plomer,

If I remember I am a few months the older — so you must unless you can catch up behave yourself if I say you must — after all as a perennial gerontophil (I am sure that word is not in the Shorter Oxford) I am always very careful about my respects to my seniors of every possible sex. But oh dear oh dear how could I have ever supposed myself a septuagenarian! From now on it will be the purpose of my life to enter my non-age.

Once is Enough seems to have gone much unnoticed. I saw virtually nothing except for a helpful piece in the Guardian — helpful yes, but it seemed to have got so badly treated at the stone that it was almost unintelligible. Oh well, who can bother, but I am sorry for my publisher. I believe the book is a handsome one — but hearsay — after 3 months I still haven't seen a copy, and my NZ publishers are cross that their order takes so long to arrive. I expect I would be cross too if it wasn't that More Than Enough is at final typescript page 126, and I think not more than 70 to go. For me perhaps short pieces to come but PLEASE God no more books! [. . .]

Your appearances and getting about interest me very much — neither of which things I do or want to do. For four years before Harry died I couldn't, and for two years since it often seems there is just my affection for little Jimmy (he was my model for M of EN), to keep me going. He has the most terrible wife on earth — but I suppose I should be grateful because of the payoff. As you would expect he is a little older than I am and very lively indeed (although lately I have helped him with the dreadful expenses of a dreadful hip operation — and the adjective is right, my doctor whom I have known so long hands me over his BMA Journals unopened these days — he is nearly 80 — and I read with horror of all that will go wrong with the new surgical technology — anyhow this little J has survived and fast becomes again the liveliest cricket).

But I seem to have nothing much to say, and am indeed much exhausted by the revisions and typing I do. But I often think of you and Charles too — and Hassocks (geog. has always been one of my best subjects), and I know the terrain — my friend the Englishwoman named K which you met in the little extract from my O is E in a book I sent you called Landfall Country was a Rodean girl, and had a vast collection of photographs.

All for now, but for you and Charles may the heavens forbid their own lightnings and thunder,

F.S.

Britten's heart made the cable news — photographs of his weight lately have troubled me. May he be well again!

To Phillip Wilson, *Wellington*

Alexander Turnbull Library

[Charles Brasch died on 20 May 1973.]

2 June 1973

Dear Phil,

Marvellously, I've been able to locate in the chaos, really just plain mess, your three letters. All for weeks has been channelled into getting my damned sequel (More Than Enough) into the post for London. A somewhat longer book than OIE, and perhaps notable for what it has to say about Fairburn Cresswell and best of all, Karl Wolfskehl. But o God what strain, my last book of any length I should say, unless I could get assistance (for typing especially).

Anyhow I hope in coming week to come right after feeling terrible from relaxation of tension.

Yes, very bad about Charles Brasch. I think he died of Hodgkin's disease. I don't know what property he left or how he disposed of it — I know only that Alan Roddick is executor (but whether just literary executor I don't know) — anyhow I expect quite right — it would have to be a poet, somebody pretty young, and of shattering probity — and R fulfils all these requirements exactly.

One worry recently resolved. Since end of March NZ edition of Once is Enough has been lost — and now found in container towed from a ship and deposited in the backyard of an importer of ironmongery. The man has had no occasion apparently to unpack. The only copy of the book I have so far seen is one I begged from a Reed salesman who had an advance copy — and I sent it to Charles Brasch as it was dedicated to him and he was dying — I believe he got it shortly before he died. If Martin Green in London posted me off my six presentation copies last January the parcel never reached me.

Incidentally, Man of England Now and Once is Enough published and finished More than Enough, and the only money I have seen so far is $400. Thank God for public lending rights, but in the name of heaven how much is it going to work out at? (PEN distinguishes itself by presenting me with half a prize the Church — *for 1971* — to mark by 70tieth birthday.) But even though I was told about this prize in Dec last not a sign of any money have I so far seen.

However your own troubles and worries more severe I am sure. I see Janet occasionally, and hope to visit her (for first time) coming week. I would like to beg her not to tell me (with the idea it's going to frighten me) that I have to die — I mean in *another* book. I hope I shall shout back at her goody goody if she does.

No more this time. Good wishes.

To Phillip Wilson, *Wellington*

Alexander Turnbull Library

17 June 1973

Dear Phil,

The best thing in your note is about the NZ Jack proofs. May they have pleased you and may all go smoothly. And may I be buying my copy before Christmas!

And you are far too generous as you always are when writing about something of mine. It would be too much to hope the book [*Once is Enough*] is as good as you say. And by the way, there are always miracles. Joe O'Neill of the Auckland Library has been on to me for years to put something on tape for their Archives, and the other day really bounced me — the idea being that there was Brasch gone, and any day it might be myself — and then where would they be (as though I would care). Anyhow he turned up one morning and I said something about Fairburn, Karl Wolfskehl and John Graham — reading I'm afraid very badly as I hadn't done any preparation. It was a whole morning's write-off for work and I wasn't in a good temper — but afterwards he surprised me by saying he would send in an invoice to the City Council, and payment had never occurred to me. Now I have a cheque for $30 — which astonishes me. I wonder what the hell it would have been like for all of us if our time during our working years had been paid for at a rate comparable to what any professional man would take for granted. I imagine I would have been demoralized. (Of course it occurs to me that Master Shadbolt functions in this section of the broad spectrum anyhow).

Oh Turnlung [in *Daughter Buffalo*] and Janet — in my view she doesn't present portraits of people, but it's part of her screwy slant on things to collect items about people she knows which she apparently has no second thoughts about using. And in her time she has taken bits of hide off her sister, Karl Stead, Ruth Dallas, and (now) Charles Brasch or myself (you can take your pick). I don't mind for myself, but it's a sheer bastard when she involves a third party. However nothing can be done. (And by the way I *can't* read Daughter Buffalo — exactly the same pattern ever since Owls Do Cry, a page beautifully done with all sorts of profound and moving sentences — and then the next page just schoolgirl's rattle or prattle, the bright literateur of the fifth form. Well, take it or leave it, but for me now without too much regret I leave it. Of course it's a bit unfortunate that lately I've been re-reading all Tolstoy's shorter work and what doesn't suffer by comparison?)

Nothing in Budget about Public Lending Rights. Up those, and down with Awards!

No more this time but all good wishes,

To H. Winston Rhodes, *Christchurch*

Alexander Turnbull Library

28 July 1973

Dear Winston,

Thank you for your letter, and I was about to write for reasons which will in a moment appear.

[. . .] [I]t's publishing questions and problems which plague me at this moment. I've lately put a cunning two and two together and decided there never was an English edition of *Once is Enough* — or if there was it amounted to no more than a few score copies (and I've never seen a copy myself). But I can't blame Martin Brian and O'Keeffe, clearly they are broke, and for this book relied very heavily on Reed's NZ edition. I don't know whether you ever see *New Society* (London): in issue May 3 there is a very interesting article about the disastrous results of the tycoon publishing which has taken over, although the article is mainly about the 'refugee' publishers who aim at survival and rejuvenation by trying to get by by publishing only 'necessary' books. Martin B and O'Keeffe figure among these.

Another point which I find enormously interesting is NZ's lead in Public Lending Rights. I think somebody will have to write a book about the Philosophy of Repercussions. Of course PLR should be for publishers too if they publish 'necessary' books — but as things are what they are going to say to writers is for them to look to PLR for their reward and cut out expectations of royalties. And what Martin Green has done for me is a good illustration of my point. Counting the time he was with MacGibbon and Kee he has been the one behind the publication of six books from me: on a preliminary survey of NZ Libraries I have more than a thousand books in circulation (full survey say 1500) — then my first year's PLR return should be between 700 and 900 dollars. And this (large by my standards even though trivial by those of most people) I owe to M.G. It seems clear to me that if he says (as I think he genuinely does) that he admires my work and wishes to publish it despite nil chances of anything over to pay me, I have to agree. I can't turn round and say I must look for another publisher (and that's apart from the cost and time-wasting nuisance of any such search).

And by the way authors who boast about their affluence (if I'm not mistaken, Shadbolt, and Billing), don't I think make it out of their books as such. I am told Shadbolt received 1500 dollars for about 3 and a half pages in Reader's Digest on dolphins. And I think Billing sold to the films, a picture which has never been made.

Anyhow, all this leads up to my saying I would be very glad if you could get round to a reading of *More Than Enough*. Green says he of course wants to publish subject to the by now usual jack-up from some publishers in NZ. (which shouldn't be terribly difficult). He speaks enthusiastically, but I am a wee bit doubtful. It is not the (in Green's words) 'more of an idyll, an evocation' of *OIE* — and indeed it is not, more an account of the plain hard work writing becomes once one is beyond the preliminary committal stage. I should be very grateful indeed for your reactions — it is quite within my capacity to let it remain among my private papers if I have fallen badly below the standard I try to write to.

I well remember your urging about a selection of my criticism. I was looking at a few things about the time I disposed of a lot of papers to the Turnbull — my notice of Davin's *Roads from Home* eg, and was surprised that perhaps there was something worth reprinting. Then the chores descended on me — and it seemed the good old last straw when a folder of about seventy or eighty notices I'd written got lost when cartons were in transit to Wellington (or rather we think they must have by bad chance remained in some carton after unpacking, hence reached the Wellington city incinerator). Those I had spoken on the air were certainly lost irretrievably and no great loss probably: those printed could probably be traced, but my God what work! But with some few exceptions I doubt whether I have written anything of value in that line, (except perhaps my pieces in unusual critical form — I mean my dialogues in Landfall).

I bought the Courage book [*Such Separate Creatures: Stories*] — I think mainly to read Charles [Brasch]'s introduction and read the stories I had never seen. Charles was very deliberately being very reticent I thought. I think I have always envied a little a certain 'magazine' quality in Courage — it used to be clear to me that editors would prefer as a rule his stories to my own on this ground. Anyhow I am glad to have the book. And yes, I agree about writing about Charles — I turned Dudding down for a piece, I could think of nothing to say just at present. And Finlayson on Cresswell — I was touched and alas a little amused, Rod is such pure gold, and D'Arcy strange as it may sound to you, surprisingly often could make you feel something of the same quality.

I shall get round to sending you the typescript sometime late this coming week, and if you wanted to stop me you could send me a wire.

My good wishes meantime,

F.S.

To Denis Glover, *Wellington*

Alexander Turnbull Library

[Glover to FS, 26 August 1973: 'I write this because of the article and photo in Heritage *where you look sagely ruminating "Babitch, Babitch, Babitch". The photo affects you as a profound philosopher, and this you are not, any more than the Ll.B you would like to be mistaken for. That's an Achilles' heel, Frank. [. . .] Drop it, lad — your name lies on other fence-posts. [. . .] That pestiferious little punk, Brian Bell, accosted me with his daemonic off-beat ribaldry. [. . .] One of his stories was that you execrated Glover because he had sold your letters to some such improbable place as Texas, and received either millions of dollars or millions of oil shares. (You'd like to think you're as important as that, wouldn't you?). The fact is, Frank me old mate, [. . .] I finally dumped them on the Turnbull Library. I have your permission in writing to have done this, though you tentatively suggested the Hocken. Get that straight, or think up more megalomania, Texas-wise. Now, Sarge, cease to confuse yourself with the Deity: there's a church along Lake Road, is it? which said, COME IN AND HAVE YOUR FAITH LIFTED. [. . .]' ATL MS-Papers-4261-068.]*

31 August 1973

Dear Glover,

You have written me a strange letter which I do not understand, at least I don't understand much of the matter in it. But apart from matter perhaps it is not so difficult to understand. It seems I affect some kind of superiority, and this you find intolerable.

Can I reassure you immediately? I think one should distinguish between what people are and what they do — and surely this is a case of what I am made to appear to be doing. How can I be responsible for what people say I have done? Or people who take snapshots of me without warning? Or write things about me?

But superiority? I concede to you immediately. I would much rather have been a poet — which you are, with a wonderful number of poems to your credit besides many which take my breath away with their achievement. Quality. And I know a good deal about poems in our language both as to number and quality. I read Shakespeare, all there is of him, every few years — I don't know I can say I've read everything of any of the others, except Wordsworth: a few years ago, and it was worth it, because besides the marvellous things there's fun of such variety in the daily-grind stuff (if you don't know a sonnet on Illustrated Papers ((a very late one)) I much recommend it).

And Shakespeare by the way — in 1927 I bought in Whitechapel for about a shilling a Shakespeare Concordance (or a kind of such thing) of 18th century. The page where the Bard's uses of the word suck are listed is a delight:

I can fuck melancholy out of a fong as a weasel fucks eggs
I have given fuck etc.
And your fair fhew shall fuck away their fouls
As I fuck blood I fhould fome mercy fhow
That from you great Rome fhall fuck reviving blood
Tell him of Nestor, one that was a man when Hector's grand-fire fucked

And one from Troilus and C which was missed

Praise him that got thee, she that gave you fuck

And now I must address myself to my tasks, alas mainly household disorder today.

Good wishes,

F.S.

[Glover to FS, 2 September 1973: 'A nice reply, when your fanmail must exceed mine by twenty times. [. . .] I applaud you for many things, Sarge — but mostly for your rather callous (but properly self-protective) retreat under your carapace. Proper pride, even arrogance, is a sine qua non, and shd belong to all. I do not see further than that one must carry on with humility and integrity. However they *can be defined. That's the novelist's business. Carry on, with compassion! You can'. ATL MS-Papers-0418-018.]*

To The Secretary, *Literary Fund Advisory Committee, Wellington*

Alexander Turnbull Library

29 September 1973

Dear Sir,

I wish to apply for the 1974 Scholarship in Letters.

And the project I have in mind is the completion of two literary works, (1) another work of fiction which I expect will run to somewhere about 60,000 words, and (2) the third and last part of my trilogy of memoirs, of which the first part, *Once is Enough*, has already been published, and the second part, *More Than Enough*, completed (publishing arrangements are now being made).

It is not possible for me to send you copies of my published works, but I enclose a biographical list, and would send whatever works might be required (but please select from more recent publications.)

Perhaps I should explain that I am in my 71st year, that financial returns from my major literary works of the sixties have been negligible, and that in writing these works I have for the most part lived on Age Benefit, latterly Universal Superannuation, and some capital resources, mainly from inheritance and now diminished, and rapidly diminishing further.

I await the results of Authors' Fund calculations with anxiety, as I am a totally professional writer and wish to complete what I conceive of as my life's work.

One of my reasons for sending you this application is that since 1963 I have had the disability of the use of one eye only, and that eye after much nursing appears to be moving rapidly to what may be a final crisis. I find myself much interested in aids for people engaged in literature with eyesight difficulties — gadgets for speaking into etc. Also it would now assist me very much if I could afford from income to pay for much typing.

But probably my main reason is that financial and other constrictions may create in me too much anxiety about my chances of rounding off my work — an anxiety which is also I believe very bad for my eyesight.

Yours sincerely,

Frank Sargeson

[FS was awarded the $4000 New Zealand Literary Fund's Scholarship in Letters in April 1974.]

To Denis Glover, *Wellington*

Alexander Turnbull Library

7 October 1973

Dear Glover,

I have been intending a note. And now it is all about a sad event. Auden yes, of course, alas (and I hope you did not miss, I forget where, when he was talking about Yeats — who spent the first half of his life writing minor poetry, and the second half as a Great Poet writing about what it is was like to be a Minor. Nobody laughed and poor Mr A suddenly went pale — so very patent — spent the first half of his life writing major poetry, and the second doing poetical exercises.)

But yes, Auden! The previous Sunday however I delayed getting out of bed until the 7 o'clock news was over — and then last item, Plomer! In his sleep at his home in Sussex — just like that! And after more than thirty years of letters we had exchanged only a week or so previously. Nothing in the printed 'media' that I could discover — if it had been some International Whore whose slip had slipped she would have been lovingly (un-)covered.

Well, it is marked on my calendar, Auden 29 Sept, Plomer 22. You met him and I never did. His letters have been like his best verse, generous, lively, macabre — and wonderfully aware of what it has been to have lived in our day and age. He admired you and your work as you know — I can remember nearly thirty years ago he said something about how one could never suppose 'from his exterior what an aesthete he is'. And true, workmanship, the right word, the exact sound — all of it.

No more just now as I have a dozen letters to catch up on,

F.S.

[Plomer actually died on 20 September, in the arms of his companion Charles Erdmann, and in considerable pain. See Peter Alexander, William Plomer, *p. 328.]*

To Robin Dudding, *Christchurch*

Alexander Turnbull Library

14 October 1973

Dear Bob,

Must knock off this in answer to your queries. Quite interesting Islands by the way — [Michael] Volkerling shows he can handle the language of criticism (I expect you know about him, he wrote The Ride of the Volkerlings, music by a Wagner disciple, I forget his name), and Gifkins within the limits of what he is up to couldn't be better, the piece gave me an authentic chill.

But my Listener stories — here am I a professional writer, and Cross behaves like the editor of the sixth form Annual. I want to be published and paid. (And incidentally am I cross about all Awards — except for the very young. My demand is for justice not pats on the head for the local boy. The last time Janet was away wasn't too long ago, and I remember it cost me a hundred dollars in help to get her home, and now off she goes again. And good luck. But where is the justice when I have not so far received one single cent for Once is Enough — I mean as a book. If Authors' Fund turns out just another flop I'll be reaching for the Prussic Acid).

In early days of Lit Fund I thought I should be content with the Heenan £4 a week pension. Then I had my row with Holcroft, and as Jim Winchester put it in one of the last numbers of Comment H had the power to deprive me of all paid employment on Listener and he exercised that power. But H sat on the Lit Fund I think, and I thought it was no good applying with him there. (Also I had been told Blaiklock had referred to my gutter writing, and that also was a bit putting off). I tell something about it in More than Enough. I don't know whether the updated Collected have applied. Anyhow I have never pocketed anything except the chicken feed stuff — Mansfield, Church. I remember in the sixties I felt surprised that nobody seemed to have thought of me for the Achievement touch — after all, Peon Hangover Worm, in my sixties if that wasn't achievement etc! (But frankly even here at this moment I am sick of the whole thing). [. . .]

No more this time. Islands is generally speaking of very good quality — I only wish more people understood what it costs you in every possible way to turn out a number so remarkable for quality.

Good wishes to family,

To Muriel Firth, *Wellington*

Alexander Turnbull Library

[FS to Phillip Wilson, 1 December 1973: '[. . .] Broadcasting has lately paid $400 for four half hour adaptations (half hour plays) from four of my stories done by Muriel Firth (whose half hour plays adapted from the Classics are pure wizard)'. ATL MS-Papers-4261-206.]

3 November 1973

Dear Muriel,

This first to acknowledge safe receipt of the Thackeray and Zola.

But I do much regret my being so busy an author — I mean when your letters interest me so much. And yes, I see now, about the irony transferred to the priest — and of course it is further evidence of the creative job you do. Let's face it, in the hands of the wrong sort of person results could be terrible; but I am reinforced in my first view of your work, that you have such a sure touch I would never dare to interfere with whatever you might do to ensure the end-result *works*. Of course it goes without saying I can discuss all this until the cows come home — except that I close up when some piece of my own is involved — the reason being *not* on account of anything you may do, but simply because after a certain time of writing any given piece of work I cannot bear to return to it. If I do I immediately see or think I see where I went wrong, or else tell myself that now I would have made quite a different approach. And the essence of all this is that past work is something cut off and detached from oneself and of no more concern. What matters in one's lifetime is forever the work under one's hand at the given moment.

Oh damn it, I sound pretentious.

And of course your literary (and more, the touch about Renoir) knowledge demands my respect. I have never been much of a Thackeray person, but I must tell you an anecdote. Before I wrote Memoirs of a Peon I was intending to read Memoirs of Barry Lyndon and never got round to it. Then soon after I wrote the Peon I did read Lyndon — with great interest/dismay when I discovered an anecdote I had used about the farmer who got into the habit of lifting and carrying a sick calf — and carried on until the creature weighed hundreds of pounds — well, there it was in Lyndon. But now at last I remembered (or thought I remembered) that I had got the anecdote from reading a Florio translation of Montaigne when I was very young. Alas, not certainly — because a copy of Barry Lyndon had been on my King Country uncle's shelves, and my uncle may well have told me the story when I was a small boy.

Anyhow, for now I must leave it all at that. [. . .]

Many grateful thanks, all as usual,

To H. Winston Rhodes, *Christchurch*

Alexander Turnbull Library

[Winston Rhodes was preparing a new edition of I Saw in My Dream, *1974.]*

11 November 1973

Dear Winston,

This just a note to say I'm at the moment plagued by so much happening so slowly I will be a little time looking into the points you raise about ISIMD. (But I will oblige you, and I was remembering the other day going through the book some years ago when MacGibbon and Kee thought they might be reissuing — I thought there was still life in the thing — and I have been remembering because I mentioned the other day this new re-issue to my friend Bruce Beaver (the Australian poet who continues to write poetry reviews in the local Herald since his return to Australia about 10 years ago) — and it interested me he had lately re-read the book and thought it stood up very well).

Anyhow I will be writing you again before too long.

I have no information yet about any arrangement made for *More than Enough* by Martin Green along with Reeds. Two other re-issues are the *Peon* (Heinemann Educational Books, contract signed and they sound very business-like — even paid $70 advance, very unusual) and the *Collected Stories* with 20,000 words added — Longman Paul (they've been frigging around since about August before last, not paying me anything yet clearly going to much expense, including extended Bibliography). I find it a piece of grim irony that at my age if only the books can be got out I stand at long last to be in possession of an income from Public Lending Fund.

I have thought of mapping out a work scheme so I can fit in the collecting together of pieces of criticism which could be of some value. I've been much preoccupied getting launched into *Sunset Village*, a fiction about pensioners (I know rather a lot, and *what* I know and can imagine has many possibilities).

Ah no, not Harry in the Listener story ['Riding High'], not anything I was conscious of — but I got a ring from a professional social worker who wanted to know what I 'meant' by my 'article' in the Listener. I assured her I thought the lady in the *story* was not offensively *handled*. I wrote that piece in July hoping that Winds of Change through the Listener might enable me to earn something after Holcroft's long interdiction — but the usual story, no pay yet. And the illustration simply reinforces the notion of some people that my stories really 'happened' instead of appearing to.

[. . .] I daresay Dr Johnson might have approved of the Public Lending Fund — rough and ready justice perhaps, but surely much to be preferred [to prizes and awards] by the truly professional worker. But of course I am very glad about Janet, as she will have a better margin for her stay in Menton. She could never have remained 'uninstitutionalized' if these things hadn't from time to time turned up. (Fortunately, mainly on account of determined endeavours by Charles Brasch, she has the equivalent to a Universal Super. pension: but one anomaly is that the National Cabinet apparently insisted it be an 'annuity' — the practical result being that it is 'fixed' and so doesn't increase along with other Benefits to keep up with cost of living. Anyhow it's very handy and diminishes the worry of a few of us). I am much in favour of all her good fortune whenever it comes, but I must confess I don't take kindly to her books. Absurd no doubt to map out another person's future, but I always hoped for some line which would derive from her little story *The Day of the Sheep*. In that she is *not* writing about herself, and for me it is significant you cannot mention that story to her without her immediately closing up. I deduce from this that one view of her work could be that it is a long elaborately worked out self-indulgence. I could say much about this view, but not now. But what it amounts to is that meeting her 'instability' in life I don't take much to finding it in her books. I find I can't read them, for her there may be something therapeutic in her 'death theme' but after the years it has become repeatedly freakish, a tiresome reiteration of her refusal to admit there are people in the world *as such*, not just a gallery of monsters transformed *into such* by her

Boschian imagination. And another point is that for those who have assumed some responsibility there is never any knowing what twists her 'instability' will take. For example last time in America when she got into financial difficulty she could readily have earned a few thousand dollars by writing for the New Yorker. Nothing doing. And I think the point I am making is that one after the years can become very exhausted trying to cope with 'disorder' of this kind.

No more just now [. . .]

From yours,

F.S.

To H. Winston Rhodes, *Christchurch*

Alexander Turnbull Library

15 November 1973

Dear Winston,

I don't know I can be much use to you, I mean ISIMD. I have a good memory, but things do get a bit mixed once I've worked material into something fictional. Though the word fictional can be a bit difficult. I shocked somebody the other day by remarking that I couldn't now remember for sure whether I ever in fact went on that journey of OIE, Part 1. (Probably not, but I went on so many journeys over that route when Peter Dawson lived at Mt Maunganui I probably tried to extract the essence of the whole lot rolled into one. For me I can satisfactorily say to myself, So what? But I would agree that I might be creating difficulty for other people).

And by the way Peter for the last eight years or so has been living in a little Norfolk village, her cottage neighbouring an old farmhouse inhabited by George Barker and family (young children who adore P who is now in her late seventies). All very handy for Janet when she is in England.

My *feeling* is that you did a very good job with ISIMD. I think it probably has some good parts, but certainly patchy. I remember that after Fairburn in 1936 had passed on to me the first number of *transition* (sic) — no sorry, it just shows, I mean James Laughlin's *New Directions* (a sort of New England *transition*) I for some years cherished it as a kind of literary Bible. There was Cocteau, Stein, Henry Miller, Wallace Stevens, all those. I thought of myself as avant-garde. I never forgot Cocteau's remark that he adored literary puzzles. Undoubtedly *When the Wind Blows* was intended to be my *Portrait of the Artist*. And ISIMD was intended to be that book with my *Ulysses* added. [Marginal note: No doubt I overlooked I hadn't Joyce's advantage of the coherent background of the Church: instead only the broken-down Puritanism. And my Bloom was missing — he didn't turn up until the Peon: Michael Newhouse was made out of 'Bake' — see dedication to my Plays.]

I think though that now, with OIE published, your task should be a little easier. I mean you can take more for granted simply by referring to it where appropriate.

I don't know whether this is any help. If you have questions just ask them. [. . .]

I think Janet appreciates a letter from you, but I suspect she has sent no reply — you will be then in good company, Patrick White wrote her some years ago but she never answered. A curious sight is to see Janet in company with Jacquie Baxter, they are like two superior peasant women who communicate by having nothing to say to each other — meaning of course they get on famously.

Good wishes,

F.S.

To Lawrence Jones, *Dunedin*

Alexander Turnbull Library

25 November 1973

Dear Lawrence Jones,

Thank you for your letter, and I remember quite well my own. I was suffering some agitation on two counts — it is rare to see a notice by somebody who has really been able to read quite a lot of one's work — but as well I had been for some weeks in a state over Dudding's having thought the Power of Thought not worthy of publication (this was shortly before he finished with Landfall) as a piece of work written by myself.

I have found this sort of thing a problem for anyone in this country trying to be wholly a professional writer. If a writer is a professional and is not without competence, then I much resent any editor presuming to 'judge' any piece of work and rejecting it on the grounds that he is 'protecting' the author from his own folly. Even the very professional in any field can have his lapses, and these must be allowed him — after all how can he hope to write the 'good ones' if he is suddenly cut off from earning on the ones that alas turn out not so good. Immediate questions of literary excellence shouldn't come into the matter — these if the past is anything to judge by will always come out in the wash long afterwards.

But I must try and forget this trouble — Bensemann after Dudding's departure from Landfall was pleased to use the story, finding it entertaining and readable (the sine qua non surely) — but the dispute with Dudding rankled and I compromised to the extent of using the pseudonym — and I am still compromising — Longman-Paul shortly published my collected stories brought up to date, grandiosely entitled The Stories of Frank Sargeson — and The Power of Thought is in the Bibliography but not in the Text. I expect when I wrote you I had in my mind that Dudding said he was getting somebody to write in Islands about my later stories, and I thought if I revealed myself as author I might discover what you thought of the story if you happened to be the person Dudding had asked to do the job.

Well, never mind, for heavens sake let me forget it!

And after all that egotism! there is much in your letter to interest me, particularly about LA and growing up there. I hear a good deal about California these days apart from what I read — Janet Frame has two painter friends, Bill Brown and Paul Wonner, she stays with them and meets with Bacardi [Don Bachardy] Isherwood, quite a gallery — all very interesting — but I think I prefer the for the most part penurious obscurity of this bit of coast here to trying to keep up with the cost of living across the Pacific. And all the connotations! my God.

Oh dear it is Sunday morning and I have been trying to knock off a few letters, and now I see my time has gone. In my 71st year I remain a writer (of what quality I wouldn't I'm afraid know, although other writers can be kind). The problem of name-dropping is terrible in a memoir, but I have finished More than Enough (although uneasy at the thought of — perhaps — Never Enough) — and perhaps it has to be that because after so long it looks as though Public Lending Rights will at long last fetch me in some income to get by on. Also I am lucky with reprints at the moment — I Saw in my Dream and Memoirs of a Peon, besides the new Collected.

But the chores are screaming at me, so all for now, and renewed thanks for a friendly letter,

To Dorothy Sutherland, *Oamaru*

Alexander Turnbull Library

16 December 1973

Dear Dorothy,

The only way to ensure I don't do as usual (send a card with a promise of a letter which I don't keep), is to omit the card and send the letter NOW.

First, nice to have your kind remarks about my book. No recriminations! And how could I blame you if there were? Authors are such parasites of a very peculiar kind, and I suppose one's only excuse is that something lively and entertaining has been made out of the material (one hopes without malice poor taste breach of confidence etc etc — or should I say without *too much* of all that.) Well anyhow, I have often said to myself and others, mankind goes in categories — at the top are the saints and who of us can compete (when of course there'd be no competition anyhow)? Next come the artists (and all of us with luck can be or become some kind of artist), who are necessarily very impure creatures (but some, lovable? — has one ever thought of any saint as *lovable*?) And then the riff-raff begins, kings and queens, presidents and politicians merchants moneybags etc etc (all the nobodies indeed, although surprisingly some of them artists, and — I would be the last to deny — sometimes a saint).

Well, having got through all that old-age tangle — I mean the preceding paragraph — it was nice to get your letter and hear about your travels. How glad I was *once* to get around — but I have never wanted to again! Very different from poor Janet. There's lately been terrible upset over her getting away to France to take up the Mansfield fellowship in Menton. Funds not really enough considering Inflation and all that jazz or whatever. But oh dear oh dear oh dear, what is one to think? — she makes use of what was Harry's room whenever so inclined and the night before she sailed slept there. I took the morning off work and everything that had to go with her was suitably packed. But at noon she decided to go to the boat from her sister's place some miles away. So all packings and herself put into taxi after I had searched the house and nothing had been overlooked. Alas, at her sister's things came unpacked — including the spectacles she can never be without. And were they re-packed? Never! So there you have it, a professional writer with Funds made available for her to go abroad and she leaves behind a most essential tool of trade. I do not myself suffer from that sort of madness — and now I can't any more suffer those people who do!

For me your son doesn't suggest your father — perhaps in ways as you say, but surely much of the character of the Don I knew came from his facial moulding (and it comes out very beautifully in the snaps I had enlarged). I can see those trout tell a story — perhaps. No Kircaldie leftover bits and pieces for that boy! Well, you can't put the clock back, they say. But the oil business does put rather a different look on things. Sometimes I wish I could take more interest in the people who surround me. I can't — they take all that I think so chancey and temporary for granted. But I am immediately interested and touched when the age old human situation is suddenly revealed beneath a smooth surface. For years a middle-aged farmer at Kaukapakapa [Murdoch McLean] brought me each winter my firewood, marvellous chunks of manuka and he never charged me nearly as much as I thought he should. After all, the journey was thirty miles here and the same back. Then this year, do what I could over the phone I couldn't get a delivery, just excuses. They didn't satisfy and I set to work to find out — and of course found the human situation which is always found when you scratch the surface. A property owned by the family for over a hundred years, and old farmhouse or homestead beginning to fall down, sons and daughters who had gone away about their concerns, and the son who had remained with mother and father — and remains although they are now dead. Before I had firewood at a bargain price, now there will be no more firewood, but I have instead a friend I much value. I can improvise for firewood — one can't do that for a friend. And the marvellous land and old house (and even though my uncle in the King Country had new land and a new house, there's a link restored which had been cut since my uncle died in 1948).

I do assiduously work at more writing. I don't bring Don into *More than Enough* at all (I try again to avoid name-dropping so far as it is possible). I tell a lot about Harry (Irish like Don, and the best snap of him I had enlarged and hope to have printed in the book). Also I tell a good deal about the German-Jewish poet, Karl Wolfskehl who became my friend during the war. (And I have just remembered, about fifteen minutes of my talk about him will be on the air, YC network at 10 pm next Tuesday evening 18 Dec).

But here I am talking of my own concerns too much. Just one bit more though — although I am writing what looks like a short novel, I call it *Sunset Village*, and it is about pensioners, I am so worried about a number of loose ends I failed to tie up (I mean in *More than Enough*), I think there will be a final memoir book called *Never Enough* — in which I will hope to say a little more about Don.

Oh, many good wishes, and may all this not be too dull to read,

F.S. [. . .]

To Marcel Aurousseau, *Sydney*

Alexander Turnbull Library

23 December 1973

Dear Marcel oh dear oh dear — meaning I was not intending to prise a letter out of you. But kind of you, and I have long been reconciled to my publishers being the sort who are hellbent on not promoting my works. Honestly, I don't mind, the thing is to get them written without which they can never get so far as to be on the knees of the gods. (You mentioned in your October letter about Patrick White [getting the Nobel Prize] — and a good many fiends have asked me what I thought about it. Well my reply is, Look in the Oxford Companion to Eng. Lit. and you will see I get 8 lines while Patrick gets only 6. But the other day this answer wasn't clever enough, because my questioner came up with, Ah, but wait until the next edition and see how many lines he gets.)

Well, well. And perhaps I should confess that except for a short story and a shot at The Tree of Man I haven't read PW's work. And of course nothing unusual about this. A practising writer may for several reasons — and one or two good ones among them — leave some of his contemporaries very much alone. You will have noted that I haven't in these few years of re-engagement showered you with my works. It was just in this instance you sounded genuinely deprived and upon impulse I sent you that book [*Once is Enough*].

I have been much disturbed lately about the death of my friend William Plomer, he died a week before Auden and the same way in his Sussex (Hassocks) home. We never met, yet for 36 years wrote to each other several times a year. I admired him very much as a poet, writer of some of the best short stories this century, his work on Kilvert's Diary, his Curlew River script for Britten's work of that name — for much else too. And of course part of our interest in each other was that we were both 'colonials' — although Plomer was not born in South Africa he lived mainly there in boyhood and on until he was in his twenties. (Among his works I should have mentioned too Turbott Wolfe, an extraordinary South African novel — I mean to be written by a boy of nineteen). It's interesting about Plomer and myself too that we each figure in the Twayne World Authors series, the volume about him being numbered 54, and about myself 75 — but although the second is I think quite well done by that admirer of yours, the Australian Winston Rhodes, the first is I think unfortunately rather poor (the poor man failed to do his homework and has Plomer having conversations with Edward Lear in London in the 1920's)!

It so turned out that after long mail-delay Plomer read Once is Enough only a few weeks before he died. And among the remarks he sent me there was 'frank without ostentation'. Which I thought rather good, and more especially when Plomer had so many MSS to read — he was Cape's reader (succeeding Edward Garnett away back (I think) in the late thirties).

It delights me to hear of your many Honours. And how deserved! But you must bear with me when I say I have not one jot of envy. I long ago assured myself that if I did what I have (maybe) done, payoff in appreciation would be very slight. (I believe in some academic circles I am thought (or my work is thought), 'not to be nice, in fact unhealthy'. It much reminds me of the man I thought the healthiest of my friends. He was A.R.D. Fairburn, a good poet and nearly six and a half feet tall. He died of cancer aged 52. Well, that was perhaps just bad luck — but I always remember that away back in the thirties he solemnly assured me that there could be little doubt that E.M. Forster was a very unhealthy man. Well, that was bad luck too, and no doubt at all, well a man who lived to his nineties. I expect it just shows that re-definitions are always necessary.

Unusually for me I have been able to turn out of my chaos two former letters from you, and attached to one is a photograph of yourself and 'my Cecily'. I have used a magnifying glass on the pair of you, and feel a little mortified to find you both look much younger then than I do now (see enclosed). Also I have few doubts you have both become even younger since.

Oh well, I was intending a Christmas letter anyhow — and now it goes off with all my fond good wishes,

[. . .] I *may* unload some more of my works on you. After all two books are reprinting, and a third, just out, is my augmented Collected Stories, done by Longman, and with the grandiose title, The Stories of Frank Sargeson (not author otherwise). NZ publishers and London ones are still bickering on terms for More Than Enough. The really sweet news is that first payment for Public Lending Rights (called Authors' Fund) will be made in March. I am all eyes expecting.

To Phillip Wilson, *Wellington*

Alexander Turnbull Library

10 February 1974

Dear Phil,

Many thanks for two letters. And you are surely being tormented about NZ Jack — I inquired again and no results yet.

I made it to Bay of Islands with my firewood subsistence farmer friend of Kaukapakapa — all in one day, began 5 o'clock Wednesday morning in little Ford utility and got home 2 am following morning. He is over sixty and myself more than 70, and yet we stood it excellently — must be pure lives or something. The Bay of I incredibly beautiful so far as it is as nature made it — for the rest shit a hot brick! We were 3 yards off where the Q disembarked from her car (some old-fashioned couple's little cook done up for a day out in lolly-papers). The boys with placards and crackers were hidden in the bushes just behind us. No Security in sight. I jested with them and they said the pakeha had taken their land, and I agree but thought they shouldn't forget they ate the Morioris out (joke took a few moments to sink in, but was then appreciated). The doings which were hard to see because of crowd were very camp (work of Dick Johnson I imagine). [. . .]

You may be right about p 239 of that Landfall story ['The Power of Thought'], but I can't see it — the passage seems to me to say what I intended.

Well, not the right weather for work, for arguments with publishers, for having to put up with prolonged visits from friends who feel one can prop them up when one can't (what is so tiring and disconcerting is that said friends don't seem to understand one can't prop up even one's own self). This as I expect you might guess refers to poor Cole (can he not understand that after an hour I can still love him, but after 5 hours from sheer exhaustion I can't help viciously hating him)?

However that last para is a vicious piece of work anyhow.

Good wishes,

F.S.

['the passage seems to say what I intended': Wilson to FS, 27 January 1974: 'I did notice what appears to be a misprint [. . .] — you say the father sees in his son a grace of moment unparalleled — & it seems to me it should read "a grace of movement unparalleled"? Just a small technical point but of some interest to me as to which is the correct word'. ATL MS-Papers-4261-183.]

To James Bertram, *Wellington*

Alexander Turnbull Library

[Bertram to FS, 2 February 1974: 'I've been asked to help as General Editor with a series of little books the Oxford University Press plan to bring out on New Zealand writers [. . .]. You will be one of the 'subjects', under prose writers: but what I want to ask first is whether you might be prepared to write yourself on Katherine Mansfield?' ATL MS-Papers-4261-026. FS replied on 5 February: 'Thank you for the offer, but what I would write would be too eccentric. [. . .] No, I think quite firmly not for me. [. . .]'. The following is a draft of a subsequent letter to Bertram in ATL 93-133-20.]

23 February 1974

Dear Jim,

Your note: I wrote suddenly upon impulse, but I haven't changed my mind as it seems you would like me to.

You wouldn't like what I would do: the fact is I have a lot of difficulty in taking Mansfield, although I find much of her easier than Frame: I have a good deal of difficulty over Sargeson too — and it was I who told Rhodes that remarkable aperçu which Rhodes concludes his book with. [Marginal note: Some anonymous young woman at question time after a talk.] Self-indulgence is surely a detestable literary vice, and probably Janet is the worst offender, after all there is so much more of her than Mansfield. (When McCormick and myself were selecting for the first Oxford Book I was puzzled to know which story we should choose from The Lagoon — until McC suddenly said, well, The Day of the Sheep. And of course! — the best thing she has written, not about herself and no self-indulgence: she *must* write about her friends nearest and dearest and most helpful, yet does not scruple to ignore all reserve and turn them into the kind of monster that at the moment suits her purpose).

I couldn't write about Mansfield without raising the question why it had to be K.M. F.S. and J.F. Henry Lawson is all right for Australia within the context of Boldrewood Henry Kingsley Xavier Herbert, perhaps too Furphy and James Tucker. (I would like to be able to relate White to Lawson, but no go, surely he's pretty spurious: and for NZ the little I've read of Shadbolt — and *can* read of him — just depresses me).

Well, there it is — and clear to me that for better/worse I must stick to plugging my own line.

Thanks for your note,

F.S.

[Marginal note: Not posted]

['that remarkable aperçu': 'New Zealand literature has had two tragedies: the first was Katherine Mansfield, and the second is Frank Sargeson'. Winston Rhodes, Frank Sargeson, *p. 168.]*

To Christine Cole Catley, *Whatamonga Bay*

Alexander Turnbull Library

3 March 1974

Dear Chris,

Many thanks for your letter, and my Public Rights cheque came to nearly $1900. It goes without saying this is a great help, and I think one should not object to publicity and the press's itch to reveal the actual figures when the money comes from the taxation which nobody is happy about paying.

But what I find extraordinary is the overall assumption that this is windfall, money from home — never a notion that this is my income. Clearly if one is in the public eye a good deal it is assumed as a matter of course that one has a pretty good week to week income and a payment of this kind is without any question *extra*. (And of course so it is — extra to Universal Superannuation, which, about $20 a week, is very handy.)

But another extraordinary thing to come out is the assumption that if one is single one has only oneself to consider and provide for. A married man supports maybe a wife and kids perhaps a mistress — apparently not a notion that a single person is not heartless, not committed in perhaps half a dozen directions where his heart leads him by the nose.

Is this a particularly NZ thing? Is it particularly an especially bone-headed NZ thing to suppose I write my stories out of nothing — out of *not* having a complex pattern of involvements which you would think everyone with even a shred of imagination would take for granted?

I must say I sometimes think the New Zealander despite his many good points evens things up a bit too drastically with some truly awful crudities.

But that's that. And David Elworthy called on me the other day. Unfortunately a little back I mentioned to Michael Foster [of Reeds] that I was writing a new fiction called *Sunset Village* — and they seemed to me to jump a little too readily to the conclusion it was about to come off the assembly line and I might agree to their having first chance instead of Martin Green in London. (I think in fact this can be done, but it's not quite as easy as that — apart from the fact that at the moment it is seeming to me very difficult to write). However things seem to have been straightened out a little.

Again thanks for your letter, and I have every confidence in Muriel Firth. After listening to so many of her tapes I think of her as a radio adapter of genius — I have complete confidence in her good taste and discretion.

To Ray Copland, *Christchurch*

Private collection

[On 11 April Copland wrote to say he had accepted the 'very pleasant task' of writing on FS for the OUP 'New Zealand Writers and their Work' series, and to ask him about his family, and the bach at 14 Esmonde Road. ATL MS-Papers-4261-034.]

20 April 1974

Dear Ray Copland,

Your note, and I am afraid there must be reservations in what I can agree to tell you. No doubt I should by now be dead, quite the decent thing to be I should think from the point of view of the literary critic.

But I am not, and indeed, besides *Never Enough!* (which I meditate), there is a fairly longish fiction called *Sunset Village* which I imagine is about half finished.

Meantime, there is *More than Enough* which has been in proof since last February, but when it will appear will be according to the grace of my publishers in London, and I think A.H. and A.W. Reed. Anyhow, this book answers your last question — the bach. Or baches — there were two in their time, the 2nd, an army hut. None now, but the book tells a good deal of their story and something of the people they sheltered.

I am sorry, but I am not willing to give you any information about surnames etc. But I advise caution, particularly with information you may suppose you are deriving from *Once is Enough*. (See young Cunningham's piece in Islands 6, p. 411.

He is right about that surname, and you have it the wrong way round).

I am afraid that generally speaking I am not much in favour of 'serious' approaches to a writer's work during lifetime. I think what a writer hopes for most is to be 'noticed' — and it doesn't matter what is said so long as the name of the book reviewed is correctly stated, the author's name correctly spelt — and of course frequently mentioned. I don't need to tell you there is no such thing as bad publicity. A 'real', that is to say a fulltime writer such as myself must from time to time hope for some relief from his chronic poverty.

Of course the writer is himself to blame if he reads serious studies. I expect I sound harsh, I know there is a sense in which we all do our best, at any rate hope for the best. But what is the writer to think and feel when it is clear the critic has not kept his eyes on the text, which (during lifetime at anyrate) is all that should concern him? So, when you spoke on the air about somebody called 'Bohun' and related him to the old clergyman of that name in *Joy of the Worm*, you were so far as I was concerned talking about somebody I have never ever known anything whatsoever about. And why attribute to me speculations about the writing of *Memoirs of a Peon* which I am not conscious of having at any time entered my mind? The 'Peon' was derived from an elderly man (he was more than twenty years older than myself) — or rather I should say, *mainly* derived. I met him in the early forties and for nearly 20 years was very pleased to spend one evening a week in his company — and for the most part because of the pleasure of his sumptuous conversation. He was a retired bank inspector, his brother (much older) had been chief inspector of schools for NZ, his father had been a last century Auckland doctor. When I came to write the *Peon* I had no conscious thoughts about a change of style theories or whatnot. I simply went ahead in the language I had become so much accustomed to. It is most flattering to be credited with having created a figure of some curious quality, but one which cannot be supposed really to belong to NZ. I would without hesitation assert that only four people knew the old man better than I did — his four daughters, and none of them has any doubts about the fidelity of my representation (if there is a reproach it is that I dropped as unsuitable some of his more bizarre stories which were as familiar to them as to me). And by the way, if this interests you, his name will be found in the dedication to my plays — 'Bake'.

Well, if you can forgive me do — and perhaps it should not be thought too much amiss if, near the end of a long literary life, I hand out a bit of sound advice to the critics. Keep your eyes on the text!

Good wishes,

Frank Sargeson

To Dorothy Sutherland, *Oamaru*

Alexander Turnbull Library

26 May 1974

Dear Dorothy,

People who bang a letter right back on you can be tiresome, but I have the excuse that if I don't write now I mightn't at all.

Yours as usual packed with most interesting detail — believe me, having nothing of the *company* of domestic life, I am always very interested particularly when comment is so intelligent & apt. You do really make me see & even better, understand, much that concerns you. My compliments on it all — you leave me in no doubt that being a committed writer is all very well, but the stuff of life one gets down on paper often will not compare with life as lived.

But perhaps you shouldn't take me too seriously — as I hope I don't myself. I have the most complicated relationships — & let me say it, for the most part with people not unlike your father: there's my firewood man a subsistence farmer with ancestral acres which he won't sell (& particularly when among his trees is a giant kauri), yet who in his early sixties lives (or would live if it wasn't for what he can eat of his land) very thinly indeed. He is tall, reserved, with handsome dignity, & control which can never be shaken. And what a world for a person of that kind to have to get by in!! Simply not interested in all the nervous ballyhoo & bustle he's surrounded by. The strain he is under from Bank & Business Demands is tremendous, yet he doesn't crack — well, not yet. However, I'm running on.

Nice of you about that $4000 [Scholarship in Letters]. But so far it is just one big question. Letters showered on me offering to help with typing, suggesting tape-recorders etc. But even if I decided along this line it would be no good until a Tax Question is solved. I am sure your husband would be interested to know I've apparently joined the H.T.C. — the Happy Taxpayers' Club. But also it's disastrous for a beginner — not sufficient provisional tax paid, more shortly due — in effect, unless I can persuade Inland Revenue, it means double tax, & I would think about $3500 & that means I am indeed in the cactus. Perhaps I can resolve it all by sending that amount to the Minister, saying he can pay it on my behalf, and I'll stick to the odd $500. All can then be finally washed up by his *un*announcing his Announcement. (And how your father would have been astounded by this High Finance of mine if he were here)!

You mention the sound radio plays — & it is interesting me to discover what Muriel Firth has made of my texts. I have never met her, but I know well her very very able work — there seems not to be a story in English or any language that she's incapable of turning into a very listenable piece of radio drama. Her liberties astound me, yet always she will move you, make you laugh, or whatever.

And such a nice person to hear from, full of the sense that life is for once, & get on & make the best of it. If I'm not mistaken a person a good deal like your good self.

May all your family matters go well with no disasters! — & of course my special interest comes from my knowledge that all goes back to Don, of dear & undiminished memory.

All for now, & may all bad fates withhold their thunders!

from,

F.S.

I seem not to hear v. much from Janet at the moment.

To Denis Glover, *Wellington*

Alexander Turnbull Library

[On 10 June Glover wrote to congratulate FS on the Scholarship in Letters: 'My regards to the admirable Dudding, who no doubt is permitted to visit you in the afternoons. [. . .] Recevez mes compliments tres agréables'. ATL MS-Papers-4261-068.]

23 June 1974

Dear Glover,

You must excuse me from writing anywhere near adequately — I could never hope to keep up with your own quality (although if you like you can interpret this remark as another way of saying it is mutually agreed that 'egotism is a thing only the worms can destroy'.)

More people come in than you might suppose, and may it please you that they too totally agree with me about your quality.

Ah well, I do seem to keep at it, and have indeed just finished a new fiction entitled *Sunset Village* (pensioners as you would guess. Grotesque etc, and perhaps the more so for being funny. Well, I hope).

If I can solve certain tax problems I may get around the country, in which case postpone any thoughts of permanent departure until I call in on you.

And talking of keeping at it — my valued doctor who is 6 years older than I am (making him nearly 78), complaining about this and that the other day, I told him a way of continuing therapeutic practice at small cost and trouble to himself yet quite profitable. He would, I said, have two cards printed, and he would not see patients only receive their letters describing their illnesses (which I further explained would certainly be rooted in their erotic troubles). On receipt of a letter he would post off Card 1, which would read, Do You Fuck Suck Pull Or Bugger? (tick all items if necessary). And upon receiving the answers he would immediately despatch Card 2 which would read, Well Keep On And Don't Worry About It. My fee two dollars.

He agreed there could be quite a lot (of money) in the idea.

I don't get up at 4, no, 6 — to address myself to the Poets (who remain an unquestioned perennial delight). Poets, I said, not poets — and you needn't guess whether the big pee covers you, IT DOES.

Janet sent me a French press cutting about a peasant who was eaten by his dogs — this enables me to match your French with my own, un petit conte épouvantable.

Rien de plus,

To Colin Maiden, *Vice Chancellor, University of Auckland*

Alexander Turnbull Library

4 August 1974

Dear Doctor Maiden,

I won't go into a large bag of mixed thoughts and feelings — after all the University is my old university college where in the early twenties I failed to get myself a degree. And if I had I imagine I would have thought of myself as getting in by the back door (my heart was never much in my law studies, a great deal more with what I could find in the Auckland Public Library).

But anyhow, now you most generously offer me the opportunity of going in by the front door — you honour me, so how can I not honour you too by accepting? And very curiously, if I did not, total honour would be over to Stratford High School, Taranaki — for by the same mail as your letter I received from 'Mr Haddock and Form 4L' a very pleasant pencil drawing and a cheque for $10 — 'we hope it will enable you to buy something to help you to continue in your work of writing such enjoyable stories and novels'.

So there you have it. Two letters on one day, and more emotion than good for me.

Thank you for your letter, and I am grateful to accept the honorary degree which you wish to confer upon me.

With my very good wishes,

from

Frank Sargeson

To Mr Haddock, *Taranaki*

Alexander Turnbull Library

4 August 1974

Dear Mr Haddock,

I do get compliments (probably more in a long lifetime than has been good for me).

But I can't remember that I have ever been touched as I am by this one. The very pleasant pencil drawing and the 10 dollar cheque both astonish me — such imagination and understanding, believe me it's not the sort of thing I run into everyday in my writing environment.

You will inform the young people how I feel, won't you? And say this too, that although I am materially a good deal better off than during most of my writing life, I have not lost touch with many many of the people from whom my stories have been made. Like myself they are that much older, and alas too, some, (unlike myself), that much poorer. I can most gratefully use the 10 dollars — where it will meet a need.

I wonder if all of you will believe me when I say I much prefer the honour of your communication to the honorary degree which Auckland University says it will shortly confer upon me. My commitment is not to the formal occasion — much more to the people mentioned above, and those who have enjoyed reading my work.

May you all too find much to enjoy in *many* of our writers,

With good wishes from,

Frank Sargeson

To Robin Dudding, *Torbay, Auckland*

Alexander Turnbull Library

[Dudding to FS, 11 September: 'I've only noticed lately that your road signs spell Esmond as 'Esmonde' — why is this?' ATL MS-Papers-4261-043.]

14 September 1974

Dear Bob,

[. . .] I would have written but for a dose of the new flu (nothing nasal or bronchial), just fantastic headache pain in the neck back and legs. Hope you don't fall for it.

Look, two things, Terry Sturm is still and for some time in Hororata Road (phone number 494,431). He has got on to a fabulous cache of papers left behind by

F.S. Anthony (like Morrieson — Hawera — and I think I told you my grandfather was elected to the Borough Council the year I was born 1903 — and I daresay it could mean for the future, Anthony Sargeson and Morrieson will be all one person). Anyhow contact him [. . .].

The other thing is Ralph Bodle, and to save myself trouble I enclose his last letter to me. (First paragraph refers to the Honorary Doctorate of Letters or Litterature, the Auckland University says it will confer on me mid-November — I camp for one evening in a red gown red hat (with feather?) I think)

Anyhow Bodle is a bit younger than I am — you will see he is highly literate in a bibliographical way. And his collection on those lines is astonishing. Lives alone — I've meant to tell you about him for nearly a year. Very nice bloke, and Oyster Point Road could make a nice Saturday or Sunday excursion on which it would please me to accompany you. Anyhow if the sound of him attracts you let me know (my phone no in case mislaid is 496,999, and Bodle incidentally can be rung up, Kaukapakapa, for about 15 cents, I think).

Esmond Road. At beginning of the twenties when I first began to haunt the original hut it was Esmonde (after Esmonde Napier you know, one of *the* Napiers — name derives I think from Napper, tastier sounding, certainly), anyhow illegitimately connected with Sir George G, and the original house on little point of land at bottom of road, interior harbour). The sign got dilapidated, and the painter painted Esmond Road — which lasted for many many years. Then new sign, and original name restored.

I can't co-ordinate, see typing, Flu I think,

So all for now,

To Ralph Bodle, *Kaukapakapa*

Alexander Turnbull Library

[Bodle, an autodidact with only a primary school education, spent many years researching comparative editions of The Swiss Family Robinson. *FS encouraged him in his efforts to find a publisher.]*

29 September 1974

Dear Ralph,

Many thanks for your letter, your very good letter I should say.

And sadly pressed for the moment for time I have just this to say. ISLANDS is now published from Torbay, and I have arranged with Robin Dudding, if you are agreeable, that he and I, in his van, and accompanied by a few of his numberless daughters, go on an excursion in your direction on Sunday afternoon, 20 October.

We will of course promise not to stay too long, but I hope he may see something of your book collection, and with luck take away some typescript which we all could be glad to see in the quarterly.

Anyhow, this just preliminary notice — if we didn't hear we would assume that you would welcome the visit.

I must also raise with you the question whether or not you would like an invitation to my doctorate ceremony (point is I'm not keen for people I know to come and see my embarrassment — I've told this to Murdoch also. But at the same time I feel appreciating people would have their invitation so as to decide for themselves even though I know which way I would prefer them to decide.)

Really rushed, literary copy to be got off to Australia and generally pressing literary chores.

More anon, that means soon,

To M.I. Aldred, *Sydney*

Alexander Turnbull Library

[In September 1974 Sargeson received a circular letter from M.I. Aldred, the President of the English Teachers' Association of New South Wales, which planned to publish a booklet about contemporary writing, and invited authors to respond to questions which would give students a glimpse of writers' 'methods and problems'. Participants would receive a fee of $25. FS typed a formal reply to the questionnaire under the heading 'ANSWERS TO ETA's QUESTIONS'.]

[29 September 1974]

[1. What can the novel accomplish that other literary forms cannot?]

1. Surely it is self-evident that we would know much less about the personal life of individuals without the insights which the great novelists can provide us with. Would we not be much poorer off if we had never, for example read Tolstoy or Dostoevsky or Henry Fielding?

[2. Does the modern novel offer more scope to the writer than earlier novels did?]

2. Who knows the answer about the modern novel? If it is a question of form (or absence of), there are attractive dangers which may be compared to 'free' verse. If the question is one of content, then I would think that human nature does not change even though its expression in behaviour may vary a great deal.

[3. What was the genesis of one of your novels? Give a description of how a particular novel took shape.]

3. My novel, *Memoirs of a Peon*, came out of a long friendship. For many years

I visited once a week a 'superior' old gentleman from motives of respect and sympathy. He was irascible and difficult, yet at the same time lovable, and I often thought of him as resembling some character or other out of some classical novel. Perhaps Smollett, perhaps Thackeray. At last I thought I would try to transform him into a present-day character of that kind. I wrote my opening paragraph, and realized it yielded nothing to the opening of many classical novels I admired. After that I could not leave off for nearly three hundred pages.

[4. What special problems did you encounter in a particular novel?]

4. There is always the same special problem with every novel — how to begin. You keep your fingers crossed until at last with luck off she goes! Then it's hard slogging plus what will from day to day float to the surface of your mind — I mean from depths which are always there even though for most of the time remaining pretty secretive.

[5. How much do you revise your work?]

5. I write in long-hand one page a morning (green quarto, the colour to spare my eyes the strain of prolonged staring at blank white paper). Before I begin the next morning I revise and type that page. That gives me the lead-in for the morning's work. The prescription is, 'repeat regularly'. Writing at this rate means that after about a year a new book is ready for final revision and typing.

[6. To what extent is conscious use made of grammatical knowledge?]

6. I think a novelist has always to be conscious of grammar. He has to speak through a variety of characters every one of which must convince the reader of his or her own reality. Words and sentences must be grammatically varied to assist in achieving this effect. When the novelist speaks in his own person however, I prefer him to be grammatically precise and formal. I do not take kindly to 'like' as a conjunction: to 'different to': to 'hanging' participles. After all, there are standards: genius as we know will break all the rules: short of that, one had best read frequently a page of Swift, or Fielding, or Boswell.

[7. How much are you influenced by other writers?]

7. When one is young influences from other writers are difficult to resist. Also there is a need for them, one does not write in a social vacuum, nor in a craft one either. One must learn. The difficulty is to know which influences will be fruitful, and which the reverse. I do not think that at my time of life I am influenced by contemporary writers. I do however remain influenced by Huckleberry Finn, by Sherwood Anderson, by Henry Lawson. Without these influences I do not think I would have ever seen my way into becoming a writer who uses English as a literary tool, yet live permanently in a country as remote from England as it is possible to be. I mean in the geographical sense.

[8. Does your work have a consciously symbolic intention?]

8. It seems to me that to think in terms of symbols before one begins to write

can turn out to be quite deadly: look *afterwards* for the symbols that may have turned up willy-nilly: a certain amount of manipulation may then be fruitful. Take heed of Goethe:

> There is a great difference between a poet who seeks the particular for the sake of the universal and one who sees the universal in the particular. From the former method comes Allegory where the particular is used only as an example, an instance of the universal; but the latter is the true method of poetry. It expresses a particular without a thought of or a reference to the universal. But whosoever has a living grasp of this particular grasps the universal with it, knowing it either not at all, or long afterwards.

[9. Which of your novels do you most value?]

9. Two of them:

Memoirs of a Peon. This one because it more or less demonstrates that a mainstream European type of novel can turn out to be convincing in a New Zealand setting: everything is there, the amorous rogue-hero, plagued by his comic misadventures and poverty — and surviving!

Joy of the Worm. Because of its sophistication. It was satisfaction, when I had remained continuously in my native country for more than forty years, to have Mr Jonathan Raban say of the book in the *New Statesman*: 'an idiosyncratic masterpiece; elegant, formal, deliciously ironic'.

[10. Have you any advice for young writers?]

10. No advice. Much sympathy. I think that Australian writers have the advantage of a context (Boldrewood, Henry Kingsley, Marcus Clarke, Xavier Herbert: within that framework Henry Lawson is right and natural). New Zealanders are not so fortunate. Katherine Mansfield was our Henry Lawson, but what context can we point to?

Frank Sargeson was born in 1903, second son of a Hamilton storekeeper. He was admitted as a Solicitor of the Supreme Court in Auckland in 1926. He spent a year travelling about England and the continent on foot, and back in New Zealand worked for a Government department until he began casual employment which enabled him to begin writing. He has written short stories novels and plays: also two volumes of memoirs. He has lived mainly in Wellington, the King Country, and Takapuna.

To Henry Cooper, *Auckland*

Alexander Turnbull Library

3 November 1974

Dear Mr Cooper,

I should have written before this to compliment you upon the honour of your own degree. Please forgive me that I have been so long in writing.

There is just one short thing I would like you to say on my behalf, and perhaps you won't mind if I put the words into your mouth:

'Mr Sargeson wishes me to say that as an independent worker in the field of the Humanities, he is grateful for the honour conferred — as much on behalf of fellow-workers in this field, as on his own. He hopes the gesture by the University will be interpreted as an endorsement of his belief, that those who may worthily practise the difficult art of Letters should always be accorded a reasonably decent place in a modern community'.

Okay? After all, I touch upon your own lifetime distinction — I mean the Humanities.

Clearly we have a date, the evening of the twentieth of the month. I look forward to meeting you.

Yours sincerely,

Frank Sargeson

To Phillip Wilson, *Wellington*

Alexander Turnbull Library

8 December 1974

Dear Phil,

[. . .] The Ceremony of the Doctorate was interesting in a way — medieval, red gown, velvet hat with hard brim and tassel (I have been told I looked rather well sitting up on the platform afterwards in drag — better than the other two, the scientist Doctor Charles Fleming, and the ex-Chancellor of the University Henry Cooper — must have all come natural to me. The most interesting thing of all was a kind of apostolic succession, a laying on of hoods (instead of hands) by the Chancellor (Mr Justice Speight by the way — sitting next to him at the preceding dinner — dinner suit, forsooth — borrowed — I was compulsively moved to inform him that I expected he should have been sentencing me instead — I expect my way of rebelling against the country's hypocrisy-inducing laws).

No more just now, but good wishes, and I must ring your daughter up on some pretext before too long.

F.S.

To Robin Dudding, *Torbay, Auckland*

Alexander Turnbull Library

[Re: Islands *obituary for Maurice Duggan, who died 11 December 1974.]*

7 January 1975

Dear Bob,

I didn't reply immediately about M.D. — I thought I could do what you wanted without too much strain. I find I can't — and God knows off and on for over a week I've tried very hard.

The right sort of note very difficult — what put in, what leave out. I think our main tie was M's intelligence, very remarkable — our main cleavage, that not only did one often suppose from what he wrote that he had nothing to write about, he often disconcerted by saying that he hadn't. I didn't agree with this attitude. Then there was the alcohol, the advertising the illness. No, I can't do it. It all needs a terrific biography and I don't doubt one will eventually be done.

But I'm sorry I can't help.

Good wishes,

To Bill Pearson, *Auckland*

Alexander Turnbull Library

[Pearson wrote to FS from Australia on 9 December 1974: 'It was July [1973] that John Reece Cole put the suggestion [about FS's honorary doctorate] to me in Christchurch, and looking into the ways and means I found that any such proposal had to come from three full (no less) professors. So approaching Keith Sinclair and Bob Chapman and then Karl Stead [. . .] I composed the letter [of 6 September 1973] which was signed by the three professors, and was only surprised [. . .] that it should have had to wait so long'. ATL MS-Papers-4261-143.]

12 January 1975

Dear Bill,

Yes, your letter did turn up before Christmas. I was much moved by it. [. . .]

Anyhow, in conventional language, it is all very handsome of you, and more particularly when I recall (which I often do with pain and embarrassment) all the pain and worry I caused you ten years ago. Not that I am wholly reconciled to being doctored (it was my joke when asked if I would make a speech to say no, my little black cat didn't — though he did — when he was doctored, so why should I?), if it wasn't that I realize it is a genuine distinction I would think of myself as sucked a little too closely to the Establishment. Also it came just as I was making decisions about a shift from Takapuna — for ten years a bachelor subsistence-farmer ten years younger than I am brought me firewood down from his place on the Kaipara. Now it looks as though we may be able to share expenses and a house a little better than the decayed last century place he lives in: the setting of bush (including one kauri tree of great dimensions) and reverted pasture is incredibly beautiful: the biggest attraction perhaps is no noise (except from 12 dogs), and only farmyard smells. Anyhow we should shortly see.

Because of bureaucratic nonsense over my Scholarship in Letters I shall soon have to go with some leisure from here to Invercargill and back, and charge it all for expenses, or else hand over about $3000 to Tax Department (trigger factor was first Authors Fund payment coinciding).

I agree that Dennis and the University Press have done a very handsome job on I Saw in My Dream [Rhodes's 1974 edition], and it plagues me that perhaps I am not as grateful as I should be. I thought I was really achieving something when I wrote that book. It seemed a super-difficult task. But reception was so mixed I got muddled and tried to forget all about it — tried far too long as it turned out (I almost destroyed myself as a writer). Result now is that all my affection goes to three, perhaps four, of the short stories, then to the Peon and Joy of the Worm (yet both of these kind of tour de force jobs — I have no notion at all what kind of future anything of mine may have).

Perhaps I am most interested of all in your last paragraph. I read again Thyrsis and the Scholar, I read too Virgil's Corydon Eclogue — and everything in those seems a long long way from Coal Flat, and yet I don't know. In late years I haven't read again the Flat, but I intend to remedy that. But 'faint and fugitive?' One writes out of the reverse — energy and pursuit?

Anyhow many thanks, Bill, I have memories —

If I may say so without more embarrassings I have still away down in my heart much love,

Frank

['your last paragraph': Pearson to FS, 9 December 1974, 'Myself I have been glad to get away from the trivialities of our little world, I mean the shop I work for, and feel stirrings of strength but they are, like the tree that stood for the gipsy for Thyrsis and Corydon, faint and fugitive, like the gipsy himself, and need exercise.' ATL MS-Papers-4261-143.]

To Felix Donnelly, *Auckland*

Alexander Turnbull Library

[Donnelly to Michael King, 10 August 1992: 'I first met Frank [. . .] when I was giving a talk night at the Presbyterian Church in Takapuna. Frank came along as one of a large audience in attendance, and stayed back at the end of the meeting to meet with me. I later drove him home and dropped him off at his little house on the Shore. He liked what I was doing apparently, and in particular standing up for homosexuals against the Church'. ATL 97-042-19/06.]

24 February 1975

Dear Father Donnelly,

Would you not perhaps agree that until there is a clearing-up of questions of terminology, chances are slight of a wide and reasonably accurate understanding of what the big question is all about.

Let me see if I can explain.

You are asked a question which should not have been put to you — I mean because, in essence, it doesn't make for any good sense at all. You answer no, and although I immediately and clearly understand what you mean, I am also dismayed. NOT for reasons you may tend to suppose. No, because if the question had properly been put the answer in my view should and perhaps would have been affirmative. Are you bi-sexual? It is an important part of our human nature for us to be bi-sexual, hence the answer you have supplied implies that you deny a large part of your human inheritance.

I think there is a very big question for the Church here — although it goes without saying one must be cautious about taking the New Zealand version of the Church as representative.

May I say that I am nearly into my 73rd year, and think of these points I make to you as byproducts of a reasonably satisfying and fruitful lifetime? Also it could interest you that in *Landfall* 80 (December, 1966) I wrote an Imaginary Conversation between William Yate and Saumel Butler. I think I threw a shaft or two of light into places where there is so often so lamentably little. [Marginal note: because of or in spite of things of this kind that the University has made me a doctor]

With every good wish to you,

Frank Sargeson

To Felix Donnelly, *Auckland*

Alexander Turnbull Library

[Donnelly to FS, 4 March: 'The question of bisexuality interests me very much. I believe that a specific orientation to either heterosexuality or homosexuality comes very much from environmental factors. It seems in many cases it is a learned process. I see man very much as pansexual in his responses and he tends to be conditioned to respond one way or another'. ATL MS-Papers-4261-040.]

17 March 1975

Dear Father Donnelly,

Tidying my writing table this morning, I see that when sending you my Conversation I overlooked sending as well a comment or two on your remarks about 'in many cases a learned process'.

I think I would say in some cases yes, but I have known those who have been sexually orthodox until quite late in life, when at last a long lived-with sense of missing out has been too powerful to deny any more, I doubt very much whether there is an environmental factor here. Not seldom I have heard, 'I always knew as far back as I can remember'. One of the most useful publicized remarks I can remember was by the Archbishop of Canterbury at the time of the Wolfenden Inquiry — as far as I know it said, 'Nature sends into the world a steady proportion of these people' (but I can't be sure it was exactly like that.)

It seems to me that environment fails to account for strength and persistence which can show up in very ordinary average orthodox practitioners, also I imagine a pretty steady proportion does not support the environment idea.

Do you know Gosse's bit about how he couldn't take it when his father wanted him to believe that God had deliberately created the fossils and left them about to try a Christian man's faith? Perhaps same with Male and Female he created them. He didn't. Why have men tits e.g.? Surely not to try a good Christian man's faith in Male and Female.

Sincerely yours good Father Donnelly,
from
Frank Sargeson

To New Statesman, *London*

Alexander Turnbull Library

27 April 1975

Dear Subs Department,

Here is something on account of sub, leaving £7.50 still to pay. It will take me about another 10 to circumvent currency regulations.

I have a grouch. I am in my 73rd year. There used to be professional writers in the NS, excellent to read despite what they might be reviewing. Now you consistently dig up a lot of dullards alleged to be experts in some field or other. You make it touch and go with me whether I renew or not.

Also, where is the liaison between subs and editorial? You did not notice my last book, and it looks as though you may overlook my current one. Damn it all, Raban said one of my books was some kind of masterpiece, and I figure in the Oxford Companion to English Literature. What other achievement do you require before one becomes worthy of being noticed? (And Christ! some of the work you *do* notice!)

Yours sincerely,
Frank Sargeson

To Ray Copland, *Christchurch*

Private collection

30 April 1975

Dear Ray Copland,

You much interest me in the *Landfall* notice [of *Once is Enough*]. A part of the monograph? Anyhow a compliment to be taken as you do take me. And I suppose this note is really to say yes, right about a 'work of imagination' (so far as I know, nobody so far has dared to say that).

How would I put it myself? A memoir is a work in which one really does 'put oneself in' as a character? And never does, quite, when writing straight fiction? I don't know, but it is something like that. And another thing is time. At this distance I would hate to be asked to cross my heart & say yes, this or that really was a 'happening'.

This is also to say that *More than Enough* has at last been shipped from England — binding was the hold-up (unfortunately I had no opportunity to remedy literals etc, many so aptly pointed out by yourself). Anyhow I expect it will be many weeks yet before the book arrives.

The new vol, *Never Enough*, seems to go surprisingly well at present (although the toughest work of the three — this probably my age). Publishers in London & Wellington think well of my little novel *Sunset Village*, but I have nagging doubts.

Good wishes,

Frank Sargeson

To Murdoch McLean, *Kaukapakapa*

Alexander Turnbull Library

8 June 1975

Dear Murdie,

[. . .] If you find time to look at the enclosed sheets (they are photocopy of the story ['The Power of Thought'] to appear in Melbourne Herald) you may see how handy to me that book you gave me turned out to be, *Think and Grow Rich*. My story is a kind of take-off or send-up of the terrible world implied by that book. Not one of my best stories, but amusing, surely. Anyhow the 100 bucks not turned up yet, nor the 60 from the Listener. But soon, maybe.

Nobody (and alas, perhaps I even include my dear dear Murdoch, and Clarrie [Tucker] certainly I think) in this country understands the awful strain work of this kind can be, a stretching almost to snapping-point. Anyhow I'm on the upgrade after my exhaustion now, and very grateful to be.

No more just now

To John Lehmann, *London*

Princeton University Library

8 July 1975

Dear John,

I am afraid at very long last. My intentions were of the best at the time of Plomer's death — but there you are, I must have been almost as early as anyone to hear of it (it was on the BBC overseas news immediately) and so much immediately flooded my mind — you, NW, all those years. But I was soon writing off to Charles [Erdmann], then came the arrangements for a complete collection of letters to go to the Turnbull Library in Wellington (and [Rupert] H[art]-Davis was very kind and helpful) — and, well, I never got around to my intended letter. But what a loss, that marvellously warm-hearted understanding man — thank heaven we have his work, and there's much of it that's yet to be cherished, and I would think for a long long time.

And you? Glover in Wellington has lately written me, rather concerned after hearing from you. I do hope things are [marginal note: *not* (a bad slip!)] sad or bad for you. I know just a little about your visits to California from my friend Janet Frame, who now lives not very far from me, (which can be very nice, my memory of the time when she lived in my army hut these days suggests to my mind that that was just a little too close).

And I suppose as one does I should tell you a little about myself. If I have an excuse for not writing you it is that although these days I can knock off my work a little more readily, I do put in an awful lot of time at it. I suppose I am something of a rarity in not really discovering what I could do until I was rising sixty. And really output, now I am rising 73, continues to astonish me. Also I confess to being quite touched by the reception I often get (though more overseas than here, NZders have a rooted objection to anybody who is supposed to be any good staying around the local scene — although they do make one exception, in favour of their All Black Rugby players). Anyhow the comments I have mostly had about my 2nd memoir vol (More than Enough) have quite moved me. And perhaps another point I should make is that over nearly 4 years of all this activity I had on hand an exacting nursing job — my friend of 36 years, ten years older. He died in 1971 in his 78th year, and he was the beall the occasion and all the rest of it for That Summer. I don't know how it is with you, but despite years, I find I can still find new friends — although eventually it all probably *must* become a little difficult (people *younger* than myself I tend to think of as honorary friends only!) Anyhow it comforts me to think the 3rd and last memoir book is not to be about myself, no, subtitle, Places and People, and really, it's the *environment* I would like at last to do something unusual about.

Denis tells me you write of Virginia Woolf, and clearly that will be something for all of us to look forward to. But meantime if *you* can get round to a note without worry and time consumed, then do let me have it. And for my part I will get round to posting you off two specimens of our two little magazines. There is the oldtimer *Landfall* (and because it is run by the Caxton Press typography and all is always very decent, even though the matter is not always well edited). *Islands* is often perhaps a bit short on what the Caxton Press can provide, but for all that there's much to it, and Lord knows I get very tired of the with-it philistinism one has to put up with. No more, dear John, but affection and gratitude (even though you may feel I'm a bit short, particularly on the latter)

From yours,

Frank S

To Patrick Evans, *Christchurch*

Private collection

[Evans wrote to FS on 3 June 1975 saying he was working on a literary-critical study of Frame for Twayne's 'World Authors' series. He mentioned that he had written to Frame, who replied 'cordially with a couple of letters over the last few years but I sense that she is unwilling to say anything committed'. Evans told FS he had 'approached a lot of people about various details' but had found that people had 'simply closed ranks at the mention of her name.' 'I'd like to be clear that I'm not after secrets. [. . .] What I'd like is confirmation of dates, movements, and so on, rather than anecdotes' after her return from England. ATL MS-Papers-4261-050.]

11 July 1975

Dear Patrick Evans,

I don't mind at all telling you about Janet — but hold on a moment, I don't mind, but my papers have built up again into a pretty mess since I disposed of so many to the Turnbull Library. What I'm saying is I can't remember any sequence, and don't imagine myself putting in days trying to reconstruct.

Anyhow here's what I remember (and be damned to her if she objects — she can be very very free with what she has to say, usually in her books, about what she knows or imagines she does about other people).

Yes, it would be c 1965 she returned from her first trip (and we had got her away in 1956 (Charles Brasch was the big helper). But I'll be damned if I can remember the number and sequence of events of the last ten years. How many times away? — I would think at very least three (after all she has been twice in Yaddo and once in the McDowell set-up — Vermont; Yaddo is at Saratoga Springs N.Y.). Or it may have been 4 times, very well have been. Or more. Each time abroad she has been fortunate in John Money (who was her psychology lecturer at Otago when she had her breakdown: he got to America, got a very good Harvard degree, and is now a professor at the Johns Hopkins in Baltimore: a Sexologist of world class — whatever the word and world class may mean — he's at anyrate always arranging world conferences of sexologists, and perhaps most appropriately he usually arranges them at Bangkok). Also in two Californian painters, Bill Brown and Paul Wonner — they used to be at Santa Barbara, Calif, but I'm not sure where now, anyhow they know their stuff — I've seen Wonners and very good ones in International Art magazines. The third person is Miss E.P. Dawson, who lives in Norfolk, England, and she is the K of the Tauranga seaside cottage which you can find in my Up Onto the Roof and Down Again.

Perhaps too I should say somewhere there is a painting or drawing of J by Don Bacardi [Bachardy] who if I am remembering rightly has for long been a very cherished pal of Isherwood.

Of course I can remember much you can't possibly use, not at this stage, such as her story about going off London Bridge and being beaten up by very formidable lesbian policewomen before being rescued by a Maudsley Hosp professor who had become a personal friend.

It was John Money who collected her stories after her first breakdown and put them to the Caxton Press. So he must be credited with launching her career. It was in my army hut that she wrote Owls do Cry which she sent on her own initiative to Albion Wright.

And my own view of her work? — there is only one thing I admire without any reserves whatsoever — The Day of the Sheep. I leave you to decide why. If you can sort out something and think I may be of more help please write. [. . .] Janet's address is now 276, Glenfield Road, Glenfield, Auckland 10. You will be surer of her opening any letter by addressing Janet Clutha (her name by deed poll: but I have not yet become Frank Waikato).

Good wishes,

F.S.

To Graeme Lay, *Auckland*

Private collection

[Lay, then teaching in Auckland, wanted to be a writer but was having difficulty breaking through to publication. He wrote to FS enclosing his story 'The Children of Wah' and asked for his advice.]

11 July 1975

Dear Graeme Lay,

I could read the story — no trouble at all. Don't be offended if I send you a few comments. If you aim at *Listener* don't, I think, run to so many words — the shorter the better. And don't do so much *thinking* — I mean on paper — let the *reader* think the feet have been *inhumanly* deformed. You state & record too much. Try instead to suggest. Make the reader work for you without his having a notion of your cunning. Let the story be its own moral, don't show your hand, let all the concentration be on the *story* so that it won't slip out of focus — as it surely will if you push yourself into it without exercising extreme caution discretion & skill. Let it seem finally to have written itself, so that there it is, a creation, absolutely, imaginatively *there* — with whatever name attached to it of little importance — the true importance is that it should remain for all time imaginatively truthful (but of course very few of us can be quite as good as all that: nonetheless we try to be). A short story is the most difficult of all literary forms (apart from poetry, that is to say). I hope you will try again & pretty often — I hope that in time you may without question bring it off.

Good wishes,

Frank Sargeson

To Graeme Lay, *Auckland*

Alexander Turnbull Library

20 July 1975

Dear Graeme Lay,

Your letter, thank you — and I don't want to become involved in a correspondence (perhaps as much for your sake as my own).

But I do want to say it would worry me if I'd somehow managed to ball you up — and particularly about the first person.

It is, surely, a device. The narrator may sometimes be the author — I mean the 'I'. Open wide your imagination to this question, I would think most of the 'I' fiction is certainly not myself — I mean the 'I' fiction I have written. Think of *I For One* as a very clear example. Indeed one advantage of the 'I' technique is that it enables the author to stay out. After all with third person it may perhaps strongly occur to the reader that there must be somebody there, and it will then be strongly suspected the author is there (which in many senses may well be right). There is of course one great disadvantage of the 'I' — only what the 'I' knows sees and experiences can be presented.

I just throw off these rather jumbled thoughts in the hope they may be of some use to you. I must say all this technical matter came very readily to me when I began writing — I never had any trouble at all. But I have often detected the trouble other story writers have let themselves in for.

And length. Well of course it all depends on what the story demands. But that is to say ideally. It goes without saying that with a paper of the NZ Listener kind you will stand more chance if you don't demand too much space. You would stand a better chance with a more spacious story in *Landfall* or *Islands* (and both these don't pay so badly at all — if you have something you think well of you might very well try them).

But there again — that's about it. A very busy tried (sorely) tired and not young professional writer is sending you this. To all who show talent I wish all the success in the world. But there's no formula — except perhaps discipline and hard work.

With many good wishes,

To Christine Cole Catley, *Whatamonga Bay*

Alexander Turnbull Library

20 July 1975

Dear Chris,

[. . .] Thanks for your remarks about Making Father Pay [*Listener* June 7] — and yes, it does seem after all my years I know how to produce my effects in a story (that one took 20 years — first I couldn't think of something sufficiently horrible for the lead in (the woman who ate her husband) to the cement business. Also I tried for many years to describe the cementing until I saw it should happen 'off' — and all finally hingeing on a knowing imaginative narrator remaining well in the background.

The winter has been really very trying, I mean for anyone my age. It seems as though for the first time in my life I have really felt the cold. But I do thank God stick to Never Enough and now have 20,000 drafted words. [. . .]

All for now,

To Vincent O'Sullivan, *Hamilton*

Alexander Turnbull Library

27 July 1975

Dear Vincent O'Sullivan,

The 114 Landfall turned up to remind me I had never sent you a note to say how much to my liking I found your *Visitors*. I have just read the story again with renewed admiration. You need not of course take seriously anything I say, but it seemed to me you could have found yourself quite undone with a ready-made Inferno on hand. But not at all — and I see now (or think I do) that in all the stories I have seen you are presenting us with the inhabitants of a modern Inferno (and all the better for us that the agony of it all comes across so memorably because of the low-key kind of presentation you manage with such skill.)

Well, I don't know whether that is what I would have written had I written months ago — at anyrate it does more or less say how it strikes me at this moment.

And the Mansfield. I have read with very great interest, and I can always admire such a thorough scholar. It's just that I am doubtful about the worth of so much work. Surely it all must hinge on the Mansfield achievement, which, God forgive me, I see as pretty meagre. A few very good stories — what else? The soul-torments are what you would expect, and which I imagine can readily be found if anyone cares to look closely (and a few years later it would have been Rupert Brooke instead of Wilde. I remember Fairburn used to say that it was rather unfair to Brooke that so many young women used to have his photograph on their dressing tables. And it goes without saying Wilde ((or should I say the best of several Wildes?)) could and can still do without colonial schoolgirl raptures. Surely the point about Mansfield is (yes, she died young, admitted) that nothing came to very much. But I concede to you without any reserves your scholarship — and perhaps you won't take it amiss if I make a few amateur points. I thought the story dug up by Margaret Scott (I mean the one published in Landfall) did the author no credit at all. To me it seemed rather terrible that I found it positively bad. Yet it greatly interested me with the name 'Evershed.' This occurs as the name of a character in Mrs Ward's *Robert Elsemere*; but Evershed was also the middle name of James Agate. As you probably know there was a Wildean slant to Agate, and it might be argued that Mansfield could have been referring to something of the kind when she made use of the name.

Just a small point to end with. On page 98 (Landfall) it looks as though you could be attributing 'though your sins be as scarlet. . .' to Wilde. I daresay I am wrong, but just in case (Chap I Prophet Isaiah) the sentence goes on, 'they shall be as white as snow.' Most certainly, it *sounds* like Wilde.

['the Mansfield': O'Sullivan's 'The Magnetic Chain: Notes and Approaches to KM', Landfall, *June 1975.]*

To Patrick Evans, *Christchurch*

Private collection

[Evans wrote to FS on 4 August asking him to verify some further points of substance relating to Janet Frame's biography. ATL MS-Papers-4261-050.]

9 August 1975

Dear Pat Evans,

I seem to have a few minutes, so here goes. And just look what by the miracle of a hand probing into Chaos came up with! A date on the back which should help you (but I don't know why the coloured wooden gentleman has no knackers — so far as I remember J discounted my suggestion that she had perhaps got up secretly in the night and bitten them off. Was it on no knacker account that we composed our limerick — was it mine or hers (and yet I have a sneaking feeling it may have been many years ago attributed to Aldous Huxley). Anyhow,

Said a man to a pretty maid please,

If you *must* explore to my knees
In return for a kiss,
Wrap your hand round *this*,
And pay less attention to *these*!

(for 2nd line of couplet, 'Close your lips round this,' may be substituted)

And you must admit nearly as good as that daddy of all limericks,

A handsome young plumber named Lee
Was plumbing a girl down by the sea.
Said the girl, 'Cease your plumbing!
There's somebody coming!'
Said the plumber still plumbing, 'IT'S ME!!'

But you know, you have started me off on all this with your 'lecherer in Psychology' — so obvious yet in all my 72 years I had never thought of that.

But ANSWERS

1 [Was Frame in the US for two years, c 1970–72?] I don't know about the two years, but the postcard shows the date September 1971.

2 [Was Frame in the US between c 1965 and 1968?] I don't hear a bell ringing, but I would say yes, between 1965 and 68.

3 [Are Frame's friends the Marquands the novelist John P Marquand and his wife?] The Marquand husband is the son of the celebrated J.P.M. The son writes novels too, but I don't know anything about them. I remember though Janet said he didn't think very well of his father's. His wife (very lately now I think, divorced) has or had a Rothschild aunt — something of the kind. Must be true I imagine, because when the French baron R came here for a heart operation for his wife, Janet got a message, and I think went to pay a call at Hotel Mon Desir (I remember too she had some difficulty discouraging her sister (Chicks) and husband from accompanying her). I seem to remember Janet met the younger Marquand when he was doing a stint on a novel at Yaddo (or it may have been at McDowell). Anyhow Janet's relation is really with his wife, Sue, who lavishes money on phone calls to her from New York, for a time set her up in an apartment in NY, also took her twice on holiday with family to Bermuda, or it may have been a Bahama. I remember I said to J it must have been a deluxe holiday fridges the entire works, and J said no, she used to get very hungry, not knowing how to open the coconuts which lay all about, but once she had learned she lived on coconuts and wasn't hungry.

4 [Evans asks about E.P. Dawson and Miss R.E. Rowlandson] Miss E.P. Dawson of near Norfolk. My friend. An Englishwoman who wrote to me when we both were contributing to *Tomorrow* in the thirties. She lived in Pelorus Sound, afterwards at Mount Maunganui, Tauranga. I often used to stay with her, a good many years older than I was. I introduced her to Janet and they clicked pretty well, Janet went on visits, and when E.P. (whom all her friends called Peter — my *Memoirs of a Peon* is dedicated to her —) at last returned to England her cottage in a village near Norwich has been a marvellous standby for Janet. Almost next door lives George Barker. The other woman Rebie Eleanor Rowlandson, yes violin, & I did have her in mind for *Memoirs of Peon*, pp 28, 29 30 — and I have always regretted I could do nothing more with her in later parts of the novel. [. . .] It was almost incredible coincidence that Janet rented for a time a Waiheke bach where she had died (Janet brought up from Waiheke a paperbacked *A Man and his Wife* which was in the bach and had been given by me to Miss R in the early forties). I told Janet her story, and I think J made use of it (not absolutely sure though as I have never read *A State of* (finding it tedious). Yes, I think you are right about the Wagner book [she found on Waiheke] and the phrase ['the room two inches behind the eyes'].

5 [Evans: 'I didn't know [. . .] that John Money was a lecherer in Psychology when [Frame] broke down. Do you have any idea *when* she broke down? I don't want any gory details, but wonder whether she was affected badly by the drowning of sister Isobel on 17 February 1947'.] Work out the approximate date, J was born 1924, and was at University and Training College when she was first committed. The story she told me was that an inspector walked into the room one day when she was teaching and she promptly walked out the other door, then she was not on view for some days until discovered — her story was a bottle of aspirin tablets. Yes J had and has a thing about water and drowning. Wasn't there another sister who was drowned though? — I seem to remember.

6 [How long did Frame stay in FS's bach?] It would be Feb or March 1955 that J started in the hut. First the hut was made available for her to come when she liked and go when she liked (back to her sister's), not seeing me except on rare days. Later though I suggested she set herself up in the hut for the year and

write a novel — and so it turned out. It became very trying for me especially during the two winters when she would become at times quite psychotic. She left for England towards the end of the second winter.

Look, thinking it over — she has been *many times* in USA. First there was John Money as anchor, also she managed to get into Yaddo and McDowell. Then since she developed her crush on one of the two Californian painters [Bill Brown] she has seized on almost any pretext to get to see him.

No doubt I am giving away too much — must rely on your discretion. But you could say 'has been many times in USA and knows California especially, also Yaddo and MacD, Boston NY and Baltimore.'

I wouldn't say J's picture of Chicks is all 'wrong'. But admittedly she *must* write much too directly, but that doesn't mean accurately, and does mean extraordinary distortions. Karl Stead Charles Brasch and myself have much reason to know this, the three of us especially, and my God at times it seems this is the penalty visited on us for being of help. Indeed, help is sometimes a signal for another rendition of what we are imagined to be. Don't ask me to explain,

Of course at her best a marvellous companion, ready wit, as intelligent as they come, never misses an allusion, literary or whatever, all PLUS.

Good wishes,

Frank Sargeson

['the coloured wooden gentleman': The photo, now lost, showed two people standing on either side of one of John Money's tribal statues. 'I remember this figure as being pretty near life-sized. [. . .] The statue had no testicles but a large penis, hence Frank's suggestion re Janet's supposed midnight feast'. Evans, personal correspondence, 5 October 2009.]

To Patrick Evans, *Christchurch*

Private collection

[Evans to FS, 3 September: 'Did she (Frame) ever, to your knowledge, read Robin Hyde's novel The Godwits Fly, *or refer to it? It seems so much like* Owls Do Cry *in parts. Can you recall anything of where she stayed in England?' ATL MS-Papers-4261-050. At the time of these letters FS was being treated for congestive heart failure.]*

18 October 1975

Dear Pat Evans,

I seem to have survived (less a stone and a half, but mainly water I think), they have taken away my oxygen cylinder, but I don't suffocate any more. At its worst a pretty narrow squeak as we used to say. [. . .]

Indeed Miss J did read The Godwits Fly — it was among the probably thousands of books she read when she was (so far as leisure went) a Hospital lady at large. I knew she read a good deal more Enzed lit. than I did — and anyhow Hyde used to trade on that stiff leg, in the early thirties turning up at my bach at 3 am, and maintaining a steady pace of about 30 yards an hour while I helped to repatriate her. [Marginal note: This somehow works like some sublime *non sequitur* — probably the result of my being dehydrated — such people can become very disorganised.] One thing I clearly remember about these two women. A spot of housework or cooking was not for them. How I remember myself mad with starvation snatching a string of sausages from the hand of Miss H, and her not noticing, being enraptured by the sound of her own voice and verse as she read aloud from the yards of script in her other hand. But compensation — so long as she could continue from more yards of script I could eat the sausages.

In England — yes, well when J made London after Ibiza via Andorra (where she ran up and down pine hills jumping in and out of pools in an endeavour to 'procure' something — which according to her she did), it was for quite some time the Maudsley (Karl Stead once when calling there to inquire after her was told they in some ways regarded her as the most interesting patient they had). Improving, she moved to lodgings in Camberwell. I think she worked for a time as a cinema usher, and she received National Assistance. Later she shifted to Camden Town. She also visited my friend Miss E.P. Dawson at Itteringham in Norfolk, and at one time bought a caravan which was established on Miss D's property. Also one holiday-time she walked with a pup tent in the Wordsworth country (I mean the Lake District, not Somerset). I remember she was amazed at lack of space in the Grasmere cottage, indeed quite obsessed with thoughts about what poor Dorothy must have suffered with William cuckolding her with his wife only a few inches away on the other side of a thin partition. She was greatly helped through London days by the man who owns or used to own W.H. Allen — what was his name, Mark somebody, perhaps Mark Goulding? [Goulden] I think he had the notion he could put her across to a big readership — but it never seemed to come off. Not as he had hoped anyhow. Also I think it was he who recommended her to her more or less dilettante millionaire publisher in America [George Braziller] who has also failed to turn her into the hoped-for popular writer.

Look, I find myself fatigued. *Aftermath* — perhaps I will call my next book that. May all this gossip be of some help.

All for now,

F.S.

To Vincent O'Sullivan, *Hamilton*

Alexander Turnbull Library

[On 10 September O'Sullivan wrote to say that he had written a story as a way of thanking FS for his earlier comments. '[. . .]I thought that the best way, perhaps, to say something in return, was to write a story about the kind of world you have marked out as so much your own, and to let you know [. . .] that it was written for you. The story will be in the next Islands *[12], a piece set in Frankton'. ATL MS-Papers-4261-139.]*

26 October 1975

Dear Vincent O'Sullivan,

Since your note I have been ill, and apart from finding myself still a bit hallucinated (the result of becoming disorganised by my having to be dehydrated), far too much literary matter has accumulated — for the time being I really do not quite know where I am.

There was the Landfall (I mean the Islands) story ['End'], and I appreciate the compliment, it is indeed the kind of world which strongly attracts me, and I was much interested to discover how you had handled it. I am inclined to believe the story is a masterpiece (but remember I am not all that right in my head at the moment). And apart from all else it is hard for me to judge — I am plagued by thoughts of how I would have handled it myself. So often in the past when asked questions about 'influences' I have mentioned Sherwood Anderson — and always I forget to mention Tolstoy, his short stories, where his use of the clear statement repeated and repeated until all is added up into something very powerful. This work was my constant reading a good many years before I tried to write, and it still is. I think what I am intending to say is that I thought of Anderson as I began to read your story.

But as I have said too much material for coping with at present. The Oxford Stories [ed. by O'Sullivan] have taken up much time (and although I knew the book was to appear I knew nothing of any work of my own to appear in it — I think Longman Paul must have slipped up about letting me know.) Anyhow too great a variety of work to prompt me into any comment meantime. (In your own Mavvy Phoenix I see again about the quick hand of friendship and the oral tradition, and I am set wondering again for some hours about 'sophistication' in writing, and to what degree it undoes one, or doesn't.

Must return to light convalescent chores, but I hope I may be writing again,

From yours, with appreciation,

To Arthur Coombes, *Physician/cardiologist, Takapuna*

Alexander Turnbull Library

27 October 1975

Dear Arthur Coombes,

I wouldn't like you to think I am ungrateful for what you did for me. Your diagnosis was dead on, and even though the dumbest GP could hardly have missed the swollen legs, I hadn't been told of water in lungs liver and I imagine from what came away every bodily cavity or whatever where it could lodge.

Nor was it your fault that the diuretic seemed not to work, and the salt-removing modern prescription poison seemed in my view a very nasty piece of work (not your fault either).

I do though have a slight complaint which applies equally to my GP (and I imagine every physician in the country). It apparently will remain for ever a question whether or not I owe my survival to a female friend actively engaged in the more humble areas of the healing profession [Barbara Duggan, a physiotherapist]. In conversation we agreed that if one assumed a diuretic would work it would be as well to put oneself into a suitable posture. After all, we agreed, if it was a bad case of water-logging, then even according to the New Physics water would probably be most reluctant to run uphill. So okay, take your medicine at say 4.30 am then go back to bed with your feet and legs propped up and a pile of pillows behind your back and head.

It worked like a charm, but of course scientifically speaking I can make no serious claims because I lacked a control.

But strangely I have lately suffered from another curious omission to provide information — I was not informed by a GP that there is a great difference between Hydrocortisone for applying to the skin which is 1 per cent and the same at ½ p.c. Further, I have never ever been told that particularly the first strength should on no account be covered (socks, for instance, and results may be checked from a glance at my lower legs, afflicted by a capillary varicose condition).

Well now, perhaps the gist of all this is that I am thinking of asking Ian Cross to allow me to write another editorial in the Listener — this time about an urgent reform required for physicians. They may prescribe only upon the condition that the patient is afterwards informed by an experienced nurse (and of course you will agree that good nurses know far far more about illness than any doctor knows or is likely to know) about how the prescribed substance is likely to behave according to proper or improper use.

But the point of this note is that I much hope I am not ungrateful for what you did for me.

Good wishes,

To Arnold Wall, *[Nelson]*

Alexander Turnbull Library

6 March 1976

Dear Arnold,

[. . .] True, I don't move much from here, indeed only a few miles away on to the unfashionable side of the Peninsula — a bachelor farmer 10 years younger than I am, a taciturn Scot whose house falls down and is infested with rats, but the reverting land is marvellous and so is the making bush (with the one great kauri the millers missed last century — and he won't sell it no matter how more and more broke he gets).

Yes, I carefully read Hooks and Feelers several times. I believe I am on record as saying I don't think I'm too good as a model for younger NZ writers — when I saw that perhaps something of S had gone into this piece of work I thought there could be something to make up my mind about. Well, never mind, I finally decided the story was worth anyone's time — indeed a skilful piece of work. I hope Keri Hulme won't mind these remarks if you report them to her. As for visits I never these days know what to say about them. But there's my unlisted phone no. (496,999), and I always try to say my piece courteously.

I wrote Sunset Village after I'd finished the 2nd instalment of my memoir. I didn't want to get my hand out with fiction — an overdose of 'fact' was a bit too much. Anyhow it didn't to me seem to turn out all that well — but it was surprise from my London man — he thought it very okay — and further surprise when your Wellington people seemed to agree. We shall see (but I wish I could be confident that the printing will arrive on time).

This is my Sunday knock-off of letters. Where's my house-keeper secretary gardener rouseabout . . .

Most kind of you to write, and many good wishes,

[Arnold Wall (1908–1998) — 'piratical one-eyed publisher/scout & grammarian' — was the son of Prof. Arnold Wall, philologist, poet and mountaineer. Keri Hulme, personal correspondence, 2 July 2011.]

To Christine Cole Catley, *Whatamonga Bay*

Alexander Turnbull Library

27 March 1976

Dearest Chris,

[. . .] No Clarrie [Tucker] here at present, and whatever happens he can't return to Murdoch's — Murdie is marrying his 20 year old girl after all. He is rising 64. I have asked him to let his Rhonda know that if she doesn't behave herself or makes him suffer in any way she will find to her very great cost that she has me to reckon with. I asked M if she knew his situation — did she know that he is utterly and hopelessly broke? — well a slow smile came on his face and he said she would have to be absolutely dumb if she didn't. So then I said where was the colour telly the electricity supply the fridg the hot water etc etc etc to come from — and again the slow smile and he said if she wanted all that she could go out and work for it. But seriously, it is all almost impossible to believe — if there is a child how could it escape being eaten by the rats? after all the chickens and puppies about the house (?) can't.

Anyhow, the entire purpose of my life at moment seems to be to get the 3rd memoir written, and it's 3 fifths finished. I mean drafted. [. . .]

To Murdoch McLean, *Kaukapakapa*

Alexander Turnbull Library

Sunday [1976]

Dearest Murdie,

I daresay that shortly these letters I send you just won't do. Never mind, I won't be losing heart, and we shall see.

It all does remind me very keenly of away back in my early twenties when I was running myself up against brick walls in attempts to solve my terrible problems.

In every direction I looked for help there was nothing doing. I remember that kind of Methodist Pope, Rev Ransom — he told me I must reconcile myself to 'doing without.' I remember some awful doctors too, one in Ponsonby Road you may remember, Dr Pettit.

And then I started developing my head to accompany my over-developed affectionate heart. My reading suddenly took in Shaw and I read day and night gulping down everything he had written. He had said that marriage is popular because it combines the maximum of temptation with the maximum of opportunity, he didn't think much of children mucked up by being reared in 'Christian' families.

And then came all my excesses when I snatched very dangerously at everything I thought I might get. And I got a load of trouble.

And then by grace by God by luck by whathave you I found Harry — and immediately lost him for 10 years — and then by super-grace, super-luck superwhathaveyou I found him again — and that was it. And for thirty five years I never had a serious complaint.

Well, that's enough — I want to be a combination of those three monkeys — but not see nothing hear nothing say nothing. Instead see everything hear everything say everything (but the last only to myself)

Dear Murdie it seems to me extraordinary beyond belief that all that I got settled pretty early in life now comes up for you so late.

Do read the piece I gave you on Henry Lawson ['Henry Lawson: Some Notes After Re-Reading']. In many ways it's one of the best things I have ever done. I think it's a good example of my perennial endeavour to yell truth that should be told — I expect that's why I have run into censure in Australia over it.

I collected your pants which are nicely taken up and I am ironing in a cuff. So bring the other ones to be done. And I will remember about pullover.

To Christine Cole Catley, *Whatamonga Bay*

Alexander Turnbull Library

[FS to Catley, 9 May: 'I go on [Max Cryer's live talk/variety show] Town Cryer next Wednesday evening (along with Frank Muir and Spike Milligan? — well so I am told, maybe [. . .]).' Catley to FS, 13 May: '[P]lainly you enjoyed yourself. [. . .] You looked most impressive; loved that scarf. But what a silly show it is. Following you with that girl singer — and the show ended with a chimpanzee — was altogether too much.' ATL MS-Papers-4261-030.]

22 May 1976

Dearest Chris,

I think I might be a little inclined to disagree with you about Maxie, he said to me before hand that his show was vaudeville and I don't know but I think it helped. I haven't a notion of what I said (being blinded with lights and a little previously deafened with noise, not to mention tripping over cable — it's done in a broken down theatre in Dominion Road, and Barbara [probably Duggan] most kindly took charge of me), so reaction has vastly surprised me — at first I didn't believe the compliments, but there have been so many from so many people I don't know (letters from as far as Invercargill etc — I expect it happens to anyone who takes up television time — and it astonished me that my time was more than

15 mins — somehow nobody got my signature to contract so I don't know yet what it was worth (?) — of course Milligan was supposed to be on but his plane couldn't get down or something). At first we thought TV1 hadn't been able to withstand the impact of Sargeson, but it was an electrical storm, quite close, so apart from me there were only the Wombles — and I thought the chumpanzee was a darling.)

Anyhow, rather hoping NOT to become a TV star. Yes! [. . .]

To Ralph Bodle, *Kaukapakapa*

Alexander Turnbull Library

[Bodle to FS, 13 June, happened to mention that James K. Baxter, 'the hippie poet', was the grandson of Professor Macmillan Brown. ATL MS-Papers-4261-020.]

20 June 1976

Dear Ralph,

Excuse again the brevity — very busy yesterday with Murdoch yesterday getting Clarrie established in a very Posh Rest Home in Albany. May all go well but fingers crossed (making it difficult for typing). [. . .]

The professor's too-brilliant too-trying grandson used to stay with me on occasions, and I liked him best as an early poet, less as a poetizing prophet patriarch (a kinder term than pseudo-religious bullshit artist). Ah but a pink and white wise dreadful dangerous baby if ever there was one!

But so sorry, no more for now.

To Maurice Gee, *Nelson*

Alexander Turnbull Library

25 July 1976

Dear Maurice,

Nearly literally only a line (I have put off writing a few days, thinking I might find time to say something not too banal).

Not a show — take advantage of your immense privileges as a married man, marvellous excuses when it seems half the world wants to claim your time & attention!

Anyhow it's about the book [*Games of Choice*] — a splendid affair! My copy turned up a week ago — & now I'm shamelessly lending it, because price puts it out of reach of a few who may get even more from it than I did. I won't name them — but they are younger, writers, and broke.

And now I can't really say anything of any account. But what top kind of pleasure (from writing, from the assurance, the fascinating *interest*, & from the first page, *knowing* you are going to bring it off.) And all after the shame of [M. K. Joseph's] *A Soldier's Tale* — Mike at his worst, & surprising worst! — the shocking brutality not resolved in any way — who does he think he is? Sophocles? An amateur self-deceiving job!

Anyhow there you are — I'm too old to know for sure, but for me your remarkablest of all achievements — and may I live long enough to enjoy a few more!

May all public appreciation & success be yours to help you along,

From,

F.S.

My very good wishes to M[argaretha]. (Did I tell you my Kaukapakapa farmer friend 64, & a bachelor (more a virgin), has lately married — a girl 20? Now there's something for someone! (Perhaps me, perhaps not.)

['Now there's something for someone': the situation features in En Route *(1979).]*

To Ray Copland, *Christchurch*

Private collection

10 October 1976

Dear Ray Copland,

I've lately at last been able to pick up the four little first Oxford studies [*New Zealand Writers and their Work*] — and forgive a typewritten personal note (with rheumatism I get on better these days this way, it's getting difficult to hold the damn pen).

My compliments upon your conscientious job. Nothing at all to complain about (my bits and pieces of criticism, if there's anything much to them, can well wait awhile — I'm meaning such things as my defence of naturalism — *Conversation in a Train* I think it was called.)

I hope much you get the appreciation you deserve — to our mutual advantage. It may be that in one matter you seem to get things rather upside down. I do sincerely believe I never had any natural ability — my ability was not for *words*, and perhaps that is the reason why all has had to be learned — my ability was and still is (putting it very loosely) for knowing how people probably behave. If I don't know I can readily imagine. But all this preliminary business, this sine qua non if you like, has little to do with words. The difficulty for me in writing is to find the right words and decide upon the right sort of sentence and discover how to write it. All this means I don't see myself as literary in the way it appears you do. You are quite wide of the mark about Smollett (yes, many years ago I enjoyed *Random* also *Clinker*, but read nothing else: I've never got more than a few pages into *Shandy*, though I remember I thoroughly enjoyed *Sentimental Journey*). Contrary to this though, I was for years closely devoted to Fielding and read many times everything I could get into my hands.

Consider this proposition. Fielding in order to be Fielding the writer must have known many people who talked and behaved in a manner which he could make the foundation of his fictions. Why then should you be so reluctant to believe (apparently) that I have proceeded in any different way with the people you meet in *Memoirs of a Peon* or *Joy of the Worm*? It so happens I am engaged in the final typing of *Never Enough!* (which will conclude my memoirs no matter how many more years I may have the misfortune to live). Anyhow, I give an account of how I came to write my *Peon*. At that time I had my reasons for believing myself at the end of my tether so to speak — so every bit and piece of experience which I had never made use of in my writing life had to go in, and all had to be tied together in the person of the chief character [. . .]. Honest to God once I'd got the thing going I never ever had one thought of Smollett Sterne or whohaveyou in my mind. Having heard dear old Bake roll out his periods over all these years my only thought was to get the true flavour of them on to the written page. Anyhow, there you are and may you find something to interest you in *Never Enough*!

I see my God time has flown and it is Sunday and I am hungry — but a word of special appreciation. I was touched by your appreciation of *Man of England Now*, which is one of my own favourites. The little sine qua non pink and white man, now lives with his wife in a pensioner flat not too far away. Whenever his wife allows him out on his own he haunts my house and pulls scores of books down from my shelves (and a surprisingly large number he reads). How at the age of 74 he can be ending up like an angel when at the age of 12 he was down a coal mine is one of the unsolved mysteries of my life.

Well, no more for now, but very good wishes,

Frank Sargeson

I think perhaps what I am trying to say is that I am not *really* 'literary' in the way you at times appear to suppose.

To Alec Pickard, *Hamilton*

Alexander Turnbull Library

19 October 1976

Dear Alec,

My congratulations on what the Herald had to say Saturday. A long time. But I never forget that when I first saw your work I thought your talents were superior to my own. And (deep in the marathon of typing my 3rd memoir vol), I say something to that effect in these *last* (I hope) of my writing pages. It goes without saying much interested also in photograph. I envy your carrying round such a living map of experience, wisdom — everything I would like show in a face — epiphany — & no hope!

Well, for now, these few lines, but again my compliments: & may all associated extensions of yourself — wife, children, grandchildren be a complex source of extra satisfaction to you.

From yours,

F.S.

[On 16 October the NZ Herald *carried a short feature article about Pickard, highlighting Auckland University Press's forthcoming edition of his stories.]*

To Eric Godley, *[Lincoln University, Christchurch]*

Alexander Turnbull Library

2 January 1977

Dear Eric,

Your nice card and 'enclosure' turned up okay, and should have been acknowledged long ago (I was under vow to finish the 3rd vol of my memoir — More than Enough! — no sorry that was 2nd vol, I mean *Never Enough!* before 1976 was out, and made it with about half an hour to spare.)

But oh yes Murdoch's kauri survives, and I think I have persuaded him — to be more cagey about it — too many people, parties of schoolchildren and such, with teacher, go for looksee and it can't be very good for it. It's pretty high up, and to me it *looks* as though over the centuries it must have tended to be water-short, anyhow, not one of those surrounded by any mound of compost (perhaps because too many feet have tramped around?) Anyhow if you pass by here I much hope we can go and see it together.

Poor Murdoch is as hopelessly broke as ever and his marriage is in some senses ridiculous, particularly as his wife is said now to be pregnant (a 21 year old wife pregnant to a 64 year old husband!) Well, I daresay risk of mongolism ruled out in that combination — but my god, to be hopelessly broke and starting a family in one's mid-sixties!! Unfortunately there is a good deal of decayed Methodism in this madness.

Anyhow, I translated the cheque into cash and sent it out, and I am sure the man will be infinitely grateful (I've lately had to break off my handouts, funds close to exhaustion — but I'd give if I had it, a very charming bloke in a dour dark way).

It would be excellent if you come near to hear from you, my phone number is 496,999.

With all my kindest wishes,

F.S. [. . .]

To Janet Frame, *Stratford*

Alexander Turnbull Library

3 January 1977

Dear J,

Thank me for yours [Marginal note: Just noticed — sinister!] [. . .]

Yes, ah yes, I should have written ages ago. Alas, I had promised on my knees myself that I would complete *Never Enough* before midnight chimes of the old year — and I kept my promise by about half an hour. Well, we shall see. Didn't Agate write eight or nine EGOS? Perhaps I have foolishly opened the door on something more with my title, *Never Enough*.

Before I forget, Clarrie, who was 'raised' in a Salvation Army Home in Wellington, has been telling me some of the rhymes they invented to contradict their daily conditioning. I think the best is the following (going clearly to the tune of Jesus loves me this I know. . .)

> Jesus loves me I don't think,
> He took me to the skating rink,
> I drank whisky, he drank rum,
> He went skating on his bum!

It surprised me that Dennis McEldowney's book [*Frank Sargeson in His Time*] is so well done (I mean as a piece of book production). I think generally the inking is a bit wonky, too heavy, but fairly right for all that. I think Dennis's part is well done but it makes me (spuriously) blush, being too complimentary. Martin Green my publisher in London described it as a splendidly concocted *mélange*, and he particularly liked E.M. Forster 'and friends' also the three young men cutting the road (which indeed it is excellent to preserve as the negative was on glass and has been broken and lost) — but my favourites are my old grandmother and my uncle and that bit of land (what you see is not his place at all, the next door neighbour's). Also I have a liking for the photo on page 45 [of Frame] and am glad it has been preserved.

Well, I suffer from reaction and a bad back. Thank you for the photographs and I envy you the tranquillity of the Taranaki small town backblocks — I am sure it would be nice if for a change you changed places with Bill and Paul — *think* what they would do with Stratford (it could even put Muldoon out of the news!)

No more for now. I assume a new book from you comes before too long. I daresay you remain a fairish number of dollars ahead of me on Authors payment — $2049, me.

Are you to be in Readers' Digest at a fabulous rate of payment? Fortunately I got your address when they inquired, just a moment or two previously.

Murdoch has sold Rhonda's jumping horse — so we think she is *enceinte*! — they married last April. But M is more broke than ever!!

Best love x

To H. Winston Rhodes, *Lyttleton*

Alexander Turnbull Library

21 January 1977

Dear Winston,

[. . .] [Y]our remarks about Sunset Village interested me because I wrote that as a kind of reaction from writing *More than Enough*. I told myself damn it I'm a fiction writer, and began to frig around with a possible opening paragraph, thought of the name Trigger and that suggested a military husband — and at that point a former pupil of yours, Bill Mitchell (he retired lately, finishing up as headmaster Kaipara College, and he's a valued friend and dropper-in, excellent wit and feeling for a phrase) appeared and in a moment or two I'd got from him o.p. plus hair trigger — and that was sufficient, another piece of fiction was launched. I rather like the thing myself, as it surprises me that I wrote it. What I like best is 'the ranked letter-boxes suggested an enterprise for the battery rearing of bantams'. It's when my ear and eye quite happily combine that I get my best effects I think.

This has been sparked off by the finish of Never Enough — no more memoirs for God's sake. May Bill appear before too long with another inspirational word!

Before Ron Mason's play was taken in hand by Bill Austin a good deal of impudent 'editing' had been done by Chris Cathcart and myself not to mention Colin McCahon. Anyhow I was glad to listen again — certainly it doesn't come out quite right, but I thought it wasn't too bad at all, less dense than I remembered it and reasonable coherence (of course it was hopeless trying to persuade Ron there should be only a touch of 'foreign language' — I think he was trying to be literally faithful to what he remembered of his grandmother's speech — and dubious thanks to the old lady).

I expect I am not the one to say so, but I was shocked by Mike Joseph's novel — it seemed to me to be all coming out Catholic marriage, tribes of kids, his wife a Dally and I think she would have preferred him to run a fish shop — I imagine if I were her with a little extra nous I would be looking at him a little warily now.

I long to lay my hands on the Xavier Herbert [*Poor Fellow My Country*] and expect I will soon now. It's been my regret for years I haven't a copy of Capricornia on my shelves, the Australian Coal Flat but not a finicky touch showing, instead bursting at the seams. I daresay the new one is just as good or even better.

Sorry the [Frederick] Sinclaire book doesn't seem to go. I never knew [William] Jellie [author of 'The Principles and Doctrines of Unitarians', Rhodes' current reading], but on one of my few attendances at the Unitarian church in Ponsonby Road I enjoyed hearing his successor (Thornhill was he?) letting the Baptists around the corner have it — because they disgraced the Greek style of building they functioned in by dealing in the language of Little Bethel. [. . .]

Good wishes,

F.S.

['I'd got from him o.p': '[I]t was [Mrs Trigger's] habit to knit while she sat comfortably at what her deceased husband would have called her o.p.; that is to say, observation post'. Sunset Village, *p. 7.]*

To Roderick Finlayson, *Weymouth, Manukau*

Hocken Library

4 February 1977

Dear Rod,

[. . .] Your letter was a ray of sunshine for me. I cross my heart when I say there are stories of yours, there are pages, which I would rather have written than anything I have written — yet I do have an affection for both books you mention — SV because it surprised me so much that at my age I could write it, and the Worm because I've always felt since that's about as good as I can do.

And I suppose 'good' for me connotes a good deal of 'literary' matter. The puzzling 'joy of the worm' is from close to the end of Antony and Cleopatra, and is spoken by the sly slave whom the Queen has engaged to procure her a viper to sting her to death. Erotic suggestion too, and of course love and death go together a lot in Shakespeare. I thought it extraordinary that somebody academic (lectures in drama) writing in Landfall about the book couldn't pick up the source of the phrase.

Anyhow it was very nice of you to say when you enjoyed — I remember I got as much delight myself when writing that book as I hoped readers, or some of them, would. I never thought when I began it I would fall so much in love with the old man by the time I was finishing. Incidentally P.J. Parker was derived from V.J. Larner — remember him? I derived the old clergyman from a Methodist, Rev Cook, who used to come and stay with my uncle and myself on the farm in the early thirties. He spent hours each time he visited explaining once again how VJL had diddled him out of his £500 — not the faintest suspicion of anything so outrageous as a little Christian forgiveness. It was because he was such a colossal bore that it surprised me so much that I made him finally kind of lovable — I suppose just an instance of the magic writers such as you and I can sometimes by divine accident make happen on paper. [. . .]

No more for now, but very good wishes,

Fx

I am glad McEldowney sent you a copy of the picture book — which I value (a) because of the picture of my grandmother (b) of the men cutting the road, (c) of Harry (d) of my uncle, — (e) 'EM Forster and friends'. — EMF left all his money to the policeman who on a visit out here with his wife came to see me.

To Christine Cole Catley, *Whatamonga Bay*

Alexander Turnbull Library

20 June 1977

Sweet Chris,

Yes, of course I have intended to write — instead have been writing painful beginnings of something new. Peon about a *male* rake, therefore 'acceptable.' But now, *2* female rakes no longer young going up and down the country in a little car looking for bachelor farmers to stay with [*En Route*]. We must wait and see.

I know nothing of [Graeme] Lay's work except I suggested he try it on you. I shall attend to this matter as delicately as I know how, and I don't doubt he will let me see his typescript. More soon anon I hope. Like Craig Harrison he too is very nice, very handsome, 2nd generation from those Italian Island Bay fishermen — slight very dark with natural Latin understanding and courtesy — 3rd child just about to be born.

Glad you see Maurice Gee — I hope he may get that $2000 award for his excellent last novel.

I saw OM's S ['Old Man's Story'] on colour up at Jean Bartlett's, and confess to being astonished. I never supposed anything so genuine could have been created. Not good notices (not much good) up here but everybody seems to have been agreeably surprised. I thought all the players did splendidly, and special mention for [Gerry] Duggan [as Bandy]. It astonished me that something so genuinely Sargeson got onto the screen. I thought the ending should have been the boy peering into the cowshed and seeing a pair of swinging feet. Anyhow much pleased you thought well of it too.

I saw the 2nd and third Joe and Koro pieces — I thought 2nd quite agreeable, but the third for me seemed not to take off, come to life etc.

Jean Bartlett was a great help to me with proof of Never Enough! and it went off back to London last Wednesday. My publisher thinks it's the best of the three Enough books (because it succeeds in rounding off my 'story'), but I'm not so sure of this. I think with luck there may be copies reach NZ before end of year — but I would doubt whether Reed's would want to publish until next year. They pay awfully slowly, I haven't had a cent yet for Sunset Village and must give them a hint.

May you be keeping well — I get along, but I sometimes have an awful lot to do for Clarrie, and no time for section and house — it doesn't matter, may I perhaps be spared until I round off the new fiction, then please the gods may it be all over to you.

[. . .]

*[*Old Man's Story*, 1977, directed for television by Yvonne Mackay. Produced by Dave Gibson.]*

To Janet Frame, *Stratford*

Alexander Turnbull Library

10 August 1977

Dear Janet,

I was touched to read about your friend Sue [Marquand]. No, I did not know — and that must have been a nasty knock for you. I don't know which is worse — lost friends who are still living or ones who are not. Poor Clarrie suffers more than I do about Murdoch — thinking of him as heartlessly throwing him over. Not so — the key to it all is that despite having managed superannuation (the married kind) he is so hopelessly broke he daren't move many yards in his van as his warrant of fitness is about eighteen months overdue. How then can either of us expect to see him? (Also I have the consolation of the comedy of his informing me — just before Rhonda appeared on the horizon — that he 'wasn't interested in that animal side of life.' When I do see the pair of them again I must remember to think of some way of asking Rhonda whether she would agree with this statement).

You should hear from PEN (I think Alistair Campbell) very soon as I have twice supplied your Stratford address plus phone number. I am very glad you will represent us in Sydney. And Oh yes, I hope you heard from a television man with Tele One (I think) — I gave him your address as he wanted to film some of your stories next year (I think it was).

Maybe about Readers Digest — but I remember hearing about Shadbolt's collecting more than a thousand dollars for 3 or 4 pages about dolphins — *his* story though I think.

I don't know how you manage financially — although I hope you do manage — although none of us do very well at present and it will get much worse yet — I hardly know how I remain here now with rates about $250 and electricity $45 each 2 months. Foolishly no gloriously I threw away nearly all I had to come and go on keeping Murdie afloat until he brought off the superannuation.

My old rakesses [in *En Route*] don't knit. They complain that Enzed cockies sometimes keep their gumboots on, excusing themselves because they are *house* gumboots — and anyhow they like everything to be wrapped up and finished with so they can roll another fag and not miss their television serial.

Filth! Good wishes,

Fx

[Sue Marquand died in January 1977.]

To Dorothy Sutherland, *Oamaru*

Alexander Turnbull Library

29 January 1978

Dear Dorothy Sutherland,

[. . .] Lately I have been keenly recalling your father, and this is because my friend Clarrie, a good deal younger than myself died in his sleep on New Year's morning. Your father comes into my mental pictures because during the days when the pair of us walked miles of Wellington streets, Clarrie probably at least 12 years younger than myself, had not quite done with the Salvation Army Home in

Newtown where he was brought up almost from time of infancy as his father and mother were both hopeless drunks. Anyhow he eventually became a ploughman cowspanker heavy-lorry driver about the Kaipara district where I first met him — and for the last 3 years or so has very much shared my house, being incapable of any more work (too much smoking too much booze). Anyhow, what a sharp lively character (whatever booze and tobacco did to lungs bronchials etc, they never did a bad thing to the sharpness of his mind nor soured the sweetness of his temper and affections).

Just one little anecdote about him (and I use another on almost the last page of my forthcoming *Never Enough!*)

At Christmas a year ago a geneticist friend of mine [Eric Godley] in the South Island sent up $50 as a Christmas present for Clarrie's friend, a Kaipara subsistence farmer whose decayed house Clarrie used to share, the reason being that this man has had for years on his property a giant kauri tree which, although he is always dead broke, he has always so far refused to sell (for timber, and the value would be very great). It was my job to send on the $50 to this man, and I could see that Clarrie was not wholly pleased. So I said, 'Surely Clarrie, you don't envy Murdy a little bit of good fortune'. And Clarrie's answer, 'No, Frank, no, I don't — but when you write to your friend in the South Island tell him that I haven't even got a kauri tree'.

How your father would have appreciated the perception and humour of that remark!

I am afraid that all and everything does get more and more if-y and difficult. Yet I have had the satisfaction of writing quite a lot of a new shortish novel. It's about two elderly female rakes (or if you like liberationists), who go up and down the countryside looking for bachelor farmers to stay with. It is intended to be pretty consistently funny — and one of the two is so elderly she dates back nearly to the time of Ettie Rout. Does that name mean anything to you? She was a Canterbury University woman who in the first World War became appalled at the awful toll of VD among New Zealand soldiers at large in Cairo, and later in Paris. Courageous Ettie got off after the troops in an endeavour to establish Clinics with advice about contraceptives and reasonably clean brothels. Etc. She was of course reviled throughout New Zealand (and my God don't I remember my mother saying what she would have done to that young lady if she could have got her hands on her)! Of course Ettie never got her *real* due in New Zealand, but a friend of mine a literary scholar, tells me that among her rewards was a temporary status as mistress of H.G. Wells and one or two other London notables of the day. Alas, she died finally, it seems a defeated woman, somewhere in the Polynesian islands.

Well, I run on and must stop.

Next time you visit North of Auckland, look for Esmond Road, when you are among the first houses after the Bridge. You would almost certainly pass by. My place would be on the right, and if in a car you have only to make a U turn and you can stop outside my place and park for hours (even though the road is a virtual motorway).

With most enthusiastic good wishes,

Frank Sargeson

To Toby Easterbrook-Smith, *Hamilton*

Alexander Turnbull Library

[Toby Easterbrook-Smith wrote to FS on 16 March to wish him a happy 75th birthday and to tell him how rewarding he had found teaching his fiction. ATL MS-Papers-4261-047.]

19 March 1978

Dear Toby Easterbrook-Smith,

And what a lovely name — a pleasure to set it out like that! [. . .]

But what a pleasant kind of birthday letter — I mainly mean because of the young people. I remember years ago, a teacher & his class wrote from Taranaki (mainly about *An Affair of the Heart*, & sent quite a huge drawing of what they imagined the sea coast & the little bach must have looked like — very touching!)

But you know — how you make me feel what one willy-nilly lets loose on the world if one writes! Yes, I do know that I have my readers, but just occasionally appreciation becomes something very much an addition to the words on the page. Almost as though there has been an echo from the time when one first wrote with a kind of 'purity' unlikely in later work to be there. I think every 'mature' writer will sometimes say to himself something like this: 'Ah! if only I could write with any *calculation*! [Marginal note: I think I mean *conscious* calculation] — as I used to in my beginnings.' Alas, that can never happen apart from a faint glimmer now & then, & here & there. What astonishes me though! — once words have been made to affect the reader, they sometimes most mysteriously retain that power. And I find this all the more astonishing when they can be words of only 2 or 3 syllables — so that if one *thinks* too much one is conscious that only by some kind of miracle has a tumble into the most awful bathos been avoided.

What really touches me in your letter, is that you totally convince me of totally real experience. It is indeed an experience to feel that I have at times moved readers to such a reality of experience. I hope I am not writing nonsense to you. I do very much appreciate your letter, & am very sincerely yours,

Frank Sargeson

To Denis Glover, *Wellington*

Alexander Turnbull Library

[Re: 'Conversation with my Uncle Sarge', Glover's contribution to Islands 21, *March 1978, a celebration of Frank Sargeson at 75.]*

2 April 1978

Dear Denis,

Nothing of the [*Islands*] occasion was my doing, but I can take it (and have indeed taken it) because of one or two really nice things. Perhaps a number of just nice things, but only a few with that word *really* to point them up — well, Karl Stead's letter, Odo's and of course your own. You astonish me no end with your quotes from my letters (I can hardly imagine them to be letters I ever wrote but perhaps I did — did I ever refer to the awful Marris as an intellectual leper? How astonishing to discover that I had such an ability).

I don't think I understand what you mean by 4 rather feeble lines. If they got into my mailbox or whatever they must have disappeared into the chaos which accompanies every household and other activity these days.

One more thing to mention — or person it should be — Bob Dudding. Surely the true and (lone?) successor (to) inheritor (of) those thirties. He has half a dozen kids and no money. What with all my material used there was a sizable cheque — in fact there was more dollars for just a few lines (so I am told) than quite a number expected. How commercial are people these days? I wouldn't know — I suspect there is a lot of 'money is money'. But I fancy a good deal of myself remains with those thirties. Are there people such as Dudding in the World today? Somehow there must be. Anyhow you can guess what I did with my cheque — and never would have if it hadn't been for those thirties. Let a few of us until the end make these gestures which it is nonsense to suppose we can afford to do.

No more now, but your Conversation a piece that touches me because of its excellence quite apart from any connection with myself.

F.S.

['4 rather feeble lines': on 24 January 1978, Glover offered Dudding some additional lines he had just sent to FS, to include or not as he saw fit:

> *FOR SARGE FRANK SARGE*
> *To help a lame*
> *Dog over a stile*
> *You would lumber a mile*
> *To borrow or claim*
> *Timber to build same.*

Dudding decided against printing. ATL 80-387-1.]

To Bill Manhire, *Wellington*

Alexander Turnbull Library

16 April 1978

Dear Bill Manhire,

It was Karl Stead who first put me right about your poetry. A poem somewhere, Mate perhaps, and I questioned your ear — but KS supplied the light (and of course light for the ear I have just seen is something of a rare howler quite surely!)

Anyhow from then on I have read with attention believe me. And now on the opening page of the beautiful little book you send me [*How To Take Off Your Clothes At The Picnic*] I have for days been reluctant to get past,

> Snow in the brain, under the skin.
> Under the covers, bark and a few branches.

Well, there's sound for anyone who can hear it, and for the meantime I send you thanks and congratulations (knowing well that when I can read on I'll find you make it and make, and no doubts at all.

Of course I do appreciate the cover, and the nether young woman reminds me so strongly of a schoolboy story that I hope if she is ever able to put her far leg down she won't find she has dislocated her hip.

But just a brief excuse for writing in this way. Time, sir, not pub time, house time — I am badly in need of a housekeeper secretary gardener (not to mention somebody to sleep with the boss). To have to do everything for myself is becoming just the wee-ist bit of a burden. But I may be writing you again before too long!

Well of course I appreciated your words on Sunset V. It goes without saying. As for birthdays, I have tried to explain that I had nothing whatsoever to do with my own — it was my parents — God er well — perhaps forgive them!

I appreciate your kindness,

[Bill Manhire's review of Sunset Village *appeared in* Islands *21.]*

To Ralph Bodle, *Kaukapakapa*

Alexander Turnbull Library

23 June 1978

Dear Ralph,

You don't say, but I have to assume that your indisposition proved not to be fatal. Very glad if you are feeling much better. The cat returned after nearly three weeks — but she has suffered some sort of sea-change. She won't come inside, will allow me only one light tentative stroke, and seems to be alert every second for some attack. She DOES however consent to appear when I call her each morning (from where I have no idea) — and she too too quickly gobbles a too too large meal of meat and fish with a 'kitvet' tablet concealed. She's a mystery but good luck to her (especially as I've discovered she began life as a Mt Eden prison-kitchen kitcat).

I don't know whether to think you happy or unhappy over unfinished [George] Bruce. My relief over En Route has been very welcome — and yet and yet I don't relish present mood of empty collapse. It seems I don't have to check with you for much about Ettie. References to her are passing thoughts in the head of my old rakish Connie — expressing admiration indignation etc. My indebtedness to you is total and shameful. Suicided on some remote Polynesian island. Admired by forward-looking thinkers of the day — and temporary bedmate of some of them. Her name not in Enc of New Zealand. Mark Fagan the Honorable not in Enc either — and his only claim to fame may be that he did pay some attention to our Ettie.

There is a terrible storm in En Route — in some places remarkably resembling a certain part of Kaukapakapa. And Peter Smart of Landfall wanted to use me for his Awards, or one of them. I agreed provided there was no suggestion I was providing any of the money (as the suggestion that I might have any to spare (except to a few of my friends) was much too much for me: and of course who gets the pay off is nothing to do with me — although if I hadn't been so busy I was thinking of an elaborate hoax and collect myself).

Well, getting my damn typescripts away to England etc. But fingers crossed. My English publisher [Martin Green] has never paid me for my last four books, and although he claims to be still my enthusiastic supporter, he has lately taken to pub-keeping in darkest and deepest Wales — I believe a pub with two doors, the front one never open and the back never shut.

No more for now dear Ralph. Thank God sun is out today after a week. I think of country and country pleasures, and perhaps I may be able to think out some kind of excursion. Murdie and Rhonda called with baby, dark-eyed dark-haired like Murdie, and how very fortunate for him! A thoughtful well-behaved little bloke while he was here. May Rhonda by some miracle learn some notion of how to ensure that he survives. Poor M very proud very worried gaunt haggard — but I imagine after a sixty odd years wait he now has something he can't conceive he could ever be without. Poor Murdie, but he has a lot of strength.

To Alec Pickard, *Hamilton*

Alexander Turnbull Library

6 July 1978

Dear Alec,

This note owes itself to my being 'between books' — hence finding myself with time for more attractive pleasures. And the best of these has been a reading of your book [*All Part of the Game: The Stories of A.P. Gaskell*, 1978]. My pleasure has been if anything keener than it was so very many years ago now. Work that is as near perfect as it can come — and *how come*?!?! Well, as a literary local bloke perhaps best keep that under your hat. Anyhow page by page there was nothing of a let-down. I know that in school I was told you can't have anything more perfect than perfect — but these stories at the very top of their form disprove that — but let us just say that here & there there is the very topmost height of perfection (and all this by the way I've been saying to Bill Manhire — just passing through: I hope he took it in — yes I do, because he embarrasses me sometimes by appearing to attribute to me attributes of GOD — it will be something achieved if I have convinced him that he should go away & attribute ELSEWHERE).

Anyhow page by page — it would be impertinent even to suppose one might fault your eye or ear. And so it all adds up to being unique & timeless so far as one can (fallibly no doubt), judge.

Renewed congratulations & gratitude.

And to finish (since I am between books), I am terribly worried these days about Janet. She *sits* on her books — typescripts, she must have half a dozen of them or more. Lately she went off to live in Stratford (Taranaki), & has now bought a little house beside the railway line. This is surpassing odd! She was born in one of those little ganger huts railway maintenance men used to live in — it looks as though next she will be disappearing into some WOMB! Better I imagine for her to depart once again for California, where she can hit it off splendidly with a bunch of male sophisticates who paint mainly, & entertain European counterparts such as Chris. Isherwood et al.

No more. Best salutes. And good wishes to yourself & family.

Frank S

The Director of Broadcasting, *Wellington*

Alexander Turnbull Library

20 July 1978

Dear Sir,

I am confirming urgent telegram sent to you this morning:

IDENTIFICATION OF MYSELF AS CHARACTER IN WEDNESDAY'S YA REVIEW OF THE MENTOR NOT APPRECIATED. SUGGEST APOLOGY AND CANCELLATION OF SUNDAY REPEAT. TRANSCRIPT OF TAPE ALSO REQUIRED.

FRANK SARGESON

14 Esmond Road, Takapuna

I trust you can let me know that you have acted in this matter.

Yours sincerely,

Frank Sargeson

['Although I invented much of the plot [of The Mentor*], at the heart of the narrative was a man very much like Frank, a literary giant who cherished his privacy, and whom I called James Paterson'. Graeme Lay, 'Affairs of the Heart' in* Speaking Frankly, *p. 136.]*

To Barbara Basham, *Radio New Zealand, Wellington*

Alexander Turnbull Library

25 July 1978

Dear Barbara Basham,

I find your letter a strange mixture of guilt and come again — but very wise of you and Mr Boyes to eliminate the offending sentences (and incidentally the review sounded a much improved piece of work without them).

I did not take exception to having my name mentioned. I could not take (and no reasonable or rational person would expect me to) 'in James Paterson one sees Sargeson' related to 'James Paterson the successful author, the literary sage and individualistic recluse . . .'

That word 'successful' in the context as you can be in no doubt implies to a New Zealander riches, all the trappings (I have just completed my tax returns and find as usual my year's income, including Author's Lending Rights and National Superannuation, is with tax deducted about $3,800: alas it never varies much — and so much for the 'successful author:' I have never owned a car or even a vacuum cleaner: a second hand fridge, yes). 'Literary sage?' — but people who read my work know that I am in essence a comic writer — and as for my conversation it becomes more and more a re-telling of bawdy stories. As for 'recluse,' my door is never locked whether I am in or out, and literally dozens of this suburb's most ordinary inhabitants know I seldom object to their comings and goings just as they please.

I read Graeme Lay's book in typescript. He did not think, and nor did I, that some of the novel's aspects pointed to myself (although probably for the purposes of publicity Mrs Cole Catley would have liked to think they did). To me the notion was laughable — until I had the unpleasant experience of listening to your reviewer. Clearly my quarrel is not with Mr Lay. But what puzzles me is why the devil you did not edit out the offending material without any prompting from me. Say for instance that your reviewer instead of picking on me had named another novelist. Ian Cross, perhaps. Can Mr Boyes put his hand on his heart and say he would not have immediately eliminated the name. There is a big question mark — what am I to suppose?

Yours sincerely,
Frank Sargeson

To Ralph Bodle, *Kaukapakapa*

Alexander Turnbull Library

17 October 1978

Dear Ralph,

[. . .] Alas, dear Ralph, nothing much to say — so I enclose a picture of the Cerne Giant from which you may derive one or two or three ideas for embellishing your Long Man of Kaukapakapa when you get round to carving him in clay. (Would you like me to write Murdie and inquire whether he would agree to stand in (ahem! perhaps stand up would be a fraction nicer.)

I notice your jokes tend to be a good deal more hetero than homo. This in New Zealand will no doubt be thought to be a healthy and wholesome preference — which remark prompts me to say I have been reading Felix Donnelly's book, Big Boys don't Cry (for the past few years I usually go out of a Saturday evening to purchase the 8 o'clock just to see what Enzed's subversive priest has had to say *this* week). Anyhow, I now surmise with this lively little book he may have finally bought it. After all how can you tear your Archbishop up for arsepaper and remain in Holy (Catholic) Orders? [. . .]

To Felix Donnelly, *Auckland*

Alexander Turnbull Library

18 October 1978

Dear Felix Donnelly,

How nice of you to have written that book (although not so nice the trouble it will land you in). What I particularly liked were the opening pieces, about Mosgiel (I used to know Sid — Father, Doctor, — Duggan, brother of our late Maurice of high literary distinction), and Waihi (how that brought back about the priests I used to know in Wellington in the twenties (and have lately written about in the third book of my Memoirs.)

Also the prose is so wonderfully well done and to the purpose in those opening passages. Later on, well, a handy tool no doubt — but how quickly matter which is to the moment can alter its character. And so much do I feel this that I have hunted out a spare copy of my *Hangover* which I am posting you. If you can find time to look at it what I want you to see is how very different the dropouts of the late fifties and early sixties were from your young people in one to me very important character. They were not to be written off as cultural hicks. When some of them appeared in my two arena plays put on in the Art Gallery it was difficult to get them concentrated on my lines when they had to tear themselves away from *The Divine Comedy* lately (inadequately) translated by Dorothy Sayers and issued by Penguin, or Pelican.

I daresay it's all the result of television, anyhow it looks to me like one of *the* disasters of the ages. There is only one thing that I fall out with you over in your book. Your Bibliography. Oh dear oh dear oh dear, where are . . . But useless going on, except to say I lately read the marvellous Swift's *Tale of a Tub* and *Battle of the Books*. What pleasure, what delight! And how could you (mind you, just here and there), write so badly if you had lately known that delight . . . (perhaps too that discipline).

But all my good wishes, good Felix Donnelly, and may whatever Lord bless protect and cherish,

from

[Donnelly to FS, 19 October: '[. . .] I regret my limited style. I wanted to formally study English when in Waihi but Dr Annie Sheppard of the University, vetoed my application to do it extra-murally, because of her Anglo-saxon requirement. So I feel I was the loser there'. ATL MS-Papers-4261-040.]

To Raymond Hawthorne, *Theatre Corporate, Auckland*

Alexander Turnbull Library

22 November 1978

Dear Mr Hawthorne,

I note that you are quoted in the introduction to the Harcourt book [*A Dramatic Appearance: New Zealand Theatre 1920–1970*] — about reading playscripts which are sent to you, and they're not good enough.

Does it occur to you to wonder where any theatre would be without its texts? Let's face it, we're Europeans, English mainly — and where would UK theatre be if one couldn't reach for many marvels of scripts? When I was younger I read hundreds, beginning from somewhere about Ralph Roister Doister. I think I learned much of my skill with lively and comic dialogue from many years persistent reading of Congreve. It's not too much to say I know much dialogue off by heart — from Marlowe and Shaks through the Restoration people to Shaw. Fortunately too I had some months in London in the twenties — and was fortunate enough to see Evans at the top of her career playing Congreve and Farquhar.

What this note intends to say is that remarks about scripts not being good enough always relates in this country to what turns up in the mail. Does it not occur to you that many texts have been published over the years, and some of them very beautifully published? (If there is a more beautifully produced book than my Wrestling with the Angel, containing my two plays A Time for Sowing, and The Cradle and the Egg, I have yet to hear of it — although Cresswell's The Forest is very nice too). But there are many worthy publications. Ian Hamilton's Falls the Shadow for example, and of course not to mention Curnow, Bruce Mason, R.A.K. Mason, and Lord knows how many.

Can you really cross your heart and say that NZ theatre is something that may appear in the future? Do you believe yourself competent enough to deny that maybe NZ theatre is already alive and kicking, and this is something you would be aware of if you forgot about your mail for say six months and examined the texts? We are currently part of the era of the illiterate theatre, yes, granted (and I guess will be for a long time to come), but just take a look at some of the texts sometime.

You could be surprised!

From yours,

Frank Sargeson

To Ralph Bodle, *Kaukapakapa*

Alexander Turnbull Library

17 February 1979

Dear Ralph,

You rock me old boy, you really do, because I seem not to suffer from *any* of the frustrations (and really shockers) which populate your letters. I *think* part of the payoff from being a (ahem! ahem!) — a 'creative' writer. Let other people and the world behave as it likes — it's all grist to my (the magic of the 'creative' literary art), mill. Why, somebody has told me today that 'official' society has just awarded me $500 for the final volume of my 'life' trilogy (and a hell of a lot of that last one was devoted to Murdie and his bit of bush and land). You may say what about Rhonda, but my cunning prompted me to reserve something like her for my forthcoming piece of fiction which is to appear in a tandem book with an odd short novel by Edith Campion (nee Hannah, a tolerably clever Jewess with a background of DOUGH). Anyhow I shall try to remember to send you a copy of Tandem, my own piece entitled *En Route*, and Edith's, *The Chain* (about a man who wakes up one morning to find himself in the middle of an immense silent forest chained to a tree. Just that — after so-so pages he's still there but dead — and a not too bad exercise of the human (female) imagination.

But all this is not to say I am not deeply sympathetic about what undoubtedly must be reckoned your sufferings — and I mean personal and literary. About publishing, always there must be an immense patience. It is I think accepted that publishing is about the chanciest activity that anyone who devotes money to it can engage in. My own practice is to exert discreet but unrelenting pressure in polite letters.

But what to do about personal frustrations which do frequently and painfully figure in your letter-prose (so lively and vivid), I am not the least bit sure. Long long ago I decided I would throughout my life make practical and satisfying arrangements, and this I have for the most part (and very much for the most part) contrived. You mentioned the twinkle (was it?) in Clarrie's eye. What was so devastating about Murdie was that there wasn't that twinkle — but then let's face it, that man surprised us all — and very good luck to him. But I was never in any doubt about Clarrie, and over a year of one week off one week on of looking after him it was immense comfort and consolation to discover we understood each other's 'arrangements' and could look outwards on what the rest of the world was up to without any of the rage which appears to plague one, Ralph, who we agreed was very dear to both of us. [. . .]

No more dear Ralph, I hope not to offend you with some of my remarks,

To Kevin Ireland, *London*

Alexander Turnbull Library

20 February 1979

Dear Kevin,

Very kind of you to keep me so well posted — and despite our (too-hot) summer I much envy you that Cornish trip (in 1927 I walked for about a fortnight in Devon and Cornwall — at Bodmin after crossing the moor I turned west again and crossed Dartmoor.)

I had better tell you something of some developments. The enclosed evidence of my ownership of my 3 best novels might be worth showing to Peter Owen sometime (although the *Peon* is out at present as it was a few years ago re-done by NZ Heinemann). *The Hangover* gets a high commendation in that most if-y *Guide to Modern World Literature* (Martin Seymour-Smith, but I don't know who the English publishers were, in America, Funk and Wagnall). And I'm just now signing a contract with a local Danish photographer and his startling Israeli-Indian wife, to make a film of *Joy of the Worm* (according to them their work will be to Karl Stead's *Sleeping Dogs*, as *Wild Strawberries* is to *Birth of a Nation*). It seems that $120,000 could be involved. Anyhow we shall see. The script has been done by a New Zealander called Roger Simpson who has a good Australian reputation, his so-far piece of resistance being something called *Hunter's Gold* — for television.

I don't hear much from Reeds at present, but they did get cracking with their *Tandem* idea and I lately attended to the proofs of my part in it. I will promptly send you a copy of the volume when I have one.

I've forgotten to mention that *The Hangover* was lately read on the air in seven parts, and I was astonished that it apparently lent itself to quite a remarkable experience.

Anyhow all for now. No doubt Reeds will come to light with some idea of what they may try to do in UK — but I get so very much exhausted these days I fear much of myself is already vegetable — indeed the sort of thing that goes on the compost heap.

I wrote a most glowing note to Maurice Gee about *Plumb* — after all his grandfather belonged very much to the world I grew up in. M has done a most fetching job — I won't make any comparisons except to say my clergyman was and remains much much funnier.

May your poetry (*as* poetry) not be anything inferior to what we had from you in the *Cartoons*.

All for now.

Fx

If it could be of any interest to Peter Owen you could say that *Joy of the Worm* was an 'idiosyncratic masterpiece' according to Jon. Raban in New Statesman.
['the enclosed': a letter of 4 December 1972 from Granada Publishing informing FS that the rights of Joy of the Worm, The Hangover *and* Memoirs of a Peon *had reverted to the author.]*

To Christine Cole Catley, *Whatamonga Bay*

Alexander Turnbull Library

6 March 1979

Dear Chris,

[. . .] There's now a formal agreement with Heller Films for Joy of the Worm. It seems there is an Enzed tycoon (literary) who has seen the script done by Roger (Hunter's Gold) Simpson and is very impressed. There is talk of perhaps something up to $120,000 made available if Govt can go 50 c to the dollar or something of the kind. Anyhow there had to be a proper formal agreement, so I got to work after photocopying the one Karl Stead had with Aardvark. For me (I haven't seen the script), I can't see a popular success [. . .] — but clearly they'll need a mint of money to give it a fair go. So although they offered me $500 down and $5000 when the cameras started turning, I decided to give them the fairest of goes by accepting only $100 down and $1000 when camera-work begins, BUT instead of 10 p.c. of profits, I provided for 2 ½ of gross takings. SEE? Not an original idea, Karl Stead had done the same, so even though Aardvark are bankrupt (so it is said) he still collects a little.

Incidentally, did I tell you that Old Man's Story has gone all round the world and I don't doubt that young man in Wellington (I even forget his name) has made something of a packet. The nicest story I heard was that in China audiences concluded that the old man and the little girl had chummed up together because they had to show a solid proletarian front when they were being exploited by their farmer boss and his wife. [. . .]

No more for now. Stinking hot day, but peppers in garden are fine.

To Michael King, *Wellington*

Alexander Turnbull Library

11 March 1979

Dear Michael,

[. . .] Clearly I should have sent you a note ages ago. You should not have sent me a copy of your book as I do buy the works of my literary colleagues. Anyhow I have no longer that copy as it was borrowed and then, or so I was told proceeded overseas. But I procured myself another copy, and had the good fortune to be within striding distance from the final page when it too was borrowed. But as near as damn it (for the first time) I read it. And my congratulations on your probity and all the rest of it (and I daresay you already know you have the sincere approval of Eric McCormick). And in fact I used myself to do something of the donkey work required for that kind of literary activity — I used to read for R.M. Burdon much in the Auckland Library about de Thierry — in the days before photocopy — I remember by God the labour of my note-taking. However I had a very soft spot for R.M.B. — if it hadn't been for his (no doubt) not terribly adequate essay on Kendall I could not have written my Time for Sowing — a play which I am conceited enough to suppose has not yet been adequately assessed — it came to life in production, though perhaps it may have been more on account of my friend Chris Cathcart assisted by Colin McCahon.

Well, there I dither on. But at least I have let you know something of what I found in and about the book.

Incidentally, about [Peter] Fraser. I first encountered him when he was speaking from a lorry in Wellington — it would be in 1928. A *very* astute speaker — and he had a double-handed gesture (bringing first one hand and then the other up to his face in front of his nose — and then suddenly disposing of interjections by suddenly flinging it out — right hand right, left hand left). What interested me the last time I saw him (electioneering in Takapuna in the 1940s) was that he used exactly the same gesture — and strangely in his black Cabinet Minister clothes it was just as even more effective. Anyhow, a very eloquent very astute electioneering person.

No more now dear Michael, but good fortune for all that you write.

From yours,

Frank Sargeson

To Ralph Bodle, *Kaukapakapa*

Alexander Turnbull Library

[Bodle to FS, 18 March: 'I have had a letter from the Swiss Nat. Library to tell me that the book is now with a leading Swiss publisher who is very interested. Who knows what may come of it?' ATL MS-Papers-4261-022.]

27 March 1979

My dear Ralph, Not a word about any other matter until I have felicitated you upon the momentous event. How indeed could 'a leading Swiss publisher' *not* be very interested! Let's not shilly-shally pretend or be coy about this. Surely you are on the very brink of a momentous event in your life — my God after a lifetime's struggle with what promises shortly to be a total of about 14 books (and all of them monstrously painful pencil — or more lately patent-pen — written jobs, and *clearly* painful as anybody who cares to inspect the great stack of MSS could not doubt), I do sometimes wonder what my fate would have been if I had never made it to that great unknown amorphous mass, the public — WELL!!!

I hardly know how I can go on typing, my fingers are so firmly crossed on your behalf. Believe me, I don't know how I can wait.

And don't be cross with me if I say that once this blessed event becomes a reality you won't any more have to engage in your ravings (comic amusing lively on-the-nail) but for all that repetitious and worrying for me (and who else?)) because of the endless and repeated suffering they must of necessity imply for one, Ralph. Well, *of course*, about Chillon and the motorway, but why dwell upon what won't be changed in your lifetime? And Chillon motorways notwithstanding my memories of my walking across are not horrors, most certainly not. I had never been in high mountains before, and my two passes (Butler's Gemmi), and Napoleon's Simplon — because of the rudeness of the Fascist soldiers on the Italian side of the Simplon nobody that year would go over by foot car or whatever, and my sudden appearance at the Italian frontier was an event. They took all my tobacco and searched for more before sending me on downhill with pretended pricks (of their pricks maybe, I didn't look, but bayonets I think — they were push-bike operating bastards with very lovely feathers hanging down their backs from their hats, and their bikes rattled as though put together with hopeless pieces of junk. But really I simply want to say I won't forget because I can't being on top of the world and finally after being finished with by the soldiers looking down on the loveliest view I have ever had, the vineyard and garden plain of Lombardy.

But to suddenly become gossipy — have you had yet an ear for the news and Murdie's next baby is well on the way (and I say Murdie in case I should be interpreted as trying to libel him by saying Rhonda). And really these aged yet pure revels. How very different from the middle-aged gent who put the question to me in the Takapuna public lavatory the other day. He displayed what I can only call a beaut standing fiercely at attention. Would I I was asked, would I like to close my lips around this. I was most polite, but thought it wiser to decline the invitation.

I think I would for the most part prefer my two black spayed she-cats to your Peppi. I know exactly how I am regarded by them. For all that I am very sorry for the daughter one, she was spayed before she had kittens — hence her unmistakable spinsterish temperament. Just the thought of trying to get her to consent to my rubbing her belly is quite impossible — but her mother invites me to engage in this mild impropriety several times a day.

But now of course the birthday streamer — which is quite a masterpiece in the well-known Bodle style. I have discovered that pinned up in front of a strong wall-light it reveals to all every fruity detail of the genuine Bodle genius in this genre. Many thanks, much appreciated.

No more this time

[Nothing came of the Swiss interest beyond the gift of a lavish volume of aerial views of Switzerland. One showed Byron's Chillon, 'dwarfed by a monstrous big motorway viaduct', Bodle to FS, 18 March 1979. Bodle deposited his manuscript in the Alexander Turnbull Library (ATL MS-Papers-9513). It remains unpublished.]

To Toby Easterbrook-Smith, *Hamilton*

Alexander Turnbull Library

27 March 1979

Dear (I hardly know how to put it, Toby, Tobias, Easty, Brookie, Smithy) — [. . .] And oh dear oh dear, you rock me with what I remember with affection and regret. Fairburn Glover! — yes, but poets, and *they* could achieve a reputation with a few pages of print. And there was I putting up with their insults while I had to run to thousands of pages, and even then I often thought, make only a very little dent.

And here I am still at it (well not quite), but literary chores are still my plague.

I must be short (and I fear, so far, dull — compared to your own elan). I must own that visitors except a very few non-literary people for whom I keep such an affection are pretty few these days.

If you travel or visit by car, please first ring me — my number not listed, but I trust you with it, 496,999. Then if I am available, as you come from town my house will be on your right, (a U turn allowable, and once achieved you may park right outside my house as long as you please). Kindly note too that although the hole in my hedge is intended to discourage visitors, knowing ones enter alongside my neighbour's car shed, and after a few yards step across into my place. Weekend days could be best, Mondays I am never available, but weekday afternoons I can be reasonably polite, except never on a Thursday.

Well, I don't know how off-putting I sound, but your letter besides being so amusing, was very kind,

from yours,

To E.H. McCormick, *Auckland*

Alexander Turnbull Library

8 April 1979

Dear Eric,

Yes, thank you for the card [from Taihape] — to look at and look at even though my country *was* north of the mountain. Before I left school it was part of me that from the hills behind my uncle's house the mountain was perfectly symmetrical, a great levelly-truncated cone. But I never thought of the country about Taumarunui as either specially wild or volcanic until one had topped the spiral — but once up there its character seemed to stay with it until one had reached Taihape and beyond. Perhaps I have got it all wrong but much, and many of the names, will always be part of me — Mangaweka because of the viaduct (am I right?), and later on the town became special for me as it figured so much in my friend Levenet Bakewell's conversation (he had been bank manager there before he was transferred to Taumarunui).

Anyhow the river at Taihape is such a memory, the curve and the pumice faces. And I think I have told you, although as little more than a baby I spent a night in *a* hotel (I haven't a notion which one it would be) with my parents on our way to Taranaki by the first through Main Trunk train, I never spent another night there until I was on my way to the Writers' Conference at Christchurch — and Lord save me, at one pub my friend Harry was a barman, and at the other my Cockney friend Jack was a porter. (He died of leukaemia last year by good fortune well looked after in a Herne Bay hospital. He even amazingly left me a few hundred dollars, some of which came in very handy, but the rest I made over to the Old People's Centre in Edinburgh St. Newton which I visited a lot over a great number of years and came much to admire because of their care for the old and the way they carried it out.

Anyhow again thanks. I am not altogether sure about the 2nd Forster vol., [i.e. P.N. Furbank's two-volume biography] but certainly it is all very interesting. I have the difficult task of writing a letter to May Buckingham in England (she is the widow of the policeman who was Forster's friend, and I met her some years ago when the pair of them were brought to see me by May's local friend, a Miss Evans a most admirable retired infant school mistress). The cop has since died, but the widow apparently wishes much to know what I thought of the biog. Help! They had their trip out here on money left them by Forster.

Well, as with everything we shall see. Good wishes to both of you,

Fx

To Janet Frame, *Stratford*

Alexander Turnbull Library

10 April 1979

Dear Janet,

Thank you for your letter (21 March), and I giggled over the telegram which you got round to sending after all — Provencal French? There was one word I couldn't translate . . . 'innombrables plans *zuel*' (my, strictly speaking *your* Dictionary doesn't run to it either.) But to your letter. A quacking dick is a brilliant invention and you should copyright it. [. . .]

Alas, I am a dull fish at present — can't get launched on new work, and quite candidly, too old now — and I'm being a bit harassed these days because of the state of the property — too many risks I'm told, fire vermin whatwouldyou, to other people's property mind you. I will candidly admit the interior has to be seen to be believed — chaos dust dirt, and of course I no longer attempt to lay a hand on books or papers I want to consult or read because I know I'll never find them. One consolation is that I am frequented by two female black cats, both spayed, but one a true-blue spinster who had never had any kittens before her operation. She has a very spinsterish nature. The other has a look in her eye, and likes nothing so much as to be rolled over and have her belly tickled. They are in and out the windows all day and night, and never on the floor, preferring anything elevated even to the tops of the books on the topmost bookshelves. It goes without saying they scorn anything to eat except fresh fish and cuts of fresh red meat, also the cream off the top of a bottle of milk. Oh well!

Have you noticed the Orsman Enzed Dictionary? *I* have noticed they have missed kafuffle (if that's how it would be spelt). But no doubt those wonder people who actually read dictionaries will find they've missed a large packet.

Oh, no more today but I'm worried that things must be pretty difficult for you — for the moment fingers crossed,

Fx

To Kevin Cunningham, *Dunedin*

Alexander Turnbull Library

[Cunningham corresponded with FS over his bibliography of FS's critical and autobiographical writing (1977), and later edited Conversation in a Train and Other Critical Writing, *AUP 1983.]*

3 July 1979

Dear Kevin,

I daresay I should be silent about the sufferings you tell me about (and perhaps don't tell me about). But piles — yes, piles and piles as it were! and it's more than half a century since my own acute miseries — the operation I refused, the doctors' (as I later came to believe) phoney warnings. All began to clear up and become of no account from the time I commenced my climbings onto lavatory seats to assume the 'natural' position (and very easy to maintain when there was so often my uncle's King Country farm, and later my great garden at the above at the time blind street address).

Yes, that has been my story (the other half of it being I think my pretty 'natural' diet — what's constipation? I just wouldn't know. I *have* found though that a daily smear of ointment helps after washing — and after many many years I swear by an (originally) German preparation, Hadenza, which any chemist seems to stock. If my talent was in the musical field I would undoubtedly compose a charming little hadenza for some solo instrument.

Anyhow there we are, and may all be well with you again before too long.

I haven't seen Kevin (Ireland) yet, but we spoke over the phone last Sunday. I haven't yet seen in the paper what accolade it was exactly that he has been accommodated with — much deserved however I don't doubt.

All for now, and please not worries on any Sargesonian matters,

To Ralph Bodle, *Kaukapakapa*

Alexander Turnbull Library

5 July 1979

Dear Ralph,

I meant to ring David Bosworth last night but forgot — I'm afraid I am a little too miserable with that very rare thing for me, a nasty cold. I'll patch things up this evening. Cultivate him a little perhaps? — he is grandson to Takapuna multi-millionaire, one Speedy, also to a grandmother of comparable riches, O'Neill — O'Neill's point, O'Neill's Avenue (I think too it's O'Neill's cemetery). A nice young bloke with a horrifying fascination for me — a so-so lawyer, and I think almost exactly what at one stage I could have so readily become. A thousand Ughs!!! (And I forgot to say a favourite grandson to both g-parents).

Alas alas, I am no great lexiconologist, but I do know that puce is flea-colour (can you with poise boast about that one?). Anyhow I do also remember that prepuce is from the Latin, praeputium — but I've always forgotten to check up on the second half of the word, but then again I do remember that the verb puteo is to stink, to rot — and my God we (no, not we, inferior people!) may have something shameful coming to us there (and oh dear that 'coming' — I think I had better dry up before I become any more nauseous).

Although to go on to a perhaps related but much more elevated (!) matter, I was visited not too long ago by a very pleasant young man from Christchurch, Robin Duff, who teaches 6th form English at Christchurch Boys' High School. He is the Big Shot in the Gay Liberation Movement, and I heard him speaking very competently on the air the other night. Anyhow I think he and other Gays had been reading my books and decided they should try to drag me in as a kind of patron saint (?). I did not at the time know your reverse word Yag or I would have informed him of it. But I did explain I disapproved of the name but thoroughly approved of the effort to have the law changed. What public ignorance! A mixed top crowd of Cabinet ministers Judges Army and Navy chiefs, Ministers of Religion and God knows what common and garden very decent folk at risk! But what a courageous young man — I asked him if he had had any repercussions from parents et al, and he said no, nothing whatsoever so far. Can we be becoming civilized after all?

Well not more this time, but may there be world-shattering and Ralph-elevating news in the post for you before too long.

To H. Winston Rhodes, *Christchurch*

Alexander Turnbull Library

29 August 1979

Dear Winston,

[...] Kind of you about En Route — I rather enjoyed myself writing it despite all that keeps happening (one of my friends who shared that derelict farmhouse I made use of died in his sleep, a great grief to me as I was much closer to him — a diminutive kind of urchin man whose childhood was spent in the Wellington Salvation Army Home for kids whose parents are hopeless drunks — than I was to 'the McGilly man' who owns the place (and he by the way, a man very much as I have depicted him, not long since married an eighteen year old girl — well, time enough for there now to be 2 little boys: daddy is about to be 70 in a year, perhaps two: nobody could have been more virginal up to the time of his wedding).

Well anyway, there it all was, and yes I did think I had perhaps too cleverly carried it all off with my 'Connie' impersonation.

I think I have decided that I would indeed like to write some more. But I've never before found the prospects of the labour and the consequent neglect of household chores etc and scene of disorder so incredible. I find the comments of callers very hard to take. [. . .]

I have, haven't I, seen the beginning of the Tomorrow story — yes! And Curnow! he's so incredible I tend to surrender (but of course you would notice too that he slightly misquoted Dante — and very bad when his ear is almost every moment so impeccable). I think it is Karl Stead's admiration for Curnow that is now making his own verse more and more 'difficult' — for all that he's a remarkable poet with a very powerful very reliable mind. I think I would most like to go into a trance for 20 years, and then revive to see how these people of very great consequence have stuck to their guns (or not) — to leave behind them — well, exactly what? But of course the names are with me. And perhaps best put Shakespeare first.

No more for now, [. . .]

['he slightly misquoted Dante': some poems from Curnow's sequence An Incorrigible Music *first appeared in* Islands *22. A typo in the first line of Section 2 of 'In the Duomo' was corrected for the book publication, AUP/OUP, 1979.]*

To Peter Wells, *Auckland*

Alexander Turnbull Library

[Wells had been working on Edward Carpenter as part of his PhD. 'I sent [FS] a letter saying I had been studying 'Edward Carpenter' in England. In the covert world of pre-liberation homosexual men, this was a definite message. He wrote back to me immediately [. . .]'. Speaking Frankly, *p. 81.]*

27 November 1979

Dear Peter Wells,

Do pardon me for bunging a hurried letter straight back — it's part of my senile bungling that if I don't write immediately I don't write at all.

But first, these days I am on the phone but not listed. The number is 496,999 — and evenings are the best times to ring.

One reason I mustn't neglect writing is that I have a copy of *Edward Carpenter*,

An Exposition and an Appreciation by Edward Lewis. I think you would be certainly familiar with the work (1915), but I expect perhaps it's not likely you own a copy — and in that event allow me to present you with the book (frontispiece photograph v.g. and in v.g. condition). Published by Methuen.

Oh yes indeed I fell heavily for the man in my young years.

You would of course know about Forster's visiting him. But I have a touching anecdote about a visit D'Arcy Cresswell paid him.

Well no more for now, but I do hope you ring — when with luck I hope we can arrange a meeting.

To Ralph Bodle, *Kaukapakapa*

Alexander Turnbull Library

[On 28 November 1979 Air NZ flight 901 crashed in Antarctica with the loss of 257 lives.]

Sunday [2 December 1979]

Dear Ralph,

[. . .] Since I began this note there has been the plane disaster, and a fascination for me I think because the Scott tragedy happened just when I was beginning to take notice of the world I found myself in — I was given for a birthday present 2 vols. Scott's last Expedition with maps — hence I've always been able to tell anybody quite accurately where Mr Erebus is, and Mt Terror etc. The entire affair seems to me such a colossal piece of stupidity I invented a horrid little sketch of last moments which went something like this:

Scene. One of stupendous luxury, the caviar lunch has been served and is being toyed with — all in a modern jet-crate.

Little Boy — (who sits on his mum's knee, and has been looking out a porthole at the fog) Mummie, I saw in the fog a big rock.

Mum — Did you darling? Well, never mind — and how about eating a teeny weeny bit of mummie's chooky?

Granny — (who sits alongside neglecting her food in favour of a fashion paper) Funny boy.

Mum — Actually mother I thought I saw something myself.

Granny — Oh, don't be silly, the pair of you — as though the Captain doesn't know what he's up to!

The scene is replaced by a great blank of blinding light.

To John Geraets, *Auckland*

Alexander Turnbull Library

[John Geraets was working on a PhD on Landfall *under Brasch.]*

16 December 1979

Dear John Geraets,

It troubles me a good deal that I must (I think) disappoint you.

I can understand your having your theories about Landfall, but it seems to me that if you had known Brasch personally you wouldn't have had them — at least by no means as you sketch them for me.

For anyone who knew Brasch Landfall was what one would expect. I think I will risk saying a piece of civilized decency functioning in a pretty barbarous environment. I don't and never did see the poetry as 'normative', and any notion that the short stories had to be cast in its light seems to me nonsense. Any notion that I felt myself obliged to shape my material in the Landfall mould seems to me laughable. I don't think Brasch ever 'directed' me in any way. I sent him what I had written that I thought he might publish, and fortunately he never (perhaps almost never), turned me down.

Certainly Charles knew he couldn't last forever, and I think an eye open for whoever it might be who would carry on his good work was always with him. And it wouldn't be what you call 'disciples' — not at all, what would concern him would be plain ability to write good English plus a handsome respect for and acquaintance with the literary wonders inherited from the past.

I find any suggestion that Charles would have not been responsive to emerging talents (Wedde Harlow et al) as quite without any serious foundation.

I can't remember the details now, but I was always drawing Charles' attention to new people *worthy* of his attention and he would always respond even though he did not always fit them into his pages. I would never have dreamt of *arguing* with him about this.

You simply astonish me with 'disciples' and the same ball game. I don't believe there is anything you are driving at — except that Landfall had cost Charles a lot of time energy and money, and naturally he would not be happy if it were finally to fall into the hands of people who might sabotage a whole complicated set of standards and achievements.

As I started off by saying I am troubled about all this. I know that 'youth must be served', find themselves in a paying job, and so on — but let past achievements be subjected to criticism of a worthy kind — reaction can so often be just that, reaction, and best soon forgotten.

Well, all for now, from

To Toby Easterbrook-Smith, *Hamilton*

Alexander Turnbull Library

3 January 1980

Dear Toby,

I was very sudden and short yesterday, finding myself much preoccupied with your so very uncomfortable illness [congestive heart failure]. Pardon my talk of how to make a diuretic work (although I have discussed the matter with one or two Enzed medicine men now disgustingly famous overseas). Have you ever seen a diuretic with anything on the label except a direction to take in the morning? Not a word about posture, and with me it has been clear for years that unless I am on my back with a pillow under my legs at the knees and my feet on a good thick book with a soft cover (I find an old Family Good Book most convenient) — well, precisely nothing happens, indeed not one drop. To be brief I owe my life to Barbara Duggan (widow of Maurice Duggan and daughter of that revered Hamilton magistrate F. (something) Platts), who owes her own life to her own discovery (and this despite her two brother quacks, one of them a distinguished venerealologist). Don't do me wrong by mentioning my name, but it would extend this valuable research of mine if you were to murmur the word posture to your own prescriber and inform me about his reactions.

But there I run on, and I have just this morning found time to read properly your most delightful letter. What pleasure to take you up on one or two literary matters about which clearly you know a great deal more than I do. I think it was probably because I became addicted to Proust at a very early age that I thought I might as well miss out on Anthony Powell (Pole to you). Yes, I have dipped, but what seemed to me a certain thinness of the material tended to put me off. Also, even at his best, he's surely nowhere near as good as Waugh — at least that's what I thought at the time, a long while ago now. And Naipaul (if I am spelling it right) — he was brought to see me by David Ballantyne some years ago (some United Nations cultural business it seemed). Anyhow we spent a few somewhat awkward hours. I remember that to get going I thought American lit. might be a good ploy, Whitman Hawthorne Twain, before going on to Latin and Negro American. Nothing much doing. I think we were both relieved when Dave returned to collect him. I expect he may have gone away making a note of having met a quite impossible modern colonial hick. For me it was perhaps something like what Forster felt on first contact with his millenium-aged Indian friends. Never mind. But you remind me that I lately read a review of the *House for Mr B[iswas]*. Kind of you, but really don't send as I can without much trouble get it from our Library.

Now time has gone despite my arthritic fingers being a little quicker on this machine than with a pen. Chores chores — I *must* sign off. But very good wishes, and may I be soon again. And may you soon be well!

F.S.

To Toby Easterbrook-Smith, *Hamilton*

Alexander Turnbull Library

20 January 1980

Dear Toby,

Well that sounds to me like excellent news, it was quite a kick to take in your first few words. But here I am being a kind of Jonah. You can stick your Heart Consultants — my God there was I paying great fees to Arthur Coombes, a revered specialist in matters of the ticker, and he was an unquestionable fraud. For one thing he was one floor above the ground, and a building without an 'elevator'!!! How I remembered [G.M.] Smith's story about the American (very rich) who came to London to consult somebody genuinely famous in heart matters. Anyhow this man's rooms were on a fifth floor, and on the day the patient was due the 'elevator' wasn't working. Doctor opens his door to a knock and there's his patient smiling (I suppose because of relief over his impending salvation). Doctor doesn't smile, he's astonished. 'Are you Mr So-and-So from New York?' — and yes he was. And how had he managed without the lift working? More smiles, no trouble he'd walked up. No smiles from doctor, he takes the man by the shoulder and walks him in the direction of the stairs. 'Well you just walk down again, you're not taking up my time, there's nothing wrong with your heart'.

The point about Coombes and myself was that it took me about fifteen minutes. I reproached the man for the absurdity of it all. I was a wreck. And he laughed!!! After that I consulted him by phone — because I was rapidly becoming solid with water, his diuretic being a complete failure. He said, well there's a new technique, I would be given tablets that would sweep out every grain of salt from my entire system. If there was no salt to hang on to the water, the water would be ever so happy to run away.

That was my last communication with this eminent specialist with a Enzed reputation and beyond. Sometimes these days when I'm struggling home with a flagon of lemora in a rucksack on my shoulder and sizeable kits packed with groceries and vegetables in each hand he glides by me in his monstrously vulgar car. I smile sweetly, he sadly.

But to finish. I manage my diuresis with the aid of my GP. Some people daily weigh themselves. I don't, I measure the urine — and if I don't pass just on half a gallon each morning between 2am and 6 am there'll be no running up stairs for me that day. I walk miles every day, refuse all rides, and carrying heavy loads is a positive therapy.

Pardon all my arrogance!!!

Alas, poor Clarrie, sweet urchin man that he was! But Murdoch's life situation is almost worse. He dare not live in his ancestral house — the local authority will execute an order for demolition if he does. So he lives in a place of city-squalor (Ponsonby Road) instead, going in his terrible old lorry out to his ancestral acres every other day to feed the doctors [Maringal note: marvellous slip! — I mean dogs]. I suspect Rhonda is pregnant again. I used to hand over to him every cent I could spare but I don't even do that now — it's all so awful, and of course quite mad. Yet he remains a tall handsome man of much dark dignity — and I love him to distraction, have for many years, and always will.

Well I expect this note may be a kind of signing off more or less. But perhaps not. Good wishes, and of course we will see.

Thanks for all the interesting matter in your own letter.

Many good wishes,

F.S. [. . .]

To Ralph Bodle, *Kaukapakapa*

Alexander Turnbull Library

20 January 1980

Dear Ralph,

Yes, I did want to fire a letter straight back at you — but perhaps you will forgive me for the thought when I say it was because you moved me with your account of SFR [*The Swiss Family Robinson*] revisions private printing etc. I remember some good time ago trying to reassure you. Patience, patience, I said, all will be well in good time. [. . .]

Well anyhow, there was another bit in your letter that made me want to fire back immediately — about buggering and fucking, and how you would prefer to be the more active party. For some reason you recall to me all the extraordinary doubt and puzzlement about sexual matters I suffered from until the time of my getting off to England at the beginning of 1927 — one hell of a long time ago now! And how lucky I was — because various experiences, and most agreeable ones seemed to be waiting for me to make them my own personal property. So that all my worries were as though magically disposed of.

Strangely, I have lately been in contact with some young Enzers who seem to have found themselves with their heads above water in much the same way as happened to myself. For example there's a young chap called Peter Wells who has had some things in Dudding's Islands. He wanted to come and see me and I agreed, and he had a tale to tell me which tells me for sure that my own youthful benightedness wasn't uniquely special to myself. Before he went off to England he had got on to Whitman, but also (and this came very much down my own street), Whitman's rather pale English reflection, Edward Carpenter. But he astonished me with the information that at Warwick University he was allowed to write his doctoral thesis on Carpenter, and since he had done his research very thoroughly he was able to supplement my own knowledge of that sadly neglected pioneer (I mean for many many people). I am obliged to believe that Carpenter has become a kind of key figure for many younger people — all of which interests me enormously. [. . .]

[Incomplete. The thread continues in the following letter.]

To Ralph Bodle, *Kaukapakapa*

Alexander Turnbull Library

10 February 1980

Dear Ralph,

How very odd that just as I was about to write you a week ago (with something more to say about that boyhood hero of mine, Edward Carpenter), I was suddenly invaded by quite a bunch of local Gays in a state of indignation over police investigation of one of their favourite Sauna outfits over in the city. Well well well. I know nothing about the Sauna outfits, and imagined they offered cubicles with private 'services.' Not so apparently. The one in question is simply what I used to patronise in London as a Turkish Bath, and any erotic sub-erotic near-erotic virtually-erotic activities are accomplished with all patrons getting pretty much of an eyeful if disposed so to do. It appears that all these invading young men were seeking from me some kind of support for their protest against police persecution. I'm afraid they didn't get any — at least in the form they sought, my signature to a protest document. But I must confess that indeed I was interested, and the more especially when it is revealed that their invasion was just a brief interruption to an excursion they were making to a Gay Beach located just south of the Wade River. They would have been pleased if I accompanied them (alas alas, my age, my wrecked and ruined figyouah). But I will admit to being flattered by their high regard for my liberal sentiments which it pleased them to take for granted.

But anyhow we live and sometimes learn — yet I am so 'literary' that what sticks in my mind most is that I was reminded of a marvellous short story by Anthony Trollope called The Turkish Bath — which later on that day I sat down to read again after perhaps forty years, and found even more satisfying than I had remembered. May the Arts Flourish! Reality can too often be a Nuisance, a Bore, a Danger! Eroticism, OK, but where is the satisfaction compared with that of having got one's books written?

Now I hear footsteps on my path — a visitor and one who habitually shares my Sunday evening dinner. So only to say next time I will really write about Edward Carpenter, who must be credited with having done a good deal to send out the news that instead of two there are at least three sexes (not to mention several more not yet invented).

May you not be laid flat by this hot weather (as I — but don't tell anyone, I would hate to be crept up on by someone — am).

Good wishes,

To Toby Easterbrook-Smith, *Hamilton*

Alexander Turnbull Library

20 February 1980

Dear Toby,

Thank you for your 7 Feb letter, all very interesting, and may convalescence (whatever that may be) be something of a pleasure to you (if any such thing is possible).

But being so literary I want immediately to say how I envy you your familiarity with what 'quality' writers are up to. I've for years neglected them — for complex reasons. I fear influence which I tell myself would do me no good, and I also fear the depression that could result from too too many discoveries that some of them are far and away beyond me in good literary quality. For all that let me say I've passed over Graeme Greene for many years (although I did read — was it The Confidential Agent? — South America — and apart from the skill of the story-telling I thought much and long on the strange and probably crucial differences when one compared the long-ago Mexican one — I forget the name, about the modern 'saint' of a priest.) As for Golding I have never read him much, and never at all after the prolonged boredom of that sailor on the rock — was he Pincher Martin? And alas alas, apart from some of Wendt's short pieces in Landall and such when he was beginning, I have not read him at all. Yes yes, many alases, but I share with Denis Glover a stubborn scepticism for grass-hut grass-skirt culture. Alas alas I am European, yes in some ways awful-English — but that implies for me the incredible riches of — well you name it, say beginning in reverse with Charles Dickens and on to Congreve Milton Shakespeare Marlow Spencer Chaucer, not to mention across the Channel, Proust Balzac Flaubert Stendhal Molière. How do I fit in Wendt or Tuwhare? or maybe even Graham Greene — or for that matter Sargeson?

Well, never mind.

And how readily one's most careful theories can be upset. I was just meditating how on earth I could have omitted Byron from my list (after all Don Juan may well be the most immediately marvellous and readable piece of literature in English), when it came back into my mind that last week I had no sooner ceased to listen to the wireless debate between Felix Donnelly and Kennedy of the Tablet when I was invaded by a tribe of intellectual Gays who I think were after my signature to a document protesting against police persecution (Turkish baths goings-on-and-off). Fortunately they did not stay long, being headed for a Gay beach beyond Tor bay. So you see in another century it may not be Wendt or Glover or whoever, it could be — well you tell me.

But meantime I have just knocked this off with the idea it may tell you how glad I am about your recovery so far.

A ton of good wishes,

F.S.

To John Geraets, *Auckland*

Alexander Turnbull Library

2 March 1980

Dear John Geraets,

I am sorry I did not get around to a reply to your second letter — I'm afraid I must have had many matters to worry me at the time it turned up.

And now yours 26 February. It's clear to me you must have put in much hard work, and I compliment you upon the matter you come to light with, also the generally apt language which says your say as graciously as precisely.

So it by no means pleases me to say I haven't the energy these days to take you up about this and that. I can't remember that I ever reacted much to Charles's Landfall — I think it very soon became my habit to accept it as a feature of the landscape, one for which I was for the most part very grateful. I seem to remember there was a good deal I kept to myself. I don't think I ever got round to telling Charles that for me *the* Enzed poets were Mason and Fairburn (and it's more or less true to say that Mason still is.) If I sometimes felt that some of Landfall's poets failed to take off in any flight which would rivet my attention — well it was hardly the sort of thing I would mention to Charles.

At the same time it did move me that for his part he seemed to have no difficulty in appreciating the worth of prose-writers such as Rod Finlayson and Alec Gaskell. Also I can't remember his ever questioning me (except perhaps on trivial points), about any piece of prose I sent him. It was this that seemed to make him so valuable to Enzed. When I remember the sheer blank incomprehension I encountered from allegedly intelligent people about what I was up to with some of my shortest and simplest pieces! (And incidentally, still do) — well, running Landfall, and apparently having the means to run it — well how could one avoid seeing him as the oasis which could alleviate the prevailing dust and drought of a Climate which (for my part at any rate) I had reconciled myself into taking for granted.

Of course we know now it didn't all finally turn out to be our Antipodean Renaissance (and so clearly the case if one looks at what passes for Landfall at the present time (although thank the Lord for *Islands*!) But in the context of the time, my God how much poorer off so many of us would have been without it!

I don't know that you would get much out of a talk with me. I don't want to harp on my years, my loss of energy and my co-ordinating abilities. It would be very dull for you, and very tiring for myself. But perhaps, I don't know — even though I seem strongly to know I would prefer that you let me off.

Good luck to you and your plans anyway, and mouths to feed as you say — may some excellent job come your way!

To Ralph Bodle, *Kaukapakapa*

Alexander Turnbull Library

16 March 1980

Dear Ralph,

Two excellently famous and entirely 'normal' letters from you — and you can have little idea how envious you make me. Of course I know something of the variety of bats that inhabit my own belfry — but it goes without saying that they can't compare with your own. Yes, such a range! How can I compare, constricted as I am in this horrid suburb. Does an umpteenth reading of Shakespeare compensate? Or Marlowe? — and do you know his Edward II? I had forgotten the unforgettable language, the sensuous glow, and all focusing on the king's camp favourite, Gaveston — yes, favourite or minion (which of course derives from *mignon*). I must remember to make my recommendation to the Gays — and one of them by the way has suddenly revealed to me his quite startling talent for 'plastic' work. He has done in some kind of (I think) new metal a head of me in the round — or rather in the flat, because although it is indubitably three-dimensional it assumes the form of a double profile. I become startlingly narrow-headed, yet the constriction doesn't matter when the eye goes right and left to the profiles he has so cleverly (from the technical viewpoint certainly) been after. Anyhow, note this young man's name, Terry Stringer — it's a name which I think will persist. [. . .]

But another thing I fancy I have always failed to speak to you about is the London Magazine. It was started by John Lehmann soon after the war when Penguin New Writing had had it — but before very long got into the hands of Alan Ross a very versatile young man who promptly ruled out the overt 'political' bias. These days, 'precious'? — perhaps in a way, but from time to time there's something with the quality which does really rivet attention — perhaps an incredibly funny story, or a reproduction of painting drawing or sculpture which really is the genuine article. There is for example in the current number a drawing by R.B. Kitaj. It is called 'Portrait of Quentin', on the face of it a simple mainly line drawing of a nude elderly man — but it has an erotic quality which is very startling. All is there, a tired wise elderly face which is in a way 'answered' by flesh of chest and belly and then by cock and balls which become a kind of final touch of serenity. I think one is fascinated because basically it is closely related to the pisshouse graffiti one has been familiar with over a lifetime, yet I defy anyone to discover one solitary hint of grossness of any kind. Clean eroticism in other words — one is grateful there is no prepuce, and the cock (not standing), has its own reserved power and graciousness. Of course I am amazed that I have been lucky enough not to have had this piece of mail (male) interfered with in the post, and open envelope for inspection, but it got here.

But alas, dinner to get and 3 mouths to feed today.

Perhaps next time I will try to write one of your sort of letter.

To Ralph Bodle, *Kaukapakapa*

Alexander Turnbull Library

Tuesday [late March or early April 1980]

Dear Ralph,

I am knocking this off in a hurry in case it should be the last. A few days before my birthday I got up in the night to take my diuretic, and having the misfortune to glance in the mirror discovered my face to be all out of shape. Felt fairly all right but the glass wasn't lying. A (mild?) stroke I told myself — or what used to be called such, as my doctor informed me they have a new name now. I'd be all right he said in a few days, and there's now a new wonder drug which stoutly discourages the heart attack which can follow. (Actually of course *now* I heartily regret I wasn't knocked clean out for good and all. But hold! — if that had happened I wouldn't have had the pleasure of 77 years and your Christmas card.)

Such wit Ralph, congratulations and my gratitude.

But what has been so extraordinary is that you revived memories of London and my 'liberation.' And round about my 24th birthday. I was in the first stage of London — simply gaping. And in about the centre of Mayfair I suddenly woke up to being in desperate need of a piss, and no place anywhere in sight. Fortunately (as it turned out) I asked a handsome youngish Guardsman in his off duty walking out clothes shrouded by an immense overcoat (it was a sharp spring day). He was most kind — he could help me. And I was astonished that a few yards on he took me down underground alongside the entrance to a great mansion where there was what seemed to me a very clean and tidy convenience. He said Go ahead which I did, and when I turned round he was smiling at me and saying, 'There's nothing else you want?' — and not waiting for an answer opened up his overcoat, and there, hanging out was the most monstrously large (and to me as it turned out, attractive) 'thing' I had ever seen. To cut the story short he had thought I had been trying to pick up *him*. Not at all I was too innocent. Anyhow he informed me I could do anything I liked with what I saw for 'a couple of quid.' Alas I hadn't that much money on me (having been told to be very cautious with my money on London streets.)

And now to cut the story *very* short — during all my stay in England (nearly a year), I was very friendly with this bloke and his very pleasant and attractive wife [Fred and Lucy Bush], visiting them often in North London, and they even arranged an excursion for me to visit his parents down in Dorset. *He* came with me, *she* stayed at home, and it proved most convenient for his mum to put him and me into the one big bed. Whoopee!

Well this touching little story after fifty years or so I had almost quite forgotten. But your drawings brought it suddenly all back. And yes, the answer is yes, yes, as the one most cherished friend left to me (and one year older than myself) can confirm, yes YES. And thank God for that!

To Toby Easterbrook-Smith, *Hamilton*

Alexander Turnbull Library

12 April 1980

Dear Toby,

I've never written since your kind sympathetic letter.

Well, of course, I suppose I have to put my prejudices on exhibition. Ian Hamilton (whose fame for *Till Human Voices Wake Us* has never been nearly so marked as it might well have been), has been very good with his car (even though smitten by rheumatic pains of awful severity I don't doubt) — without his assistance in getting home my weekend shopping I don't know what I would have done for meals which have remained remarkably square. No alas, what I writhed with fear over were the varied services offered by two remarkable women — 1, Barbara Duggan, Maurice's widow who used to be a Hamilton girl, Barbara Platts: 2, Jean Bartlett née Alison, the great-granddaughter of the 'chippy' on board the *Beagle* of the famous Voyage — he returned to Enzed to found Devonport and the Ferry Coy. Anyhow perhaps enough said — a Hamilton magistrate's daughter and a woman of local aristocracy — well, OF COURSE it is to be taken for granted that yield an inch and no, no I don't mean the other five or six inches will be taken for granted, no *no* not at all — simply that my house will be springcleaned, not a spot of dust surviving, and not one paper which I *do* know *now* where to be found, ever to be found again PLUS a long list of admonitions, advice, warnings, let it be a lesson to you . . .

But enough enough, I survive.

And from a chemist friend I have borrowed a Martindale, and read all about the Anturan I am taking. Quite a story. It came in as a new drug about 10 years ago — a specific for gout. But about a year ago it was discovered (in Adelaide) that it shows a remarkable capacity for unclotting the vascular set-up, and indeed in America they are getting worried — millions of the elderly who should be decently dead are now returned into public circulation on Anturan, growing older and older, sending up the Inflation and being generally a God-damned nuisance. I was most moved by this reading, I have been going about making humble apologies for myself.

But to finish, my face has straightened up, I feel shaken, tend to bump into objects on my left, but except that I have to proceed about my shopping a bit more slowly, and have had to dust and use the trundler I bought about six or seven years ago when I filled up with water (the problem disposed of when I discovered the diuretic would work only when I lay propped with my feet up) well I'm the same bloody old nuisance to myself and other people as formerly.

Two top spots of reading lately which I won't forget. I passed over Shaks, being conceited enough to think I could hardly now improve on my reading. So it was Marlowe — ah, if he had lived Shaks' nose could have been put out of joint. Anyhow, *Edward II*, and I've been delighted to find in the Oxford *Companion* a note which says it is his best play. And fair enough, yes, *play* — but only a sprinkling of *lines* which can compare with his best — which in many many works take one's breath away — they come so thick and fast.

But I had to read a modern work too, and by good fortune lighted upon Tom Driberg's *Ruling Passions*. Well, of course one knows about Driberg, but here he is at his most lively (I don't doubt you know he was William Hickey of the Daily Express, who cost Beaverbrook a lot of libel money when he was rash enough to refer to Liberace as 'a fruit.') Anyhow in this book is quite a wealth of the atmosphere which suggests people like Auden and Isherwood, Evelyn Waugh, Spender, Labour Wilson and Gaitskill — and Driberg supposes he might have himself readily become a Labour PM if it hadn't been for the 'heterosexual dictatorship'. One of his most outrageous anecdotes is about Hugh Walpole (who for a time when I was young was my and my sister's favourite novelist). Driberg and Walpole were in Rome to report a Papal coronation — and at lunch one day the latter was in such a state of exultation that he was asked what it was all about. Walpole replied that that morning a handsome young attendant at the Borghese gallery had insisted upon pinning him against a wall and buggering him. Oh dear oh dear, perhaps I'd better not tell my sister.

Well, no more for now, but may your own élan and all the rest of it be flourishing.

Many good wishes anyhow,
from,
F.S.

To Ralph Bodle, *Kaukapakapa*

Alexander Turnbull Library

[Bodle to FS, 23 April: 'When I turned the wireless on there were Edith Evans and Larry Olivier at 4 50 a.m. reciting Bill the Birthday boy — Shakespeare. I don't care much for the lady — too mannered — but Olivier's Fear no more the heat o' the sun has made my day'. ATL MS-Papers-4261-022.]

7 May 1980

Dear Ralph,

[. . .] [A]las although I have delayed answering your letter I am still troubled by your Edith Evans blasphemy. Although perhaps I should be delighted as you recalled to me London, 1927, Wyndhams theatre — the divine Evans playing Millamant to Godfrey Tearle's Mirabell. What an evening — I had for companion a young Enzed architect I had shared a cabin with from Australia. We became literally drunk with the wonders of theatrical art. A few weeks later we went out to the Lyric Hammersmith to see Farquhar's *The Beaux' Stratagem* with the same pair doing their magic stuff. For myself I remember I wept over the thought F had died at about 29 and yet had proved himself no lesser man than Congreve. Would you mind folding your hands across your heart and repenting of your sin?

(Indeed I think I can say without exaggeration that it was my experience of the performances of these 2 plays that prompted me into my vows to become a word artist — Enzed words into the bargain and every sentence thought out and imperishably wrought — well, if you ever get time read *Joy of the Worm* — I think it has been there where I came closest to proving myself not altogether an imposter).

And carrying on from there, no dissolute imposter either — indeed in these my latter days, it is my daily great sorrow that I seem not to approach the dissolution I yearn for with footsteps that do not falter. In other words I find life now a bastard (and this is no doubt tied up with my conviction that my work in this world is DONE! — I must confess however that over many past years I used to try to convince my dearest and my closest companions such as Harry my racehorse man (and my more lately little Jimmy, my little Pommy street-cleaner man) that it is indeed the case — and neither would ever believe a word I said. Alas for Harry he's dead these ten years now — but Jimmy thank God remains to be a Comforter I can never be too grateful for.

Well dear Ralph, there I am at the moment, Lord how I've had it. *I* am perfectly prepared to say that and act on it — but woe is me there's just one or two things about me which refuse to agree with plain-speaking.

No more for now, good wishes, I envy you the Marlowe vols.

To John Macalister, *Wellington*

Alexander Turnbull Library

[Macalister wrote to FS on 3 May asking about A.R.D. Fairburn's friendship with Geoffrey Potocki de Montalk, and about the attempt on D'Arcy Cresswell's life mentioned in More than Enough. *ATL MS-Papers-4261-125.]*

8 May 1980

Dear John Macalister,

It could perhaps be something of an advantage if I send you some sort of reply immediately (I have lately been visited by what used to be called a 'stroke', and although I don't feel too bad at the moment I imagine some possible future is at present much on the knees of the gods — as it used to be said).

Anyhow, thank you — and just to say in passing that I sometimes think what I value most among my writings is my novel, Joy of the Worm. Perhaps I am mistaken, but I sometimes think that the more outrageous my comic talent becomes, the better it is for what I write.

But about your questions. I never met Potocki de Montalk although I must have come close to it in the early twenties before I left for England. Fairburn a kind of 'natural' aristocrat (at his best) himself was always sympathetic to him, and as he was fortunate in having a little money to spare it was much to Monty's advantage to tag along when they went off to England. I never myself came much into the picture until the thirties when Fairburn was back and a hopelessly tied-up family man working for that Farmers' organisation. Monty's letters and publications were I think always read to me (or lent) and of course Rex admired the panache and gesture of it all. I don't think their friendship ever 'ended' — but over many years there was greater and greater increase of eccentricity (sometimes very very funny apart from all else and finally very tenuous communication. And I am afraid that's about all I can tell you, although among Fairburn's papers there must have been many, many items of very great de Montalk interest. I'm afraid I don't know what happened about F's papers after his death, but I think you could find out from an inquiry at the Turnbull Library.

Now about Cresswell and the Mayor of Wanganui, a lawyer married to one of the upper-crust Duncans of the Wairarapa. C was lately returned from World War I, and Mackay the Mayor was president of the local R.S.A. C thought the man, because of his private character, unfitted for this presidency and presented him with an ultimatum to resign. He later called on the man at his office premises, and after some talk the Mayor took from a drawer and fired a revolver at C. Now all this you could check from newspaper reports (early twenties, 1921-22, or thereabouts) but what exactly was behind these happenings? Well, alas, I can't at present persuade myself to tell you anything more. A tragic business — and all round as it were. Mackay a good many years later was killed in a riot in Berlin. And Cresswell, God help him, seemed always to cling to the belief that he had not in anyway behaved badly.

['Cresswell and the Mayor of Wanganui': Chris Brickell recounts the details of 'the Wanganui Affair', in which Charles Mackay's political enemies paid Cresswell to entrap him in a homosexual scandal. See Mates and Lovers, *pp. 115–117.]*

To Toby Easterbrook-Smith, *Hamilton*

Alexander Turnbull Library

[Easterbrook-Smith to FS, 12 May: 'The late Sir Thomas More lived his life, I understand, believing that his urine smelt of violets, and that this was a special mark of divine favour'. ATL MS-Papers-4261-047.]

12 May 1980

Dear Toby,

I don't know about violets, but I *have* known people with diabetes whose very attractive smell I have always attributed to their sugar — but since I have in old-age become myself mildly diabetic it sometimes occurs to me that I must inquire from one or other of my intimates whether or not I smell like a bag of lolly-pops. (A bag? — probably yes, but I daresay I shall remain in doubt about anything further. Safest to restrain my curiosity.)

But how lively you sound — and I have crossed my fingers (hence my atrocious typing) against any falling-off. Also, much that you say touches a good deal on my own situation about 40 years ago. TB it was said — in my ribs, in my groin (with a troubles me undescended testicle involved. The (alas) unpaid services of Douglas Robb did little to improve matters, and for years I very perfunctorily attended to the leaking holes in chest and groin — and yet I never seemed to pick up any infection from pretty unsterile swabs of meths. However it was something to get over — although never quite, as I to this day will occasionally 'break out' anew.

But apart from this chatter I perhaps have something of interest to say. I am about to review for Bob Dudding's ISLANDS a remarkable first book of short stories by one Owen Marshall (but a pseudonym), called Supper Waltz Wilson. The author a note tells me teaches at Waitaki BHS, and he would be about 40. Anyhow, nothing amateurish, a remarkable and startlingly original maturity, and I must without exaggeration hand out my praises without any reserves at all. But of course one can always be stupidly mistaken. The gist of what I am saying is that praises or not, would you have been interested in noticing this book (assuming I could have got Dudding to agree) — because if so the next chance I get I will gladly pass it on to you. Of course just as you please — but my professional career in letters has lasted quite long enough, and I have no wish whatsoever to prolong it — and whatever the quality. Anyhow perhaps you might give me some indication sometime.

Also, my friend (whom I have never actually met), James Laughlin, who publishes New Directions books from Norfolk, Connecticut (but whose grandfather established in Pittsburgh the Jones-Laughlin Steel Corporation which now has on its payroll greater numbers of workers than the entire working population of Enzed) — books with authors such as Ferlinghetti (Landscapes of Living and Dying) or

Elaine Kraf (The Princess of 72nd Street) or Alphabetical Africa, by Walter Abish, etc, etc. Laughlin loves comment and if you felt you could provide him with some I could readily send you a selection.

[FS's review of Owen Marshall's Supper Waltz Wilson *(1979), the last piece of his writing to be published, appeared in* Islands *8: 3, 1980, p. 284.]*

To Julie Falkner, *Auckland*

Alexander Turnbull Library

[Falkner to Jim Traue, Turnbull Librarian, 12 June 1982: 'Two years ago, as a sixth form English student, I was given the task of preparing a seminar on a New Zealand writer. [. . .] I wrote to [Sargeson] and asked him several questions about his writing'. ATL MS-Papers-4201.]

10 June 1980

Dear Julie Falkner,

I expect I should be delighted to be 'done' by you — perhaps I am.

'A story which you consider your best?'

I expect you mean by story short story? And there is a difficulty. I don't know that it is any less difficult (for me, I mean) to write a novel than a short story — all I know is that except in very few instances I have found it *always* difficult (although the labour and doubt and worry is certainly less prolonged with the short form).

Alas, I think it's a question with me which story I would think my best. But I do know the ones which other people prefer, and among them I think I would plump for *An Affair of the Heart* and perhaps I say this because years ago I was touched to be so sincerely complimented by an entire class of children in a Taranaki School. I must warn you though that I have sometimes been told (by adults I regret to say) that this story is one of my worst. ('Sentimental' 'A stupid old crone' 'Etc') So you see!

I think I slowly drifted into devoting my life to writing. And I think what eventually drove me on and on was the wish to do my part in creating what might come to be recognised as a valid kind of Enzed language for the stories I had to tell.

Stories don't always turn out to be the exact story with its exact way of telling that one had in mind. Fortunately however what finally comes to light appears sometimes to be plainly superior to what one had had in mind to begin with. This is a kind of natural largesse which I am always grateful for. Sometimes however the reverse happens, and I am not grateful.

I think my writing style is a kind of concealed (perhaps) literary variation of New Zealand speech — but the speech of the ordinary Nzer who has been fortunate enough not to be too much tampered with by bad literary language such as one too often finds in newspapers and magazines.

Now perhaps that is the best I can do for you at the moment (and I say 'at the moment' because I have lately been unwell from what Enzers call a stroke, but Americans (now) 'a circulatory accident.'

Anyhow good wishes, and most especially if literary adventures of your own are ahead of you, *very* good hopes & wishes.

From,

Frank Sargeson

To John Ower, *University of South Carolina at Columbia*

Alexander Turnbull Library

4 August 1980

Dear John Ower,

A string of excuses for my never having written would be tedious. This goes off to you very pronto, and may I be able to say something that could interest you!

Yes of course it interested me very much to read your Landfall piece — and yesterday interested me more now that I have read it again after 8 years. I just don't know about Adler. He was no more than a name to me up to the time I was in London in 1927, but among the readers I up to a point (and I mean by readers the mainly young people I mixed with in the Museum Library) woke up to my having focused probably much too much on Freud and Jung. But alas, I was never very conscious that any of these three had made much of an impression upon my virgin mind. Alas! I early became addicted to the poets, assuring myself that the *pleasure* of such as Shaks. or Byron, Spenser or Browning would do for me as much and more than I would derive from the psychologists. Chaucer for good example — how could anyone do more for me than he could? — and to this day I believe that.

Another point is that I think of the *Peon* as a kind of late early beginning. Perhaps I managed it rather better than I ever supposed I could — I expect because I had at last discovered how to write fiction (or shall I say a longish work of fiction) and almost totally keep myself out of it. I think I can be no more identified with Michael Newhouse than Cervantes can be with the Don. If I had not made the discovery of the Peon I think it very unlikely I could ever have gone on to what I regard as my best work. I mean Joy of the Worm (as the best example), but there's also The Hangover. And among other things these two books made possible the late novellas, Man of England, A Game of Hide and Seek, Sunset

Village, and En Route. Also it was the Peon that enabled me to see that a good deal of my strength as a writer derived from my ability to write comedy. And of course I then reminded myself that the essence of the pleasure of my London days was not to be located in my Brit Museum reading — no, in seeing performances of Congreve (The Way of the World with Edith Evans and Godfrey Tearle), of Farquhar (The Beaux' Stratagem, with Edith Evans) of Getting Married (Shaw) with Esmé Percy — Each of these a supreme delight.

But alas, this must be all for now. (I have this year suffered some kind of 'stroke' which has impaired large areas of my memory and virtually made it impossible for me to write anymore. But if I have said anything of value to me, write if you think I could be of any further use to you.

And do forgive the long silence, when, so very busy and so much of my life taken up in chores, I simply could never get round to it.

F.S.

['your Landfall piece': John Ower's 'Wizard's Brew: Frank Sargeson's Memoirs of a Peon', Landfall, *December 1972.]*

To John Ower, *University of South Carolina at Columbia*

Alexander Turnbull Library

24 August 1980

Dear John Ower,

Your letter August 9. And I keep telling myself how fortunate I am to have such an appreciating person write me letters. Honestly though I don't know how I can help you much — I expect mainly because there is a sense in which you are most perceptive about *That Summer*. I expect all writers have some particular piece of work (whether their own, or somebody else's which cuts very close to the knuckle, I mean their own knuckle). So far as I know, I mean that insofar as I can separate TS from all that surrounded it, I think when I was occupied with it I was gripped by 2 obsessions — the first was that it had to be the best by far of anything I could do — because I would die soon and write nothing else: and the second was that the 'Terry' would die — and that would certainly imply that my own life would be finished as well. Yes, indeed, it was all as powerful and for me as terrible as that. I expect you will understand — so let me go on and say what happened in the event. I didn't die — so there were years and years of writing to get on with, much of it of quite some quality, I thought, and still think: but by far the most of it had only a very tenuous connection with the 'Terry' who had been so crucial and vital for TS (God knows what I am telling — or should I say 'trusting' you with). But having got so far perhaps I should go on. The point is that Terry didn't die either — or rather until some eight or so years ago, and all the years it was assumed that I would go on putting him first in my life. It did not irk me. Indeed it gave me steady satisfaction so to do — but in at times *very* 'straightened' circumstances I found it a strain nearly to the limit of what I could do and endure. After all almost to the time when Terry did in fact die we lived in the tiny convenience-lacking bach hardly big enough for one, let alone two. One of the eventual ironies was that I could never suppose myself surviving him — and yet here I am, I have survived (and until the last 2 years or so thrived up to a point). It costs me much to be honest and write that.

I wonder if I can theorize. Up to the time I wrote *That Summer* I could scarcely imagine at all that I would ever write anything that would closely relate to myself. So the greatest discovery of a literary lifetime was my finding that I could marvellously and almost totally rely on my imagination to supply me with what I wanted to write book after book.

If anything is coming out of this for you, it will be pretty clear that I doubt much that I would have written anything at all (though I expect I really mean anything of any consequence) if I had never met that one and only Terry. And once met it was the finish. The strangest thing of all was that it was mutual — when, given the sort of world we lived in, chances of anything beyond a day or two would be impossible.

It plagues me to think that the whole of this letter could be a sad mistake — which instead of ditching I am sending on to you. The US has such a fascination for me — I mean most the US of Twain (on the one hand), and Hawthorne for contrast. Then too Janet Frame and myself have a Enzed-born friend who occupies a Johns Hopkins Chair (he's almost this very moment visiting, and giving us the 'word' on the air — God forgive me for not being able to take him altogether seriously. He's a professional psychologist and no doubt a very able one according to modern patterns, but I distrust (mainly secretly). His name is John Money. I admire very much the courage of his ambitions from the time of humble Morrinsville beginning to Otago university (where as a psychology lecturer he encountered in his class Janet — and much to his credit was in no doubt about her potential genius. From Otago he worked his sea-passage to America and somehow got into Harvard which I think bestowed upon him an exceedingly useful degree. His relations with me these days are mainly limited to his sending me his erudite (and often for me embarrassingly illustrated pamphlets — which I hastily and anonymously send on to the Auckland Hospital Medical Library, though drawing attention to the author as an exported Enzed genius — (but *I* don't think — why should he embarrass me with postal communications containing super photographic illustrations of surgical operations for the relief of priapism — after all this *is* Enzed, hence prying postal censors of 'indecent' material? Ah well.)

Anyhow this page and the preceding one goes into the post to you for what it is worth.

Forget all I write — or not, just as you please. But much good will & good wishes for your good self.

F.S.

To Frank Sargeson, *Salford, Lancashire*

Alexander Turnbull Library

5 October 1980

Dear Mr Sargeson,

Goodness me, yes, I am most interested. Thank you for your letter, but I would be very doubtful about any family connection — although oddly enough the family I belong to in these parts appear to be singular in spelling the name as you do — the names I know are usually spelt with an i or perhaps double s.

My grandfather Sargeson was an east Anglia man who emigrated twice late last century — first across to Belfast, and then on to New Zealand. He was a painter and paperhanger. I am not myself a Sargeson by birthname — My mother was a Sargeson daughter who married my Davey father. The Daveys however were not craftsmen, instead shopkeepers — so when I began my long and painful avocation of (against many difficult odds) transforming myself into a writer of fiction I assumed the maternal name.

I am nearly eighty now and have something of a small reputation about the world (you did not tell me which book of mine you were referring to — there is about 20), but financial returns have always been meagre.

However I did get to England once, in the mid-twenties, but I am afraid I preferred to remain mainly in London where I could make use of the British Museum Reading Room.

Another coincidence is that my parents were Methodist — but alas as I grew up I preferred not to commit myself — which I have never regretted. Nor do I regret never having married.

I daresay my grandfather may have been in or close to Salford once he probably passed through Manchester-Liverpool where he got off to Belfast.

Well anyhow, I have never before known of another Frank Sargeson, and now I do — and may I wish you all that's well in this more and more difficult contemporary world,

With affection, from

To Ralph Bodle, *Kaukapakapa*

Alexander Turnbull Library

18 November 1980

My dear and dearest Ralph,

Pardon what may sound an over-affectionate beginning (after my late long long silence, what may sound insincere and affected) — but alas alas a letter, any letter (even one of 3 or so lines telling some tiresome widow, NO, I do not lend my books and moreover I know it is not books you are after — on the contrary it is my person — or rather indeed a very certain private part of it that you would be much more interested in — visually and tangibly if I'm not VERY MUCH MISTAKEN.

Well anyhow yes yes indeed, with my particular brand of what might justly be called palsy I'm really quite close to being a write-off (for typing, literary composition and human relations of any kind (although it astonishes me how comforting I find my two black monsters of cats who blessedly continue to accept me for what I am — which blessedly comforts me no end (although with the slight reservation that it is provided I arrive home from the shops with — meat? alas no, but loads of fish and RIVAL — this last a meat substitute for Jellymeat — and very good stuff with cat vits.

I have been profoundly disturbed by your description of a seatful of bus-awaiters who failed to respond to a request for MONEY. Pardon me, but it throws light on the present replacement of one 'culture' by another. I can't remember a time when I wasn't moved by being touched — to have the agonies of mankind suddenly thrust upon one. How moving — and for a writer of fiction how fruitful for his daily labours (which, not being able to do anymore I find myself ever more infinitely grateful for. Any how instructive — what's a dollar — shit! So there you have it both ways. You get rid of the shit that's sticking to you — and satisfying your resentment by sticking it onto somebody else.

Before this becomes too much a head-splitting chore I must say that Janet (Frame) was with me a few days lately. Exhausting — but marvellously worth it as always. Also she very kindly gave me a copy of *Living in the Maniototo* — I suppose the last word could mean Plain of Blood. Anyhow she finally clinches her hold on the literary world with a masterpiece. God knows where her comic genius derives from, but there it is. Staggeringly original, disturbingly probing — may the Lord preserve her for a few decades yet. Strangely I was telling her about your own mode of life — she never forgets anything she's told, so cherish life at least until you see yourself Frame-print-preserved for all time.

No more for now dear Ralph, [. . .]

To Janet Frame, *Wanganui*

Private collection

December 9 (I think) [1980]

Dear Janet,

My morale is boosted by a letter from the author of *Maniototo*. But this note goes because it worries me you may be inconvenienced by the delay in the payment from Authors' Fund. I've decided not to anticipate — but I will gladly do so if it puts you in a jam. *Do* say.

I'll have to ask you shortly what *sort* of cuckoo I'd be classed as now. I simply on some days can remember nothing — nothing in itself, but it rapidly becomes worse. I think I told you I for far too long thought I was *Jack Nobilo* & this flattering illusion was not shattered until the butcher (fortunately, perhaps) called me Doc. — it looks like paranoia, I suppose, but whatever it gets rapidly worse. Trouble is I *know* a Jack Nobilo & I'd like very much to be him. (or should I say 'he').

Never mind. And thanks for the interesting letter.

F.

To Alison Pollard, *Gisborne*

Alexander Turnbull Library

31 March 1981

Dear Alison Pollard,

I think there really must be a Enzed literature. Otherwise how come that so many of us have worked for so long and so painfully over contributing to it? My God, how I remember Janet Frame, on leave from Mental Hospital, living in my backyard bach and slavishly labouring *Owls Do Cry*. Instead of the cups of tea I used to take along to her I used to have cups of cold water on my mind. I thought they could be needed to quench the flames that could break out as her typewriter ran hotter and hotter.

You see, we do it and do it. And slavery! Yes, that! And after all. *What* we do! You've read *Owls Do Cry*? And Enzed lit? — yes very naturally I would say. And I haven't done so badly myself, surely. You've never read my comic novel, *Joy of the Worm*? Well! — and we'll get round to discussing it further when you have.

And talking of patterns of style — in verse, say? Do you need to look further than Denis Glover. What wit, what variety, what marvellous use of every style of prosody!

And what *pleasure*! And there's the nub of your question. Who wants to bother a moment with Enzed Lit. unless there is PLEASURE — And nowhere exactly duplicated in any another Lit.

No more for now, but thanks for your letter and particularly the stamp.

Good lit. pleasure for you in years to come

PS Of course the phonies are legion — I could tell you a host of names. But you tell me!

To Janet Frame, *Wanganui*

Private collection

['Kaleidoscope: Conversations with Frank Sargeson', in which Gordon McLauchlan talked to FS about his life and work, screened on 14 August 1981.]

20 September 1981

Dearest Janet,

My ignorant cat doesn't even know she's been on TV. But alas all that was a mistake. I was ignorant too, I thought we were all having fun & games — if the PUBLIC had entered my head I would have gone all self-conscious. What interested me though was the way pieces & bits could be strung together to have something coherent emerge. The genius of that thing was Morison, part Polynesian, who clearly knew what he was up to.

Well, well, But my obsession at the moment is my Hospital Adventures. Lately emerged from the *Dept. of Nuclear Med.* (sic, believe it or not — & made me *so* sick.) I walked out on them before they were through (I could not stand being virtually enclosed by a terrifying machine, making — I assume — nuclear movies. But I gave as my excuse it was too painful for my damaged ribs — previously, in Hosp I fell out of bed one night — I told the dr. I thought I had broken some ribs, but he looked & with pooh-poohs said he could find nothing but a scratch — eventually xray revealed 3 broken ribs.)

Anyhow they were aiming at a 'bone scan', which follows a prostate op because they believe p. malignancy moves next to bones BUT no more co-op. from me.

All too depressing to write about.

I have thoroughly read *Maniototo* now, & what an excellent piece of work!!!! How nice for you to be reviewed in T.L.S. by a woman called Jennifer UGLOW

All the Stead family have been prosecuted & fined over the Springbucks — even down to the little girl — most improper!!!

All for now (I can't maintain my back for long in sitting position.

Much love (& reverence)

Fx

[This appears to be FS's last dated letter. His health deteriorated rapidly, and he was hospitalised again on 21 December. He died on 1 March 1982.]

Bibliography

Alexander, Peter, *William Plomer: A Biography*, Oxford University Press, Oxford and New York, 1989.

Beveridge, Michael, 'Conversation with Frank Sargeson', *Landfall*, vol. 24, no. 1, 1970, pp. 4–27 and vol. 24, no. 2, 1970, pp. 142–160.

Birtles, Birt, 'Marcel Aurousseau: Poetry, People and Places', *Meanjin Quarterly*, vol. 27, no. 4, Summer 1968, pp. 409–417.

Brickell, Chris, *Mates and Lovers: A History of Gay New Zealand*, Godwit, Auckland, 2008.

Calder, Alex, *The Settler's Plot: How Stories Take Place in New Zealand*, Auckland University Press, Auckland, 2011.

Catley, Christine Cole, 'Frank the Bank: The Unending Generosity of Frank Sargeson', in Sarah Shieff (ed.), *Speaking Frankly: The Frank Sargeson Memorial Lectures 2003–2010*, Cape Catley, Devonport, 2011, pp. 97–119.

Challis, Derek, & Gloria Rawlinson, *The Book of Iris: A Life of Robin Hyde*, Auckland University Press, Auckland, 2002.

Copland, R. A., 'The Goodly Roof: Some Comments on the Fiction of Frank Sargeson', in Wystan Curnow (ed.), *Essays on New Zealand Literature*, Heinemann, Auckland, 1973, pp. 43–53.

—, *New Zealand Writers and Their Work: Frank Sargeson*, Oxford University Press, Wellington, 1976.

Cunningham, Kevin, *Frank Sargeson's Critical and Autobiographical Writings: An Annotated Bibliography*, Library School, Wellington, 1977.

Curnow, Allen, *An Incorrigible Music: A Sequence of Poems*, Auckland University Press/Oxford University Press, Auckland, 1979.

—, *Whim Wham's New Zealand: The Best of Whim Wham, 1937–1988*, Terry Sturm (ed.), Vintage, Auckland, 2005.

Curnow, Wystan (ed.), *Essays on New Zealand Literature*, Heinemann, Auckland, 1973.

Davin, Dan, *Cliffs of Fall*, Nicholson and Watson, London, 1945.

—, *Crete*, Historical Publications Branch, Wellington, 1953.

— (ed.), *New Zealand Short Stories*, Oxford University Press, London, 1953.

—, *The Gorse Blooms Pale: Dan Davin's Southland Stories*, Janet Wilson (ed.), University of Otago Press, Dunedin, 2007.

Dudding, Robin (ed.), 'Frank Sargeson at 75', *Islands*, 21, vol. 6 no. 3, March 1978.

—, *Beginnings: New Zealand Authors Tell How They Began Writing*, Wellington, Oxford University Press, 1980.

Evans, Patrick, *Janet Frame*, Twayne, Boston, 1977.

—, *The Long Forgetting: Post-colonial Literary Culture in New Zealand*, Canterbury University Press, Christchurch, 2007.

Fairburn, A.R.D., *The Letters of A.R.D. Fairburn*, Lauris Edmond (sel. and ed.), Oxford University Press, Auckland, 1981.

Frame, Janet, 'A Last Letter to Frank Sargeson', *Islands*, new series, vol. 1, no. 1, July 1984, pp. 17–22.

—, *An Autobiography*, Century Hutchinson, Auckland, 1989.

—, 'The Silkworms', *Granta*, vol. 105, Spring 2009, pp. 113–122.

—, *In Her Own Words*, Denis Harold and Pamela Gordon (eds.), Penguin, Auckland, 2011.

Franke, Norman, 'The Last European and the First New Zealander: Karl Wolfskehl Meets Frank Sargeson', *Span*, vol. 47, October 1998, pp. 57–71.

Gaskell, A.P., *The Big Game and Other Stories*, Caxton, Christchurch, 1947.

—, *All Part of the Game: The Stories of A. P. Gaskell*, R. A. Copland (ed. and introd.), Auckland University Press, Auckland, 1978.

Hamilton, Stephen, 'Charles Brasch, 1909–1973', *Kotare* 2008: Special Issue: Essays in New Zealand Biography Series Three: 'The Early Poets' http://www.nzetc.org/tm/scholarly/tei-Whi073Kota-t1-g1-t18.html [accessed 7 June 2011].

Harcourt, Peter, *A Dramatic Appearance: New Zealand Theatre 1920–1970*, Methuen, Wellington, 1978.

Holman, Dinah, & Christine Cole Catley (eds.), *Fairburn and Friends*, Cape Catley, Devonport, 2004.

Ireland, Kevin, 'Mr Sargeson at Home: A Glimpse at the Domestic Arrangements and Literary Carry-on at 14 Esmonde Road, Takapuna', in Sarah Shieff (ed.), *Speaking Frankly: The Frank Sargeson Memorial Lectures 2003–2010*, Cape Catley, Devonport, 2011, pp. 49–71.

Jones, Lawrence, 'Frank Sargeson (Norris Frank Davey), 1903–1982' *Kotare* 2008: Special Issue: Essays in New Zealand Biography Series Two: 'Early Male Prose Writers'. http://www.nzetc.org/tm/scholarly/tei-Whi072Kota-t1-g1-t18.html [accessed 7 June 2011].

—, 'The Wrong Bus: The "Sons of Sargeson", Dan Davin and the Search for the Great New Zealand Novel, 1943–56', in Sarah Shieff (ed.), *Speaking Frankly: The Frank Sargeson Memorial Lectures 2003–2010*, Cape Catley, Devonport, 2011, pp. 27–48.

King, Michael, *Frank Sargeson: A Life*, Viking, Auckland, 1995.

—, *Wrestling with the Angel: A Life of Janet Frame*, Viking, Auckland, 2000.

—, 'A Conversation with my Uncle: Frank Sargeson and Hamilton', in Sarah Shieff (ed.) *Speaking Frankly: The Frank Sargeson Memorial Lectures 2003–2010*, Cape Catley, Devonport, 2011, pp. 12–26.

Lay, Graeme, 'Affairs of the Heart', in Sarah Shieff (ed.), *Speaking Frankly: The Frank Sargeson Memorial Lectures 2003–2010*, Cape Catley,

Devonport, 2011, pp. 119–142.

Lay, Graeme & Stephen Stratford (eds.), *An Affair of the Heart: A Celebration of Frank Sargeson's Centenary*, Cape Catley, Devonport, 2003.

McEldowney, Dennis, *The World Regained*, Chapman Hall, London, 1957.

—, *Frank Sargeson in His Time*, John McIndoe, Dunedin, 1976.

Millar, Paul (ed.), *New Selected Poems: James K. Baxter*, Auckland, Oxford University Press, 2001.

—, *No Fretful Sleeper: A Life of Bill Pearson*, Auckland University Press, Auckland, 2010.

Murray, Stuart, '"A New Tramp Abroad": Sargeson in Europe', *Journal of New Zealand Literature*, vol. 8, 1990, pp. 66–73.

Ogilvie, Gordon, *Denis Glover: His Life*, Godwit, Auckland, 1999.

Ovenden, Keith, *A Fighting Withdrawal: The Life of Dan Davin, Writer, Soldier, Publisher*, Oxford University Press, Oxford and New York, 1996.

Pearson, Bill, *Coal Flat*, Paul's Book Arcade, Auckland and Hamilton, 1963.

—, *Fretful Sleepers and Other Essays*, Heinemann Education Books, Auckland, 1974.

Reid, Bryan, *After the Fireworks: A Life of David Ballantyne*, Auckland University Press, Auckland, 2004.

Reid, J.C., *Creative Writing in New Zealand: A Brief Critical History*, Whitcombe and Tombs, Auckland, 1946.

Rhodes, H. Winston, *Frank Sargeson*, Twayne Publishers, New York, 1969.

Richards, Ian, *To Bed at Noon: The Life and Art of Maurice Duggan*, Auckland University Press, Auckland, 1997.

Sargeson, Frank, *Conversation with my Uncle and other Sketches*, Unicorn Press, Auckland, 1936.

—, *A Man and His Wife*, Caxton, Christchurch, 1940.

—, *When the Wind Blows*, Caxton, Christchurch, 1945.

— (ed.), *Speaking for Ourselves*, Caxton, Christchurch, 1945.

—, *That Summer and Other Stories*, John Lehmann, London, 1946.

—, *Cet été-là* [*That Summer*], Jeanne Fournier-Pargoire (trans.), Editions du Bateau-Ivre, Paris, 1946.

—, *I Saw in My Dream*, John Lehmann, London, 1949.

—, *I For One . . .*, Caxton, Christchurch, 1954.

—, *Wrestling with the Angel: Two Plays. A Time for Sewing* and *The Cradle and The Egg*, Caxton, Christchurch, 1964.

—, *Collected Stories 1935–1963*, Bill Pearson (introd.), Blackwood and Janet Paul, Auckland, 1964.

—, *Memoirs of a Peon*, MacGibbon and Kee, London, 1965.

—, *The Hangover*, MacGibbon and Kee, London, 1967.

—, *Joy of the Worm*, MacGibbon and Kee, London, 1969.

—, *Man of England Now*, [with '*I For One . . .*' and *A Game of Hide and Seek*], Martin Brian and O'Keeffe, London; Caxton, Christchurch, 1972.

—, *Once is Enough: A Memoir*, Martin Brian and O'Keeffe, London; A.H. and A.W. Reed, Wellington, 1973.

—, *I Saw in My Dream,* H. Winston Rhodes (ed. and introd.), Auckland University Press, Auckland, 1974.

—, *More than Enough: A Memoir*, Martin Brian and O'Keeffe, London; A.H. and A.W. Reed, Wellington, 1975.

—, *Sunset Village*, Martin Brian and O'Keeffe, London; A.H. and A.W. Reed, Wellington, 1976.

—, *Never Enough!*, Martin Brian and O'Keeffe, London; A.H. and A.W. Reed, Wellington, 1977.

—, *Tandem: The Chain* by Edith Campion and *En Route* by Frank Sargeson, A.H. and A.W. Reed, Wellington, 1979.

—, *Sargeson*, Penguin, Auckland, 1981.

—, *The Stories of Frank Sargeson*, Penguin, Auckland, 1982.

—, *Conversation in a Train and Other Critical Writing*, Kevin Cunningham (sel. and ed.), Auckland University Press, Auckland; Oxford University Press, Oxford, 1983.

—, *The Hangover and Joy of the Worm: 2 Short Novels*, Penguin, Auckland, 1984.

—, *Frank Sargeson's Stories*, Janet Wilson (ed.), Cape Catley, Devonport, 2010.

Shaw, Helen (ed.), *The Puritan and the Waif: a Symposium of Critical Essays on the Work of Frank Sargeson*, Hofmann, Auckland, 1955.

Shieff, Sarah (ed.), *Speaking Frankly: The Frank Sargeson Memorial Lectures 2003–2010*, Cape Catley, Devonport, 2011.

—, 'Risotto with Pipis: Frank Sargeson in Italy', *Journal of New Zealand Literature*, vol. 26, 2008, pp. 41–58.

Stead, C.K., *In the Glass Case: Essays on New Zealand Literature*, Auckland University Press, Auckland, 1981.

—, 'Allen Curnow's Poetry: Poet of the Real' [1963], *In the Glass Case: Essays on New Zealand Literature*, Auckland University Press, Auckland, 1981, pp. 189–206.

—, *All Visitors Ashore*, Harvill, London; Collins, Auckland, 1984.

—, *New Zealand Short Stories* [2nd series], C.K. Stead (sel. and introd.), Oxford University Press, London, Wellington and Melbourne, 1996.

—, *The Writer at Work: Essays*, University of Otago Press, Dunedin, 2000.

—, *Book Self: The Reader as Writer and the Writer as Critic*, Auckland University Press, Auckland, 2008.

—, *Poems 1951–2006*, Auckland University Press, Auckland, 2008.

—, *South-West of Eden: A Memoir 1932–1956*, Auckland University Press, Auckland, 2010.

Wells, Peter, 'The Hole in the Hedge: Landscape and the Fragility of Memory', in Sarah Shieff (ed.), *Speaking Frankly: The Frank Sargeson Memorial Lectures 2003–2010*, Cape Catley, Devonport, 2011, pp. 72–96.

Wotherspoon, Garry, *City of the Plain: History of a Gay Subculture*, Hale and Ironmonger, Sydney, 1991.

Index by correspondent

Abbreviations:

ATL: Alexander Turnbull Library, Wellington, New Zealand.
Harry Ransom: Harry Ransom Humanities Research Center, University of Texas at Austin.
Hocken: Hocken Collections/Uare Taoka O Hakena, University of Otago, Dunedin, New Zealand.
Houghton: Houghton Library, Harvard University.
JFLT: Janet Frame Literary Trust, PO Box 6160, Dunedin, New Zealand.
Princeton: Lehmann Family Papers, Manuscripts Division, Department of Rare Books and Special Collections, Princeton University Library.
Special Collections, ACL: Sir George Grey Special Collections, Auckland City Libraries.
Special Collections, UoA: Special Collections, The University of Auckland Library.

The following lists the correspondent's name, each letter in date order, the location of the original, and the page reference for this book.

2 March, 1980. MS-Papers-4261-222, ATL. 588-589.
Glover Denis, 13 Nov, 1935. MS-Papers-0418-018, ATL. 7-8.
3 June, 1936. MS-Papers-0418-018, ATL. 10-11.
26 Jan, [1937]. MS-Papers-0418-018, ATL. 11-12.
27 June, [1937]. MS-Papers-0418-018, ATL. 13.
9 Aug, [1937]. MS-Papers-0418-018, ATL. 14-15.
28 Aug, [1937]. MS-Papers-0418-018, ATL. 15-16.
26 Sept, [1937]. MS-Papers-0418-018, ATL. 16.
29 Dec, 1937. MS-Papers-0418-018, ATL. 18.
2 Feb, 1938. MS-Papers-0418-018, ATL. 19–21.
8 July, [1940]. MS-Papers-0418-018, ATL. 33.
10 Feb, 1943. 80-387-2, ATL. 57-58.
9 Sept, 1943. 80-387-2, ATL. 60-61.
22 April, 1953. MS-Papers-0418-018, ATL. 158-160.
19 Oct, 1954. MS-Papers-0418-018, ATL. 181-182.
25 Feb, 1956. MS-Papers-0418-018, ATL. 219-221.
3 March, 1956. MS-Papers-0418-018, ATL. 221-224.
21 Sept, 1956. MS-Papers-0418-018, ATL. 241-243.
31 Aug, 1973. MS-Papers-0418-018, ATL. 502-503.
7 Oct, 1973. MS-Papers-0418-018, ATL. 504-505.
23 June, 1974. MS-Papers-4261-208, ATL. 521-522.
2 April, 1978. 80-387-1, ATL. 562.
Godley Eric, 2 Jan, 1977. MS-Papers-2376, ATL. 553-554.
Graham John, 10 Nov, 1957. MS-Papers-4235, ATL. 260-261.
Green Martin, 7 Dec, 1963. MS Papers-0432-140, ATL. 317.
15 Aug, 1965. MS-Papers-4261-192, ATL. 363.
Grindlay Lionel, 22 Nov, 1945. MS-Papers-0432-140, ATL. 85-87.
Haddock Mr, 4 Aug, 1974. MS-Papers-4261-208, ATL. 523.
Harris Max, 1 May, 1946. MS-Papers-0432-198, ATL. 90-91.
Hawthorne Raymond, 22 Nov, 1978. MS-Papers-4261-219, ATL. 569.
Heenan Joseph, 29 Dec, 1948. MS-Papers-1132-204, ATL. 113-114.
Henderson Kennaway, 10 Aug, 1935. MS-Papers-0432-168, ATL. 5-6.
Henderson W. H [Mayor], [August, 1960]. MS-Papers-0432-140, ATL. 284.
Hill David, 14 Feb, 1971. MS-Papers-4216, ATL. 446.
22 Feb, 1971. MS-Papers-4216, ATL. 447-448.
Holcroft Monte, 28 Dec, 1940. MS-Papers-1186-22, ATL. 38-39.
Horsman Alan, 21 May, 1966. MS-2452, Hocken. 382-383.
Insley Marie, 10 Feb, 1949. MS-Papers-4256, ATL. 116.
Ireland Kevin, 23 July, 1959. MS-Papers-3920, ATL. 277-278.
26 June, 1965. MS-Papers-3920, ATL. 358.
20 Feb, 1979. MS-Papers-3920, ATL. 571-572.
Jones Lawrence, 24 Dec, 1972. MS-Papers-4261-202, ATL. 493-494.
25 Nov, 1973. MS-Papers-4261-206, ATL. 510-511.
Kennedy Rodney, 23 May, 1955. Misc-MS-1284, Hocken. 202-203.
King Michael, 11 March, 1979. MS-Papers-4261-220, ATL. 573.
Laughlin James, 26 Dec, 1937. bMS Am 2077 (1495), Houghton. 17.
17 Jan, 1938. bMS Am 2077 (1495), Houghton. 19.
28 June, 1944. bMS Am 2077 (1495), Houghton. 76.
5 April, 1948. bMS Am 2077 (1495), Houghton. 104-105.
24 July, 1963. bMS Am 2077 (1495), Houghton. 301-302.
20 Aug, 1963. bMS Am 2077 (1495), Houghton. 307-308.
Lay Graeme, 11 July, 1975, Lay and Stratford, *An Affair of the Heart* pp. 33–34. 537-538.
20 July, 1975. MS-Papers-4261-211, ATL. 538.
Lehmann John, 23 March, 1939. John Lehmann Collection, Harry Ransom. 21-22.
9 May, 1940. CO746Box 44 f.7, Princeton. 27-28.
22 Jan, 1941. John Lehmann Collection, Harry Ransom. 39-41.
30 April, 1944. CO746Box 44 f.7, Princeton. 71-72.
[25 Nov, 1944]. CO746Box 44 f.7, Princeton. 77-78.
7 July, 1945. CO746Box 44 f.7, Princeton. 80-82.
8 July, 1975. CO746Box 44 f.7, Princeton. 534-535.
Literary Fund [Secretary], 29 Sept , 1973. MS-Papers-4223, ATL. 503-504.
Macalister John, 8 May, 1980. MS-Papers-4261-223, ATL. 594-595.
Maiden Colin, 4 Aug, 1974. MS-Papers-4261-208, ATL. 522.
Manhire Bill, 16 April, 1978. MS-Papers-4261-217, ATL. 563.

15 Sept, 1957. MS-Papers-0432-186, ATL. 257-258.
11 May, 1958. MS-Papers-0432-186, ATL. 266.
21 Sept, 1958. MS-Papers-0432-186, ATL. 272-273.
23 Oct, 1959. MS-Papers-0432-186, ATL. 278-279.
3 Feb, 1961. MS-Papers-0432-186, ATL. 286-288.
24 Dec, 1962. MS-Papers-0432-186, ATL. 298-299.
30 July, 1964. MS-Papers-0432-187, ATL. 338-339.
1 Oct, 1964. MS-Papers-0432-187, ATL. 342-344.
15 Nov, 1964. MS-Papers-0432-187, ATL. 348-349.
5 Sept, 1965. MS-Papers-0432-187, ATL. 365-366.
10 April, 1967. MS-Papers-0432-187, ATL. 396-397.
5 Nov, 1967. MS-Papers-0432-187, ATL. 404-405.
14 April, 1968. MS-Papers-0432-187, ATL. 406-407.
30 March, 1969. MS-Papers-0432-187, ATL. 417-419.
8 July, 1969. MS-Papers-0432-187, ATL. 420-421.
24 Aug, 1969. MS-Papers-0432-187, ATL. 422-423.
29 March, 1970. MS-Papers-0432-187, ATL. 429-430.
6 June, 1970. MS-Papers-4247, ATL. 430-432.
25 Aug, 1970. MS-Papers-4247, ATL. 434-436.
16 Sept, 1970. MS-Papers-4247, ATL. 436-437.
27 Oct, 1970. MS-Papers-4247, ATL. 440-441.
15 Nov, 1970. MS-Papers-4247, ATL. 443-444.
14 March, 1971. MS-Papers-4247, ATL. 448-450.
9 Jan, 1972. MS-Papers-4247, ATL. 469.
25 March, 1972. MS-Papers-4247, ATL. 473-474.
30 April, 1973. MS-Papers-4247, ATL. 497-498.

Pollard Alison, 31 March, 1981. MS-Papers-4261-225, ATL. 603-604.

Powell Mr, 20 Feb, 1964. MS-Papers-0432-140, ATL. 321-322.

Rations Dept [Dept of Labour], 21 Oct, 1935. MS-Papers-0432-140, ATL. 6-7.

Read Mr [Internal Affairs], 5 June, 1965. MS-Papers-0432-141, ATL. 356-357.

Rennie Bruce, [Oct, 1965]. MS-Papers-4234, ATL. 370.

Rhodes H. Winston, 1 June, 1964. MS-Papers-0424-23, ATL. 328-330.
21 Sept, 1964. MS-Papers-0424-23, ATL. 341-342.
19 Feb, 1966. MS-Papers-0424-23, ATL. 382.
15 Jan, 1967. MS-Papers-0424-23, ATL. 393-394.
26 March, 1967. MS-Papers-0424-23, ATL. 395-396.
18 July, 1967. MS-Papers-0424-23, ATL. 399-400.
20 Aug, 1967. MS-Papers-0424-23, ATL. 403-404.
21 Aug, 1968. MS-Papers-0424-23, ATL. 409-411.
1 Dec, 1968. MS-Papers-0424-23, ATL. 413-415.
18 Jan, 1971. MS-Papers-0424-23A, ATL. 445.
7 Oct, 1972. MS-Papers-0424-23A, ATL. 485-486.
4 Nov, 1972. MS-Papers-0424-23A, ATL. 487-488.
28 July, 1973. MS-Papers-0424-23A, ATL. 500-502.
11 Nov, 1973. MS-Papers-0424-23A, ATL. 507-509.
15 Nov, 1973. MS-Papers-0424-23A, ATL. 509-510.
21 Jan, 1977. MS-Papers-0424-23A, ATL. 555-556.
29 Aug, 1979. MS-Papers-4261-221, ATL. 579-580.

Ryan Kevin, 11 April, 1973. MS-Papers-4261-203, ATL. 496-497.

Sargeson Frank [UK], 5 Oct, 1980. MS-Papers-4261-224, ATL. 601.

Scott Margaret, 21 Oct, 1970. MS-Papers-4221, ATL. 439.

Shaw Helen/Frank Hofmann, Tuesday, [1949]. MS-Papers-7642-131, ATL. 119.

Shaw Helen, 9 Dec, 1954. MS-Papers-7642-131, ATL. 185.
30 March, 1955. MS-Papers-7642-131, ATL. 196-197.

Shaw Jim, [30 Sept, 1969]. MS-Papers-4261-193, ATL. 424.

Sinclair Keith, 4 Oct, 1953. Private Collection, Raewyn Dalziel. 165-166.
8 July, 1954. Private Collection, Raewyn Dalziel. 177-178.
23 Nov, 1954. Private Collection, Raewyn Dalziel. 183-184.

Smith Mr [Health Inspector], 1 March, 1973. MS-Papers-4261-203, ATL. 495.

Smithyman Kendrick, 15 Dec, 1949. MSS and Archives 2009/3. Special Collections, UoA. 119-121.
22 Jan, 1950. MSS and Archives 2009/3. Special Collections, UoA. 127-128.

Somerville Dora, 3 Dec, 1972. 73-161-6/10, ATL. 490-491.
[10 Dec, 1972]. 73-161-6/10, ATL. 491-492.

State Advances Corporation, 3 June, 1947. MS-Papers-0432-140, ATL. 97-98.

Stead C.K., 14 May, 1954. MS-Papers-8220-01, ATL. 171-172.
30 June, 1956. MS-Papers-8220-01, ATL. 232-233.
10 Aug, 1958. MS-Papers-8220-01, ATL. 270-271.
Mon [Aug, 1958]. MS-Papers-8220-01, ATL. 272.
12 Aug, 1963. MS-Papers-8220-01, ATL. 307.
7 Oct, 1964. MS-Papers-8220-01, ATL. 344-345.
21 Nov, 1964. MS-Papers-8220-01, ATL. 350-351.
19 Oct, 1965. MS-Papers-8220-02, ATL. 369.
26 June, 1966. MS-Papers-8220-02, ATL. 386-388.
16 June, 1968. MS-Papers-8220-02, ATL. 408-409.
30 April, 1972. MS-Papers-8220-02. ATL. 476-477.
21 May, 1972. MS-Papers-8220-02, ATL. 477-478.
13 Aug, 1972. MS-Papers-8220-02, ATL. 482-483.
9 Nov, 1972. MS-Papers-8220-02, ATL. 489-490.
17 Dec, 1972. MS-Papers-8220-02, ATL. 492-493.

Stead K and K, 11 Nov, 1956. MS-Papers-8220-01, ATL. 243-244.
22 Jan, 1957. MS-Papers-8220-01, ATL. 246-249.
28 May, 1957. MS-Papers-8220-01, ATL. 254-256.
8 April, 1972. MS-Papers-8220-02, ATL. 474-476.

Styles-McLeod Catherine, 8 Jan, 1971. MS-Papers-4261-196, ATL. 444.

Sutherland Dorothy, 27 June, 1971. MS-Papers-4232, ATL. 457-458.
3 Oct, 1971. MS-Papers-4232, ATL. 461-462.
14 Nov, 1971. MS-Papers-4232, ATL. 466.
12 Feb, 1972. MS-Papers-4232, ATL. 470-471.
2 June, 1972. MS-Papers-4232, ATL. 479-481.
16 Dec, 1973. MS-Papers-4232, ATL. 511-513.
26 May, 1974. MS-Papers-4232, ATL. 520-521.
29 Jan, 1978. MS-Papers-4232, ATL. 559-561.

Texidor Greville, 16 Oct, 1950. MSS and Archives A-198 Box 1 f.2, Special Collections, UoA. 131-132.

Volkerling Ngahuia, 25 March, 1973. MS-Papers-4261-203, ATL. 496.

Wall Arnold, 6 March, 1976. MS-Papers-4261-213, ATL. 547.

Weir John, 13 June, 1971. MS-Papers-4261-197, ATL. 456.

Wells Peter, 27 Nov, 1979. MS-Papers-4261-221, ATL. 580-581.

Wilson Phillip, 9 March, 1969. MS-Papers-7685-014, ATL. 416-417.
13 July, 1971. MS-Papers-7685-014, ATL. 459-460.
12 Sept, [1971]. MS-Papers-4261-221, ATL. 460-461.
24 Oct, 1971. MS-Papers-7685-014, ATL. 462-463.
2 June, 1973. MS-Papers-4261-204, ATL. 498-499.
17 June, 1973. MS-Papers-4261-204, ATL. 499-500.
10 Feb, 1974. MS-Papers-7685-033, ATL. 515-516.
8 Dec, 1974. MS-Papers-7685-033, ATL. 528-529

Index of Sargeson's works

short story anthologies:

Index